W9-AMU-913

Within the Social World

Essays in Social Psychology

Jeffrey C. Chin
Le Moyne College

Cardell K. Jacobson
Brigham Young University

Boston • New York • San Francisco
Mexico City • Montreal • Toronto • London • Madrid • Munich • Paris
Hong Kong • Singapore • Tokyo • Cape Town • Sydney

Jeff dedicates this book to his father who was a psychologist and his mother who was a sociologist. So naturally he had to be a social psychologist.

Cardell dedicates this book to Rosanne and those who have followed from our union.

With a special dedication to Bernie N. Meltzer, Oct. 17, 1916–Jan. 29, 2008.

Executive Editor: *Jeff Lasser*
Editorial Assistant: *Lauren Macey*
Senior Marketing Manager: *Kelly May*
Production Supervisor: *Roberta Sherman*
Editorial-Production and Electronic Composition Services: *Pine Tree Composition*
Manufacturing Buyer: *Debbie Rossi*
Cover Administrator: *Linda Knowles*

For related titles and support materials, visit our online catalog at www.ablongman.com.

Copyright © 2009 Pearson Education, Inc.

All rights reserved. No part of the material protected by this copyright notice may be reproduced or utilized in any form or by any means, electronic or mechanical, including photocopying, recording, or by any information storage and retrieval system, without written permission from the copyright owner.

To obtain permission(s) to use material from this work, please submit a written request to Allyn and Bacon, Permissions Department, 501 Boylston Street, Suite 900, Boston, MA 02116 or fax your request to 617-671-2290.

Between the time website information is gathered and then published, it is not unusual for some sites to have closed. Also, the transcription of URLs can result in typographical errors. The publisher would appreciate notification where these errors occur so that they may be corrected in subsequent editions.

Library of Congress Cataloging-in-Publication Data

Chin, Jeffrey C. (Jeffrey Chuan-che)
Within the social world : essays in social psychology / Jeffrey C. Chin, Cardell K. Jacobson.
p. cm.
ISBN-13: 978-0-205-49888-8
ISBN-10: 0-205-49888-4
1. Social psychology. I. Jacobson, Cardell K. II. Title.
HM1033.C45 2008
302—dc22

2008011382

Printed in the United States of America

10 9 8 7 6 5 4 3 2 1 RRD-VA 12 11 10 09 08

Contents

Preface

We hope this book will appeal to sociologically trained social psychologists and their students. We approached this project the way most textbook authors approach their projects. We were dissatisfied with what was available for instructors of sociological social psychology, and we wanted to bring a more sociological orientation to social psychology classes. We thought, perhaps arrogantly, we could fill this void. Ultimately you will determine whether this book fulfills this goal.

The goal of this project from the very beginning was to produce an edited volume of work in sociological social psychology that would be accessible to undergraduate students. There are many excellent edited volumes on sociological social psych (e.g., Burke, 2006, Cook et al., 1995; Delamater, 2003), but they are for graduate students and professionals and we never intended to compete with them. There are also many excellent readers for social psychology students, but they tend to focus on popular culture articles and primarily to have a psychological or exclusively symbolic interactionist focus. We believe the interactionist perspective is important in a sociological social psychology text, and there are already many good readers that focus on symbolic interactionism. We wanted to emphasize both symbolic interaction and House's (1977; 1990) third "face" of social psychology (personality and social structure, psychological sociology or our preferred term, structural social psychology).

We found that classifying articles and chapters within even these broad groupings was not easy. As with any classification system, there will be some disagreement about placement. The field of social psychology is indeed rich and diverse. While psychological social psychology textbooks almost uniformly address a standard set of topics, there is no standard set of topics or theories within sociological social psychology. So, to a certain extent, this book represents only our view of the field.

About the Organization and Reading Selections

We have divided the book into five sections with no assumptions that they follow an agreed-upon progression of topics in sociological social psychology. Clearly some chapters draw from more than one theoretical tradition or cover more than one area and could arguably be placed in a different section. We rely on the good sense of instructors to decide first what their student learning goals and objectives are, and second how the course and the book can help students achieve them.

Section 1 The Sociology of Social Psychology

In 1977 **James S. House** wrote his landmark article on the three "faces" of social psychology. In this volume, we reprint an update of his article published in 1990. This article provides a bridge between his 1977 article and his presentation as recipient of the ASA/Social Psychology section's 2007 Cooley-Mead Award. (Unfortunately, we were not able to include that article as it was not available at the time we had to go to press.) In these articles he describes the landscape of social psychology which provides the structure for this volume. Students of social psychology and readers of House's work know that social psychology in psychology relies heavily on the experimental method to collect data. Symbolic Interaction has a long history within the sociology side of social psychology with its reliance on observation as a method. The final face of social psychology is social structure and personality. This perspective emphasizes how the social structure affects interpersonal behavior, attitudes, and outcomes. Social psychologists from this tradition usually gather data through surveys.

Marcie Goodman presents a short history of social psychology and the concepts central to the discipline. She demonstrates that social psychology has deep historical roots. While the field of social psychology itself is quite young, perhaps dating to only a century or so ago when academic disciplines in the social science were being formed, she shows that many earlier writers were thinking about what we now know as social psychology.

The third article in this section by **Carl Hovland** is a reprint of a classic article that describes methodological differences between the two major "faces" of the discipline. When it comes to attitude change, psychologically based social psychologies tend to rely on experimental design to show how attitudes can be changed while sociologically orientated social psychologies, particularly from the structural social psychological "face," tend to use surveys as the preferred research design to show the distribution of attitudes in the population and how they vary among different demographic groups.

Michael Shanahan, Scott M. Hofer, and **Stephen Vaisey** examine the relationship between social structural arrangements and biology. They show that biology and social arrangements interact to produce social outcomes and that social factors sometimes override "hard" genetic factors. While social scientists have long acknowledged that genetics plays a factor in human behavior, this research shows how structural arrangements in society also affect outcomes.

Finally **Jonathan Turner** presents a general theory of interpersonal processes. His sophisticated analysis, while focusing on interpersonal processes, integrates many of the perspectives that appear in more specific chapters later in the book. Instructors may want to return to this chapter after the students have had the opportunity to read the later chapters.

The later sections of this book are grouped to an extent based on their method, as well as their theoretical perspective. Thus, the essays in the section that we call **Experimental Social Psychology** are there primarily because they use experimentation as a method of data collection. As sociological social psychologists, however, the authors in this section draw their theories and perspectives from sociology.

Section 2 Experimental Social Psychology

Diane Felmlee draws on exchange theory in her chapter on fatal attractions. She examines how attributes of others that initially attract us may become tiresome. Later partners may find them bothersome enough that they terminate the relationship. Felmlee shows how these kinds of fatal attractions can occur in a variety of relationships.

Christine Horne's chapter on social norms is firmly grounded in the experimental tradition, but it also draws on sociological literature. She discusses the problems and approaches associated with studying norms and how social structure is associated with norm enforcement. She also presents her own experimental research on sanctioning and norms.

Section 3 Symbolic Interaction

Most sociology students will find this section on **Symbolic Interaction** reassuringly familiar. Symbolic Interaction is one of the principle theories used in essentially all introduction to sociology and social problems texts. Symbolic Interaction has a long and storied tradition within sociology. Its adherents date back to the 1920s and 1930s; this emphasis was especially strong at the University of Chicago and later at many other institutions. One of the central figures in symbolic interaction (sometimes simply referred to as SI theory or SI), was George Herbert Mead. One of the authors in this section, Bernie Meltzer, was a student of Mead's. Both George McCall (with J.L. Simmons) and Bernie Meltzer present some of their early work on symbolic interaction, reworked specifically for this volume.

George McCall and **J. L. Simmons** published what is now a classic work on symbolic interaction (McCall and Simmons, 1966). This chapter presents some of the work of a pioneer in the field of symbolic interaction—George Herbert Mead. Both McCall and Simmons and Meltzer emphasize the differences between human behavior and other primate behavior. Much of the difference is in intention. While animal behavior is reactive, human behavior is intentional-with thought. The "self" is critical for the interactionist with the self evolving out of human interaction.

For **Bernard N. Meltzer**, all group life is a matter of cooperative behavior that evolves out of consensus. Thus, ascertaining the intention of others' acts is critical. Gestures as well as spoken language are symbolic and must be interpreted. We also learn to respond to our own gestures and form a sense of self from our interactions with others. Meltzer also discusses the genesis of the self that occurs first in childhood. Those already familiar with symbolic interaction will also recognize Mead's conceptions of the "I," the "Me," and the development of the "Mind."

Lynn Smith-Lovin draws upon portions of her address as the 2006 Cooley-Mead Award winner to the social psychology section of the American Sociological Association (ASA) to present an ecological theory of how the self develops within social structure. She argues that we live in multiplex relationships, but that they are becoming increasingly segregated in modern society with different audiences and different selves being expressed in each network.

The chapter by **Robert Young** presents an updated example of research from the symbolic interaction tradition from his book *Understanding Misunderstandings.* In it, he argues that some common form of communication is required for human interaction and symbolic interactionists long have examined language, and gestures are part of the rich interaction that humans have. Young portrays some of the difficulties that can arise from misunderstandings and how we attempt to correct them.

Section 4 Socialization

While we include socialization as a separate section, the authors in this section draw from the symbolic interaction tradition, as well as other sociological theory. Socialization is the process by which individuals become aware of society, their relationships with others. It is also the process through which individuals acquire the norms, values, beliefs, roles, and general competency necessary to negotiate their way in society. Much socialization occurs in childhood, but it also continues throughout our lives as we change occupations and move into new spheres throughout our lives.

Gil Musolf summarizes much of the literature on childhood socialization and presents the major authors who have written on the topic. Musolf draws much of his research from the symbolic interaction perspective and also provides examples from international research.

Angela O'Rand and **Glen Elder** have updated their important work on socialization across the life span. Their chapter in this volume provides a broad perspective on the factors that influence individual's life courses. This includes historical factors, as well as ongoing events. Some of the factors are the changing age structure of society, changes in family formation and dissolution, changes in work careers, and even changes in health that allow individuals to live longer and healthier lives.

Finally, we present an example of socialization in a total institution by reprinting a chapter from **Gywnne Dyer**'s (1985) work on war. This chapter, originally written after the Vietnam War, focuses on the study of socialization in the military services. He illustrates how individuals leading ordinary lives can be turned into effective and efficient participants in the military services in a relatively short but intensive period of time.

Section 5 Social Structural Approaches to Social Psychology

The final section of the volume presents articles written primarily from the perspective of structural social psychology. These chapters focus on how social structure affects individuals in a multiplicity of ways. We include some articles on race and gender. While race and gender are not part of social structure per se, they are characteristics that affect members of society. They are master statuses or statuses that often override other statuses that individuals may occupy. Members of society treat males and females and members of racial and ethnic groups differently because of their ethnicity and gender. The authors of other chapters in this section portray the effects of social structure on emotions, health, and a variety of other outcomes.

The social psychologists whose works appear in this section use a variety of data sources, as well as theoretical perspectives. These include national surveys, but also intensive structured interviews. How social structure affects the lives of individuals has been apparent in many of the earlier chapters. Since sociologists focus on social structures, many of the chapters in other sections of this book could have been placed here as well. But the chapters here focus specifically on how microlevel interactions are affected by the larger social structures.

Roxanna Harlow focuses on race in the classroom, not race of the students but of the instructor. Utilizing recent work on the sociology of emotions, she presents substantial evidence that African American professors teaching at predominantly white universities often have to do more "emotion work" than white professors. White professors in the same universities seldom think about dynamics of their own race in the classroom. Harlow garners these conclusion using intensive interviews.

W. E. B. DuBois, a past president of the American Sociological Association (previously called the American Sociological Society), wrote this entry just over one-hundred years ago. In it he illustrates the double-consciousness that many minorities and African Americans in particular feel as a result of their status in American society. We present it here as a companion article to the Harlow chapter since both illustrate the persistence and difficulty that racism can present for minorities.

Phyllis Baker and **Martha Copp** also use intensive interviews, as well as teacher ratings, to examine the effects of Professor Baker's own role in the classroom when she becomes pregnant. Baker's role expectations while teaching feminist theory clearly change as a result of changing definitions. Several other authors in the book incorporate gender as an important factor in their analysis, but none address the changing expectations that pregnancy brings.

In her chapter on emotion, **Peggy A. Thoits** examines the social origins and functions of emotion norms. She illustrates how adults undergo emotional socialization and pressures in service and professional jobs. These processes are in turn used to sustain the social order.

Raechel Lizon and **Mikaela Dufur** use nationally representative data on adolescents to examine how participation in extracurricular activities affects students' popularity. They find that participation in exclusive activities generally reinforces popularity. Participation in activities that are not exclusive can actually decrease participants' popularity, however.

Bryan R. Johnson and **Cardell K. Jacobson** also utilize nationally representative poll data to examine white attitudes about interracial marriage. They argue that the social structure affects opportunities for interracial contact, which in turn affects support for interracial marriage. These social structural effects persist even when interracial friendship is taken into account

How we make attributions for success or errors is a traditional topic in psychological social psychology. In their chapter in this book **Jeannine Gailey** and **Matthew T. Lee** present work on how attributions are made in corporations and other complex organizations. Their chapter is a synthesis of literature from sociology, psychology and organizational studies on the attribution processes.

The concluding chapter is by **Catherine E. Ross** and **John Mirowsky** who are well known for their extensive writing and work on social structure and well-being. They provide a comprehensive review of how the social structure influences cognitions, emotions, and behaviors. Socioeconomic status, family status, and work relations prove to be critical factors here as they are in much of social life. They examine their influence on sense of control and well-being, and they examine factors the moderate potentially negative influences.

We are pleased with the breadth and soundness of the scholarship exhibited in each chapter in this volume. Much of the work is cutting edge, written by important scholars in the field. We trust that you will gain an appreciation of the richness and complexity of human interaction from your exposure to the sociological social psychology in this volume.

Acknowledgments

We thank those who have written chapters for this volume. We have learned much from each of the authors as we completed this book. Many of the contributors are well-established scholars who have been willing to summarize, rewrite, and update their work for us. Others are bright young scholars who are just now making their mark in the field. All have been professional and cooperative. All have been supportive and helpful, and we appreciate their making our deadlines. Finally we thank Jeff Lasser and the staff at Allyn Bacon for supporting this project.

References

Burke, Peter J. 2006. *Contemporary Social Psychological Theories*. Stanford, CA: Stanford University Press.

Cook, Karen S., Gary Alan Fine, and James S. House. 1995. *Sociological Perspectives in Social Psychology.* Boston: Allyn and Bacon.

Delamater, John. 2003. *Handbook of Social Psychology.* New York: Kluwer Academic/Plenum Publishers.

Dyer, Gwyne. 1985. *War*. New York: Crown Publishers.

House, James S. 1977. "The Three Faces of Social Psychology." *Sociometry* 40: 161–177.

House, James S. 1990. "The Nature of Social Psychology and Its Place in the Curriculum of Sociology and the Social and Natural Sciences." In Jeffrey Chin and Judith K. Little (Eds.), *The Introductory Social Psychology Course: Syllabi and Related Materials*, pp. 10–22. Washington, DC: American Sociological Association Teaching Resources Center.

McCall, George J., and J. L. Simmons. 1966. *Identities and Interactions*. New York: Free Press.

Rubin, Zick. 1973. *Liking and Loving*. New York: Holt Rinehart and Winston.

Young, Robert L. 1999. *Understanding Misunderstandings: A Guide to More Successful Human Interaction.* Austin: University of Texas Press.

About the Editors

Jeffrey Chin is a Carnegie National Scholar and Professor of Sociology at Le Moyne College in Syracuse, New York where he teaches courses on social psychology: Sociological Perspectives in Social Psychology and Group Dynamics and Interpersonal Communication. He was editor of the ASA/Teaching Resources Center's *Teaching Undergraduate Social Psychology*, 2e, (1991) and he has facilitated a number of ASA Teaching Workshops including "Teaching Social Psychology Courses." He served as Editor of *Teaching Sociology*, an official journal of the American Sociological Association from 1997–1999. He has published in *Teaching Sociology* and other ASA publications devoted to teaching and was lead editor for *Included in Sociology: Learning Climates that Cultivate Racial and Ethnic Diversity* (ASA/AAHE, 2002). He and Cardell have published together in *Perspectives on Social Problems* (2001), and *Research in the Social Scientific Study of Religion* (1999). He can be reached at:

Jeffrey Chin
Department of Sociology and Anthropology
Le Moyne College
1419 Salt Springs Rd.
Syracuse, NY 13214-1399
Email: chin@lemoyne.edu
Department's home page: http://www.lemoyne.edu/sociology anthropology/index.htm
Personal web page: http://web.lemoyne.edu/~chin.htm

Cardell Jacobson is Professor of Sociology at Brigham Young University where he teaches and does research on social psychology, race and ethnic relations and the sociology of religion. His recent research has examined factors that predict inter-group marriage in the United States and other countries. His interest in social psychology has long focused on how events, social change, and social structure affect attitudes. In recent years he published *All God's Children: Racial and Ethnic Voices in the LDS Church* (Bonneville Books, 2004), (with Tim B. Heaton and Stephen J. Bahr) *The Health, Wealth, and Social Life of Mormons* (Mellen Press, 2004), and *Revisiting Thomas F. O'Dea's The Mormons: Contemporary Perspectives* (University of Utah Press, 2008). He can be reached at:

Cardell Jacobson
Department of Sociology
Brigham Young University
Provo, UT 84602
Phone: 801-422-2105
Email: Cardell_Jacobson@byu.edu
On the Department Website: http://sociology.byu.edu/fac/JacobsonC.html

Section I

The Sociology of Social Psychology

1

*The Nature of Social Psychology and Its Place in the Curriculum of Sociology and the Social and Natural Sciences**

James S. House
The University of Michigan

It is both a pleasure and a challenge to introduce this second edition of "The Introductory Social Psychology Course: Syllabi and Related Materials," which has been from its inception in 1984 a joint venture of the ASA Teaching Resources Center and the ASA Section on Social Psychology. The study of social psychology as an undergraduate first attracted me to social science, and then to graduate work in the interdisciplinary social psychology program at the University of Michigan. Forced to choose on taking my first job between the "two social psychologies" (Stryker 1977; Stephan and Stephan 1986 & 1991), I became and remain a sociological social psychologist of the "social structure and personality" variety (about which more below). The perspective, theories, and methods of social psychology have shaped all of my teaching research, and professional work. Thus, I am pleased to contribute to an enterprise which seeks to improve the teaching of social psychology and hence its ability to impact the life and work of others as it has mine.

Having recently spent much more time on research and administration than I ever envisioned on entering academia, it is also a pleasure to affirm the central value that teaching has had for me, and must have for social psychology and the social sciences if they are to continue to prosper. Teaching in all its forms is the process which attracts, develops, and

*I am grateful to Jeylan Mortimer and Howard Schuman for comments on a prior draft, and to Marie Klatt and Sue Meyer for assistance in preparation of the manuscript.

sustains practitioners of our disciplines. It also diffuses knowledge and appreciation of these disciplines into the larger society. Finally, good teaching involves creative thought on the part of the teacher as well as the student, and thus informs and enhances the scholarly and other professional work of the teacher as well as the student. My own thinking and writing on the nature of social psychology (e.g., House 1977 and 1981) has grown out of my teaching of it, particularly my attempt to articulate how the kind of social psychology which has been most interesting and focal for me relates to the larger field of social psychology and its parent disciplines of psychology and sociology. In all of these ways, what and how we teach is central to the development of any discipline.

It is also a challenge for me to write about current nature or state of social psychology, at least as a teaching enterprise, since I have not taught social psychology to undergraduates for some time. I have regularly taught basic sociological social psychology to graduate students, however, and maintained a continuing interest in the nature and state of social psychology as a field and its relations to psychology, sociology and the other social sciences (House 1977; 1981; 1991). I will not presume to offer guidance on specific texts, activities, or methods of teaching undergraduate social psychology. Rather, I would like to suggest from several perspectives how and why social psychology is fundamentally important to education at both the undergraduate and graduate levels: (1) the perspective of any curriculum of study of human behavior and social life; (2) the perspective of the disciplines of psychology and especially sociology; (3) the perspective of an individual student and (4) the perspective of our larger society. In the process, I will draw some general implications for teaching and research in social psychology.

My basic argument is that social psychology is an interdisciplinary field formed by the intersection of two of the three basic sciences of human behavior and social life—psychology and sociology.[1] As such, social psychology is a broad and basic foundation subfield within the disciplines of psychology *and* sociology. Because it offers the most unified perspective available for understanding human behavior and social life, a social psychological perspective is essential to understanding the phenomena and problems of individual and social life. Thus, social psychology deserves to be at the center of undergraduate liberal education, as well as more concentrated undergraduate or graduate education in sociology, psychology and the other social sciences. The study of social psychology could and should also be more closely articulated with the study of biology which is the third basic science of human behavior and social life.

Some of my discussion of the nature of social psychology and its place in educational curricula will be general and abstract. What must not be lost sight of, however, is that the ultimate justification and utility of social psychology (or any social science) as a field of study and inquiry is its ability to enhance our insight into and understanding of concrete and consequential individual and social phenomena or problems. Thus, social psychology courses must attempt to bring the general theoretical and methodological tools of the field to bear on such meaningful and important phenomena or problems, and suggest how and why these phenomena can only be properly and fully understood from a social psychological perspective.

[1]As is already evident, I do believe unabashedly that social psychology is one of the social *sciences*. I also believe that conceptual and theoretical work in science is a creative process, influenced by values and intuition as well as logic and empirical analysis. Similarly the empirical methods of science are broad, ranging from qualitative and clinical observation or interviewing to highly quantified measurement and analysis.

In sum, the study of social psychology should be *broad* and *integrative* in its overall theoretical and methodological framework, but also problem-focused in its substantive content. This is true for research and scholarship as well as for teaching. It is the ability to identify and understand, and sometimes even solve, socially and scientifically important problems which makes social psychology, or any field, vital, interesting, and valuable. Breadth of theoretical and methodological perspective is important because it facilitates effective identification and understanding or solution of important problems.

The Central Place of Social Psychology in Sociology, Psychology and the (Biopsycho) Social Sciences

As Sewell (1989) and Cartwright (1979) have argued, the 1930s, 1940s, 1950s, and 1960s were generally halcyon decades for social science, especially social psychology and other interdisciplinary social science. The growth and progress of that period was, however, never fully institutionalized, and the decades of the 1970s and 1980s witnessed increasing uncertainty and skepticism about the nature or utility of social science within the fields themselves and within the larger academy and society. This has been especially true for the newest of these fields, including sociology and social psychology. The sources and solutions of these problems of the disciplines are broader than this essay, and progress is being made (see House 1991). What and how we teach, must, however, constitute part of both our problems and their solutions.

A number of the social forces that contributed to the growth and development of social psychology and related social sciences in the halcyon decades are reemerging as we enter the last decade of the twentieth century. These include growing populations of students in primary and secondary schools, and soon in colleges and universities as well; increased interest in the social sciences among students; and increased concern with the social bases and potential social solutions of a wide range of personal and social problems. We have yet to see the increases in resources for teaching and research which accompanied similar trends in the 1950s and 1960s, though we are seeing a growing call for support for graduate education in social sciences (Bowen and Sosa 1989) in anticipation of a potential shortage of college and university faculty in these fields. It is thus an opportune time for social psychology and the social sciences to consider how they might capitalize on potential new opportunities to advance their fields in terms of teaching, research, and applications.

Among the problems confronting social psychology, as well as sociology and much of the social sciences today, is the lack of a coherent and reasonably consensual *curriculum* at both the graduate and undergraduate levels. Students, and hence ultimately faculty, in the same field and even the same department, often do not share a core of educational experience or a common sense of the field or its relation to other fields. The variety of the syllabi in this volume reflect the current diversity of views on the nature of social psychology. This complaint has been raised about education more generally, at least in the United States in recent years, and the proposed solution is often a return to education as it was before the 1950s or 1960s.

I doubt the validity of this general diagnosis and proposed solution, especially for the social sciences. What we have as curricula in sociology, social psychology, and much of the social sciences are largely products of the relatively recent emergence, and great post–World War II growth, of these disciplines. It is not surprising that sharply defined and consensual curricula did not emerge in the social sciences in this period. The general trends in education were toward increasing variety and flexibility in curricula. The social sciences were also growing rapidly, and often focused more heavily on issues of graduate education and research than on developing undergraduate programs and curricula. Thus, the social sciences tend to be at this point less organized and coherent curricularly than those fields which have a much longer history of existence as distinct academic fields. We need to solve our curricular problems in the here and now, though with proper cognizance and reverence for our origins.

Social psychology, and teachers and students of it, stand especially to gain from increased efforts to delineate the nature and intellectual and curricular structure of social psychology, its parent disciplines of sociology and psychology, and the social sciences more generally. Despite its many inherent virtues, social psychology has suffered from internal fractionation (House 1977; Stryker 1977) and from dangers of increasing marginality or dissipation in relation to its parent disciplines of sociology and psychology (Liska 1977; Steiner 1986; Stryker 1989). Yet social psychology is arguably the queen of the social sciences, coming closest to approximating the true "final science" which Auguste Comte sought to create toward the end of his life (Allport 1968:670) and which remains an appropriate goal—a combination of sociology, psychology and biology. More clearly articulating the full nature of social psychology and its central place in the intellectual structure of the social sciences, and the emerging biopsychosocial sciences, should enhance the quality of education and scholarship in social psychology and its centrality to any coherent curriculum in sociology (as well as psychology or the social sciences).

The Structure of the Social Sciences (in Relation to Natural Sciences and Humanities)

In contrast to the natural sciences, and to the lesser degree the humanities, the social sciences are, as suggested above, younger and less coherent both as individual disciplines and as a set. No one would dispute that physics, chemistry, and biology are the core natural sciences, with other fields being largely defined by the intersections of these three (e.g., physical chemistry, biochemistry, biophysics) or by their application to particular more molar phenomenon (e.g., geology, astronomy, or physiology, which are often subdivided into more physical, chemical, or biological subfields). The structure of the humanities is not quite so clear and consensual, but the foci are certainly language and literature, philosophy, art and music, and history. Again other humanities fields are largely defined as intersections of these fields (e.g., history of art) or particular national, ethnic, regional or chronological foci (e.g., classics, various area studies, medieval studies, Afro-American studies, etc.).

These conceptions of core disciplines have long histories and are reflected in the institutional and intellectual structure of education and inquiry at all levels. The *core* or basic natural science and humanities fields are almost always represented in the organizational and curricular structure of education at all levels, while those disciplines defined by the intersection of these core fields or their application to particular phenomena will be variably and selectively represented and organized. Because one can count on the presence of these core disciplines, and on their having certain inherent intradisciplinary structure, it is possible for training in one discipline to be coordinated with or presuppose training in others. This curricular structure is most evident in the natural sciences.

The situation is very different in the social or behavioral sciences, which have been recognized as distinctive fields of study only within the last two centuries, and mainly in this century and even past half century. There is much less consensus as to the nature and structure of the social sciences as a whole, as individual disciplines, and in relation to the humanities and natural sciences. Beyond history, which is sometimes classed with the social sciences and sometimes with the humanities, no social science disciplines are necessarily and certainly included in educational curricula at any level, and until recently the major disciplines represented at the post-secondary level (anthropology, economics, political science, psychology, and sociology) were seldom represented as such in elementary, secondary curricula, and are still somewhat haphazardly included. Even at the post-secondary levels, the organization and structure of the social sciences as disciplines and as a whole are more variable than is true in the natural sciences and humanities.

Economics and political science are probably the most senior and visible of the social sciences, based on their respective foci on central phenomena of social life—the economy and the polity. By virtue of its age and its possession of a basic monetary metric, economics is also the most internally coherent and paradigmatic of the social sciences. Yet I would argue that from a purely analytic perspective there are *two basic social sciences* of human behavior and social life—psychology and sociology—just as physics and chemistry are the basic natural sciences. Linking the natural and the social sciences is *biology*, which has as its focus the emergent phenomenon of life itself—nonhuman as well as human.

Figure 1.1 provides a schematic diagram of how these five basic sciences of nature and life—physics, chemistry, biology, psychology and sociology—interrelate, and the central place of social psychology in this scheme. Social psychology is properly conceived of as the intersection of sociology and psychology. The intersection of social psychology with biology produces Comte's "final science"—here termed biopsychosocial science—which is the comprehensive science of human behavior and social life. Thus, social psychology and biopsychosocial science are, just as Comte argued, at the pinnacle of the sciences when they are ordered in terms of their focus on the most elemental (physics) to the most molar (sociology) aspects of the natural and human world.

The Central Place of Social Psychology in Sociology and the Social Sciences

This conception of the structure of the social (and natural) sciences suggests several things about the nature and teaching of social psychology. First, social psychology is one of the basic subfields of each of its parent disciplines. Within sociology I would argue that there are three basic meta-theoretical paradigms and approaches to which all students of sociology should be exposed—(1) the organizational or structural, (2) the social psychological, and (3) the demographic. The first embodies what is unique to sociology as a discipline—its focus on the emergent organizational or structural properties of the interdependent behavior of human beings. Such structural properties emerge from and then constrain or influence the behavior of individuals, and this behavior is also influenced by psychological and biological forces. Social psychology is the

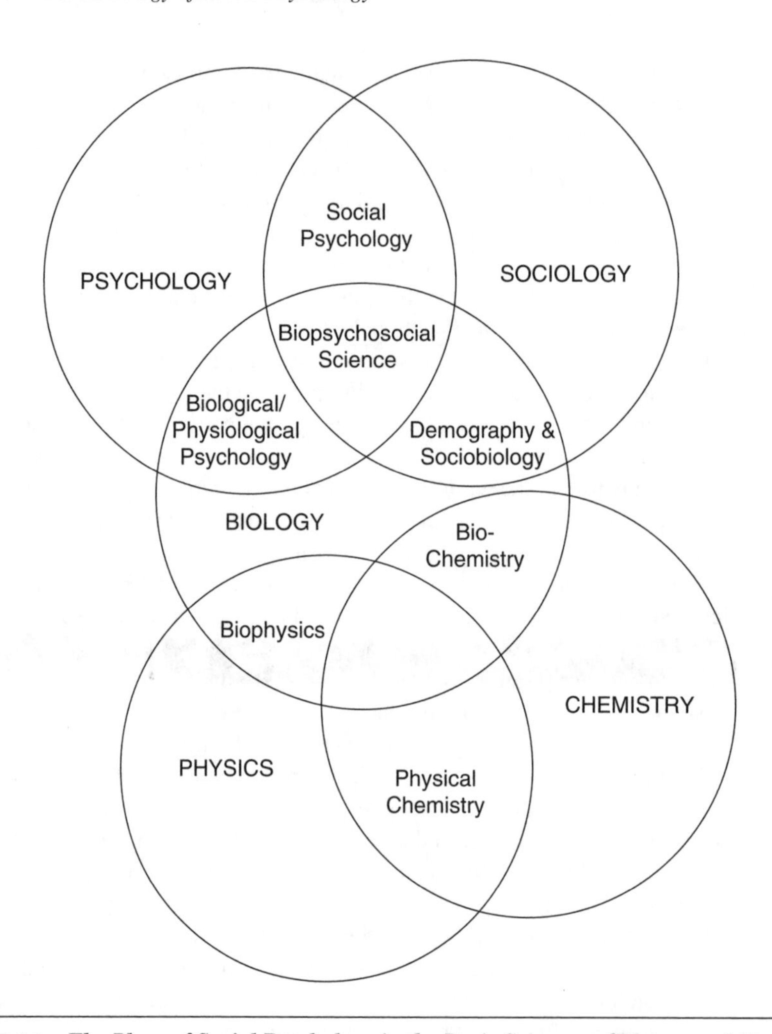

FIGURE 1.1 ***The Place of Social Psychology in the Basic Sciences of Nature and Humanity***

broad subfield of sociology which attends to and makes manifest the way in which organizational and structural phenomena influences and are influenced by psychological variables and processes. Demography (and more recently sociobiology) has similarly attended to and made manifest the ways in which social forces influence and are influenced by biological variables and processes (e.g., fertility and mortality). The study of any social phenomenon, institution or process (e.g., the family, race and ethnicity, work and organizations, social stratification, etc.) can and has been addressed from each of these perspectives, and major paradigmatic shifts in each of these areas usually reflect the increasing dominion of one perspective—witness the shifts over time in the study of that most sociological of topics, organizations, from more structural to more social psychological to current more demographic approaches.

Thus, I would argue that training in social psychology must be part of any curriculum in sociology, and should be required as a part of the training of any concentrator or specialist in sociology. That this is not self-evident to many sociologists is well-known, at least to social psychologists, and was manifested again recently in the self-conscious neglect of social psychology in the new *Handbook of Sociology* (Smelser 1988:17). Yet, any tendency to marginalize or dissipate social psychology within the curriculum of sociology is a tendency to weaken the core foundations of the field. The recent revival of interest in micro-macro linkages in sociology attests to the centrality of social psychology to the field of sociology (e.g., Alexander et al. 1987), though this is not yet recognized by either social psychologists or analysts of micro-macro relations (House and Mortimer, 1990). Social psychology is, of course, equally central to the field of psychology.

Social psychology is not only a component of each discipline, it is also an interdisciplinary field. Thus, one cannot (or at least should not) either study or teach social psychology without also studying and interrelating basic aspects of sociology and psychology.[2] This means that any social psychology course should be interdisciplinary in content and concerns, though a social psychology course in sociology ought to emphasize the distinctively sociological aspects of the field.

Finally, the conception developed here suggests that the study of social psychology, and its parent disciplines, must increasingly attempt to interact with biology, the third basic science of human behavior and social life. Social psychology courses provide a good avenue for at least beginning this process, if only in a limited way. Social psychology provides a context in which it should be evident that the understanding of human behavior and social life can never be reduced to one or the other of these disciplines, but rather will increasingly require the articulation of all three (see the syllabus of Doby for ideas on points of articulation with biology, though I would not advocate such a thoroughgoing biological or biopsychosocial orientation).[3]

The Nature of Social Psychology

The Three Faces of Social Psychology

By its very nature, the study of social psychology should be a unifying experience in which students bring the insights of at least two disciplines (sociology and psychology) and perhaps others (biology, anthropology, economics, and political science) to bear on understanding consequential phenomena of individual behavior and social life. I and others, however, have argued that over the last half-century social psychology has experienced the same tendencies toward fractionation and specialization which have characterized much of the social sciences and other disciplines as well. Stryker (1977) and others (e.g., Stephan and Stephan 1991) have depicted the division between sociological and psychological social psychology. I have argued further that there are two distinct variants of sociological social psychology—symbolic interactionism and the study of social structure and personality—and hence a total of three major branches or faces of social psychology as shown in Figure 1.2 (House 1977).

[2]Since social psychology is a core part of each discipline, it also follows that one cannot or should not study either sociology or psychology without studying the other. One cannot study any of the natural sciences in depth at the post secondary level without also studying at least the basic of the others. That the same is not true in the social sciences is a sign of their immaturity.

[3]Intersecting with biology provides a nonhuman baseline or comparison point for social psychology. Jeylan Mortimer (personal communication) correctly suggests that it is also important to use cross-cultural and cross-national comparisons to understand the full variability of social psychological phenomena, and to avoid tendencies to view necessarily as universal what we observe in our own society.

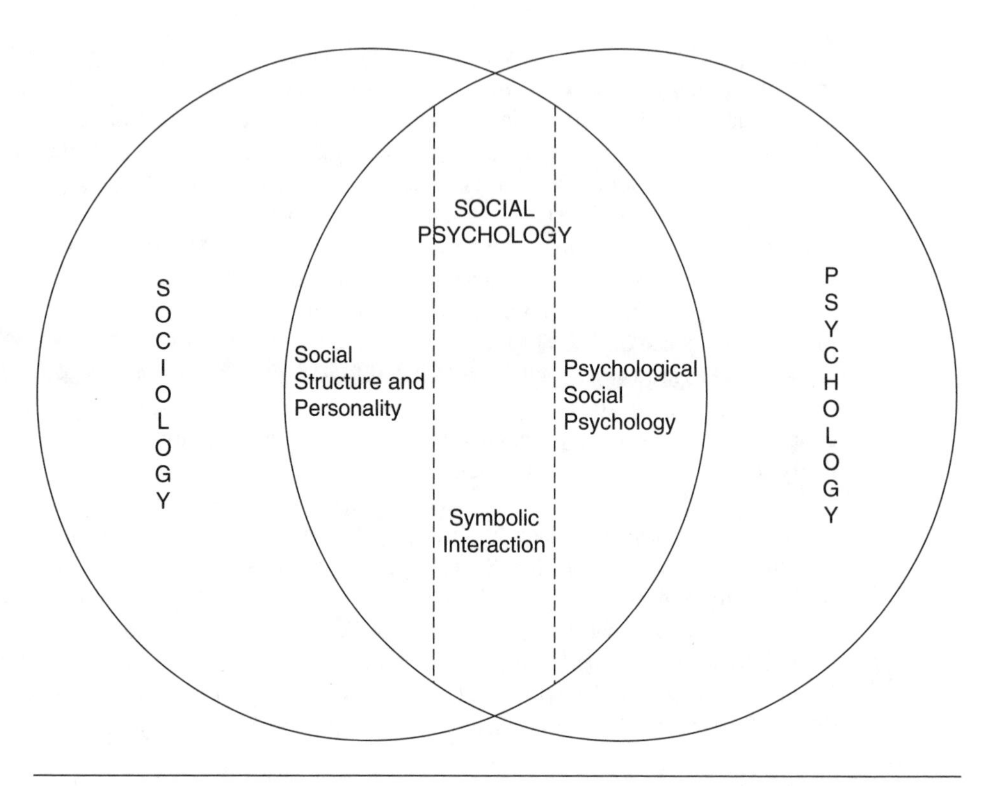

FIGURE 1.2 ***Social Psychology as the Intersection of Sociology and Psychology***

Psychological social psychology focuses on how a broad array of properties of individuals are influenced by any social stimuli, usually the actual or implied presence or action of one or a few individuals (cf. Allport 1968:3; Jones and Gerard 1967). Thus, as indicated in Figure 1.2 its concerns lie close to the center of psychology, as does its emphasis on experimental method. Analogously, the concerns of the *social structure and personality* face of sociological social psychology focus on the relation of macroscopic properties of social organization (e.g., "class," "modernization," "urbanicity," etc.) to a limited range of individual attributes, using largely survey methods, thus lying close to the center of the discipline of sociology in terms of both substance and methods (again, see Figure 1.2). With its focus on studying social interaction and the microscopic properties of social situations using largely qualitative observational methods, *symbolic interactionism* is more on the fringe of both sociology and psychology.

Sociological Social Psychology

No single course in social psychology can adequately cover all three faces. Any course should, however, cover at least the basic substantial and methodological aspects of each face, and clearly locate itself in relation to these three faces. (The syllabi of Chin, Kearl, Mortimer, and Rothenberg are among the most balanced in this regard.) Social psychology courses in sociology should place greater emphasis on the sociological faces, thus balancing the more psychological emphasis of social psychology courses in psychology. There is an established tradition of courses and texts in sociology in the symbolic interactionist tradition, some represented in this collection of syllabi (e.g., those of Holstein and Miller, O'Brien, and Stimson). Teaching from the tradition of social structure and personality will require a more personalized organization of the course and readings by the instructor, although a number of text-readers have appeared in this tradition (e.g., Stoodley 1962; Smelser and Smelser 1970) and general discussions of the tradition can also be helpful (Inkeles 1959; House 1977; 1981).

I believe the most important contribution that a sociological social psychology course can make is to elucidate the reciprocal relation between macro social structures and individual thought, feeling and behavior. This is the focus which Comte (quoted in Allport 1968:9) posed for his "true final science":

> "How can the individual be both a cause and a consequence of society? That is to say: How can his nature depend indisputably upon the prior existence of cultural designs and upon his role in a predetermined social structure while at the same time he is clearly a unique person, both selecting and rejecting influences from his cultural surrounding, and in turn creating new cultural forms for the guidance of future generations?"

This focus is important because it reminds students of sociology that social structures and culture (see House 1981 for definitions of social structure vs. culture) are after all only the emergent outcome of patterns of individual thought, feeling and behavior; yet these structures then powerfully shape individual thought, feeling and behavior. It reminds psychologists, including psychological social psychologists, that individuals think, feel, and behave not only in the context of immediate social stimuli, but also in the context of a larger structure of social relationships.

In sum, a basic course in social psychology should introduce students to the basic substance *and* methods of all three faces of social psychology, though any course, reflecting the interests and aptitudes of its instructor, will emphasize certain of these faces more than others. Within sociology the emphasis should be particularly on the unique contribution of sociology to social psychology—the nature of macrosocial structures and their reciprocal relations with both microsocial structures or processes and individual thought, feeling, and behavior.

A Focus on Consequential Social Phenomena

The utility of a more unified approach to social psychology and social science, the complementary value of the three faces of social psychology, and the importance of considering macrosocial phenomena in social psychology can best be demonstrated by focusing the course on a variety of consequential social phenomena, each of which can be understood and illuminated by a social psychological perspective. This may be achieved in a number of different ways, or combinations thereof. One approach is to identify a set of generic social phenomena and theories with which social psychology is concerned, (e.g., exchange, attribution, influence and conformity, altruism, self-justification, attraction, etc.)—an approach commonly taken in more psychologically-oriented social psychology courses and texts (e.g., texts by Aronson 1984; Brown, 1986; Michener et al. 1986 and syllabi which use them). A second approach, characteristic of many symbolic interactionist courses and texts is essentially to follow the process of individual development from a neonate through childhood development and socialization to adulthood, and the parallel processes of increasing social interaction and engagement. A third approach is to identify more macrosocial phenomena and problems (e.g., racial-ethnic prejudice and inequality; sex and gender differences and inequality; other socioeconomic stratification and inequality; health and illness; urban life; crime and deviance; etc.) and to show how social psychology can help to understand these phenomena. These different strategies can be and often are mixed in the syllabi and texts presented in this collection.

Both instructors and students will differ on which issues or phenomena engage them most. Instructors must opt for those things that engage them most and about which they can be more engaging. At the same time, they should try to include a range of topics so as to engage a wider variety of students. I and many others were personally engaged during the 1950s and 1960s by social psychology's contribution to understanding phenomena such as prejudice and discrimination, crime and deviance, the commission of crimes of obedience, social stratification, political behavior (from voting to social movements), and the vicissitudes of urban life. I was also intrigued by what social psychology could not then explain, but might be able to. In graduate school I discovered that social psychology could illuminate a whole range of issues I had previously relegated to the domain of biomedical science—problems of health and illness, physical as well as psychological.

Many of these topics remain currently important, though we understand and deal with them differently than we once did. To them have been added major issues of sex and gender, the operation of the legal system, and others. I believe social psychology and social science prosper most as both teaching enterprises and scientific disciplines when they directly engage and focus on "*understanding, explaining, and predicting specific social phenomena or problems* . . . having some *ultimate applied values*" (House 1990). Stanley Schacter has given a similar prescription for doing high quality and innovative social psychology.

> . . . if I were forced to give advice, I'd say get problem-oriented, follow your nose and go where the problems lead you. Then if something opens up that's interesting and that requires techniques and knowledge with which you're unfamiliar, learn them. (Quoted in Evans 1976:168)

Again, teaching and research are more complementary endeavors than is often assumed.

I have argued elsewhere (House in press) that we have seen over the last decade an increasing focus in social psychology on such problem-focused research, and this has tended to counteract the fractionation and malaise which was so evident in the 1970s, thus increasing the unity, vitality and strength of the field (see also House 1977, for some earlier discussion of potential focal problems or phenomena). This is reflected also in the kinds of syllabi and texts which have increasingly characterized teaching of social psychology in the 1980s, as can be seen in this volume.

The reemergence of a stronger sense of problem-focus, then, represents a major avenue through which both teaching and research in social psychology have been, and can continue to be, strengthened. We must recognize that focusing on issues and problems of great personal and social relevance can be difficult and complicated, especially if and when these issues and problems are especially politically and emotionally charged. It should also be recognized, however, that teaching and research in social science (or really any field) can never be completely divorced from issues of social and personal values. Handled sensitively, research and teaching that illuminate significant personal and social issues and problems remain the best way to demonstrate the utility and relevance of social psychology for liberal education, for the parent disciplines of sociology and psychology, for the broader biopsychosocial sciences, and for both individuals and society. In this way, good teaching is ultimately as crucial as good research to advancement of any academic or scientific discipline or field.

References

Alexander, Jeffrey C., Bernhard Giesen, Richard Munch, and Neil J. Smelser. 1987. *The Micro-Macro Link.* Berkeley: University of California Press.

Allport, Gordon. 1968. The Historical Background of Modern Social Psychology. In *Handbook of Social Psychology*, 2nd ed., Vol. 1, edited by G. Lindzey and E. Aronson. Reading, MA: Addison-Wesley.

Aronson, Elliot. 1984. *The Social Animal*, 4th Ed. San Francisco: W. H. Freeman.

Bowen, William G. and Julie Ann Sosa. 1989. *Prospects for Faculty in the Arts and Sciences*. Princeton, NJ: Princeton University Press.

Brown, Roger. 1986. *Social Psychology*, 2nd Ed. New York: Free Press.

Cartwright, Dorwin. 1979. Contemporary Social Psychology in Historical Perspective. *Social Psychology Quarterly* 42:82–93.

Evans, R. I. 1976. *The Making of Social Psychology: Discussions with Creative Contributors*. New York: Knopf.

House, James S. 1977. The Three Faces of Social Psychology. *Sociometry* 40:161–177.

———. 1981. *Work Stress and Social Support*. Reading, MA: Addison-Wesley.

———. 1991. Sociology, Psychology and Social Psychology (and Social Science). *The Future of Social Psychology*, edited by Thomas Pettigrew, Cookie White Stephan, and Walter Stephan. New York: Springer-Verlag, pp. 45–60.

House, James S. and Jeylan Mortimer. 1990. Social Structure and the Individual: Emerging Themes and New Directions. To appear in a Special Issue of the *Social Psychology Quarterly* 53(2), June 1990.

Inkeles, Alex. 1959. Personality and Social Structure. Pp. 525–571 in *Sociology Today*, edited by R. K. Merton, L. Broom and L. Cottrell.

Jones, Edward E. and Harold B. Gerard. 1967. *Foundations of Social Psychology*. New York: Wiley.

Liska, Alan E. 1977. The Dissipation of Sociological Social Psychology. *American Sociologist* 12:2–8.

Michener, H. Andrew, John Delamater, and Shalom Schwartz. 1986. *Social Psychology*. San Diego: Harcourt Brace.

Sewell, W. H. 1989. Some Reflections in the Golden Age of Interdisciplinary Social Psychology. *Annual Review of Sociology* 15:1–16.

Smelser, Neil J. (ed.). 1988. *The Handbook of Sociology*. Newbury Park, CA: Sage.

Smelser, Neil J. and William T. Smelser. 1970. *Personality and Social Systems*, 2nd Ed. New York: Wiley.

Steiner, I. D. 1986. Paradigms and Groups. Pp. 251–289 in *Advances in Experimental Social Psychology*, Vol. 19, edited by L. Berkowitz. Orlando, FL: Academic Press.

Stephan, Cookie White and Walter G. Stephan. 1986. *Two Social Psychologies: An Integrative Approach.* Homewood, IL: The Dorsey Press.

———. 1991. *The Future of Social Psychology.* New York: Springer-Verlag.

Stoodley, Bartlett H. 1962. *Society and Self: A Reader in Social Psychology*. New York: The Free Press.

Stryker, Sheldon. 1977. Developments in "Two Social Psychologies": Toward an Appreciation of Mutual Relevance. *Sociometry* 40(2):145–160.

———. 1989. The Two Psychologies: Additional Thoughts. *Social Forces* 68:45–54.

2

Once upon a Time in Social Psychology: A Short History

Marcie N. Goodman

Weber State University

Once upon a time the human story of social psychology began in antiquity. One may find revealing evidence of social psychology when viewing primitive cave drawings, tracing hieroglyphics, pondering Plato's *Republic*, or simply reading the Quran. As long as people have lived together they have wondered about everyday activities in social groups as demonstrated through love, persuasion, power, jealousy, attitudes, games, aggression, imitation, emotion, authority, deviance, and countless other common experiences. Seneca, Shakespeare, or Sun Tzu may not have termed their favorite subject as social psychology, but their inquisitiveness about the how and why of life were the fodder for noteworthy literature throughout ages and across cultures. Long after the advent of the Enlightenment, when scientism came to rule the nomenclature of psychology and sociology, ordinary folk continued to examine the dynamics of their daily doings among one another, as we do at this time. Undergraduates today enjoy social psychology because they are already familiar with its general concepts before opening a textbook. Students possess this acquaintance from a lifetime of absorbing social information on how people relate to one another from such nonacademic sources as Aunt Helen, Hollywood, or Harry Potter.

First and foremost, the narrative of social psychology is a record that is written upon the pages of all humankind, including those most humble or illiterate, as well as the erudite few who conduct the experiments or officially name the processes. Each of us breathes and moves within a world of people, whether or not we wish to learn the more formal terminology about those activities. So, as we embark on a brief overview of this scientific discipline,

Author's note: While many excellent sources are available on the history of social psychology, three volumes have been of particular help in this endeavor and are highly recommended to those wishing a more detailed or in-depth analysis than can be provided in this article: 1) *Currents of Thought in American Social Psychology* (1991) by Gary Collier, Henry Minton and Graham Reynolds; 2) *Social Psychology, Past and Present: An Integrative Orientation* (1988) by Jay Jackson; and 3) *The Roots of Modern Social Psychology: 1872–1954* (1996) by Robert Farr.

keep in mind that you are part of the social world, and are already acquainted with many concepts from social psychology. When relating this story, if I have erred in reducing complex issues too severely or oversimplifying too drastically, interested parties may find sources at the conclusion of this article leading them to more thorough expositions. With this in mind, please settle down in a comfortable chair and let me tell you a tale of how and why the fascinating subject of social psychology became what we study today.

Early Influences in Europe and England

Wilhelm Wundt

Academic histories are often considered so dry and boring that university librarians serve large pitchers of water to patrons perusing such documents. Wilhelm Wundt, however, lived in a German intellectual world of the nineteenth century that was anything but dull. At the time scholars throughout Europe and Britain were competing to establish intellectual preeminence. Wundt dedicated his time to *experimentalism* (Jackson 1988) and became a central figure of early social psychology. Many students today are competent using the *scientific method*, but Wundt was a real innovator in this emerging field (Danzinger 1985). He set up the world's first experimental psychological laboratory in Leipzig in 1879 (Pepitone 1976, 1981). He asserted that the natural and social worlds were one and the same in spite of rather spirited opposition to these ideas (Farr 1996). In his mind psychology was merely an indicator or extension of the natural world, impacting social and linguistic aspects. According to Danziger (1985), Wundt was "the first German writer to present a comprehensive treatment of social psychology," and his work was highly prominent "in the development of the social sciences at the turn of the century, especially cultural anthropology, sociology and linguistics" (Farr 1983). Wundt's ideas influenced some of Europe's most recognized figures, including Sigmund Freud, who also intermingled his focus between groups and individuals—a hallmark of social psychology. Freud endeavored to understand behavior, personality, motivation, emotion, gender, and group dynamics, to name a few (Freud 1953). Freud is often better remembered in social psychology than Wundt (an interesting historical irony), in spite of the latter's importance to a number of key theorists of this age, including the preeminent sociologist Emile Durkheim.

Emile Durkheim

Durkheim visited several German universities during the height of his career in 1885–1886. The early theorist "used Wundt's distinction between experimental and social psychology as the basis for his claim that sociology could not be explained in psychological terms" (Collier et al. 1991). Durkheim's most noted biographer, Lukes (1973) contends that the French thinker greatly admired Wundt's experimental work in psychology, with its concentration on "precise and restricted" problems (Lukes 1973). France, like Germany, was socially and politically unstable at the time. Durkheim responded to this chaos by thoroughly exploring a number of pivotal subjects such as religion, suicide, the *group mind* (or *collective representations*), social influences, norms (and *normlessness*, or *anomie*), and the social construction of symbols.

AUGUSTE COMTE

Another Frenchman, Auguste Comte, preceded Durkheim and is the first theorist to use the term *sociology.* Comte advocated a scientific or *positivist* base for understanding knowledge, history, and how people behave in social settings. Compte also provided insights into society through objective experience and observation. Gordon Allport, a modern American scholar, noted that: "if it were possible to designate a single deliberate 'founder' of social psychology as a science we should have to nominate Comte for this honor" (1954). In addition to Comte and Durkheim, several other French thinkers of the period made vital contributions, most notably Le Bon and Widener (1979) and Tarde (1969). Concurrently, academics in England worked in complimentary areas of inquiry as impressive amounts of social psychology developed in France and Germany.

Early Influences in England

England's growth and challenges resulting from the industrial revolution and subsequent urbanization spawned its own brand of social ideas by the end of the nineteenth century. Collier (1991) concludes that: "British social theory was based on Charles Darwin's theory of evolution." One might be curious how ideas from a preeminent biologist influenced social analysis, but Darwin's work on human (and animal) instincts and survival profoundly impacted a number of English academics, especially in the areas of social evolution, *laissez-faire,* and *utilitarianism.* "Even in social psychology it would require a volume to trace all of the varied effects of his doctrine of natural selection, survival, and evolution of species, and his theory of emotional expression and recognition" (Jackson 1988). Herbert Spencer also accentuated the connections between biology and society. He developed several highly controversial ideas concerning "evolution as the master societal process" (Turner et al. 2007), and actually coined the phrase, "survival of the fittest," that is often erroneously attributed to Darwin. Spencer's ability to recognize that individual self-interest and competition functioned within a larger societal realm may be his most enduring contribution to social psychology. He saw that weaker persons within the group were frequently eliminated or marginalized, either economically or socially. Along with Spencer and Darwin, the important ideas of Galton (Bulmer 2003) and McDougall (1908) added to the British pantheon of thought around the turn of the last century. With European and English social psychology in place by the 1860s, those from across the pond soon added to the budding field of inquiry.

Early Influences in America

The Civil War took a terrible toll on the United States, but in the decades that followed, universities began to focus on the business at hand: teaching a new cadre of students about an increasingly complex world. The industrial revolution sweeping England and Europe was also in full force in America. New ideas and inventions seemed to be springing up almost overnight. The monumental *second wave* of immigration through ports like Ellis Island brought a host of people from many distant lands, languages, and cultures to create their own brand of the American dream. Indigenous social observers soon made their mark in theoretical circles. In fact, as the new century dawned, eight key figures substantially contributed to the newly ploughed ground of social psychology:

- *James M. Baldwin* After graduating from Princeton and studying with Wundt in Leipzig, Baldwin turned to *developmental* social psychology. Strongly influenced by Gabriel Tarde, Baldwin focused on imitation, invention, and how the self develops through social interaction. Taking cues from Darwin, Baldwin felt humans differed from animals in their ability to learn from social contact and from self-consciousness. Baldwin cofounded the American Psychological Association and was very highly regarded during his time (Broughton & Freeman-Moir 1982).
- *Charles H. Cooley* A product of the University of Michigan in sociology and economics, Cooley began making an impact on sociology with three primary ideas: 1) general social theory; 2) differences between primary and secondary groups; and 3) the social or *looking-glass* self. He believed that children learn about themselves through envisioning how others view them. He is frequently seen as a social commentator as well as a theorist and sometimes became embroiled in criticisms of urban life, community disintegration, and social malaise (Jacobs 2006).
- *Charles S. Peirce* Receiving numerous degrees from Harvard in mathematics and chemistry, Peirce founded the doctrine of *pragmatism* as the concrete solution to a long list of societal and human ills. He concerned himself with questions of reality and consciousness, and conceived a person to be an instrument of thought, with truth based on a kind of *collective opinion* (Peirce 1955). He remained a rather obscure figure until William James introduced him to the academic world as the father of pragmatism.
- *William James* Also a product of Harvard, James trained in medicine and taught there from 1872 to 1910. James's ideas centered predominantly on *behaviorism,* habits, purposeful activity, reasoning, self-consciousness, and pragmatism. Highly influential in psychology, James was a charismatic and outgoing figure who impacted the work of important theorists such as Weber, Husserl, Bergson, Dewey, and Mead (Richardson 2006).
- *John Dewey* A student of philosophy at Johns Hopkins University, Dewey earned his doctorate in 1884. He published his first textbook (about psychology) while teaching at Michigan. He is best remembered for his work on the *reflex arc,* creativity, education, logic, and the need of social networks. In a treatise in 1917 entitled *The Need for Social Psychology*, he commented: "all that is left of our mental life, our beliefs, ideas and desires, falls within the scope of social psychology" (Dewey 1917, 1922). During his long career Dewey substantially contributed to sociology, pragmatism, psychology, experimentation, and educational reform.
- *George Herbert Mead* Mead received several degrees from Harvard, deciding to focus on experimental psychology. He traveled to the Leipzig laboratory of Wundt in 1888, and spent two years at Berlin, studying vision, touch, and spatial perception with Wilhelm Dilthey. He taught philosophy (and later psychology) at Chicago until 1931. Mead's theorizing centered on the process of interaction, patterns of social organization, gestures, mind, self, role taking, behavior, self-reflection, cooperation, the nature of prejudice, personal development, and *micro*-sociology in general (Mead 1934). Mead is recognized as one of the most prominent figures in social psychology

through what came to be known as *Symbolic Interactionism*, and led the University of Chicago to preeminence during the first half of the twentieth century. For more on the symbolic interactionist perspective see the chapter in this volume by Meltzer and also McCall.

- *W. I. Thomas* Another member of the Chicago School, Thomas finished his first doctoral training at Tennessee in 1888, and a second doctorate in sociology at Chicago. During his extensive travels he became interested in Europeans immigrating to America and received a $50,000 grant to research this phenomenon. Thomas teamed up with another scholar at Chicago, Florian Znaniecki, to investigate immigrant culture and conditions in Chicago. *The Polish Peasant* was a pioneering project focusing on subjects such as: values, achievement, self-indulgence, conflict, solidarity, leadership, and most importantly, attitudes (Thomas & Znaniecki 1918). "Thomas' work was instrumental in establishing *attitudes* as the central concept within social psychology and a direct forerunner of the culture and personality studies carried out during the 1930s and 1940s" (Collier 1991).
- *Robert Park* An additional bright light from the Chicago School, Park centered his interests in urban sociology and its impacts on the individual. Park studied with Dewey at Michigan, was awarded a Masters from Harvard in 1899, and garnered a doctorate from Berlin in 1904. He worked with William James after returning to America and also with Booker T. Washington from 1905 to 1914. He made important contributions in areas such as status, crowd behavior, fashion, manners, group dynamics, community analysis, delinquency, values, and interactions of the individual in the urban setting (Park et al. 1984). Park's work at Chicago during the 1920s and 1930s also contributed in establishing that university as a hub for urban studies and sociological inquiry. He authored many noteworthy textbooks and supervised a number of doctoral projects in social psychology, as well as countless dissertations in urban studies.

The work of these eight innovative scholars is representative of many others who, at the time, were earning degrees and conducting research in subjects that were in their infancy. The groundbreaking ideas in social psychology produced by American theorists at the turn of twentieth century until World War I became the solid foundation for a new scholarly discipline.

Social Psychology after World War I

Like any new enterprise, there were missteps and controversies in early social psychology, but the fledging field sputtered ahead nonetheless. After the Great War, American universities were more willing to develop their own doctoral programs in the social sciences rather than rely on European training. As Farr reports, "The international emphasis was still there but one did not need to travel abroad in order to find it" (1996). As part of that development and undoubtedly reflective of the emphasis on scientism at prestigious colleges, social psychology during this period began to embrace *experimentation* on a much broader scale with improved and more precise measurement techniques. *Psychophysicists* such as Likert (1932), Thurstone (1927), and Guttman (1941) enhanced the methodologist's ability to measure previously nebulous concepts such as attitude, social distance, and opinion. Many key researchers conducted a number of early studies using meticulous analysis (including the Chicago project by Thomas and Znaniecki [1918]) that became classics in social psychology, such as:

- *Middletown* Robert Lynd and Helen Lynd sought to reveal daily life in an average community (1929, 1937).
- *The Hawthorne Studies* Harvard School of Business researchers experimented on groups of industrial workers' responses to observations (Roethlisberger 1941; Roethlisberger & Dickson 1939).
- *Yankee City Series* Yale University scholars W. Lloyd Warner and others used observations coupled with interviews to expose stratification in Southern, Midwest, and New England communities (Warner & Low 1947; Warner & Lunt 1941).
- *Street-Corner Society* William Foote Whyte watched gang behavior in Boston slums for several years analyzing composition, dynamics, influence, group processes, and structure (1943).
- *Bennington Study* Theodore Newcomb implemented a longitudinal inquiry concerning women at a small college to discern relationships, attitudes, roles, and community groups (1943, 1950).
- *Autokenetic Experiment* Muzafer Sherif measured factors leading to the formation and maintenance of social norms (1936, 1948, 1961).
- *Iowa Child Research Station Program* Kurt Lewin researched goal setting and frustration in young children (1935/6).

Additionally during this period, Gordon Allport established *The Journal of Abnormal and Social Psychology (JASP)* as the preeminent social psychology publication within the developing discipline. Building upon their predecessors, such academics added a number of critical aspects to the growing body of work within the subject, but it was after World War II when social psychology truly gained its niche.

Social Psychology Blossoms during and after World War II

Wars typically bring both positive and negative consequences to the societies and people engaged in such hostilities. Farr observed that much of the research done "during the Second World War laid the basis for the modern era in social psychology after the war" (1996). Indeed, this period marked a radical shift in the overall importance of social psychology as a respected academic field. Researchers proceeded to explore such diverse topics as attitude, persuasion, troop and civilian morale, patriotism, collective behavior, psychological warfare, propaganda, and perception. Money for significant social inquiry was available due to exigencies the conflagration presented. Social scientists were used during the war in a variety of ways. *The American Soldier*, a four-volume treatise published in 1949 (Stouffer et al.), evidenced extensive efforts to understand human issues. In 1943, an article on life in concentration camps by Bettelheim (who had actually been in Dachau and Buchenwald) appeared in *JASP.* General Dwight Eisenhower, Supreme Allied Commander in the

European theater, ordered soldiers who were liberating such camps to read this article. Dorwin Cartwright (1949) investigated why people would or would not buy war bonds. Attitude surveys were conducted on the effects of mass bombing (Krech & Crutchfield 1948). Kurt Lewin, who had sought asylum from Germany, established *action research* during this period. Jackson (1988) relates that during the war the attitude and opinion survey techniques "came to maturity and won acceptance as a prime tool of large-scale administration and policy formation." In fact, internal bickering over prominence began to diminish after WWII (one of the more positive outcomes on the academic community). Interdisciplinary collaboration between sociologists, psychologists, anthropologists, government technicians, and other specialists promoted a synergistic approach to inquiry, serving to enhancing the value of a hybrid entity like social psychology. The increased cooperation, however, would not endure.

After WWII ended, optimism and activity seemed the order of the day. The spirit of cooperation established during the 1940s invigorated the discipline (Murray 1938, 1949), and a number of permanent research organizations took root along with graduate programs in social psychology at many major universities, with Michigan and Harvard both offering doctorates in the field. Several organizations with a predominantly military focus morphed into postwar centers of inquiry. Rensis Likert and Angus Campbell headed the new Survey Research Center, which had been the Bureau of Program Surveys under the Department of Agriculture. Later joined by Lewin's Research Center for Group Dynamics, the two merged to become the influential Institute for Social Research. The era overflowed with projects, conferences, programs, and money. The federal government, along with other interested parties, poured vast amounts of resources into understanding and solving the complex social problems brought into sharp view during the war. A decade after the world conflict's end, however, such optimism and cooperation began to wane. Collaboration between interested parties lessened as each resumed emphasis in their specific area of expertise. Sociology and psychology tended at the time (and subsequently) to invest their own visions in teaching. Even Harvard and Michigan discontinued their interdisciplinary graduate programs to the dismay of many participants. Still, "social psychology in the first two postwar decades had become a well-established, productive scientific field by almost all criteria" (Jackson 1988). Not only had the number of those receiving doctorates in related areas increased (Cartwright 1979), public support, professional societies and journals, texts, and graduate training had all substantially expanded. Overall, the postwar period was noteworthy for prosperity and general technological advancement in many arenas. As thousands of returning veterans evidenced a desire to extend their learning, education became a more prominent factor, with social psychologists anxious to contribute their brand of knowledge.

A number of consequential contributions occurred after WWII. Here I mention only a select few of the most prominent. Theodore Adorno et al's (1950) milestone view into prejudice and discrimination was one of the early efforts. Ronald Lippett (1951) and colleagues at the Research Center for Group Dynamics introduced *T-groups* and sensitivity training, while expanding study in large-group techniques and leadership abilities (Bradford et al. 1964). Leon Festinger (1950, 1957) extended Lewin's experimental study of groups at Michigan, especially adding to understanding in *cognitive dissonance,* cohesiveness, and hierarchical structure. Solomon Asch (1940) conducted what would become one of social psychology's most noted experiments in conformity and group dynamics. Asch's work led to many subsequent projects, including the controversial but now-famous exercises on obedience by Stanley Milgram (1963) and Philip Zimbardo's (1972) well-known study of a mock prison set up in the basement of the psychology building on the campus of Stanford University. Thibaut and Kelley (1959) (and George Homans [1950—the human group]) developed *social exchange* theory during this period, examining social interactions predominantly within dyads and small groups. Additionally, offerings by Fritz Heider (1944, 1946, 1958) on interpersonal perception were among the most influential contributions of the era (Jackson 1988). Along with research, many publications were becoming of use to those interested in this subject area. In 1954, Lindzey published a dual-volume hallmark titled *The Handbook of Social Psychology*. By 1968, the update of this handbook required five large volumes to contain a reasonable overview of various research findings, theoretical aspects, applied literature, and history (Lindzey and Aronson 1968). Textbooks flowed off the presses at impressive levels, and by 1965 over 100 were available with about one-third written by sociologists and two-thirds by pyschologists (Allport 1968). New methodological tools became increasingly common, especially with the advent of computers, offering exponentially more powerful ways to analyze and manipulate social data. Scott (1968) relates that "a large variety of creative methods for measuring attitudes and opinions transformed that traditional area." By 1970, the growth and fragmentation of social psychology was in full swing, and Volkart (1971) observed that the discipline appeared to be "a rather vast umbrella under which a number of different theorists and researchers huddle together for protective reasons; but few of them know how to talk to each other." In the succeeding years, what had once been a fairly homogenous endeavor disintegrated into several major schisms that would impact social psychology well into the twenty-first century.

Social Upheaval and The Crisis *in Social Psychology*

Ironically reflecting the overall societal unrest of the period, social psychology faced a number of difficulties by the late 1960s, which came to be known as *The Crisis*. Few argued that psychologists had long been dominating the field. Two-thirds of the textbooks published were written from this perspective. Few sociologists invested much time or interest in experimentation, a primary methodology in psychology. Some commentators of the age even predicted that sociological social psychology would disappear entirely (Burgess 1977; Liska 1977). Additional rancor emerged when a number of psychologists began to reject the mainstay theoretical school informing the sociological approach—symbolic interactionism (Stryker 1980). Utilizing the ideas of Blumer (1986), Goffman (1983), and other notable theorists, Symbolic Interactionism (SI) appeared to many sociologists to be methodologically superior to psychological experimentalism (Gergen 1985). Collier argued that SI included that "mental processes are culturally derived," and second, that it "focused on interaction—that is, communication and coordinated activity—rather than cognitive processes taking place within individuals." Conversely, some psychologists complained that key notions of SI were inherently vague, overly rational, difficult to operationalize, and generally not testable. For many, sociological social psychology based on SI had degenerated into merely "intuitive insights and long rambling journalistic descriptions" (Collier 1991).

Adding to the battle over sociological versus psychological dominance, a number of highly censorious critics appeared. The main critique of these observers concerning social psychology included: 1) questionable ethical practices, violations of personal privacy, and use of deception in laboratory settings (Kelman 1967: 2) "theoretical retardation" in the entire field (Tajfel 1972: 3) impossibility of realistic isomorphism (define or reword) in research (Gergen 1973: 4) sociopolitical bias and cultural ethnocentrism (Moscovici 1972); and 5) institutional pressure to publish that often produced substandard results (Jackson 1988). In general, the era from 1965 to 1980 was one of introspection, infighting, and dissatisfaction. In spite of such divisiveness, this period may have produced a more viable form of social psychology, better prepared for new directions the discipline would soon follow.

The confrontation and self-doubt that swirled about social psychology during *The Crisis* years slowly gave way and cooler heads prevailed with better scholarship emerging. New initiatives in theory, method, and application took form leading to a number of revisions within the discipline. *Attribution theory,* which is primarily concerned with comprehending people's behavior, gained prominence (Bem 1965, 1967, 1972; Kelley 1972; Kelley & Michela 1980; Kelley & Thibaut 1969, 1978) with help from Jones and Davis conducting inquiry on *correspondent inference theory* (1965). Although first introduced by Heider in the mid 1940s, attribution theory "emerged during the 1970s as the most researched topic in American social psychology and remained one of the most popular topics throughout the 1980s as well" (Collier, 1991). *Social cognition* (how people perceive, process, and organize information about others) emerged as a significant idea (Gergen 1973, 1989; Joan Miller 1984; Ross [1977] 1984; Sampson 1981; Taylor 1981). Albert Bandura's (1982) research in *reciprocal interaction, self-schemas,* and *causal attribution* made significant links between SI and attribution theory. Symbolic interactionism also found new pathways with enhanced and less ambiguous approaches with significant efforts by Goffman (1983), Kemper (1978), Turner (1976), Strauss (1978), and Stryker (1980), and Stryker and Statham (1985). Biological perspectives grew in prominence through *ethology* (studying animals in natural environments) and *sociobiology* (with emphasis on genetic predisposition and evolutionary theory). American social scientists became more open to the importance of physiological, biological, genetic, hormonal, and evolutionary factors as critical in understanding human behavior. Theories once advanced by McDougall (1908), Freud (1953), and Watson (1925) became more sophisticated and tenable through the work of ethologists such as Lorenz (1965), Tinbergen (1984), and Hinde (1987, 1988). Edward O. Wilson (1975) emerged as the primary spokesperson for sociobiology, supported by other practitioners such as Hamilton (1964), Sahlins (1976), and Rosenthal (1969, 1978). *Applied* social psychology also began a strong period of growth building on old ideas by Lewin and Festinger. According to Collier (1991), "the relevance crisis of the late 1960s and 1970s rejuvenated the need for an applied social psychology; . . . there was also a growing recognition of the importance of the larger social context and a shift toward field research." Fisher (1981, 1982) produced a landmark text in this subject (*Social Psychology: An Applied Approach*), augmented by other scholars such as Severy (1979), Taylor (1978), Gergen and Basseches (1980), Konecni and Ebbesen (1982), and Stephenson (2001). Such revisionist trends encouraged a diverse and enthusiastic attitude toward contemporary scholarship, substantially expanding the growth period of the 1980s.

Complexity Reigns Supreme since 1980

Social psychology from about 1980 through the early nineties became a massive and complex theater of operation, including such widely divergent schools as *postmodern discourse analysis* (Potter & Wetherell 1987), *critical theory* (Sampson 1989; Sullivan 1984), *poststructuralism* (Morawski 1986; Parker 1989), *meta-analysis* (Segall 1986), *social representativeness* (Moscovici 1981), and *ethogenics* (Potter & Wetherell 1987). Following Jackson (1988), we can divide the areas of emphasis into six major trends that were pivotal in the discipline which can offer greater understanding of the subject:

- *Expansion of the unit of analysis* A growing movement began toward including the individual in a larger social context or situation and away from viewing the psychological process or personality as a subject. Research conducted in these topics includes Brislin's (1983) examination of *achievement motivation* and Berscheid's (1985) inquiries into *natural social contexts.* Questions that increased the scope of social psychology to include the environment and circumstances became much more commonplace and pertinent.
- *Change in the model of a person* Over the course of many decades a distinctly *unified* model of a person evolved from experimentalism that presented the individual as passive, reflexive, and autonomous, with the external world activating behavior. In the eighties, old paradigms gave way to new assumptions that included the person as being active, reflexive, and interdependent with others (Gergen 1982, 1984; Howard 1985; Koch 1981). The inclusion of agency into the new model added the dimensions of *choice* and active intelligence to the picture (see work by Bandura [1982] and Krebs & Miller [1985]).
- *Toward self as a reflexive, multiplex process* Queries concerning the *self* have often presented challenges. Explanations from the 1980s continued to hold *self* as central to understanding social psychology, but moved their definitions to the *self* being more pliable, dynamic, and reflexive than previous theorists allowed (Berkowitz 1984; Loevinger & Knoll 1983; Tyler 1981). Even multiple identities for divergent purposes and situations were proposed (Brewer & Kramer 1985; Stryker & Statham 1985). Consistency of self was not forgotten but the new emphasis settled on *social identity* instead.
- *Increased inclusion of a complex reference process* Ideas concerning *reference groups* have floated about the discipline almost from its inception, but work in this subject during the 1980s advanced the notion that "reference groups are an intrinsic part of all social behavior" (Jackson 1988). Such *social referencing* becomes critical to a human being at an early age according to Klinnert et al. (1982). In 1985, Stephan probed interracial behaviors that explored these processes. Jackson relates that: "We see a development and broadening, concomitant with the changing unit of analysis in social psychology, from an individual reference process, perceptual or judgmental, to an interactive, reciprocal one" (1988).
- *Increased inclusion of complex normative processes* Norms and values have often been rather peripherally included within the context of social psychology especially following the many contributions of Sherif (1948). Research in the eighties, however,

placed normative processes more into the mainstream (Campbell 1978; Krebs & Miller 1985). Such structures were more seriously considered in studying attitudes (Cialdini et al., 1981), social exchange (McClintock et al. 1984), aggression (Schwartz & Howard, 1981), and role theory (Stryker & Statham 1985).

- *From a static time frame toward a bounded unitary period* An amazing number of projects in social psychology were snapshots in time. Too frequently the social world froze into a glacially static portrait, unchanging and unforgiving. The trend in inquiry during the 1980s tended to revise these theoretical orientations to be more fluid in their models. No longer were scholars simply satisfied to ignore longitudinal projects that required substantial commitments of time and effort to complete. Many investigators began to delve into the *life course* instead of the *life moment* (Altman, Vinsel, & Brown 1981). Serious investment in long-range vision and research steadily overcame the fragmentation endemic to cross-sectional analysis.

Conceptualizing social psychology through the lens of these six categories offers some cohesion when reviewing the 1980s. Along with scholarship in the axial period of the 1980s, researchers tackled a huge array of subjects in the last decade of the twentieth century, as well.

A dizzying amount of dynamic, stimulating, and varied scholarship has emerged in the kaleidoscopic period since 1990. Even though this brief recapitulation cannot do even the slightest justice to the broad range of contemporary research available a short recital of a very few notable efforts may be helpful. Since the early 1990s, Adler et al. (1993), Adler et al. (2003) has contributed a number of projects in health and *socioeconomic* topics. Baron et al. (1992), Baron et al. (2000) has been prolific in studying personality, as well as experimental aspects of the discipline. Glick et al. (1996), Glick et al. (2000), Glick et al. (2001), Glick et al. (2004) continues to produce excellent insights into aspects of gender, as well as personal ambivalence. A. G. Miller et al. (1990), Miller et al. (2004), who began research in the 1980s on some of the more challenging methodological issues in social psychology, continues to be fruitful. Attachment and romance are key themes for the work of Shaver et al. (1988), Shaver et al. (1993), Shaver et al. (1994), and Sheppard et al. (1991), Sheppard et al. (1995), Sheppard et al. (1999) has made some interesting insights into anxiety, incentive, and performance. Lord et al. (1984), Lord et al. (1991) has provided information in the realm of social judgment, Williams et al. (1991), Williams et al. (1992) on social loafing, and Eisenberger (1999, 2001) on characteristics of motivation. As students become aware of current labors within social psychology, they are typically impressed with the tremendous number of subjects under investigation. In fact, most scholars consider the multifaceted strains of interests as signs of a healthy science successfully moving into the twenty-first century and its concomitant technology, including the World Wide Web.

The Internet provides a conduit to thousands of references concerning social psychology, including one of the best general sites on peer-reviewed journal activity and other dimensions of the profession: www.socialpsychology.org/journals. A resource such as this offers a good clue to activities within the discipline. At first glance, the pesky division between a psychological and sociological emphasis appears to persist, but such an arbitrary bifurcation is no longer the only way to define the situation. Not only are many countries separately represented in present-day publications, international collegiality also seems to be alive and well. Areas of emphasis listed include old favorites such as personality, social cognition, small group research, aggression, emotion, language, prejudice, self and identity, social influence, and applied aspects, among others. Coupled with the old standards, though, many new and intriguing topics have also found their way into mainstream, peer-reviewed periodicals, including journals devoted to individual differences, economics, heuristics, group facilitation, organizational, industrial, and vocational behavior, human decision processes, forecasting, conflict resolution, social neuroscience, nonverbal behavior, and violence against women, to name a few. In other words, contemporary social psychology seems to be a hotbed of activity. Indeed, a further exploration of the Internet reveals that graduate programs are thriving, symposia are commonplace, grant monies are finding their way into worthy projects, various levels of government continue to be interested in key research, and countless students are enrolling in university courses to learn about the subject. All of which brings us back to the premise that began this short adventure: an assertion that the history of the discipline should be studied along with social psychology itself.

And They All Lived Happily Ever After

Most reasonable people agree that history does matter. Cultures, nations, communities, families, and individuals are at least a partial product of the events that have preceded them and the societies that have borne them. The vast majority of us do not grow up in isolated environments, with wolves as mothers or hermits as fathers. For the profession of social psychology, the years since Wundt set up his laboratory in Leipzig have been filled with a cacophony of concepts and theories about how individuals relate to their social worlds. In these few pages we have explored a basic overview of how social psychology historically developed. While the path has not always been smooth, many efforts, visions, and individuals have brought the discipline to where it is today: a jumble of ideas wrapped around the basic premise that a person is inexorably linked to the society he or she inhabits. As a human being functioning in just such circumstances, you already know this to be true. Your social psychology professors and textbooks will teach you to name (in official-sounding terminology) the aspects that transpire every day in our social worlds and will seek to explain how and why they occur. Add a dash of history to that mix and the picture will be complete—you will have a touch of understanding and excitement in an already fascinating subject—one you may continue to enjoy and apply throughout your lifetime.

Appendix A

Some Notable Contributors to Social Psychology

Alfred Adler (1870–1937) personality; learning; psychotherapy
Nancy Adler health; socioeconomic issues; stress
Floyd Allport (1890–1971) consciousness; social situations; behaviorism
Gordon Allport a "father" of social psychology; established the *Journal of Abnormal and Social Psychology;* personality; prejudice

Michael Argyle (1925–2002) social skills; nonverbal communication
Elliott Aronson coauthor of *Handbook of Social Psychology;* cognitive dissonance; jigsaw classroom
Solomon Asch (1907–1996) social conformity; obedience; group dynamics; halo effect
James Baldwin (1861–1934) developmental studies; social contact; self-consciousness
Albert Bandura social learning theory; self-efficacy; modeling
Robert Baron personality; social influence; experimentalism
Roy Baumeister self; social rejection; self-control
Howard Becker deviance; labeling theory
Daryl Bem self-perception; attitude; sexuality; personality
Ellen Berscheid natural social contexts
Michael Billig power; extremism; discursive social psychology
Alfred Binet (1859–1911) cognition; visual memory; intelligence; IQ measurement
Herbert Blumer (1900–1987) Symbolic Interactionism; collective behavior; personal perspective
Marilyn Brewer social identity; social cognition
Roger Brown (1925–1997) linguistic analysis; flashbulb memories
Ruth Byrne reasoning; cognition
Donald Campbell (1916–1996) methodology; normative processes; founder of the Survey Research Center
Merrill Carlsmith cognitive dissonance; attribution
Robert Cialdini normative processes; attitudes; social influence
Auguste Compte (1798–1857) scientific understanding of society; coins term sociology
Charles Darwin (1809–1882) evolution, instincts, survival; adaptation
Kingsley Davis (1908–1997) comparative studies; demography; group behavior
John Dewey (1859–1952) creativity; education; reflex arc; social networking
Emile Durkheim (1858–1917) empirical study on suicide; division of labor; religion; societal cohesion
Derek Edwards communication; discourse; rhetoric
Phoebe Ellsworth cultural bias; justice; efficacy
Erik Erikson (1902–1994) psychosocial development; personality; role confusion
Leon Festinger (1919–1989) originator of cognitive dissonance theory and social comparison theory
Sigmund Freud (1856–1939) founder of psychoanalysis; behavior within groups; personality; motivation
Kenneth Gergen applied social psychology; methodology; rationality; social constructionism
Thomas Gilovich decision making; behavioral economics; clustering illusion; spotlight effect
Peter Glick gender; personal ambivalence
Erving Goffman (1922–1982) Symbolic Interactionism; dramaturgy; presentation of self
Louis Guttman (1916–1987) scale and factor analysis; facet theory
William Hamilton sociobiology; parasitic behavior

Elaine Hatfield close relationships; emotion; interpersonal processes
Fritz Heider (1896–1988) balance theory; attribution theory; interpersonal perception
Carl Hovland (1912–1961) attitude; persuasion; social judgment theory
George Howard reflexivity; independence; reproductive responsibility
William James (1842–1910) behaviorism; habits; self-consciousness; pragmatism; epistemology
Irving Janis (1918–1990) creator of the concept of groupthink; behavior; conformity; sleeper effect
Edward Jones (1927–1993) co-authored first paper on fundamental attribution error; correspondent inference theory; actor-observer bias
Daniel Kahneman behavioral finance; heuristics; prospect theory
Harold Kelley (1921–2003) social exchange; social interaction; co-creator of concept of attribution theory
Mary Klinnert social referencing; diversity; ethnicity
Vladimir Konecni applied social psychology; creativity; aggression
Robert Krauss gestures; communication; social representation; cognition
Dennis Krebs agency; active intelligence; selfishness
Ziva Kunda (1955–2004) social cognition; group interactions
Bibb Latane bystander effect; social learning; dynamic social impact theory
Gustav LeBon (1841–1931) racial interaction; herd behavior; crowd psychology
Mark Lepper attribution theory; belief perseverance
Kurt Lewin (1890–1947) a father of social psychology; group dynamics; organizational development; founder of Iowa Child Research Station Program
Rensis Likert (1903–1981) scaling; surveys; methodology; organizational behavior
Gardner Lindzey (1925–1989) coauthor of *Handbook of Social Psychology;* personality; sex differentiation
Jane Loevinger dynamic self-image; ego development
Charles Lord social judgment; attitude
Konrad Lorenz (1903–1989) sociobiology; ethology
Robert Lynd (1892–1970) *Middletown Studies;* community life
Abraham Maslow (1908–1970) hierarchy of human needs; humanism; self-actualization
David McClelland (1917–1998) motivation; personality; social change
William McDougall (1871–1938) crown psychology; motivation; instinct
George Mead (1863–1931) pragmatism; sociology; mind; self; leading theorist of Symbolic Interactionism
Stanley Milgram (1933–1984) obedience; conformity; authority
Arthur Miller active intelligence; agency
Walter Mischel impulse control; personality; human traits
Serge Moscovici social representation; conformity
Gordon Moskowitz social cognition; stereotyping; motivation
Theodore Newcomb *Bennington Studies;* relationships; attitude
Richard Nisbett culture; social class; cognition; personal bias
Robert Park (1864–1944) status crowd behavior; fashion; manners; urban studies
Charles Pierce (1839–1914) pragmatism; collective opinion; reality
Jonathan Potter ethogenics; poststructuralism

Lee Ross pioneer in fundamental attribution error research; hostile media effect
Stanley Schachter role theory; identity; emotion; affiliation
Lawrence Severy applied social psychology; cross cultural studies
Muzafer Sharif (1906–1988) *Robber's Cave Studies;* social norms; autokenetic experiement
Philip Shaver attachment; romance
Herbert Spencer (1820–1903) evolutionary theory; intelligence; coined phrase "survival of the fittest"
Claude Steele stereotype threat; self-image; addictive behaviors
Walter Stephan interracial social referencing; experimentalism
Geoffrey Stephenson applied social psychology; industrial studies
Robert Sternberg triangular theory of love; creativity; leadership
Sheldon Stryker Symbolic Interactionism; multiple identities; role theory
William Swann self; self-esteem; group processes; self-verification theory
Henri Tajfel (1919–1982) prejudice; social identity theory
Gabriel Tarde (1843–1904) imitation; innovation; group mind
Carol Tavris egalitarian feminist social psychology
Paul Thibault social exchange; social interaction; cocreator of concept of attribution theory
William Thomas (1863–1947) *Polish Peasant Studies;* achievement; self indulgence; attitude
Louis Thurstone (1887–1955) scaling; psychometrics
Nikolaas Tinbergen (1907–1988) sociobiology; ethology
Norman Triplett (1861–1931) social facilitation; sport psychology; competition
Amos Tversky (1937–1996) cognition; prospect theory
Margaret Whetherall postmodern social psychology; ethogenics; poststructuralism
William Whyte (1914–2000) *Street Corner Society Studies;* group dynamics
Kip Williams social loafing; group dynamics
Edward Wilson sociobiology; environmentalism
Wilhelm Wundt (1832–1920) groundbreaking experimentalism; first social psychological laboratory in Leipzig, Germany
Robert Zajonc social facilitation; social behavior; mere exposure effect
Phillip Zimbardo Stanford Prison Experiment; attitude; conformity; shyness
Florian Znaniecki (1852–1958) *Polish Peasant Studies;* achievement; self-indulgence; attitude

References

Adler, N. E., W. T. Boyce, M. A. Chesney, S. Folkman, and S. L. Syme. 1993. "Socioeconomic Inequalities in Health: No Easy Solution." *Journal of the American Medical Association* 269:3140–4145.

Adler, N. E. and Alana C. Snibbe. 2003. "The Role of Psychosocial Processes in Explaining the Gradient between Socioeconomic Status and Health." *Current Directions in Psychological Science* 12: 119–123.

Adorno, Theodor W., Else Frenkel-Brunswik, Daniel J. Levinson, and R. Nevitt Sanford. 1950. *The Authoritarian Personality.* New York: Harper and Row.

Allport, Gordon W. 1954. "The Historical Background on Modern Social Psychology." Pp. 3–56 in *Handbook of Social Psychology,* vol. 1, edited by G. Lindzey. Cambridge, MA: Addison-Wesley.

———. 1968. "The Historical Background on Modern Social Psychology." Pp. 1–46 in *The Handbook of Social Psychology,* 2nd ed, vol. 2, edited by G. Lindzey. Reading, MA: Addison-Wesley.

Altman, Irwin, Anne Vinsel, and Barbara B. Brown. 1981. "Dialectic Conceptions in Social Psychology: An Application to Social Penetration and Privacy Regulation. Pp. 107–160 in *Advances in Experimental Psychology,* vol. 14, *Theorizing in Social Psychology: Special Topics,* edited by L. Berkowitz. New York: Academic Press.

Asch, Solomon E. 1940. "Studies in the Principles of Judgment and Attitudes: II. Determination of Judgments by Group and Ego Standards." *Journal of Social Psychology* 12:433–465.

Bandura, Albert. 1982. "The Self and Mechanisms of Agency." Pp. 5–29 in *Psychological Perspectives on the Self,* vol. 1, edited by J. Suls. Hillsdale, NJ: Lawrence Erlbaum Associates.

Baron, Robert S. 2000. "Arousal, Capacity, and Intense Indoctrination." *Personality and Social Psychology Review* 4:238–254.

Baron, Robert S., Norbert L. Kerr, and Norman Miller. 1992. *Group Process, Group Decision, Group Action.* Pacific Grove, CA: Brooks/Cole.

Bem, Daryl J. 1965. "An Experimental Analysis of Self-Persuasion." *Journal of Experimental Social Psychology* 1:199–218.

———. 1967. "Self Perception: An Alternative Interpretation of Cognitive Dissonance Phenomena." *Psychological Review* 74:183–200.

———. 1972. "Self-Perception Theory." Pp. 1–62 in *Advances in Experimental Psychology*, vol. 6, *Theorizing in Social Psychology: Special Topics*, edited by L. Berkowitz. New York: Academic Press.

Berkowitz, Leonard, ed. 1984. *Advances in Experimental Social Psychology,* vol. 18. New York: Academic Press.

Berscheid, Ellen. 1985. "Interpersonal Attraction." Pp. 413–484 in *The Handbook of Social Psychology,* 3rd ed., vol. 2, edited by G. Lindzey and E. Aronson. New York: Random House.

Bettelheim, Bruno. 1943. "Individual and Mass Behavior in Extreme Situations." *Journal of Abnormal and Social Psychology* 38:417–452.

Blumer, Herbert. 1986. *Symbolic Interactionism: Perspective and Method.* Berkeley, CA: University of California Press.

Bradford, Leland P., Jack R. Gibb, and Kenneth D. Benne. 1964. *T-Group Theory and Laboratory Method.* New York: Wiley.

Brewer, Marilynn B. and Roderick M. Kramer. 1985. "The Psychology of Intergroup Attitudes and Behavior." Pp. 219–243 in *Annual Review of Psychology*, vol. 32, edited by M. R. Rozenzweig and L. W. Porter. Palo Alto, CA: Annual Reviews.

Brislin, Richard W. 1983. "Cross-Cultural Research in Psychology." Pp. 363–400 in *Annual Review of Psychology*, vol. 34, edited by M. R. Rozenzweig and L. W. Porter. Palo Alto, CA: Annual Reviews.

Broughton, John M. and D. John Freeman-Moir. 1982. *The Cognitive Development Psychology of James Mark Baldwin: Current Theory and Research in General Epistemology.* Norwood, NJ: Ablex Publishing.

Bulmer, Michael. 2003. *Francis Galton: Pioneer of Heredity and Biometry*. Baltimore, MD: Johns Hopkins University Press.

Burgess, Robert. 1977. "The Withering Away of Social Psychology." *American Sociologist* 12:12–13.

Campbell, Donald T. 1978. "On the Genetics of Altruism and the Counterhedonic Component in Human Culture." Pp. 39–57 in *Altruism, Sympathy, and Helping,* edited by L. Wispe. New York: Academic Press.

Cartwright, Dorwin. 1949. "Basic and Applied Social Psychology." *Philosophy and Science* 16:198–208.

———. 1979. "Contemporary Social Psychology in Historical Perspective." *Social Psychology Quarterly* 42:82–93.

Cialdini, Robert B., Richard E. Petty, and John T. Cacioppo. 1981. "Attitudes and Attitude Change." Pp. 357–404 in *Annual Review of Psychology,* vol. 36, edited by M. R. Rozenzweig and L. W. Porter. Palo Alto, CA: Annual Reviews.

Collier, Gary, Henry Minton, and Graham Reynolds. 1991. *Currents of Thought in American Social Psychology*. New York: Oxford University Press.

Danzinger, Kurt. 1985. "The Origins of the Psychological Experiment as a Social Institution." *American Psychologist* 40:133–140.

Dewey, John. 1917. "The Need for Social Psychology." *Psychological Review* 24:266–277.

———. 1922. *Human Nature and Human Conduct: An Introduction to Social Psychology.* New York: Holt.

Eisenberger, Robert and Linda Rhoades. 2001. "Incremental Effects of Reward on Creativity." *Journal of Personality and Social Psychology* 81:728–741.

Eisenberger, Robert, Linda Rhoades, and Judy Cameron. 1999. "Does Pay for Performance Increase or Decrease Perceived Self-Determination and Intrinsic Motivation? *Journal of Personality and Social Psychology* 77:1026–1040.

Farr, Robert M. 1983. "Wilhelm Wundt (1832–1920) and the Origin of Psychology as an Experimental and Social Science." *British Journal of Social Psychology* 22:289–301.

———. 1996. *The Roots of Modern Social Psychology: 1872–1954.* Cambridge, MA: Blackwell.

Festinger, Leon. 1950. "Laboratory Experiments: The Role of Belongingness" Pp. 31–46 in *Experiments in Social Process,* edited by J. Miller. New York: McGraw-Hill.

———. 1957. *A Theory of Cognitive Dissonance.* Stanford, CA: Stanford University Press.

Fisher, Ronald J. 1981. "Training in Applied Social Psychology: Rationale and Core Experience." *Canadian Psychology* 22:250–259.

———. 1982. *Social Psychology: An Applied Approach.* New York: St. Martin's.

Freud, Sigmund. 1953. *The Psychopathology of Every Day Life*, edited and translated by J. Strachey. London: Hogarth Press.

Gergen, Kenneth J. 1973. "Social Psychology and History." *Journal of Personality and Social Psychology* 26:309–320.

———. 1982. *Toward Transformation in Social Knowledge.* New York: Springer-Verlag.

———. 1984. "Theory of the Self: Impasse and Evolution." Pp. 49–115 in *Advances in Experimental Pscyhology,* vol. 17, *Theorizing in Social Psychology: Special Topics,* edited by L. Berkowitz. New York: Academic Press.

———. 1985. "The Social Constructionist Movement in Modern Psychology." *American Psychologist* 40:266–275.

———. 1989. "Social Psychology and the Wrong Revolution." *European Journal of Social Psychology* 19:463–484.

Gergen, Kenneth J. and Michael Basseches. 1980. "The Potentiation of Social Psychological Knowledge." Pp. 25–46 in *Advances in Applied Social Psychology,* edited by F. Kidd and M. Saks. New York: Academic Press.

Glick, Peter, et al. 2004. "Bad but Bold: Ambivalent Attitudes toward Men Predict Gender Inequality in 16 Nations." *Journal of Personality and Social Psychology* 86:713–728.

Glick, Peter and Susan T. Fiske. 1996. "The Ambivalent Sexism Inventory: Differentiating Hostile and Benevolent Sexism." *Journal of Personality and Social Psychology* 70:491–512.

———. 2001. "An Ambivalent Alliance: Hostile and Benevolent Sexism as Complementary Justifications for Gender Inequality." *American Psychologist* 56:109–118.

Glick, Peter, Susan T. Fiske, et al. 2000. "Beyond Prejudice as Simple Antipathy: Hostile and Benevolent Sexism Across Cultures."*Journal of Personality and Social Psychology* 79:763–775.

Goffman, Erving. 1983. "The Interaction Order." *American Sociological Review* 48:1–17.

Guttman, Louis. 1941. "The Quantification of a Class of Attributes: A Theory and Method of Scale Construction." Supplementary Study B-2 in *The Prediction of Personal Adjustment,* edited by P. Horst. New York: Social Science Research Council, Bulletin No. 48.

Hamilton, William D. 1964. "The Evolution of Social Behavior: I & II. *Journal of Theoretical Biology* 1:1–52.

Heider, Fritz. 1944. "Social Perception and Phenomenal Causality." *Psychological Review* 51:358–374.

———. 1946. "Attitudes and Cognitive Organization." *Journal of Psychology* 21:107–112.

———. 1958. *The Psychology of Interpersonal Relations.* New York: Wiley.

Hinde, Robert A. 1987. *Individuals, Relationships and Culture: Links between Ethology and the Social Sciences.* Cambridge: Cambridge University Press.

———. 1988. "Ethology and Social Psychology." Pp. 1–17 in *Introduction to Social Psychology,* edited by M. Hewstone, W. Stroebe, J. P. Codol, and G. M. Stephenson. Oxford: Blackwell.

Homans, George C. 1950. *The Human Group*. New York: Harcourt, Brace and World.

Howard, George S. 1985. "The Role of Values in the Science of Psychology." *American Psychologist* 40: 255–265.

Jackson, Jay M. 1988. *Social Psychology, Past and Present: An Integrative Orientation*. Hillsdale, NJ: Lawrence Erlbaum.

Jacobs, Glenn. 2006. *Charles Horton Cooley: Imagining Social Reality.* Boston: University of Massachusetts Press.

Jones, Edward. E. and Davis, Keith E. 1965. From "Acts to Dispositions: The Attribution Process in Person Perception." Pp. 219–266 in L. Berkowitz (Ed.), *Advances in Experimental Social Psychology,* vol. 2 (1984). New York: Academic Press.

Kelley, Harold H. 1972. *Casual Schemata and the Attribution Process.* Morristown, NJ: General Learning.

Kelley, Harold H. and John L. Michela. 1980. "Attribution Theory and Research. Pp. 457–501 in *The Annual Review of Psychology,* vol. 31, edited by M. R. Rozenzweig and L. W. Porter. Palo Alto, CA: Annual Reviews.

Kelley, Harold H. and John W. Thibaut. 1969. "Group Problem Solving." Pp. 1–101 in *The Handbook of Social Psychology,* 2nd ed., vol. 4, edited by G. Lindzey and E. Aronson. Reading, MA: Addison-Wesley.

———. 1978. *Interpersonal Relations: A Theory of Interdependence.* New York: Wiley.

Kelman, Herbert C. 1967. "Human Use of Human Subjects: The Problem of Deception in Social Psychological Experiments. *Psychological Bulletin,* 67:1–11.

Kemper, Theodore D. 1978. *A Social Interactional Theory of Emotions.* New York: Wiley-Interscience.

Khalifa, Rashad. 2005. Quran: The Final Testament, Authorized English Version with Arabic Text (Revised edition IV). Submission.org Press.

Klinnert, M. D., Campos, J. J., Sorce, J. F., Emde, R., and Svejda, M. 1982. "Emotions as Behavior Regulators: Social Referencing in Infancy." Pp. 57–85 in *Emotion: Theory, Research, and Experience,* vol. 2, edited by R. Plutchik and H. Kellerman. New York: Academic Press.

Koch, Sigmund. 1981. "The Nature and Limits of Psychological Knowledge: Lessons of a Century Qua 'Science.'" *American Psychologist* 36:257–269.

Konecni, Vladimir J. and Ebbe B. Ebbesen, eds. 1982. *The Criminal Justice System: A Social Psychological Analysis.* San Francisco: CA: W. H. Freeman

Krebs, Dennis L. and Dale T. Miller. 1985. "Altruism and Aggression." Pp. 1–71 in *The Handbook of Social Psychology*, 3rd ed, vol. 2, edited by G. Lindzey and E. Aronson. New York: Random House.

Krech, David and Richard S. Crutchfield. 1948. *Theory and Problems of Social Psychology.* New York: McGraw-Hill.

Le Bon, Gustave and Alice Widener. 1979. *Gustave Le Bon, The Man and His Works: A Presentation with Introduction, First Translated into English, and Edited Extracts.* New York: Liberty Press.

Lewin, Kurt. 1935/6. *A Dynamic Theory of Personality.* New York: McGraw-Hill.

Likert, Rensis. 1932. "A Technique for the Measurement of Attitudes." *Archives of Psychology* 40:1–55.

Lindzey, Gardner, ed. 1954. *The Handbook of Social Psychology.* Reading, MA: Addison-Wesley.

Lindzey, Gardner and Elliot Aronson, eds. 1968. *The Handbook of Social Psychology*, 3rd ed. New York: Random House.

Lippett, Ronald. 1951. "A Program of Experimentation on Group Functioning and Group Productivity." Pp. 14–49 in *Current Trends in Social Psychology,* edited by W. Dennis. Pittsburgh, PA: University of Pittsburgh Press.

Liska, Allen E. 1977. "The Dissipation of Sociological Social Psychology." *American Sociologist.* 12:2–8.

Loevinger, Jane and Elizabeth Knoll. 1983. "Personality: Stages, Traits, and the Self." Pp. 195–222 in *The Annual Review of Psychology,* vol. 34, edited by M. R. Rozenzweig and L. W. Porter. Palo Alto, CA: Annual Reviews.

Lord, Charles G., Donna M. Desforges, S. L. Ramsey, G. R. Trezza, and Mark R. Lepper. 1991. "Typicality Effect in Attitude-Behavior Consistency: Effects of Category Discrimination and Category Knowledge." *Journal of Experimental Social Psychology* 27:550–575.

Lord, Charles G., Mark R. Lepper, and Elizabeth Preston. 1984. "Considering the Opposite: A Corrective Strategy for Social Judgment." *Journal of Personality and Social Psychology* 47:1231–1243.

Lorenz, Konrad. (1965). Introduction. In *The Expression of Emotion in Man and Animals,* by C. Darwin. Chicago: University of Chicago Press.

Lukes, Steven. 1973. *Emile Durkheim: His Life and Work—A Historical and Critical Study.* London: Lane.

Lynd, Robert S. and Helen Merrell Lynd. 1929. *Middletown.* New York: Harcourt Brace.

———. 1937. *Middletown in Transition.* New York: Harcourt Brace.

McClintock, Charles G., Roderick M. Kramer, and Linda J. Keil. 1984. "Equity and Social Exchange in Human Relationships." Pp. 183–228 in *Advances in Experimental Psychology,* vol. 17, edited by L. Berkowitz. New York: Academic Press.

McDougall, William. 1908. *Introduction to Social Psychology.* London: Methuen.

Mead, George H. 1934. *Mind, Self, and Society.* Chicago: University of Chicago Press.

Milgram, Stanley. 1963. "Behavioral Study of Obedience." *Journal of Abnormal and Social Psychology* 67:371–378.

Miller, Arthur G. 1986. *The Obedience Experiments: A Case Study of Controversy in Social Science.* New York: Praeger.

———. 2004. "What Can the Milgram Obedience Experiments Tell Us about the Holocaust? Generalizing from the Social Psychological Laboratory." Pp. 193–239 in *The Social Psychology of Good and Evil,* edited by A. G. Miller. New York: Guilford.

Miller, Arthur G., William A. Ashton, and Mark Mishal. 1990. "Beliefs Concerning the Features of Constrained Behavior: A Basis for the Fundamental Attribution Error." *Journal of Personality and Social Psychology* 59:635–650.

Miller, Joan G. 1984. "Culture and the Development of Everyday Social Explanations." *Journal of Personality and Social Psychology* 46:961–978.

Morawski, Jill G. 1986. "Contextual Discipline: The Unmasking and Remaking of Sociality." Pp. 47–66 in *Contextualism and Understanding in Behavioral Science,* edited by R. L. Rosnow and M. Georgoudi. New York: Praeger.

Moscovici, Serge. 1972. "Society and Theory in Social Psychology." Pp. 17–68 in J. Israel & H. Tajfel (Eds.), *The Context of Social Psychology: A Critical Assessment,* London: Academic Press.

Moscovici, Serge. 1981. "On Social Representations." Pp. 181–209 in *Social Cognition: Perspectives on Everyday Understanding,* edited by J. P. Forgas. London: Academic Press.

Murray, Henry A. 1938. *Explorations in Personality.* New York: Oxford University Press.

———. 1949. "Research Planning: A Few Propositions." Pp. 195–212 in *Culture and Personality,* edited by S. S. Sargent and M W. Smith. New York: Viking Fund.

Newcomb, Theodore M. 1943. *Personality and Social Change.* New York: Dryden.

———. 1950. "Social Psychological Theory: Integrating Individual and Social Approaches." Pp. 31–59 in *Social Psychology at the Crossroads: The University of Oklahoma Lecture Series in Social Psychology,* edited by J. H. Rohrer and M. Sherif. New York: Harper.

Park, Robert E., Ernest W. Burgess, and Morris Janoswitz. 1984. *The City* (Heritage of Sociology Series). Chicago: University of Chicago Press.

Parker, Ian. 1989. "Discourse and Power." Pp. 56–69 in *Texts of Identity,* edited by J. Shotter and K. J. Gergen. London: Sage.

Pepitone, Albert. 1976. "Toward a Normative and Comparative Biocultural Social Psychology." *Journal of Personality and Social Psychology* 34:641–653.

———. 1981. "Lessons from the History of Social Psychology." *American Psychologist* 36: 972–985.

Plato. 1992. *Republic.* Translated by G. M. Grube. Indianapolis: Hackett Publishing.

Potter, Jonathan and Margaret Wetherell. 1987. *Discourse and Social Psychology.* London: Sage.

Richardson, Robert D. 2006. *William James: In the Maelstrom of American Modernism.* Boston: Houghton Mifflin.

Roethlisberger, F. J. 1941. *Management and Morale.* Cambridge, MA: Harvard University Press.

Roethlisberger, F. J. and William J. Dickson. 1939. *Management and the Worker: An Account of a Research Program Conducted by the Western Electric Company, Hawthorne Works, Chicago.* Cambridge, MA: Harvard University Press.

Rosenthal, Robert. 1969. "The Volunteer Subject." Pp. 59–118 in *Artifact in Behavioral Research,* edited by R. Rosenthal and R. Rosnow. New York: Academic Press.

———. 1978. "Combining Results of Independent Studies." *Psychological Bulletin* 85:185–193.

Ross, Lee. [1977] 1984. "The Intuitive Psychologist and His Shortcomings: Distortions in the Attribution Process." Pp. 174–220 *Advances in Experimental Social Psychology,* vol. 10, edited by L. Berkowitz. New York: Academic Press.

Rowling, J. K. 2006. Harry Potter Paperback Box Set (Books 1–6). College Point, NY: Scholastic, Inc.

Sahlins, Marshall D. 1976. *The Use and Abuse of Biology: An Anthropological Critique of Sociobiology*. Ann Arbor: University of Michigan Press.

Sampson, Edward. E. 1981. "Cognitive Psychology as Ideology." *Amercian Psychologist,* 36:730–743.

Sampson, Edward E. 1989. "The Deconstruction of the Self." Pp. 1–19 in *Texts of Identity,* edited by J. Shotter and K. J. Gergen. London: Sage.

Schwartz, Shalom H. and Judith A. Howard. 1981. "A Normative Decision-Making Model of Altruism." Pp. 189–211 in *Altruism and Helping Behavior: Social, Personality, and Developmental Perspectives,* edited by J. Rushton and R. M. Sorrentino. Hillsdale, NJ: Lawrence Erlbaum Associates.

Scott, William A. 1968. "Attitude Measurement." Pp. 204–273 in *The Handbook of Social Psychology,* 2nd ed., vol. 2, edited by G. Lindzey and E. Aronson. Reading, MA: Addison-Wesley

Segall, Marshall H. 1986. "Culture and Behavior: Psychology in Global Perspective." Pp. 523–564 in *The Annual Review of Psychology*, vol. 37, edited by M. R. Rozenzweig and L. W. Porter. Palo Alto, CA: Annual Reviews.

Severy, Lawrence J. 1979. "Graduate Research Training Internships in Social Psychology." *Personality and Social Psychology Bulletin* 5:507–510.

Shaver, Phillip R. and Cindy Hazan. 1993. "Adult Romantic Attachment: Theory and Evidence." Pp. 29–70 in *Advances in Personal Relationships,* vol. 4, edited by D. Perlman and W. Jones. Greenwich, CT: JAI.

———. 1994. "Attachment." Pp. 110–130 in *Perspectives on Close Relationships,* edited by A. L. Weber and J. H. Harvey. Boston: Allyn & Bacon.

Shaver, Phillip R., Cindy Hazan, and Donna Bradshaw. 1988. "Love as Attachment: The Integration of Three Behavioral Systems." Pp. 68–99 in *The Psychology of Love,* edited by R. J. Sternberg and M. L. Barnes. New Haven: Yale University Press.

Sheppard, James A. and Robert M. Arkin. 1991. "Behavioral Other-Enhancement: Strategically Obscuring the Link between Performance and Evaluation." *Journal of Personality and Social Psychology* 60: 79–88.

Sheppard, James A., Robert M. Arkin, and Jean Slaughter. 1995. "Constraints on Excuse Making: The Deterring Effects of Shyness and Anticipated Retest." *Personality and Social Psychology Bulletin* 21: 1061–1072.

Sheppard, James A. and Kevin M. Taylor. 1999. "Ascribing Advantages to Social Comparison Targets." *Basic and Applied Social Psychology* 21:103–117.

Sherif, Muzafer. 1936. *The Psychology of Social Norms.* New York: Harper.

———. 1948. *An Outline of Social Psychology.* New York: Harper.

Sherif, Muzafer, O. J. Harvey, B. Jack White, William R. Hood, and Carolyn W. Sherif. 1961. *Intergroup Conflict and Cooperation: The Robbers Cave Experiment.* Norman: University of Oklahoma Press.

Stephan, Walter G. 1985. "Intergroup Relations." Pp. 599–358 in *The Handbook of Social Psychology,* 3rd ed., vol. 2, edited by G. Lindzey and E. Aronson. New York: Random House.

Stephenson, Geoffrey M. 2001. "Applied Social Psychology." Pp. 480–492 in *Introduction to Social Psychology,* edited by M. Hewstone, W. Stroebe, J.-P. Codol, and G. W. Stephenson. Oxford: Blackwell.

Stouffer, Samuel A., Edward A. Suchman, Leland C. Devinney, Shirley A. Star, and Robin M. Williams Jr. 1949. *Studies in Social Psychology in World War II: The American Soldier, Adjustment during Army Life.* Princeton, NJ: Princeton University Press.

Strauss, Anselm L. 1978. *Negotiations: Varieties, Contexts Processes, and Social Order.* San Francisco: Josey-Bass.

Stryker, Sheldon. 1980. *Symbolic Interactionism: A Social Psychological Version.* Menlo Park, CA: Benjamin/Cummings.

Stryker, Sheldon and Statham, A. 1985. "Symbolic Interaction and Role Theory." Pp. 311–78. In G. Lindzey and E. Aronson (eds.), *The Handbook of Social Psychology,* (3rd ed., vol. 1) New York: Random House.

Sullivan, Edmund V. 1984. *A Critical Psychology.* New York: Plennum.

Tajfel, Henri. (1972). "Experiments in a Vacuum." Pp. 1–13 in H. Israel & H. Tajfel (Eds.), *The Context of Social Psychology*, London: Academic Press.
Tarde, Gabriel. 1969. *On Communication and Social Influence: Selected Papers.* Chicago: University of Chicago Press.
Taylor, Shelley E. 1978. "A Developing Role for Social Psychology in Medicine and Medical Practice." *Personality and Social Psychology Bulletin* 4:515–523.
———. 1981. "The Interface of Cognitive and Social Psychology." Pp. 189–211 in *Cognition, Social Behavior, and the Environment,* edited by J. H. Harvey. Hillsdale, NJ: Lawrence Erlbaum.
Thibaut, John. W. and Harold H. Kelley. 1959. *The Social Psychology of Groups.* New York: Wiley.
Thomas, William I. and Florian Znaniecki. 1918. *The Polish Peasant in Europe and America* (5 vols.). Boston: Badger.
Thurstone, Louis L. 1927. "Attitudes Can Be Measured." *American Journal of Sociology* 33:529–554.
Tinbergen, Niko. 1984. *Curious Naturalists.* Boston: University of Massachusetts Press.
Turner, Jonathan H., et al. 2007. *The Emergence of Sociological Theory.* Belmont, CA: Thompson.
Turner, Ralph H. 1976. "The Real Self: From Institution to Impulse." *American Journal of Sociology* 81: 989–1016.
Tyler, Leona E. 1981. "More Stately Mansions—Psychology Extends Its Boundaries." Pp. 1–22 in *Annual Review of Psychology,* vol. 32, editedy by M. R. Rozenzweig and L. W. Porter. Palo Alto, CA: Annual Reviews.
Volkart, Edmund H. 1971. "Comments in Review Symposium on the *Handbook of Social Psychology.*" *American Sociological Review* 36:898–902.
Warner, W. Lloyd and Josiah O. Low. 1947. *The Social System of the Modern Factory.* New Haven: Yale University Press.
Warner, W. Lloyd and Paul S. Lunt. 1941. *The Social Life of a Modern Community.* New Haven: Yale University Press.
Watson, John B. 1925. *Behaviorism: Psychology and Physiology.* New York: People's Institute.
Whyte, William F. 1943. *Street Corner Society.* Chicago: University of Chicago Press.
Williams, Kipling D. and Steven J. Karau. 1991. "Social Loafing and Social Compensation: The Effects of Expectations of Coworker Performance." *Journal of Personality and Social Psychology* 61:570–581.
Williams, Kipling D., Jeffrey M. Jackson, and Steven J. Karau. 1992. "Collective Hedonism: A Social Loafing Analysis of Social Dilemmas." Pp. 117–141 in *Social Dilemmas: Social Psychological Perspectives,* edited by D. A. Schroeder. New York: Praeger.
Wilson, Edward O. 1975. *Sociobiology: The New Synthesis.* Cambridge, MA: Harvard University Press.
Zimbardo, Phillip G. 1972. "The Stanford Prison Experiment." A slide/tape presentation produced by Philip G. Zimbardo, Inc., P.O. Box 4395, Stanford, CA 94305.

3

Reconciling Conflicting Results Derived from Experimental and Survey Studies of Attitude Change

Carl I. Hovland
Yale University

Two quite different types of research design are characteristically used to study the modification of attitudes through communication. In the first type, the *experiment*, individuals are given a controlled exposure to a communication and the effects evaluated in terms of the amount of change in attitude or opinion produced. A base line is provided by means of a control group not exposed to the communication. The study of Gosnell (1927) on the influence of leaflets designed to get voters to the polls is a classic example of the controlled experiment.

In the alternative research design, the *sample survey*, information is secured through interviews or questionnaires both concerning the respondent's exposure to various communications and his attitudes and opinions on various issues. Generalizations are then derived from the correlations obtained between reports of exposure and measurements of attitude. In a variant of this method, measurements of attitude and of exposure to communication are obtained during repeated interviews with the same individual over a period of weeks or months. This is the "panel method" extensively utilized in studying the impact of various mass media on political attitudes and on voting behavior (cf., e.g., Kendall & Lazarsfeld 1950).

Generalizations derived from experimental and from correlational studies of communication effects are usually both reported in chapters on the effects of mass media and in other summaries of research on attitude, typically without much stress on the type of study from which the conclusion was derived. Close scrutiny of the results obtained from the two methods, however, suggests a marked difference in the picture of communication effects obtained from each. The object of my paper is to consider the conclusions derived from these two types of design, to suggest some of the factors responsible for the frequent divergence in results, and then to formulate principles aimed at reconciling some of the apparent conflicts.

Divergence

The picture of mass communication effects which emerges from correlational studies is one in which few individuals are seen as being affected by communications. One of the most thorough correlational studies of the effects of mass media on attitudes is that of Lazarsfeld, Berelson, and Gaudet published in *The People's Choice* (1944). In this report there is an extensive chapter devoted to the effects of various media, particularly radio, newspapers, and magazines. The authors conclude that few changes in attitudes were produced. They estimate that the political positions of only about 5% of their respondents were changed by the election campaign, and they are inclined to attribute even this small amount of change more to personal influence than to the mass media. A similar evaluation of mass media is made in the recent chapter in the *Handbook of Social Psychology* by Lipset and his collaborators (1954).

Research using experimental procedures, on the other hand, indicates the possibility of considerable modifiability of attitudes through exposure to communication. In both Klapper's survey (1949) and in my chapter in the *Handbook of Social Psychology* (Hovland 1954) a number of experimental studies are discussed in which the opinions of a third to a half or more of the audience are changed.

The discrepancy between the results derived from these two methodologies raises some fascinating problems for analysis. This divergence in outcome appears to me to be largely attributable to two kinds of factors: one, the difference in research design itself; and, two, the historical and traditional differences in general approach to evaluation characteristic of researchers using the experimental as contrasted with the correlational or survey method. I would like to discuss, first, the influence these factors have on the estimation of overall effects of communications and, then, turn to other divergences in outcome characteristically found by the use of the experimental and survey methodology.

Undoubtedly the most critical and interesting variation in the research *design* involved in the two procedures is that resulting from differences in definition of exposure. In an experiment the audience on whom the effects are being evaluated is one which is fully exposed to the communication. On the other hand, in naturalistic situations with which surveys are typically concerned, the outstanding phenomenon is the limitation of the audience to those who *expose themselves* to the communication. Some of the individuals in a captive audience experiment would, of course, expose themselves in the course of natural events to a communication of the type studied; but many others would not. The group which does expose itself is usually a highly biased one, since most individuals "expose themselves most of the time to the kind of material with which they agree to begin with" (Lipset et al. 1954). Thus one reason for the difference in results between experiments and correlational studies is that experiments describe the effects of exposure on the whole range of individuals studied, some of whom are initially in favor of the position being advocated and some who are opposed, whereas surveys primarily describe the effects produced on those already in favor of the point of view advocated in the communication. The amount of change is thus, of course, much smaller in surveys. Lipset and his collaborators make this same evaluation, stating that:

> As long as we test a program in the laboratory we always find that it has great effect on the attitudes and interests of the experimental subjects. But when we put the program on as a regular broadcast, we then note that the people who are most influenced in the laboratory tests are those who, in a realistic situation, do not listen to the program. The controlled experiment always greatly overrates effects, as compared with those that really occur, because of the self-selection of audiences. (Lipset et al. 1954)

Differences in the second category are not inherent in the design of the two alternatives, but are characteristic of the way researchers using the two methods typically proceed.

The first difference within this class is in the size of the communication unit typically studied. In the majority of survey studies the unit evaluated is an entire program of communication. For example, in studies of political behavior an attempt is made to assess the effects of all newspaper reading and television viewing on attitudes toward the major parties. In the typical experiment, on the other hand, the interest is usually in some particular variation in the content of the communications, and experimental evaluations much more frequently involve single communications. On this point results are thus not directly comparable.

Another characteristic difference between the two methods is in the time interval used in evaluation. In the typical experiment the time at which the effect is observed is usually rather soon after exposure to the communication. In the survey study, on the other hand, the time perspective is such that much more remote effects are usually evaluated. When effects decline with the passage of time, the net outcome will, of course, be that of accentuating the effect obtained in experimental studies as compared with those obtained in survey researches. Again it must be stressed that the difference is not inherent in the designs as such. Several experiments, including our own on the effects of motion pictures (Hovland et al. 1949) and later studies on the "sleeper effect" (Hovland & Weiss 1951; Kelman & Hovland 1953), have studied retention over considerable periods of time.

Some of the difference in outcome may be attributable to the types of communicators characteristically used and to the motive-incentive conditions operative in the two situations. In experimental studies communications are frequently presented in a classroom situation. This may involve quite different types of factors from those operative in the more naturalistic communication situation with which the survey researchers are concerned. In the classroom there may be some implicit sponsorship of the communication by the teacher and the school administration. In the survey studies the communicators may often be remote individuals either unfamiliar to the recipients, or outgroupers clearly known to espouse a point of view opposed to that held by many members of the audience. Thus there may be real differences in communicator credibility in laboratory and survey researches. The net effect of the differences will typically be in the direction of increasing the likelihood of change in the experimental as compared with the survey study.

There is sometimes an additional situational difference. Communications of the type studied by survey researchers usually involve reaching the individual in his natural habitat, with consequent supplementary effects produced by discussion with friends and family. In the laboratory studies a classroom situation with low postcommunication interaction is more typically involved. Several studies, including one by Harold Kelly reported in our volume on *Communication and Persuasion* (Hovland et al. 1953), indicate that, when a communication is presented in a situation which makes group membership salient, the individual is typically more resistant to counternorm influence than when the communication is presented under conditions of low salience of group membership (cf. also, Katz & Lazarsfeld 1955, 48–133).

A difference which is almost wholly adventitious is in the types of populations utilized. In the survey design there is, typically, considerable emphasis on a random sample of the entire population. In the typical experiment, on the other hand, there is a consistent overrepresentation of high school students and college sophomores, primarily on the basis of their greater accessibility. But as Tolman has said: "College sophomores may not be people." Whether differences in the type of audience studied contribute to the differences in effect obtained with the two methods is not known.

Finally, there is an extremely important difference in the studies of the experimental and correlational variety with respect to the type of issue discussed in the communications. In the typical experiment we are interested in studying a set of factors or conditions which are expected on the basis of theory to influence the extent of effect of the communication. We usually deliberately try to find types of issues involving attitudes which are susceptible to modification through communication. Otherwise, we run the risk of no measurable effects, particularly with small-scale experiments. In the survey procedures, on the other hand, socially significant attitudes which are deeply rooted in prior experience and involve much personal commitment are typically involved. This is especially true in voting studies which have provided us with so many of our present results on social influence. I shall have considerably more to say about this problem a little later.

The differences so far discussed have primarily concerned the extent of overall effectiveness indicated by the two methods: why survey results typically show little modification of attitudes by communication while experiments indicate marked changes. Let me now turn to some of the other differences in generalizations derived from the two alternative designs. Let me take as the second main area of disparate results the research on the effect of varying distances between the position taken by the communicator and that held by the recipient of the communication. Here it is a matter of comparing changes for persons who at the outset closely agree with the communicator with those for others who are mildly or strongly in disagreement with him. In the naturalistic situation studied in surveys the typical procedure is to determine changes in opinion following reported exposure to communication for individuals differing from the communicator by varying amounts. This gives rise to two possible artifacts. When the communication is at one end of a continuum, there is little room for improvement for those who differ from the communication by small amounts, but a great deal of room for movement among those with large discrepancies. This gives rise to a spurious degree of positive relationship between the degree of discrepancy and the amount of change. Regression effects will also operate in the direction of increasing the correlation. What is needed is a situation in which the distance factor can be manipulated independently of the subject's initial position. An attempt to set up these conditions experimentally was made in a study by Pritzker and the writer (1957). The method involved preparing individual communications presented in booklet form so that the position of the communicator could be set at any desired distance from the subject's initial position. Communicators highly acceptable to the subjects were used. A number of different topics were employed, including the likelihood of a cure for cancer within five years, the desirability of compulsory voting, and the adequacy of five hours of sleep per night.

The amount of change for each degree of advocated change is shown in Figure 3.1. It will be seen that there is a fairly clear progression, such that the greater the amount of change advocated the greater the average amount of opinion change produced. Similar results have been reported by Goldberg (1954) and by French (1956).

But these results are not in line with our hunches as to what would happen in a naturalistic situation with important social issues. We felt that here other types of response than change in attitude would occur. So Muzafer Sherif, O. J. Harvey, and the writer (1957) set up a situation to simulate as closely as possible the conditions typically involved when individuals are exposed to major social issue communications at differing distances from their own position. The issue used was the desirability of prohibition. The study was done in two states (Oklahoma and Texas) where there is prohibition or local option, so that the wet-dry issue is hotly debated. We concentrated on three aspects of the problem: How favorably will the communicator be received when his position is at varying distances from that of the recipient? How will what the communicator says be perceived and interpreted by individuals at varying distances from his position? What will be the amount of opinion change produced when small and large deviations in position of communication and recipient are involved?

Three communications, one strongly wet, one strongly dry, and one moderately wet, were employed. The results bearing on the first problem, of *reception*, are presented in Figure 3.2. The positions of the subjects are indicated on the abscissa in letters from A (extreme dry) to H (strongly wet). The positions of the communication are also indicated

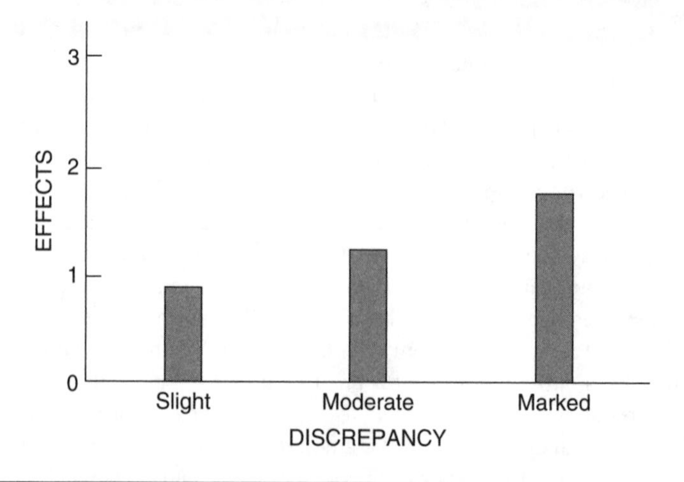

FIGURE 3.1 ***Mean opinion change score with three degrees of discrepancy (deviation between subject's position and position advocated in communication). [From Hovland & Pritzker 1957]***

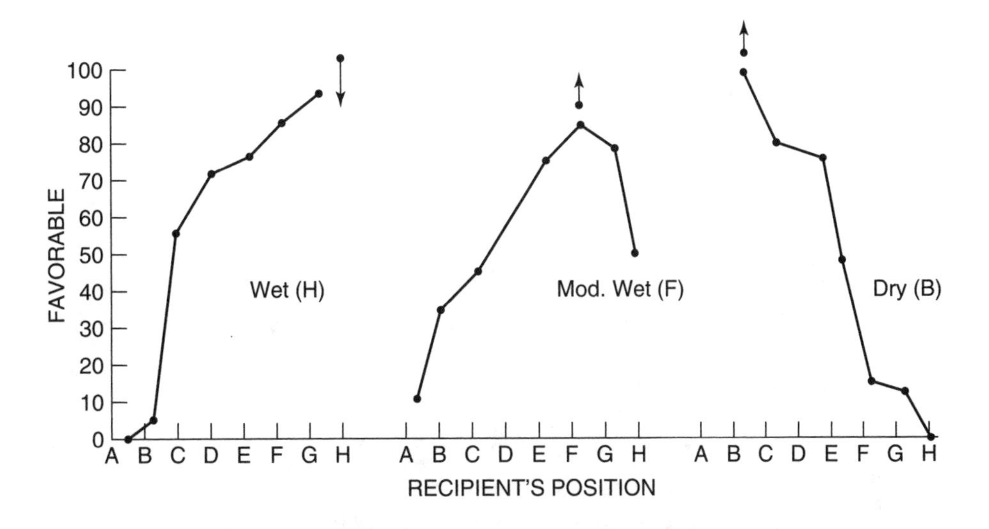

FIGURE 3.2 ***Percentage of favorable evaluations ("fair," "unbiased," etc.) of wet (H), moderately wet (F), and dry (B) communications for subjects holding various positions on prohibition. Recipients position range from A (very dry) to H (very wet). Position of communications indicated by arrow. [From Hovland, Harvey, & Sherif 1957]***

in the same letters, *B* indicating a strongly dry communication, *H* a strongly wet, and *F* a moderately wet. Along the ordinate there is plotted the percentage of subjects with each position on the issue who described the communication as "fair" and "unbiased." It will be seen that the degree of distance between the recipient and the communicator greatly influences the evaluation of the fairness of the communication. When a communication is directed at the pro-dry position, nearly all of the dry subjects consider it fair and impartial, but only a few percent of the wet subjects consider the identical communication fair. The reverse is true at the other end of the scale. When an intermediate position is adopted, the percentages fall off sharply on each side. Thus under the present conditions with a relatively ambiguous communicator one of the ways of dealing with strongly discrepant positions is to *discredit* the communicator, considering him unfair and biased.

A second way in which an individual can deal with discrepancy is by distortion of what is said by the communicator. Thus is a phenomenon extensively studied by Cooper and Jahoda (1947). In the present study, subjects were asked to state what position they thought was taken by the communicator on the prohibition question. Their evaluation of his position could then be analyzed in relation to their own position. These results are shown in Figure 3.3 for the moderately wet communication. It will be observed that there is a tendency for individuals whose position is close to that of the communicator to report on the communicator's position quite accurately, for individuals a little bit removed to report his position to be substantially more like their own (which we call an "assimilation effect"), and for those with more discrepant positions to report the communicator's position as more extreme than it really was. This we refer to as a "contrast effect."

Now to our primary results on opinion change. It was found that individuals whose position was only slightly discrepant from the communicator's were influenced to a greater extent than those whose position deviated to a larger extent. When a wet position was

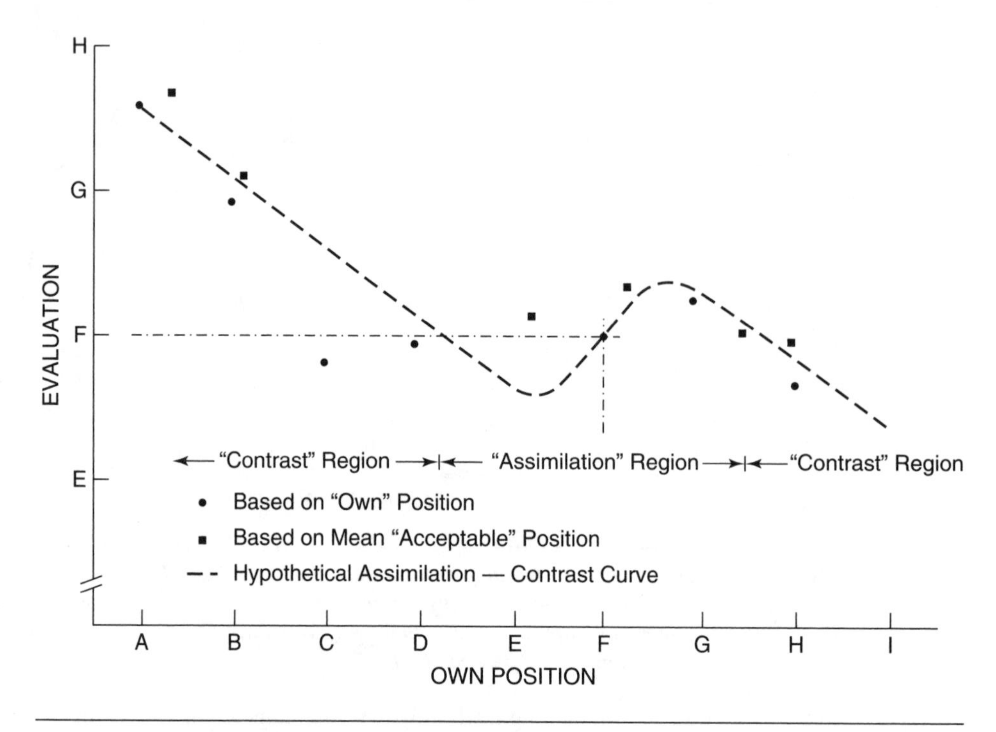

FIGURE 3.3 ***Average placement of position of moderately wet communication (F) by subjects holding various positions on the issue, plotted against hypothetical assimilation-contrast curve. [From Hovland, Harvey, & Sherif, 1957]***

espoused, 28% of the middle-of-the-road subjects were changed in the direction of the communicator, as compared with only 4% of the drys. With the dry communication 14% of the middle-of-the-roaders were changed, while only 4% of the wets were changed. Thus, more of the subjects with small discrepancies were changed than were those with large discrepancies.

These results appear to indicate that, under conditions when there is some ambiguity about the credibility of the communicator and when the subject is deeply involved with the issue, the greater the attempt at change the higher the resistance. On the other hand, with highly respected communicators, as in the previous study with Pritzker using issues of lower involvement, the greater the discrepancy the greater the effect. A study related to ours has just been completed by Zimbardo (1959) which indicates that, when an influence attempt is made by a strongly positive communicator (i.e., a close personal friend), the greater the discrepancy the greater the opinion change, even when the experimenter made a point of stressing the great importance of the subject's opinion.

The implication of these results for our primary problem of conflicting results is clear. The types of issues with which most experiments deal are relatively uninvolving and are often of the variety where expert opinion is highly relevant, as for example, on topics of health, science, and the like. Here we should expect that opinion would be considerably affected by communications and furthermore that advocacy of positions quite discrepant from the individual's own position would have a marked effect. On the other hand, the types of issues most often utilized in survey studies are ones which are very basic and involve deep commitment. As a consequence small changes in opinion due to communication would be expected. Here communication may have little effect on those who disagree at the outset and function merely to strengthen the position already held, in line with survey findings.

A third area of research in which somewhat discrepant results are obtained by the experimental and survey methods is in the role of order of presentation. From naturalistic studies the generalization has been widely adopted that primacy is an extremely important factor in persuasion. Numerous writers have reported that what we experience first has a critical role in what we believe. This is particularly stressed in studies of propaganda effects in various countries when the nation getting across its message first is alleged to have a great advantage and in commercial advertising where "getting a beat on the field" is stressed. The importance of primacy in political propaganda is indicated in the following quotation from Doob:

> The propagandist scores an initial advantage whenever his propaganda reaches people before that of his rivals. Readers or listeners are then biased to comprehend, forever after, the event as it has been initially portrayed to them. If they are told in a headline or a flash that the battle has been won, the criminal has been caught, or the bill is certain to pass the legislature, they will usually expect subsequent information to substantiate this first impression. When later facts prove otherwise, they may be loath to abandon what they believe to be true until perhaps the evidence becomes overwhelming. (Doob 1948, pp. 421–422)

A recent study by Katz and Lazarsfeld (1955) utilizing the survey method compares the extent to which respondents attribute major impact on their decisions about fashions and movie attendance to the presentations to which they were first exposed. Strong primacy effects are shown in their analyses of the data.

We have ourselves recently completed a series of experiments oriented toward this problem. These are reported in our new monograph on *Order of Presentation in Persuasion* (Hovland et al. 1957). We find that primacy is often *not* a very significant factor when the relative effectiveness of the first side of an issue is compared experimentally with that of the second. The research suggests that differences in design may account for much of the discrepancy. A key variable is whether there is exposure to both sides or whether only one side is actually received. In naturalistic studies the advantage of the first side is often not only that it is first but that it is often then the only side of the issue to which the individual is exposed. Having once been influenced, many individuals make up their mind and are no longer interested in other communications on the issue. In most experiments on order of presentation, on the other hand, the audience is systematically exposed to both sides. Thus under survey conditions, self-exposure tends to increase the impact of primacy.

Two other factors to which I have already alluded appear significant in determining the amount of primacy effect. One is the nature of the communicator, the other the setting in which the communication is received. In our volume Luchins presents results indicating that, when the same communicator presents contradictory material, the point of view read first has more influence. On the other hand, Mandell and I show that, when two different communicators present opposing views successively, little primacy effect is obtained.

The communications setting factor operates similarly. When the issue and the conditions of presentation make clear that the points of view are controversial, little primacy is obtained.

Thus in many of the situations with which there had been great concern as to undesirable effects of primacy, such as in legal trials, election campaigns, and political debate, the role of primacy appears to have been exaggerated, since the conditions there are those least conducive to primacy effects: the issue is clearly defined as controversial, the partisanship of the communicator is usually established, and different communicators present the opposing sides.

Time does not permit me to discuss other divergences in results obtained in survey and experimental studies, such as those concerned with the effects of repetition of presentation, the relationship between level of intelligence and susceptibility to attitude change, or the relative impact of mass media and personal influence. Again, however, I am sure that detailed analysis will reveal differential factors at work which can account for the apparent disparity in the generalizations derived.

Integration

On the basis of the foregoing survey of results I reach the conclusion that no contradiction has been established between the data provided by experimental and correlational studies. Instead it appears that the seeming divergence can be satisfactorily accounted for on the basis of a different definition of the communication situation (including the phenomenon of self-selection) and differences in the type of communicator, audience, and kind of issue utilized.

But there remains the task of better integrating the findings associated with the two methodologies. This is a problem closely akin to that considered by the members of the recent Social Science Research Council summer seminar on *Narrowing the Gap between Field Studies and Laboratory Studies in Social Psychology* (Riecken 1954). Many of their recommendations are pertinent to our present problem.

What seems to me quite apparent is that a genuine understanding of the effects of communications on attitudes requires both the survey and the experimental methodologies. At the same time there appear to be certain inherent limitations of each method which must be understood by the researcher if he is not to be blinded by his preoccupation with one or the other type of design. Integration of the two methodologies will require on the part of the experimentalist an awareness of the narrowness of the laboratory in interpreting the larger and more comprehensive effects of communication. It will require on the part of the survey researcher a greater awareness of the limitations of the correlational method as a basis for establishing causal relationships.

The framework within which survey research operates is most adequately and explicitly dealt with by Berelson, Lazarsfeld, and McPhee in their book on *Voting* (1954). The model which they use, taken over by them from the economist Tinbergen, is reproduced in the top half of Figure 3.4. For comparison, the model used by experimentalists is presented in the lower half of the figure. It will be seen that the model used by the survey researcher, particularly when he employs the "panel", method, stresses the large number of simultaneous and interacting influences affecting attitudes and opinions. Even more significant is its provision for a variety of "feedback" phenomena in which consequences wrought by previous

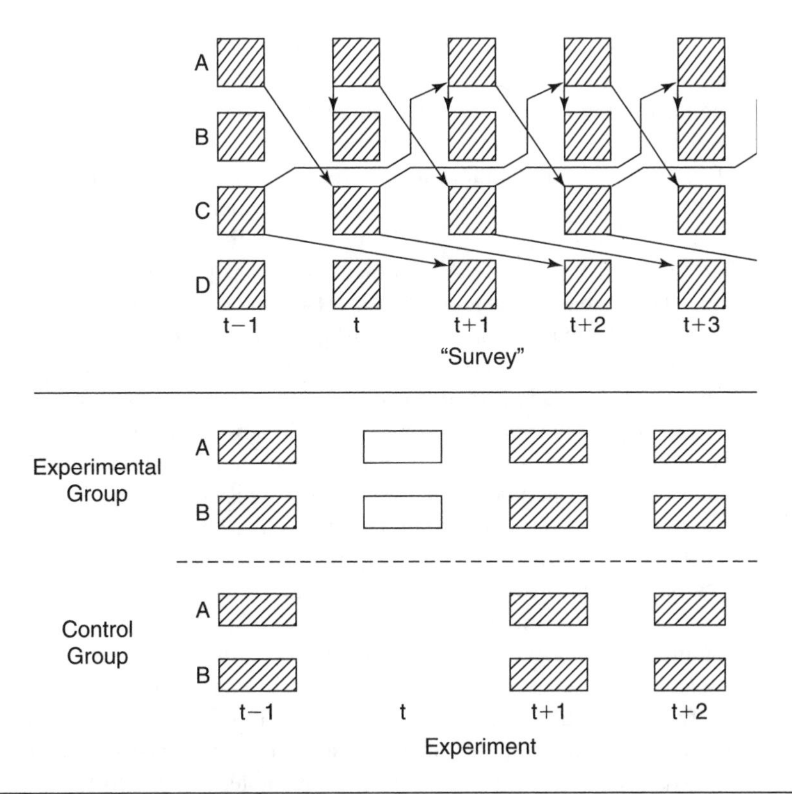

FIGURE 3.4 ***TOP HALF: "Process analysis" schema used in panel research. (Successive time intervals are indicated along abscissa. Letters indicate the variables under observation. Arrows represent relations between the variables.) [From Berelson, Lazarsfeld, & McPhee 1954]***
BOTTOM HALF: Design of experimental research. (Letters on vertical axis again indicate variables being measured. Unshaded box indicates experimentally manipulated treatment and blank absence of such treatment. Time periods indicated as in top half of chart.)

influences affect processes normally considered as occurring earlier in the sequence. The various types of interaction are indicated by the placement of arrows showing direction of effect. In contrast the experimentalist frequently tends to view the communication process as one in which some single manipulative variable is the primary determinant of the subsequent attitude change. He is, of course, aware in a general way of the importance of context, and he frequently studies interaction effects as well as main effects; but he still is less attentive than he might be to the complexity of the influence situation and the numerous possibilities for feedback loops. Undoubtedly the real life communication situation is better described in terms of the survey type of model. We are all familiar, for example, with the interactions in which attitudes predispose one to acquire certain types of information, that this often leads to changes in attitude which may result in further acquisition of knowledge, which in turn produces more attitude change, and so on. Certainly the narrow question sometimes posed by experiments as to the effect of knowledge on attitudes greatly underestimates these interactive effects.

But while the conceptualization of the survey researcher is often very valuable, his correlational research design leaves much to be desired. Advocates of correlational analysis often cite the example of a science built on observation exclusively without experiment: astronomy. But here a very limited number of space-time concepts are involved and the number of competing theoretical formulations is relatively small so that it is possible to limit alternative theories rather drastically through correlational evidence. But in the area of communication effects and social psychology generally the variables are so numerous and so intertwined that the correlational methodology is primarily useful to suggest hypotheses and not to establish casual relationships (Hovland et al. 1949, pp. 329–340; Maccoby 1956). Even with the much simpler relationships involved in biological systems there are grave difficulties of which we are all aware these days when we realize how difficult it is to establish through correlation whether eating of fats is or is not a cause of heart disease, or whether or not smoking is a cause of lung cancer. In communications research the complexity of the problem makes it inherently difficult to derive causal relationships from correlational analysis where experimental control of exposure is not possible. And I do not agree with my friends the Lazarsfelds (Kendall & Lazarsfeld 1950) concerning the effectiveness of the panel method in circumventing this problem since parallel difficulties are raised when the relationships occur over a time span.

These difficulties constitute a challenge to the experimentalist in this area of research to utilize the broad framework for studying communication effects suggested by the survey researcher, but to employ well controlled experimental design to work on those aspects of the field which are amenable to experimental manipulation and control. It is, of course, apparent that there are important communication problems which cannot be attacked directly by experimental methods. It is not, for example, feasible to modify voting behavior by manipulation of the issues discussed by the opposed parties during a particular campaign. It is not feasible to assess the effects of communications over a very long span of time. For example, one cannot visualize experimental procedures for answering the question of what has been the impact of the reading of *Das Kapital* or *Uncle Tom's Cabin*. These are questions which can be illuminated by historical and sociological study but cannot be evaluated in any rigorous experimental fashion.

But the scope of problems which do lend themselves to experimental attack is very broad. Even complex interactions can be fruitfully attacked by experiment. The possibilities are clearly shown in studies like that of Sherif and Sherif (1953) on factors influencing cooperative and competitive behavior in a camp for adolescent boys. They were able to bring under manipulative control many of the types of interpersonal relationships ordinarily considered impossible to modify experimentally, and to develop motivations of an intensity characteristic of real-life situations. It should be possible to do similar studies in the communication area with a number of the variables heretofore only investigated in uncontrolled naturalistic settings by survey procedures.

In any case it appears eminently practical to minimize many of the differences which were discussed above as being not inherent in design but more or less adventitiously linked with one or the other method. Thus there is no reason why more complex and deeply-involving social issues cannot be employed in experiments rather than the more superficial ones more commonly used. The resistance to change of socially important issues may be a handicap in studying certain types of attitude change; but, on the other hand, it is important to understand the lack of modifiability of opinion with highly-involving issues. Greater representation of the diverse types of communicators found in naturalistic situations can also be achieved. In addition, it should be possible to do experiments with a wider range of populations to reduce the possibility that many of our present generalizations from experiments are unduly affected by their heavy weighting of college student characteristics, including high literacy, alertness, and rationality.

A more difficult task is that of experimentally evaluating communications under conditions of self-selection of exposure. But this is not at all impossible in theory. It should be possible to assess what demographic and personality factors predispose one to expose oneself to particular communications and then to utilize experimental and control groups having these characteristics. Under some circumstances the evaluation could be made on only those who select themselves, with both experimental and control groups coming from the self-selected audience.

Undoubtedly many of the types of experiments which could be set up involving or simulating naturalistic conditions will be too ambitious and costly to be feasible even if possible in principle. This suggests the continued use of small-scale experiments which seek to isolate some of the key variables operative in complex situations. From synthesis of component factors, prediction of complex outcomes may be practicable. It is to this analytic procedure for narrowing the gap between laboratory and field research that we have devoted major attention in our research program. I will merely indicate briefly here some of the ties between our past work and the present problem.

We have attempted to assess the influence of the communicator by varying his expertness and attractiveness, as in the studies by Kelman, Weiss, and the writer (Hovland & Weiss 1951; Kelman & Hovland 1953). Further data on this topic were presented earlier in this paper.

We have also been concerned with evaluating social interaction effects. Some of the experiments on group affiliation as a factor affecting resistance to counternorm communication and the role of salience of group membership by Hal Kelley and others are reported in *Communication and Persuasion* (Hovland et al. 1953).

Starting with the studies carried out during the war on orientation films by Art Lumsdaine, Fred Sheffield, and the writer (1949), we have had a strong interest in the duration of communication effects. Investigation of effects at various time intervals has helped to bridge the gap between assessment of immediate changes with those of longer duration like those involved in survey studies. More recent extensions of this work have indicated the close relationship between the credibility of the communicator and the extent of postcommunication increments, or "sleeper effects" (Hovland & Weiss 1951; Kelman & Hovland 1953).

The nature of individual differences in susceptibility to persuasion via communication has been the subject of a number of our recent studies. The generality of persuasibility has been investigated by Janis and collaborators and the development of persuasibility in children has been studied by Abelson and Lesser. A volume concerned with these audience factors to which Janis, Abelson, Lesser, Field, Rife, King, Cohen, Linton, Graham, and the writer have contributed will appear under the title *Personality and Persuasibility* (1959).

Lastly, there remains the question on how the nature of the issues used in the communication affects the extent of change in attitude. We have only made a small beginning on these problems. In the research reported in *Experiments on Mass Communication*, we showed that the magnitude of effects was directly related to the type of attitude involved: film communications had a significant effect on opinions related to straight-forward interpretations of policies and events, but had little or no effect on more deeply intrenched attitudes and motivations. Further work on the nature of issues is represented in the study by Sherif, Harvey, and the writer (1957) which was discussed above. There we found a marked contrast between susceptibility to influence and the amount of ego-involvement in the issue. But the whole concept of ego-involvement is a fuzzy one and here is an excellent area for further work seeking to determine the theoretical factors involved in different types of issues.

With this brief survey of possible ways to bridge the gap between experiment and survey I must close. I should like to stress in summary the mutual importance of the two approaches to the problem of communication effectiveness. Neither is a royal road to wisdom, but each represents an important emphasis. The challenge of future work is one of fruitfully combining their virtues so that we may develop a social psychology of communication with the conceptual breadth provided by correlational study of process and with the rigorous but more delimited methodology of the experiment.

References

Berelson, B. R., Lazarsfeld, P. F., & McPres, W. N. *Voting: A study of opinion formation in a presidential campaign*. Chicago: Univer. Chicago Press, 1954.

Cooper, Eunice, & Jahola, Marie. The evasion of propaganda: How prejudiced people respond to anti-prejudice propaganda. *J. Psychol.*, 1947, 23, 15–25.

Doob, L. W. *Public opinion and propaganda*. New York: Holt, 1948.

French, J. R. P., Jr. A formal theory of social power. *Psychol. Rev.*, 1956, 63, 181–194.

Goldberg, S. C. Three situational determinants of conformity to social norms. *J. abnorm. soc. Psychol.*, 1954, 49, 325–329.

Gosnell, H. F. *Getting out the vote: An experiment in the stimulation of voting*. Chicago: Univer. Chicago Press. 1927.

Hovland, C. I. Effects of the mass media of communication. In G. Lindzey (Ed.), *Handbook of social psychology*. Vol. II. *Special fields and applications.*, Cambridge, Mass.: Addison-Wesley, 1954. Pp. 1062–1103.

Hovland, C. I, Harvey, O. J., & Sherif, M. Assimilation and contrast effects in reactions to communication and attitude change. *J. abnorm. soc. Psychol*, 1957, 55, 244–252.

Hovland, C. I., Janis, I. L., & Kelley, H. H. *Communication and persuasion*. New Haven: Yale Univer. Press, 1953.

Hovland, C. I., Lumsdaine, A. A., & Sheffield, F. D. *Experiments on mass communication*. Princeton: Princeton Univer. Press, 1949.

Hovland, C. I., Mandell, W., Campbell, Enid H., Brock, T., Luchins, A. S., Cohen, A. R., McGuire, W. J., Janis, I. L., Feierabend, Rosalind L., & Anderson, N. H. *The order of presentation in persuasion*. New Haven: Yale Univer. Press, 1957.

Hovland, C. I., & Pritzker, H. A. Extent of opinion change as a function of amount of change advocated. *J. abnorm. soc. Psychol.*, 1957, 54, 257–261.

Hovland, C. I., & Weiss, W. The influence of source credibility on communication effectiveness. *Publ. opin. Quart.*, 1951, 15, 635–650.

Janis, I. L., Hovland, C. L, Field, P. B., Linion, Harriett, Graham, Elaine, Cohen, A. R., Rife, D., Abelson, R. P., Lesser, G. S., & Kino, B. T. *Personality and persuasibility*. New Haven: Yale Univer. Press, 1959.

Katz, E., & Lazarsfeld, P. F. *Personal influence*. Glencoe, Ill.: Free Press, 1955.

Kelman, H. C., & Hovland, C. I. "Reinstatement" of the communicator in delayed measurement of opinion change. *J. abnorm. soc. Psychol.*, 1953, 48, 327–335.

Kendall, Patricia L., & Lazarsfeld, P. F. Problems of survey analysis. In R. K. Merton & P. F. Lazarsfeld (Eds.), *Continuities in social research: Studies in the scope and method of "The American Soldier."* Glencoe, Ill.: Free Press, 1950. Pp. 133–196.

Klapper, J. T. *The effects of mass media*. New York: Columbia Univer. Bureau of Applied Social Research, 1949. (Mimeo.)

Lazarsfeld, P. F., Berelson, B., & Gaudlt, Hazel. *The people's choice*. New York: Duell, Sloan, & Pearce, 1944.

Lipset, S. M., Lazarsfeld, P. F., Barton, A. H., & Linz, J. The psychology of voting: An analysis of political behavior. In G. Lindzey (Ed.), *Handbook of social psychology*. Vol. II. *Special fields and applications.* Cambridge, Mass.: Addison-Wesley, 1954. Pp. 1124–1175.

Maccoby, Eieanor E. Pitfalls in the analysis of panel data: A research note on some technical aspects of voting. *Amer. J. Social.*, 1956, 59, 359–362.

Riecken, H. W. (Chairman) Narrowing the gap between field studies and laboratory experiments in social psychology: A statement by the summer seminar. *Items Soc. Sci. Res. Council*, 1954, 8, 37–42.

Sherif, M., & Sherif, Carolyn W. *Groups in harmony and tension: An integration of studies on intergroup relations*. New York: Harper, 1953.

Zimdardo, P. G. Involvement and communication discrepancy as determinants of opinion change. Unpublished doctoral dissertation, Yale University, 1959.

4

"Biofantasy" and Beyond: Genetics, Social Psychology, and Behavior*

Michael J. Shanahan
University of North Carolina, Chapel Hill, NC

Scott M. Hofer
Oregon State University, Corvallis, OR

Stephen Vaisey
University of North Carolina, Chapel Hill, NC

Do genetic factors cause cancer or cardiovascular diseases? Do they cause complex behaviors like alcoholism, addiction to tobacco products, mental illnesses, or even how well people do in school? Many people—perhaps most people—have developed an understanding of genetics based on the popular media, including articles in newspapers and magazines (Conrad 1997). The headline reads "Gene for Cancer Identified" or "Alcoholism Gene Discovered" and catches your attention. You read the article with great interest and marvel at the progress that science is making.

*Prepared for an edited volume on social psychology edited by Jeffrey C. Chin and Cardell Jacobson. This essay draws on data from the Add Health Study designed by J. Richard Udry, Peter S. Bearman, and Kathleen Mullan Harris and the Add Health Wave IV Program Project directed by Kathleen Mullan Harris (Grant 3P01 HD031921), funded by the National Institute of Child Health and Human Development with cooperative funding from seventeen other agencies. We gratefully acknowledge support from NICHD to Glen H. Elder Jr. and Michael J. Shanahan through their subproject to the Add Health Wave IV Program Project (Grant 3P01 HD031921). Direct correspondence to Michael Shanahan, Department of Sociology, University of North Carolina at Chapel Hill, CB 3210, Hamilton Hall, Chapel Hill, NC, 27599-3210; e-mail: mjshan@unc.edu.

This is not a bad thing. Studies show that the popular media does well at getting the facts right (Bubela and Caufield 2004), so you can learn a fair amount about genes and how they are related to diseases and behaviors from reading *Time* magazine and the *New York Times* and stories in your local newspaper written by the Associated Press (to name a few examples).

On the other hand, this reliance on the popular media is not entirely good, either. Studies also show that while reporting is usually factually correct, it tends to be overly optimistic in its tone. Peter Conrad (2001) calls this "genetic optimism," by which he means that articles often follow an optimistic "plotline": a gene for a disorder exists, it will be found, and then good things like therapies and cures will result. As Conrad notes, this plotline is rarely true, although many articles report the "facts" within this "frame." His analysis of newspaper articles on mental illnesses, for example, found that newspapers reported studies showing a link between a gene and an illness with great excitement; later, when other studies failed to show the same link, newspapers tended to not carry the "negative news" or to even spin the disconfirmation in a positive way. The result can often be that nonspecialists think genetic breakthroughs are just around the corner, while specialists recognize the deep complexity involved in linking genes to diseases.

Similarly, Alan Petersen (2001) calls this overly optimistic tone "biofantasy," by which he means that although articles are usually factually correct, the facts are construed in a very positive way. Accordingly, "discoveries" of "promise" create "hope," "mysteries" are "unlocked," and genes for all sorts of diseases and behaviors are "identified," "pinpointed," and "isolated." The point is that the use of such plotlines and phrasings creates what is almost certainly a misimpression: that once genes for X (some disease or behavior) are identified, we understand X and should be able to prevent X fairly soon. But the truth is that, typically, linking genes to diseases and behaviors is a very complicated business and, at this point in history, a thorough understanding of the links between genetic activity and illnesses or behaviors is almost always more of an aspiration than an imminent reality. Jennifer Singh and her colleagues (2007) call this disconnect between media representations and reality "geno-hype."

So while people who rely on the popular media tend to be factually well informed about genetics and diseases and behaviors, these facts are typically construed far too optimistically. From a sociological point of view, one of the major reasons for this misplaced optimism is that the link between genes and diseases or behaviors oftentimes will depend on the environment. Perhaps you were taught in school that genes are the "building blocks of life." How do they work? The standard answer is that genes encode for proteins and these proteins are ultimately involved in every biological process associated with life. This explanation is the backbone of the "central dogma" of genetics, but it is overly simplistic, for many reasons. In this essay, we focus on one such reason that is of special interest to sociologists: people's environments often affect how genes work. That is, genes "turn on" and genes "turn off" and how genes work is greatly shaped by people's social settings. Not everyone with a strong genetic predisposition for alcoholism becomes an alcoholic, and not everyone who is an alcoholic has a strong genetic predisposition for alcoholism. Rather, it is a combination of genetic predispositions and socially based experiences that makes specific behaviors such as alcoholism (or, likely, any complex behavior) more or less likely.

This last sentence is a source of great excitement in genetics and in the study of genes and behaviors. Obviously, sociologists should be excited about this last sentence, because it suggests that social context plays an important role in how genes are related to behavior. In fact, a growing body of research explores this idea. In this essay, we explore how genes and social context combine to make specific behaviors more or less likely. First, we review some basic social psychological mechanisms that help understand how genes and social context combine to produce behaviors. Then we explore one of these mechanisms with an empirical example. The overarching theme of this essay is that the link between genetic factors and behaviors often depends on patterns of interactions among people. Obviously, social psychology can make important contributions to the study of this important and rich topic.

Social Psychology and Gene-Environment Interactions[1]

One of the major ways that genes and social context combine is called a gene-environment interaction (a "GxE"), which refers to situations in which the effect of genetic factors on behavior depends on social context, or the effect of social context on behavior depends on genetic factors. An example will illustrate the basic idea. Richard Rose and his colleagues (2001) observed that genetic factors predicted the use of alcohol among youth, but that these genetic factors were more powerful predictors of drinking in urban than in rural settings from age 16 to 18.5 years old. Danielle Dick and her colleagues (2001) conducted a study to learn why genetic factors were stronger predictors of drinking in urban than in rural settings. Of special interest, she looked at differences in migration into and out of the municipalities in each region, reasoning that as migration in an area increases, community monitoring and personal accountability decreases. That is, people who live in areas with high migration perceive themselves as less embedded in their communities and hence less accountable to their fellow citizens for their behaviors. So, to illustrate her argument, imagine four hypothetical people:

1. Person A has a high genetic propensity for drinking alcohol and lives in an area with a high migration rate. This person may have a strong desire to drink alcohol, and is in no way deterred by his community. He has the highest likelihood of drinking alcohol among the four hypothetical people.
2. Person B has a low genetic propensity for drinking alcohol and lives in an area with a low migration rate. This person has very little desire to drink alcohol and is strongly embedded in her community. She has the lowest likelihood of the four hypothetical people of drinking alcohol.
3. Person C has with a high genetic propensity for drinking alcohol and lives in an area with a low migration rate. This person may have a strong desire to drink alcohol but she is embedded in her community and feels a heightened sense of responsibility to her neighbors for her actions. She has a medium likelihood of drinking alcohol.

[1]This section of the essay is based on Shanahan, M. J. and Hofer, S. M. (2005). Social context in gene-environment interactions: retrospect and prospect. *Journal of Gerontology: Social* 60B (Special Issue I): 65–76 (Special Issue on The Future of Behavioral Genetics and Aging, edited by Jennifer Harris).

4. Finally, Person D has a low genetic propensity for drinking alcohol and lives in an area with a high migration rate. This person has little desire to drink but he is not embedded in his community and he has a sense of anonymity, not being responsible to anyone for his behaviors. He has a medium likelihood of drinking.

Based on these four hypothetical cases, would you say that genetic factors predict who is most likely to drink alcohol? No. Person A and Person C both have the same, high genetic risk for drinking, but Person A is most likely to drink and Person C has only a medium probability. Do genetic factors predict who is least likely to drink alcohol? Again, no. Person B and Person D both have the same low genetic risk for drinking, but Person B is least likely to drink and Person D has a medium likelihood of drinking. In fact, Person C and Person D have very different genetic propensities to drink, but a roughly equal likelihood of drinking.

To predict who is most (or least) likely to drink alcohol, we need to know the person's level of genetic risk and the migration rate of their community because, as these cases illustrate, there is a gene-environment interaction. In fact, Dick and her colleagues observed just such a pattern. In her study of Finnish youth, she observed that the percentage of migration varied from 2 percent to 16 percent across the municipalities, and migration was strongly, positively correlated with urban areas. How were genetic factors related to drinking across these settings? To answer this fascinating question, the authors estimated "heritability" or (h^2), which is a measure of how much variance in a behavior reflects variance in genetic factors. h^2 can vary from 0 (meaning that genetic factors have nothing to do with the behavior) and 1 (meaning that genetic factors can fully explain or predict a behavior). This is a very important idea in this essay, so please reread the last few sentences if you are not sure what "heritability" means.

The heritability in the area with the highest migration was .60 and the heritability in the area with the lowest migration was .16. That is, genetic factors are substantially more related to drinking alcohol in the areas with high migration when compared with the areas of low migration. The authors speculate that when people live in a stable community, when they have a sense of belonging and accountability for their actions, and when they sense that their actions are being watched by people they know well, they are not that likely to drink alcohol even if they have an appreciable genetic propensity to do so.

Beyond this example, there are many studies that provide evidence for gene-environment interactions, and they are of great interest to sociologists who have an interest in how social context can influence human behavior. In fact, we can develop a typology that describes them. A typology refers to a set of categories that describe something complex. In other words, a typology is a way to simplify matters. In this case, we can identify four such categories or types that make up a typology of gene-environment interactions. Each category represents a social psychological mechanism by which social context interacts with genetic factors to influence behavior.

Type 1: Social Control

Social control refers to social norms and structural constraints that are placed on people to limit their behavior and their choices. Broadly conceived, social control refers to any social arrangement that maintains the social order. Through ties to significant others and social institutions, people are socialized to engage in behaviors that tend to promote the stability of social arrangements or socially desired outcomes at both the micro- and macrolevel.

The sociologist makes no judgment as to whether specific behaviors should be desired or subject to disapproval. The main point is that in all social settings, a consensus emerges about behaviors that should be encouraged and behaviors that should be extinguished, and social control refers to a wide array of processes by which people seek to extinguish "undesirable" behaviors. For example, in the former Communist Soviet Union and its satellite countries, participation in public religious activities was officially disapproved and mechanisms of social control attempted to discourage such behavior. In other countries of Europe at the same time, public festivals organized around religious themes were commonplace, and such behaviors were encouraged. As a social scientist, the sociologist is interested in mapping out and explaining such differences, not in deciding which system is "better."

Studies of gene-environment interactions involving social control point to a general rule of thumb: As social control increases, the additive genetic effect decreases. In other words, in circumstances marked by high levels of social control, a large percentage of the sample—irrespective of their genetic diversity—behaves similarly; conversely, in settings marked by low social control, people's choices and behaviors are more apt to reflect their genetic predispositions.

Perhaps it has already occurred to you that the study just discussed, involving drinking alcohol and migration, is a case of social control. In areas of low migration, people feel "controlled by other people," that is, they feel embedded in a community that shares expectations and norms, they feel responsible to other people to observe, honor, and obey these expectations, and they sense that if they violate these expectations, they may be caught and even punished. So drinking (especially excessively), public drunkenness, drunken rowdy behavior, and so forth—all of these behaviors would be less likely in a high social control setting, even if people had a genetic predisposition for them. In other words, social control can "override" genetic predispositions for socially undesirable behaviors.

Another example will help to drive home the point of social control and genetic influence. Dunne and his colleagues (1997) reported that birth cohort (i.e., the year that someone is born) interacts with genetic factors to predict age of first sexual intercourse. The authors were specifically interested in two groups in a study of Australians: those youth born between 1922 and 1952 (the "older cohort") and youth born between 1952 and 1965 (the "younger cohort"). Which of these two groups do you think was exposed to higher levels of social control with respect to sexual intercourse? Most likely the older cohort. Why? We can only guess, but here are a few differences between the groups: Compared with the younger cohort, the older cohort was more likely to grow up in less populated areas, more likely to be involved in religious activities, and more likely to grow up in a household with two parents. All these factors suggest that the older cohort were monitored more closely by adults and were more subject to normative controls than the younger cohort. Indeed, Dunne and his colleagues found that h^2 accounted for 0 percent of the variance in age of first intercourse for men born between 1922 and 1952, but 72 percent of the variance for men born between 1952 and 1965. A similar pattern (though less dramatic) was observed for women. Further, the groups differed substantially in their mean levels of age of first sexual intercourse: among the younger cohort, the mean age was 18.9 years, which was significantly earlier than the mean age of 21.1 for the older cohort.

Assuming that the two groups have the same genetic diversity (which is a reasonable assumption), these statistics suggest two conclusions that together illustrate social control. First, heritability (i.e., proportion of variance due to genetic factors) is highest in situations of low social control. For the boys in the older cohort, *no* variance in age of first sexual intercourse was associated with genetic factors, compared with a substantial 72 percent in the younger cohort. Second, as might be expected, boys in the older cohort delayed first sexual intercourse when compared with boys in the younger cohort.

The authors suggest that earlier-born cohorts were constrained by the higher levels of social control when compared with the content and force of social controls encountered by youth in later-born cohorts. Unfortunately, how social controls of sexual behavior changed between the earlier and later historical periods is unknown. It may be, for example, that when compared with the later period, the earlier period's prohibition of precocious sexual behavior was more uniformly observed; that adult monitoring of youth was more thorough; and that engagement with nonfamilial adults (school, extracurricular activities, voluntary associations) was more commonplace or more extensive. In any event, the results suggest that changes in mechanisms of social control can lead some youth who are otherwise prone to engage in early sexual activity to delay intercourse.

Type 2: Social Stressors

According to the stress-diathesis model, environmental stressors interact with personal vulnerabilities (or diatheses) to produce disease states, illness, and changes in well-being. This is a fancy way of saying that stressors are bad for you. Stressors like too much work and not enough sleep, poor nutrition, substance abuse, conflictual relationships, such as a difficult boss or coworkers, and so on. But the effect of such stressors depends on characteristics of the person, or diatheses; a diathesis is basically a point of vulnerability. So the idea is that two people might be exposed to the very same stressors, but only one person changes for the worse (e.g., she gets a cold, binge drinks, or becomes irritable) because that person has a diathesis. Although diatheses encompass a wide range of personal characteristics (e.g., cognitive patterns, mood, history of emotional disturbance), the model is believed to apply to the activation of genetic predispositions for at least some outcomes. That is, specific genes can act as a diathesis and help explain why some people react to stressors but not other people. We call this pattern a "triggering interaction" because the social stress acts to "pull the genetic trigger."

Many studies provide examples of triggering interactions. One example is Avshalom Caspi and colleagues' (2002) study of adult antisocial behavior. Animal studies show that maltreatment during childhood leads to alterations in neurotransmitter systems (norepinephrine [NE], serotonin [5-HT], and dopamine [DA]) that, in both mice and humans, continue into adulthood and are positively related to aggressive behavior. Basically, child abuse changes how the brain works, and these changes are related to antisocial behavior into adulthood. Is this true for humans?

Caspi and his colleagues focused on the MAOA gene, which encodes for the MAOA enzyme, which metabolizes neurotransmitters such as NE, 5-HT, and DA. The authors reasoned that low MAOA activity would be insufficient to "counteract" maltreatment-induced changes in these neurotransmitters, and these changes would increase the likelihood of antisocial behavior in later life. In effect, childhood maltreatment coupled with a particular genotype related to lowered levels of MAOA activity alters these neurotransmitters, which in turn predisposes persons to adult antisocial behavior. You may need to reread this paragraph to get the basic idea, but it's worth the effort!

Drawing on males in a sample from New Zealand, Caspi and his colleagues examined how this particular genetic risk and childhood maltreatment (characterized as none, probable, and severe) predicted four indicators of antisocial behavior (conduct disorder, convictions for violent offenses, disposition toward violence, and antisocial personality disorder symptoms). For all four dimensions, a significant interaction was observed such that low levels of MAOA activity coupled with severe maltreatment led to significantly elevated levels of antisocial behavior. Roughly 80 percent (10 of 13 boys) of the severely maltreated, low MAOA boys exhibited adolescent conduct disorder, compared with roughly 40 percent (8 of 20 boys) of the severely maltreated high MAOA boys.

This is truly a remarkable study. The upshot is that if a child is abused and has the gene associated with low levels of MAOA, his odds of being antisocial in young adulthood are substantially elevated. In other words, the MAOA gene acts as a vulnerability, or diathesis, and the stressor is the child abuse. Combined, they lead to a form of distress (antisocial behavior). In isolation, however, neither the MAOA gene nor child abuse could fully explain variability in antisocial behavior.

Type 3: Social Complexity

Among people without a genetic diathesis, social context can also interact with genes to promote higher levels of developmental functioning. That is, given a genetic predisposition or potential (which would not be considered a diathesis for a poor behavioral outcome), some contexts can lead to significantly higher levels of functioning than might otherwise be achieved. Uri Bronfenbrenner and Stephen Ceci's (1994) bioecological model suggests that proximal processes—enduring forms of social interactions characterized by progressive complexity—encourage the actualization of genetic potential: as proximal processes improve, the genetic potential for positive development is increasingly actualized. We refer to these proximal processes as "social complexity" because ultimately they refer to opportunities to interact with people and learn in increasingly complex ways. That is, heritability (as indicated by h^2) will increase as proximal processes (or social opportunities for complexity) are enhanced. One should also observe mean level differences such that positive functioning is enhanced by better proximal settings.

Actually, there are not a lot of examples of Type 3. But consider these examples involving education. Andrew Heath and his colleagues (1985) examined the heritability of educational attainment in Norway before and after educational reforms that made it easier to continue one's education. They compared the h^2 across groups defined by birth cohorts that correspond to the progressive opening up of the educational system to larger percentages of the population. This progressive opening up should, in turn, be related to increases in social complexity at the population level. That is, earlier born cohorts have restricted choice with respect to education when compared with later cohorts. Heath and colleagues report an h^2 for educational attainment for Norwegians born between 1915 and 1939 of .41; between 1940 and 1949 of .74; and between 1950 and 1960 of .67. These last two numbers (.74 and .67) are not that different, so the "before" is about .41 and the after is about .70. The main point is that heritability increased after educational reforms that enhanced, rather than limited, opportunities.

The evidence therefore suggests that the heritability of educational attainment increases as more people face a realistic choice between continuing school or entering the labor market. As the authors conclude, "Increased educational opportunity has led to an increased dependence of educational attainment on innate ability" (p. 736). Assuming that proximal processes were not significantly different between the age cohorts, the results suggest that a broader context of enriched resources is more likely to actualize genetic potential for positive development.

Focusing on a research topic directly linked to proximal process, David Rowe and his colleagues (1999) focused on how the family of origin influences vocabulary intelligence. They report that the heritability of verbal intelligence is significantly greater among high education households (i.e., the average educational level attained by both residential parents exceeded high school) than among low education households (.74 and .26, respectively). Heritability increases from about 25 percent in offspring whose parents have less than a high school degree to about 74 percent in offspring whose parents have more than a high school degree. These results suggest that the genetic potential for verbal intelligence is more fully realized in homes of better-educated parents, who are assumed to provide better proximal processes.

Thus, although no research has directly examined how within-family proximal processes moderate gene expression, research does suggest that proximal family processes realize genetic potential for intellectual development. Enhancement (or complexity) is also likely to explain trends such as increases in average height and weight, or the trend toward earlier puberty. In all of these instances, recent historical changes probably reflect improvements in nutrition and other health-related factors, not changes in the gene pool. That is, for example, people with the same genetic potential are growing taller because of changes in context (such as improved nutrition and a lightening of the manual labor) that may be construed as enhancers.

Type 4: Social Compensation

While the social stress interaction refers to a detrimental context combining with a genetic risk or vulnerability, a social compensation interaction refers to a positive, possibly enriched, setting that prevents the expression of a genetic diathesis. In some instances, compensation and triggering are ends of a continuum. Absent significant stressors, people with a diathesis do not exhibit distress (compensation), but as the level of stressors increases, the likelihood of distress increases (triggering). In some cases, however, compensation may refer to situations in which only pronouncedly enriched settings can neutralize a genetic diathesis. In these cases, compensation refers not to an absence of a detrimental context (e.g., life-events or childhood maltreatment), but rather to the presence of markedly positive features in the environment. In such cases, the interaction refers to diathesis that might well lead to a behavior but for the presence of a compensatory mechanism in the social environment. This is an interesting possibility, because it suggests that social context can "override" genetic propensities for problematic behaviors.

Like the social complexity interaction, there are not many examples. Let's begin with a study involving rats. Studies with nonhuman animals are often very useful because the scientist can perform experiments that would not be possible with humans. Here's just such an example. First, two lines of rats were bred, one each for poor and good maze performance.

That is, one line (or family) of rats could find their way through a maze very well (the "good performers"), while another line of rats had great difficulty (the "poor performers"). Then, poor performers were raised in an enriched setting, which means that their cages were filled with toys. Normally, their cages were not filled with toys. And it was found that poor performers raised in enriched settings could get through the maze as well as the good performers. In other words, the social context (i.e., presence of toys) could compensate for a genetic propensity to perform poorly in the maze.

In fact, recent studies have actually identified a specific gene that can help explain these results, *and* they have linked this gene to differences in brain structure that would also explain these results. These studies are quite amazing because what they suggest is that people can be born with genetic factors that would be associated with low levels of performance, but this genetic propensity can be overridden by social factors, which actually rewire the brain.

Do these results really suggest anything for humans? That is, from a sociological point of view, could we identify social factors that are analogous (or comparable) to the presence of toys that created the enriched setting for the rats? These are very intriguing questions, and the answer is almost certainly. We now turn to an example.

A Human Example of Social Compensation: Going to College[2]

Some rats are born with a genetic propensity to get through a maze quickly, other rats slowly. Similarly, are some humans born with a genetic propensity to go to college, or to not go to college? Obviously there is no "gene for going to college," but some behaviors make continuing one's education more or less likely. Intelligence is one example. Often overlooked, however, is "educational comportment," which refers to behaviors that are appropriate to and expected in educational settings such as sitting still and listening, not fighting, participating in an orderly manner, being respectful of other people, and so on. Above all, a good student is someone who can learn by building on rewarded behaviors (like studying) and by extinguishing punished behaviors (like speaking out of turn). Interestingly, there are genes associated with one's ability to learn from rewards and punishments. The evidence for this assertion is complex, but one such gene, called DRD2, is associated with dopamine receptors (hence "DR") in the brain, especially in an area of the brain associated with processing rewards and punishments.

Imagine for a moment being an elementary school student named Aaron, who is very good at learning from cues from the teacher, the teacher's aide, other students and their experiences, the principal, coaches, his parents and other parents, and so on. Through interacting with all of these people, he learns very quickly what is and is not appropriate behavior in the classroom, on the playground, in the lab, during study time at home, at the library on the weekend, and so on. Now imagine another student, called Zachary, who is identical

[2]This section of the paper is based on: Shanahan, Michael J., Erickson, Lance D., Vaisey, Stephen B, & Andrew Smolen. In press. Helping Relationships and Genetic Propensities: A Combinatoric Study of DRD2, Mentoring, and Educational Continuation. Twin Research and Human Genetics (Special Issue, "Integration of Genetics and Social Environments and Behaviors," edited by Jennifer Harris).

in all respects to Aaron except that Zachary is very bad at learning from cues from the teacher, the teacher's aide, and so on. Interacting with all of these same people with whom Aaron interacts, Zachary never seems to realize what are and are not expected behaviors.

As you might guess, Aaron will fare far better in school than Zachary. Same intelligence, same looks, same everything, except for the ability to learn from rewards and punishments. And in the long run, who is more likely to continue schooling beyond high school? The answer is obvious: Aaron is more likely because, year after year, grade level after grade level, he has been able to perform better than Zachary in educational settings.

Now let's look at some actual data. Table 4.1 shows boys and girls from a sample of American youth that is very close to being nationally representative, the genetic subsample of the National Longitudinal Study of Adolescent Health, often called "Add Health." This table shows the percent students continuing their educations beyond high school (i.e., beyond secondary school to the tertiary level) by race, sex, and whether they have the genetic variant of DRD2 associated with a good ability to learn from rewards and punishments (like Aaron) or a poor ability to learn from rewards and punishments (like Zachary). The bottom row of the table reports statistical tests (based on the z-statistic) that tell us whether the percentages in the columns are statistically different from each other. If the p-value associated with the z-statistic is less than about .05, we would conclude that the two percentages in the column are statistically different from each other.

Let's look at females first. Among white females with DRD2 risk, 57.6 percent continue their educations past high school, while 61.4 percent without DRD2 risk continue their educations. The p-value of .28 indicates that those two numbers are not statistically different from each other. So the conclusion would be that the variant of the DRD2 gene does not seem to matter for whether white females continue their educations past high school. Now let's look at black females. Among black females with DRD2 risk, 47.1 percent continue their educations, compared with 51.8 percent among black females without DRD2 risk. Two observations. First, it looks like black females are less likely to continue their educations than white females. That is of course interesting, but it is not presently our main concern. Our main concern is whether DRD2 risk status seems to make a difference. Once again, however, the p-value of .49 indicates that DRD2 risk status does not matter for the black females. So the overall conclusion is that whether a female has DRD2 risk or not is of little consequence for whether she continues her schooling.

TABLE 4.1 ***Continuation to Tertiary Level by Race, Sex, and DRD2 Risk Status, % and n***

	White		*Black*	
	Male	*Female*	*Male*	*Female*
DRD2 Risk ("Zachary")	44.4, 360	57.6, 363	34.7, 121	47.1, 153
DRD2 Non-Risk ("Aaron")	59.3, 513	61.4, 581	51.5, 99	51.8, 114
z statistic, p	3.90, .000	1.07, .283	2.54, .011	.68, .493

Now let's look at males. For the white males with DRD2 risk (like Zachary), 44.4 percent continue their schooling, compared with the 59.3 percent of white males without DRD2 risk who continue. That difference—between roughly 45 percent and 60 percent—looks big and the p-value of .00 indicates that those two numbers are significantly different. That is, DRD2 risk status seems to matter greatly for whether the white males continue their schooling past high school. Actually, a similar pattern is observed for the black males. For the black males with DRD2 risk, 34.7 percent are continuing their educations compared with 51.5 percent for black males without the DRD2 risk. The p-value indicates that this is a significant difference. The bottom line of Table 4.1 is that DRD2 risk status predicts educational continuation beyond high school, but only for the males.

Getting back to the questions posed at the beginning of this section, just as rats were identified that had a genetic predisposition for poor maze performance, it appears that we can identify a group of males with a genetic predisposition not to continue their schooling. But, as with the enriched environments of the rats, could we identify socially compensatory mechanisms by which the effect of DRD2 risk is nullified? That is, can we identify a source of social compensation that would lead males with DRD2 risk status to have the same probability of continuation as males without DRD2 risk?

The answer is yes, specifically whether the student has a mentor who is a teacher. (For the sake of simplicity, we will focus on the white males only. Both white and black males are examined in our original essay.) What is a mentor? A wise and trusted advisor. In fact, mentoring represents a form of social capital, which means that it joins (or links) people together (in this case, the student and the mentor) and these links make things happen (in this case, educational continuation) (Portes 1998). Prior research distinguishes between formal and informal mentoring. *Formal mentors* usually are adults who participate in special mentoring programs to help youth who have a high risk of failure, at least in terms of their educational prospects (see Rhodes et al. 2000) or their social disadvantage (e.g., Rhodes et al. 1994). That is, sometimes students who are doing very poorly in school will be assigned a mentor who is part of a mentoring program. Of course, it is hoped that this mentor, or trusted advisor, will help the student do better in school. On the other hand, *informal mentors* are relatives, friends, and other community members with whom youth have developed relationships through their existing social networks.

The distinction between formal and informal mentors maps onto the distinction between bridging and bonding social capital. *Bridging social capital* connects actors who differ with respect to salient resources, and it is believed to be especially important in reducing socioeconomic inequalities (including education). Thus, formal mentors are likely to represent bridging capital because programs assign people with special skills and knowledge to assist students in need. Teachers who are mentors, although they are not typically formal mentors, also represent bridging capital because they possess a high level of experience with and insight into the educational system. In contrast, *bonding social capital* connects people who do not differ appreciably in the kinds of resources that might matter for facilitating a particular outcome. Accordingly, informal mentors who are not teachers are likely to lack expertise in the educational system and thus constitute bonding capital.

These distinctions suggest that teachers as mentors may be especially salient forms of bridging social capital with respect to educational continuation. Because of their expertise with the educational system and personal knowledge of the student, a mentor who is a teacher may contribute to school continuation in the presence of DRD2 risk (Hypothesis 1) by encouraging appropriate behavioral comportment and good decisions about schooling. On the other hand, a non-teacher mentor, lacking these insights and skills, may be of little assistance (Hypothesis 2).

We can test these ideas with data from the National Longitudinal Study of Adolescent Health. The white males with DRD2 risk are referred to as the "A1+" group, and the white males without this risk are designated "A1–," following a convention in genetics. The figure summarizes a set of analyses that are explained in detail in the original article that we are now summarizing. What does Figure 4.1 show? About 50 percent of the males without DRD2 risk and without a mentor continue in their schooling. The percentages increase significantly if they have a non-teacher mentor (about 63%) and again if they have a mentor who is a teacher (about 70%). Thus, among the males without DRD2 risk, having a mentor helps, especially if the mentor is a teacher.

What about the males with DRD2 risk? About 44 percent of the nonrisk boys without a mentor continue their education and that number barely changes if they have a non-teacher mentor. The asterisks in Figure 4.1 also indicate that DRD2 risk and DRD2 nonrisk boys differ significantly in whether a non-teacher mentor helps. The DRD2 risk males simply do not benefit from mentors who are not teachers, while the nonrisk males do benefit. Turning our attention to perhaps the most important comparison: about 65 percent of the DRD2 risk males with a mentor who is a teacher continue beyond secondary school, and this number is not significantly different from the 70 percent continuation among DRD2 nonrisk males. That is, a teacher who is a mentor completely compensates for DRD2 risk with respect to the probability of continuing past high school. (The data support Hypotheses 1 and 2.) Just as the enriched setting of the poor performer rats compensated for their genetic

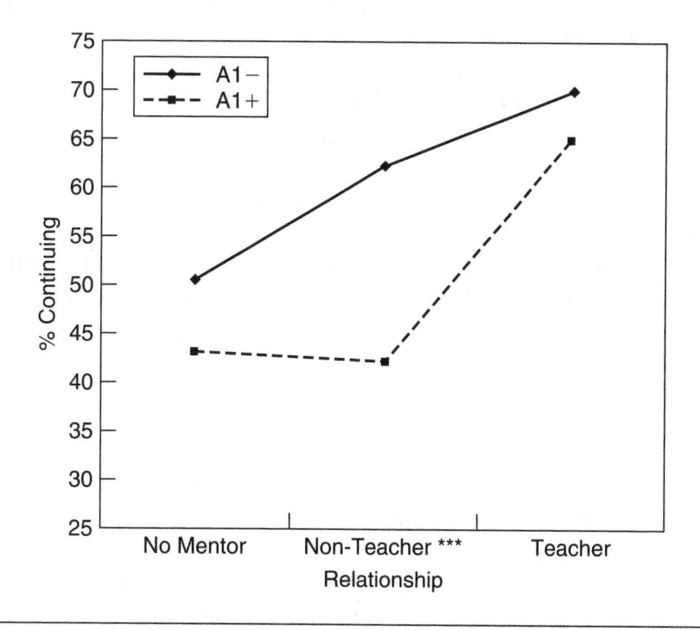

FIGURE 4.1 ***Continuation Rates for White Males by DRD2 Genotype***

propensity to be slow in mazes, teachers who are mentors can compensate for a genetic propensity not to continue one's education past high school.

Who is the Teacher's Pet?

Thus far, we have considered how genes and social context interact to make specific behaviors more or less likely. We have identified the basic social psychological mechanisms by which genes and social context interact, and we have presented an extended empirical illustration of the compensatory mechanism. The basic idea has been that the association between genetic factors often depends on social factors. As in, the association between DRD2 risk and school continuation depends on whether the student has a mentor who is a teacher.

But there is a wrinkle to the story, and the wrinkle is called a "gene-environment correlation," which refers to situations in which individuals have a genetic propensity for a specific behavior, and they are more likely to be in a social context that encourages the expression of that behavior. Once again, that may be a sentence worth rereading. It's a tricky idea, but an important one, too. A classic example is the newborn infant who has a genetic propensity for irritability, cries a lot, and upsets his parents, whose frustrated and exhausted behaviors strengthen the newborn's irritable behaviors. Another example: a young woman has a genetic propensity for substance abuse and chooses to "hang out" with friends who smoke marijuana. Soon, these friends are encouraging her to smoke marijuana and she does so.

Now let's return to our example of DRD2 and teachers who are mentors. We know that teachers can compensate for DRD2 risk, and we strongly suspect that DRD2 risk is associated with inappropriate behaviors in the classroom. Would males with DRD2 risk have teacher-mentors in the first place? Maybe DRD2 risk is associated with not continuing in school, and boys with DRD2 risk are unlikely to have teacher-mentors—a classic gene-environment correlation. In fact, a statistical analysis shows that this is true: of 360 white males with DRD2 risk, only 46 have teacher-mentors. In other words, DRD2 risk decreases the likelihood that a person will have a mentor who is a teacher. This makes sense. Teachers are not likely to establish and maintain a close relationship with a problematic student.

The upshot of all of these analyses and all of these numbers is this: compared with males without DRD risk, males with DRD2 risk are less likely to continue their educations beyond high school. However, teachers can compensate for the DRD2 risk, such that DRD2 risk and DRD2 nonrisk boys have the same probability of continuation. Note that boys with DRD2 risk are less likely to have a mentor who is a teacher than boys without DRD2 risk.

Beyond Biofantasy

In the final analysis, the connections among DRD2 risk status, mentoring, and educational continuation are fairly complex. Actually, we have simplified matters greatly for the sake of readability. For example, had we included black males, the story would have been similar, but more complex. In principle, we could add several additional layers of complexity as well. First, people have dozens (maybe hundreds, maybe thousands) of genes that might bear on school continuation. And if one defines a gene as a sequence of DNA that encodes for a protein (a standard definition), then there may be many more genetic factors—beyond genes themselves—that contribute to the biological processes by which some behaviors are more likely. Second, there are dozens of sociological factors that are known to predict school continuation. Parents' expectations and behaviors, kin networks, peer influences, school characteristics, birth cohort patterns, economic factors, and so on. We have looked at one gene and one sociological factor—a massive simplification. In truth, how genes are connected to school continuation is likely to be exceedingly complex, far beyond the complexity of our example. And we suspect that our example is representative of the complexity one would encounter in linking any genetic factor with social context and human behavior.

All these considerations suggest caution when the urge for a biofantasy sets in. Perhaps a gene for a complex disease or behavior has been discovered, and perhaps this breakthrough will lead to treatments. We hope so. But as the examples in this essay suggest, many (perhaps most or even all) complex behaviors and diseases are likely to reflect complex combinations of genetic and social factors. These combinations can not be fully understood without recourse to basic social psychological mechanisms that link people to each other: social control, social stress, social complexity, and social compensation. Social psychologists have long appreciated that these processes (sometimes referred to with different terms) are central to the human condition, and we now also know that they are central to gene-environment interplay.

References

Bronfenbrenner, Urie and Stephen J. Ceci. 1994. "Nature-Nurture Reconceptualized in Developmental Perspective—A Bioecological Model." *Psychological Review* 101:568–586.

Bubela, Tania M. and Timothy A. Caulfield. 2004. "Do the Print Media 'Hype' Genetic Research? A Comparison of Newspaper Stories and Peer-Reviewed Research Papers." *CMAJ : Canadian Medical Association Journal = Journal De l'Association Medicale Canadienne* 170:1399–107.

Caspi, Avshalom, et al. 2002. "Role of Genotype in the Cycle of Violence in Maltreated Children." *Science* 297:851–854.

Conrad, Peter. 1997. "Public Eyes and Private Genes: Historical Frames, News Constructions, and Social Problems." *Social Problems* 44:139–154.

———. 2001. "Genetic Optimism: Framing Genes and Mental Illness in the News." *Culture Medicine and Psychiatry* 25:225–247.

Dick, Danielle M., Richard J. Rose, Richard J. Viken, Jaakko Kaprio, and Markku Koskenvuo. 2001. "Exploring Gene-Environment Interactions: Socioregional Moderation of Alcohol Use." *Journal of Abnormal Psychology* 110:625–632.

Dunne, M. P., et al. 1997. "Genetic and Environmental Contributions to Variance in Age at First Sexual Intercourse." *Psychological Science* 8:211–216.

Petersen, A. 2001. "Biofantasies: Genetics and Medicine in the Print News Media." *Social Science & Medicine* (1982) 52:1255–1268.

Portes, A. 1998. "Social Capital: Its Origins and Applications in Modern Sociology." *Annual Review of Sociology* 24:1–24.

Rhodes, J. E., Grossman, J. B. and Resch, N. L. (2000). "Agents of Change: Pathways through which mentoring Relationships Influence Adolescents' Academic Adjustment." *Child Development,* 71:1662-1671.

Rhodes, J. E., J. M. Contreras, and S. C. Mangelsdorf. 1994. "Natural Mentor Relationships among Latina Adolescent Mothers—Psychological Adjustment, Moderating Processes, and the Role of Early Parental Acceptance." *American Journal of Community Psychology* 22:211–227.

Rose, R. J., D. M. Dick, R. J. Viken, and J. Kaprio. 2001. "Gene-Environment Interaction in Patterns of Adolescent Drinking: Regional Residency Moderates Longitudinal Influences on Alcohol Use." *Alcoholism, Clinical and Experimental Research* 25:637–643.

Rowe, D. C., K. C. Jacobson, and E. J. C. G. Van den Oord. 1999. "Genetic and Environmental Influences on Vocabulary IQ: Parental Education Level as Moderator." *Child Development* 70:1151–1162.

Singh, J., J. Hallmayer, and J. Illes. 2007. "Science and Society—Interacting and Paradoxical Forces in Neuroscience and Society." *Nature Reviews Neuroscience* 8:153–160.

5

Toward a General Theory of Interpersonal Processes

Jonathan H. Turner

University of California

Social psychology examines the relationship between the thoughts, emotions, and actions of individuals, on the one side, and the properties of social structure and culture, on the other side. Typically, research and theorizing in sociological variants of social psychology are specialized, exploring how individuals are influenced by a particular aspect of social structure or a dimension of culture. In this chapter, I take a somewhat different tact and lay out a more general theory of interpersonal processes that contains a more robust conceptualization of the person, social structure, and culture. In a very real sense, my goal is to integrate many of the more specialized theories in social psychology into a more global theory that explains the dynamic relations among persons, social structure, and culture.

The Nature of Social Structure

In most theories in social psychology, social structure is conceptualized at the microlevel, examining how people behave in status and roles within groups or more transitory encounters. This emphasis makes a great deal of sense because the direct interface between persons and their social worlds is typically face-to-face interaction of people in strips of interaction within small-scale structures like groups. True, people often interact with larger audiences when they think about their entire society or plug themselves into diverse social worlds through media, ranging from televisions to the Internet and gaming. Here, people take account of larger-scale dimensions of social structure and culture, using these macrolevel social settings to guide their thoughts and actions. There is, then, a macrolevel social universe in which microlevel encounters and groups are embedded, and so a general theory of interpersonal processes needs to include a conceptualization of social structure and culture at all levels of social reality. Figure 5.1 lays out a very simple view of social structures.

As Figure 5.1 outlines, social reality can be viewed as layered at three basic levels: micro, meso, and macro. At the microlevel are *encounters* of face-to-face interactions among individuals in groups. At the mesolevel are two basic kinds of social structures denoted by the terms *corporate units* and *categoric units*. A corporate unit is one where there is a division of labor organized to achieve goals, even goals that are somewhat vague. An organization such as a university is a corporate unit, and so is a community, because these kinds of middle-level structures evidence a division of labor designed to accomplish particular goals. Categoric units—the other basic type of mesolevel structure—are composed by distinctions that people make and use as a basis for evaluations of, and responses to, those placed into a particular social category. For example, gender, ethnicity, age, and social class are all social categories because they mark persons as having a particular nature and serve as a basis for responding to them. Oftentimes, categoric units reflect positions in the division

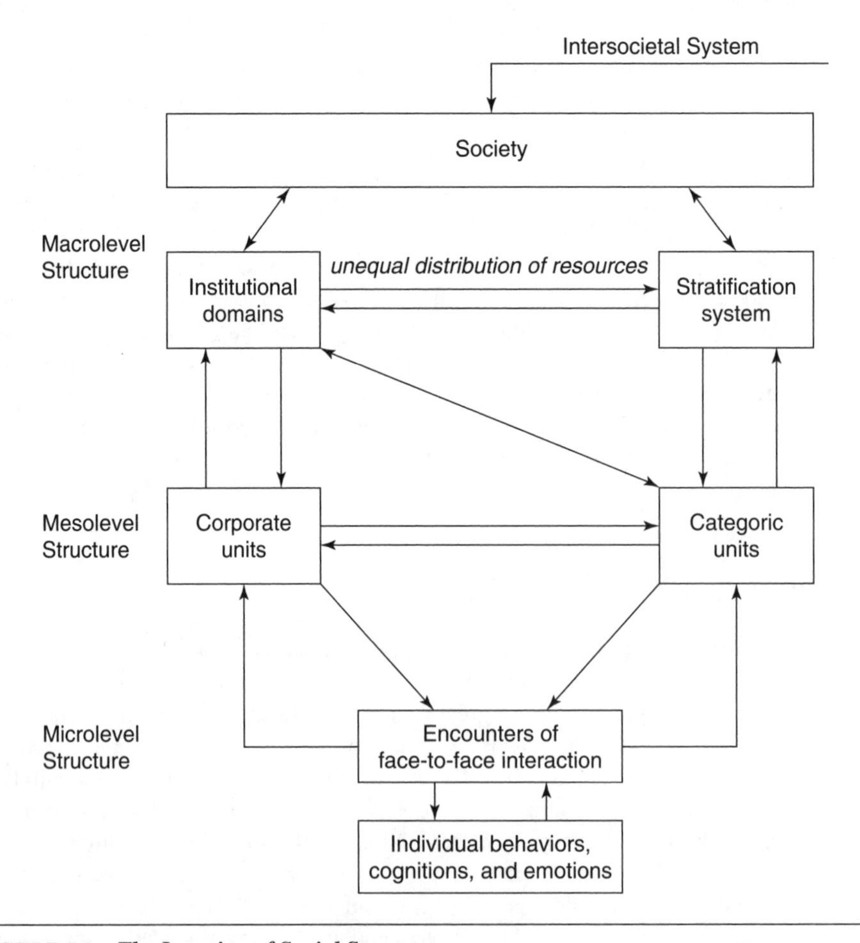

FIGURE 5.1 ***The Layering of Social Structure***

of labor. For instance, the category of "student" is generated by the position and role of student in a corporate unit—a school or university. Similarly, for some purposes, the category of mother is important, and this categoric unit is generated by the division of labor in a corporate unit, the family. This effect of corporate units in generating social distinctions that, under some circumstances, can serve as categoric units is marked by the arrow in Figure 5.1 from corporate units directed at categoric units. The reverse is also true; oftentimes, the division of labor in corporate units is affected by categoric unit membership. For example, slaves in the old plantation system (a corporate unit) in the pre–Civil War south were all members of a categoric unit: African-origin persons with dark skin. The plantation's division of labor was thus built around two basic categoric units—whites and blacks. Similarly, the division of labor within a business may be organized around other kinds of categoric units—age, gender, and ethnicity. Most secretaries, for instance, are women whereas a high proportion of senior management is composed of men as a category—a pattern reflecting long-standing (but changing) patterns of gender discrimination.

Encounters in small groups are almost always embedded in corporate and categoric units. For instance, encounters within classrooms are lodged inside of a school structure, a more mesolevel corporate unit. The same is true of encounters and categoric units. It may at first be difficult to visualize encounters of face-to-face interaction as embedded inside of categoric units, but such is almost always the case. Imagine, for example, a face-to-face encounter among all males and compare that with one among all females. The interactions will be very different because they are lodged in two different categoric units—women and men. Or, imagine an encounter of both males and females, comparing it with one of only one gender; the two types of encounters will reveal very different patterns of thought and action because they are embedded in different types of categoric units. Indeed, the categories that people use have very large effects on how they think about themselves and others, as well as how they are prepared to act toward members of diverse categoric units.

Since the most immediate social structure for any episode of interaction is almost always a corporate unit and a categoric unit(s), the properties of these two types of mesolevel social structures constrain people's thoughts, emotions, actions, and interactions. Indeed, encounters in small groups are inevitably constrained by the nature of the mesolevel structures in which they are embedded. We will all, for instance, act very differently in a school, family, church, or business because the structure and culture of these corporate units vary enormously; similarly, we will behave differently depending on the categoric units in which an encounter is embedded, as can be seen when people of different or the same gender, similar or divergent ages, the same or different social classes, or the same or divergent ethnic backgrounds interact. A general theory of interpersonal processes must, therefore, explain how this embedding of interpersonal processes inside of mesolevel corporate and categoric units affects individual thoughts, emotions, and actions. Conversely, we should also seek to explain the effects of what people do in encounters on the structure and culture of corporate and categoric units.

At the macrolevel of social structure, there are two basic kinds of structures within a society: *institutional domains* and *stratification systems* (Turner 2007). An institutional domain is a set of corporate units devoted to solving fundamental problems of adaptation in a society (Turner 2003). For example, the economy is a set of corporate units (and often social categories as well) that is devoted to securing resources, producing goods and services, and distributing these; the kinship domain is composed of corporate units (families) with the purpose of solving problems of reproduction; the polity or government is a complex of corporate units for coordinating and controlling activities in a society; and the same could be said for other institutional domains, such as education, religion, science, medicine, sport, recreation, and law. Each is composed of corporate units (and typically categoric units) dedicated to solving particular kinds of problems facing populations.

A stratification system is built around the unequal distribution of valued resources—money, power, prestige and honor, health, education, and virtually any resource that bestows value. As a result of inequalities in resource distribution, distinctive social strata or classes tend to emerge in a society. People with similar levels of resources tend to live together, interact frequently, think in similar ways, intermarry, and in general converge in their behaviors and lifestyles. As a result, they can be distinguished from each other as members of different categoric units (that is, as a member of a particular social class), but we must remember that this categoric unit is part of a larger system of such units, or in other words, a stratification system.

As the arrows in Figure 5.1 denote, institutional domains are constructed from corporate units and stratification systems from categoric units. Any particular institutional domain is composed of corporate units that are interrelated in ways that allow them to resolve particular problems of adaptation facing a population, whereas a stratification system almost always has class, ethnic, gender, and age dimensions because members of these different categoric units generally receive different shares of resources. As the arrow flowing from institutional domains to stratification system emphasizes, the unequal distribution of resources generally occurs as a result of the structure and culture of an institutional domain. The economy distributes incomes and wealth differentially; the polity distributes power; the educational domain distributes prestige-giving knowledge (and credentials); the family bestows love and affection; the legal system gives entitlements to property and other resources; and so on for most institutional domains. The reverse arrow from stratification system to institutional emphasizes that, once inequalities and strata exist, members of different social categories participate in the corporate units of each domain differentially, thereby reinforcing their position in the stratification system. Thus, if the plantation system (an element of the economy) of the pre–Civil War south distributed virtually all resources unequally to blacks and whites, the existence of these two distinct categoric units (built on ethnic markers like skin color) determined the respective chances of blacks and whites in the southern economy. Or, if women have less money or power than men because of discriminatory practices in the economy and political domains, this additional layer of difference on top of the obvious differences between the sexes has worked historically to channel men and women into different positions in corporate units of institutional domains like the economy and polity but others as well, such as family and education. Much of this "channeling" has, of course, been the result of gender discrimination.

Finally the last two macrolevel structures are *society as a whole* and *system of intersocietal relations*. A society is composed of its institutional domains and stratification system, and an intersocietal system is generally structured around relations between the institutional domains or stratification systems of two or more societies. For example, a political alliance or treaty is a relation between the polities and legal systems of two or more societies, or a pattern of trade is between the economies of societies. Migration patterns from one society to another often occur as a result of stratification, with the poor and lower classes of one society migrating to another in search of opportunities.

We should also consider institutional domains and stratification systems as embedded in a society and its culture or even a system of societies. For example, it would be difficult to understand the American economy today or the shifting demographics of the stratification system without knowledge of dynamic relations of America in the world economic system. Similarly, moving down the layers of social reality portrayed in Figure 5.1, we should also recognize that any corporate unit at the mesolevel is embedded in an institutional domain and often the stratification system as well. For instance, we could not understand the actions of a corporation without knowledge of the structure and culture of the economy in which it is embedded, or the class composition of its workforce. Similarly, we could not fully understand the properties and dynamics of categoric units without recognizing the effects of the institutional domains generating the inequalities that structure the stratification system. To illustrate, gender as a category is produced by corporate units in the kinship and economic domains, that, in turn, generate a pattern of gender inequality. Or, ethnicity is sustained by discrimination in institutional domains and by the inequalities that these domains generate; as a consequence, interpersonal processes are influenced not only by the categoric unit of ethnicity but also in the structure and culture of the institutional domains that have produced a stratification system with an ethnic dimension.

The key insight to be gained from the layering of different levels of social structure is that microlevel interpersonal processes are embedded in mesolevel structures which, in turn, are embedded in macrostructures. The most immediate structural units constraining encounters are, of course, the division of labor in a corporate unit and the differential evaluation of members in categoric units. Yet, these mesolevel units are lodged inside in institutional domains, stratification systems, societies, and even systems of intersocietal relations. To illustrate, much of what occurs in encounters in a corporate unit embedded in the American economy is constrained by the structure of the American economy and the larger world economic system. Even among students in college, meso- and macrolevel structures are affecting what occurs in the classroom; encounters in the classroom, for example, are not only constrained by the structure and culture of the university or college, but also by the macrolevel institutional domain of education and, increasingly, the competition of this domain with that in other societies that are educating workers. Thus, even as you think about your major and future career, you are also probably calculating the prestige of your university, the value of degrees in various majors, and the level of competition in job markets (national and international) among individuals with the skills that you will possess, especially in an age of outsourcing where jobs can be exported to other societies. Thus, as you ponder these matters, your thoughts and later your actions are being constrained by embedding from the world system down to you as single person and eventually to your actions in encounters lodged in mesostructures that, in turn, are embedded in macrostructures.

By comparing this conceptualization of the "social" portion of social psychology with that offered by other perspectives within social psychology, it is immediately evident that my portrayal is more global. Yet, I address many of the same issues as more specialized perspectives because people's thoughts, emotions, and actions are constrained by the immediate mesolevel units in which any episode of interpersonal behavior is embedded. And once focus is on these meso-units, the processes that I describe are much the same as other approaches because the focus is on status, roles, expectations, norms, and status characteristics like gender or ethnicity.

The Layering of Culture

Culture can be defined as *systems of symbols* that humans create and use to regulate social life. Like social structure, culture operates at micro-, meso-, and macrolevels. In Figure 5.2, I outline a very simple way to conceptualize the layering of culture. At the level of society as a whole, there is a language and, in some societies, languages that provide the basis for

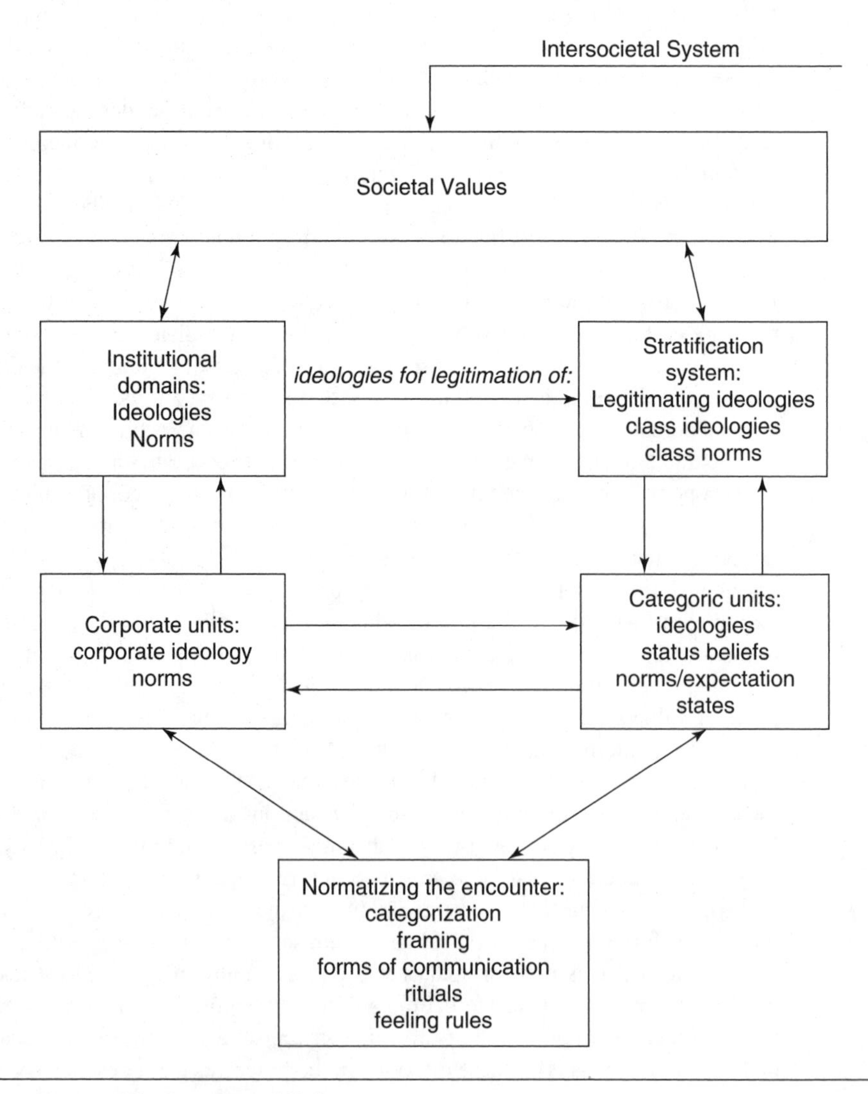

FIGURE 5.2 ***The Layering of Culture***

all other symbol systems, whereas in more developed societies, additional symbol systems, such as mathematics, computer algorithms, and logics, are also used to build culture. In terms of what transpires at the level of interpersonal behavior, however, we can narrow our focus in this chapter, and concentrate on *general values* that denote what is right and wrong, appropriate and inappropriate. Values are the standards of morality that filter down through institutional domains to corporate units and, then, to encounters of face-to-face interaction. Similarly, these values filter down as evaluations and legitimations for the overall stratification systems and, then, down to particular categoric units providing evaluations of members from diverse categoric units during the course of face-to-face interactions.

This top-down process involves taking general values and converting them into *ideologies* that specify what ought and should occur within each institutional domain and that legitimate the unequal distributions of resources and the respective resource shares of strata comprising the stratification system. These ideologies thus take the moral premises of values and apply them to institutional domains and social strata. For example, in American society, there is a general value emphasizing achievement and doing well; this value premise is then applied somewhat differently through ideologies to specific institutional domains, such as the economy (work hard to achieve), family (try to be a good parent), education (get good grades to succeed), polity (legislate in ways that increase the success of citizens and society as whole), science (success is in discovering new knowledge), sports (success in winning), and so on for all domains. Likewise, the overall stratification system is legitimated by the combination of these institutional ideologies, especially those institutions that distribute resources. Thus, typically, a stratification system is legitimated by the ideologies guiding actions of corporate units in the economy, polity, and education which are most responsible for the distribution of money, wealth, power, and prestige. Then, depending on where a categoric unit is located within the overall stratification system, there will be a differential evaluation of this category as more worthy than other categoric units located at lower places in the stratification systems. Obviously this is not "fair," but it is a fact of social life. Thus, because whites and males are higher in the stratification system than some ethnic minorities and, to a lesser degree, women, white males receive more positive evaluations and prestige that influences what transpires in interactions in encounters. Again, this dynamic is not fair, and indeed can be challenged by general values and ideologies emphasizing equality of opportunity and fairness, as has been done in efforts to reduce discrimination. But, for our purposes now, the key idea is not to focus on fairness but, rather, to recognize that culture is layered, with general values providing the premises for ideologies that, in turn, evaluate members of categoric units and serve as underlying premises for the norms that regulate conduct.

Norms operate at a number of levels. One is the institutional level, where there are expectations for how actors in a particular institutional domain are to behave. Thus, workers, students, parents, scientists, politicians, religious practitioners, doctors, and other positions and roles in corporate units of distinctive institutional domains are regulated by general norms that most people in a society understand. Similarly, there are general norms for diverse strata within the stratification system that guide conduct of people located at different positions and that hold diverse categoric unit memberships. Then, there are more specific norms that regulate behaviors in the division of labor in corporate units and among members of categoric units. And finally, as we will come to see, various levels of norms, ideologies, and values are all assembled in face-to-face interactions as a set of expectations on individuals for how they should behave during moment-by-moment interactions in face-to-face encounters. We will term this process "normatization" because it involves individuals taking the various layers of culture and applying them to particular interactions in ways that generate a set of expectations on each individual.

There are, then, layers in culture numerated in Figure 5.2 that roughly correspond to the layers of social structure portrayed in Figure 5.1. Together, these layers of social structure and culture can be seen as the "social" side of social psychology. The psychology part concerns the characteristics of individuals as they negotiate face-to-face interactions and as they think about, and have emotions over, their experiences in these interactions lodged in encounters and small groups that, in turn, are embedded in mesolevel structures (corporate and categoric units), successively embedded in more macrolevel institutional domains, stratification systems, societies as whole, and systems of societies.

Microdynamic Processes

When people interact, certain dynamics always unfold. Each of these is summarized in Table 5.1 for easy reference. These dynamics are constrained by the embedding of virtually all encounters in corporate and categoric units which, in turn, are lodged in institutional domains and stratification systems that are part of whole societies and, potentially, systems of societies. Just how these dynamics unfold, then, is constrained by embedding. Conversely, as interaction unfolds, it can work to change the structure and culture of corporate and categoric units, and potentially, macrostructures. Still, most of the time, the power of social structure and culture is top down, coming from macro to meso to constrain the microlevel processes. Let us now review how each of these dynamics processes operates in interpersonal relations.

TABLE 5.1 ***Microdynamic Forces Driving Interpersonal Behavior in Encounters***

Normatizing: The application of culture so as to categorize others and the situation, develop frames delimiting and specifying what is to transpire in the situation, use rituals (open, close, form, and repair interactions) to regulate the flow of interaction, establish forms of communication (talk and body language) in the situation, calculate and assess just shares of resources in a situation, and establish feelings to be felt and displayed by persons in a situation.

Transactional Needs: The activation of needs to verify self and identities, to receive positive exchange payoffs, to sense group inclusion (in the ongoing interpersonal flow), to achieve a sense of trust (predictability, respect, and sincerity) from others, and to achieve a sense of facticity (intersubjectivity and sense that things are as they appear).

Emotions: The arousal of variants and combinations of satisfaction-happiness, aversion-fear, assertion-anger, and disappointment-sadness in individuals.

Roles: The presentation of sequences of gestures marking a predictable course of action (role making) by an individual as well as the reading and interpreting of the gestures emitted by others to understand the course of action of others in a situation (role taking).

Status: The placement and differential evaluation of individuals in positions vis-à-vis other positions occupied by others in a situation.

Normatizing the Encounter

In almost all episodes of interaction, individuals bring to the encounter normative expectations about how individuals should and will behave. These expectations revolve around several considerations, summarized briefly in Table 5.1. Figure 5.3 outlines the dynamics of establishing expectations for an encounter in a more process form that unfolds over time. In some encounters, normative expectations are not clear, or at least not fully known; and under these conditions, individuals will interact in ways to establish normative expectations. As they do so, people always are cognizant of the corporate unit in which an encounter is embedded, and the distribution of individuals in various categoric units such as age, gender, or ethnicity. Thus, individuals are not free to construct expectations at will; they typically must do so within the cultural constraints—norms and ideologies—of the mesolevel corporate and categoric units in which the encounter is lodged. Let us now turn to outlining in more detail the dimensions of normatizing listed in Table 5.1 and diagrammed in Figure 5.3.

Categorizing. One of the first things that individuals do in an interaction is to place self and others into a categoric unit. All categoric units are differentially evaluated (by values and ideologies) and all carry with them expectations for how people in this category should behave. Thus, expectations on men and women, old and young, members of diverse ethnic groups, or people occupying different class positions are generally known by parties to an interaction. If, however, the expectations are not clear or if people in various categoric units violate expectations for how they should behave, then the interaction will prove awkward; and it will be breached because individuals cannot normatize the situation in terms of this fundamental dimension. Indeed, as Figure 5.3 outlines, if categorization fails, all other dimensions of normatization are in jeopardy because categorization is typically the first step in normatizing an encounter. If mutual categorization fails, then communication,

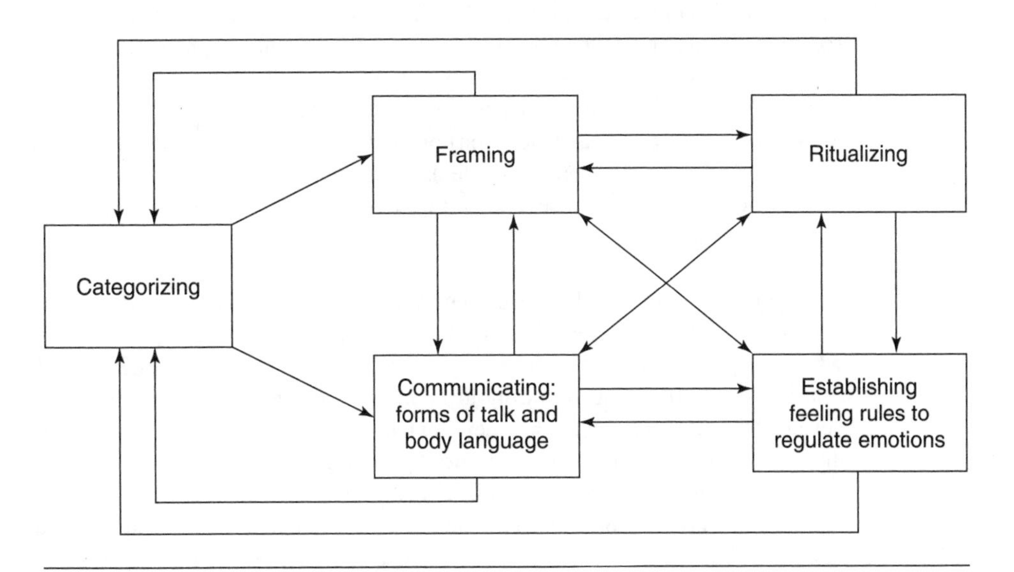

FIGURE 5.3 ***The Process of Normatizing the Encounter***

framing, ritualizing, and feeling rules are all thrown into doubt. For example, if a member of a gender category does not abide by expectations, the interaction becomes strained, making it difficult to normatize other dimensions of the encounter. People will feel stressed and be on guard about their behaviors.

People also categorize situations along at least two other dimensions. One is assessing the relative amounts of (a) *work-practical*, (b) *social*, or (c) *ceremonial* content to the interaction (Collins 1975; Goffman 1967; Turner 1988, 2002). For example, a job at a company is mostly work-practical, with social content and perhaps even a bit of ceremonial activity mixed in. The expectations that people have in this situation, then, would be expectations for how work is to be performed, how social relations in the context of work are to be played out, and what (as well as when) ceremonial actions are expected in the flow of work activities. If a person tries to act too social in a work situation or if this person refuses to honor simple ceremonies (such as greeting rituals to colleagues), then the interaction will be stressful because norms about the situation are being violated, with the result that individuals feel anxious or annoyed.

A third dimension of categorizing an encounter is the level of appropriate intimacy. For each level, there are expectations for how individuals should behave (Schutz 1967 [1932]; Turner 2002). The least intimate categorization is to see individuals as *personages*, or as nonpersons, who represent a social category or general role toward which little or no personal information is owed, or to be gleaned from the other. A clerk at a store, for example, will be treated as a clerk more than a person, with virtually no personal information exchanged. Indeed, if a customer or clerk tries to be intimate and reveal personal accounts, such actions violate expectations and place the person receiving more intimate information in an awkward position. Of course, if a customer and clerk interact frequently, then the interaction may move to the next level of intimacy which is to treat the other as *a person* toward whom some revelations about self, and from whom these same revelations are expected, but without becoming too intimate. Finally, there is the level of *intimates* where each person is expected to reveal details of his or her respective biography and feelings. Thus, individuals enter an encounter with expectations about whether others and self are to be treated as personages, persons, or intimates; and if one party violates these expectations by being too intimate (in a personage situation) or by not being sufficiently intimate (in a situation calling for interaction among intimates), the normative expectations of the encounter will be breached, causing one or several parties to become anxious and perhaps angry at the violation of norms.

Framing. Individuals also develop normative expectations about what is to be included and excluded from an interaction. This process has been termed *framing* as a metaphor for what transpires in all interactions (Goffman 1974; Turner 1988, 2002:156–158). Interaction is like the frame surrounding a picture in the sense that individuals enter, or soon develop, expectations about what they can talk about and what they can reveal to each other; these expectations constitute the frame. What is inside the frame can be a basis for communication; what is outside cannot be addressed, unless the interaction is *rekeyed* by shifting the boundaries of the frame (Goffman 1974). For example, in most interactions, details of a person's sex life reside outside the frame and, hence, are not to be addressed, but at times the frame can be shifted to include such matters. What framing accomplishes is to carve out from the virtually unlimited information that could be addressed in an interaction a delimited amount of information that can be safely communicated.

Frames are, of course, constrained by the categorization of the interaction; and so, as soon as participants in an interaction have mutually categorized each other and the situation, they have gone a long way to establishing a frame for the interaction. Frames can shift, however, as situations are recategorized; and when individuals want to shift the frame, they tend to do so in a *ritualized* manner. For example, when a person utters a highly ritualized phrase like "can I ask you a personal question?" this individual is recategorizing the other as an intimate and, at the same time, is informing the other that he or she is rekeying the new frame to include more personal information. Once the situation is reframed, new normative expectations about what is to be included and excluded as a topic in the interaction are put into place.

Communication. There are always normative expectations in an encounter about how individuals are to communicate. There are rules about the form that talk should take, whether, for example, it should be formal or informal. When a student addresses a professor, to take an obvious example, the talk is more formal and deferential compared with how a student would talk with another student. There are also expectations about body language, from the presentation of face, the alignment of bodies, or the countenance of body. Categorization and framing help to select the appropriate norms for communication. If, for instance, another is categorized as a child (or young), this will help establish what can be talked about (the frame), and how talk and body language are to be used in communicating.

When individuals violate the expectations for communication by, say, being too informal and glib when addressing a superior, the interaction will be breached because norms have been violated. Others watching this breach of norms will also be stressed because now they must reestablish the appropriate form of talk and body language and, perhaps, reframe and recategorize the situation—all of which are stressful.

Ritualizing. All interactions typically begin with greeting and end with closing rituals. The way in which these rituals are enacted is greatly constrained by how the encounter is categorized and framed (Goffman 1967; Turner 2002). For example, a student does not generally greet a professor with a ritual such as "hey, dude, how's it going?" or end the interaction with a closing ritual like "see you later, dude." Rituals put the interaction on track and then mark when it has ended, but the closing ritual also sets the stage for how the next interaction with another will occur, beginning with the greeting ritual.

Rituals also structure and form at the interaction as it proceeds between the opening and closing rituals. As noted earlier, rekeying a frame is often done with a ritual so that the other knows than the frame is being shifted. Or if someone is violating the frame, this is usually done in a ritualized way, such as "don't go there" or similar ritual response, that marks resistance to changing the frame. If you observe any strip of interaction, there is a constant verbal flow and use of body in communication, but you will also notice that this interaction will be punctuated by stylized sequences of speech or even body language (like patting someone on the back or other stylized tactile gestures). These are rituals that structure the flow, keeping individuals on track so that they can sustain categorization of others and the situation, maintain the frame or change it, and use the proper forms of communication. These rituals are not as spontaneous as they often seem because there are clear normative expectations about which rituals can be used and when they can be emitted; and if people violate them, then the interaction will be breached.

Feeling Rules. A very special kind of normative expectations concerns what have been termed "feeling rules" (Hochschild 1979, 1983). These normative expectations indicate to a person which emotions should be expressed in a situation (even if not actually felt) and what emotions should be experienced by individuals in the situation. Since humans establish relationships through emotions, abiding by these feeling rules is critical for the smooth flow of interaction. Categorizing, framing, use of proper forms of communication, and emission of appropriate rituals at the right time work to establish the expectations for what emotions a person can display and what feelings they should experience. At times individuals must engage in considerable "emotion work" to display emotions that they do not feel, or work at generating within themselves the proper feelings (Hochschild 1983).

To violate feeling rules immediately breaches the interaction, forcing a person and others to employ repair rituals to sew the encounter back together. For instance, if a person emits an emotional outburst of anger at another that violates the feeling rules, the interaction is breached not just with respect to feeling rules, but also with respect to all other aspects of normatizing arrayed in Figure 5.3. As a result the person will need to initiate a repair ritual, such as "I am so sorry, I had no right to say such a thing," to which others will respond with another repair ritual that indicates that they have accepted the apology (a ritual such as, "that's okay, we know you didn't mean it").

Emotions are a powerful force in interaction, as we will explore later; and as a result, they must be regulated. Humans can become highly emotional, and as a result, interactions can hang by a thread when emotions are running high. Feeling rules work to keep a lid on the expression of inappropriate emotions because, once the wrong emotions slip out, the interaction will be seriously breached, and the breach cannot be ignored because it generally causes others to feel more intense emotions. The result is for the interaction to fall apart, ending in hostilities; or if repairs are undertaken, there are clear rules about which *repair rituals* are to be employed, and how they are to be emitted.

In sum, these dimensions of normatizing—categorizing, framing, communicating, ritualizing, and feeling—help to guide the flow of interaction. Moreover, they are often the most important link to the meso-level structures—corporate units and categoric units—in which an encounter is embedded. The ideologies and norms of these units constrain the expectations on individuals as they normatize the encounter; and as individuals engage in normatizing, they connect people in the encounter to these mesostructures and, by extension, to the institutional domains and stratification systems in which meso-level units are embedded. The norms arising from categorization are guided by the ideologies and norms attached to members of particular categoric units and to the ideologies and norms of the division of labor in corporate units. Since these ideologies and norms are constrained, respectively, by the ideologies and norms legitimating the system of stratification and by the norms and ideologies of distinctive institutional domains, normatizing the encounter not only structures the flow of interaction, it also plugs people into mesostructures and macrostructures and culture.

Emotional Arousal in Encounters

The Palate of Human Emotions. At virtually every moment people are emotionally aroused. Sometimes this state of arousal is low-key and hardly noticeable beyond a sense of being at ease, but at other times, people experience more intense and negatively valenced emotions. There are at least four primary emotions that are hardwired into our neuroanatomy: satisfaction-happiness, assertion-anger, aversion-fear, and disappointment-sadness. (Turner 2000, 2002, 2007; Turner and Stets 2005:7–22). Variants of these primary emotions are summarized in Table 5.2. In addition to variations of primary emotions, humans also experience and express emotions that appear to be combinations or "mixes" of primary emotions (Kemper 1987; Plutchik 1980; Turner 1999, 2000, 2002, 2007). Just

TABLE 5.2 ***Variants of Primary Emotions***

	Low Intensity	*Moderate Intensity*	*High Intensity*
SATISFACTION-HAPPINESS	content sanguine serenity gratified	cheerful buoyant friendly amiable enjoyment	joy bliss rapture jubilant gaiety elation delight thrilled exhilarated
AVERSION-FEAR	concern hesitant reluctance shyness	misgivings trepidation anxiety scared alarmed unnerved panic	terror horror high anxiety
ASSERTION-ANGER	annoyed agitated irritated vexed perturbed nettled rankled piqued	displeased frustrated belligerent contentious hostility ire animosity offended consternation	dislike loathing disgust hate despise detest hatred seething wrath furious inflamed incensed outrage

(continued)

TABLE 5.2 Continued

	Low Intensity	*Moderate Intensity*	*High Intensity*
DISAPPOINTMENT-SADNESS	discouraged downcast dispirited	dismayed disheartened glum resigned gloomy woeful pained dejected	sorrow heartsick despondent anguished crestfallen

how this occurs, neurologically, is unclear at this point, but Table 5.3 outlines some of what can be termed *first-order elaborations* of primary emotions which blend (in some unknown manner) a greater amount of one primary emotion with a lesser amount of another. The resulting set of emotions, when coupled with variations of the primary emotions outlined in Table 5.2, gives humans a rather large repertoire of emotional states.

Humans can also experience some emotions that appear to be mixes of the three negative primary emotions—that is, mixes of anger, fear, and sadness. The resulting emotions are, I have hypothesized (Turner 2002, 2007), the emotions of shame, guilt, and alienation. It is the *relative ordering* of the intensity of the three negative primary emotions that determines whether a person will experience shame, guilt, or alienation. Table 5.4 outlines the rank-ordering of the emotions that lead to shame, guilt, or alienation. Shame and guilt are particularly important emotions because they are painful, and so, people seek to avoid experiencing them. When a person feels shame, this individual will have a sense of being incompetent in the eyes of others; and this is probably the most painful emotion a person can experience about self. And so, in order to avoid feeling this emotion, people monitor themselves and seek to abide by norms so as to appear competent. Guilt is an emotion that people experience when they have violated a moral code, like a core value or an ideology; and guilt motivates individuals to make amends and to behave in moral ways (Shott 1979; Tangney and Dearing 2002). The potential for guilt operates like shame because it leads individuals to monitor their actions and to conform to moral codes contained in values and ideologies. Alienation is not an emotion like shame and guilt that promotes social (self) control because alienation is a feeling of being detached from social relations and social structures. Yet, it does alert others to the fact that a person feels distanced from a situation, potentially causing them to act in ways to reduce another's alienation.

The Arousal of Emotions. There are two basic conditions that cause the arousal of emotions: (1) expectations and (2) sanctions. In any encounter people have expectations about what should transpire between self and others. Some of these expectations come from norms, but they also come from the other microdynamic forces that we will examine later—that is, transactional needs, roles and status (see Table 5.1). Let me summarize in more detail what is involved in these two emotion-arousing conditions.

TABLE 5.3 ***First-Order Elaborations of Primary Emotions***

Primary Emotions		*First-Order Elaborations*
SATISFACTION-HAPPINESS		
Satisfaction-happiness + *aversion-fear*	→	wonder, hopeful, relief, gratitude, pride, reverence
Satisfaction-happiness + *assertion-anger*	→	appeased, calmed, soothed, relish, triumphant, bemused
Satisfaction-happiness + *disappointment-sadness*	→	nostalgia, yearning, hope
AVERSION-FEAR		
Aversion-fear + *satisfaction-happiness*	→	awe, reverence, veneration
Aversion-fear + *assertion-anger*	→	revulsed, repulsed, antagonism, dislike, envy
Aversion-fear + *disappointment-sadness*	→	dread, wariness
ASSERTION-ANGER		
Assertion-anger + *satisfaction-happiness*	→	condescension, mollified, rudeness, placated, righteousness, vengeance
Assertion-anger + *aversion-fear*	→	abhorrence, jealousy, suspiciousness
Assertion-anger + *disappointment-sadness*	→	bitterness, depression, betrayed
DISAPPOINTMENT-SADNESS		
Disappointment-sadness + *satisfaction-happiness*	→	acceptance, moroseness, solace, melancholy
Disappointment-sadness + *aversion-fear*	→	regret, forlornness, remorseful, misery
Disappointment-sadness + *assertion-anger*	→	aggrieved, discontent, dissatisfied, unfulfilled, boredom, grief, envy, sullenness

1. *Emotions and Expectations.* When expectations are realized, individuals experience variants of satisfaction-happiness; and when expectations are not realized, individuals feel variants as well as first-order and second-order elaborations of negative emotions. If a situation is important to individuals and they have invested much of themselves in the encounter, their failure to meet expectations will lead to shame if they feel that they are responsible for the failure to meet expectations. They will also feel guilt if they perceive that they have also

TABLE 5.4 ***The Structure of Second-Order Elaborations of Primary Emotions: Shame, Guilt, and Alienation***

Emotion	*Rank-Ordering of Constituent Primary Emotions*		
	1	*2*	*3*
Shame	Disappointment-sadness (at self)	Assertion-anger (at self)	Aversion-fear (at consequences for self)
Guilt	Disappointment-sadness (at self)	Aversion-fear (at consequences for self)	Assertion-anger (at self)
Alienation	Disappointment-sadness (at self, others, situation)	Assertion-anger (at others, situation)	Aversion-fear (at consequences for self)

violated moral codes. When others violate expectations, an individual will experience variants and first-order elaborations of anger, and if the person violating expectations is powerful, then this individual may also experience variations and elaborations of fear and perhaps sadness. And if a person must consistently endure failure by self or others at meeting expectations, they may feel alienated from the encounter and perhaps the meso-level structure in which it is embedded and, by extension, the institutional domain and stratification system.

2. *Emotions and Sanctions.* When a person experiences positive sanctions from others—that is, signs of their approval—this person will experience variants and first-order elaborations of satisfaction-happiness; and if the individual had some fear about receiving positive sanctions, this person will experience pride, which is the opposite of shame. If, however, a person must endure negative sanctions—that is, disapproval by others—then variants, first-order elaborations, and second-order elaborations of the three negative emotions are more likely. If a person put self on the line and failed to receive positive sanctions, this individual will likely experience shame, and guilt as well if the failure is seen as a moral lapse. If a person sees others as unfairly imposing negative sanctions, then this person will experience variants and first-order elaborations of anger, but if the individuals imposing the negative sanctions are powerful, then the person will experience fear and sadness, and if sadness, anger, and fear are combined, this person will also experience alienation if negative sanctions from the powerful are persistent.

The Activation of Defense Mechanisms. Emotional arousal in encounters is complicated by the fact that individuals often seek to protect self against perceptions that they have failed to meet expectations or received negative sanctions. Sigmund Freud's (1900) key insight into the process of repressing unpleasant emotions is critical to understanding emotional dynamics in interpersonal behaviors. When self is on the line, negative emotions like shame are extremely painful; and individuals will often repress this and other negative emotions about self.

When emotions are repressed, however, they intensify. Freud's great insight was that, once out of consciousness, the emotions do not disappear. Instead, they grow in intensity, particularly when a person must consistently repress negative emotions over a period of time. As the emotions remain repressed, they can break through the neurological censors;

and when these negative emotions erupt, they often come as sudden and unexpected spikes of emotionality, whether these be sudden feelings of inadequacy, rage, intense fear and anxiety, or extreme depression.

Not only do emotions become more intense when repressed, they often transmute into new emotions, often pulling out only one of the constituent negative emotions of a first-order or second-order elaboration. For example, it has often been observed by clinicians that people who have repressed shame are often very angry and aggressive. Here, the shame transmutes into the anger component of shame and targets others or social structures. People who have experienced chronic guilt, but repressed this guilt, often have anxiety disorders (a variant of fear) which signals that the fear component of guilt has been pulled out and allowed to escape the neurological censors responsible for repression. It has often been noted that alienated people seem sad and depressed, but at times, they have episodes of intense anger, signaling that the anger component has been let free.

Defense mechanisms complicate the analysis of emotions because they often hide the underlying emotions that are at work. A person may seem happy but feel shame and guilt in ways that neither this person nor others recognize. An individual can be angry at someone, but repress this emotion and transmute it through a process called *reaction formation* into positive emotions for the hated person (for example, a son may hate his father but what emerges are declarations of great love for the father as a way of managing the guilt of hating the father). An individual may feel angry about what he is required to do on the job and repress this emotion into positive feelings about work (what is termed *sublimation*). A person may feel shame or anger at self but impute this shame or anger onto others, seeing them as humiliated or aggressive (through a process called *projection* in the clinical literature). A person may feel anger or some other negative emotion toward self but this emotion is transmuted to become anger at others (through a process termed *displacement*).

Defense mechanisms generally operate only for negative emotions because it is these kinds of emotions that hurt self, whereas positive emotional arousal is pleasurable and, hence, allowed to flow freely in an encounter. Down the left column of Table 5.5 is a list of the negative emotions that are most likely to be repressed. The next column lists the defense mechanisms involved, and then the third column lists the most likely emotion that emerges from transmutation of the repressed emotions. The final column denotes the potential target of the transmuted emotion.

At the bottom of Table 5.5 is a cognitive process not typically seen as a defense mechanism: attribution. *Attribution* is the process of making judgments as to who or what is the *cause* of certain outcomes. For example, if a person blames self for behaving incompetently, this person is making a self-attribution and will experience shame and perhaps guilt as well if incompetent behaviors are seen in moral terms. In this case, it is likely that the attribution is correct, and so attribution is not operating as a defense mechanism. But, if the shame is repressed, the emotion will be transmuted into anger, and as a consequence, the person will make an external attribution, blaming others or social units and seeing them as the cause for negative outcomes. In this case, attribution is operating as a defense mechanism, because it takes the repressed shame, transmutes this shame into anger, and then targets social objects—other people, a corporate unit, or members of a categoric unit.

Attribution processes are critical to what occurs in encounters. When people make self-attributions for not meeting expectations and for receipt of negative sanctions, they will

TABLE 5.5 ***Repression, Defense, Transmutation, and Targeting Emotions***

Repressed Emotions	*Defense Mechanism*	*Transmutation to:*	*Target of:*
anger, sadness, fear, shame, guilt, and alienation	displacement	anger	others, corporate units* and categoric units**
anger, sadness, fear, shame, guilt, and alienation	projection	little, but some anger	imputation of anger, sadness, fear, shame or guilt to dispositional states of others
anger, sadness, fear, shame, guilt, and alienation	reaction formation	positive emotions	others, corporate units, categoric units
anger, sadness, fear, shame, guilt, and alienation	sublimation	positive emotions	tasks in corporate units
anger, sadness, fear, shame, guilt, and alienation	attribution	anger	others, corporate units, or categoric units

*Corporate units are structures revealing a division of labor geared toward achieving goals.

**Categoric units are social categories that are differentially evaluated and to which differential responses are given. Members of categoric units often hold a social identity.

experience sadness at the minimum. They may also experience fear about the consequences to self of failing to meet expectations and for being negatively sanctioned. They may be angry at self, and when they experience all three negative emotions simultaneously, they will experience shame (see Table 5.4). This experience will motivate them to make amends and to take corrective actions to behave more competently. Repair rituals may also be initiated at the same time that the corrective behaviors are instigated. In this scenario, the self-attributions work to repair breaches and to reestablish social relations that will allow the person to meet expectations and receive positive sanctions (Scheff 1979, 1988). But, if the same is repressed and transmuted into anger, then the display of anger will disrupt the encounter. The person will negatively sanction others who, in turn, may become angry in a cycle of mutually escalating anger that further breaches the encounter.

Sometimes individuals pick safe targets for making attributions that are not in a position to "fight back." Social structures—whether the mesolevel corporate unit or members of categoric units—are a convenient target because they do not generally incite counteranger and cannot fight back in the way a person can. Thus, people often blame the social structures in which an encounter is embedded, seeing a corporate unit as the root of this person's anger (repressed and transmuted shame) or members of a categoric unit, such as Jews, women, or ethnic minorities, as causing their distress. As they do so, individuals generally articulate prejudicial beliefs and ideologies about the "evil" qualities of a corporate unit or members in a categoric unit. The shame may also translate into alienation since the same three emotions in the same rank order are involved (see Table 5.4), with persons being both angry at others or social structures and disaffected from these others and social structures.

These dynamics are critical to understanding the emotional flow in encounters. The more painful the negative emotions aroused, the more likely are defense mechanisms to be activated. As defense mechanisms are employed, the underlying emotion is hidden to a person; and as a result the emotion(s) will become more intense and transmute to a new emotion(s) that are directed at a number of available targets, typically those in the encounter itself (other people) or the meso-level structure in which the encounter is embedded (corporate and categoric units).

The Circulation and Targeting of Positive Emotions. Most of the time in most encounters, it is positive emotions that are aroused because these are far more rewarding to others and self than the expression of negative emotions. People generally try to bestow positive sanctions on each other, and as they do so, they arouse positive emotions in those who have received positive sanctions. There is a proximal bias to positive emotional arousal, and so, individuals will generally make self-attributions for meeting expectations and receiving positive sanctions (Lawler 2001; Turner 2007). They may also, however, make external attributions to those who have positively sanctioned them, giving off positive emotions to these others and thereby arousing positive emotions among these others. This process of mutual positive sanctioning and positive emotional arousal will cause positive emotions to circulate through an encounter, making it highly rewarding to all.

When people experience positive emotions in this way, they sometimes make more distal attributions to the social structures in which the encounter is embedded. If they see the structure and culture of a corporate unit as facilitating their ability to meet expectations and as allowing them to receive positive sanctions, they may develop positive emotions toward this structure and commitments to its culture. If they see members of a categoric unit as responsible, they will feel positive sentiments toward these members in the encounter and perhaps in other encounters as well.

It is this ratcheting up of the positive emotional flow that generates commitments of people to larger-scale social structures. If encounters produce a consistent flow of positive emotions, these emotions will begin to target mesostructures; and if the emotions are sufficiently intense and consistent across iterated encounters, macrolevel institutional domains and the stratification system may also be the target of positive emotions. For example, a student who has been consistently successful in encounters within classrooms will develop commitments to schools and their culture (the mesostructure) in which these encounters are embedded and, further out, to the macrolevel ideology and norms of the institutional domain of education. The same would be true of people experiencing consistent positive emotional arousal in encounters embedded in other types of mesostructures and macrostructures like workplaces, families, religious communities, politics, members of a social class or ethnic minority.

Thus, what happens emotionally in an encounter can have large effects when sufficient numbers of people experience positive emotions that break out of the proximal bias of such emotions and target ever-larger social structures. Of course, the converse is true. Negative emotions evidence a distal bias and target mesostructures and macrostructures with anger that works to delegitimate the ideologies and norms governing the operation of these structures. For example, it should not be surprising that members of the lower social classes who must experience daily degradations target the ideologies of the class system and the institutional domains that distribute resources unequally; and as they do so, they withdraw legitimacy from these macrostructures and, at times, become so angry as to mobilize against these structures. Emotions are thus a driving force in human affairs. They can bring people together and lead them to develop commitments to social structures and culture.

But, emotions are a double-edged sword, especially when we remember that three of the four primary emotions are negative; and so, they can cause people to disrupt social relations, delegitimate ideologies, and at times, angrily attack social structures (often intensified when fueled by repressed shame and humiliation).

Transactional Needs

When people interact in encounters, they seek to realize what I term *transactional needs*. Indeed, much of what motivates people and gives their actions direction revolves around efforts to meet five fundamental needs: (1) the need to verify and confirm self; (2) the need to receive positive exchange payoffs; (3) the need to experience trust; (4) the need to experience group inclusion; and (5) the need to have a sense of facticity (Turner, 1987, 1988, 2002, 2007). Let me briefly review each of these.

Needs to Verify Self. People have a sense of self that operates at several levels. One level evolves around situational and *role-identities*, such as the identity of being a parent, student, worker, citizen, worshiper, athlete, and any identity that arises when people play particular roles. These identities are activated when a person is playing a role, with individuals presenting this identity to others with the hope and expectation that others will verify this identity (Burke 1991, 1996; McCall and Simmons 1978; Stryker 2004). A second, deeper dimension of self is what I term *core self-conception* which is an emotionally valenced set of cognitions about self as a person. This level of self is trans-situational, with individuals carrying this identity with them at all times and presenting it to others for verification. A third layer of identity is a *social identity* that emerges by virtue of being a member of a categoric unit (Hogg 2006; Tajfel and Turner 1979). Thus, people can have a variety of social identities revolving around their gender, age, ethnicity, or class position; and in most encounters one or potentially all of these social identities can be presented to others.

When self presentations at any level—role identity, core self-conception, or social identity—are verified by others, they experience positive emotions and initiate the emotional dynamics summarized earlier. When their identity is not verified, however, the emotional reaction can become more complex, depending on whether the negative emotions are repressed and on the attributions made. When self is not verified, it becomes more likely that the negative emotions will be repressed to some degree and that external attributions for the cause of these negative emotions will be made.

The level of identity that is confirmed or not confirmed also has effects on the emotions aroused. When a core self-conception is not verified, the emotional reaction will be much greater than is the case when a role or social identity is not confirmed in an encounter, although role and social identities that go consistently unverified will also generate more intense emotional arousal. Still, the core self-conception is the center of a people's sense of what they are, and so failure here is seen as an attack on the essence of a person, thus arousing intense emotions. It is not so easy to change a core self-conception, and hence, the failure to verify this level of self puts a person in perpetual emotional tension. Role identities when consistently not verified will be a source of emotional pain, but it is easier to change these identities. For example, if a father has come to the conclusion that he is not a very good father, it is easier to accept this conclusion than the view that he is not a worthy human being, as would be the case when the father's core self-conception was not confirmed. Similarly, a person may come to realize that their ethnic identity leads to negative sanctions, and under these conditions, this identity can be discarded or at the very least made less salient.

Of all the transactional needs, the verification of self is the most powerful. It always guides the behaviors of individuals in situations. People are particularly sensitive to the self that they present and to the selves that others present, and they will almost always try to verify the selves of others because they implicitly recognize the emotional powder keg that self represents. Of course, if we choose to cause a person pain, we can deliberately go out of our way to negate another's self-presentation, but this is a risky gambit because of the potential for an extreme emotional reaction.

Needs to Receive Positive Exchange Payoffs. All interaction involves the exchange of valued resources. People give up a resource of value—time, energy, information, emotions, or anything that is valued by others—in exchange for valued resources from others. Humans are always assessing payoffs, implicitly calculating whether the resources received from others exceed the value of those given up (Turner 2002). Thus, if you help someone with their homework (your time and knowledge as valued resources given up), you will likely demand implicitly more valuable resources in return, such as approval but perhaps more valuable emotions like gratitude or even more valuable resources like deference and prestige. When the resources received exceed those given up, a person will experience positive emotions and be likely to positively sanction others and be willing to continue the encounter, now and at a future time. If, however, the person perceives that he or she has not received resources in excess of those that have been given up, then variants and first-order elaborations of anger are the most likely reaction, with the result that the encounter may be breached or, if not breached, not repeated in the future.

This process of calculating payoffs can become more complicated because there is almost always a standard of "what is just" operating as a normative expectation. This standard may reflect the ideologies of meso- and macrolevel structures. Thus, people first calculate whether their receipt of resources exceeds their costs in the immediate exchange; then, they make a comparison to see if their profit (rewards less costs) meets or exceeds a standard of what is fair and just. Thus, even if a person recognizes that they have made a profit in the exchange of resources, the standard of justice tells them if this level of profit is sufficient or insufficient. A profit can lead to negative emotional arousal when this profit is not seen as meeting the justice standards. So, if you help someone with their homework, and they express gratitude, you will make one additional calculation about whether the receipt of gratitude is fair (as determined by a standard of justice) in light of the time and energy you have given to provide help. If it is not, you may demand implicitly a larger payment, such as receiving prestige and honor from another.

The data on justice indicate that it takes more of an overreward (by justice standards) to arouse negative emotions than an underreward (Jasso 1993, 2006). A person will feel negative emotions more rapidly and intensely for a small amount of underreward or profit than if they received the same amount of overreward beyond what the justice standard might dictate. For example, if you have helped someone with homework and did not receive an expected payback by justice standards, it will take far less of underreward to arouse your anger; in contrast, if a person reciprocates by overrewarding (say, by giving your approval, gratitude, prestige, and perhaps money), you will not feel very guilty until this overreward is very high.

Thus, in any encounter, people are constantly assessing the flow of resources in terms of the resources they must give up to receive resources in return measured against a standard of justice. When a person receives a profit that meets the justice standard, then this person will positively sanction others. When, however, the person does not receive rewards that yield a profit and that also fall below the justice standard, this person will experience anger and, depending on the attributions made (to self, others, or social structure), will target and vent this anger. However, if this anger cannot be expressed because others are powerful or a person has fears of what anger might do to success in future encounters, then the anger may be repressed, initiating one or more of the defense mechanisms summarized in Table 5.5. Since people always implicitly recognize that justice is always being calculated, they generally try to assure that the justice standard has been met in order to avoid negative emotional arousal and the tensions that inevitably ensue.

Needs to Experience Trust. In any encounter, individuals need to feel that the actions of others are predictable, sincere, and respectful of self. Without this sense, the interaction immediately becomes strained, and individuals experience negative emotion such as anger or, if untrustworthy others have power, fear as well. Conversely, when people perceive that others' actions are predictable, that they are sincere in their actions, and that they are respectful of self (by verifying self), positive emotions ensue and sustain the encounter as long as this sense of trust persists. Con artists are particularly adept at creating the illusion of trust for their selfish purposes, but most of the time, people are quite adept at reading gestures of others and imputing a degree of trust to their actions. Naturally, trust is easier to achieve when others verify self and bestow positive exchange payoffs; and conversely, when self is not verified and/or exchanges are not profitable, trust is very difficult to achieve, thus breaching the encounter or, if an outright breach does not occur, leading to very cautious and wary interactions with untrustworthy others.

Needs for Group Inclusion. In all episodes of face-to-face interaction, individuals need to feel that they are part of the interpersonal flow. They do not need to feel high solidarity with others, only the sense that they are included in the rhythmic pattern of the interaction. If they feel excluded, people will get angry; if others have power, they may also experience fear; and if they cannot escape the interaction, they may experience sadness. If they blame themselves for not being part of the interpersonal flow, they may experience shame at their ineptitude and guilt if group inclusion was seen in moral terms.

When self is not verified, when exchange payoffs are too low to yield a profit, and when others are not trusted, it is difficult to develop this sense of group inclusion. Conversely, if a person does not feel part of the rhythmic flow, they will generally sense that they cannot verify self, receive profits in exchanges, or trust others, thus arousing negative emotions that cause persons to breach or leave the encounter. If they vent their anger or leave the encounter, individuals may experience all three negative emotions as well as shame at their lack of options that may be repressed and converted into alienation and role distance when in the encounter.

Needs for Facticity. During the course of an interaction, individuals need to feel that they share a common world with others for the purposes of the interaction, that the situation is really as it appears, and that the reality in which individuals find themselves has an obdurate quality. If these outcomes can be achieved, then the encounter has a "facticity" that gives individuals mild positive emotions, whereas if they cannot derive this sense of facticity, they will express anger at others for not providing the information and responsiveness that tells them that all participants in the encounter are experiencing a similar, real, and solid reality (Garfinkel 1967; Turner 1987, 1988, 2002). We all know people, for example, with whom it is awkward to interact because they do not say enough or say things that do not make sense or seem out of place; we generally get angry at them because they undermine the subtle sense of facticity that is needed to keep all interactions on a firm footing.

When this need for facticity cannot be met, it becomes difficult to meet other transactional needs. Conversely, when other needs are not being met, achieving a sense of facticity with others becomes problematic. Facticity is a quiet and subtle need state, but the anger that comes when it cannot be realized indicates how fundamental it is for the viability of interpersonal behavior.

Roles

Roles are sequences of behaviors that give direction to a person's actions and that allow others to understand why an individual is acting in certain ways. At one time it was common to talk about roles as the "behavioral" component of individuals occupying a position in the division of labor of a corporate unit, or as the behavior of individuals acting in accordance with normative expectations. Both of these views of roles are not incorrect; rather, they are incomplete and do not fully take into account that roles, per se, are a driving force in interpersonal behavior.

The Phenomenology of Roles. Phenomenology is the study of how individuals develop meanings about the social world, or how they think about and orient themselves to the external world. There is a phenomenological dimension to roles that is very important in understating interactions in micro encounters. One phenomenological dimension of roles is the fact that individuals assume that the behaviors of individuals in a situation mark an underlying role. Behaviors are assumed to be consistent with each other and to be part of a syndrome of behaviors signaling to others the role that a person is asserting in a situation (R. Turner 1962, 1968, and 2002). Thus, individuals engage in what Ralph Turner has termed *role-making*, whereby they orchestrate the signals and gestures that they send out to others in order to present self as being in a particular role; at the same time, others observing these role-making efforts operate under a "folk assumption" that gestures received do indeed mark a role and that discovering this role is possible.

This "folk assumption" works in conjunction with another phenomenological dimension of roles. People hold in their stocks of knowledge large inventories of potential roles that people can play. We all know the behaviors signaling various roles, such as worker, mother, student, shopper, and the like. These inventories can be quite refined and nuanced, as is the case when we recognize that a person is "an anxious mother" or some other fine-grained aspect of an institutional (kinship) role like that of mother. Thus, when individuals emit gestures, individuals assume for the purposes of the interaction that these gestures mark a role, and by searching their stocks of knowledge, the underlying role(s) of others will be discovered.

Types of Roles. There are, I believe, certain types of fine-grained roles that people carry in their inventory of role conceptions. There is, first of all, an inventory of *preassembled roles*. These are roles that members of a society generally know and understand because people play them in corporate units within basic institutional domains. We all know, for instance, the roles of worker, father, mother, worshiper, student, and other such roles; and we have fine-grained understandings of these roles, such as lazy worker, aggressive father, and strict mother. These roles are preassembled in the sense that the role conception is robust and contains understandings about most of the elements of the role. As a result, it is rather easy to understand these roles when we confront them.

Second, there are *combinational roles*. These roles represent combinations of two or more roles that are put together for a particular encounter. For example, a woman who is hosting her family for a dinner party combines several roles—one associated with her gender, another set of roles associated with her place in the kinship system (e.g., as mother, wife, daughter, granddaughter, aunt), and finally, her role as host. Often people are very "stressed" by family gatherings because they must combine a number of roles, and they worry that they may not be able to assemble roles together in the right manner. Generally, people are able to be successful in combining these roles since this set is often assembled in a society; and moreover, those responding to this combinational role easily understand the diverse elements of various roles that have been pieced together.

Third, there are *generalized roles* that can be added to other roles, as the situation dictates. For example, we all know the roles of being upbeat, social, aggressive, shy, serious, diligent, and reserved; the gestures marking these roles are clear in most cases. These generalized roles are usually attached to a another role or roles, such as being a serious student, a highly social and upbeat partier, a diligent worker, and the like. In fact, virtually all preassembled roles and combinational roles also are blended with one or several of these generalized roles in ways that others can readily observe and that a person can usually effect without undo stress.

Finally, there are *trans-situational roles* that people carry with them and enact each and every time they enter an encounter. These roles are typically associated with membership in categoric units. Thus, a male behaves differently from females in most situations and so, these roles are carried from situation to situation and combined with the other roles being played out in an encounter.

Verification of Roles. In any strip of interaction, people assert a role and trust that others will verify the role by accepting its performance and responding in ways that confirm that, indeed, the role has been embraced. A great deal can be at stake when verification of a role determines whether various levels of self are confirmed. Roles are the mechanisms by which people present self, and they are also the principle vehicle for meeting other transactional needs. Thus, people are not just verifying a role in an encounter; they are also confirming self, while indicating to a person if other transactional needs for profitable exchange payoffs, trust, group inclusion, and facticity can be met by playing a particular role.

Embedding of Roles. Most roles enacted in face-to-face encounters are embedded in corporate and categoric units. As a result, the relevant norms and ideologies are generally clear, and these circumscribe how a situation will be normatized and how roles will be played. Others observing roles also rely upon the fact that roles are embedded in mesostructures and macrostructures; by knowing the culture and structure of the more inclusive structure and culture, it is relatively easy to focus attention on some elements of a person's behavior and ignore others. For instance, by knowing that an interaction between students and professors occurs in a classroom, embedded in a larger corporate unit like a college which, in turn, is embedded in an institutional domain, it is relatively easy to know what gestures are markers of what roles. And, if categoric unit membership is relevant—age, gender, ethnicity, for example—the ideologies and norms for these categoric units can also be used to sensitize people to the relevant gestures that are emitted by people playing roles. Embedding thus makes roles less ambiguous for both the person presenting a role and for others trying to determine the role being presented.

Roles and Emotions. Roles are the means for acting in accordance with feeling rules, or normative prescriptions and prohibitions for what emotional states are appropriate in the encounter. Equally important, emotions are aroused when roles are being played. When people play roles that are accepted and verified by others, they are more likely to experience positive emotions. When, however, individuals play the wrong role or a role that others are not willing to verify, negative emotions will be aroused. Embedding will increase the chances of playing the right role that others will accept, whereas when roles are not clearly embedded, individuals will need to work at presenting a coherent role, while those observing a person's role-making efforts will need to search their stocks of knowledge more diligently to "discover" the role being made.

The emotional reactions to role making can be intense because so many other interpersonal dynamics are tied up with roles. Meeting transactional needs is generally accomplished by playing successful roles that others will verify; and so, failure in roles means that basic needs motivating individuals will go unmet—thus raising the emotional stakes. For instance, a person who conceives of herself as an intellectual but fails to play this role correctly or adequately will not only become emotional over the failure to have this role verified, she will also find herself in a situation where her identity (as an intellectual) and perhaps her core self-conception are called into question. She will also not receive positive exchange payoffs, nor will she feel that she can trust others, that she is included in the group, or that she understands the reality of the situation. Moreover, because the role has failed, the normatization of the encounter is called into question. Thus, because roles are the basic conduit by which other microdynamics forces play out, efforts to make roles and to verify them will generate intense emotional reactions; and when the emotions aroused are negative and revolve around shame and guilt, then the dynamics of repression are set into motion—as I enumerated earlier.

Status

The concept of status has ambiguous meanings in sociological analysis. For some it represents a position in a social structure connected to other positions. For example, the status of mother is a position in the network structure of the family that contains other positions, such as children and husband/father. Similarly, student is a position in a college or university structure that is connected to other positions (e.g., other students, faculty, and administrators). For other sociologists, status denotes the honor or prestige that individuals can claim. Thus, high status refers to having high prestige, whereas low status signals the opposite.

For still others, status refers to the amount of authority or power, with those having high status also having high power, and vice versa. These uses of the term *status* do not have to be contradictory; rather, they denote somewhat different dimensions of status.

Clarity of Status. When positions are clear and unambiguous, all other interpersonal processes are much easier to activate. When each person knows his or her "place" in a structure, each will have a clear idea of how to normatize the encounter, how to go about meeting transactional needs, and how to present roles to others. As a student, for example, you know that this position places you into a category—student, perhaps refined by other categories such as your age, gender, ethnicity, and social class background. As you recognize the relevant categories for you, you do the same for others, such as the professor; and then you will generally further categorize the situation as work-practical with ceremonial elements. Next, it becomes easier to frame what is to be discussed and not discussed, what the forms of talk will be, and what rituals are to be used in opening, closing, forming, and adding ceremonial flourishes to the encounter. And the final element of normatization—feeling rules—tells you how to exhibit emotions in the encounter. As you normatize the encounter by using status as your guideline, you also come to understand how to meet transactional needs. You will understand how to present self—your role identity as a student, your general self-conception, and your social identity (as a member of a categoric unit)—can be verified. In turn, with status as your guide, you know what resources are available in the encounter and which resources in what amounts are likely to be derived from the encounter. Status also guides you in forming a sense of trust, group inclusion, and facticity. Thus, status operates to direct your actions as you go about trying to meet transactional needs. Finally, the kinds of roles that you can make for yourself are highly constrained by your status as a student; this role is preassembled and known to all in a college, but you can still add new elements, such as generalized role elements (enthusiasm, seriousness, and diligence), as well as roles associated with being in a categoric unit, such as your gender or age. But, even as you add these additional elements, status determines which elements and in what amounts you can add to the basic preassembled role of student.

Status thus provides guidelines for all other interpersonal dynamics. Indeed, it is immediately evident that when status is not clear, problems of normatizing the encounter, meeting transactional needs, and making roles will arouse emotions. Without the guidelines provided by status, people have to work very hard at figuring out what they are supposed to do, what they can do, and just how they are to meet expectations in the encounter. When status is ambiguous, it is very likely that individuals will make mistakes, offend someone, become embarrassed, and feel even more intense emotions like shame if not humiliation.

The Embedding of Status. If an encounter is embedded in corporate and categoric units, it is more likely that status will be clear. People know each other's place in the division of labor in a corporate unit, and they also know which, if any, categoric units are relevant to the situation. Status as a position places a person within the division of labor of a corporate unit, and in so doing, it may also bring forth power/authority and prestige/honor aspects of status. Thus, the position of CEO in a business is a status position that reveals networks to other positions in the business, but it also carries the power/authority to tell others what to do while also allowing its incumbent to claim prestige and receive honor as well as deference. The embedding of status in corporate units increases the clarity of status, thereby increasing the likelihood that encounters will proceed smoothly and arouse positive emotions as individuals normatize the situation, make roles for themselves, and meet transactional needs within the context of that status order.

Status also plugs individuals into categoric units. There is a large literature on the effects of what are called *diffuse status characteristics* on people's expectations in encounters (Berger et al. 1977; Berger and Zelditch 1985, 1998). A diffuse status characteristic is what I am calling membership in a categoric unit—that is, characteristics such as age, gender, ethnicity, and social class position—that carry different degrees of evaluation and expectations for performance. These characteristics are also status in several senses. They locate people in a categoric unit which, in turn, is generally embedded within the stratification system and, hence, determines the resources that members of a unit can claim. Second, for any status within a categoric unit, there is generally a relatively clear set of normative expectations for how members of this unit should behave. Third, there are also general beliefs or ideologies about the characteristics and qualities of individuals with status in a categoric unit, and these ideologies almost always carry evaluations of people. These ideologies often suggest how much prestige and honor or power and authority people in various categoric units can and should command.

When categoric units are discrete with clear markers as to who is and who is not a member, the clarity of status is increased. For example, if gender is a salient status characteristic, one is either a male or female (granted, there are people who are in-between, but these are comparatively rare); and as a result, the expectations on, the prestige of, and power that goes to members of these two categoric units is typically clear. People can proceed to play roles, normatize, and meet transactional needs in terms of constraints imposed by their status. In contrast, when status characteristics do not have clear boundaries, there is more ambiguity and hence less certainty about how to make roles, normatize, and meet transactional needs. For example, years of education or level of income are continuous; and while there are implicit categories of "highly educated" (or "poorly educated") and of "rich" (and "poor"), the boundaries for these categories are ambiguous and open to different interpretations. When is someone to be considered rich and poor or categorized as educated or uneducated? The answer can vary and thus these kinds of categoric units do not provide the clarity that more discrete categories provide, with the result that people will need to work much harder at normatizing, making roles, and meeting transactional needs.

As status plugs individuals into corporate and categoric units, it also places them in institutional domains and the stratification system. As a result of this embedding in more macrostructures, status contains elements of institutional norms, norms for members of diverse social classes, and ideologies of institutional domains and ideologies of the stratification system. Thus, when you occupy the status of student, this status locates you within a corporate unit (your university or college) and, by extension, in the institutional domain of education where institutional norms and the ideology of this domain (as it translates general societal values) become part of the expectations upon you as you make roles, normatize, and meet transactional needs. Similarly, persons who are seen as poor (always with some ambiguity of what defines poverty), membership in this categoric unit also places them at the bottom strata of the stratification system and, thereby, brings the norms and ideologies legitimating the stratification system into play when evaluating the poor and when developing expectations for how they should behave. Generally, those who are poor cannot claim resources, and they are given little prestige and honor. Moreover, there are typically sets of status beliefs about the characteristics and qualities of the poor (mostly derogatory) that also influence the evaluation of people in this status. As individuals interact and use these beliefs and ideologies to guide conduct, they reinforce the beliefs about the poor and, in this way, implicitly legitimate the larger stratification system and the institutional domains that generate this system by distributing valued resources unequally.

Status and Emotions. Because status often marks inequalities in the division of labor of corporate units or in the differential evaluation of membership in categoric units, it should not be surprising that emotions often run high as status dynamics play themselves out (Ridgeway 1994, 2000, 2001; Ridgeway and Johnson 1990). Generally, people in low status will experience negative emotions—sadness, anger, fear, shame, humiliation—because they are subject to the authority of superordinates in corporate units and to the stigma of devalued categoric units. The converse is true for those with high status; they will experience positive emotions—satisfaction, happiness, pride, confidence—and by virtue of positive emotional arousal will often be able to make claims for more status.

Just how these emotions affect interaction depends on the clarity of expectations for high- and low-status persons and the acceptance of beliefs about the characteristics of high- and low-status individuals. In general when expectations are clear and beliefs are accepted by both high- and low-status persons, interactions proceed smoothly. If, however, higher-status individuals force lower-status persons to experience shame, then the emotional dynamics become more volatile, in accordance with the propositions outlined earlier when I reviewed emotions as a basic microdynamic force. When anger, righteous anger, and vengeance emerge, individuals will question the status order, the expectations associated with this order, and the beliefs or ideologies legitimating differential evaluation of status.

A New Social Psychology

Human behavior has a direction because it is embedded in layers of social structure and culture and because there are certain forces always pushing individuals to act along certain paths. As individuals take cognizance of the structure and culture of their situation, they normatize encounters by categorizing each other and the situation, imposing frames, using particular forms of communication, emitting rituals, and engaging in emotion work to abide by feeling and display rules. People are also driven to satisfy transactional needs for verifying several levels of self, making a profit in exchange payoffs, achieving a sense of trust, feeling included in the group, and establishing a baseline sense of facticity. Status and roles plug individuals into social structures, providing further guidance for how to normatize and meet transactional needs. Emotions pervade all aspects of human thought and action. When people know their status relative to others, can make roles for themselves, can successfully normatize the encounter, and can meet all transactional needs, they will experience positive emotions; and when they cannot do so, negative emotions will be aroused and disrupt the encounter. Moreover, because negative emotions are painful, especially those like shame and guilt that make people feel self-aware and degraded, the activation of defense mechanisms like repression, intensification, transmutation, and targeting of the transmuted emotions will reshuffle the emotional dynamics, often making them more volatile and disruptive to the flow of interaction in the encounter.

This more robust vision of culture and social structure as successive layers of embedding and of individuals as being pushed in certain directions by microdynamic forces—that is, emotions, normatizing, meeting transactional needs, role making, and establishing status—draw from existing approaches in social psychology, but the view of social structure and culture is more general and more macro, and the vision of the individual is more multidimensional. This is a new kind of social psychology that removes the traditional limitations of research and theorizing, and it is the kind of social psychology that makes possible integration of diverse theory-research traditions—many of which have been summarized in this volume.

This is also a social psychology that holds out some potential for understanding how microdynamic processes can, on occasion, change mesostructures and macrostructures. In general, social structure and culture work in a top-down fashion constraining microdynamic processes in encounters, but there is always the potential for the actions of individuals in encounters to change social structures and cultural norms and ideologies. If such were not the case, the social world would be static. What, then, are some of the basic conditions increasing the power of microdynamic to change meso- and macrolevel social reality?

One condition is the power of individuals in encounters lodged in corporate and categoric units with varying degrees of power. The more such encounters push for change, the more likely are mesostructures to change; and when these mesostructures have power or prestige, they can transform institutional domains and stratification systems. Another condition is the centrality of encounters in a network of encounters that push for change; here change in one encounter will radiate out changing the dynamics of all those other encounters to which it is connected directly and indirectly. Still another condition comes from embedding; the more encounters are embedded in mesostructures, the more potential they have to transform the division of labor in corporate units and beliefs about the characteristics of members in categoric units. Another condition relates to the institutional domain in which encounters are embedded; the more an institutional domain distributes valued resources, the greater changes in the corporate units in this domain will alter the unequal distribution of resources and, hence, the stratification system. Visibility of change-oriented encounters (via media) and the number of people who can see these changes, make it more likely that changes at the microlevel will have larger-scale effects on culture and social structure. And finally, the level of emotional energy generated in encounters increases their power to effect social change. When people are mobilized by negative emotions, they target social structures and culture, often changing them in significant ways.

Still, it is difficult for encounters to change more macrolevel social structures rapidly. Change must occur over iterated encounters, pulling ever-more individuals into their orbit and perhaps resulting in formation of a new, change oriented corporate unit that can then push for macrolevel changes. For example, the civil rights movement or the environmental movement worked slowly as emotionally mobilized individuals have created corporate units that seek to exert pressures for changes in social structure and culture. In big and complex societies, changes at the level of encounters typically take time to radiate outward, although at times a small set of encounters can make large changes, as is the case when a few key members of an army take the reins of power in a society, or when a charismatic leader can mobilize repressed shame and humiliation in ways that push large numbers of people into sudden collective action at strategic points in a society. Yet, most of the time, encounters reinforce mesostructures and macrostructures because of embedding which constrains and channels microdynamic processes—normatizing, meeting transactional needs, emotions, roles, and status—in ways that reproduce meso- and macrolevel social structures and culture norms, ideologies, and values.

The outline of the theory summarized in this chapter provides a way to get a handle on these complex relations between individual-level cognitions, emotions, and behaviors, on the one side, and the reproduction or change in meso- and macrolevel sociocultural realities of societies, on the other side (for more detailed version of this theory, see Turner [2002, 2007]). The key is to have a grander view of social structure and culture, coupled with individuals who exhibit complex patterns of thought, emotion, and action.

References

Berger, Joseph, M. Hamit Fisek, Robert Z. Norman, and Morris Zelditch Jr. 1977. *Status Characteristics and Social Interaction: An Expectation States Approach.* New York: Elsevier.

Berger, Joseph and Morris Zelditch, eds. 1985. *Status, Rewards, and Influence*. San Francisco: Jossey-Bass.

———. 1998. *Power and Legitimacy: Strategies and Theories*. New Brunswick, NJ: Transaction.

Burke, Peter J. 1991. "Identity Processes and Social Stress." *American Sociological Review* 56:836–849.

———. 1996. "Social Identities and Psychosocial Stress." Pp. 141–174 in *Psychosocial Stress: Perspectives on Structure, Theory, Life Course, and Methods*, edited by H. B. Kaplan. Orlando, FL: Academic Press.

Collins, Randall. 1975. *Conflict Sociology: Toward an Explanatory Science* New York: Academic Press.

Freud, Sigmund. 1900. *The Interpretation of Dreams*. London: Hogarth Press.

Garfinkel, Harold. 1967. *Studies in Ethnomethodology*. Englewood Cliffs, NJ: Prentice-Hall.

Goffman, Erving. 1967. *Interaction Ritual*. Garden City, NY: Anchor Books.

———. 1974. *Frame Analysis: An Essay on the Organization of Experience*. New York: Harper and Row.

Hochschild, Arlie Russell. 1979. "Emotion Work, Feeling Rules and Social Structure." *American Journal of Sociology* 85:551–575.

———. 1983. *The Managed Heart: Commercialization of Human Feeling*. Berkeley: University of California Press.

Hogg, Michael. 2006. "Social Identity Theory." Pp. 111–136 in *Contemporary Social Psychological Theories*, edited by Peter J. Burke. Stanford, CA: Stanford University Press.

Jasso, Guillermina. 1993. "Choice and Emotion in Comparison Theory." *Rationality and Society* 5:231–274.

———. 2006. "Distributive Justice Theory." *Handbook of the Sociology of Emotions*, edited by J. E. Stets and J. H. Turner. New York: Springer.

Kemper, Theodore D. 1987. "How Many Emotions Are There? Wedding the Sociological and Autonomic Components." *American Journal of Sociology* 93:263–289.

Lawler, Edward J. 2001. "An Affect Theory of Social Exchange." *American Journal of Sociology* 107: 321–352.

McCall, George J. and J. L. Simmons. 1978. *Identities and Interactions*. New York: Free Press.

Plutchik, Robert. 1980. *Emotion: A Psychoevolutionary Synthesis*. New York: Harper and Row.

Ridgeway, Cecilia. 1994. "Affect." Pp. 205–230 in *Group Processes: Sociological Analysis*, edited by Martha Foschi and Edward J. Lawler. Chicago: Nelson-Hall.

———. 2000. "The Formation of Status Beliefs: Improving Status Construction Theory." *Advances in Group Processes* 17:77–102.

———. 2001. "Inequality, Status, and the Construction of Status Beliefs." Pp. 323–342 in the *Handbook of Sociological Theory*, edited by Jonathan H. Turner. New York: Kluwer Academic/ Plenum.

Ridgeway, Cecilia L. and Cathryn Johnson. 1990. "What Is the Relationship between Socioemotional Behavior and Status in Task Groups?" *American Journal of Sociology* 95:1189:1212.

Scheff, Thomas J. 1979. *Catharsis in Healing, Ritual, and Drama*. Berkeley: University of California Press.

———. 1988. "Shame and Conformity: The Deference–Emotion System." *American Sociological Review* 53:395–406.

Shott, Susan. 1979. "Emotion and Social Life: A Symbolic Interactionist Analysis." *American Journal of Sociology* 84:1317–1334.

Schutz, Alfred. [1932] 1967. *The Phenomenology of the Social World*. Evanston, IL: Northwestern University Press.

Stryker, Sheldon. 2004. "Integrating Emotion into Identity Theory." *Advances in Group Processes* 21:1–23.

Tajfel, Henri and John C. Turner. 1979. "An Integrative Theory of Intergroup Conflict." Pp. 33–47 in *The Social Psychology of Intergroup Relations*, edited by W. G. Austin and S. Worchel. Monterey, CA: Brooks/Cole.

Tangney, June Price and Rhonda L. Dearing. 2002. *Shame and Guilt*. New York: Guilford Press.

Turner, Jonathan H. 1987. "Toward a Sociological Theory of Motivation." *American Sociological Review* 52:15–27.

———. 1988. *A Theory of Social Interaction*. Stanford, CA: Stanford University Press.

———. 1999. "Toward a General Sociological Theory of Emotions." *Journal for the Theory of Social Behavior* 29:132–162.

———. 2000. *On the Origins of Human Emotions: A Sociological Inquiry into the Evolution of Human Affect*. Stanford, CA: Stanford University Press.

———. 2002. *Face to Face: Towards a Sociological Theory of Interpersonal Behavior*. Stanford, CA: Stanford University Press.

———. 2003. *Human Institutions: A Theory of Societal Evolution*. Boulder, CO: Rowman and Littlefield.

———. 2007. *Human Emotions: A Sociological Theory*. London: Routledge.

Turner, Jonathan H. and Jan E. Stets. 2005. *The Sociology of Emotions*. New York: Cambridge University Press.

Turner, Ralph H. 1962. "Role Taking Process versus Conformity." Pp. 20–40 in *Human Behavior and Social Processes*, edited by A. Rose. Boston: Houghton Mifflin.

———. 1968. "Roles: Sociological Aspects." *International Encyclopedia of the Social Sciences*. New York: Macmillan.

———. 2002. "Roles." *Handbook of Sociological Theory*, edited by J. H. Turner. New York: Plenum.

Section **II**

Experimental Social Psychology

6

Fatal Attraction: Disenchantment in Intimate Relationships[1]

Diane H. Felmlee

Were you ever attracted to someone because of a particular quality, only to be later repelled by that same trait? Perhaps they were very funny, highly independent, or super sexy, for example, and then you later found that they never took anything seriously, always had to have their own way, or were just plain lascivious? If so, you have had a *fatal attraction*. The purpose of this chapter is to examine this type of relationship disenchantment in more detail. To better understand the process of fatal attraction, we will: 1) define what is meant by fatal attraction, 2) provide illustrations of fatal attractions, 3) examine what causes them and their underlying themes, 4) discuss social exchange theory and dyadic group processes that help in accounting for fatal attraction, 5) explain the process of fatal attraction, and 6) discuss implications of research on this topic for furthering an understanding of the social psychological underpinnings of intimate relationship behavior.

Fatal Attractions

A fatal attraction occurs when a quality that an individual comes to dislike in an intimate partner relates closely to one that was attractive and initially appealing. The disliked quality is often an exaggerated version of the originally attractive characteristic. This process is a fatal attraction, not in the sense of "deadly," but because it foretells a sequence in which the initial attraction unlocks an inevitable progression that ends with disenchantment. A quality that was initially considered attractive becomes undesirable. Fatal attractions are relatively common in intimate encounters, and research finds they occur in 29.2 percent

[1]This chapter draws on data and analyses that are described in more detail in the following sources: Felmlee 1995, 1998a, 1998b, 1998c, 2001a; Felmlee, Flynn, and Bahr 2007; and Felmlee, Fortes, and Orzechowicz 2007. The author would like to thank Scott Gartner for his helpful comments and suggestions.

(Felmlee 1995) to 66.7 percent of intimate relationships (Felmlee et al. 2007), depending on the sample and research design. Several social psychology textbooks (e.g., Aronson et al. 2005), popular media sources (e.g., Morin 1995), and relationship self-help gurus (e.g., www.doctorsingle.com) address this topic.

Illustrations of Fatal Attractions

Now that we have a definition of fatal attraction, in the next part of this chapter we will describe some examples of these types of romantic reversals. Below are several illustrations of fatal attractions taken from information gathered from real romantic relationships and marriages. In each case, individuals describe the qualities about their partner that initially attracted them, and then later report the qualities that they now dislike about that same person. Additional illustrations are shown in Table 6.1.

Caring to Clinging. One young man wrote that in addition to a woman's good looks, he found the fact that she cared about him particularly attractive. Now he dislikes that she is "clingy" and that she "holds on too tightly" to their relationship. The qualities that disturb him about his girlfriend, such as clinginess, are closely related to the personality quality

TABLE 6.1 ***Illustrations of the Light Side (Rewarding Dimension) of a Partner Quality and Its Corresponding Dark Side (Costly Dimension)***

Light Side: Rewards	*Dark Side: Costs*
Attentive	Possessive
Confident, assertive	Arrogant, haughty
Intelligent	Analytical, elitist
Lighthearted	Didn't care about anything
Opposite	Too different
Spontaneity	Too flighty
Strong-willed, persistent	Domineering, persistent
Charming	Deceptive and dishonest
Social, partier	No goals, unemployed
Sexually unrepressed	Involved with friend
Independent, individualistic	Too wrapped up in own activities
Considerate	Says sorry too much
Sensitive	Too emotional
Impulsive	Blow at any moment
Easygoing	Immature, undirected
Mature	Older
Sexy	Slut

that first attracted him, her caring about him. Clinginess, and holding on tightly to a relationship, are apt to be the possible downsides to having a partner who is very caring.

Nice to Fake. One woman was attracted to a man because he was "sweet, sensitive, soft-spoken," and he cared for her. Now she views him as being "too nice," as well as "boring and fake." In other words, it appears that this sweet, sensitive, soft-spoken, and caring man is now seen as having traits that are the consequence of being *too* sweet, sensitive, soft-spoken, and caring.

Confident to Cocky. A man reported that the confidence and intelligence of his wife was initially attractive, but he now dislikes that she can be "egotistical." It seems that he is interpreting his spouse's desirable quality in a negative manner. Originally she exuded confidence, but now that confidence is seen as displaying an ego.

Fun to Foolish. Another type of disenchantment involves qualities related to fun or humor. For instance, one young woman reported that her boyfriend's sense of humor initially attracted her, but then she complained that he now jokes excessively and that he fails to take other people's feelings seriously. Here we see that having a particularly good sense of humor is both the source of attraction, as well as the source of friction later in this relationship. This is a relatively common type of fatal attraction in college romances, in particular (Felmlee 1995).

Shy to Secretive. In another example, the following qualities drew a man to his partner of nine years: "quiet, a bit shy," (also smile and "hairy legs"). He dislikes, however, that this man is: "Too much of a lone wolf, secretive, seemed ashamed to be seen in public with me." In other words, this partner who was attractive in part because he was quiet and shy in the first place, is now viewed as "secretive," too much of a loner, and too shy in public. Here again it appears that the originally attractive qualities of a mate eventually are a source of relationship distress.

Friendly to Flirty. The personal quality that one woman liked best about her boyfriend initially was his friendliness. Subsequently she became disturbed by his tendency to be "too friendly with other girls." Apparently the desirable characteristic of gregariousness in her partner developed an undesirable side effect.

Laid-back to Lazy. One woman was drawn to a man because he was good looking, rebellious, a good skateboarder, and he "didn't go to school." Yet she became distressed because this rebellious young man smoked, didn't wear nice clothes, lacked a good job and had "no $." Once again, the same qualities that interested her in this person are implicated in the characteristics that doomed the relationship. To an outsider, at least, it does not seem surprising that a rebellious, young, skateboarder who doesn't attend school also smokes, and is lacking in money, nice clothes, and a job.

Sexy to Slut. One man was attracted to a woman because she is a "slut" and says that what he most dislikes about her currently is that she is a "slut." In response to the question regarding what attracted him to his partner, another young man provided the following list (Felmlee 1998a, p. 248):

> (1) A cute face, (2) Gams that wouldn't stop, (3) Long smooth legs, (4) A hard tight body, (5) Hard firm bresis [breasts] not too big or too small, (6) A tight booty, (7) Beautiful hair, (8) Wild in bed.

Nevertheless, he disliked a number of her characteristics (e.g., her "whining voice of complaint") and he broke up with her because "the [relationship was] based too much on physical aspects. No true love just lust." In other words, he became involved with a woman because of her numerous beautiful and sexy qualities, but eventually found the relationship with her to be too physical and lustful.

Predictors of Fatal Attraction

We have seen that there are many different types of relationship disenchantment that transpire among men and women. However, we have yet to address the important question: When is a fatal attraction is likely to occur? In the following section of the chapter, we will summarize research that examines several factors that influence the incidence of these disillusioning relationships.

Certain romantic relationships are more susceptible to disenchantment than are others, in particular, those in which the basis of attraction is differences. Differences in romantic companions may be appealing initially, that is, "opposites attract" (Winch 1955), in part because involvement with a dissimilar other makes a person feel special (Snyder and Fromkin 1980). Yet, disparities between couples can be problematic and are often cited as the basis for divorce and breakup (e.g., Hill et al. 1976). It seems likely that tolerance for dissimilarity between mates runs thin over time, and that it is prone to evolve into a source of stress and conflict.

Dissimilar, Strange or Unique, and Extreme Attractors

A romantic partner could have attractive characteristics that are "different" in several ways. First, a partner may possess a trait that is dissimilar from an individual's own characteristics (i.e., different from self). Second, a partner may have a quality that varies from the average; it is unusual or unique, because most people do not possess that particular characteristic (i.e., different from average). Or a quality could be exhibited in an extreme manner (i.e., different from the average degree of expression, that is, immoderate, or extreme). An attraction to any of these three types of differences in a partner is particularly susceptible to disillusionment. On the other hand, a relationship in which similarity is the basis of attraction is less prone to disenchantment.

There is substantial evidence of the connection between these three differences and disenchantment when examining empirical data. As shown in Table 6.2, the chance of a fatal attraction relates significantly to all three types of differences and similarity, based on findings from a statistical analysis of 301 intimate relationships. A fatal attraction is over six times more likely when the basis of attraction is dissimilarity between partners. It is

TABLE 6.2 ***The Degree to Which Attractive Partner Qualities Significantly Multiply the Likelihood of a Fatal Attraction***

Partner Quality	*Odds Ratio*
Dissimilar Quality	6.6**
Extreme Quality	4.1***
Strange or Unique Quality	11.5*
Similar Quality	.19*
Number of Traits	1027
Chi-Square	475.01; df = 290

Note: Findings derived from a multivariate, fixed-effects logistic regression analysis of nonphysical traits; controls not shown (all nonsignificant): gender, atypical gender quality, number of attracting traits.

*p≤.05; **p≤.01; ***p≤.001; one-tailed test.

over eleven times as prevalent when someone is drawn to characteristics in another that are unusual or strange, and it is four times more likely when the appealing partner trait is an extreme, rather than one that is more moderate. Cases in which individuals find similarity in a romantic partner particularly desirable, on the other hand, are significantly *less* prone to fatal attractions than those in which similarity is not an attractor; an attraction to similarity is less than 20 percent (one-fifth) as likely to result in disenchantment. These findings are consistent with those of previous research (Felmlee 1998a).

In sum, there are patterns in the types of attractions that are prone to result in subsequent disillusionment. Individuals often become irritated with the desirable qualities of their partner that are either dissimilar from their own, extreme, unique, or strange, and they are less apt to be disturbed later by the similar, attractive qualities of another. We have yet to address the theoretical underpinnings of this process of romantic disenchantment, however. In the next section we describe social psychological explanations of fatal attractions.

Theoretical Explanations

Why might fatal attractions occur in the first place? Why would someone come to dislike qualities to which they once were attracted? There are at least two possible social psychological explanations for the process behind this type of disenchantment—one involving relationship rewards and costs, and the other concerning contradictory dyadic tensions.

Social Exchange Theory: From Relationship Rewards to Relationship Costs

Social exchange theory is one of the major theoretical perspectives in the field of social psychology (e.g., Cook 1987; Homans 1974; Molm 1997), and it is useful in explaining the phenomenon of relationship disenchantment. This perspective views many types of social interaction as an interchange of rewards and services. It assumes that actors are interested in maximizing socially mediated rewards in their interactions, such as money, goods, services, prestige, and approval, and at the same time actors attempt to minimize costs, such as a loss of either money, social approval, or other resources.

Individuals participate in interactions only if they find that these interactions produce positive outcomes in which the rewards outweigh the costs. In making a decision as to whether to continue a particular course of action, people compare their outcomes in a current interaction with their own expected outcomes, based largely on past experiences. They also compare their outcomes with the level of outcome available in alternative interactions of the same type. The outcome that exists in alternative, possible interactions is termed the *comparison level for alternatives* (Thibaut and Kelley 1959). Individuals may remain in a relatively unrewarding job, for example, if their expectations are low, based on their experience with prior, similarly unsatisfying jobs. Or they may stay in such a position because they fail to locate a better employment opportunity, that is, their comparison level for alternatives is low.

Concepts in social exchange theory apply not only to actions in the world of work, but also to personal relationships (e.g., Sprecher 2001). According to the perspective of social exchange, individuals attempt to maximize the outcomes they gain from their intimate encounters, and satisfying relationships are apt to be those in which the perceived rewards greatly exceed the costs. Disenchantment with a partner's characteristics is likely when the costs associated with those qualities exceed the inherent rewards. For example, a committed relationship with a mate who is attractive because of his or her drive, motivation, and success at work is likely to have rewarding aspects, such as the possible prestige and money the person can bring to the couple, as well as the potential for stimulating conversations. Yet if the mate's ambitions interfere with a couple's time spent together, and intrude on their emotional and physical intimacy, disillusionment is likely, because the relationship becomes high in costs.

Furthermore, individuals are apt to be drawn to the noticeable strengths of another person, and those strengths are often closely related to a person's weaknesses and therefore entail relationship costs. Philosophers dating back to Aristotle maintain that possessing an extreme degree of a positive trait is just as likely to have a downside as possessing too little of a desirable quality; it is moderation in character, not excess, that represents virtue, according to Aristotle's notion of the "Golden Mean." Thus an attraction to the intense positive characteristics of another, regardless of the type of quality, is likely to have its costs. See Table 6.1 for illustrations of the potential rewards (the light side) connected to a partner's characteristics and the associated costs (the dark side).

Dyadic Group Processes: Confronting Relationship Tensions

According to the classic, social psychology work of Georg Simmel (1955), individuals in small groups confront ongoing strains between the forces of anomie and solidarity, with people desiring the solidarity represented by group membership, but at the same time wanting to preserve their autonomy. Members of groups continually encounter opposing tensions, in other words. Likewise, couples face strains between pairs of contradictory relationship forces, such as those of autonomy and connection, openness and closedness, and novelty and predictability, according to a dialectical perspective (e.g., Baxter and

Montgomery 1996). Disenchantment occurs when individuals are drawn to partner qualities that represent one of two opposing forces (e.g., openness), but then they discover that their relationship is lacking in the other dimension (e.g., closedness).

Next we will examine these, and additional, oppositional relationship themes in fatal attractions, using data from individuals who are dating, cohabiting, or married. The examples demonstrate the various dilemmas faced by people in everyday relationships and the ways in which partner disenchantment reflects these dilemmas.

Illustrations of Contradictory Relationship Tensions

There are a number of contradictory, dyadic tensions inherent in fatal attractions. For example, there are cases that reflect the central opposing strain, that between anomie and solidarity (Simmel 1955), or *autonomy and connection* (e.g., Baxter and Montgomery 1996). In some instances individuals are attracted to aspects that heighten the connectedness, or solidarity, that they experience with another, but then evaluate the relationship as coming up short in autonomy. For example, a man reports being drawn to his girlfriend because she is "caring and faithful," but what concerns him now is her tendency to be extremely jealous. In other cases, people like the autonomy reflected in their partner's qualities, but then experience a lack of connectedness. One woman was interested in her boyfriend because he was "very self-reliant," and yet her relationship broke up, in part because he "didn't show that I was important or needed in his life."

Several other contradictory relationship strains appear in relationships characterized by this type of disenchantment. One represents tensions between *relaxation and drive*. For example, one woman became interested in her husband of seventeen years because he was "career-oriented and very smart," but she is distressed now because he is "too career driven." Her spouse exhibits a good deal of drive, in other words, but he comes up short when it comes to relaxation. In other instances, individuals are interested initially in the qualities in a mate that represent the dimension of relaxation ("easygoing"), but then long for additional drive or motivation in their relationship ("flaky; too easygoing"). See Table 6.3 for illustrations of additional contradictory dyadic tensions in fatal attractions.

We see, therefore, that fatal attractions reflect a number of ongoing tensions that arise in ordinary relationships, such as that between maintaining one's individual freedom and at the same time achieving connectedness with a significant other. Next we examine the range of fatal attractions and discuss the extent to which this process takes place among various groups and personality types—married couples, same-sex relationships, differing ethnic and racial groups, varying nationalities, and personality dimesnions.

Fatal Attractions in Marriages

Do married couples and cohabiting partners experience fatal attractions, or are these types of attractions located primarily in relatively short, college relationships? Pines (2005) finds evidence of fatal attractions among almost all the married couples in her interview sample of over one hundred couples undergoing therapy. She views these as "wise unconscious choices," in that they provide couples with an opportunity to face unresolved childhood

TABLE 6.3 ***Oppositional Dyadic Themes in Fatal Attractions***

Theme	*Attracting Quality*	*Disliked Quality*
Fun vs. Seriousness	funny and fun sense of humor	constant silliness jokes
Connection vs. Autonomy	nurturing cared about me	smothering clingy; held on too tightly
Strength vs. Vulnerability	strong-willed spunk	domineering and macho arguing ability
Novelty vs. Predictability	strange spontaneity	too different flighty
Sexual vs. Chaste	sexual experience knew she would have sex	sexual experience couldn't say no (to sex)
Relaxation vs. Drive	relaxed successful and very focused	constantly late work commanded him
Closedness vs. Openness	shy openness	too shy too open to others
Social vs. Personal	very outgoing and social friendly	too social too concerned with pals
Maturity vs. Youth	older; looked up to him older	age treated me as younger

Adapted from Felmlee, 1998c.

conflicts that influence their intimate relationship. In one example, a couple describes the following bases of attraction and tension in the marriage (p. 188):

> ***Attraction: Wife:*** He was like a rock, strong, someone you can lean on.
>
> ***Husband:*** She was warm and sensitive, very gentle.
>
> ***Stress: Wife:*** He is like a block; you can't change his mind about anything.
>
> ***Husband:*** She is too sensitive, too gentle.

Felmlee, Flynn, and Bahr (2007) also find fatal attractions in a sample of 208 middle-aged adults, most of whom are either married or in long-term, committed relationships. This study uses closed-ended scales, rather than relying solely on qualitative data, to investigate disenchantment more systematically and to avoid the possibility of biases associated with coding open-ended responses. Participants rated their level of attraction to a set of twenty-six partner attributes (e.g., caring, confident, attractive) and then reported the degree to which they now believe that their partner possesses "too much" of that same positive attribute. In a series of multivariate analyses, the researchers find that the intensity of an initial attraction to a particular appealing quality is significantly and positively related to the tendency toward disenchantment (i.e., viewing a mate as having "too much" of that quality). Approximately two-thirds of the adults (66.7%) report this pattern of attraction and subsequent disaffection with their spouse or partner.

Fatal Attractions in Same-Sex Dyads

The bulk of research on fatal attraction relies on data from heterosexuals. One study, however, reveals evidence of this same phenomenon among gays and lesbians (Fortes, 2005). In a follow-up investigation with both qualitative and quantitative data, Felmlee, Fortes, and Orzechowicz (2007) find that lesbians and gays exhibit the same basic types of attraction and disenchantment processes as heterosexuals. In particular, the more intense the initial attraction to a particular quality in an intimate same-sex partner, the stronger is the tendency to assess that person as subsequently exhibiting "too much" of that same quality. As is true in research with heterosexual couples (Felmlee et al. 2007a), this pattern of disenchantment with otherwise desirable partner traits is statistically significant for all the twenty-six partner qualities examined.

In one illustration (Felmlee et al. 2007), a lesbian reports that the qualities that originally attracted her to her committed partner of eight years were that she was "spontaneous and funny." On the other hand, she dislikes that her partner is: "crass and inappropriately loud in social situations (embarrassing)." In other words, this woman appears to experience some degree of disenchantment with the qualities that originally drew her to her partner, and this occurs in spite of the fact that she is highly committed to the relationship. The otherwise desirable qualities of spontaneity and humor in her partner have a downside, that of embarrassing behavior.

Fatal Attractions in Various Ethnic/Race and Nationality Types

This pattern of disenchantment occurs among individuals from various ethnic and racial backgrounds as well. For instance, there are fatal attractions among Asian Americans, African Americans, and Latinos (e.g., Felmlee 1995, 2001a). Statistical analyses to date find no significant differences in the likelihood of disenchantment between Caucasians and individuals of color (e.g., Felmlee 2001a). Furthermore, disillusionment is not a phenomenon solely relegated to the United States. Fatal attractions take place among couples in Israel (Pines 2005), and there is recent evidence of this phenomenon among New Zelanders, as well. There are probably some culturally specific attractors and detractors among intimate pairs from varying ethnic and cultural backgrounds, yet couples from different backgrounds and cultures appear to be subject to this same pattern of romantic reversal. More research is needed along these lines, however, with larger, and more representative samples to further investigate the extent to which cultural and racial diversity influences disillusionment.

Disenchantment with a Variety of Personality Types

Disenchantment is also widespread in the sense that it involves a broad spectrum of partner personality types. There are fatal attractions in each of the dimensions of established personality inventories (e.g., agreeableness, conscientiousness, extraversion, openness, and emotional stability), as well as in the additional dimensions of physical attractiveness and motivation, as demonstrated by both quantitative and qualitative analyses (Felmlee et al. and Bahr, 2007). In other words, individuals can become disenchanted with traits in another that are captured by any of the major personality factors, such as agreeableness, conscientiousness, and emotional stability. This perception that an otherwise desirable characteristic is excessive is more pronounced for some types of qualities in a mate than others (e.g., agreeableness, extraversion). Yet all genres of appealing characteristics are significantly prone to disenchantment. No strength, it seems, is completely immune from being recast in a negative light, or no strength lacks a possible corresponding weakness.

The Fatal Attraction Process

We see herein that there are themes and instigating factors in fatal attractions. We find, too, that disenchantment occurs in a variety of types of attractions and individuals. In the next section we discuss what may occur in the actual unfolding of such an attraction over time. There are several likely processes: 1) time will tell, 2) sour grapes, 3) rose-colored glasses, and 4) people-pleasing.

Time Will Tell

One possible scenario is that people are initially drawn to certain aspects of another, but the costly, negative sides of those qualities are not revealed until some amount of time has passed. Presumably individuals try to put their "best face" forward, and attempt to hide, or alter, the less attractive elements of their personality at the initiation of a romantic liaison, but they may be unable to maintain this facade over time.

Sour Grapes

A second possibility is that individuals attempt to reduce the cognitive distress (Festinger 1957) generated by the demise (or imminent demise) of a once close, intimate relationship by denigrating their former partner's character. Of course they could disparage an ex-partner in many ways that would not be defined as fatal attractions. Nevertheless, it may be easier cognitively to recast a former partner's attractive qualities in a negative light (i.e., a fatal attraction), than it would be to claim that a partner never possessed those qualities at all, or than it would be to maintain that a partner had entirely unrelated weaknesses.

Rose-Colored Glasses

A third potential scenario is that individuals are romantically drawn to the strengths of another person, and that they are aware of the associated weaknesses from the very beginning, but choose to ignore or downplay them. When infatuation fades, however, it becomes difficult to overlook the other person's weaknesses and to overlook related relationship tensions. Certain vices also are probably harder to disregard than others (e.g., those that differ from one's own, those that are extreme), and so disenchantment with an intimate is especially likely in such cases.

People-Pleasing

Another possibility for an explanation of fatal attraction is that people in a relationship actually do change, and that they may even alter in ways that cause their own attractive trait to turn into a liability. Suppose, for instance, that individuals unwittingly, or intentionally, reinforce the appealing qualities and actions of a mate, by complimenting and giving attention to those qualities. Their partner may then attempt to intensify, or amplify, these characteristics and related behaviors. Someone aware that his romantic companion likes humor, for example, may then tell so many jokes and act so funny, that he appears silly. Another may exude arrogance and a "know it all" attitude when she attempts to further impress a boyfriend who originally found her intelligent and confident manner pleasing.

Each of these processes may contribute to relationship disenchantment, with some more central to certain types of couples and contexts. Research to date provides the most support for the third scenario, the "rose-colored glasses" hypothesis. For example, fatal attractions are significantly more frequent when individuals themselves initiate the ending of a relationship, rather than when they are on the receiving end of a breakup. Someone who terminates a romantic liaison is likely to be uninfatuated and well aware of the downsides of a partner's attractive characteristics, unlike one who is the breakup "victim." Furthermore, research finds that those in a state of infatuation are able to correctly evaluate a potential partner, but this evaluation is more positive than that of those not infatuated (Gold et al. 1984; McClanahan et al. 1990). The negative features of a love object are seen, but ignored (Tennov 1979).

There is some support for the first scenario, "Time will Tell," as well. Fatal attractions can be more frequent in relatively lengthy relationships and marriages (Felmlee et al 2007). This tendency occurs for only certain types of attractors, however, such as those related to high motivation and competence. It may take time for the negative aspects of certain virtues to surface. For example, the costs associated with a highly motivated and aspiring mate may be apparent only after his or her work decisions begin to conflict with a well-developed family life.

In sum, of all four possible explanations of the fatal attraction process, the one that receives the most empirical support is the "rose-colored glasses" argument. Yet none of the four can be ruled out completely, and they are not mutually exclusive. More than one could take place in the same relationship. Note, too, that none of these processes are likely to unfold at the individual or couple level alone. Friends and family members can aid in the removal of rose-colored glasses, for example, according to studies on the effects of social networks on intimate couples (Felmlee 2001b). Moreoever, contemporary social exchange perspectives emphasize the structural and network embeddedness of exchange interactions (e.g., Cook and Emerson 1978; Molm 1997).

Implications

In this chapter we see that fatal attractions are a relatively common experience in a wide variety of close relationships and marriages. Attractions to dissimilar, strange, and extreme characteristics in another are particularly prone to this pattern of disillusionment. Dissimilar, strange, and extreme partner qualities are likely to generate relatively high relationship costs, at least as compared with those connected with similar and more moderate partner characteristics. According to the perspective of social exchange theory, disenchantment is apt to occur when the costs associated with a partner's otherwise appealing qualities outweigh the rewards. Fatal attractions also reflect the inevitable dilemmas faced by couples and other small groups, such as the need for both connectedness and autonomy, and both novelty and predictability. Furthermore, we see that the process of disenchantment is apt to take place when infatuation with a loved one recedes, that is, the "rose-colored glasses" scenario. These findings have a number of theoretical and practical implications for the expanding field of the study of close relationships.

Opposites Attract and Then Repel

First, the phenomenon of relationship disenchantment informs the theoretical debate as to whether "opposites attract" (e.g., Winch 1955). There are cases here in which respondents report being attracted to a dissimilar, or "different" individual, but these instances are less common than those in which similarity is the basis of appeal. Furthermore, differences are more apt than similarities to result in fatal attractions. The dark side of the quality of "different" that appears in such instances is that of "strange," and it implies a lack of mutual understanding among members of a couple. In some situations, thus, opposites may initially attract, but they later repel.

Beginnings Predict Endings

The findings discussed here also have potential ramifications for the dissolution of relationships. Many accounts of breakups imply that these endings are circumstantial and out of an individual's control. Yet fatal attraction research indicates that for a substantial proportion of couples, individuals may play a instigative role in the demise of their relationship, by selecting as a partner someone whose strengths they will eventually find annoying.

The potential battlegrounds for couples are also evident. The troublesome partner qualities in fatal attractions indicate that common complaints about a mate that are likely to appear in couples' disagreements include, for example, a lack of seriousness, domineering ways, or unpredictable and irresponsible behavior. The puzzle, of course, is that these types of grievances about a loved one seem so closely related to the features initially found pleasing. The ideas discussed in this chapter, therefore, raise the intriguing possibility that such objections, and related dyadic conflict, are predictable from the very initial stages of a relationship.

Not So Fatal Attractions

Note that fatal attractions are not limited to romantic breakups or divorces; they also appear in ongoing, stable marriages and relationships. Couples can remain together in spite of the fact that both members dislike aspects of the qualities that caused them to gravitate to each other. Attracting characteristics are still "fatal" in such cases, but the overall relationship is not.

Social exchange theory is informative in addressing the question as to why individuals may have a fatal attraction, and yet remain in a marriage or relationship. According to this perspective, commitment to an intimate relationship is a function not only of the relative rewards and costs of a relationship, but also a number of other factors. These additional factors include an individual's own expectations for relationship outcomes, personal investments in a relationship, and one's comparison level for alternatives, that is, the viability of alternative relationships (Rusbult 1980). Thus, someone may remain in a relationship that has costs associated with disenchantment because they know from their previous experiences that other relationships have downsides as well, and that the downsides currently experienced are less severe. Individuals also are likely to stay with a partner, in spite of some degree of disenchantment, when they believe that their current relationship is superior to the alternatives currently available to them.

How do some couples successfully negotiate an intimate encounter and at the same time remain cognizant of the trying dimensions of each other's desirable features? The responses of research participants who are involved in such situations can further inform an answer to this question.

In one example, a man writes about the qualities that attracted him to his wife of six and a half years and emphasizes her strong personality: "She says what she believes no matter what." Nevertheless, her tendency to be "extremely stubborn and pigheaded," is what he finds least attractive about her (i.e., "Strong to Stubborn" type of fatal attraction). In his answer to the question regarding how long he thinks his marriage to this woman will last, he answers, "Forever." This case demonstrates that it is possible to find the dark side of a loved one's merits troublesome, and yet remain completely committed to that person.

How is it that this man can dislike aspects of the qualities that once attracted him to his wife and yet remain satisfied with the relationship? In the first place, he recognizes that there are connections between the positive and negative attributes of his spouse. When asked whether the characteristics that he finds least attractive about her are very different from, or very similar to, those that first attracted him, he replies, "They are related. Her stubborn nature comes from her strong sense of self-worth and her personal beliefs." He also acknowledges his own similar strengths and weaknesses, which may make it easier to appreciate his spouse's particular combination of positive and negative traits.

Wanting Everything

Relationships involve trade-offs, and such trade-offs mean that one experience is sacrificed at the expense of another. As indicated earlier, a common opposing theme in fatal attractions occurred in cases involving a fun or funny partner. An abundance of fun in a relationship, however, may mean that there is less time for seriousness. On the other hand, an attraction to a solemn, responsible partner may imply loss, too, since such a relationship may suffer from an excess of weightiness and an absence of lightheartedness or playfulness.

There is also a subtle implication embedded in these themes that people "want it all," that is, they do not want to experience any type of loss in romance. There is a tendency to want a partner who is extremely laid-back and at the same time highly motivated and successful. Or others wish for someone who is outgoing and social, but who spends plenty of exclusive time as a couple or family. Some want a partner who is confident and strong, and yet at the same time modest and self-effacing. Perhaps certain individuals have the flexibility to fulfill such desires, allowing situations to determine the appropriateness of their behavior. In theory, such an ideal mate would be extremely easygoing and relaxed on weekends and vacations, for instance, but highly driven and motivated in the workplace. They would be outgoing and friendly at parties, and yet focus exclusively on their partner on joint outings or within the home. Realistically, however, such desires for a loved one are probably inherently contradictory and are likely to remain unmet. To the extent that personality and behavioral tendencies are relatively stable and difficult to alter, the average person is unlikely to switch from one style of behavior to its opposite, situation by situation. Choosing a partner, thus, means embracing certain qualities in another at the expense of others. Furthermore, even if a companion was capable of shifting behavior to fit every occasion, that person no doubt would be at risk of being seen as "wishy-washy." Every virtue has its vice.

Minimizing the Pitfalls of Fatal Attractions

So how do you avoid a fatal attraction? What does this mean for you and your relationships? There are several procedures that could be helpful in circumventing some of the most obvious of fatal attractions. First and foremost, "be careful what you wish for." To the extent possible, be aware of what you are searching for in a partner or spouse. In particular, if you are enticed by dissimilar, strange, or extreme qualities in another, research suggests that you are also particularly likely to be disturbed later by these same traits. At the very least it should not be surprising that those differences between you and a partner are the source of some conflict.

On the other hand, one of the lessons here is that it is probably impossible to avoid some degree of partner disenchantment altogether. Fatal attractions can occur with respect to just about any quality you can name. For instance, attractions to similarity, as compared to dissimilarity, in a prospective partner are less prone to be disillusioning. Yet there are instances of such fatal attractions. One man, for example, liked the many ways in which he and his girlfriend were similar, but at the same time, he believed that the relationship was "too boring" and suffered from a lack of excitement, that is, excessive similarity. Thus, it is likely that there are no types of attractions that are completely impervious to subsequent disaffection.

What do you do when you and your partner uncover fatal attractions? How do you keep something that kills the attractiveness of a particular quality about your mate from killing the entire relationship? As discussed earlier, at least some committed, long-term couples appear to be aware that a mate's liabilities stem from his or her strengths; presumably this awareness helps in accepting a partner as he or she is, with both pluses and minuses. In addition, committed pairs readily acknowledge their own shortcomings, some of which may be related to those of the partner. Thus, being aware of the light and dark sides of one's own character, as well as one's partner, may assist in coping with disenchantment in an ongoing relationship. Yet it is easier for most of us to uncover such relationship contradictions in the lives of others, it is not always as simple to obtain an objective view of our own. A number of satisfied couples note that friends, family members, and sometimes others, such as therapists, assist in helping them arrive at a balanced evaluation of the pros and cons of their intimate relationship.

In conclusion, it is said of many famous men and women that their great strengths were also their major weaknesses. Napoleon was tenacious and confident but also "stubborn and cocky." Cleopatra was considered clever and ambitious and yet manipulative and power hungry. The yin and yang of personality, however, are not reserved for the elite. Everyone, in every relationship, has traits that initially attracted them to their partner, and frequently, these traits generate qualities viewed as unattractive. Relationships represent complex processes. What was rewarding can produce costs. But what was once troublesome also might become rewarding. The key is to be aware of inherent relationship paradoxes. It is frequently said that in relationships, you have to take the bad with the good. Fatal attractions suggest that sometimes the good and the bad are deeply intertwined, and that obtaining one means embracing the other.

References

Aronson, Elliot, Timothy D. Wilson, and Robin M. Akert. 2005. *Social Psychology*. Upper Saddle River, NJ: Prentice Hall.

Baxter, Leslie A. and Barbara M. Montgomery. 1996. *Relating: Dialogues and Dialectics*. New York: Guilford Press.

Cook, Karen S. (Ed.) 1987. *Social Exchange Theory*. Newbury Park, CA: Sage.

Cook, Karen S. and Richard M. Emerson. 1978. "Power, Equity, and Commitment in Exchange Networks." *American Sociological Review* 43:721–739.

Felmlee, Diane H. 1995. "Fatal Attractions—Affection and Disaffection in Intimate-Relationships." *Journal of Social and Personal Relationships* 12:295–311.

———. 1998a. "Be Careful What You Wish For . . . ": A Quantitative and Qualitative Investigation of "Fatal Attractions." *Personal Relationships* 5:235–253.

———. 1998b."Fatal Attraction." Pp. 3–31 in *The Dark Side of Close Relationships*. Hillsdale, NJ: Lawrence Erlbaum.

———. 1998c. "Loss and Contradictions in Intimate Relationships." in *Perspectives on Loss: A Sourcebook*. Washington, DC: Taylor and Francis.

———. 2001a. "From Appealing to Appalling: Disenchantment with a Romantic Partner." *Sociological Perspectives* 44:263–280.

———. 2001b. "No Couple Is an Island: A Social Network Perspective on Dyadic Stability." *Social Forces* 79:1259–1287.

Felmlee, Diane H., Heather Flynn, and Peter Bahr. 2007a. "Too Much of a Good Thing: Fatal Attraction in Marriages and Intimate Relationships." Paper presented at The Annual Meetings of the American Sociological Association. New York City, NY.

Felmlee, Diane H., Carmen Fortes, and David Orzechowicz. 2007b. "Fairy Tales: Attraction in Same Sex Relationships." Paper presented at The 78th Annual Meeting of the Pacific Sociological Association.

Festinger, Leon. 1957. *A Theory of Cognitive Dissonance*. Evanston, IL: Row, Peterson.

Fortes, Carmen. 2005. "Myths and Enchantment Tales: Attraction and Disillusionment in Same-Sex Romatic Relationships." *McNair Scholars Journal* 8:1–11.

Gold, Joel A., R. M. Richard M. Ryckman, and N R. Mosley. 1984. "Romantic Mood Induction and Attraction to a Dissimilar Other—Is Love Blind." *Personality and Social Psychology Bulletin* 10:358–368.

Hill, C. T., Z. Rubin, and L. A. Peplau. 1976. "Breakups before Marriage—End of 103 Affairs." *Journal of Social Issues* 32:147–168.

Homans, George C. 1974. *Social Behavior: Its Elementary Forms,* Rev. ed. New York: Harcourt, Brace, & World.

Kelly, Harold H. and John W. Thiebaut. 1978. *Interpersonal Relations: A Theory of Interdependence*. New York: Wiley.

McClanahan, K. K., J. A. Gold, E. Lenney, R. M. Ryckman, and G. E. Kulberg. 1990. "Infatuation and Attraction to a Dissimilar Other—Why Is Love Blind?" *Journal of Social Psychology* 130:433–445.

Molm, Linda D. 1997. *Coercive Power in Social Exchange*. Cambridge, UK: Cambridge University Press.

Morin, Richard. 1995. "Unconventional Wisdom: New Facts and Hot Stats from the Social Sciences." In *The Washington Post*, Washington, DC.

Pines, Ayala M. 2005. *Falling in Love: Why We Choose the Lovers We Choose*. New York: Taylor & Francis Group.

Rusbult, Caryl E. 1980. "Committment and Satisfaction in Romantic Associations." *Journal of Experimental Social Psychology* 16:172–186.

Simmel, Georg. 1955. *Conflict and the Web of Group Affiliations*. Glencoe, IL: Free Press.

Snyder, C. R. and Howard L. Fromkin. 1980. *Uniqueness, the Human Pursuit of Difference*. New York: Plenum Press.

Sprecher, Susan. 2001. "Equity and Social Exchange in Dating Couples: Associations with Satisfaction, Commitment, and Stability." *Journal of Marriage and the Family* 63:599–613.

Tennov, Dorothy. 1979. *Love and Limerence: The Experience of Being in Love*. New York: Stein and Day.

Winch, Robert F. 1955. "The Theory of Complementary Needs in Mate-Selection: A Test of One Kind of Complementariness." *American Sociological Review* 20:52–56.

7

Social Norms

Christine Horne

Department of Sociology, Washington State University

For centuries, women in China practiced foot binding. Foot binding involved folding the foot of a young girl under itself and wrapping it tightly with bandages. The result was that the foot grew no more than a few inches long. Women with bound feet were unable to walk normally. They experienced pain and complications—including gangrene, amputation, and even death. Despite these damaging effects, women perpetuated the practice, making sure that their daughters' feet were bound. Foot binding was almost universal among the Chinese and persisted for hundreds of years. Numerous reform efforts failed. Laws against foot binding did nothing to discourage it. Efforts to educate the Chinese and to inform them of world opinion about the practice also failed. But then, almost overnight, it disappeared (Mackie 1996).

Why, given its painful and damaging effects, and the efforts to stop it, was the practice of foot binding so widespread? And why, after all the failed efforts, was it finally eliminated—in only a generation?

Often, when confronted with such seemingly irrational behavior, researchers turn to social norms as an explanation. Why do individuals do things against their own self-interest? Why do other cultures do things we do not understand? Why do groups engage in self-destructive behavior? Norms provide an answer. They make the irrational comprehensible.

Foot binding in China provides just one graphic example of such a norm. We can think of many more. Norms are ubiquitous. They affect a range of behaviors—voting, drinking, eating disorders, human rights violations, violence and crime, pregnancy, fashion, parenting practices, and many, many others. In fact it may be that most, if not all, of the behaviors that we care about have a normative component. Norms can encourage people to do things that we think are good but they also can lead people to do things that are harmful or foolish.

If norms matter, then we need to understand them. Sociologists have long been interested in social norms, but early research focused on their effects. Recently scholars across a range of disciplines—including not only sociology, but also political science, economics, anthropology, law, and psychology—have begun trying to understand social norms themselves. Where do norms come from? What causal factors and mechanisms account for them? In this chapter I describe some of the recent norms research (primarily in sociology) that seeks to answer these questions.

What Are Norms?

A norm is a rule accompanied by social sanctions. Norms are externally enforced. Those who obey a normative rule are treated more positively than those who do not. This external enforcement distinguishes norms from other kinds of evaluations like values, morals, principles, ideals, or meaning. These other evaluations are similar to norms in that they identify what is good or bad, acceptable or unacceptable. But they differ in that they are internally enforced. When our behavior is inconsistent with what we believe, we feel guilty, but when our behavior violates norms, others sanction us. They reward good behavior and punish bad behavior. Social sanctions are the distinguishing feature of norms.

In order to understand norms, therefore, we need to explain why groups enforce them. It is, of course, important to understand the source of evaluative statements—the source of rules about what is good and bad. But this issue is not unique to the study of norms. Norms are norms because they are socially enforced. Accordingly, this chapter focuses on research that contributes to our understanding of norm enforcement.

Studying Norms

Researchers studying norms must be able to measure them. How do they know if a norm exists? This issue is a problem not only for scholars, but also for individuals trying to figure out how to behave, particularly in new situations. Just as an individual in an unfamiliar social situation looks for clues as to what they should do, researchers must also look for indicators of norms.

Patterns of Behavior

One possible strategy is to observe patterns of behavior. This is probably what many of us do as we try to succeed in a new situation. We look at others and use their behavior as a starting point for determining how we should behave. Similarly, researchers may look at patterns of behavior and from those patterns, infer the existence of a norm.

But for scholars studying norms, this approach is problematic. They cannot just assume that if many people are engaging in a behavior, there is a norm regulating it. People might engage in a behavior either because it is normative, or because it is a smart thing to do. When it is −40 degrees outside and the wind is howling, we wear a hat because we want to stay warm and avoid frostbitten ears, not because people will react negatively to us if we do not. There may be patterns of behavior without norms. If individuals can deviate from whatever is typical without any social consequences, then there is no norm.

Consider age "norms," for example. Are there age norms? We know that Americans tend to do certain things (move out of their parents' house, get married, have children, and so forth) at particular ages. Those who do not follow the pattern are atypical. Does this mean that they are violating a norm? Not unless people react negatively. If deviations are not sanctioned, then there is no norm. While we know a lot about age-related patterns of behavior, we know relatively little about social reactions to deviations (Macmillan 2005:11–14; Marini 1984). Age-related patterns of behavior do not necessarily imply age-related norms.

To ascertain the existence of norms, we need more. "Normal" behavior (behavior that everyone does) is not necessarily normative (subject to social sanction). A statistical regularity does not equal a norm.

Normative Rules

A second approach to measurement is to ask people about the norms in their community. One problem with this method is that people may not consciously know what the norms are. There are rules of behavior that we do not think about until someone violates them. We are not consciously aware of the rules governing walking down the sidewalk. We do not think about our expectations regarding personal space. Even if people are honestly trying to answer the researcher's questions, they may not be able to respond reliably to a question out of the blue.

In addition, when identifying behaviors that are seen as good or bad, people may be describing ideals, not norms. For example, church members might say that the norm is that everyone ought to love one another and treat others as they would like to be treated. But if people do not actually react negatively when others fail to be kind, then the rule is an ideal that may or may not have any behavioral consequences. Just as behavior is not equivalent to a norm, rules alone do not establish the existence of a norm.

Sanctions

A third approach to identifying norms is to look at reactions to behavior. Sanctions are the key element of norms that distinguishes them from other kinds of evaluations. They are also arguably the best indicator of whether a norm exists. If a male college student drinks a vodka cran instead of a beer, does he get made fun of? If a woman wears clothes that are in hopelessly bad taste, or outdated, do people react to her less favorably? If so, then we know that norms govern alcohol consumption and fashion. The best indicator of norms is to look at reactions to behavior.

Obtaining information about such reactions is tricky, however. In real life we often do not know if a behavior is sanctioned. The researcher may not be there to see it happen. Further, people do not necessarily tell the researcher about sanctioning. They might or might not want to tell a stranger about how they were made fun of. They might or might not describe how they treated others. They might not even know whether sanctioning occurred.

Measuring sanctioning therefore is a challenge. For this and other reasons, some researchers have turned to laboratory experiments—where, unlike in naturally occurring settings, they can observe every sanction. Such experimental research programs are very useful for developing theoretical understanding of norms.

Other researchers have been ingenious in coming up with ways to measure norms using traditional survey instruments. Mollborn, for example, uses self-reports of how embarrassed a respondent would be if they became pregnant, or if someone in their family became pregnant. If people are embarrassed when others find out about their behavior, this suggests that they expect others to react negatively. In other words, Mollborn measures norm enforcement not by measuring sanctions themselves, but by looking at individuals' expectations of others' reactions (Mollborn 2007a, 2007b). Creative efforts like these can be useful in helping researchers to identify and study norms.

Social Structure and Norm Enforcement

Why do groups enforce norms? It is not at all obvious why people sanction. After all, sanctioning is risky. The person who is punished may retaliate. Sanctioning can take time and energy, and put one at risk of a range of negative consequences—from embarrassment to personal injury. People may be reluctant to try to control the behavior of a strong, athletic teenager or of someone in their workplace who controls their promotion. They may not want to risk being ridiculed or verbally attacked; they may not want to risk losing a friend.

The problem inherent in sanctioning is illustrated in one of Aesop's fables, "The Mice in Council" (Coleman 1990:270–271). The mice lived a very good life, in a home with plenty of food. Their one problem was the cat who would eat the mice when they ventured out of their holes. The mice got together to decide what to do. They all agreed that the best approach would be to put a bell around the cat's neck so that they would be able to hear the cat approaching in time to get to safety. All the mice enthusiastically applauded this suggestion until one wise old mouse asked, "Who is going to put the bell around the cat's neck?" There were very large costs associated with attaching the bell to the cat. Similarly, there can be large costs associated with sanctioning. Why do people sanction given these costs?

To answer this question, sociological explanations of norm enforcement focus on the social structural features of the situation. These features include the characteristics of behavior (in particular, its consequences for others), the characteristics of social relations (including ties between individuals within groups and conflict across groups), and the distribution of behavior across social space (in particular, the frequency of behavior).

Characteristics of Behavior

In general, people do not like it when an individual's behavior produces negative consequences for others. When someone engages in a behavior, that behavior affects not only them, but potentially others as well. And when others are affected by a behavior, they have an interest in it (Coleman 1990; Heckathorn 1988, 1989). That is, they have a *regulatory interest* in the behavior. If the behavior has positive consequences for others, then those others would like to see more of it. If the behavior has negative consequences, then they would like to see less of it. There is a demand for a norm (Coleman 1990). People want to see harmful behavior punished.

This idea is illustrated in Figure 7.1. White face is doing something he likes, but that affects all the gray faces. Those gray faces then have an interest in that behavior and react to it.

FIGURE 7.1 ***Characteristics of Behavior Approach.***

Our legal system functions in a way that is consistent with this view. It treats behaviors that cause serious harm more severely than those that do not. Longer prison sentences are associated with serious crimes—murder and rape as compared with shoplifting, for example. Research shows that both lay people and judges want those who cause great damage to be punished severely. And people care about more than just physical harm. They also care about emotional injury (Nadler and Rose 2003). When people have information regarding the emotional harm to a victim, they feel sympathy, and think that the defendant deserves more severe punishment.

We see similar dynamics operating in informal groups and networks. When people have information about the negative consequences of a behavior, they begin to sanction those who engage in it.

The rise of a norm against smoking is a good example (Ellickson 2001). Americans used to think that smoking was acceptable. Famed news anchor Edward Murrow smoked cigarettes during his broadcasts; movie stars smoked on screen. Doctors were even known to advise people to smoke. Smoking was seen as cool. But now, views of smoking have changed. We think of smoking as an unhealthy habit and we react negatively to smokers. How did this norm arise, and why did it only emerge recently?

Americans used to be ignorant of the health consequences of smoking, and we certainly did not understand the dangers of secondhand smoke. Government publications started to tell Americans about the results of studies showing that smokers damaged not only their own lungs, but also those of their family members and others sharing the same breathing space. People therefore began to care about others' smoking habits—they were not just the smoker's business anymore. People began reacting negatively to smoking. Eventually, they not only enforced norms against smoking, but also took action to get smoking banned from work environments, airports, restaurants, and even from traditionally smoky bars. Americans accepted smoking when they did not understand its consequences, but when they learned that it hurt people other than the smoker, then they had an interest in it and did something about it.

This argument can be used to explain norms regulating a range of behaviors. In addition to explaining reactions to specific concrete behaviors (like smoking) that cause harm to others, it is useful for understanding regulation of more general categories of behavior. In particular, the approach suggests that norms arise in response to social dilemmas.

A social dilemma is a situation in which the interests of the individual conflict with those of the group. For example, everyone might want to live in a clean and safe neighborhood, but individuals may not have the time or energy to help make it happen. Americans might think it is important to vote, but be dissuaded from going to the polls by bad weather, long lines, or an emergency at work. Of course, if everyone behaves in this self-interested way, then nobody contributes. Neighborhoods deteriorate and voter turn out is low. Everyone is worse off.

Individual behaviors that contribute to or detract from the collective good (a nice neighborhood, a vibrant democracy, and so forth) affect others. Social dilemma situations, by their very nature, trigger regulatory interests. Therefore, we might expect that such situations will lead to strong regulatory interests that in turn motivate norm enforcement. When seen in this way, norms are a potentially important tool for encouraging people to contribute to the collective good. Sanctions provide a means of overcoming social dilemmas. If people are punished for their self-interested behavior, then they are more likely to behave cooperatively. The question is, then, do social dilemma situations actually lead to sanctioning?

Social psychologists have used laboratory experiments to see if social dilemmas do indeed produce norms discouraging free-riding. Yamagishi (1988) argued that the seriousness of a social dilemma affected people's willingness to contribute to a sanctioning system. He predicted that the more people benefitted from group member cooperation (and the more they lost if people failed to cooperate), the more they would contribute to a collective sanctioning system.

Yamagishi conducted an experiment in which he brought subjects into a laboratory. Subjects participated in groups of four. Each individual had opportunities to contribute points to the group, but at a personal cost. Yamagishi created two conditions—a weak social dilemma condition and a strong social dilemma condition. In the weak social dilemma condition, any points subjects contributed to the group were doubled. In the strong condition they were tripled; people had more to gain if others contributed to the group, and more to lose if they did not. In other words, the social dilemma was more serious. Yamagishi's results showed that when the stakes were higher, people supported sanctioning systems that punished failures to contribute.

Later I did a study that produced similar results (Horne 2007a). Instead of looking at subjects' contributions to a sanctioning system, this research looked at actual punishments—how people treated those who contributed points to the group compared with those who did not. Like Yamagishi, I also brought subjects into the lab in groups of four. Participants had opportunities to contribute to the group. These contributions produced benefits for all group members, but they produced different amounts of benefit in different conditions. In the low benefit condition, every group member received only two points if someone contributed to the group. In the high benefit condition, they received six points.

After making decisions about contributing to the group, participants were able to exchange with each other. They did this by giving points to other group members. These exchange opportunities gave subjects a means of expressing their approval or disapproval of their fellow group members' behavior. They could express approval by giving more points to those who contributed to the group and disapproval by giving fewer points to those who did not. Sanctioning was measured by calculating the difference between the points that subjects gave to those who contributed to the group and to those who did not contribute. The bigger the difference, the stronger the norm favoring contribution to the group.

The results showed that (at least under certain conditions) subjects imposed more severe punishments for more consequential failures to contribute. When individual contribution decisions had only small effects on fellow group members, their self-interested behavior was rarely sanctioned, but when these decisions had larger consequences for group members, failure to contribute was punished more severely.

This line of research suggests that norms may help to solve social problems. When behavior produces negative consequences, people have reason to punish it. Norms encourage behavior that increases group welfare.

The explanation is not fully satisfying, however. It is not clear why people would sanction even if they really wanted damaging behaviors to stop. While any rational individual would like others to behave in prosocial ways, they also would prefer not to have to bear the costs of getting them to do so. People hope that someone else will ask the smoker at the next table to stop smoking. They hope that someone else will confront a belligerent coworker. They hope that someone else will put the bell around the cat's neck. They want someone to take action, but they would prefer not to do it themselves.

Fehr and Gächter (2002) find evidence that people get angry at free-riders. Free-riders enjoy the benefits they receive when others contribute to the collective good, even though they themselves do not contribute. Such free-riding naturally makes people angry. (Think how frustrating it is when a fellow student does not pull their weight on a group project.) That anger motivates punishment. If people fail to contribute to the collective good, other group members become angry, and in turn impose sanctions. This research suggests that human beings are motivated by emotion that drives them to sanction—even when doing so is irrational. For Fehr and Gächter then, human beings are motivated by emotion. Emotions lead people to punish at personal expense.

Even if Fehr and Gächter are right, and people have internalized tendencies to react negatively to harmful behavior, this does not explain norms supporting behaviors like foot binding. Foot binding not only caused harm to the women who experienced it, but also, because the women were handicapped, it reduced the productivity of families and communities. Foot binding provides an example of norms that actually encouraged harmful behavior. Why would people enforce norms that were so clearly damaging?

The characteristics of behavior approach to explaining sanctioning also does not explain norms regulating behaviors that have no significant consequences. Many trivial behaviors are associated with strong normative pressures. It is hard to see how the fashion choices of an individual high school student produce any great damage—yet normative pressure is certainly there. We have only to look around us to see that people enforce norms even when the benefits of doing so appear small or nonexistent.

The characteristics of behavior alone are not sufficient to explain all that we observe. In order to improve understanding of norm enforcement, researchers have turned to other factors.

Social Relations

Social psychologist Homans (1951, 1974) argued that group cohesion increased pressure for conformity. His research on small work groups showed that people in cohesive groups were more likely to meet obligations than those in less cohesive groups. He argued that they did so because they cared about others' opinions. Individuals contributed to the group in order to get approval from others, and they particularly cared about getting approval from those on whom they were dependent.

Homans's work is consistent with other sociological research demonstrating the importance of social relations. Recent norms research has built on this fundamental insight—exploring the particular characteristics of social relations that affect norm enforcement and the mechanisms through which they do so.

Relations between Individuals within Groups. People depend on others to get things that they want and need. If we think about all the things we would like out of life—love, money, status, and so forth—relatively few of them can be attained alone. Most require some level of cooperation from others. This means that people need to demonstrate to others that they are good actors—that they would be good people with whom to interact (Posner 2000). Because human beings need others, they will try to behave in ways that will maintain relationships and lead others to treat them positively rather than negatively. Individuals typically try to avoid behaviors that will get them fired, or lose friends.

What can people do to demonstrate that they are good exchange partners and good group members? One thing they can do is follow norms. When individuals obey group norms, they demonstrate that they know how to behave. Their behavior provides evidence of their reliability and trustworthiness. This is particularly true if the behavior is costly.

Another thing that people can do is to enforce norms. If an individual sanctions behavior that other group members would like to see punished, then that individual is demonstrating that they understand what the group norms are. Further, they are providing evidence of their commitment to the norm, and they are showing that they are willing to make personal sacrifices to enforce those norms. Enforcement provides further (potentially stronger) evidence that the individual is a reliable and trustworthy actor. One reason to sanction is to let others know that one is a good actor—in hopes that they will respond positively.

In other words, people who are considering sanctioning are affected by *metanorms,* the reactions of others to sanctioning efforts. Metanorms are a particular kind of norm that regulate enforcement. They tell people whether they should sanction, how severely, and so forth. Potential sanctioners anticipate these reactions and make sanctioning decisions accordingly.

Consider, for example, President George W. Bush's visit to the United Nations shortly after the U.S. invasion of Iraq in 2003. President Bush spoke. He was followed by French President Jacques Chirac. Chirac was very critical of the U.S. invasion. His criticism can be seen as enforcement of an international norm. Chirac's remarks were vigorously applauded by others in the room. That applause was a form of metanorm enforcement—a reward given to someone who sanctioned President Bush.

In another Iraq related incident, consider the furor that erupted when the Dixie Chicks, in a London concert, criticized President Bush for his decision to invade. Like Jacques Chirac, they were enforcing a norm. The concert audience applauded—enforcing a metanorm that rewarded such criticisms of the American president. But, many people at home in the United States responded differently. They were deeply offended by the Dixie Chicks' comments. They responded by refusing to buy their music and asking radio stations not to play it. Whereas the concert goers enforced a metanorm favoring sanctioning, American country music listeners enforced an opposing metanorm—one that says that it is not okay to publicly criticize the president of the United States in a war situation.

At a more mundane level, consider people waiting in a long line to get tickets to a sporting event. Everyone will be angry if someone cuts into line. If somebody actually does something about it—in essence, sanctioning the inconsiderate person—others in line will be grateful. If they give positive feedback to the person who took action, they are enforcing a metanorm that says that we ought to punish people who cut into line in front of those who have been standing there for hours.

People who care about others' opinions will take metanorms into account. Chirac no doubt at least considered the likely reactions of the international community to his criticisms of Bush. If he had expected to be booed, he might not have acted as he did. When people expect their sanctioning efforts to be followed by positive reactions, then they are more likely to enforce norms.

If metanorms motivate sanctioning, then we need to understand why people enforce them. Just as people would prefer to get the benefits of sanctioning without bearing any of the costs, so to would they prefer to get the benefits that result from giving support to sanctioners without actually having to make any effort themselves. Why then do people enforce metanorms?

Coleman (1990) argued that if people in a group know each other—if networks are "closed"—then people can coordinate to provide support to sanctioners. When each individual makes just a little effort to encourage someone to punish deviance (or to discourage them from doing so), the cumulative impact can be large. (Consider the Dixie Chicks' precipitous loss in sales resulting from many country music listeners doing relatively little.) All of the separate voices of approval aggregate to increase the incentives for an individual to sanction.

In other words, according to Coleman, people in "closed" networks reward sanctioners because, if they can coordinate, the costs of doing so are small relative to the benefits they expect to get if deviance is punished. This argument suggests that people weigh the benefits of rewarding the sanctioner against the cost. In closed networks this cost is small. If we think back to the UN delegates who applauded Jacques Chirac, this argument suggests that they applauded because it was relatively easy to do so and because they were hopeful that Chirac would be effective in getting the United States to change its behavior.

Country music listeners exchanged the small cost of refusing to listen to the Dixie Chicks for the larger benefits of persuading American entertainers to be patriotic by supporting the president's war efforts.

In essence, Coleman argues that metanorm costs are lower in closed groups in which people know each other and can coordinate to react to the sanctioner. Groups with a closed network structure therefore will have stronger metanorms and, in turn, be more able to enforce norms than when people do not know each other.

People may enforce metanorms for another reason. Like sanctioners, metanorm enforcers consider their social relations. If they value their relationship with the sanctioner, then they will want to maintain it. This means that they need to provide support when the sanctioner experiences costs. In other words, people enforce metanorms for the same reason that they enforce norms. They want social approval. And they care more about maintaining their relationships when they are dependent—when their relationships are valuable. This approach suggests that the UN delegates applauded Chirac's speech, not so much because they cared about U.S. action, but because they cared about their relations with Chirac and wanted to maintain them.

This argument is illustrated in Figure 7.2. In the group connected with thin lines, people have only weak ties with each other. They do not value their relationships. In turn, metanorms are weak, and norm enforcement is also weak. In the group connected with thick lines, people have strong ties with each other. They care about maintaining their relationships with each other. In groups like this, metanorms and norm enforcement will be stronger.

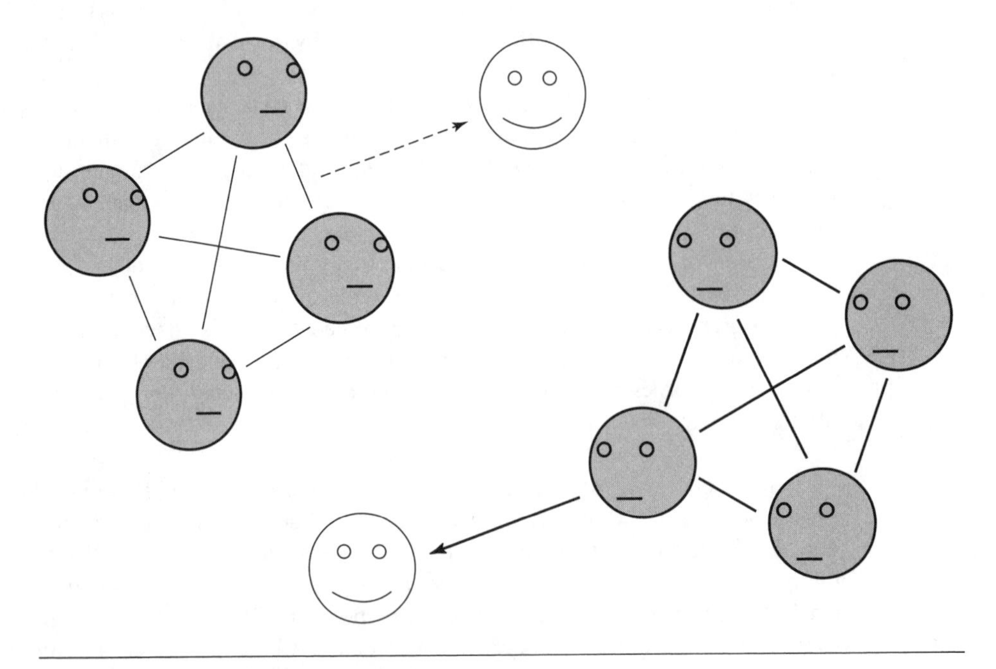

FIGURE 7.2 ***Social Relations Approach.***

To test this idea, I conducted a series of experiments looking at how dependence between group members affected metanorms, as well as how it affected sanctioning itself (Horne 2001, 2004). Initially, I was interested in the effects of dependence alone. I conducted an experiment in which I brought people into the lab in groups of four. Participants interacted with each other over networked computers; they could not see each other face-to-face. In addition to these four human actors, the group also included a computer simulated thief who the participants thought was a fellow subject like themselves. People in the group had opportunities both to punish the thief, and to react to others' punishment decisions. And they could interact by giving points to each other. Participants made money based on the experimental condition to which they were assigned and the decisions that they and others made. They made less money if the thief stole from them. They made less money if they used their resources to sanction. They made more money if they engaged in profitable exchange with others and if others responded positively to their sanctioning decisions.

Because I was interested in how a structural feature of social relations—dependence—affected sanctioning, I manipulated dependence and randomly assigned participants to either a high- or low-dependence condition. In the low-dependence condition, people could do just as well alone as they could by interacting with others. In this condition, people had little reason to care about others' opinions and little motivation to exchange with them. In the high-dependence condition, subjects could do much better if they exchanged with others. In this condition, they had reason to want to maintain productive exchange relations.

What happened? I found that, as predicted, groups in high-dependence conditions gave more support to sanctioners. Sanctioners in these high-dependence groups received larger rewards when they sanctioned the thief than did people in low dependence groups. Further, these rewards were associated with increased sanctioning. Dependence strengthened metanorms, and metanorms encouraged norm enforcement.

Experimental research finds that dependence increases metanorm enforcement. When people have a strong relationship with others, they are more likely to reward those who sanction deviance. Dependence may also increase potential sanctioners' concern about those metanorms. Consider the high school classroom, for example. One of the major challenges facing teachers is student resistance and disruption (McFarland 2001). Analysis of this problem using norms suggests that students act out more if others in the classroom encourage them to do so. When students enforce norms that are disruptive to learning, little learning occurs. Why do students enforce anti-education norms? Presumably because they think other students will approve of their actions, and they care about peer approval. High school students place high value on their relationships with their peers. Peer opinion matters. Students enforce disruptive norms, anticipating that others will respond positively to their actions.

What about the opinion of the teacher? We might think that students would enforce pro-education norms in order to get the approval of their teachers. But often they do not. The social relations argument suggests that students will only be concerned with teacher reaction if they are dependent on that teacher—if they value their relationship with the teacher and what that teacher has to offer. What do teachers have to offer students in today's America? Relatively little. Teachers do not control access to jobs, or even to college. Far more important to many high school students are the peers who can make their lives miserable. A social relations approach to norms would suggest that if we want high school students to enforce pro-achievement norms, we should increase their dependence on their teachers and the value they place on teacher approval.

According to the social relations approach, dependence matters for norm enforcement—people consider their social relations in making sanctioning decisions. How do these concerns with social relations intersect with the characteristics of the deviant behavior? If a deviant behavior is very harmful, then presumably punishing that behavior will result in large benefits. If it is relatively harmless, then sanctioning will produce only small benefits. How do concerns with social relations operate in conjunction with these costs and benefits?

To investigate this question, I conducted several experiments (Horne 2007). This time, in addition to manipulating dependence, I also manipulated the costs and benefits associated with sanctioning. In one condition, the costs outweighed the benefits for the individual, but the benefits to the group as a whole outweighed the costs. It was costly for the individual to sanction, but beneficial for the group. In this condition, sanctioning contributed to group welfare. Everyone in the group would be better off if the deviant was punished.

In another condition, the costs were greater than the collective benefit to the group. Not only was sanctioning costly for the individual, it also did not make any sense from the group's perspective. The group would be better off if no sanctioning occurred; it would be worse off if the deviant was punished.

I found that in high-dependence conditions, people sanctioned even when it did not make sense. When people valued their relationships with other group members, they were more likely to sanction. This was true even when the group as a whole suffered as a result. Dependence between group members created a dynamic that encouraged sanctioning. People treated the same theft differently depending on their social relations.

These experiments showed not only that explanations that rely only on the characteristics of behavior are incomplete, but also that they may lead to inaccurate predictions. The *characteristics of behavior* approach to explaining norms suggests that norms address social problems. They reduce antisocial behavior. Accordingly norms increase group welfare. The research on social relations provides evidence that norm enforcement does not necessarily increase group welfare. Social dynamics can lead to norm enforcement decisions that are bad for the group. They can lead groups to be overly zealous. The characteristics of behavior intersect with the characteristics of social relations to affect norms.

Findings about the importance of social relations are not just of academic interest. They also have implications outside the lab. Consider, for example, judges' use of shame as a sanction for convicted criminals. The idea is that instead of, or in addition to, relying on incarceration and fines, the legal system can take advantage of informal social controls. Judges try to do this by imposing sentences that involve publicizing the individual's offense. The research reported here suggests that members of the community who see this information will react differently depending on their relations with each other. The extent to which they depend on fellow community members might well lead them to over- or under-react to the deviant. Informal sanctions that judges trigger may be uncorrelated with the severity of the crime.

In addition to dependence, other characteristics of social relations also matter. Social status is an important component of social relations that can both increase and decrease norm enforcement.

McAdams (1997) argues that when people sanction, others reward them by giving them higher status. Human concern with social status facilitates sanctioning.

In contrast, Kitts (2006) argues that status concerns can impede norm enforcement. Under some conditions, while we might want people to contribute to the collective good (because we want a share of it) we also might not want to reward them because we do not want them to get higher status at our expense. In the workplace, for example, if everyone works hard, the company prospers. But individuals might not want to praise others who work hard, because they want praise and advancement for themselves. If only a few can succeed, the individual might not want others to be successful at his or her expense. The individual wants to be the one who comes out on top—he does not want to lose to others. Status competitions between individuals can reduce the likelihood that they will enforce norms that benefit the group.

Sanctioning occurs in the context of social relationships. If we want to explain norm enforcement, we need to understand how characteristics of social relationships, like dependence and status, matter.

Relations across Groups. Connections between individuals within groups are just one kind of social relationship. Do other types of relations also affect sanctioning?

There is lots of evidence that human beings are group oriented creatures—that group membership means a lot to us. Research shows that people tend to treat fellow group members better than they do outsiders, even when the differences between groups are minimal. Tajfel and his colleagues did a series of experiments in which they assigned people to minimally different groups. For example, they showed participants pictures of paintings by Klee and Kandinsky and asked them which one they preferred. Participants were then assigned to a group based on their preference. Researchers also tried simply flipping a coin to decide which group subjects would be in. In these experiments, people were more generous to people in their own group than to those in the out-group—even thought there was little, if any, difference between them (Billig and Tajfel 1973; Tajfel 1982).

Additional work demonstrates particular sensitivity to group membership in conflict situations. Researchers conducted an experiment in which they showed subjects pictures of two black and two white individuals (Cosmides et al. 2003). They found that if subjects just saw the individuals, they paid attention to their race. But, when the researchers created competing "teams" wearing different colored jerseys, and put one white and one black person on each team, subjects no longer paid attention to race. Membership in competing teams apparently erased the effect of race. These findings provide further evidence that people care about group membership—particularly in situations of conflict.

Sherif (1966) not only suggests that people care about group conflict, but also points to a possible connection between intergroup conflict and sanctioning. In his famous "Robbers Cave Experiment," Sherif brought eleven- and twelve-year-old boys to summer camp. He divided them into two groups and had the groups compete with each other. He found that the boys reacted negatively to members of their team who sought to alleviate the conflict and reacted positively toward fellow members who behaved aggressively toward the other team.

In the Robbers Cave Experiment, boys enforced norms within their group in order to encourage their group members to behave in ways that would help them win. But suppose that the result of sanctioning is no different in conflict or no-conflict situations. Does intergroup conflict itself increase the tendency of groups to sanction their members?

In order to answer this question, Benard (2007) designed an experiment looking at how conflict between groups affects the extent to which people punish free-riding of fellow group members. Each experimental session included two 3-person groups. Individuals were able to contribute to their own group at a personal cost. In the conflict condition, groups were better off if their group had more contributions and worse off if the competing group had more contributions. In the no conflict condition, contributions simply contributed to the group's welfare. Everyone in the group was better off if people contributed, but the well-being of one group was unrelated to that of the other.

In addition to contributing to the group, subjects had opportunities to give to a punishment fund. The points in the punishment fund determined the size of the sanction directed at noncontributors in the individual's group. Benard looked at this sanctioning behavior across conflict and no-conflict conditions. In both conditions, sanctioning produces the same monetary payoffs for subjects. Would conflict affect sanctioning even though there was no difference between the payoffs in the two conditions?

Benard found that individuals differed in their reaction to the experimental conditions. He identified two kinds of people—vertical individualists and vertical collectivists. Vertical individualists value individuals and individual success. Such people typically are self-oriented; they do not contribute to the group and do not punish failures to contribute. In situations of intergroup conflict, however, their sanctioning increases. This is because they care about winning. When their group is in conflict with another group, they want their group to come out on top. They sanction so that their group will win.

In contrast, vertical collectivists value groups. Typically, they are group oriented and more likely to contribute to the group than are individualists. In situations of intergroup conflict, however, their sanctioning efforts decline. This is because collectivists recognize that intergroup conflict is bad for everyone. Even if their group comes out ahead, it does so at an overall cost. Because they see the downsides for all, collectivists are not inclined to exacerbate the situation. They do not sanction failures to contribute.

Benard's results suggest that intergroup conflict does affect sanctioning within the group, but that the effect varies depending on individual characteristics (Benard 2007). Accordingly the effect of intergroup conflict on norm enforcement may vary. If there are more individualists, intergroup conflict would increase norm enforcement within the group. But if the group includes more collectivists, intergroup conflict would have the opposite effect.

The research shows that relations across groups matter. More remains to be done to explore the precise mechanisms at work and to identify the conditions under which intergroup conflict affects norms.

Everybody's Doing It

In addition to looking at the characteristics of behavior and social relations, researchers are also interested in the relation between typical behavior and norms (Opp 1982). Some suggest that typical behavior becomes normative, and deviations become subject to sanction (Opp 1982; Ullmann-Margalit 1977).

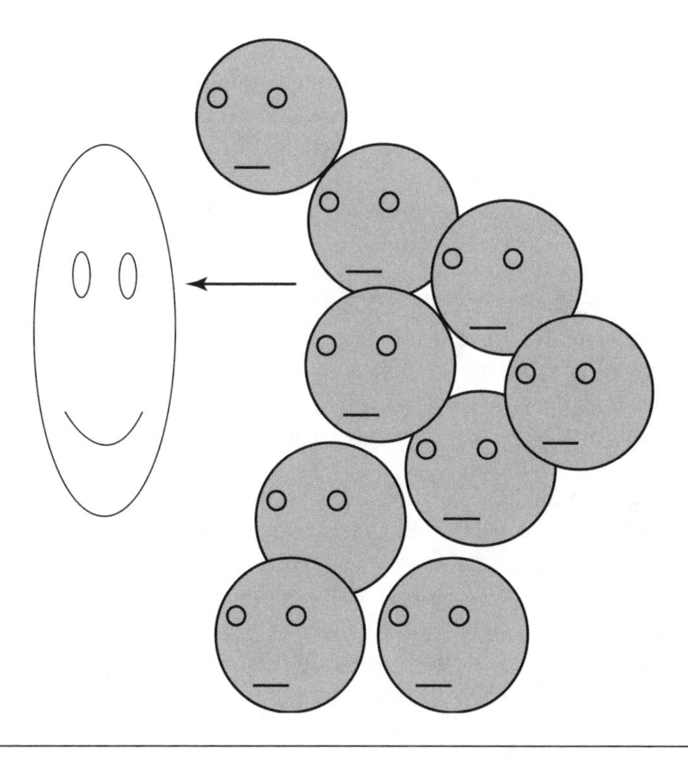

FIGURE 7.3 ***Typicality Approach.***

This idea is illustrated in Figure 7.3. White face is doing something different from everyone else. The gray faces see that they are all doing the same thing. Accordingly, gray faces will punish white face for doing something atypical. But why would people do this, and under what conditions?

Classic social psychological research on norms focused on the tendency of people to conform with others. A famous study done by Sherif (1936) examined this tendency. He shone a light on a screen and asked subjects to evaluate how much it moved. In reality, the light did not move at all. Any apparent movement was merely an optical illusion. Sherif found that individuals' estimates of this illusory movement tended to converge. Estimates that individuals gave when they were part of a group were very similar, while those that isolated individuals gave (without knowledge of others' judgments) were much more diverse. This work showed that in conditions of uncertainty, people tended to look to others.

Later, Asch (1951) showed that people would mimic others' choices, not only under conditions of uncertainty, but even if those choices were clearly wrong. He showed subjects a set of three lines and asked them to match a fourth line to the one that was closest in length. Before they made their decision, seven other ostensible participants (actors pretending that they were subjects while they were actually confederates of the experimenter) made their choices. Asch found that when all the confederates chose the wrong line, subjects were more likely to choose the wrong line as well.

This research demonstrates a tendency to conform. It tells us about patterns of behavior. But, as we know, a pattern of behavior in and of itself does not mean there is a norm. These studies do not provide evidence as to whether atypical behavior produces negative reactions. Are people who choose something different from the group treated more negatively than those who go along?

Schachter's (1951) well-known Johnny Rocco experiment provides some early relevant evidence. In that experiment subjects discussed the appropriate punishment to apply to a delinquent. A confederate of the experimenter persisted in sticking to an opinion that differed from that of the group. Schachter observed how other group members treated that confederate. He found that at first, people tried to convince the confederate to change his mind. After a time, however, they stopped talking to him. There, the person who did not go along with the group was ostracized. Group consensus on the appropriate punishment led subjects to treat negatively those who expressed a different opinion.

Recent norms research builds on these earlier conformity studies to explicitly examine the relation between typical behavior and norms. Younts (2008) looks at approval of deviance in the context of deviant subcultures. He focuses on how subgroups maintain norms that contradict those of mainstream society. In order to address this question, he conducted an experiment in which subjects had opportunities to cheat. After they completed the experiment, subjects then instructed future participants on how to do the experiment. Even though cheating clearly violated university rules, were there conditions under which subjects would encourage newcomers to cheat?

Younts finds that people in his experiments are more likely to instruct future subjects to be deviant if their fellow participants were deviant or if they themselves were told by a high-status person that deviance was a good idea. He explains this outcome by suggesting that when people know that others engage in deviance, they internalize the message that deviance is okay. They start to think that deviance is justifiable, and they communicate that belief to others.

Other researchers suggest an alternative mechanism. Rather than focusing on internalization, they suggest that people want to sanction behavior in ways that they think others will approve. If they anticipate positive reactions from others for their sanctioning efforts, then they are more likely to sanction (Centola et al. 2005). In other words, these researchers think that metanorms motivate sanctioning. People try to anticipate others' reactions to their sanctioning decisions.

How do people know whether sanctioning efforts are likely to be rewarded? How do they know what others will approve? If a behavior is harmful—like smoking or free-riding—then the problem is relatively straightforward. It is reasonable to assume that others will approve of sanctions directed against behaviors like these that create costs for group members. But what about behaviors that are not harmful? Can metanorms alone produce sanctions directed against such behavior? How can individuals tell what the metanorms are likely to be?

One possibility is that people look at others' behavior. If the individual observes everyone else engaging in behavior A and avoiding behavior B, then they might well assume that those others approve of A and not B. In turn, they would also tend to do A—at least when others are likely to see them—because they want to get their approval. Note that people's perceptions of support for a particular behavior are not necessarily accurate (Kitts 2003). We do not see every behavior that every member of the group does, so we do not necessarily know what they really prefer. Instead, we base our assessment on what we know, or think we know. Regardless of the accuracy of these assessments, if an individual thinks that others approve of A and not B, it would make sense for them to infer that others would approve of those who punished behavior B. In turn, we might expect them to sanction.

Willer, Kuwabara, and Macy (2006) conducted an experiment to see if metanorms would lead people to sanction nonconforming behavior. They had students engage in a wine-tasting experiment. Students had to decide which wine was superior. When making their choice, they could see what all but one other participant had chosen. After ranking the wines, they also then had to rate the wine-tasting abilities of the other participants. In other words, they could sanction others for making poor wine-ranking decisions.

Willer, Kuwabara, and Macy were interested in the sanctioning decisions of people who had conformed with the majority. They expected that conformers would be more likely to sanction those whose wine rankings were inconsistent from the majority if they knew that their sanctioning decisions would be seen by others. To test this hypothesis, the experiment compared a condition without metanorms (sanctioning decisions were private) with one with metanorms (sanctioning decisions were public).

The researchers found that metanorms did have an effect. Conformers sanctioned nonconformity more when their sanctioning decisions were observed by others. When conformers' sanctioning decisions were public, they were more likely to punish those who made different wine-ranking decisions than the majority. When sanctioning decisions were private, conformers did not sanction atypical behavior.

In this experiment, participants knew that the others (actually computer-simulated actors) preferred a particular wine. They also knew that others would see their judgments of others' wine-tasting ability, and they were explicitly instructed about the likelihood of social reactions. Their expectations regarding those reactions affected their sanctioning decisions. In other words, metanorms encouraged sanctioning.

If metanorms really do lead people to sanction nonconforming behavior, then we would expect that typical behavior would be associated with norms. Changes in the frequency of a behavior would produce a change in norms. This is because individuals who engage in a behavior will sanction those who do not. Accordingly, the frequency of a behavior would produce norms. Typical behavior would become normative.

Some graduate students and I conducted an experiment to look at this issue (Horne et al. 2007). We used a framework similar to that of the wine-tasting experiment, but we focused on a different behavior. We thought that wine-tasting might well be associated with expectations the subjects brought into the lab from their regular lives. We wanted to look at a behavior that was not associated with norms, or status, or good taste, outside the lab. So, we had students engage in a meaningless behavior—choosing between two letters of the alphabet, X and W. The X-W choice was as arbitrary at it sounds. Subjects simply chose one letter or the other. The behavior was specifically designed to be as meaningless as possible—something that would not be governed by norms outside of the lab and that in and of itself had no consequences.

In one condition, the majority of group members chose X; in the other, most chose W. After making their X-W choice, subjects could react to the choices of others by giving points. The larger the gap between the number of points they gave to conformers relative to nonconformers, the stronger the sanction.

If people use others' behavior as a clue to what the metanorms are, then we would expect conformers to punish nonconformers. In majority W groups, individuals who chose W would punish those who chose X; in majority X groups, people who chose X would punish those who chose W.

The results were not consistent with this prediction. Conformers did not punish nonconformers. We then repeated the experiment, this time giving participants information that made the X-W choice more socially meaningful. This time, consistent with the Willer, Kuwabara, and Macy (2006) study we found that conformers punished those who did not go along. The results suggest that typical behavior in and of itself does not make a behavior normative. Rather, if a behavior is already socially meaningful, then the typicality of a behavior may lead to increased sanctioning.

Research provides evidence that if a behavior is socially meaningful, and if a majority of group members engage in that behavior, and if sanctioning decisions are public, then conformers will punish those who deviate. Under certain conditions, then, the typicality of behavior may indeed be related to norms. But, one should not assume that typical behavior is necessarily normative.

Conclusion

What have we learned about norms? They emerge in response to three factors: the characteristics of behavior, social relations, and the frequency of behavior. In sum:

- People punish behavior that is *harmful.*
- People punish behavior *they think others want* to see punished.
- People punish more if their group is in a *conflict* with another group than if it is not.
- People who *conform* with the majority punish those who deviate (but only under certain conditions).

Concern with social relationships intersects with the characteristics and frequency of behavior to affect norm enforcement, producing the diverse and sometimes bewildering array of norms we observe.

Foot binding ended in China when people changed the norm—when they eliminated the negative social consequences of natural feet (Mackie 1996). Mothers who bound their daughters' feet were not purposely hurting their daughters. Rather they were doing what they thought was best—protecting their children's marriage prospects. A foot-bound girl had a better chance at a good marriage than a natural-footed girl. There were social repercussions for failing to bind feet. These repercussions were large. They outweighed the threat of legal sanctions or international disapproval. No mother wished to risk her daughter being unable to marry.

Only when reformers were able to assure mothers that their daughters would have marriage opportunities was foot binding eliminated. In other words, only when social sanctions directed against natural-footed girls were eliminated, did mothers stop binding their daughters' feet. Reformers provided this assurance by creating anti–foot binding societies. Families who joined the societies pledged both that they would not foot bind their daughters and that their sons would marry women who were not foot bound. These societies dramatically reduced the social sanctions associated with failure to foot bind by providing natural-footed girls with appropriate marriage partners. Mothers no longer had to worry that if they did not bind their daughters' feet, they would not find good husbands.

The mothers who had their daughters' feet bound were rational people who cared about the well-being of their children. They were responding to more than the obvious costs of foot binding—pain and poor health. Their behavior was also affected by their expectations of social reactions. Part of ensuring that their daughters would survive as adults was following and enforcing social norms.

As the foot binding example and the research described in this chapter illustrate, social dynamics can intersect with the characteristics of a behavior to produce variable results. Rational people can and do produce irrational norms. Norms can lead to bad outcomes—both for the individual and for the group in which they are upheld. They can mandate frivolous behavior. But, they can also help to solve collective problems and move groups forward. In China, reformers stumbled on a norms-based solution to a serious social problem—and produced one of the greatest social transformations of the twentieth century. If we understood norms well enough to harness their power, what further potential might there be for social change?

References

Asch, Solomon E. 1951. "Effects of Group Pressure upon the Modification and Distortion of Judgments." Pp. 177–190 in *Groups, Leadership, and Men,* edited by H. Guetzcom. Pittsburg, PA: Carnegie Press.

Benard, Stephen. 2007. "Group Conflict, Cultural Values, and the Emergence of Norms and Hierarchies." Unpublished manuscript.

Billig, Michael and Henri Tajfel. 1973. "Social Categorization and Similarity in Intergroup Behavior." *European Journal of Social Psychology* 3(1):27–52.

Centola, Damon, Robb Willer, and Michael Macy. 2005. "The Emperor's Dilemma: A Computational Model of Self-Enforcing Norms." *American Journal of Sociology* 110(4):1009–1040.

Coleman, James S. 1990. *Foundations of Social Theory*. Cambridge, MA: Harvard University Press.

Cosmides, Leda, John Tooby, and Robert Kurzban. 2003. "Perceptions of Race." *Trends in Cognitive Science* 7(4):173–179.

Ellickson, Robert C. 2001. "The Evolution of Social Norms: A Perspective from the Legal Academy." Pp. 35–75 in *Social Norms,* edited by Michael Hackifer and Karl-Dieter Opp. NY: Russell Sage.

Fehr, Ernst and Simon Gächter. 2002. "Altruistic Punishment in Humans." *Nature* 415:137–140.

Heckathorn, Douglas. D. 1988. "Collective Sanctions and the Creation of Prisoner's Dilemma Norms." *American Journal of Sociology* 94:535–562.

———. 1989. "Collective Action and the Second Order Free Rider Problem." *Rationality and Society* 1:78–100.

Homans, George C. 1951. *The Human Group*. New York: Harcourt Brace Jovanovich.

———. 1974. *Social Behavior: Its Elementary Forms*. New York: Harcourt Brace Jovanovich.

Horne, Christine. 2001. "The Enforcement of Norms: Group Cohesion and Meta-norms." *Social Psychology Quarterly* 53:253–266.

———. 2004. "Collective Benefits, Exchange Interests, and Norm Enforcement." *Social Forces* 82(3):1037–1062.

———. 2008. "Norm Enforcement in Heterogeneous Groups." *Rationality and Society.* 20(2): 147–172.

———. 2007a. "Explaining Norm Enforcement." *Rationality and Society* 19(2):139–170.

Horne, Christine, Chien-Fei Chen, Justin Berg, and Katie Evermann-Druffel. 2007b. "Norm Enforcement: Coordination, Conflict, and Consensus." Unpublished manuscript.

Kitts, James. 2003. "Egocentric Bias or Information Management? Selective Disclosure and the Social Roots of Norm Misperception." *Social Psychology Quarterly* 66(3):222–237.

———. 2006. "Collective Action, Rival Incentives, and the Emergence of Antisocial Norms." *American Sociological Review* 71:235–259.

Mackie, Gerry. 1996. "Ending Foot binding and Infibulation: A Convention Account."*American Sociological Review* 61(6):999–1017.

Macmillan, Ross. 2005. "The Structure of the Life Course: Classic Issues and Current Controversies." *Advances in Life Course Research.* 9:3–24.

Marini, Margaret Mooney. 1984. "Age and Sequencing Norms in the Transition to Adulthood." *Social Forces* 63(1):229–243.

McAdams, R. 1997. "The Origin, Development, and Regulation of Norms." *Michigan Law Review* 96(2): 338–433.

McFarland, Daniel. 2001. "Student Resistance: Howe the Formal and Informal Organization of Classrooms Facilitate Everyday Forms of Student Defiance." *American Journal of Sociology* 107(3):612–678.

Mollborn, Stefanie, 2007a. "Who Says It's So Bad? The Influences of Racial/Ethnic Cultures and Neighborhood Socioeconomic Context on Teenage Pregnancy Norms." Unpublished manuscript.

———, 2007b. "American Adults' Norms about Nonmarital Pregnancy and Their Influence on Willingness to Provide Resources to Parents." Unpublished manuscript.

Nadler, Janice and Mary R. Rose. 2003. "Victim Impact Testimony and the Psychology of Punishment." *Cornell Law Review* 88:419–460.

Opp, Karl-Dieter. 1982. "The Evolutionary Emergence of Norms." *British Journal of Social Psychology* 21:139–149.

Posner, Eric A. 2000. *Law and Social Norms*. Cambridge, MA: Harvard University Press.

Schachter, Stanley. 1951. "Deviation, Rejection, and Communication." *Journal of Abnormal Social Psychology* 46:190–207.

Sherif, Muzafer. 1936. *The Psychology of Social Norms*. New York: Harper Torchbooks.

———. 1966. *In Common Predicament: Social Psychology of Intergroup Conflict and Cooperation*. Boston: Houghton Mifflin.

Tajfel, Henri. 1982. "Social Psychology of Intergroup Relations." *Annual Review of Psychology* 33:1–39.

Ullmann-Margalit, Edna. 1977. *The Emergence of Norms*. Oxford: Clarendon Press.

Willer, Robb, Ko Kuwabara, and Michael Macy. 2006. "The Emperor's Dilemma II: False Enforcement of Unpopular Norms." Unpublished manuscript.

Yamagishi, Toshio. 1988. "Seriousness of Social Dilemmas and the Provision of a Sanctioning System." *Social Psychology Quarterly* 51(1):32–42.

Younts, Wesley. 2008. "The Effects of Status and Peer Support on the Approval and Transmission of Justifications for Deviance." In *Experimental Studies in Law and Criminology*, edited by Christine Horne and Michael Lovaglia. Lauham, MD: Rowman and Littlefield.

Section III

Symbolic Interactionist Approaches to Social Psychology

8

*Symbolic Interaction: Core Concepts and Principles**

George J. McCall
University of Missouri–St.Louis (emeritus)

J. L. Simmons
University of California at Santa Barbara (emeritus)

We believe that perhaps the most important thing about man's situation is that he lives simultaneously in two very different "worlds." In the first place, man is a mammal, of quite ordinary properties, and is subject to all the blind determinisms of his anatomy, chemistry, and physiology—the heritage of eons of mammalian selection and evolution. He must ingest nutrient substances and evacuate waste products; he must sleep; he must maintain a specified range of body temperature and blood pressure. Like every other animal, he is subject to the ups and downs of his hormones and neurohumors—he is subject to all the animal lusts and fears that are concomitants of mammalian machinery.

Yet, at the same time, man lives in a symbolic universe not unlike Plato's realm of ideals. There man is a conscious, self-conscious, reasoning being—a creature of ideas, evaluations, and volitions. His actions are not the result of blind causal forces but of his own considered and willed choices. Consequently, he is a creature of responsibility, pride, and dignity, which in turn implies that he is also a creature of guilt, shame, and humiliation.

In fact, man finds this very situation of having to live simultaneously in two such disparate "worlds" most embarrassing in itself. Therefore he struggles mightily to free himself from the fate of his fellow animals, to live solely in the world of ideas. He finds it most inconvenient that his noblest actions need to be interrupted to satisfy such elemental animal

*Modified slightly from pages 39–62 of McCall and Simmons, *Identities and Interactions*, New York: Free Press, 1966. In view of the age of that source, we ask your indulgence of language that might now seem to be sexist in nature but was quite conventional at that time.

urges as evacuation. He finds it rather embarrassing that he can discover no other way to reproduce himself than by the grotesque posturing of copulation. He finds it terrifying that his existence in the world of ideas is unconditionally dependent on his continued existence and functioning in the animal world. The prospect of decline, death, and decay is a most cruel one to a being who aspires to live in a timeless world of ideals.

The strategy that man has typically adopted to deal with this embarrassing animal existence is to ignore it as far as possible, to blind himself to the facts until they force themselves upon him at irregular intervals. We all try to restrict our attention to those aspects of our lives that are consonant with our view of ourselves as gentlemen and ladies who regulate their conduct in accordance with the very highest moral, legal, and spiritual codes, not as animals. We pursue one another in the manners prescribed by these codes, scoring points—hopefully enough to make it into heaven as well as to succeed on earth. Pursuing one another in these moral and social games, we scarcely notice (except in rare moments of jaundice reflection) that the conventional goals of these games turn out to involve the very animal directions we had hoped to escape—alimentary engorgement, genital friction, mild toxic delirium, and all the rest.

But, *as* men, social theorists must take man as man is. Our task must be to grapple with the fact of man's double existence, to try to describe and explain the peculiar relationship between his two "worlds." As men, we can hardly hope to escape man's proclivity to emphasize the degree to which he lives in the world of ideals; if we exaggerate this degree, it is because we too are subject to the all the frailties and blindnesses of our peculiar species.

Still, we should try to remember the considerable extent to which man's actions are the result of forces other than the conscious, reasoned choices based on ideal considerations. Despite all a person's thinking and pondering, he is constantly doing things of which he is only partially aware and doing them for reasons still more obscure to him. These kinds of action he is always having to legitimate after the fact, having to interpret in some fashion to make them consonant with the various ideal codes and prescriptions that have dominion over him. At all costs, as we shall see, he must preserve his picture of himself as an ideal being. Among these costs are those of selective attention and inattention, of rationalization and projection, of ambivalence, alienation, and mistrust, of conscience and guilt.

Man is, then, a brooding animal, concerned about his past actions and looking forward to the future with mingled hopes and fears. Anxiety and ambivalence are for him a way of life. Acting always on inadequate and biased information, man makes his crucial life choices and allocates his very limited resources. His most vital choices must, perforce, be made almost completely in the dark. He must choose today, knowing but little of the alternatives or the consequences of his choice. This discomfiting fact lies at the base of tragedy and of comedy. Man does his best to grapple with this truth and spends an amazing amount of time constructing alternative lives from which to choose at any point, although his subjective sense of freedom to choose among them is often unrealistic and illusory.

Although man is an introspective creature, he is not solitary. It would be easier for him, as an ideal being, if he were. For it is perhaps not so hard to legitimate our actions to ourselves, from our egocentric perspectives, but our fellows remain harsh judges. They are not so easily taken in by our alibis, our yarns and tall tales. They shake us out of our reveries and demand that we convince them that we are indeed what we claim to be, that things are indeed as we seem to think they are. If we are to maintain our shaky hold on our ideals, we are forced to become rhetoricians—experts in forensic disputation. We must persuade others, *as well as ourselves,* that things are indeed as we construe them.

Reality, then, in this distinctively human world, is not a hard, immutable thing but is fragile and adjudicated—a thing to be debated, compromised, and legislated. Those who most succeed in this world are those who are most persuasive and effective in having their interpretations ratified as true reality. Those who do not are relegated to the fringes of the human world are executed as heretics or traitors, ridiculed as crackpots, or locked up as lunatics. The vast majority of us occupies the middle ground on most issues of social reality, climbing aboard the bandwagons of the leading "parties," voting for the incumbents, so to speak. Consequently, for we who are passively oriented, reality seems given, in the nature of things. It is only when confronted with inescapable conflict that most of us come to question the accepted order of things. In other times, we fail to see all the little interstices of arbitrariness and ambiguity that could be seized upon to legislate reality *in our own favor.*

It is precisely this flexibility of the ideal realm that makes man—for all his animal weakness, ignorance, self-pity, ambivalence, and arbitrariness—a heroic figure fit to play the leading role in the drama of human life. Like the gods, he creates and shatters whole worlds. He decrees new spiritual codes of the highest order, creates out of nothingness and chaos new orders of men. Out of lusts he creates passions and noble strivings; out of discomforts he creates agonies and degradations. Out of animal existence on earth he creates both heaven and hell and strives to lift himself bodily, by his bootstraps, out of the "hell" of animal existence into the "heaven" of his ideal realm.

> The lower animals have neither words nor symbols; nothing, for them, has what we may describe as meaning. The lower animals have, in the words of Durkheim, no "collective representations." They do not organize processions and carry banners; they sing, and sometimes, we are told, even dance, but they do not celebrate; they acquire habits which are sometimes transmitted as a kind of social tradition, but they have no customs, and for them nothing is either sacred or lawful. Above all, the animals are natural and naïve, and not concerned, as human beings are, about their reputations and their conduct. (Park 1927:737)

It is *just* the symbolic abilities of human beings that lead them to agonize over their reputations and their souls that is also the basis for the mode of social organization that has set man so far above the other animals in the evolutionary scheme. Symbols, language, and the role-taking ability that these imply transform man's behaviors into an entirely different level of behavior, which we regard as the special *province* of social psychology, that is, *conduct.*

> One consequence of the fact that man is (a symbolic), political animal is that human behavior is fundamentally neither reflexive, instinctive, nor even habitudinal merely, but conventional and rational, that is to say governed by rules, codes, and institutions; controlled by fashion, etiquette, and public opinion. Thus man turns out to be a sophisticated animal, keenly conscious of himself, knowing good and evil, calculating and casuistic, concerned at once about his reputation and his soul. Behavior of this sort is what we ordinarily call conduct, when that word is given an ethical connotation. Conduct is that form of behavior we expect in man when is conscious of the comment that other men are making, or are likely to make, upon his actions. Conduct, in short, is behavior that is sophisticated. (Park 1931:36, italics added)

In human society every act of every individual tends to become a gesture, since what one does is always an indication of what one intends to do. The consequence is that the individual in society lives a more or less public existence, in which all his acts are anticipated, checked, inhibited, or modified by the gestures and the intentions of his fellows. It is in this social conflict, in which every individual lives more or less in the mind of every other individual, that human nature and the individual may acquire their most characteristic and human traits. (Park 1927:738)

Some Core Concepts

In order to set forth what we consider the basic principles of symbolic interaction,[1] we will first need to discuss briefly certain key concepts. These include (1) the concept of interaction itself, (2) the intertwined concepts of social act and social object, (3) the concept of the self, and (4) the dramaturgical perspective.

Interaction

For most students, one of the greatest obstacles to achieving a thorough grasp of social psychological theories is learning to think in terms of interaction, a concept that seems foreign to ordinary ways of thinking. Perhaps the best way to approach this troublesome idea is to consider why it has this reputation.

To begin, let us take a familiar physical example, the law of gravity. We have all learned that the earth attracts the moon, and those of us who have seen tides on the ocean may know that the moon also exerts attraction on the earth. Each physical body generates a gravitational field in relation to every other body in the universe, affecting the momentum of each of those bodies. Newton's law of universal attraction says that

$$F = G\frac{m_1 m_2}{r^2}$$

That is, the force of attraction between two bodies equals some constant times the ratio of the product of the masses of those bodies to the square of the distance between them.

Is the mass of body 1 the cause of the acceleration of body 2, or is the mass of body 2 the cause of the acceleration of body 1? The question is clearly absurd, for Newton's law says that there is only *one* force and that it is a joint function of *both* bodies. Attraction is a reciprocal or mutual kind of influence. There is not a one-sided dependence of effect upon cause but a two-sided dependence—an *inter*dependence—between two events. From one side of this dependence, event *A* is cause and event *B* effect, but, from the other side of the dependence, event *B* is cause and event *A* effect.

Whenever a relationship of deterministic influence between two events cannot be resolved into a simple function of one but must instead be treated as a *joint* function, as a mutual or reciprocal influence, we have a case of interaction (McCall 2004).

One can see, then, why in physics causal laws are preferred to interaction laws and why causal laws are easier to grasp. We have a long cultural heritage concerning causation, making it seem more intuitive to us than does interaction.

[1]The ancient history and the protracted conceptual development of the symbolic interaction tradition are further recounted in McCall (2006).

Similarly in human affairs we have a long cultural tradition that predisposes us to think in terms of causation rather than of interaction. Our systems of morals, ethics, and law, from the times of the Jews, Greeks, and Romans, have been predicated on a sort of simple, causal type of psychology. Western culture has viewed man as an individual, self-determining psyche, which (for good or evil) causes the body in which it resides to carry out certain actions. Each person, as an independent agent, must therefore be responsible for the actions of the body he controls. From our earliest years, this picture has been drummed into our heads until it is second nature to us. But, just as a simple causal picture of physical reality does not begin to cover the facts, this simple causal picture of man does not cover the facts. Other types of determinism are operating in the social world, one of the most important of which is interaction.

What are some examples of social interaction? A conversation, a knife fight, a chess game, lovemaking. None of these things can be done by one. It takes two to tango, just as it takes two bodies to produce gravitational attraction or two electrons to produce electrostatic repulsion. None of these things can be viewed simply as a result of two independent units simultaneously unwinding their self-determined lines of action. The action of one unit is dependent on the action of the other, *and vice versa.* One person shoving pieces over a chessboard plus another person shoving pieces over a chessboard does not constitute a chess game. Unless the shoves of one person are made in a specific fashion, dependent on the actions of the other, and vice versa, there is only piece-shoving, not chess. There must be mutual influence, not mere additive concatenation.

Social Acts and Social Objects

The next ideas we must assimilate are those contained in George Herbert Mead's theory of acts and objects.

According to Mead, any act of any animal consists of three components, or stages:

1. There are in the animal *impulses* (incipient acts) seeking enactment.
2. The animal then encounters *stimuli* favoring one or another of these incipient acts.
3. There follows, then, a *response* to these stimuli in terms of the favored impulse. (Mead 1938:65)

Acts, in this view, are present in latent form in the animal and are *released*, not "stimulated," by configurations of stimuli that the animal *seeks out* in order to fulfill these impulses, or incipient acts. The animal is thus not a passive robot merely reacting to the environment of stimuli but an active agent seeking to *act upon* that environment—Mead would say, to *create* the objects of his environment (Mead 1912).

The reader should not allow himself to become confused by this claim about the animal creating his environment. Mead was perfectly aware that *things*—the bundles of stimuli the animal encounters—exist prior to and independent of the animal. Mead was simply drawing a distinction between such "things" and what he called *objects*, which exist only in relation to acts. In brief, "things" are converted to "objects" through acts.

Perhaps the best way to wrestle with this point is by example. What is the object of a given act? Let us take eating. The object of the act of eating is *nutrition.* Therefore, if one is hungry (has an impulse to eat), he seeks out stimuli that will release the act of eating. If, in this seeking, he comes across a tomato, he picks it up, puts it in his mouth, chews it, and swallows it. The object of this act is nutrition.

But if he has a different impulse—if he is angry at someone nearby—and he comes across that same tomato, he may suddenly snatch it up and throw it at his tormentor. And what is the object of that act? Expression of his anger.

Really to grasp Mead's concept of objects, we have to play on his *double-entendre*. Let us take our tomato, which is simply a red, leathery, firmly soft, juicy spheroid with a mildly pungent smell and a slightly acid taste. This same bundle of stimuli, this one "thing," releases two very different acts (eating and throwing) with two very different objects (nutrition and expression of anger). Now, this tomato *serves* as both of these objects of acts. It is nutrition when eaten, and it is an expression of anger when hurled at someone. A thing thus *becomes* an object, through the completion of an act. The tomato is not nutrition until it is eaten, nor is it an expression of anger until it is thrown.

Thus, in Mead's theory, "things" are made to serve as various "objects" (in an enriched sense of that word), objects of acts—that is, the *consummations* of those acts (Mead 1932).

But this usage is somewhat confusing as long as we confine ourselves to what we ordinarily think of as *physical* objects. The strength of Mead's notion is more apparent when we consider *social objects*, which are the objects of *social acts* (acts involving the coordinated activity of a plurality of persons) (Mead 1932). Let us consider one admittedly bizarre act. A rather young man, in a park in the Bronx, is standing quietly but very alertly in the afternoon sun. Suddenly he tenses and scurries a few tentative steps to his right, still rather frozen, his gaze locked on a man only a few feet away. This other man makes a sudden movement with his right arm, and the first fellow breaks into sudden flight. Twenty or thirty yards away, still another fellow starts to run to cut him off, and the first man falls flat on his face, skidding and bouncing roughly along the ground for several feet as a result of his great momentum.

What object has this act created? What was the object of the act? Male readers, at least, may have recognized this common social object for what it is, a "stolen base." It has no physical structure but is simply a social object, a symbolic structure generated by a cooperative social act. A stolen base cannot be touched, smelled, or tasted, but it does exist, through the joint efforts of human actors. No one person can create a stolen base all by himself. It takes at least eleven men, laboring together under a common rule, to do so.

Such social objects are insubstantial, but they are extremely abundant and important. Most of the things we officially strive for—marriage, academic degrees, occupational positions, grades—do not exist in nature but are created jointly by the persons involved. Perhaps the reader has never pondered the metaphysical status of these social objects, but it is sobering to do so, and it raises profound theoretical questions as to why we should be so exclusively oriented to such "insubstantial" objects. We shall have many occasions to return to these concepts and this question.

The Social Self

The third concept we shall need in our preliminary armamentarium is the concept of the self. For this idea, we again turn to Mead's influential formulations, in his theory of mind and self.

The key concept in Mead's theory of mind is the *gesture*, which is originally the first element of some act but comes eventually to serve as a *sign* of the whole act (Mead 1934:76). If we see a television cowboy's hand stiffen near his holster, that is a sign that pretty soon he is going to go for his gun and "drill" the outlaw in the black hat. Why is this gesture a sign of that act? Because it is the first component and presages the rest of it. When we see that first component, we need not wait to see the rest of it—in fact, a gunslinger had better not. He knows what is coming, and he had better go for his own gun. This first component of the act, then, has become a gesture.

The meaning of a gesture is the response of the audience *to* that gesture. This response in turn serves as a gesture to the original actor, and his response to it serves as a further gesture, and so on, ad infinitum, in a "conversation of gestures" (Mead 1934:43).

If a gesture elicits the same response from the actor and his audience, it is said to be a "significant gesture," or a *symbol* (Mead 1934:45–46). Vocal gestures, as opposed, for instance, to facial gestures, are especially important in this connection, for one hears his own voice in the same fashion as his audience does, so that he is more nearly able to respond to his vocal gestures in the same way the audience does. By means of these vocal symbols, one can in fact carry on a conversation with himself, first uttering something and then responding (like an audience) to what he has said, and this response is in turn a meaningful gesture to which he himself responds, and so forth.

In fact, the initial phases of uttering those vocal gestures come themselves to serve as signs *of* those gestures, so that a solitary conversation of vocal gestures can take place *internally*, without anything actually being uttered aloud. This kind of internal conversation is of the utmost importance to intelligent behavior, for it makes possible elaborate vicarious trial-and-error activity. Mead claimed that intelligence arises when an act is blocked and ways must be found to circumvent the block. Instead of physically trying out impulses that come to mind in this effort, the intelligent creature can react to his own verbal formulations of these impulses, and, because the symbols call out the same responses in him that they would call out in an audience of his fellows, he has a social check on his immediate impulses. And this inner social check is, of course, the basis of *conduct*, and it leads us directly to Mead's ideal of self.

The individual achieves selfhood at that point at which he first begins to act toward *himself* in more or less the same fashion in which he acts toward other people. When he does so, he is said to be "taking the role of the other toward himself." It is important not to become confused by this phrase. The individual, John Doe, *is* still himself, and others act with respect *to* him. But when he too begins to act toward John Doe in some similar fashion, he can be said to serving *in the role of* an other, an alter. This concept is all that is meant by that harried phrase, "taking the role of the other toward oneself" (Mead 1932:189). It is nothing more than responding to oneself, quite as other people might respond to one. It is still he who is doing this responding, even though he is also the object *toward* which he is responding.

This reflexiveness is what William James (1892) meant when he wrote that the self as subject and the self as object—the "I" and the "me"—are not distinct entities but merely analytically separable aspects of the same thing.

Mead used the terms "I" and "me" in a similar but importantly different sense. Both James and Mead took over Kant's definition of the "I" as the essentially unknowable active agent of the personality—that which *does* the thinking, the knowing, the planning, the acting.

But, whereas James meant by the "me" all those aspects of the personality that the "I" knows and cares about, Mead meant all those *perspectives* on oneself that the individual has learned from others—the *attitudes* that the "I" assumes toward his own person when he is taking the role of the other toward himself (Mead 1934).

If the "I" and the "me" constitute the totality of the self, this self is best seen in what Mead called the "inner forum," the silent internal conversation that is continually going on inside the human organism. But the reader should avoid the fallacy of thinking of this conversation as a simple dialogue between something called the "I" and something called the "me." Many people have tried to think of the internal conversation as going something like this: The person, as "I," says something; then, assuming the role of other toward himself, the person responds to what the "I" has said; then the "I" in turn responds; and so forth. This conception is too simple, although on occasion it does seem to work this way.

More generally, the person does *not* act out, successively, the parts of a model dialogue. The human mind is not so simple and monolithic. Ordinarily, one's mind is reacting to what one is saying or thinking *as one is saying or thinking it*. One does not wait until he has said something to see just what it is that he was going to say. One monitors oneself *throughout* the process and from a multiplicity of perspectives and contexts. And it is this organization of multiple perspectives and contexts for reaction that is the "me," in Mead's terms. The "me" is best thought of, not as the antagonist in a dialogue with the "I," but as an *audience*, all the people in a *multiperson discussion* who are temporarily silent while the "I" holds the floor. But though they are politely silent, they are evaluating and criticizing all the while that the "I" is talking. Each has a somewhat different reaction, corresponding to his unique perspective, and, when the "I" has finished and relinquished the floor, so to speak, every member of this metaphorical audience strives to inform him of his own personal reaction to what was said. It is not accidental that Mead chose the metaphor of "inner *forum*." And, of course, if any of the "audience" objects really strongly to what the "I" is saying or doing, he may not restrain himself until the "I" has completed his act but may instead rudely interject his reactions and disrupt or suspend the ongoing action.

But of course metaphors are merely crutches, and we must not allow ourselves to hypostatize this picture of the self as inner forum. We recognize that there is not really any formal gathering of little men—learned homunculi—convened inside the head. *The "me" is merely the organized cognitive frames of reference in terms of which the mind appraises and evaluates and monitors the ongoing thought and action of its own person, the "I."* And if this statement sounds much duller than Mead's metaphor, we must nevertheless avoid underestimating the profound importance of this continual self-appraisal, which is carried on in terms of standards internalized from significant others and individually elaborated. As Mead and others have suggested, this process is the basis for that intelligent, controlled, socialized behavior of which we are so proud, the singular accomplishment of the human animal.

> One thing that distinguishes man from lower animals is the fact that he has a conception of himself, and once he has defined his role he strives to live up to it. He not only acts, but he dresses the part, assumes quite spontaneously all the manners and attitudes that he conceives as proper to it. Often enough it happens that he is not fitted to the role which he chooses to play. In any case, it is an effort for any of us to maintain the attitudes which we assume; all the more difficult when the world refuses to take us at our own estimates of ourselves. Being actors, we are consciously or unconsciously seeking recognition, and failure to win it is, at the very least, a depressing, often a heartbreaking, experience. This is one of the reasons why we all eventually conform to the accepted models and conceive ourselves in some one or other of the conventional patterns.

> The consequence of this, however, is that we inevitably lead a dual existence. We have a private and a public life. In seeking to live up to the role which we have assumed, and which society has imposed upon us, we find ourselves in a constant conflict with ourselves. Instead of acting simply and naturally, as a child, responding to each natural impulse as it arises, we seek to conform to accepted models, and conceive of ourselves in some one of the conventional and socially accepted patterns. In our efforts to conform, we restrain our immediate and spontaneous impulses, and act, not as we are impelled to act, but rather as seems appropriate and proper to the occasion.
>
> Under these circumstances our manners, our polite speeches and gestures, our conventional and proper behavior, assume the character of a mask (Park 1927:738–739). (It is probably no mere historical accident . . . . that the word "person," originally meant a mask) (738). . . . In a sense, and in so far as this mask represents the conception which we have formed of ourselves, the role we are striving to live up to, this mask is our "truer self," the self we should like to be. So, at any rate, our mask becomes at last an integral part of our personality; becomes second nature. We come into the world as individuals, achieve character, and become persons. (739)

The Dramaturgical Perspective on Life

These concluding remarks on the self by Park suggest that there is more than a little of the theatrical in ordinary human conduct. Indeed, this idea has been a prevalent theme in symbolic interactionism from Mead's early writings on role down to the elaborate "dramaturgical" frameworks of Goffman (1957), Burke (1945), and others. We too shall make heuristic use of a good many of these similarities of the theater to life.

The key concepts here are character, role, and audience. The first two are very closely intertwined and must be carefully differentiated. In the fullest sense, a *character* is a person with a distinctive organization of such personal characteristics as appearance, mannerisms, habits, traits, motives, and social statuses. A *role*, on the other hand, is the characteristic and plausible line of action truly expressive of the personality of that character.[2] If the actor's performance (all those of his actions that can be construed as relevant to the role) is congruent with that role, the audience attributes to him the corresponding character. The audience is taken in by the act and is absorbed in the emergent dramatic reality. If, however, the actor's performance is *not* congruent with that role, is incongruous, the audience regards him as "out of character."

Of course, the success or failure of a performance is not entirely in the hands of the actor himself. The props and supporting cast can often make or break an actor's performance, whatever his own ability. In an important sense, then, the success of an actor's performance depends on whether or not each entire *scene* of the play is well staged, "comes off" dramatically.

Even the audience is a factor in the actor's success. No matter how brilliant the script, characters and their roles are always largely implicit; much of the art in acting and directing

[2] Note that "role" in this sense—an "interactive role"—must not be confused with the notion of role as an element of social structure—a "social role." This distinction is clarified in later pages of McCall and Simmons (1966), where we go on to elaborate their combination in our central notion of a "role-identity"—the character and role that an individual devises for himself as an occupant of a particular social position.

lies in making out the nascent anatomy of characters and roles as they are suggested in the meager lines and stage directions. Audiences, as well as actors, differ widely in their ability to see plausible characters and roles in what are merely parts, in their ability to clothe these parts with dramatic reality. The same performance may strike one audience as overdrawn and entirely unconvincing, yet it may impress a more naïve audience as nightmarishly gripping.

All this is theater, yet it serves to illuminate much of human conduct. If each of us has a part to play in the larger human drama, in terms of the positions we occupy in the web of societal institutions, we must first conceive the role implicit in that part and perform in a manner expressive of that role if we are at last, in Park's terms, "to achieve character and become persons." We shall have occasion later to consider props, supporting casts, scenes, and audiences in ordinary human conduct. Before leaving our consideration of the dramaturgical perspective, however, let us make use of it briefly to take another look at the structure of the social self.

In this perspective, what we have been referring to as the "I," the active agent of the personality, can be thought of as the *performer* or actor. And, as we have already hinted, what we call the "me" can profitably be thought of as a very important internal *audience* of that performer. We want now merely to add that, if an actor is successful, he is never seen by his audience as an actor but as the character he strives to represent. Accordingly, then, we want to distinguish yet a third component of self, the self as *character*.

These components, of course, are not distinct entities or homunculi within the person but are merely *aspects* of the person that can be distinguished for analytic purposes:

1. The self qua performer;
2. The self qua audience to that performer; and
3. The self qua character. (See Goffman 1957:80–81, 253–255)

Some Basic Principles

Let us conclude this prefatory review by setting out, very baldly, some important propositions about parts of man's behavior that underlie one key interactive process, the process of *symbolic* interaction. There are, of course, many other processes simultaneously involved in any concrete interaction (processes of exchange, task performance, social control, and so forth), but in most instances these additional processes take place within the arena carved out by symbolic interaction. Therefore, we take time here to consider this important process.

1. *Man is a planning animal.* Man is a thinker, a planner, a schemer. He continually constructs plans of action (what Mead called "impulses" out of bits and pieces of plans left lying around by his culture, fitting them together in endless permutations of the larger patterns and motifs that the culture presents as models. This ubiquitous planning is carried on at all levels of awareness, not always verbally but always conceptually.

2. *Things take on meanings in relation to plans.* The meaning of a "thing" (as a bundle of stimuli, in Mead's sense) can be taken as its implications for these plans of action we are always constructing. Its meaning can be thought of as the answer to the question, "Where does it fit in the unfolding scheme of events?" If a plan of action is visualized in the form of a flowchart, things may be regarded as the nodes or choice points, which always require that choices be made between alternative course of action: "Where do we go from here?" It can be seen from this description that the same "thing" can present different meanings, in this sense, relative to different plans of action. An ordinary beer bottle, for instance, means two very different things, depending on whether one is contemplating a cool drink or barroom violence. But insofar as we have all absorbed the same plans of action from the culture, the thing can yet have consensual meaning, in our sense. A beer bottle, after all, is still a beer bottle, whatever our momentary proclivities may be.

3. *We act toward things in terms of their meaning for our plan of action.* Or, better stated, the execution of our plan of action is contingent upon the meaning *for that plan* of every "thing" we encounter. If we bend down to pick up a stick and that stick turns out to be a dead snake—or vice versa—the chances are that that plan of action will be suspended and superseded by some other plan.

4. *Therefore, we must identify every "thing" we encounter and discover its meaning.* We have always to be identifying (categorizing, naming) the "things" we encounter and interpreting (construing, reconstructing) them to determine their meanings for our plans of action. "No longer in a merely physical universe, man lives in a symbolic universe. . . . Instead of dealing with the things themselves man is in a sense constantly conversing with himself. . . . What disturbs and alarms man,' said Epictetus, 'are not the things, but his opinions and fancies about the things" (Cassirer 1944:25). Until we have made out the identity and meaning of a thing *vis-à-vis* our plans, we have no bearings; we cannot proceed.

5. *For social plans of action, these meanings must be consensual.* If a plan of action involves more than one person and we encounter a "thing" whose meaning for this plan of action is unclear—not consensual among those involved—the meaning must be hammered out by collective effort in the rhetoric of interaction.

As the consummation of a social act, the resulting attributed meaning is a "social object." It is this process of arriving at a meaning for a problematic "thing," of structuring an unstructured situation, that lies at the core of that fascinating subject we call "collective behavior." This meaning will seldom be clear and identical in the minds of all concerned, yet it will still be consensual, in the pragmatic sense that the understanding will at least be sufficiently common to permit the apparent mutual adjustment of lines of action, whether in cooperation or conflict.

6. *The basic "thing" to be identified in any situation is the person himself.* For each actor there is one key "thing" whose identity and meaning must be consensually established before all else—namely, himself. "Who am I in this situation? What implications do I have for the plans of action, both active and latent, of myself and of the others?" The answers to these questions, if *consensually* arrived at as already described, constitute what we have called the *character* of that person. Self qua character, then, is not alone a personal thing but also a *social object*.

In these terms, the study of symbolic interaction is the study of how social acts generate social objects—especially that important class of social objects we call "selves" (as characters). It is largely an attempt to account for the dynamics of this process of arriving at social consensus on the identities and meanings of all the warm bodies on the scene, after which the various plans of action of the performers can ripple more or less smoothly together into a stream of behavior. This process of achieving consensus is conceived of an interaction, as we have so laboriously defined that term.

This process of symbolic interaction is progressively complicated as we attempt to predict and explain the WHO, WHAT, WHEN, and WHERE of human behavior. Symbolic interaction is important, not because it take place on the plane of symbols and ideals, but precisely because it is this process that *links* man's two worlds, the world of physical "things" and the world of symbolic "objects." It is this process that transposes behavior into conduct, thus setting the stage for still other processes that assume the possession of selves and that, in turn, have considerable effect on our dependent variables.

References

Burke, Kenneth. 1945. *The Grammar of Motives*. Englewood Cliffs, NJ: Prentice-Hall.

Cassirer, Ernst. 1944. *An Essay on Man*. New Haven, CT: Yale University Press.

Goffman, Erving. 1957. *The Presentation of Self in Everyday Life*. Garden City, NY: Doubleday Anchor.

James, William. 1892. *Psychology: The Briefer Course*. New York: Holt.

McCall, George J. 2004. "Interaction." Pp. 327–348 in *Handbook of Symbolic Interactionism*, edited by L. T. Reynolds and N. J. Herman. Walnut Creek, CA: AltaMira Press.

———. 2006. "Symbolic Interaction." Pp. 1–23 in *Contemporary Social Psychological Theories,* edited by P. J. Burke. Stanford, CA: Stanford University Press.

McCall, George J., and J. L. Simmons. 1966. *Identities and Interactions*. New York: Free Press.

Mead, George Herbert. 1912. "The Mechanism of Social Consciousness." *Journal of Philosophy* 9:401–406.

———. 1932. *The Philosophy of the Present*. Chicago: Open Court.

———. 1934. *Mind, Self, and Society*. Chicago: University of Chicago Press.

———. 1938. *The Philosophy of the Act*. Chicago: University of Chicago Press.

Park, Robert E. 1927. "Human Nature and Collective Behavior." *American Journal of Sociology* 32:733–741.

———. 1931. "Human Nature, Attitudes, and Mores." In *Social Attitudes*, edited by K. Young. New York: Holt.

9

*Symbolic Interactionism**

Bernard N. Meltzer
Central Michigan University (Emeritus)

About thirty-five years ago, a survey of sociological theories (Mullins and Mullins 1973: 98) quite erroneously predicted that symbolic interactionism, as "the loyal opposition" to the period's mainstream of sociology, was nearing its demise. Reflecting the current popularity of symbolic interactionism, however, two periodicals (*Symbolic Interaction* and *Studies in Symbolic Interaction*) devote themselves almost entirely to that social psychological perspective. This contradiction of the pessimistic prediction is further supported, as David Maines (2001) claims, by the incorporation of several elements of symbolic interactionism into the body of contemporary sociology. He argues that many "unaware interactionists" employ concepts and ideas from the interactionist frame of reference apparently without realizing that they are doing so (2001: 16–25).

The earliest exponents of the perspective (John Dewey, William James, Charles S. Peirce, Josiah Royce, Charles Horton Cooley, and George Herbert Mead) were adherents of the American philosophy known as Pragmatism, which emphasized, among other pertinent ideas, the potential creativity of each human being, thereby opposing the more widely held view that prior conditions determine human behavior. Mead, particularly in the lectures and articles composing his *Mind, Self, and Society* (1934), was the leading founder of the theoretical framework of symbolic interactionism. His influential student, Herbert Blumer, was the major expounder of Mead's ideas, particularly in his collection of essays titled *Symbolic Interactionism* (1969). Blumer is credited with originating the designation "symbolic interactionism."

Blumer (1969: 2) also expressed the following three fundamental premises of symbolic interactionism: (1) human beings act toward things on the basis of the meanings that the things have for them; (2) the meaning of such things is derived from the social interaction that one has with other people; and (3) these meanings are handled in, and modified through, an interpretative process used by the person in dealing with the things one encounters.

*This report draws heavily upon Meltzer (1987).

Sometimes termed "social behaviorism," this framework starts, as does psychological behaviorism, with the observable actions of individuals; but, unlike the latter, social behaviorism (symbolic interactionism) concerns behavior in broad enough terms to include—in fact, emphasize—*covert* activity (thought and feeling). This inclusion is deemed necessary to understanding the distinctive, unique character of human conduct. Psychological behaviorism, on the other hand, reduces human behavior to the very same mechanisms as are found on the nonhuman level. As a corollary, such thinking sees the social dimension of human behavior as merely a sort of external influence upon individuals. Symbolic interactionism, by contrast, views human behavior, in general, as *social* behavior. For this perspective, both the content and the very existence of distinctively human behavior are accountable only on a social basis. These distinctions should become more clear in the course of this report.[1]

Society

According to symbolic interactionists, all group life is essentially a matter of cooperative behavior. We must distinguish, however, between nonhuman society and human society. Insects—whose society (e.g., beehives or ant colonies) closely approximates the complexity of human social life—act together in certain ways because of their biological makeup. This is shown by many facts, among which is the fixity, the stability, of the relationships of insect-society members to one another. Insects, according to the evidence, go on for countless generations without any difference in their patterns of association. This picture of nonhuman society remains basically valid as one ascends the scale of complexity of animal life until we arrive at the human level.

In the case of human association, the situation is fundamentally different. Human cooperation is not brought about by mere physiological factors. The very diversity of the patterns of human group life makes it quite clear that human cooperative activity cannot be explained in the same terms as that of insects and other nonhuman animals. The fact that human patterns are not highly stabilized and cannot be explained in biological terms leads to another basis of explanation of human association. Such joint activity can be brought about only by some process wherein: (a) each acting individual ascertains the *intention* of the acts of others, and then (b) makes her or his own response on the basis of that inferred intention. What this means is that, in order for human beings to cooperate, there must be present some sort of mechanism whereby each acting individual: (a) can come to understand the lines of action of others and (b) can guide his or her own behavior to fit in with those lines of action. Thus, human conduct is not a matter of responding directly to the activities of others. Rather, it involves responding to the *intentions* of others, that is, to the future, intended behavior of others—not merely to their present actions.

We can better understand the nature of this uniquely human mode of interaction between individuals by contrasting it with the nonhuman mode of communication, what Mead called the "conversation of gestures." For example, two hostile dogs, in the prefight stage, may go through an elaborate conversation of gestures (snarling, growling, baring fangs, walking stiff-leggedly

[1]Symbolic interactionism differs so greatly, both theoretically and methodologically, from other prevalent social psychologies as to call for special efforts at clarification. One such effort is frequent repetition of key ideas.

around one another, etc.). The dogs are adjusting themselves by responding to one another's gestures. (A gesture is that part of an act that represents the entire act; it is the initial, overt phrase of the act, which summarizes it, for example, shaking one's fist at someone.) Now, in the case of the dogs, so far as we can ascertain, the response to a gesture is dictated by preestablished tendencies (innate or conditioned) to respond in certain ways. Each gesture leads to a direct, immediate, automatic, and unthinking response by the recipient of the gesture, the other dog. Neither dog responds to the *intention* of the gestures. Further, each dog does not make its gestures with the intent of eliciting certain responses in the other dog. Thus, nonhuman animal interaction is devoid of conscious, deliberate meaning.

To summarize: gestures, at the nonhuman, nonlinguistic level, do not carry the connotation of conscious meaning or intent, but serve merely as cues, or stimuli, for the responses of others. Gestural communication takes place immediately, without the intervention of meaning. Each organism adjusts automatically to the other; it does not stop and figure out what response it will give. Its behavior is, largely, a series of direct responses to stimuli, without the insertion of meaning between the stimuli and responses to them.

Human beings, on the other hand, respond to one another on the basis of the intentions, or meanings, of gestures. This renders the gesture *symbolic*; that is, the gesture becomes a symbol to be interpreted—something that, in the imaginations of the participants, stands for an entire act. Thus, individual A begins to act, making a gesture; for example, draws back an arm. Individual B (who perceives the gesture) completes, or fills in, the act in her or his imagination; that is, B imaginatively projects the gesture into the future: "A will strike me." In other words, B conceives what the gesture represents, thereby understanding its meaning. Thus, human behavior involves responses to *interpreted* stimuli, to definitions of the situation.

The foregoing points can also be expressed in terms of the differences between "signs," or "signals," and symbols. A sign stands for something else because of the fact that it is present at approximately the same time and place with that "something else." A symbol, on the other hand, stands for something else because people in a given language community have come to let it stand for that "something else." Thus, signs are directly and intrinsically linked with present or proximate situations; while symbols, having arbitrary and agreed-upon, rather than intrinsic meanings, may go beyond the immediate situation. Signs (sometimes called "natural signs") have intrinsic, or inherent, meanings that induce direct reactions; symbols have arbitrary meanings that require interpretations by the actor prior to his or her response or action. The former, it will be recalled, are "tied to" the immediate situation, while the latter "transcend" the immediate situation. Hence, symbols may refer to past or future events, to hypothetical situations, to nonexistent or imaginary objects, to falsehoods, etc.

Bernard Berelson and Gary Steiner (1964) report the following early experiment illustrating the difference between signs and symbols:

> A hungry animal is taught to go to whichever of three bulbs is lighted in order to get food—an easy matter for him after repeated trials in which food is always present behind the lighted bulb. In the critical "delayed response" test, the light is flashed and turned off while the subject is restrained; after a short delay he is released and permitted to choose. Under these conditions rats and cats can usually delay successfully for a matter of seconds, and dogs for a few minutes. A young child, of course, has no trouble finding the right bulb after half an hour, and an adult could choose correctly after many years. (44–45)

Berelson and Steiner (1964: 45) also point out that although nonhumans can "understand" or obey commands, they do so only by an immediate, or almost immediate, specific response to a specific sound after the sound and their action have been paired many times. Dogs cannot comply with "Come here in two minutes," or "From now on, come whenever I say 'stay.'" As James A. Forte (2001: 34) asserts, "Humans [in contrast to nonhumans] can psychologically stretch the present to incorporate large amounts of past or future . . . and transcend a spatial here and now. . . . [They] can extend the time between stimulus and response." Contrast this symbolized behavior with such sign behavior as the dog or cat going to its food dish upon hearing the operation of a can-opener, or going to the outer door to signal its wanting to go outside. Similarly, note the flight or cries of alarm by animals in the wild to signal danger to the herd or flock.

As we have seen, then, people respond to one another on the basis of imaginative activity. In order to engage in concerted, joint behavior, however, each participating individual must be able to attach the same meaning to the same symbol. Unless interacting persons interpret symbols similarly, unless they fill out the imagined portion in more or less the same way, there can be no cooperative action. This is another way of saying what has become a truism in sociology and social psychology: Human society requires *consensus*, that is, the sharing of meanings in the form of common understandings and expectations.

In the case of the human being, each person has the ability to respond to her or his own gestures; and, thus, it is possible to have the same meaning for the gestures as other persons. For example: as I say "chair," I present to myself the same image as to my hearer; moreover, this is the same image as when someone else says "chair." This ability to stimulate oneself as one stimulates another, and to respond to oneself as another does, may be attributed largely to the human vocal-auditory mechanism. That is, the ability to hear oneself implies at least the potentiality for responding to oneself. When a gesture has a shared, common meaning, when it is—in other words—a *language* element, we may designate it as a "significant symbol." For example, take the words, "Open the window"; the pattern of action symbolized by these words must be in the mind of the listener as well as the speaker. That is, each must respond, in imagination, to the words in the same way. The speaker must have an image of the listener responding to the words by opening the window, and the listener must have an image of her or his opening the window.

The imaginative completion of the act, which we may call "meaning" and which constitutes mental activity, necessarily takes place through *role-taking*, through putting oneself in the shoes of someone else. The earliest beginnings of role-taking occur when an already established act of another individual is stopped short of completion, thereby requiring the observing individual to fill in, or complete the activity imaginatively.

The relation of human beings to one another, then, arises from their developed ability to respond to their own gestures. This ability—in contrast to a dog's response to another dog's growl, but not to its own—enables people to respond in the same way to the same gesture, thereby sharing one another's experience.

This latter point is of great importance. Behavior is viewed as "social" not simply when it is a response to others, but rather when it has incorporated in it the behavior of others. Human beings respond to themselves much as other persons respond to them, and in so doing they imaginatively share the conduct (thinking, feeling, and acting) of others. These processes of symbolization and role-taking are, of course, essential to the development of culture and of socialized individuals. Indeed, they are, to a large extent, what is meant by the term "socialization."

Self

To state that we can respond to our own gestures necessarily implies that we possess selves. Having a self means that the individual may act socially toward oneself, just as toward others. One may praise, blame, or encourage oneself; one may become disgusted with oneself, may seek to punish oneself, and so forth. Thus, individuals may become the object of their own actions. The self is formed in the same way as other objects—that is, things that can be designated—through the "definitions," or interpretations, made by others.

The mechanism whereby individuals become able to view themselves as objects is that of role-taking, involving the process of communication, especially vocal gestures or speech. (Such communication, as we have seen, necessarily involves role-taking.) It is only by taking the standpoint of others that individuals can come to see themselves as others see them. The standpoint of other people provides a platform for getting outside oneself and thus viewing oneself. The development of the self is concurrent with the ability to take roles.

The crucial importance of language in this process must be emphasized. It is through language (significant symbols) that the child acquires the meanings, or definitions, of those around it. By learning the symbols of one's groups, one comes to internalize, or accept, their definitions of events and things, including their definitions of one's own conduct.

It is quite evident that rather than assuming the prior existence of selves and explaining society thereby, symbolic interactionists start out from the prior existence of society as the context within which selves arise. This view contrasts with the position of various individualistic psychologies.

Genesis of the Self

The relationship between role-playing and various stages in the development of the self is described below.

1. *Preparatory Stage.* This stage is one of meaningless imitation by the infant (for example, "reading" the newspaper). The child does certain things that others near it do without any understanding of what it is doing. Such imitation, however, implies that the child is beginning to take the roles of people around it, and is on the verge of putting itself in the position of others and acting like them.

2. *Play Stage.* In this stage the actual playing of roles occurs. The child plays mother, teacher, mail carrier, Mr. Jones, and other people. What is of central importance in such play-acting is that it places the child in the position where it is able to act back toward itself in such roles as "mother" or "teacher." In this stage, then, the child begins to form a self, that is, to direct activity toward itself—and it does so by taking the standpoints of others. This is clearly indicated by its use of the third person in referring to itself instead of the first person: "John wants . . . ," "John is a bad boy."

However, in this stage the young child's configuration, or set, of roles is unstable; the child passes from one role to another in unorganized, inconsistent fashion. It has, as yet, no unitary standpoint from which to view itself, and hence, it has no unified conception of itself. In other words, the child forms a number of separate and discrete objects of itself, depending on the specific roles in which it acts toward itself.

3. *Game Stage.* This is the "completing" stage of the self. In time, the child finds itself in situations wherein it must respond to the expectation of several people at the same time. This sort of situation is exemplified by the game of baseball. To use Mead's illustration: each player must visualize the intentions and expectations of several other players. In such situations the child must take the standpoints of groups of individuals as over against particular standpoints. The child becomes enabled to do this by abstracting a "composite" role out of the concrete roles of particular persons. In the course of its association with others, then, it builds up a *generalized other*, a generalized role or standpoint from which it views itself and its conduct. This generalized other represents, then, the set of standpoints common to the group.

Having achieved this generalized standpoint, individuals can view themselves from a uniform position and conduct themselves in an organized, consistent manner. This means, then, that individuals can transcend, or go beyond, the local and present definitions and expectations with which they come in contact. An illustration of this point would be the stereotyped British gentleman who "dresses for dinner" in an isolated outpost. Thus, through developing a generalized other, the individual becomes emancipated from the pressures of the norms of the immediate situation. He or she can act with a certain amount of consistency in a variety of situations because he or she acts according to a generalized set of internalized meanings and expectations.

The "I" and the "Me"

The self is essentially a social process within the individual involving two analytically distinguishable phases: The "I" and the "Me." The "I" is the impulsive tendency of the individual. It is the initial, spontaneous, unorganized aspect of human experience; it represents the undirected tendencies of the individual. The "Me" represents the incorporated, or internalized, others within the individual; it comprises the organized set of attitudes and definitions, understandings and expectations—or simply meanings—common to the group. In any given situation, the "Me" comprises the generalized other and, often, some particular other(s).

Every act begins in the form of an "I" and usually ends in the form of the "Me." For the "I" represents the initiation of the behavior prior to its coming under control of the definitions or expectations of others (the "Me"). The "I" thus gives *propulsion* while the "Me" gives *direction* to the act. Human behavior, then, can be viewed as a perpetual series of initiations of acts by the "I" and of acting-back-upon the act (that is, guidance of the act) by the "Me." Behavior is a result of this interplay.

The "I," being spontaneous and propelling, offers the potentiality for new, creative behavior. The "Me," being regulatory, disposes the individual to both goal-directed activity and conformity. In the operation of these aspects of the self, we have the basis for, on the one hand, social control and, on the other hand, novelty and innovation. We are thus provided with a basis for understanding the mutuality of the relationship between the individual and society.[2]

Implications of Selfhood. Some of the major implications of selfhood in human conduct are as follows:

1. Possession of a self makes of the individual a society in miniature. That is, individuals may engage in interaction with themselves just as with other, different individuals. In the course of this interaction, one can come to view oneself in a new way, thereby bringing about changes in oneself.
2. The ability to behave (think, feel, act) toward oneself makes possible an inner experience that need not reach overt expression. That is, the individual, by virtue of having a self, is thereby endowed with the possibility of having a mental life: one can indicate things to oneself—which constitutes *mind.*
3. Individuals, possessing selves, are thereby enabled to direct and control their behavior. Instead of being subject to all impulses and stimuli directly playing upon them, individuals can check, guide, and organize their behavior. They are, then, not mere *passive* agents.

All three of these implications of selfhood may be summarized by the statement that the self and the mind (mental activity) are twin emergents, or developments, in the social process.[3]

Mind

To discuss the self almost inevitably leads us to consideration of the mind.

[2]At first glance, the "I" and the "Me" may appear to bear a close affinity with the psychoanalytical concepts of Id, Ego, and Superego. The resemblance is, for the most part, more apparent than real. While the Superego is held to be harshly frustrating and repressive of the instinctual, libidinous, and aggressive Id, the "Me" is held to provide necessary direction—often of a *gratifying* nature—to the otherwise undirected impulses constituting the "I." Putting the matter in figurative terms: Freud views the Id and the Superego as locked in combat upon the battleground of the Ego; Mead sees the "I" and "Me" engaged in close collaboration. This difference in perspective may derive from different preoccupations: Freud was primarily concerned with tension, anxiety, and pathological behavior; Mead was primarily concerned with behavior in general.

It is true, on the other hand, that the Id, Ego, and Superego—particularly as modified by such neo-Freudians as Karen Horney, Erich Fromm, and Harry S. Sullivan—converge at a few points with the "I" and the "Me." This is especially evident in the emphasis of both the Superego and "Me" concepts upon the internalization of the norms of *significant others* (those persons who significantly influence the individual's self) through the process of identification, or role-taking. Incidentally, it should be noted that both sets of concepts refer to processes of behavior, *not* to concrete entities or structures.

[3]Charles Horton Cooley (1922: 184) describes an aspect of the self that concerns reflected feelings. The "looking-glass self" has three principal components: (a) one's imaginations of how we appear to the other person; (b) one's imagination of the other person's judgment of that appearance; and (c) some sort of self-feeling, such as pride or mortification.

Development of Mind

As in the instance of the consideration of the self, symbolic interactionists reject both individualistic psychologies and the Social Contract theories of Thomas Hobbes, John Locke, and Jacques Rousseau, in which the social process (society, social interaction) is viewed as preceded by, and being a product of, mind. In direct contrast is the interactionist view that mind is preceded by, and is a product of, the social process. Mind is seen as developing concurrently with the self, constituting (in a very important sense) the self in action.

The mind, like the self, emerges out of the development of human-ness through communication. The mind is present only at certain points in human behavior, namely, when significant symbols are used by the individual. This view dispenses with the notion of mind as a boxlike container in the head, or as some kind of fixed, ever-present entity, such as the brain. Mind is viewed as a *process*, which manifests itself whenever the individual is interacting with herself or himself.

Interactionists begin discussion of the mind by considering the relation of organisms to their respective environments. The central principle in the behavior of all organisms, as both evolutionists and pragmatists maintain, is that of continuous adjustment, or adaptation, to environing fields. We cannot accurately regard the environment as having a fixed character for all organisms, as being the same for all organisms. All behavior involves selective attention and perception. The organism accepts certain events or things in its field, or vicinity, as stimuli and rejects or overlooks certain others as irrelevant to its needs. (For example, an animal battling for its life ignores food.) Bombarded constantly by stimuli, the organism selectively attends to those stimuli or aspects of its field that relate to, are functional to, the acts in which the organism is engaged. Thus, the organism has a hand in determining the nature of its environment. What this means, then, is that all life is ongoing activity, and that stimuli are not, in themselves, initiators of activity but, rather, elements selected by the organism in the furtherance of that activity.

Perception is thus an activity that involves selective attention to certain aspects of a situation, rather than a mere matter of something entering the individual's nervous system and leaving an impression. Visual perception, for example, is more than a matter of just opening one's eyes and recording what falls on the retina.

The determination of the environment by the biologic individual (nonhumans and the unsocialized human infant) is not a cognitive activity. It is selective, but does not involve consciousness in the sense of reflective intelligence. At the distinctively human level, on the other hand, there occurs a hesitancy, an inhibition of overt conduct, which is *not* involved in the selective attention of animal behavior. In this period of inhibition, mind is present. That is, human behavior entails keeping an act in check and trying out varying approaches in imagination. For symbols, as Forte (2001: 33) reminds us, "allow us to . . . use remembered pasts and imagined futures in our deliberations." This contrasts, as we have seen, with the acts of the biologic individual, which are relatively immediate, direct, and made up of innate or habitual ways of reacting. In other words, the unsocialized organism lacks consciousness of meaning. This being the case, the organism has little or no means for the abstract analysis of its field when it encounters new situations, and hence little or no means for reorganizing its action-tendencies in the light of that analysis. True, some nonhumans (e.g. chimpanzees) can produce and use certain tools, or can mark their paths for other troop members to follow; but the time-span between occurrence of the situation requiring the tool and the actual production of the tool, or between occurrence of the trail-marking and its use by troop-members is quite extremely limited in comparison with what is possible for humans.

Minded behavior arises around problems. It constitutes, to repeat an important point, a temporary restraint of action whereby the individual is attempting to prevision the future. It entails presenting to oneself, tentatively and in advance of overt behavior, the different possibilities or alternatives of future action with reference to a given situation. The future is, thus, present in the form of images of prospective lines of action from which the individual can make a selection. The mental process is, then, one of delaying, organizing, and selecting a response to the stimuli of the environment. This implies that human individuals *construct* their acts, rather than respond in predetermined ways. Mind makes it possible for humans to purposively control and organize their responses. Needless to say, this view contradicts the stimulus-response conception of human behavior.

When the act of a nonhuman is checked, it may engage in overt trial and error or random activity. In the case of blocked human acts, the trial and error can be carried on covertly, implicitly. Consequences can be imaginatively "tried out" in advance. This is what is primarily meant by "mind," "reflective thinking," or "abstract reasoning."

The mind is social in both origin and function. It arises in the social process of communication. Through interaction with the members of their groups, people come to internalize the definitions, or interpretations, transmitted to them through linguistic symbols, learn to adopt the perspectives of others, and thereby acquire the ability to think. When the mind has arisen in this process, it operates to maintain and adjust people in their society; and it enables the society to persist. The persistence of human society depends, as we have previously noted, upon consensus (although conflicts may also be present), and consensus necessarily entails minded behavior.

The mind is social in function in the sense that individuals continually indicate things to themselves from the standpoint of others and control their activity with reference to the definitions provided by others. In order to carry on, they must have some standpoint from which to converse with themselves. They obtain this standpoint by importing into themselves the role of others.

By "taking the role of the other," as pointed out, we see ourselves as others see us, and arouse in ourselves the responses that we call out in others. It is this conversation with ourselves, between the representation of the other (in the form of the "Me") and our impulses (in the form of the "I") that constitutes the mind. Thus, what the individual does in minded behaviors is to carry on an internal conversation. By addressing ourselves from the standpoint of the generalized other, we have a universe of discourse, a system of common, shared symbols and meanings, with which to address ourselves. These provide the context for minded behavior. Thus, mental activity is a particular type of activity that goes on in the experience of the person. The activity is that of individuals responding to themselves, of indicating things to themselves.

To repeat, mind originates in the social process, in interaction with others. There is little doubt that human beings lived together in groups before mind ever evolved. But there emerged, because of certain biological developments, the point where human beings were able to respond to their own acts and gestures. It was at this point that minded behavior emerged.

Similarly, mind comes into being for *individuals* at the point where they become capable of responding to their own behavior, that is, when they can designate things to themselves.

Summarizing this brief treatment of mental activity, we may say that it is a matter of making indications of meanings to oneself as to others. This is another way of saying that mind is the product of using significant symbols. For thinking goes on when we use symbols to elicit in ourselves the responses that other people would make. Mind, then, is symbolic behavior. As such, mind diverges from nonsymbolic behavior and is fundamentally irreducible to the stimulus-response activity that characterizes the latter form of behavior. Thus, the interactionist perspective avoids both the traditional behavioristic fallacy of equating nonhuman and human behavior and the individualistic fallacy of taking for granted the cognitive phenomenon that is to be explained.

Objects

Returning to our discussion of the organization-in-environment, we can now give more explicit attention to the interactionist concept of *objects*. As we have shown, we cannot regard the environment as having a fixed, stationary character for all organisms. The environment is a function of the animal's own characteristics, being greatly determined by the makeup of the animal. Each animal largely selects its own environment: it selects out the stimuli toward which it acts, its makeup and ongoing activity determining the kinds of stimuli it will select. Importantly, the qualities of the objects toward which the animal acts arise from the kinds of experiences that the animal has with the objects. To illustrate, grass is not the same phenomenon for a cat and for a cow. The environment and its qualities, then, are always related to the structure and experience of the animal.

As one passes to the human level, the relation of the individual to the world becomes markedly more complicated. This is because of the ways in which humans form objects. For humans, objects have to be detached (abstracted), pointed out, "imaged" to themselves. The human's environment is constituted largely by such objects.

Now let us examine the relation of the individual to these objects. The object represents an implied plan of action. That is, the object, as previously shown, doesn't exist for the individual in some preestablished form. Perception of the object has telescoped in it a series of experiences that one would have if one carried out the plan of action toward that object. The object has no significant qualities for the individual aside from those that would result from the carrying out of a plan of action. In this respect, the object is constituted by one's activities with it. For example, chalk is the sum of the qualities that are perceived as a result of one's actions: a hard, smooth implement for writing on a chalkboard.

Thus, the objects that make up the "effective environment," the individual's experienced environment, are established by the individual's activities. To the extent that one's activity varies, one's environment varies. In other words, objects change as activities with them change. Chalk, for instance, may become a missile. This does not mean that interactionists deny the existence of a "real world" apart from the meanings people hold. However, interactionists emphasize that *meanings* are the basis upon which people conduct themselves.

Objects, which are constituted by the activities of the human individual, are largely *shared* objects. They usually represent patterns of activity that are held in common among individuals. This is true by virtue of the fact that objects arise, and are present in experience, only in the process of being indicated to oneself (and hence, explicitly or implicitly, to others). In other words, the perspective from which one indicates an object implies definitions by others. Needless to say, these definitions involve language, or significant symbols. The individual acquires common perspectives with others by learning the symbols by which they designate aspects of the world.

The contrast between this view of learning and the neo-behavioristic "learning theory" of some psychologists should be clearly evident. Basically, as previously indicated, the neo-behaviorists attempt to reduce human socialization to the mechanisms found in nonhuman learning. This is reflected in their tendency virtually to ignore the role of linguistic symbols in human conduct, their conceptualization of human activity in terms of stimulus-response couplets, and the equating of learning with conditioning.

The Act

All human activity, other than reflexes and habitual action, is built up in the course of its execution. That is, behavior is constructed as it goes along, for decisions must be made at several points. The significance of this fact is that people act—rather than merely react.

For symbolic interactionists, the unit of study is "the act," which comprises both covert and overt aspects of human behavior. Within the act, all the separate categories of the traditional, orthodox psychologies find a place. Attention, perception, imagination, reasoning, emotion, and so forth are seen as parts of the act—rather than as more or less extrinsic, extraneous influences upon it. Human behavior presents itself in the form of acts, rather than of chains of minute responses.

The act, then, encompasses the total process involved in human activity. It is viewed as a complete span of action: its initial point is an impulse and its terminal point some objective that gives release to the impulse. In between, individuals are in the process of constructing, organizing, even rehearsing their behavior. It is during this period that the act undergoes its most significant phase of development. This period is marked by the play of images of possible goals or lines of action upon the impulse, thus directing the activity to its consummation.

In pointing out that the act begins with an impulse, interactionists mean that organisms experience physiological or other disturbances of equilibrium. In the case of nonhuman animals, their biological makeup or conditioned responses channelize the impulse toward appropriate goals. In the case of the human being, the mere presence of an impulse usually leads to nothing but mere random, unorganized activity. This is most clearly witnessed in the case of the behavior of infants. Until the defining actions of others set up guidance and goals for it, the infant's behavior is unchannelized. It becomes the function of images to direct, organize, and construct, or form, this activity. The presence in behavior of images implies, of course, a process of indicating something to oneself, or mind.

The act may have a short span (for example, attending a particular class meeting, or starting a new page of lecture notes) or may involve the major portion of a person's life (for example, trying to achieve a successful career). Moreover, acts are parts of an interlacing of previous acts, and are built up, one upon another. This is in contradistinction to the view that behavior is a series of discrete stimulus-response bonds. Conceiving human behavior in terms of acts, we become aware of the necessity for viewing any particular act within its larger psychosocial context.

Emergence

Knowing that human actors *construct* acts in the course of their execution enables us to understand the phenomenon of *emergence*, or unexpected innovation in human behavior and interaction. As Anselm Strauss (1959: 36) asserts: "Unless a path of action has been well traversed, its terminal point is largely indeterminate [or unpredictable]. Both ends and means may be reformulated in transit." Whether in the thinking by an individual or the deliberations of a committee, the outcome may be an unanticipated one.

How common are emergent events in everyday life? We observe emergence in instances when individuals find that their actual behavior in given situations may not conform to what they may have expected to do. Moreover, persons performing social roles engage in "role-making," or modifying the roles (Turner 1962); participants in organizations may negotiate their behavior (Strauss 1978), even in situations marked by their subordination, rather than simply conforming to organizational norms or external pressure; collective behavior (including social movements) frequently give rise to "emerging norms" (Snow et al. 1981; Turner and Killian 1987); and new social forms (for example, widespread cohabitation of unmarried couples) constantly emerge in societies and cultures (Greer 1969). Plummer (1991) describes the omnipresent nature of emergence:

> In the world of the interactionist, meaning is never fixed and immutable; rather, it is always shifting, emergent, and ultimately ambiguous. Although we may regularly create habitual, routine, and shared meanings, these are always open to reappraisal and further adjustment. . . . Lives, situations, and even societies are always and everywhere evolving, adjusting, emerging, becoming. (x)

Hence, the behavior that emerges from the interactions within or between individuals is not a necessary product of culture, social roles, past experiences, or preestablished inclinations or meanings held by the actors. The behavior, whether individual or collective, frequently is an unpredictable emergent constructed in the thought processes of the actor or actors, processes in which the "I" plays a crucial role. Given these processes, group life assumes the character of a continuing matter of fitting developing lines of conduct to one another in negotiated, shifting, and emergent ways. This does not mean that social structure plays little or no part in these processes. Structural features, however, do not *determine* the processes; rather, they *influence* behavior and interaction by providing frameworks of both constraints and opportunities within which behavior takes place.

Thus, interactionists hold that human acts are emergent, in a state of "becoming," rather than determined by preexisting internal dispositions or external events. Both individual conduct and joint activity are not simply expressions or products of what people bring to the situation or of conditions that exist prior to the act. Moreover, human beings become able to act in ways that "confront, negotiate, renegotiate, and remake social institutions and social selves" (Forte 2001: 36).

Summary

At several points in this chapter the reader must have been aware of the extremely closely interwoven character of the various symbolic interactionist concepts. In the discussion of society, of self, of mind, of objects, and of emergence, certain ideas seemed to require frequent (and, perhaps, overly repetitious) statement. A brief summary of the theoretical framework may help to reveal more clearly the way in which the key concepts interlock, logically implying one another.

Human beings are born into a society characterized by *symbolic interaction*. The use of *significant symbols* by those around them enables them to pass from the conversation of gestures—which involves direct, unmeaningful responses to the overt acts of the other people—to the occasional, incipient *taking of the roles* of the others. Eventually, role-taking enables them to *share* the perspectives of others. Concurrent with role-taking, the *self*—that is, the capacity to act toward oneself—develops. Action toward oneself comes to take the form of viewing oneself from the standpoint, or perspective, of the *generalized other* (the composite representative of others, of society, within the individual). This implies defining (giving meaning to) one's behavior on the basis of the understandings and expectations of others. In the process of such viewing of oneself, one must carry on symbolic interaction with oneself, involving an inner dialogue between one's impulsive aspect (the "I") and the incorporated perspectives of particular others or the generalized other (the "Me"). The *mind*, or mental activity, is present in behavior whenever such internal conversation goes on—whether one is simply thinking (in the everyday sense of the word) or is also interacting with another person. (In both cases one must indicate things to oneself.) Thus, minded behavior necessarily involves *meanings*, which attach to, and define, *objects*. The meaning of an object or event is merely an image of the pattern of activity that defines the object or event. That is, the completion in one's imagination of an act, or the mental picture of the actions and experiences symbolized by an object, define (give meaning to) the act or object. In the unit of study called "*the act*," all of the foregoing processes are usually entailed. We construct our acts, a fact that opens the door to *emergent*, often unforeseen, novel (that is, innovative) conduct.

The concluding point is the one introducing this summary: many symbolic interactionist concepts intertwine and thereby mutually imply one another. Underlying this point is the idea that human society (characterized by symbolic interaction) both precedes the rise of individual selves and minds and is maintained by the rise of individual selves and minds. This means, then, that symbolic interaction is both the medium for the development of human beings and the process by which human beings associate as human beings. Finally, it should be clearly evident that any distinctively human act inescapably involves: symbolic interaction, role-taking, meaning, mind, self, objects, and emergence. When one of these concepts is involved, the others are also inescapably present. Here we see, unmistakably, the close coherence, or unity, of the interactionist frame of reference.

Basic Propositions of Symbolic Interactionism[4]

The present section of this report briefly indicates several basic statements, or propositions, that further clarify the complexities of symbolic interactionism. Each of the following propositions identifies an essential element of the perspective. These elements are: (1) the meaning component in human conduct; (2) the social sources of humanness; (3) society as process; (4) the voluntaristic component in human conduct; (5) a dialectical, or interactive, conception of mind; (6) the constructive, emergent nature of human conduct; and (7) the necessity of sympathetic introspection (role-taking by the researcher) in the study of human conduct.

1. *Distinctively human behavior and interaction are carried on through the medium of symbols and their meanings.* This is the central idea in symbolic interactionism. It entails the recognition that human beings insert interpretations (meanings) into the stimulus-response behavior common to other animals, thereby transforming such behavior into stimulus-interpretation-response acts.
2. *The individual becomes humanized through interaction with other persons.* Interaction with others gives rise to the ability to imagine how others feel and think in given situations, the use of symbols (thinking, or mind), and the ability to behave toward oneself as toward others (self)—the distinctively human attributes.
3. *Human society is most usefully conceived as consisting of people in interaction.* The features (structures) of society are maintained and changed by the *actions* of people toward one another within larger networks of social networks; but such networks (society, social organization) do not determine the ongoing actions.
4. *Human beings are active in shaping their own behavior.* Given the ability to interact with themselves (that is, to engage in thought), humans can form new meanings and new lines of action—a fact that both enmeshes them in society and frees them somewhat from society.
5. *Consciousness, or thinking, involves interaction with oneself.* Through the use of socially derived symbols, individuals engage in a process of internal conversation between the "I" and the "Me," rehearsing alternative lines of behavior.
6. *Human beings construct their behavior in the course of its execution.* Human behavior is an elaborate process of interpreting, choosing, rehearsing, and rejecting possible lines of action, rather than a necessary, inescapable product of external forces or past events and experiences.
7. *An understanding of human conduct requires study of the actor's covert behavior.* As human beings act on the basis of their interpretations, or meanings, it is essential to get at these meanings in order to comprehend their conduct—an undertaking that involves sympathetic introspection, or taking the position of the subjects through such techniques as interviews, participant observation, ethnographic studies, personal documents, and other procedures that illuminate the rich internal development of acts.

[4]This section draws upon Manis and Meltzer (1978, pp. 5–9).

Conclusion

Symbolic interactionism, according to its exponents, clearly represents the most sociological of social psychologies. It directs attention to the social derivation of the human being's unique behavioral attributes; it describes mind and self as society in microcosm; it delineates how the members of any group develop and form a common world; it illuminates the nature of human association by showing that humans share the meaning of one another's behavior instead of merely responding to each other's overt behavior; and, in numerous other ways, it implicates the individual with society and society with the individual. These achievements apply to both individual and collective conduct.

The high volume of published work within this framework suggests its usefulness and viability. Several collections of theoretical and empirical studies have become available. Relatively recently, Larry T. Reynolds and Nancy Herman-Kinney (2003) have edited a *Handbook of Symbolic Interaction*, and a number of textbooks currently expound the framework. In addition, some new social-psychological perspectives (e.g., ethnomethodology and dramaturgical sociology) are considered to be derived from symbolic interactionism.

References

Berelson, Bernard and Gary A. Steiner. 1964. *Human Behavior: An Inventory of Scientific Findings*. New York: Harcourt, Brace and World.

Blumer, Herbert. 1969. *Symbolic Interactionism: Perspective and Method*. Englewood Cliffs, NJ: Prentice-Hall.

Cooley, Charles H. 1922. *Human Nature and the Social Order*, Revised edition. New York: Charles Scribner's Sons.

Forte, James A. 2001. *Theories for Practice: Symbolic Interactionist Translations*. Lanham, MD: University Press of America.

Greer, Scott. 1969. *The Logic of Social Inquiry*. Chicago: Aldine Press.

Maines, David R. 2001. *The Faultlines of Consciousness: A View of Interactionism in Sociology*. New York: Aldine De Gruyter.

Manis, Jerome G. and Bernard N. Meltzer eds. 1978. *Symbolic Interaction: A Reader in Social Psychology*. Boston: Allyn and Bacon.

Mead, George H. 1934. *Mind, Self and Society: From the Standpoint of a Social Behaviorist*. Chicago: University of Chicago Press.

Meltzer, Bernard N. 1987. *The Social Psychology of George Herbert Mead*, 6th printing. Mt. Pleasant: Central Michigan University Press.

Mullins, Nicholas C. and Carolyn J. Mullins. 1973. *Theories and Theory Groups in American Sociology*. New York: Harper and Row, Publishers.

Plummer, Ken (Editor). 1991. *Symbolic Interactionism*, 2 volumes. Brookfield, VT: Edward Elgar Publishing.

Reynolds, Larry T. and Nancy J. Herman-Kinney (Editor). 2003. *Handbook of Symbolic Interactionism*. Walnut Creek, CA: Altamira Press.

Snow, David A., Louis A. Zurcher, and Robert Peters. 1981. "Victory Celebrations as Theater: A Dramaturgical Approach to Crowd Behavior." *Symbolic Interaction* 4: 21–42.

Strauss, Anselm. 1959. *Mirrors and Masks*. Glancoe, IL: Free Press.

———. 1978. *Negotiations: Varieties, Contexts, Processes, and Social Order*. San Francisco: Jossey-Bass.

Turner, Ralph. 1962. "Role-taking: Process vs. Conformity." Pp. 20–24 in *Human Behavior and Social Processes*, edited by A. M. Rose. Boston: Houghton Mifflin.

Turner, Ralph and Lewis Killian. 1987. *Collective Behavior*, 3rd ed. Englewood Cliffs, NJ: Prentice-Hall.

10

*To Thine Own Self Be True? Social Structural Sources of Self, Situation, and Emotional Experience**

Lynn Smith-Lovin
Duke University

ABSTRACT
A recent study showed that Americans have fewer really close confidants now than they had in 1985 (McPherson et al. 2006). These Americans aren't really isolated from others. It's more likely that they just have more, weaker connections and fewer truly close ties than people used to have. What are the implications of a society with fewer strong ties and more weak ties for how we live? What do these changes mean for our emotional experience in everyday life? In this chapter, I outline an ecological theory of self, identity, and emotion. I argue that a society of weaker ties leads people to have more fluid, changeable selves and to spend most of their time in situations with people who view them in only one way. But in those few situations where they have multiple audiences or complex relationships with their interaction partners, they will feel mixed emotions that could lead to personal and social change.

*This chapter is based on my Cooley-Mead address, presented to the Social Psychology section of the American Sociological Association on August 13, 2006, at the Association's annual meetings in Montreal and later published in *Social Psychology Quarterly* (June 2007). Grants that supported specific findings mentioned in this address include National Science Foundation Grants SES-9008951 and SES-0347699.

In Shakespeare's *Hamlet*, Polonius advised his son Laertes "to thine own self be true." It seems like a simple idea. We should be authentic, rather than duplicitous. We should reflect some inner reality rather than attempting to please others. Our actions should embody our core values.

It might surprise you to find out that Polonius's advice might not have made sense to someone a few hundred years before Shakespeare's time. Historic evidence suggests that humans didn't think of themselves as having an individualized, separate, inner being as recently as the Dark Ages (Baumeister 1987). When everyone that a person interacted with knew all of the experiences that s/he had had, there was not as much of a distinction between the inner and outer presentation of self. Much of our sense of being a distinct individual comes from the fact that we know things about ourselves that are different (and much more elaborated) than people with whom we interact. So, our sense of who we are is intricately tied to who we interact with. Sociologists conceptualize the self as a set of identities that we use to think about ourselves as an individual, some of which are more important to us than others (Stryker 1980).

Viewed this way, the person we become depends on the interpersonal networks in which we are embedded. One person can be a son, a father, a student, a softball player, and many other things. The actions we take and the emotions we experience depend on these relationships. These relationships are, in turn, shaped powerfully by the social systems in which we live. Therefore, it makes sense to think about how our social system is changing. What impact will those changes have on the types of people we become, and the ways in which we think about ourselves? In this chapter, we will make some observations about the direction that our society is moving, and discuss how this might affect our sense of self and our emotional lives.

A Glass Half Full

The ecology of our social encounters depends more on the structure of our environment than on individual choice. When we think about our lives, we often stress the choices that we make among identities (e.g., if "student" is high in the salience hierarchy of our self-structure, we might study instead of having a beer). But many things do not depend much on choice at all. I emphasize here that social structures around us often lead us to enact identities that are not central to our self-structure. Who wants to be a "traffic violator" when driving? Is "customer" really part of our core selves, when we are standing in line at the supermarket? Those situational identity enactments, while not central to our definitions of self, still influence our emotional lives in a profound way. In fact, the most common situation that evoked anger in the 1996 Module on Emotions in the General Social Survey was waiting in line at the grocery store.

Stryker's (1980) classic statement of symbolic interaction argued that *society shapes self which then shapes social interaction*. Society does shape selves. It also shapes interactions through the ecology of our encounters with others. But I argue that in much of everyday life, how we think about our core selves does not dominate what we do from moment to moment. Instead, I propose that the social environment (especially our connections to other people) shapes both the self and social interaction, and creates a somewhat spurious relationship between the two. So, as experienced in everyday life, selves are probably more important to how we think and feel about ourselves than to our choices and actions. We spend much time in identities that are not central to our self-structure. When we are enacting identities that are central to the self-structure, it is more likely to be a function of the institutional environments (e.g., school or work) in which we are embedded than any immediate choices we make.

Many of our modern institutional settings segregate us into environments where we occupy a single identity. Relatively few people know us in more than one important type of relationship. Sociologists call these multiple-identity ties "strong ties" because you are tied to one person in several different ways. For example, if you grew up in a small town and worked in a family business with your sister, you might relate to her as a sister, a coworker, and a neighbor. But the fact that few people live in those types of environments in a postmodern society makes multiple identity enactments quite rare.

Here, I dissect the broad question of the multiple-identity self into a set of more specific issues. This dissection allows me to use some well-formed ideas from other research traditions to link social structure and individuals into an ecology of encounters and identities. I present some data—from an experiential sampling study and from a nationally representative survey—that illustrate some features of modern identity structure. I then argue that the rare simultaneous experience of multiple identities with very different cultural meanings can produce mixed emotions.

I focus on four basic questions. First, what social structures determine available identities? Second, how do these identities combine into selves as individuals internalize them? Third, when do people occupy two or more identities within the same social situation? Fourth, how do those simultaneously held identities produce emotional response?

What Is an Identity?

I use the term *identity* in a fairly broad way. MacKinnon and Heise (2008) define "cultural theories of people" as the set of categories that a culture provides for labeling types of people, as well as the logical implications among those categories. For example, the identity Supreme Court Justice implies Lawyer, which implies College Graduate, and eventually implies more abstract levels like Adult and Human. Notice that these cultural theories of people can change. Thirty years ago the same identity, Supreme Court Justice, might have implied the more abstract identity Man. While that might still be a part of the prototypical Justice, the strength of that implication has softened in the past three decades.

Here, I deal with identities that are the nouns that people use spontaneously (or when asked) to name themselves or others within a situation. So, both Friend and Rival would be identities, because they are ways in which I could label someone with whom I have an interaction. They make sense within my culture, and the act of labeling someone communicates much to others in the culture who share those words and their social meanings.

Cultural identity labels include: (1) the role-identities indicating positions in the social structure, (2) the social identities indicating membership in groups, and (3) the category memberships that come from identification with some characteristic, trait, or attribute

TABLE 10.1 ***Situations from an Experiential Sampling Study (N = 578 Situations)***

Of 200 multiple identity situations
69 had no self-structure identities
77 had one self-structure identity and one purely situational identity
54 had two self-structure identities
Of 378 single identity situations
181 involved self-structure identities
192 involved purely situational identities

(Smith-Lovin 2003). For example, when we asked thirty-eight members of the university community at Arizona about their identities in a 1995 experiential sampling study, they reported 328 distinct identities. Those identities included roles within the social system, activity-based identities, social identities based on group membership and salient personal characteristics (see Table 10.1). I argue that this wide range of social labels should be studied together because they represent the ways that people think about themselves and others in situations.

Social Structure and Possible Identities

What social structural features determine the "cultural theory of people" available to actors? All three types of identity—role-identities, group memberships, and differentiating characteristics—have networks as their source. In the case of role-identities, a relationship with another person defines a position within a social structure. You are a parent because you have a child. That position has rights, responsibilities, and behavioral expectations *vis-à-vis* some other position (Merton 1957). In the case of group membership, the tie is a connection to a named group of others (Breiger 1974; McPherson 1983). You are a member of the Girls Scouts if you meet with a certain group of girls on a regular basis. In the case of personal-characteristic identities, interactions with people different from us lead us to notice salient social categorizations (Berger et al. 1977). We only know we are intelligent if we compare ourselves with someone we think is less smart. Once network connections generate identities, we know that meanings (like status) will inevitably follow (MacKinnon 1994). When we think of ourselves as an honor student, we feel better than if we think of ourselves as a cheater.

The fact that identities depend on network connections is very useful, because sociologists know a lot about them. First, we know there is a strong relationship between size and differentiation, the tendency for a system to break into subparts (e.g., Mayhew 1974; Mayhew et al. 1972). In virtually any domain—from the entire social system to a voluntary association—larger size leads to increased internal differentiation. Relations between actors shift from connection based on similarity to connections based on a division of labor. In smaller systems, we interact with those who are similar to us. Our neighbor is our coworker, our friend, a member of our church, the parent of our children's friends. In larger systems, we interact with those who are functionally interrelated but different from us. We may not live near any members of our church, and our place of work might be contacted through the Internet. More differentiation means more role identities, more membership groups, and more salient distinctions among those who interact within the system.

Miller McPherson (2004) notes that there are few characteristics distinguishing individuals in small, technologically simple societies (primarily age, sex, and physical capabilities). As society grows in size and scope, the system acquires other dimensions, such as wealth and education, to organize social interaction. More importantly, McPherson (2004) argues that salient dimensions of social differentiation become less correlated in large systems. This unfolding of the multidimensional social space leads not just to greater diversity in the system as a whole; it also allows the development of many more distinctive regions (niches) within the social system. These niches affect the size and composition of membership groups within the larger social structure (McPherson 1983; McPherson and Rotolo 1996). In a large city, you could have a book club that read only a certain type of German literature; in a small town you might have a book club that reads any bestseller. In turn, the composition of groups and their social environments have profound implications for the network ties of their members (McPherson and Smith-Lovin 1981, 1986, 1987, 2002) and their self-identities (Smith-Lovin 2003, 2007).

Proposition 1: System size will be positively related to the number of identities in the system.

Identities into Selves: The Internalization of Structure

Now that I have described the social space within which selves are formed, I can proceed to the next question: what determines the complexity and stability of selves? The differentiation in larger systems creates lower density of interactions among actors and greater segmentation of that interaction. This lower density of interactions has implications for the ways that social actors within the system think about themselves.

We know that social systems are characterized by homophily, the increasing probability of interaction as actors become more similar on almost any characteristic, from physical distance to sociodemographic features to information (McPherson, Smith-Lovin, and Cook 2001). Birds of a feather flock together. When membership groups, cultural tastes, or beliefs compete for people's energy in this network that connects similar others, they become localized in social space. Different kinds of people do different kinds of things. Entities as wide ranging as voluntary group memberships, occupations, musical tastes, and religious practices have been successfully analyzed using this framework (Chaves 2004; Mark 1998, 1999; Rotolo and McPherson 2001).

Homophily affects the overlap of groups and diversity of groups, both of which should make for a more complex self. Homophily within a social system is likely to be created when sociodemographic dimensions are more correlated, since homophily becomes stronger when we are similar to someone else on multiple dimensions (e.g., race, sex, political attitudes, extracurricular interests). Under such conditions, groups (and other social entities like communities that hold similar tastes, engage in similar activities, etc.) will tend to be small and less diverse, leading to a simpler self.

> *Proposition 2: Complexity of self-structures will be positively related to system size.*
>
> *Proposition 3: Complexity of self-structures will be negatively related to the correlation of salient social distinctions within the social system.*
>
> *Proposition 4: Complexity of self-structures will be negatively related to the level of homophily in a social system.*

Like most symbolic interactionists, I argue that we need to look at the social structures in which individuals are embedded to see how their selves are formed. By looking at the system as a whole, we can see that some niches in social space imply more complex selves than others. Without examining the broader system-level phenomena, we risk viewing complex selves as something akin to a personality characteristic (an individual attribute), rather than a reflection of the social system and an individual's location within it.

By focusing on the dependence of selves on network connections, I can generate some relatively straightforward predictions, based on what we know about the density and diversity of networks in different regions of social space. For example, we know from Peter Blau's (1977) structural analysis that numerically smaller categories of people will have more out-group ties than those in larger categories (e.g., African Americans have more ties with European Americans than European Americans do with African Americans). Actors higher in the stratification system are likely to have diverse networks that range further through the social system than those who are lower in the stratification system (Lin 2001). Each of these well-established findings leads to a corresponding proposition about self complexity.

> *Proposition 5: Individuals occupying numerically smaller categories will have more complex selves than individuals from numerically larger categories.*
>
> *Proposition 6: Higher status actors will have more complex selves than lower status actors.*

These structural phenomena can tell us something about self-concepts held by respondents in different social niches. For example, Turner (1976) argued that society was undergoing a shift from the perception of self as an institutionally motivated actor toward a more impulsively, personally motivated one. We are less likely to see ourselves as a son now (with all of those rights and obligations), and more likely to see ourselves as an extroverted, but responsible person (who is tied to parents, peers, and acquaintances in different ways). When people serve as a single bridge between different groups, they are more likely to perceive themselves in an individuated, autonomous way (Pescosolido and Rubin 2000). They are less likely to see themselves as part of a collective, with an institutional role that is submerged in the social group. I suggest that structural positions (e.g., connections to isolated audiences or embeddedness in overlapping groups) directly influence how people see themselves and their motivations.

Proposition 7: People with more complex selves will be more likely to self-describe in attribute terms and less likely to self-describe using group-membership or role-occupancy terms.

I now turn to the domain of interaction to suggest how these system level properties will be reflected in actual social interactions.

Complexity of Situated Encounters

A complex self is a necessary condition for multiple identities to be enacted simultaneously in a situation. But just because we have complex selves doesn't mean that we spend a lot of time in complex situations. Modern interactions are highly segregated into isolated audiences. This segregation leads complex selves to be played out in relatively simple single-identity interactions.

Sociologists have two types of data that indicate this fact. The first is a national survey of Americans' reports of their close confidants, collected in the 2004 General Social Survey. These close ties are rarer in 2004 than they were in a 1985 survey (McPherson, Smith-Lovin, and Brashears 2006). The average number of confidants had dropped almost a third, from 2.08 to 2.96. More strikingly, almost a quarter of people said that they had no one with whom they discussed matters that were important to them.

What strikes me about these data, however, is how few multiplex (multiple relationship) ties we found. We know that these data measure very, very close ties (McPherson et al. 2006: 354–356). The respondents and the confidants with whom they discuss important matters have known each other for an average of seven years and interact almost five times a week (McPherson et al. 2006: 360). Close ties are more likely than more distant ones to be multiplex. Yet when we look at the very close tie of spouse in the 2004 data, we find that 58 percent of the spouses mentioned do not share any other structural link with their partners. These spouses are not designated as coworker, comember of a voluntary group, or other kind of relation. Of the 42 percent that *did* have some serious multiplexity in their relationship with their spouse (that is, other than labeling their spouse a "friend"), only 13 percent had more than two types of relations with their spouse. Of the 1,467 respondents that we surveyed, only thirty-three had a spouse who was also a friend, advisor, coworker, and group comember—the kind of complex, multiplex relationship that I have with my husband, Miller McPherson, and which many academic couples assume is typical.

Non-kin ties were even simpler. Among non-kin relations, very few people in the 2004 data were neighbors and coworkers, or coworkers and comembers in a voluntary group. Only about 6 percent of the non-kin ties were multiplex in a seriously structural way, linking more than one institutional or group context. More data about the kinds of relationships that we spend most of our time in come from experiential sampling data collected in 1995.

The experiential sampling study measured the self-structure of individuals at the beginning of the study. We asked respondents to list up to ten "more important" and ten "less important" self-identities in a questionnaire. We then asked what identities that they were actually enacting in situations that we sampled at random by paging them during an eight-day period.

Here, I focus on two features of our respondents' identities. First, of the 224 identities that respondents mentioned in the first self-structure questionaire, only 105 appeared in the situations that were sampled later in the study. Almost as many identities (104) appeared only as situational identities, but did not appear in the self-structure. Clearly, respondents were spending much of their time (roughly 50 percent) in identities that were elicited by their situational contexts, but were not an expression of "who they were." This picture of the interactional environment is somewhat at odds with our traditional views of self-structure enactment, which would lead us to expect a large number of self-identities in interactional situations (Stryker 1980; Thoits 2003). People are not acting as "themselves" a lot of the time.

When we turn our view to the situation level, this tension is reinforced. Of the 578 situations observed, 261 involved no self-structure identities at all (see Table 10.1). The majority of situations (378 of 578 or 65.4 percent) involved only a single identity. Over half of those (192 of the 378) involved a single identity that was not central to the respondent's self-structure. While multiple-identity situations were not rare (200 out of 578), they were as likely to involve two non-self-structure identities or a self-structure identity and a purely situational identity as they were to involve the combination or clash of two salient identities that were a part of the core self-structure.

These empirical findings lead me to question whether an increasingly complex social system really leads to increasingly complex social interactions. Multiplex (multiple identity) relationships do not seem extremely common, even in the context of very close ties. In fact, our experiential sampling data indicate few situations where multiplex relationships lead to multiple-identity interactions with a significant other. When multiple-identity situations did occur in our experiential sampling study, they seemed more likely (1) to result from unusual situations with multiple audiences (in a group of several people), (2) as the result of enacting a situationally elicited nonsalient identity while mentally occupying a salient self-structure identity, or (3) as the result of ruminating over noninteractional identity conflicts. For example, a student reports worrying about a test while he is lunching with some friends (occupying both the student and friend identities). A respondent reports worrying about which family member to stay with on an upcoming trip while she is interacting with strangers in a laundromat. Stryker's point about the central importance of selves may have more force when we *think* about our lives, rather than in our actions.

Complex selves did not seem to come from acting with people with whom we had complex relationships. They generally did not lead to complex situations: instead, they were mostly features of the mind—the process of ruminating about our lives, making plans, being "out of" the current situation and cognitively (or emotionally) in "another place" that is important to us.

Rethinking the Situational Self: Complex Selves and Simple Situations

Neil MacKinnon's and David Heise's (2008) book begins with an extensive discussion of the postmodern self. In much of this literature, the self is a local, experientially based one. Postmodernists argue that we are now many people to many audiences, but not necessarily at the same time. In such a postmodern world, where most network ties are bridging ties between groups that don't know each other, individuals would have complex selves but would seldom encounter situations in which multiple salient identities were relevant.

Pescosolido and Rubin (2000) suggest that the main mechanism driving the post-modern "spoke" network structure, where individual actors act as bridging ties between otherwise unconnected groups, is the declining stability of ties. If ties are stable, long-term relations, the fact that most group memberships are recruited through network ties should lead one bridging tie to become many. Social groups will become cross-cutting social circles if ties persist long enough for new ties to build on the old connection. There is a strong positive relationship between tie stability and the membership overlap of groups. Ties that persist for longer periods of time are more likely to evoke multiple, overlapping group memberships and to result in the simultaneous operation of multiple identities.

> *Proposition 8: Interactions with alters with whom one has a longer history of interaction are more likely to involve multiple identities than interactions with those with whom one has a shorter term relationship.*
>
> *Proposition 9: Interactions between alters with a multiplex relationship will more likely evoke multiple identity standards than interactions between alters who are connected by only a single relation.*

An example from the experiential sampling study helps to illustrate this point. The respondent is an administrative assistant with three children. She is polled while in her university office, where she is "speaking with a soccer mother." She occupies the identities of Coach, Mother, and Friend in the conversation (she volunteers the third identity, when the questionnaire only gives room for two). She is the coach of her neighborhood friend's child's soccer team, and all three of these identities are part of her self-structure (as recorded in the survey at the beginning of the study). Her embeddedness in this multiplex relationship, spawned in neighborhood, voluntary association, and family institutional contexts, has potential for discomfort. There are different expectations and cultural meanings for each role-identity.

But these close, complex ties *are increasingly rare* (McPherson et al. 2006). Instead, we are increasingly able to segregate our audiences. The implications of the increasing proportion of weak ties and the scarcity of deep, embedded ties and cross-cutting social circles is actually quite profound. Research shows how weak and strong ties influence our stability of memberships in groups (McPherson, Popielarz, and Drobnic 1992). Strong ties shared with those in a group dramatically lengthen our stay in that group. Multiplex relationships tend to become more multiplex, as their shared information increases and people pull their friends into shared activities. Dense networks inside a group make the meanings of identities shared within the group move together (Keeton 1999). These processes increase the clarity of group boundaries.

Interacting in sparser, less interconnected networks of weak ties exposes us to new information, and makes us more likely both to leave current groups and to join new ones. This, in turn, affects our identities. Experimenters have found that people who interact in less dense networks adopt more identities in an experimental computer chat situation (Robinson et al. 2002). If our world has a higher proportion of weak ties, we also have more complex, less stable selves—but not necessarily more complex situations.

I have generated a series of predictions, derived mostly from social ecology and network theory, about when multiple indentities will be available in self-structures and operative within situations. I now move onto more familiar social psychological terrain to discuss how multiple identities when simultaneously held will lead to actions and emotions in situations.

How Multiple Identities Create Lines of Action

Much research shows that identities have meanings, and that people try to maintain those meanings while interacting with others. When identities are relatively close in meaning, they can be maintained simultaneously by similar actions. They are effectively the same identity. (A computer simulation program that shows how this works is described in Heise 2007, and is available on the web at http://www.indiana.edu/~socpsy/ACT/).

Consider, however, the relatively unusual case where two identities are quite different in meaning, but simultaneously evoked by the situation. In this case, actions that maintain one identity will be disruptive to the other.

If identities that are very different in meaning are processed in parallel, maintenance in one will result in disturbance for the other. Since that disturbance is experienced psychologically as a sense that the world is unpredictable or unreal, one would expect stress to result. There also might be a heightened probability of leaving the interaction. Our experiments show that people are more likely to select away from interactions with those who fail to confirm their identities even when those identities are negative in evaluation (Robinson and Smith-Lovin 1992).

Proposition 10: Interactions involving disparate identity meanings simultaneously held by one actor will create more stress than interactions involving a single identity standard.

Proposition 11: Actors will terminate interactions in which they simultaneously enact disparate identity meanings at a higher rate than interactions involving a single identity.

One phenomenon that this parallel multiple-identity processing could explain is the common experience of mixed emotions. If our identity-maintenance models are correct, emotions are experienced primarily as the result of the confirmation or disconfirmation of identities. If an actor is occupying more than one identity simultaneously, and experiencing events from those multiple perspectives, it is natural that a mixture of emotions would result from events. For example, a directive action that would support the identity of "judge" might seem less positive and more powerful that the act that would support the identity of "woman" for the female who occupies that position. This might produce a mixture of feelings of being humble (from the perspective of someone thinking of themselves as a judge) and being contemptuous (from the perspective as a woman). (The predictions are from the computer simulation program INTERACT.)

Proposition 12: Emotions experienced in interactions with multiple-identity meanings simultaneously held by one actor will be more variable in their affective meaning than emotions experienced in interactions while occupying a single identity.

We often feel mixed emotions when there has been social change in our society. Many of the multiple-identity situations in our experiential sampling study are focused on work or family settings where people have relatively little control over their (multiple) audiences. These are institutional domains that have undergone major demographic changes in the last decades, as women have entered the labor force and families have been reshaped through divorce and non-marital childbearing.

For example, one situation with substantial distance between two identities occurs in a family setting where a woman readies her family for church attendance. The distance between her wife and mother identities occurs almost entirely in the power domain and is substantial. She feels quite powerless as a wife, but relatively powerful as a mother. The interesting thing about this situation is the inability of the actor to segregate audiences, given the multiple roles present within the institutional setting. These settings are the ones in which people are likely to experience mixed emotions and stress.

Conclusions

I argue here for an ecological theory of self and identity, where large-scale social structures (population distributions, correlation of social dimensions, homophily) influence the availability and occupancy of identities. These identities get incorporated into selves as they are enacted in networks of stable, recurring relationships. But they also get elicited by situations, even when they are not part of a self-structure. The decline of stable, long-term, multiplex relationships over the evolution of human society, added to the increasing differentiation and expansion of social space, has led to more complex selves but simpler situations. Our complex selves are available mostly in introspection, as we ponder autobiographical narrative and conflicting role obligations. Weak ties pull us into and out of institutional and group settings at a higher rate. Selves are complex but fluid.

On the other hand, situations are largely simple. Our traditional models of meaning maintenance within the context of a well-defined situation do a remarkably good job of handling everyday interaction. Only institutions that restrict our ability to segregate audiences (like family and work) confront us with situations in which multiplex relationships, multiple interaction partners, or other features force the simultaneous occupancy of identities that have distinctly different meanings.

References

Baumeister, Roy F. 1987. "How the Self Became a Problem: A Psychological Review of Historical Research." *Journal of Personality and Social Psychology* 52:163–176.

Berger, Joseph, M. Hamit Fisek, Robert Z. Norman, and Morris Zelditch Jr. 1972. *Status Characteristics and Social Interaction: An Expectation States Approach.* New York: Elsevier.

Blau, Peter M. 1977. *Inequality and Heterogeneity*. New York: Free Press.

Breiger, Ronald L. 1974. "The Duality of Persons and Groups." *Social Forces* 53:181–189.

Chaves, Mark. 2004. *Congregations in America*. Boston, MA: Harvard University Press.

Heise, David R. 2007. *Expressive Order: Confirming Sentiments in Social Actions.* New York: Springer.

Keeton, Shirley. 1999. "To Thine Own Self (and One's Associates) Be True: The Strategic Management of Competing Identities among Academic Women." Ph.D. dissertation, Louisiana State University, Baton Rouge, LA.

Lin, Nan. 2001. *Social Capital: A Theory of Social Structure and Action*. New York: Cambridge University Press.

MacKinnon, Neil J. 1994. *Symbolic Interactionism as Affect Control*. Albany, NY: State University of New York Press.

MacKinnon, Neil J. and David R. Heise. 2008. *Identities, Selves, and Social Institutions.* Book manuscript. Department of Sociology, Indiana University.

Mark, Noah P. 1998. "Birds of a Feather Sing Together." *Social Forces* 77:455–485.

———. 1999. "Beyond Individual Differences: Social Differentiation from First Principles." *American Sociological Review* 63:309–330.

Mayhew, Bruce H. 1974. "Baseline Models of Social Structure." *American Sociological Review* 39:137–143.

Mayhew, Bruce H., Roger L. Levinger, J. Miller McPherson, and T. F. James. 1972. "System Size and Structural Differentiation in Formal Organizations: A Baseline Generator for Two Major Theoretical Propositions." *American Sociological Review* 37:629–633.

McPherson, Miller. 1983. "An Ecology of Affiliation." *American Sociological Review* 48:519–532.

———. 2004. "A Blau Space Primer: Prolegomenon to an Ecology of Affiliation." *Industrial and Corporate Change* 13:263–280.

McPherson, Miller, Pamela A. Popielarz, and Sonja Drobnic. 1992. "Social Networks and Organizational Dynamics." *American Sociological Review* 57:153–170.

McPherson, Miller and Tomas Rotolo. 1996. "Testing a Dynamic Model of Social Composition: Diversity and Change in Voluntary Groups." *American Sociological Review* 61:179–202.

McPherson, Miller and Lynn Smith-Lovin. 1981. "Women and Weak Ties: Sex Differences in the Size of Voluntary Associations." *American Journal of Sociology* 87:883–904.

———. 1986. "Sex Segregation in Voluntary Associations." *American Sociological Review* 51:61–79.

———. 1987. "Homophily in Voluntary Organizations: Status Distance and the Composition of Face-to-Face Groups." *American Sociological Review* 52:370–379.

———. 2002. "Cohesion and Membership Duration: Linking Groups, Relations, and Individuals in an Ecology of Affiliation." *Advances in Group Processes* 19:1–35.

McPherson, Miller, Lynn Smith-Lovin, and Matthew Brashears. 2006. "Social Isolation in America: Changes in Discussion Networks over Twenty Years." *American Sociological Review* 71:353–375.

McPherson, Miller, Lynn Smith-Lovin, and James M. Cook. 2001. "Birds of a Feather: Homophily in Social Networks." *Annual Review of Sociology* 27:415–444.

Merton, Robert K. 1957. "The Role-set: Problems in Sociological Theory." *British Journal of Sociology* 8:106–120.

Pescosolido, Bernice A. and Beth A. Rubin. 2000. "The Web of Group Affiliations Revisited: Social Life, Postmodernism and Sociology." *American Sociological Review* 65:52–76.

Robinson, Dawn T., Shirley A. Keeton, and Christabel Rogalin. 2002. "Network Density and the Organization of Social Identities." Presented at the annual meeting of the International Network for Social Network Analysis, New Orleans, LA.

Robinson, Dawn T. and Lynn Smith-Lovin. 1992. "Selective Interaction as a Strategy for Identity Maintenance: An Affect Control Model." *Social Psychology Quarterly* 55:12–28.

Rotolo, Thomas and Miller McPherson. 2001. "The System of Occupations: Modeling Occupations in Sociodemographic Space." *Social Forces* 79:1095–1130.

Smith-Lovin, Lynn. 2003. "Self, Identity and Interaction in an Ecology of Identities." Pp. 167–178 in *Advances in Identity Theory and Research,* edited by Peter J. Burke, Timothy J. Owens, Richard T. Serpe, and Peggy A. Thoits. New York: Kluwer/Plenum.

———. 2007. "The Strength of Weak Identities: Social Structural Sources of Self, Situation and Emotional Experience." *Social Psychology Quarterly* 19:106–124.

Stryker, Sheldon. 1980. *Symbolic Interactionism: A Social Structural Version*. Menlo Park, CA: Benjamin Cummings.

Thoits, Peggy A. 2003. "Personal Agency in the Accumulation of Multiple Role-Identities." Pp. 179–194 in *Advances in Identity Theory and Research,* edited by Peter J. Burke, Timothy J. Owens, Richard T. Serpe, and Peggy A. Thoits. New York: Kluwer/Plenum.

Turner, Ralph H. 1976. "The Real Self: From Institution to Impulse." *American Journal of Sociology* 81:989–1016.

11

*Modest Actions, Monumental Misunderstandings**

Robert L. Young
University of Texas at Arlington

> *Great literature is simply language charged with meaning to the utmost possible degree.*
>
> —Ezra Pound

That which makes great literature often makes unfortunate discourse. During a speech to the American Enterprise Institute on December 5, 1996, Federal Reserve Chair Alan Greenspan posed the following questions:

> How do we know when irrational exuberance has unduly escalated asset values which then become the subject of unexpected and prolonged contractions as they have in Japan over the past decade? And how do we factor that assessment into monetary policy?

In the fascinating psychological world of the stock market, the mere suggestion by someone of Greenspan's economic power that the market might be due for a fall can produce a familiar self-fulfilling prophesy, whereby stockholders attempting to sell before their current holdings became devalued, produce that very devaluation. As a result, those somewhat slower on the draw suffer the consequences. No doubt stock brokers, who stand to gain whether stocks are bought or sold, do little to quell such fears. Whether Greenspan anticipated the far-reaching effect of his comments is unknown, but it is unlikely that even he imagined just what a dramatic and immediate impact his words would have. It is often the unfortunate plight of those in positions of authority that casual comments are accorded significance well beyond their intentions, although it is also true that such individuals can occasionally exploit this fact to their advantage.

*For a more elaborate treatment of this topic see Young (1995).

The problem of assessing the significance of action also produces the opposite effect; words and deeds that are intended to carry great significance are sometimes ignored or casually dismissed. Although this can happen to anyone, it is more often the dilemma of those of lesser status. All actions—verbal and nonverbal, serious and facetious—can be intended to carry messages of great significance or of very little import, and can likewise be interpreted at multiple levels. The result is that many misunderstandings occur because observers over- or underinterpret the actions of others (Young 1995). In order to clarify what I mean by levels of action, it will first be necessary to explain, in a general sense, the kinds of things actions accomplish.

Meanings and Effects: What Actions Do

John is walking down the street when he recognizes Kathy from a distance and waves. Kathy hesitates, then tentatively returns the gesture as they continue on their respective paths. How do we make sense of this hesitant and under-enthusiastic response to such a common action? A number of plausible explanations could be offered, but the answer is likely to lie in the meaning Kathy attributed to the wave. Did John actually wave his arm, or was he simply raising his hand to block the sun? If he was waving, was he waving to Kathy or someone else? If he was waving to Kathy, did she recognize him, and if she did, did she fear that returning the gesture would lead to a lengthy conversation she had no time for? Suppose the two had had an unpleasant exchange the day before. Was the wave intended sarcastically, repentantly, or casually?

This particular interaction illustrates the fact that all actions can be interpreted at different levels of meaning. At the most basic level, actions can be interpreted and described in purely *physical* terms. The action of hailing a cab, for example, could be described thus: I stepped forward placing my right foot on the street leaving the left on the sidewalk, looked directly at the oncoming cab, raised both hands above my head, lowered them approximately forty-five degrees, and repeated this motion rapidly three times. Actions that are interpreted in purely physical terms are likely to elicit quite different responses than those interpreted at a more social level. Cab drivers who observe this kind of gesturing but do not interpret such actions as they are intended will leave frustrated would-be passengers stranded. Likewise, if I see a student raise her hand in class but interpret it as a purely physical action, such as stretching, I will not acknowledge the student as someone who has something to say. Actions interpreted as purely physical acts are not perceived as attempts to communicate social messages; thus we are inclined to pay them little attention.

In contrast, what I will call *generalized* actions are those that are seen as attempts to communicate something specific. The problem with generalized actions, however, is that the observer is unsure of precisely what they are supposed to mean. Suppose that during an office meeting Frank notices Jim look at Beth and nod. Does this nod of the head signal that Jim agrees with the point the speaker just made, or does it signal the initiation of some strategic plan he and Beth have worked out in advance? Frank might be fairly certain that it signals something of social significance (that is, Jim is not simply falling asleep) but without more information and interpretation he cannot be sure what it means. Likewise, simple utterances such as "yes" can signal agreement or simply indicate that the listener is paying attention. Because generalized actions are assumed to communicate something the observer cannot interpret, they tend to grab and hold our attention as we struggle to make sense of them.

The third level of action is the *implicative* level. Unlike ambiguous generalized actions, implicative actions are those to which we are able to attribute precise meaning. Often, more important than the meaning itself is the fact that implicative actions are assumed to indicate specific motives or states of mind on the part of actors. To say that John flirted with Kathy, for example, is to suggest that John's actions were motivated by a desire to let Kathy know that he found her attractive. For actions to be interpreted at the implicative level, observers must do a fair amount of interpretation. Noticing that John blinked one of his eyes while looking at Kathy (a physical action) requires no interpretation. Concluding that this action constituted a wink (generalized action) requires some interpretive work. Concluding, on the basis of a wink, that John was flirting with Kathy involves even more interpretation. After all, a wink can also indicate, among other things, that the two share knowledge of which others are not aware. Whether observers interpret a wink as meaning one thing or another, depends on other information available to them.

Analyzing all the information necessary to interpret an action at the implicative level is a complex cognitive process. However, because our culture supplies us with a large set of standardized scripts with which we can quickly compare individual actions, categorizing an action as having one implication or another is greatly simplified. The downside of such categorical interpretations, however, is that misunderstandings are likely to develop if actions deviate much from standard scripts. For example, if John were twenty-five years old and Kathy were sixty, most observers would interpret John's wink as something other than a romantic gesture, since our cultural scripts for flirtatious winks do not readily accommodate the possibility of romantic relationships between twenty-five year-old men and sixty-year-old women.

Once actions have been interpreted they may have dramatic effects on observers or they may have little or no effect at all. Ordinary actions, such as saying hello to those we encounter, paying for things we have purchased at the grocery store, or performing routine tasks at work do little to alter the future of those to whom they are directed. Other times, however, actions can have profound effects on others. Saying hello to someone we have refused to speak to for years, paying for a major purchase to an individual who stands to make a considerable personal profit on the sale, or performing work tasks that can mean the difference between being promoted and being fired are all actions that are likely to have significant consequences for ourselves and/or others involved. Thus, I use the term *consequential* actions to represent the highest or most complex level of action. Consequential actions share all the characteristics of implicative actions. However, they are not defined solely by their meaning, but also by the effects they have on observers. Greetings are consequential if and only if they are interpreted as more than just routine, thereby making those who are greeted happy, honored, suspicious, or in some other way mentally or emotionally different than they were before the greeting.

Actions of this sort can produce two types of consequences. *Personal consequences* are those that somehow affect the life of the observer but do not alter the relationship between the actor and observer. If people we love pay us compliments they are likely to make us feel good, but they are unlikely to alter our relationships with them. After all, we expect occasional compliments from those we love. Complements from those we perceive as especially objective or critical, however, can make our day. In addition to such personal effects, actions often have *interpersonal consequences*; that is, they affect the relationship between the actor and the observer. Receiving a complement from someone we don't particularly like, for example, might increase our liking for them and thus influence our future relationship.

To summarize, all actions can be described and may be interpreted at a physical, generalized, implicative, or consequential level. As we move from the physical to the generalized, to the implicative, more information is necessary and additional interpretation is involved. Finally, consequential actions are distinguished from others by virtue of the significance of the effects they have on observers or the relationship between actors and observers.

Intentions, Interpretations, and the Creation of Misunderstandings

It is clear that actions intended at one level are sometimes interpreted at another level. Likewise, many misunderstandings are the result of the fact that actions intended at one level are interpreted at another. All the possible types of misunderstanding that can result from over- or underinterpretation are displayed in Table 11.1. As the table shows, observers might recognize any action on the part of actors in physical, generalized, implicative or consequential terms. However, actors do not normally intend for their actions to be interpreted at a generalized level. Most physical actions are performed with little or no regard for the way others might interpret them. All social actions, however, are performed with the expectation that others will interpret them in a particular way. For example, I might move my head in a nodding fashion to relieve neck tension, or place my hand in a waving position in order to block the sun, but I do not nod or wave at or to another person unless I intend it to have a particular meaning to someone. Thus, although actions may be interpreted at any of the four levels discussed earlier, actions are never intended at a generalized level. As a result, there is a certain asymmetry between the levels at which actions may be intended by actors and the levels at which they might be recognized by observers.

This asymmetry between levels of intention and levels of interpretation is reflected in Table 11.1. The cells of the table designated by two capital letters represent the types of

TABLE 11.1 ***Intended versus Recognized Level of Action***

	Level of Action Assumed or Intended by Actor		
Level of Action as Interpreted by Observer	*Physical (P)*	*Implicative (I)*	*Consequential (C)*
Physical	Possible Understanding	IP	IP
Generalized	Understanding	Nonunderstanding	Nonunderstanding
Implicative	PI	Possible Understanding	CI
Consequential	PC	IC	Possible Understanding

misunderstandings that can result from the mismatch between actors' intentions and observers' interpretations. Before discussing these different types of misunderstanding, a few other points should be made. First, as discussed, no actions are intended as generalized actions. Second, any actions interpreted as generalized actions result in non-understandings. This is because, in contrast to non-understandings, both understandings and misunderstandings imply that the action has a particular meaning for observers. Because generalized actions are completely ambiguous to observers they cannot be misunderstood, they can only be not understood. Finally, although understanding can exist only when actions are interpreted at the same level at which they were intended, interpreting an act at the appropriate level does not guarantee that the act has been correctly understood. For example, if John's flirtatious wink is correctly perceived as an implicative action, the observer might still be wrong about exactly what it implies. Thus, I have used the term *possible understanding* to describe situations in which intention and interpretation levels match.

The cells in the table representing misunderstandings are identified with the first letters of the level of intention and the level of interpretation respectively. The two misunderstanding cells in the upper right corner of the table (IP and CP) and the CI cell represent situations in which the actions of the actor have been underinterpreted, whereas the three cells in the lower left (PI, PC, and IC) are all the result of overinterpretations on the part of observers. For example, an IP misunderstanding would be one in which an actor intends the action to have specific social meaning, but the observer misinterprets the action as being purely physical. If a listener clears her throat to signal to the speaker to beware of what he says, but the speaker interprets the gesture as nothing more than an effort to cope with a congested throat, he has misunderstood the gesture by underinterpreting it. On the other hand, a PI misunderstanding would result if a speaker interpreted a purely physical clearing of the throat as a signal by the observer that the speaker should watch what he says. Likewise, an IC misunderstanding suggests that the observer has overinterpreted an action that was intended to imply something of relatively minor personal or interpersonal consequence to mean something more consequential. The following is an example of a PC misunderstanding described by a student.

> The other night in class I hiccuped during a presentation being given by another girl in the class. You have to understand that my hiccups can sound very strange, sort of like a gasp. That would have been embarrassing enough, but it just so happened that I hiccuped right when she was giving her opinion on something kind of controversial, so she was probably feeling a little self conscious about it anyhow. Well, it was clear from her reaction and the reaction of others that they thought my hiccup was a gasp expressing my disapproval or disagreement with what she said. That made me feel really embarrassed, so I was quick to apologize and assure her that it was just a hiccup.

As this story suggests, producing inadvertent bodily noises in public can be embarrassing enough on its own. What is also clear, however, is that the major source of embarrassment here was the fact that the physical act of hiccupping was interpreted as the social act of vocally disapproving, an act that would have had negative consequences for both the self-esteem of the speaker and for the future relationship of the two individuals.

Because physical actions are usually easy to distinguish from social ones, they are less likely to be interpreted at another level. Distinguishing between levels of social action, however, is somewhat more difficult. Consider the following example of an IC misunderstanding supplied by another student.

> About 2 years ago, New Year' Eve, a male friend and I had a terrible misunderstanding concerning our relationship that night. First of all, I asked him if he wanted to go out. He said he had never been out on NYE before. I had not made any plans, so I thought it would be fun to go celebrate together. The night was a disaster. He assumed that we were on a date. We were not. I was only concerned about being a good friend. I did not want a serious relationship with him. Everything I did he took as a sign that I liked him. I was just being nice. I was treating him as I treated everyone else. I even told him point blank that I didn't like him in that way. To this day, I don't know how to act around him. If I'm nice, I feel he thinks I like him [romantically], and if I'm mean, I feel like he thinks I'm weird. Needless to say, we are not the friends we use to be.

In this example, the act of asking an opposite-sex friend to go out on New Year's Eve was not expected to have significant interpersonal consequences. The narrator was simply suggesting that since neither had plans, maybe they should celebrate the new year together. Unfortunately, her friend interpreted the invitation as an act that had significant consequences for their relationship. Ironically, because of the misunderstanding the evening did have lasting consequences for their relationship, but not of the kind initially imagined by the friend.

Am I Paranoid or Just Powerless? Over-interpreting and Under-interpreting Actions

There are many specific reasons why a particular action might be over- or under-interpreted. In a general sense, however, there are two types of causes: personal and interpersonal. By personal causes, I mean that some individuals are more inclined than others to have difficulty finding the appropriate level of interpretation. People who suffer from paranoia, for example, have a persistent tendency to overinterpret the actions of others. Believing that the actions of others have serious personal consequences for oneself is a major part of paranoia. This is not to say that anyone who has a tendency to overinterpret the actions of others is paranoid. Often there are understandable interpersonal reasons for such interpretations. As Charles Berger (1979) suggests, individuals who are highly dependent on others are likely to attach great significance to the actions of those on whom they are dependent, and justifiably so. Young children, for example, often act as though dire consequences would ensue if their parents left them alone, even momentarily. Although adults often laugh at such reactions, from the point of view of the dependent child, who does not know when the parent will return or what might happen while they are gone, such concerns are not unreasonable. Dependent or insecure adults may react similarly to the idea of their partner leaving them to spend time with others, regardless of how legitimate the reason. Dependence is often linked to powerlessness, and the actions of powerful individuals really do tend to have more significant consequences than those of the less powerful individuals. For example, although most of the actions of patients have relatively minor consequences for the physicians on whom they depend, the actions of the doctors can have life and death consequences for their patients.

As a result of the greater consequentiality of the acts of the more powerful interactant, situations that involve interactions between subordinates and those with power over them tends to motivate the less powerful individuals to closely monitor their own actions and those of the other. Such monitoring is motivated by the desire to avoid being misunderstood and the parallel need to understand the full implications of the other's actions. Situations that tend to produce these kinds of misunderstandings are found in the lower left corner of Table 11.1. In contrast, situations that are less personally consequential for the observer will be more likely to produce under-interpretations and lead to the type of misunderstandings found in the other cells of the table.

The Problem with Fixing it

Actors and observers don't always devote the same measure of attention to an interaction. As a result, as actors we do not always consciously think about our intentions before we act. Before we sigh, yawn, or stretch, for example, we are not likely to think about how such physical acts will be interpreted by others. However, upon realizing that our actions have been misinterpreted, we become acutely aware of what impressions we did not intend to give. Thus, whether or not we consciously intended an action to carry a particular level of meaning, we are quick to declare that certain meanings were not our intention.

In general, the diligence with which we monitor actions, both our own and those of others, is related to the importance of the interaction for us. As I suggested in the previous section, in situations that we expect to be highly consequential we tend to be especially attentive to the more subtle aspects of the other's behavior and are thus more sensitive to the implications of all of his or her actions. On such occasions we also tend to be more careful in orchestrating our own acts, choosing our words carefully, and plotting our moves more methodically than usual. Because of this enhanced attention to detail and subtlety, we are more likely than our less invested interaction partner to recognize misunderstandings when they do occur.

Whether a misunderstanding is first recognized by an actor or an observer has important implications for the future of the interaction. Observers who realize they have misunderstood the actions of another can simply adjust their thinking to bring it into line with newly discovered information. When actors are the first to recognize that they have been misunderstood, however, they must take concrete action in order to rectify the situation, and sometimes this can be a traumatic realization. As the work of psychologist Arnold Buss (1980) suggests, the realization that we must actively work to correct a misunderstanding is likely to produce a degree of anxiety. In order to take corrective actions, we often must disrupt the flow of interaction and take it in a new and probably uncomfortable direction. This alone can make us somewhat uneasy, but such uneasiness will be exaggerated by any uncertainty we might have over whether or not the action we are contemplating will be considered appropriate. This is one of the reasons why realizing that we have been misunderstood is normally more bothersome than realizing that we have misunderstood someone else. In the face of such a dilemma, whether or not we take any action at all depends largely on whether the anxiety of allowing the other's misunderstanding of our actions to persist is greater or less than the anxiety created by imagining the other's reaction to our efforts to clarify the situation.

Conclusion: Truth and Consequences

Actions can be intended as physical, implicative, or consequential and can be interpreted as either physical, generalized, implicative, or consequential. When words or deeds are intended at one level but are interpreted at another—that is, when we read too much or too little into each other's actions—misunderstanding results. Casual or innocent comments that are over-interpreted can result in such interpersonal problems as embarrassment, resentment, or out-right conflict. Although discovering that their actions have been underinterpreted is likely to be somewhat less problematic at the interpersonal level, this kind of misunderstanding nevertheless can be extremely frustrating for actors who might be left wondering just how obvious they have to be to get their point across.

Whether we recognize such discrepancies between our intentions and others' interpretations depends largely on how closely we monitor the situation, and that often depends on how much we have to gain or lose from the interaction. In general, interactions among those with different amounts of social power are more consequential for less powerful individuals. As a result, they will typically monitor their own actions and those of the other more carefully, and, as a result, will be more likely than the other to recognize when they have been misunderstood. Although such a realization is beneficial in that it allows them the opportunity to clarify things, it may, for that very reason, create extreme anxiety. After all, actions aimed at clarification could also be misunderstood, thus making bad matters worse. Moreover, if actors are wrong in their perception that they have been misunderstood clarification efforts will be inappropriate, which in turn might make the other feel insulted or make the actor appear foolish. Thus, while problematic for anyone, the perception of having been misunderstood can be especially traumatic for those of a subordinate status.

A common way of alleviating some of the anxiety associated with face-to-face interaction is to provide feedback to the other. Feedback allows actors to assess whether or not they are being understood. We have all had the unpleasant and somewhat intimidating experience of interacting with the type of person who provides little or no feedback as we struggle to express ourselves. When conversing with anyone, but especially those of lower status, we should be aware of the need to occasionally reassure them that we understand what they are communicating. However, it is wise to be aware of how we express our understanding. A common way of doing so is by nodding and using such verbal affirmative responses as "yes" or "OK" Unfortunately, such responses can be interpreted as signs of agreement rather than interest or understanding. The work of Maltz and Borker (1982) suggests that women are more likely to use such affirmative responses to indicate that they are paying attention, whereas men are more likely to interpret such responses as indications of agreement. Thus, this seemingly minor distinction can be especially important in interactions between men and women. More explicit responses, such as "I understand" or "I see what you mean," are less likely to be misunderstood. Likewise, we should be willing to politely ask for clarifications when necessary. Avoiding misunderstandings is often easier and almost always less stressful than attempting to correct them. This assumes of course that we want to reduce the stress of those with whom we interact.

References

Berger, Charles R. 1979. "Beyond Initial Interaction: Uncertainty, Understanding, and the Development of Interpersonal Relationships." in *Language and Social Psychology*, edited by Howard Giles and Robert N. St Clair. Baltimore, MD: University Park Press.

Buss, Arnold H. 1980. *Self-Consciousness and Social Anxiety*. San Francisco, CA: W. H. Freeman.

Maltz, Daniel N. and Ruth A. Borker. 1982. "A Cultural Approach to Male-Female Miscommunication." in *Language and Social Identity*, edited by John J. Gumperz. Cambridge: Cambridge University Press.

Young, Robert L. 1995. "Intentions, Interpretations, and Misunderstandings." *Sociological Spectrum* 15:161–180.

Section IV

Socialization

12

Childhood Socialization

Gil Richard Musolf
Central Michigan University

Socialization was a foundational concept in sociology. From 1890 to 1934, the concept of socialization developed toward an interactionist perspective in the works of William James (1890, 1892), James Mark Baldwin (1895, 1897, 1910), Charles Horton Cooley (1902, 1908, 1909), John Dewey (1906, 1922), and George Herbert Mead (1934). A number of questions emerge from the study of socialization: How do infants become human through a socially grounded process from which emerges a self, mind, conscience, identity, and the ability to engage in social interaction? How do we become like all other human beings, like some other human beings, and like no other human beings (Kluckhohn and Murray 1948: 35)? How does culture become internalized (i.e., enculturation) and individuality emerge? Needless to say, this process presupposes the existence of culture, which itself arises out of social interaction. Childhood socialization is a process that "includes all of one's tendencies to establish and maintain relations with others, to become an accepted member of society-at-large, to regulate one's behavior according to society's codes and standards, and generally to get along well with other people" (Damon 2006, 3–4). It has three dimensions: "efforts to shape behavior, moral values, and cultural styles" (Brint 2006, 158). Human beings are made, by others and by themselves, that is, socialization "is essential in creating the human person and in shaping the identity, outlook, skills, and resources of the evolving person" (Handel 2006: xviii). Socialization agents such as the family, schools, religion, peer groups, and the media (TV, movies, and the Internet) endeavor to accomplish such goals; however, such agents may offer "conflicting [values,] goals, standards, and expectations" (Handel 2006: xviii) rendering childhood a trying time for children and adults. In this process, the child is a fully active player in his or her own socialization and defines situations and acts accordingly, accepting, creatively reproducing, resisting, and even defying socialization agents. Class, race, and gender affect the child as both a receiver and producer of its own socialization, so that one of the saddest aspects of stratification is the denial of life-chances to children, their opportunities at "becoming." Such children are painfully aware of their negations in family and schools. I observed one extreme yet poignant instance in London in 2006 in a street youth wearing the patch "born dead."

Cooley (1902, 1908) studied his own children to assess the self-objectification process, thereby formulating such concepts as the looking-glass self, and the way in which sentiments, especially self-esteem, are socially derived through our imagination of others' judgments. Yet the symbolic interactionist (SI) paradigm did not come to fruition until Mead, heavily influenced by James and Cooley, formulated a more elaborate theory of the self-as-object. His theory emphasized that the self develops through the social and cognitive processes of role-taking and language acquisition, and this proved to be a foundational perspective for American sociology. A framework for theorizing childhood socialization had been established. An SI research agenda emerged with the publication of John F. Markey's ([1928] 1978) and W. I. Thomas and D. S. Thomas's work (1928). Subsequent research, however, primarily focused on adult socialization. Thus, until the 1970s, children and their social worlds were slighted in SI scholarship. At present, a more complex and nuanced perspective on childhood socialization has emerged, which emphasizes agency, "meaning-making," and the "doing" of gender and race in children's constructions of peer cultures.

My focus is on the processes of socialization in early childhood and peer culture. Still, this area is too vast and unwieldy to cover without further circumscribing this chapter by limiting my review to Spencer E. Cahill, William A. Corsaro, Norman K. Denzin, and a few others, who have had an enormous impact on the reconceptualization of childhood socialization. Other interactionists work in this area, but this chapter is directed to an in-depth exposition of a few scholars, rather than an extensive review.

Denzin's (1971, 1972, 1977, 1979, 1982) dialectical conceptualization of the emergence of self and mind is a comprehensive contribution from an SI perspective. Cahill's (1980, 1983, 1986a, 1986b, 1987, 1989, 1990, 1994) research generates insights into the self-acquisition and gender-identity process, utilizing the work of Mead, Garfinkel, and Goffman. Corsaro draws not only on the seminal work of Cooley and Mead but also on the theories of Piaget, Vygotsky, Youniss, and, especially, Aaron Cicourel. In various publications, Corsaro and his associates (Corsaro 1979a, 1979b, 1985, 1986, 1988, 1992, 1997; Corsaro and Eder 1990; Corsaro and Rizzo 1988, 1990) have examined the concept of peer culture and its influence on the genesis of self, mind, and collective identity. Corsaro shares with Denzin and Cahill the following similarities: a critique of the stage model of development, a strong emphasis on the idea that children are active in their own socialization, rather than just passive vessels internalizing an adult-given normative order, and the view that socialization is a collective process (i.e., one entailing social interaction). Corsaro (1992), however, has extended the interactionist perspective through his conceptualization of "interpretive reproduction," that is, children creatively incorporate yet transform adult culture to collectively reproduce peer cultures.

My purpose is to review how these interactionists conceptualize socialization and the emergence of peer culture during childhood—its period of maximum efficacy. The authors reviewed share thematic similarities which will be organized under the following rubrics: (1) stages: automatic or contingent? (2) play and games, (3) peer groups and peer culture, (4) doing gender and race, and (5) public behavior.

Stages: Automatic or Contingent?

Denzin (challenging Piaget) and Cahill (challenging no one in particular) question the natural progression of developmental stages, even the one interactionists (following Mead) advance—the sequence of the play and game stages. "The movement from one stage to another is contingent on the development of sufficient language skills and on the presence of interactive experiences" (Denzin 1977: 89). "Nowhere does Mead attach age specifications" to the play and game sequence, and "implicit in [Mead's] formulations is the suggestion that some persons may never progress to the generalized other phase of taking the other's attitude" (Denzin 1977: 163). Cahill (1986a: 170) shares with Denzin the view that "childhood socialization does not consist of empirically discrete, easily identifiable stages." There is a "sequential pattern" to this process, and one can give names to the elements of that process, but these names are merely "analytic constructs" (Cahill 1986a: 170). Corsaro (1985, 73) accepts aspects of Piaget's model, yet he is critical of stages because of their linearity. Rather than discard stages, Corsaro's (1985: 74) interpretive model "extends the notion of stages by viewing development as a productive-reproductive complex in which an increasing density and reorganization of knowledge marks progression." This interpretive model, as did Cooley's and Mead's, attends to the importance of language (74). Self-development, dependent on language acquisition, is thus problematic.

Denzin's rejection of Piaget's stage theory, which, to him, entailed biological determinism, advances another differentiating tenet of SI: the age at which the self dawns. Social behavior, which presupposes a self, emerges earlier than previously thought. Cooley tied social behavior to the use of personal pronouns, while Gordon Allport linked it to understanding one's personal name or identity (Denzin 1977: 92). But Denzin's (96) ethnography on preschool children establishes that "children are social interactants far before the appearance of systematic pronoun usage, even before names are fully understood." The self is also adduced by "behaviors [that] go beyond verbal declarations," since much nonverbal behavior, also, is used "to communicate self" (Denzin 1972: 309). Denzin (1977: 21) argues that "by the age of three children are able systematically to take one another's roles, present definitions of self, construct elaborate games, and manipulate adults in desired directions." The emergence of self and mind is not determined by stages of growth, nor by attained age at which maturational processes allegedly "take off." Its course is shaped by environmental factors, the most significant of which is the character of the processes of interaction involving the child. Yet the distinguishing sign of selfhood is that the child "must be able to see himself as both object and subject" (Denzin 1972: 306).

As noted, Denzin observes that three-year-olds "are able" to engage in social interaction, and it is important to consider that phrase. What is critical for Denzin (1977, 1982) is not alleged stages of development tethered to chronological age, but *interactional* age and experience; thus, the pace and progress one makes toward self-development and language acquisition are contingent. How fully the child's self, identity, or conscience develop (that is, whether they are marred or enhanced) is contingent upon the social context of socialization. In short, context dispenses interactional life-chances, which lead to "differential levels of reflexivity" (Denzin 1972: 299). If children experience exceptional interaction, then the self emerges more rapidly than previously understood in the role-taking process characterizing interaction. Outstanding interaction and differential reflexivity are evidenced by sophisticated language behavior as well as the use of personal pronouns and personal names. Thus childhood is profoundly unfair.

Although interaction and language acquisition are important to the pace of self-development, interactionists now emphasize that "contrary to Mead, children evidence a rudimentary sense of self in interaction with others even before they acquire language" (Cahill 2003: 861). Bergesen (2004: 358) advances an even more anti-Median argument that a "preinteractional mental architecture exists," evidenced by "numerous studies identifying quite complex mental operations that are performed by infants of only a few months of age, which suggest that 'the existence of mind' exists prior to, not after, interaction." The child's self and mind are argued as developing very early and that social interaction may not be as crucial or generative of an incipient self and mind as previously argued, although interaction and language acquisition are still viewed as indispensable in self development. Although traditionally adjudicated an antilearning heresy in interactionist orthodoxy, Bergesen (368) nevertheless argues that "a more complete account of symbolic interaction [requires] an innatist component." No act of uniformity has appeared.

Play and Games

Play and games contribute fundamentally to the emergence of self and mind by cultivating the ability to take the roles of others (Denzin 1977: 143). They function as forms of anticipatory socialization through which children learn to interact with each other. Play and games are similar in some respects, but they are different from each other in fundamental ways. Games constrain by rules, authority, space, and time; play promotes creativity. Both furnish essential learning experiences that are required for adult life.

Games are forms of social interaction performed by one or more players. They familiarize children with rules, engender skill acquisition, and habituate them to competition and cooperation, as well as authority, goals, plans of action, and chance, all of which significantly contribute to the unfolding of adult lives (Denzin 1977: 150). Children are swiftly exposed to the fact that life is not fair. An awareness of inequality tinges consciousness early, not only through variation in skill but also through aleatory factors beyond human control. The power of social constraints is imparted through the experience of being assigned "undesirable roles" to play; through realization that winners and losers are inevitable in any game; and through recognition that time, place, and circumstance govern life-chances (150). Games also involve pretense, bluffing, alignments, even rule breakers and cheaters—all part of everyday adult life.

Play is much less structured than games. Pretense characterizes play; skill and chance are less requisite. All the authors emphasize that play promotes cooperation and creativity through which children actively construct their own social worlds. Corsaro's project underscores play's shared, collective, and interactive features, maintaining that it is in peer play that children develop a sense of social identity as children (Corsaro 1985, 66).

Cahill, expanding on Goffman's (1959) work, highlights how play helps children learn to fashion their gender identities and appearance through the management of "personal fronts." Since gender recognition is anatomically concealed, and often misidentified by both adults and peers, sartorial displays and bodily adornment signify to the world one's gender identity. Children conceive of such items as hats and bows as signifying gender, ignoring anatomical features, even when visible (Cahill 1989).

Cross-dressing is a process of learning appearance management and sex-appropriate gender display. Adults scrutinize such behavior and direct their children to more suitable sartorial symbols. Even peers criticize overwrought cross-gender exhibitions. Girls are allowed more sartorial freedom, while boys whose attire smacks of femininity are ridiculed. This is the beginning of a long march through childhood, where boys dissociate themselves from anything feminine, thereby contributing to the social reproduction of gender and the sexist evaluation of women in adult life.

Sartorial requirements enhance and limit behavioral repertoires. Girls are instructed to be careful about how they play because of how they are dressed. Gender-socialized behavior (e.g., play) is then adduced as evidence of human nature, justifying the sexist treatment of boys and girls.

One type of play is "spontaneous fantasy." It involves "becoming" all types of creatures (both people and animals) and the creation of social worlds "through [the child's] manipulation and animation of various play objects and materials" (Corsaro 1986: 91). Spontaneous fantasy is different from role-play proper. In this form of activity, children create novelty by expanding on the inspirational behavior of peers, thereby providing an ever-spiraling social world of imagination and invention.

Corsaro (1985, 193–208; 1986, 91) has found that three tension-saturated themes dominate this type of play: lost-found, danger-rescue, and death-rebirth. Through these themes, play teaches serious lessons for adult life. These fantasies generate play during which the skills of interpersonal behavior (for example, cooperation, trust, gratitude, and coping with anxiety) are sharpened. Two essential adaptive skills, the "control" of fear and the ability to "communally share" this control with peers, is produced. Spontaneous fantasy stimulates training in strategies for coping with the uncertainties, dilemmas, quandaries, and exigencies of everyday life with responses such as contingencies, plans of action, novelty, cooperation, and leadership. Children acquire these interactional skills through "communicative strategies," or "discourse abilities," such as turn-taking and topic selection, thereby establishing group cohesion (Corsaro 1986, 98–99). Thus, children's construction of social worlds through spontaneous fantasy underscores how children, through language, play an active role in their own socialization. And, recursively, by participating in spontaneous fantasy, children develop language skills (Corsaro and Rizzo 1988, 880).

Besides spontaneous fantasy, Corsaro's (1985, 219–250; 1988) comparative ethnography of American and Italian nursery schools has led him to identify another common pattern of play: approach-avoidance. The structure of the approach-avoidance routine involves a "threatening agent" (monster) who is identified, approached, and avoided (Corsaro 1988: 5). Corsaro contends that in this routine, where threat is personified, children are learning how to cope with fear by devising escape plans. Furthermore, he argues that, collectively, these routines generate communicative strategies that prepare the child for the adult world (9). Two communicative skills that children learn are interpretation and role-taking, whereby they "link specific signals or cues (voice intonation, facial expression, avoidance behavior, and so on) to shared knowledge about monsters, mad scientists, etc., to participate competently in the routine" (Corsaro 1985: 71). Children learn to control their environment so that they are not victims of it. Other lessons include the formation of friendship and taking care of oneself without adult interference (i.e., independence).

Cahill, Corsaro, and Denzin realize that play is an *adult* term for children's social interaction. It has the trivializing connotation that the interaction is not serious. Their respective ethnographies enable them to assert that play is reflective work by children and requires a self in order to be accomplished. In fact, play is children at work; it "involves such serious matters as developing languages for communication, defining and processing deviance, and constructing rules of entry and exit into emergent social groups" (Denzin 1977: 185). Thus, a child's world is not totally derivative from the adult world; children construct their own peer culture.

Peer Groups and Peer Culture

The most significant public arena for children is the peer group, through which children make meaning and produce a peer culture. One of the first to explore this process was Fine's (1987) study of Little Leaguers. His concept of "idocultures" was fitting, but the word did not endure. The phrase "peer culture" arose, which Corsaro (1992, 162; 1988: 3) defines as "a stable set of activities or routines, artifacts, values, and concerns that children produce and share." A routine is an element of peer culture that is repetitive; it is a joint production, and it is predictable. Peer culture emerges through interaction in which children appropriate adult culture but transform it so that it fits the situation at hand, as exemplified in a "garbage man" routine that was even transmitted to the following year's class (Corsaro 1985: 250–254). Appropriation and transformation are clearly adducible from "animal family" role-play, whereby children, through shared knowledge of family role-play, adopt an external culture and alter it to mesh with the context of the ongoing peer group (105–120). They reproduce representative family performances—such as the enactment of power differentials—but recast them in order to produce recognizable but imaginative behavior (that is, novelty). A cross-cultural example is provided by Corsaro and Rizzo's (1988) research on another adult cultural routine specific to Italian culture: the *discussione*. Again, children appropriate adult culture and transform it so that the *discussione* is suitable for the needs of a peer culture. A form of public debate emerges among three or more children that involves making claims and counterclaims, stating beliefs, arguing, and disputing the history of shared experience. *Discussione* consists of the dramatization of opposition, where each child engages in a stylized ritual of providing "supporting evidence for one's positions within the debate" (Corsaro 1988: 886). The *discussione* is a verbal performance that spawns sophisticated communication skills, solidarity, and friendship. Children acquire social knowledge, interpersonal skills, and the ability to create social worlds through this ritual of debate. Through cultural routines, children exemplify their ability to role-take and role-make.

Corsaro's (1985: 272; emphasis in original) research has revealed two themes of peer culture: children's attempt to "gain *control* over their lives through the *communal production* and *sharing* of social activities with peers." Two major activities socially organize peer interaction: access to social participation and protecting interactive space, and both of them are initiated by children's conceptions of friendship (122–170). This parallels Denzin's (1977: 155) finding that "play is limited by the number of persons present and by the relationships the players have with one another." Access rituals allow children to gain entry to ongoing play in a peer culture. Corsaro enumerates many strategies that children use to enter and exit an interaction sequence. The most common feature of children's access strategies is that they are indirect and nonverbal, while adult access rituals tend to be direct and verbal. Children may imitate the ongoing behavior, circle the interaction until invited to participate, make reference to friendship, or just enter. Being defined as either a friend or not is one basis for inclusion or exclusion—a way of protecting interactive space. As children mature, they engage in more direct and verbal access strategies, such as greetings, questioning participants, or just requesting access.

Gaining access is no easy affair; sometimes children have to employ several access strategies before gaining entry to ongoing interaction. In the protection of interactive space, children establish play areas and activities, thereby dissuading others from entering the areas or engaging in the play. By studying the transition from indirect to direct access strategies, one can discern the emergence of communicative competence, especially the art of negotiation.

Corsaro's (1979b: 53) research reveals how status is a ubiquitous aspect of peer culture, especially in "language use." Children clearly "display knowledge of status as power" (57). Cross-status interaction between superordinate and subordinate is typified by the superordinate's use of imperatives. Subordinates use informative statements, requests for permission to do something, and entreaties to engage in joint action. Same-status interaction—among superordinates or subordinates—is characterized by tag questions and requests for joint action. A tag question such as, "We're playing army, right?" is meant to confirm intersubjectivity or a shared definition of the situation. Since children recognize status as power, higher-status interactants are able to maintain control over the flow of interaction. They exert authority by giving orders, receiving deference, and (here the research is only suggestive) inflicting "discipline scripts" (Corsaro 1985: 77–100).

Deviance is also a part of peer cultures. Corsaro (1985: 255–268; 1992, 173) draws on Goffman's (1961) concept of "secondary adjustments" to describe the ways children actively resist adult rules and expectations—ways that constitute the underlife of the nursery school. Secondary adjustments contribute to children's sense of self, identity, and, especially for Corsaro, their collective identity qua children *vis-à-vis* adults. Nursery schoolers "worked the confront" by resisting the rules concerning play areas and materials, guns and shooting, bad language, and clean-up time. The social knowledge they gain through resisting adult norms and organizations will help them with analogous aspects of working the system as adults: office politics, climbing the corporate ladder, and the general dissemblance of contemporary life.

As a complement and contrast to Corsaro's research, case studies of infant-toddler day care centers have shown that they "sometimes [can be] sites of struggle and contestation, where children often 'lose' as their own meanings and constructions of the world are undermined, as their identities are constructed within relations of power" (Leavitt 2006: 115). Leavitt (127) has shown that children's resistance to routinization in day care centers confronts "discipline and power," leaving children "in a kind of 'culture of silence' where the oppressed are mute, prohibited from 'naming' and transforming their world" (127). Caregivers, who are under multiple constraints, fail to perceive children as "subjects [that is, as] active, reflective, interpreting participants in the day care environment" (129). We need "empowering caregivers" and caregivers who are empowered through an enhanced cultural valuation of children and their caregivers. In a cross-cultural comparison, Lewis (2006: 140) found four ways that Japanese caregivers in nursery schools embrace and cultivate agency to obtain their overall control strategy, demonstrating that "children are most likely to internalize rules when they receive the least external pressure in the course of obeying these rules." Caregivers accomplished this by (1) "minimizing the impression of teacher control" by "tolerat[ing] a wide latitude of child behavior" and keeping "a low profile as classroom authorities," (2) "delegating control to children" by making them "responsible for calling the class together, overseeing class projects, and even managing disagreements," (3) "providing opportunities to develop a good-child identity" by giving children "visible leadership roles [such] as leading the class in greetings and distributing tea at lunch" and fostering peer-based efforts at cooperation, and (4) "avoiding the attribution that children intentionally misbehave" by defining misbehavior as "strange" or a failure in understanding, or asking children "naive questions" to help the child awaken to a realization of the consequences of taken or prospective action (143–149).

What these studies generally show is that by participating in peer culture, friendships are seasoned and interaction skills are honed. Children develop "solidarity," "mutual trust," and "communal sharing." Taking the role of others cultivates children's ability to share intersubjectivity and cooperate at joint action, collective definitions of the situation, and the construction of common meanings through which social worlds are built. Peer cultures are constituted in which children not only reproduce but also challenge and transform the world of adults so as to achieve self-control and a measure of autonomy, two defining characteristics of agency. Communicative competence or discourse ability (at turn-taking rules, access rituals, and role-playing) are matured in peer cultures, where we find the child's active contribution to his or her own socialization (Corsaro 1986: 84).

Doing Gender and Race

Moore (2002), drawing on West and Fenstermaker, explains the interactionist perspective of "doing" race and gender. "Conceptualizing race [and gender] as something we 'do' allows us to see kids as active agents who form their own constructions of race [and gender] and who influence and are influenced by their peers, adults, and the larger social structures around them. It allows us to see how concepts of race [and gender] *emerge* in the children's interactions" (59; emphasis in original).

Gender

Through taking the role of the generalized other, a child learns the rules of public conduct and acquires skill in applying those rules in everyday interaction (Cahill, 1986a, 164). Social control must be largely self-control in a democratic society that promotes civility, liberty, and freedom. Cahill's research sets out to answer the question how one acquires self-regulation by emphasizing the emergence of gender identity, a fundamental aspect of self and society.

One learns to act, think, and feel either as a male or female. Gender development is a process of recruitment into a gender identity. External genitalia, of course, do not provide the cultural equipment necessary so that one is recognized as masculine or feminine; such recognition involves a process of social construction. Consequently, interactionists reject essentialism, the idea that gender identity is biologically determined in favor of the theory that identity is socially anchored (Cahill 1980: 125; 1983, 2).

Caretakers, especially those connected with schools, recruit children into gender identities so that they internalize gender ideals and exhibit a range of competence at displaying those ideals in everyday behavior (Denzin 1971: 67). Self-regulation through gender socialization means a more or less loose conformity to gender ideals and rules of conduct that display masculinity or femininity (Cahill 1986a, 166).

Gender identity is constructed as others reproduce sexually differentiated behavior by reinforcing interaction that is in keeping with gender ideals. The social construction of gender continues as children respond to others' expectations in a process of unwitting participation—a process that centers on children's active, but unaware, participation in fashioning gender.

Cahill (1983: 5), suggests, following Denzin, that the self-labeling process is important in the ripening of gender identity. The child reacts to his or her self as others would by trying to "confirm" or "ratify" the identity of male or female. Gender confirmation dwells in others' responses. If the child elicits gender-appropriate reactions, then he or she is treated as a boy or girl; gender identity is established. In order to elicit the confirming responses, the child models same-sex others from a variety of referents, such as TV, movies, stories, and parents (Cahill 1980, 1983, 1986a); however, in this media era, parents may be less influential as significant others (Cahill 1983: 8–9).

Claims and behavior are not always supported by others. This teaches children that they should be circumspect with their identity avowals and behavior. In other words, the labeling of behaviors as gender-appropriate is a matter of social control and the social reproduction of gender (Cahill 1983: 10–11; 1986b: 304; 1989). Children must behave as others expect them to; otherwise, they may not have their gender identities ratified. What the child considers appropriate will depend on the cues and expectations she or he has learned from the adults, peers, and general culture in her or his social world. During this period of interaction, the most important affirmation is one of "big boy" or "big girl," since the child tends to want to discard the label of "baby," a despised identity (Cahill 1986b: 302). As a result of labeling by others, as well as self-labeling, there is a strong relationship "between language practices and gender identity acquisition" (297).

In large measure, children learn to become self-regulating participants in society by displaying masculine and feminine behavior, thereby conforming to the gender ideals of society and claiming a gender identity. Gender-segregation behaviors are rehearsed in childhood and performed in adulthood (Cahill 1994: 467). Yet both structure and agency are clearly visible as each generation modifies gender ideals, for example, through innovative sartorial expressions. Today, some men wear earrings while some women wear suits; however, a man wearing makeup and a dress would be deviant in any corporation.

Race

Hill (2001: 498) shows that doing gender is less circumscribed in black children because "flexible gender roles and shared child rearing [are] normative and key features" of socialization. Structural forces such as "economic deprivation and racism have made it impractical if not impossible for many Black people to create sharp divisions between male and female roles or to divide family labor into gendered categories of economic and domestic work" (501). Structural inequality has also made the recruitment to success problematic for black males' gender identity. "Understanding that their sons face many obstacles and even dangers in expressing masculinity, parents may develop higher expectations for daughters than for sons [and] support competence and self-reliance more in daughters than in sons" (503), all because daughters have "greater opportunity to survive and succeed in mainstream society" (504). Discerning these subtleties through role-taking from their parents as a looking-glass might lead to a self-fulfilling prophecy as some black males may develop a self that acts, thinks, and feels as a failure in a society that affords little opportunity and much discrimination.

Moore (2002) studied how preadolescents collaboratively "do" race in two summer day camps, one camp mostly white and the other multiracial. Both camps employed essentialist notions of race, which in the white camp socially reproduced traditional conceptions of hierarchy and association in clique structures, especially treating minorities as invisible "nonpersons" (65). Clique structures in the multiracial group were more unstable and fluid in their "conceptions of race, thus disrupting easy definitions of in-group and out-group membership, and affecting the social negotiation of identity" (59). In a number of instances (69–70), children in the multiracial camp *through definition and action* deconstructed the prevailing essentialist notion of race based on physicality by excluding blacks who were defined as not "cool" and therefore deemed "not black enough" or including a white counselor defined as "trustworthy" and therefore deemed "not white." However,"coolness" could not achieve inclusion for a "cool" white girl who failed to achieve the status of "not white." Thus the kids were doing race by "appropriating, but creatively shifting, the criteria by which adult culture establishes race categorization" (68). Criteria other than skin color, such as "coolness" and "trustworthiness," resulted in both exclusion and inclusion. In another example, Latino and black kids who usually "identified themselves as part of the same group, the more inclusive, 'kids of color'" (70) lost intergroup solidarity when Latino kids spoke Spanish. On such occasions, the black kids excluded the Latinos from their group, which "involved a loss of power for the Latino kids" (70), since the black kids' group was larger. Latinos negotiated their clique status by refraining from speaking Spanish. Blacks and Latinos thus defined language as a racial marker. White girls in the multiracial camp also disrupted and "deligitimize[d] the race categorization process" (72) when a white girl leader did not allow a black girl to play. The white girls refused to play until "democratic" and "egalitarian" norms prevailed. The white girls later engaged in a "bias intervention" by interrogating the leader's values. Moore's research underscores the social construction of race, its arbitrary basis in physicality, how nonphysical criteria emerge when doing race, and, important for social stratification, how the level of diversity can lead to variation in the fluidity of in- and out-group memberships, that is, how "splits and alliances" can "form along panethic lines" when a "wider range of people from different race categories [are] present" (75). However, preadolescents create other categories of hierarchy, exclusion, and inclusion.

Public Behavior

Cahill (1987, 1990) and Denzin (1971) have emphasized the arduous task of socializing children to the normative expectations of behavior in public places. Drawing on the work of Durkheim and Goffman, Cahill describes the rituals necessary to constitute and maintain civil society. Parents or caretakers must instruct children in public etiquette and the ceremonies necessary to maintain a moral order. Children are not considered morally responsible people; therefore, they must be accompanied, while in public, by an adult who is held morally liable. Taking children to public places is a socializing experience (and often a harrowing one) for both the adult and child. The child must be taught the rules of public behavior. Since these rules are "unspoken," the child can learn only through a hands-on experience, such as by practicing public behavior under the tutelage of a caretaker and observing how others in the situation behave. If the child does not conform to the normative expectations of public etiquette, then the caretaker must discipline the child, since others stand ready to reaffirm society's expectations if the caretaker is found to be incapable of doing so. Any irresponsibility on the caretaker's part will elicit negative sanctions from the surrounding adults as well as the label associated with a negative moral identity. A child who misbehaves shapes the moral identity of the parent or caretaker; the young child is excused, though older children also are held morally accountable. Thus, children are not allowed to participate freely in public life but are under constant scrutiny so that they do not disrupt it. Until a child can behave in public—signifying that he or she has internalized the moral order—the child will be held captive by his or her parents. Allowing one's child to gambol in public expresses faith that one's child is bridled by the normative order against untoward acts.

The Interactionist Perspective: Structure and Agency

What seems clear is that socialization is not a "structurally determined process whereby the values and goals of social systems are instilled in the child's behavior repertoires" (Denzin 1977: 2–3). Children are cultural, social, historical, political, and economic products (15–27), but structural constraints are not deterministic. For example, socialization reproduces gender ideals, boundaries, and behavior, just as it reproduces the "natural and moral order" of society (Cahill 1986a: 181). However, Cahill's work also shows us how adults forget that children and adults coauthor gender.

Interactionists emphasize that socialization is an active process, accomplished through taking the attitude of others. While significant others are influential, because of their function as the child's first looking glass, children contribute to the social construction of their own worlds. Witness their participation in the formation of peer cultures through which they transform what is at hand into castles, spaceships, alien worlds—into make-believe social worlds where monsters lurk and heroes save the day. Climbing bars can be defined as a prison, a burning house, a restaurant, a circus, a home, or a den (Corsaro 1985: 184). This is the most fundamental example of bricolage. Like some South American writers, children create a world of magical realism; their play and peer culture are full of personification, anthropomorphism, zoomorphism, and animism; it is a world of the sacred and the profane.

Corsaro emphasizes children's transformative power through their appropriation of adult culture, creatively interpreted and reproduced within peer culture. He also highlights children's culture making that is nonderivative from adults. In contrast, Cahill's work on children's gender identity and public behavior and Denzin's work on speech communities emphasize the environmental, internalization, and social reproduction aspects of socialization. The socialization process entails a tension between continuity and change. Acquiring competence as a social actor involves a dialectic between the role-taking (reproductive/thesis) and role-making (productive/antithesis) qualities of the self (synthesis). SI has always conceptualized this dialectic as an *inter*generational process. What Corsaro's project underscores is that becoming a social actor is also a process of *intra*generational routines in a progression of peer cultures. For example, Hadley (2003: 196) has portrayed both intergenerational and intragenerational interaction through children's word play in which they "both resisted and accommodated the Confucian values" to be good students and good peer group members. In a Tiawanese kindergarten class, children through word play made fun of their teachers' names and the name of their class in front of an administrator, simultaneously demonstrating their resistance to always be respectful of adults as well as their good-student literacy skills of "word structure, vocabulary, and word placement" (204). In addition, students "inserted bathroom humor" into group-participation "word plays to achieve a sense of collective identity and sharing with peers, a Confucian value instilled in them by the teachers during their socialization efforts" (203). Children resisted authority through word play yet acquired *adult-intended* intellectual and social skills.

Many other interactionists have focused on the structure and agency aspects of socialization. Marjorie Harness Goodwin (1990: 308) and Barrie Thorne (1993: 176) also argue that socialization theory has privileged internalization and viewed children as those "who are acted upon more than acting" (3). Goodwin's (1990: 283) ethnography has shown that children not only shape themselves but also shape others through peer interaction. Thorne argues that for too long socialization has conveyed the idea that adults are active while children are passive. Children are not just learners; they are more than passive, incomplete, or incompetent adults; they are makers of fashion, gender, social identity, and selves. "There is much to be gained by seeing children not as the next generation's adults, but as social actors in a range of institutions. Children's interactions are not preparation for life; they are life itself" (Thorne 1993: 3).

But social structure is also featured in Goodwin's (1990: 49) ethnography of a peer group of working-class black children and the social organizational features of their talk—in stories, gossip, and argument. She shows that, in the absence of structural constraints or directives from caretakers, girls and boys spontaneously talk to and play with one another. Goodwin's peer group consisted of an unfocused gathering in which gender asymmetry was generally absent. She found that many activities promote equality and solidarity (284–285); nevertheless, children segregate when conflict arises over what is defined as exclusively girls' or boys' play. Eder and Hallinan (1978) observed that girls' dyadic friendships were more exclusive than boys' (that is, girls rejected newcomers more frequently). Boys' play tends to require a larger number of participants, which helps to explain their orientation toward nonexclusivity. Teachers may reinforce gender separateness, however, through notions of what is appropriate play for girls and boys. Furthermore, children who are already cognizant of gender ideals may self-select gender-typed play (238). When the structure of the situation was an open classroom, boys and girls interacted together more often. Thus, context (interaction other than play) and structure (the open classroom) are factors that must be taken into account (247). Different types of play may lead to differentially valorized social skills. If males acquire group-leadership skills while females acquire skills at self-disclosure, then their play is socially reproducing gender inequality (247). This theme is further amplified by Eder and Parker (1987: 209) in their study of the effects of extracurricular activities: sports socialize males to competitiveness, achievement, and aggressiveness; cheerleading socializes females to the importance of attractiveness, glamour, and emotion management.

Thorne (1993: 161) also underscores the influence of structure in noting that teachers structure conflict into academics, which "ratified the gender divide by pitting boys against girls in math and spelling contests." This "harness[es] gender rivalry as a motivation for learning," debases competition into "hostility," and reproduces "polarization," by associating gender with opposition, antagonism, and conquest. Classrooms, the cafeteria, and playgrounds have "gendered turfs," which create two distinct social worlds wherein teachers "police gender boundaries" and aides "shooed children" away from places they thought exclusively girls' or boys' territory (Thorne 1989: 74–76). Thus, Thorne's (1993: 161) ethnography reveals how gender-segregated academic contests and play, structured by teachers and school aides, "perpetuates an image of dichotomous difference" and "encourages psychological splitting." These findings corroborate Cahill's insights. School practices that divide boys and girls institutionalize gender struggle. Extrapolating from how girls and boys are differentially directed (Cahill 1983, 1986a, 1986b, 1989; Eder and Hallinan 1978; Eder and Parker 1987), we come to understand how a gendered opportunity structure arises that reproduces inequality across generations (power, education, occupation, and income).

Summary

Interactionists have shown that children, in their appropriation and transformation of adult culture, construct selves, gender and race, social identities, and peer cultures. Stages of self-development are seen as contingent, dependent on the quality of socialization. Play and games engender intellectual and social skills fundamental to successful adulthood. Parents and caregivers must prepare children for independent, self-controlled, public behavior. Arguments that the self emerges before language acquisition are now accepted. An argument that language has an "innatist" component that does not undermine SI has been propounded. No longer playing bit parts on the proscenium, children now appear center stage in that collective rather than individual, sociological rather than psychological, active rather than passive, drama known as socialization. The interactionist reconceptualization of children as agents who construct a variety of peer cultures, make meaning, do gender and race, and develop contingently provides a powerful platform for the continued study of childhood socialization.

References

Baldwin, James Mark. 1895. *Mental Development in the Child and the Race.* New York: Macmillan.

———. 1897. *Social and Ethical Interpretations in Mental Development.* New York: Macmillan.

———. 1910. *The Story of Mind.* New York: D. Appleton.

Bergesen, Albert J. 2004. "Chomsky versus Mead." *Sociological Theory* 22: 357–370.

Brint, Steven. 2006. "Schools and Socialization." Pp. 157–173 in *Childhood Socialization.* Edited by Gerald Handel. Piscataway, NJ: AldineTransaction.

Cahill, Spencer E. 1980. "Directions for an Interactionist Study of Gender Development." *Symbolic Interaction* 13:123–138.

———. 1983. "Reexamining the Acquisition of Sex Roles: A Social Interactionist Approach." *Sex Roles* 9:1–15.

———. 1986a. "Childhood Socialization as a Recruitment Process: Some Lessons from the Study of Gender Development." Pp. 163–186 in *Sociological Studies of Child Development, Volume I,* edited by Peter Adler and Patricia Adler. Greenwich, CT: JAI Press.

———. 1986b. "Language Practices and Self Definition: The Case of Gender Identity Acquisition." *Sociological Quarterly* 27:295–311.

———. 1987. "Children and Civility: Ceremonial Deviance and the Acquisition of Ritual Competence." *Social Psychological Quarterly* 50:312–321.

———. 1989. "Fashioning Males and Females: Appearance Management and the Social Reproduction of Gender." *Symbolic Interaction* 12:281–298.

———. 1990. "Childhood and Public Life: Reaffirming Biographical Divisions." *Social Problems* 37:390–402.

———. 1994. "And a Child Shall Lead Us: Children, Gender, and Perspectives by Incongruity." Pp. 459–469 in *Symbolic Interaction: An Introduction to Social Psychology,* edited by Nancy J. Herman and Larry T. Reynolds. Dix Hills, NY: General Hall Press.

———. 2003. "Childhood." Pp. 857–874 in *Handbook of Symbolic Interactionism.* Edited by Larry T. Reynolds and Nancy J. Herman-Kinney. Walnut Creek, CA: AltaMira Press.

Cooley, Charles Horton. 1902. *Human Nature and the Social Order.* New York: Charles Scribner's Sons.

———. 1908. "A Study of the Early Use of Self-Words by a Child." *Psychological Review* 15:339–357.

———. 1909. *Social Organization.* New York: Charles Scribner's Sons.

Corsaro, William A. 1979a. "'We're Friends, Right': Children's Use of Access Rituals in a Nursery School." *Language in Society* 8:315–336.

———. 1979b. "Young Children's Conception of Status and Role." *Sociology of Education* 52:46–59.

———. 1985. *Friendship and Peer Culture* in *the Early Years.* Norwood, NJ: Ablex Publishing.

———. 1986. "Discourse Processes within Peer Culture: From a Constructivist to an Interpretive Approach to Childhood Socialization." Pp. 81–101 in *Sociological Studies of Child Development. Volume* 1, edited by Peter Adler and Patricia Adler. Greenwich, CT: JAI Press.

———. 1988. "Routines in the Peer Culture of American and Italian Nursery School Children." *Sociology of Education* 61:1–14.

———. 1992. "Interpretive Reproduction in Children's Peer Cultures." *Social Psychology Quarterly* 55:160–177.

———. 1997. *The Sociology of Childhood.* Thousand Oaks, CA: Pine Forge Press.

———. and Donna Eder. 1990. "Children's Peer Cultures." *Annual Review of Sociology* 16:197–220.

———. and Thomas A. Rizzo. 1988. "Discussions and Friendship: Socialization Processes in the Peer Culture of Italian Nursery School Children." *American Sociological Review* 53:879–894.

———. and Thomas A. Rizzo. 1990. "An Interpretive Approach to Childhood Socialization." *American Sociological Review* 55:466–468.

Damon, William. 2006. "Socialization and Individuation." Pp. 3–9 in *Childhood Socialization.* Edited by Gerald Handel. Piscataway, NJ: AldineTransaction.

Denzin, Norman K. 1971. "Children and Their Caretakers." *Transaction* 8:62–72.

———. 1972. "The Genesis of Self in Early Childhood." *Sociological Quarterly* 13:291–314.

———. 1977. *Childhood Socialization.* San Francisco, CA: Jossey-Bass.

———. 1979. "Toward a Social Psychology of Childhood Socialization." *Contemporary Sociology* 8:550–556.

———. 1982. "The Significant Others of Young Children: Notes toward a Phenomenology of Childhood." Pp. 29–46 in *The Social Life of Children in a Changing Society,* edited by K. M. Borman. Hillsdale, NJ: Erlbaum.

Dewey, John. 1906. *The Child and the Curricula.* Chicago: University of Chicago Press.

———. 1922. *Human Nature and Conduct: An Introduction to Social Psychology.* New York: Henry Holt.

Eder, Donna, and Maureen T. Hallinan. 1978. "Sex Differences in Children's Friendships." *American Sociological Review* 43:237–250.

Eder, Donna, and Stephen Parker. 1987. "The Cultural Production and Reproduction of Gender: The Effect of Extracurricular Activities on Peer-Group Culture." *Sociology of Education* 60:200–213.

Fine, Gary Alan. 1987. *With the Boys*. Chicago: University of Chicago Press.

Goffman, Erving. 1959. *The Presentation of Self in Everyday Life.* Garden City, NY: Doubleday.

———. 1961. *Asylums: Essays on the Social Situation of Mental Patients and Other Inmates.* Garden City, NY: Doubleday.

Goodwin, Marjorie Harness. 1990. *He-Said-She-Said.* Bloomington: Indiana University Press.

Hadley, Kathryn Gold. 2003. "Children's Word Play: Resisting and Accommodating Confucian Values in a Taiwanese Kindergarten Classroom." *Sociology of Education* 76:193–208.

Handel, Gerald. 2006. *Childhood Socialization.* Piscataway, NJ: AldineTransaction.

Hill, Shirley A. 2001. "Class, Race, and Gender Dimensions of Child Rearing in African American Families." *Journal of Black Studies* 31:494–508.

James, William. 1890. *Principles of Psychology.* New York: Henry Holt.

———. 1892. *Psychology: Briefer Course.* New York: Henry Holt.

Kluckhohn, Clyde, and Henry Murray. 1948. "Personality Formation: The Determinants." Pp. 35–48 in *Personality* in *Nature. Society, and Culture,* edited by Clyde Kluckhohn and Henry Murray. New York: Alfred A. Knopf.

Leavitt, Robin Lynn. 2006. "Power and Resistance in Infant-Toddler Day Care Centers." Pp. 115–136 in *Childhood Socialization.* Edited by Gerald Handel. Piscataway, NJ: Aldine Transaction.

Lewis, Catherine C. 2006. "Cooperation and Control in Japanese Nursery Schools." Pp. 137–153 in *Childhood Socialization.* Edited by Gerald Handel. Piscataway, NJ: Aldine Transaction.

Markey, John F. [1928] 1978. The *Symbolic Process and Its Integration in Children: A Study in Social Psychology.* Chicago: University of Chicago Press.

Mead, George Herbert. 1934. *Mind, Self and Society.* Chicago, IL: University of Chicago Press.

Moore, Valerie Ann. 2002. "The Collaborative of Race in Children's Play: A Case Study of Two Summer Camps." *Social Problems* 49:58–78.

Thomas, W. I., and D. S. Thomas. 1928. *The Child in America: Behavior Problems and Programs.* New York: Knopf.

Thorne, Barrie. 1989. "Girls and Boys Together . . . But Mostly Apart: Gender Arrangements in Elementary Schools." Pp. 73–84 in *Feminist Frontiers* II, edited by Laurel Richardson and Verta Taylor. New York: Random House.

———. 1993. *Gender Play: Girls and Boys in School.* New Brunswick, NJ: Rutgers University Press.

13

Changing Societies and Changing Lives

Angela M. O'Rand
Duke University

Glen H. Elder, Jr.
University of North Carolina at Chapel Hill

This chapter follows up on an earlier one we published over a decade ago (Elder and O'Rand 1995) in another handbook of social psychology. That chapter provided a summary of the life course perspective, its intellectual roots in several disciplines such as demography, life span psychology and social history, and current directions in research. We return to this topic again, in part because this perspective has diffused across the social sciences to inform research in new areas, such as criminology and health, and in part because the life course perspective is a progressive research program that continues to generate new questions. Its implications for social psychology are well in evidence and are addressed below.

The life course perspective reveals the dynamic interdependence of history and biography. Just as historical circumstances and opportunity structures shape the courses of individual lives, the aggregate impact of individual responses to historical and structural conditions also leads to institutional and social change. This dynamic is revealed by the multilevel consideration of time—time as history at the societal level and time as aging, development, and change across the life span at the individual level. The centrality of time to the life course perspective probably accounts for its well-established influence across the social and behavioral sciences because lives are best understood in the context of their past, present, and prospective future and by the temporal linkages among these.

In this chapter we will examine selected aspects of the interdependence of history and biography at the turn of the twenty-first century and their relevance for future research on the life course. First, we will examine some of the demographic, historical, and technological changes in recent decades that are exerting strong new forces on individual lives, with potentially multidirectional effects that either precipitate changes in lives or amplify and accentuate persistent life patterns. We will also argue that the choices of individuals in response to life demands, including those related to fertility, union formation, educational participation, work careers, marital dissolution, and health behaviors (among others), can erode or change social institutions that are historically associated with earlier life course patterns across these domains. Arguably, the paces of change in societies and in the patterns of individual lives have accelerated in recent decades and rendered the life course an increasingly variable phenomenon. These changes are motivating new agendas for research.

Second, we will summarize major elements of the life course perspective presented in our earlier chapter and in the considerable literature on the life course that has appeared since that time. We will review the life course mechanisms that have been demonstrated to influence the course of lives. Social origins, situational conditions, linked lives, individual agency, and lifelong cumulative processes, among other mechanisms, anchor and direct the courses of lives and represent the intersections of historical context and individual biography. These intersections produce heterogeneity and inequality within and across cohorts and societies.

Finally, we will consider several frontiers of life course research that are motivated by the life course paradigm and by social change, including research on cumulative processes, time perspectives, risk and uncertainty, role complexity and conflict, identity, and health. Notably, recent developments in life course research have (re)introduced "biology" as an integral component of individual-environment interactions over time with implications for longevity and general well-being.

Historical Change and a "Runaway World"

Anthony Giddens (2003) has characterized the late modern era as a "runaway world" with consequences for the life course. He cites globalization, demographic shifts, and cultural change as drivers of an increased individualization of lives that are both less closely attached to proximal primary relationships and more vulnerable to distal events. They are also less stratified by age and gender and more sensitive to real-time changes in the social environment. Individualization thus implies an increasing destandardization of the life course by statuses traditionally related to putatively universal categories such as age and gender and the ascendance of risk and unexpected events in people's lives.

Life course research has emphasized the importance of sociohistorical locations for people's lives for over forty years. Depressions, other economic transformations, demographic changes, and wars at the societal level and ascribed statuses and socioeconomic locations at the individual level have shaped the courses of lives (Elder 1999), especially at critical points in the life course such as childhood and the transition to adulthood (Conger and Donnellan 2007; Crosnoe and Elder 2003). In the case of childhood, the formative and fateful impacts of childhood conditions have enduring effects, which we are still uncovering. In the transition to adulthood, the movement of individuals from families of origin to more independent adult lives appears to be formative also, as individual dispositions begin to become hardened and life trajectories are anchored by early achievements and failures (Shanahan 2000). The diverse life course characteristics of different birth cohorts also exemplify the impact of sociohistorical locations and track the course of social change as individuals make choices in their day-to-day lives that can influence social change (Hughes and O'Rand 2004).

In the modern context described by Giddens (2003), demographic changes are responses to both economic transformations and independent influences on economic change. Long-term declines in fertility in western countries have reached levels below population replacement rates in most western countries. The United States still reaches the replacement level of 2.1 children per woman over her reproductive years, but most of Europe and former English colonies hover below 1.5 with the lowest rates nearer 1.2 (Bond et al. 2007). At the same time, average life expectancy across developed and developing countries alike is increasing—resulting in patterns of population aging that are challenging economic and national policies (Bongaarts 2004).

Women are choosing to have fewer children. These life course choices are transforming the age structures of populations and challenging social policies developed over a long time to sustain populations that exceeded the current rates of population growth. From a life course perspective, this pattern is an illustration of the aggregate impact of individual choices on social structure. Lower fertility is correlated with higher rates of educational participation and employment, increased rates of cohabitation, and lower and later transitions to marriage (Lesthaeghe 1995). As such, the institutional grounding of gender role socialization has shifted from the traditional family to the market and broader material culture that promote individualism and personal accomplishment.

Alternatively, global economic transformation is disrupting employment institutions that once sustained nuclear families. The shift to price competition and financial capitalism has broken traditional employer-employee ties and shifted employers' allegiances from workers to shareholders (Berg and Kalleberg 2001). This has generated and sustained a trend toward impermanent employment relations, wage compression, and the retrenchment of employee benefits targeted for the support of families. The consequences of these structural trends for the life course have been felt directly in the workplace, where economic restructuring and job instability have become commonplace and where the demand for women's labor exceeds that for men in many economic sectors. They have also been felt indirectly in the family, where economic strains have influenced marital and childbearing patterns and where family support policies related to income and health maintenance once provided by the workplace are disappearing as employers abandon traditional pensions and health insurance policies (Jacoby 2001).

This withdrawal of structural supports for family and individual well-being is, arguably, a primary cause of the increasing individualization of the life course. Individuals' experiences without work, family, and government institutions are becoming less standardized. Consequently, life course risks are increasing across the life course and being transmitted across generations. This devolution of risk increasingly places responsibility on individuals or individual families to plan for or protect themselves against unexpected health and income decline without the support of collective organizations once associated with employers, labor unions, and national welfare policies. Certainly in the case of the United States, these collective institutions never attained the level of solidarity and generosity of some European states, but they have nevertheless contracted over the twenty-year period that ended the twentieth century.

In short, global changes in fertility, population aging, and labor markets have added new uncertainties to the structure of the life course. Adulthood has become a more problematic construction than in the past. And patterns of individualization have consequently elevated the importance of understanding individuals' capacities and propensities to make choices and manage their lives in the face of uncertainties.

The Life Course Perspective

In general, the life course perspective is a framework for studying lives in contexts over time. Lives are comprised of sequentially contingent social transitions across multiple life contexts that include family, schooling, work, health, and other areas. These sequences of social transitions are interdependent across life contexts in the sense that transitions or exposures to events in one area of life can trigger changes in other areas. As such, these are conceptualized as interlocking trajectories or pathways across the life span, which are marked by variable sequences of expected and unexpected social transitions and events that are not always strongly correlated with age. The variability in the timing and ordering of these transitions/events produces quite diverse trajectories and patterned differences across biographies. These trajectory differences, in turn, mean that specific transitions do not carry universal meanings across lives, since they may occur in diverse sequences relative to other transitions and since their meanings are framed by the biographies of which they are a part.

The Life Course as a Lifelong Cumulative Process

Research over the past forty years has repeatedly documented several general principles of the life course and their social implications (Elder et al. 2003). These principles and their implications are summarized below in a review of recent literature. The first principle identifies the life course as a relatively continuous, multidimensional, and cumulative lifelong process graded in some respects by normative standards related to age and gender, but increasingly variable *viz* these standards over time. The triphasic life course that emerged in association with industrial society was conceptualized as comprised by relatively disjunctive phases associated with youth, adulthood, and old age. Transitions associated with education, work and family, and retirement, leisure, and health were associated, respectively, with these age grades or life phases and served to standardize lives and largely segregate women and men in separate spheres.

However, changes over recent decades reveal increasing heterogeneity in the trajectories of these transition patterns both between cohorts and within cohorts as they age (Shanahan 2000). Transitions once strictly associated with specific life phases, such as educational attainments among youth, are now observable at later phases; similarly, transitions in work and family once typically restricted to midlife now extend to later years. For example, in the case of education, which is commonly presumed to end during the first twenty years or so of life, there is mounting evidence that larger proportions of succeeding cohorts in the United States stay in longer or return to school (often more than once) well into adulthood. A study that tracked two baby boom cohorts into middle age by the 1990s found that delays and interruptions in school completion increased in the late twentieth century (Bernhardt et al. 2001) showing persons completing education well into their fourth decade. Some of these school reentries and completions in adulthood are motivated by job loss or job insecurity (Elman and O'Rand 2002); or by desires to complete higher credentials to improve wages (Elman and O'Rand 2004); and still others by marital dissolution and other disruptive transitions or events (Bernhardt et al. 2001; Jacobs and King 2002). These patterns display the multidimensionality of the life course, in which transitions can occur across ages and traditional life phases and in response to transitions in other life contexts over time, but they also underscore the idea of lifelong processes not necessarily linked to specific age ranges.

Similarly, adult family roles are not limited to a restricted range of adult reproductive ages, but can extend over a longer period of the life course beginning prior to adulthood and extending to older ages. Early and delayed marriage, early and late childbearing, childlessness, marital dissolution and remarriage, and other changing household arrangements occur and recur across ages and have become nontrivial variations in the biographies of recent cohorts in the United States and elsewhere in advanced countries (Hughes and O'Rand 2004; Mason and Jensen 1995). These patterns have produced complex family life trajectories encompassing four to five decades of life. They have, in part, been attributed to women's increased participation in education and work over the life course and decreased motivations for larger families and more years spent as caregivers (Mason and Jensen 1995). Delays in marriage and fertility have extended the child-rearing years past the traditional middle-age range to preretirement years when late-born children's educational completion remains a parental responsibility. Similarly, adult children's educational, marital, and work transitions often delay nest-leaving or precipitate returns to the nest. Children's life transitions also often bring new child care responsibilities related to grandchildren. Finally, increased life expectancy among older generations has introduced more prevalent responsibilities among older adults for caring for parents (Bengtson 2001). Hence, as nuclear family relations have diversified rapidly, intergenerational relationships have gained (or perhaps regained) a new importance.

Some demographers refer to these changing family careers across generations since 1960 as "the second demographic transition," an accelerating trend that is leading to faster fertility decline and increased population aging (Lesthaeghe 1995). In the U.S. context, this trend takes two class-related forms: first, women with higher levels of education increasingly choose to work and to delay or forgo marriage and childbearing and invest in themselves and their careers while, second, women from less advantaged backgrounds experience higher rates of nonmarriage and divorce during childbearing. A major consequence is the growing divergence of the well-being of the children of these two groups, respectively (McLanahan 2004).

These trends also signal broader changes in gender socialization in response to the expansion of choices for women and men alike across their lives. The well-being of earlier cohorts of women was tied principally to family because of the centrality of the caregiver role for women and the breadwinner role for men. However, recent cohort studies of gender differences in the predictors of depression and global happiness reveal that women's well-being is less tied to family relationships than in the past, although men's well-being continues to be influenced significantly by socioeconomic status and wealth (e.g., Salari and Zhang 2006).

This complexity challenges research on the family, particularly if longitudinal observations of individuals and their families over long periods of their lives are not available (Uhlenberg and Mueller 2003). Changes in gender role attitudes have not made the family an extinct institution, but have reconfigured the family system over time. Not only have spousal and parent-child relationships been affected by these changes, but also intergenerational relationships. Families still matter, but family dynamics appear to have changed. Their implications for individual well-being are increasingly evident. Disruptions in families of origin influence the later economic and social well-being of individuals (O'Rand

and Hamil-Luker 2005). Disruptions of marriages affect the mental health of individuals (Barrett 2000). And the later years of life now may include more intergenerational familial responsibilities than those that retirement and leisure can deliver (Bengtson 2001).

Like family transitions, work transitions are not limited to adulthood. They can extend from adolescence to the later years typically associated with normative retirement ages (Hallinan 2000; Parnes and Somers 1994). Among recent cohorts, adolescents are working more while still in high school and the long-term trend toward early retirement have stalled, if not reversed (Quinn 1997). In between adolescence and retirement, the work career has undergone changes and variations equivalent to those observed in the family career. In the post-1970s era of globalization and economic restructuring, which has ushered in greater voluntary and involuntary job mobility, the work career has changed in its configuration. Women work more. But both men and women experience more employer changes, shifts between full-time and part-time work, and spells of unemployment in adulthood than any workforce since the Great Depression in the United States (Berg and Kalleberg 2001). The implications of these multiple transitions for the life course include the extension (or contraction, as the case may be) of the work career and ramifications of work transitions for other life transitions such as those in education and the family and for the general well-being of workers and their families (Singh-Manoux et al. 2004). More stable career paths are associated with positive well-being and better health; less stable (and now normative career paths) have more negative effects on well-being and health (Moen and Roehling 2005). As such, the work career—like educational and familial careers—has become more variable and less age-graded for recent cohorts and potentially more problematic for psychological well-being.

Cumulative Advantage and Disadvantage. These complex lifelong trajectories bring gains and losses to people's lives and can have cumulative effects on well-being across life contexts. Indeed, the accumulation of advantages and disadvantages over the life course is influenced by patterns of gain and loss from multiple life transitions that are initiated in early life and accumulate via sequences of educational attainment or interruption, marriage or marital dissolution, job mobility or job loss, health decline, and so on. The idea of cumulative advantage/disadvantage has become attached, implicitly or explicitly, to the longitudinal study of variability and stratification over the life course (Dannefer 2003). It originated in a Mertonian framework to study processes of professional recognition and reward in science. It was formulated to apply to quasi-economic, Pareto-optimal situations in which inequality increases in a population over time and is biased in the direction of early or initial inequalities. Inequalities increase as the advantaged minority accumulates a growing disproportionate share of the rewards in a system. As the minority gets richer, the majority gets relatively poorer.

This idea has been applied explicitly to the study of economic stratification and increasingly to the age-related distribution of health and well-being in aging cohorts (Di Prete and Eirich 2006). Education-dependent wage and retirement income inequality in middle-aged and older populations support the cumulative advantage argument. Earlier attainments condition later attainments. Advantaged origins increase opportunities for accessing additional advantages and buffer individuals against shocks and unexpected life events that can reverse fortunes. Disadvantaged origins set individuals on more vulnerable paths in which exposures to sequentially threatening life events or potentially derailing transitions across life domains levy penalties that cumulatively dissipate resources (Elman and O'Rand 2004).

Growing physical and mental health disparities within aging cohorts follow similar patterns of divergence over time and have been linked to economic stratification (Mirowsky and Ross 2003). Poverty and economic strains have pervasive effects across life domains. Family, education, work, and health transitions are influenced negatively by persistent economic strains leading to lower levels of education, less stable family and work histories, and poorer health over time. Cumulative disadvantage in health has been characterized as a pathway of stress proliferation (Pearlin et al. 2005), in which disparities in morbidity and mortality can be traced to undesired changes in relationships, to repeated exposures to trauma and strain, and to out-of-sequence transitions in early life.

The social psychology of economic and health disparities focuses on how inequality "gets under the skin" (Schnittker and McLeod 2005) and affects individual personalities, perceptions, dispositions, behaviors, and physiology. Obesity, depression, and susceptibility to illness have all been linked to subjective assessments of status and self-worth, which when they are negative can compound the effects of disadvantage or when positive can attenuate the effects of objective disadvantage. Hence, some social psychological variables appear to mediate the impact of objective indicators of inequality. Thus, for example, a higher perceived sense of control can have a stronger relationship with physical and mental health among those with fewer economic resources (Lachman and Weaver 1998).

Persistence and Change. These cumulative processes are also linked to patterns of persistence and change. Cumulative processes by their very nature are conditioned on past experiences, but these experiences include both exposures to stressors of various kinds, such as childhood adversity or the loss of a job or a spouse, and patterns of response to and coping with these experiences. Cumulative exposures to stressors are, therefore, accompanied by relatively consistent patterns of coping and response that have been traced to relatively persistent personality structures (Caspi et al. 2005). Arguably, the patterns of response to life events over time are related to long developing characteristics that lead individuals to selected experiences of loss or gain in the first place. Coping patterns and personal dispositions can be particularly accentuated when confronting traumatic and extremely disruptive life events, such as combat, severe economic loss, or the death of a loved one (Elder and Caspi 1990; Elder and Clipp 1988a, b).

Some debate continues over the effects of the life course on personality change (Ardelt 2000). Many studies of the five higher-order personality traits (neuroticism, extraversion, openness to experience, agreeableness, and conscientiousness) suggest that these traits are relatively stable after the age of thirty—or following the period of perhaps the greatest change in disposition associated with late adolescence and the transition to adult roles. One study, for example, reported that ill-tempered adolescent boys became ill-tempered men who are subsequently vulnerable to divorce and unemployment (Caspi et al. 1989). Other studies find similar patterns of persistence across more and less traumatic experiences, but also detect some change or stress-related growth in adulthood (Elder and Clipp 1988a, b; Elder et al. 1991). One critic of this literature argues that what is required to adjudicate this debate is more research using long-term longitudinal data that permit the examination of multiple social exposures over time to gains and losses in the life course (Ardelt 2000).

The life course as a lifelong process also supports the idea that social psychological change and other forms of individual change are possible because of the plasticity of the life course, especially in times of change. The social environment over time has formative effects, but individuals also select and influence their environments (Elder and Caspi 1990). This is especially evident in studies of health over the life course. The rate at which people age is affected by health habits and psychosocial factors, both of which are readily changeable over time by individuals (Aldwin et al. 2006). One of the long-term positive trends of the twentieth century has been the extension of life expectancy and the more recent lengthening of healthy or active life expectancy. These patterns have emerged in part in response to improved public health policies and practices and in part from changing individual habits (such as the decline of smoking, the improvement of education, etc.). Active life expectancy—or the portion of the life span that is disability-free—is being rescheduled or has moved the average onset of disablement to later ages (Crimmins and Saito 2001).

In summary, the lifelong development of the life course reveals patterns of continuity and discontinuity within lives and variability in these patterns across lives. As a cumulative process of gains and losses, it serves as a stratifying process driven by the linkages among earlier and later experiences and by the responses of individuals to expected and unexpected social circumstances. The requirements for the study of these patterns include repeated observations of individuals over time across life contexts consisting of education, family, work, leisure, and health, to name a few.

Other Principles of the Life Course

Several other principles are intrinsic to the life course as a lifelong process with patterns of cumulation, persistence and change. These include the following (Elder et al. 2003: 11–14):

> *The Principle of Time and Place:* The life course is embedded and shaped by historical times and places experienced by individuals over a lifetime. Individuals are born into social circumstances with formative effects on their lives and experience historical change from different vantage points of their lives at the times that changes occur. Biographies intersect with historical changes to produce heterogeneity in the life course.
>
> *The Principle of Timing:* The developmental antecedents and consequences of life transitions, events, and behavioral patterns vary in their timing in persons' lives. Lives do not conform to a single chronological clock, but rather to the accumulation of diverse experiences which potentiate life transitions at different times in people's lives. The timing, sequencing, and co-occurrence of life transitions distinguish the courses of lives. In processes of cumulative advantage and disadvantage, the early timing of positive achievements increases the likelihood of later high achievements; lower early achievement or stigmatized status can lead to a lifetime of cumulative disadvantage.
>
> *The Principle of Linked Lives:* Lives are lived interdependently, and sociohistorical influences are expressed through networks of shared relationships. Individuals experience history in and through their relationships with others. Primary, long-standing relationships are influential in the development of the self and of patterns of response

to life conditions. New relationships can become turning points and resources for change in the pattern of lives.

The Principle of Agency: Individuals construct their own life course through their choices and actions within the opportunities and constraints of history and social circumstance. Persons formulate and pursue goals and select themselves into situations and contexts. These patterns develop over the life course and are linked to earlier experiences and to psychosocial patterns of coping and response.

These principles motivate current research on the life course that is introducing new concepts that extend and refine the life course perspective and reintroducing older concepts in the context of new data and methods for their analysis. The section of this chapter summarizes highlights of current research at these frontiers.

Frontiers in Life Course Research

The Long Arm of Childhood

The well-being of individuals at any point in the life course reflects cumulative processes that begin in childhood, if not at conception. This is a long-standing premise of lifespan development theory. However, new research is identifying the joint effects of early childhood health and family circumstances on later life well-being using extensive longitudinal data spanning five to six decades of life. Several aspects of childhood conditions influence development over the life course. Childhood health, socioeconomic conditions, family structure, and parental values have all been implicated in lifetime trajectories across education, family, work, and health. A variety of subjective health assessments, depression, and chronic diseases such as cancer, lung disease, cardiovascular conditions, and arthritis and rheumatism in late middle-age have been linked to early life conditions (Hamilton and O'Rand 2007; Hayward and Gorman 2004; O'Rand and Hamil-Luker 2005; Hamil-Luker and O'Rand 2007).

Economic hardship in childhood is clearly associated with lower adult socio economic status, and poorer physical and mental health in adulthood (Conger and Donnellan 2007; Palloni 2006). Childhood family instability and distress are also implicated in later life transitions. Divorce and marital distress among parents creates an unstable environment of mistrust, distraction, and parental inattention that appears to recur in the lives of children as they become parents. Resources for the support and nurturance of healthy and unhealthy children are stretched thin by family distress, even in intact households. The consequences of these early life exposures in later life include poor health, marital and occupational instability, and lower self-esteem.

These early structural influences are accompanied by others that stem from parental values and their transmission to children. Again, for sociologists and social psychologists it is not news that parental values matter. The new information is that these values extend well beyond the young adult years to old age as they influence lifelong patterns of goal-setting and goal-attainment beyond young adulthood (Hitlin 2006; Shanahan 2000). Children's values and aspirations are largely anchored in their experiences and are tested in new life situations as they move across the life course. They shape educational attainments, occupational successes and failures, marital stability, health behaviors, and other life experiences. Childhood circumstances clearly reflect the principle of time and place and the principle of linked lives, but they are also relevant for later patterns of choice and agency in later adulthood.

The Role of Biology and Health in Person-Environment Interactions

The recent confluence of life course research with medical sociology has promoted new interests in the relationship between social and biological characteristics. Once considered unorthodox in the social sciences, interests in genetics and behavioral endocrinology are developing rapidly. Longitudinal research projects are integrating social survey data with data on biological markers of health and DNA samples. These developments are motivated by at least three assumptions about the relationship of biology to human behavior: (1) biological traits interact with social environments to influence specific behavior patterns; (2) gene-environment interactions over the course of human evolution have generated a range of adaptive human behaviors which are only beginning to be understood; and (3) social environments, especially stressful ones, induce biological responses in human beings (Shanahan, Hofer, and Shanahan 2003).

Three areas of life course research are leading edges of these interests. One is the area reviewed immediately above, focused on the persistence of the effects of childhood conditions on long-term patterns on behavior and health. The persistent effects on the life course of childhood adversity, including poor health and family conditions, may be transmitted through dispositions and patterns of response to environmental circumstances experienced in childhood that anchor and direct later patterns of response (Freese, Li, and Wade 2003). Early persistent exposures to strains or stress from childhood to adolescence may influence the course of personality and sexual development and establish problem-solving patterns and emotionally reactive patterns that persist into adulthood.

The second area is stress research. The so-called stress process examines the influence of exposures to traumas and sustained stress in the social environment on patterns of health; the mediating mechanisms are considered to be biological, that is, to implicate the neuroendocrine system that regulates emotional and reactive behaviors such as fear and aggression (Pearlin et al. 2005). Stress processes produce gains and losses and thus are multidirectional in their effects over the life course (McLeod and Almazan 2003; Schnittker and McLeod 2005), although sustained negative strains have been found to be disadvantageous for well-being.

The third area focuses on sex differences in patterns of physical and mental health and in patterns of association. While the genetic bases for these differences are far from established, the "unshared environments" of girls and boys in childhood and men and women in adulthood probably generate distinctive interactions between environments and developing individuals. Gendered patterns of health and mortality demonstrate that women experience worse health than men over their lives, but men face earlier mortality—a phenomenon referred to as the health-survival paradox. This is still a puzzle, but a share of the answer will be discovered at the intersection of biological and social experience.

A yet unexplored area in life course research which has clear implications for future research addresses the impact of recent biological technologies on the life course. New technologies in genetic testing and assisted reproduction have implications for family transitions and for personal identity (Richards 2004). DNA technologies can be used to identify biological kin relations with relative certainty. As a result, adopted children, those conceived by assisted reproductive technologies that included anonymous germ cell donors, and those conceived without full knowledge of parentage have new access to information about their biological origins. This knowledge can have medical implications in the case of testing for genetically heritable diseases and social psychological implications for personal identity. These new forms of identification can redefine the meaning of family. But they can also create what have been referred as "persons genetically at risk," that is, self-identities that have among their salient features the sense of susceptibility to illness and death. These are new self-identities associated with modernity with implications for lives. As Richards (2004, 491) concludes, "We are living in the future, where we have never been before."

Chance, Uncertainty, and Agency in the Life Course: Emotions and Time Perspectives

The "runaway world" described by Giddens (2003) includes the spread of technologies like those mentioned earlier that both improve life planning but also introduce new risks. It also places chance and uncertainty at the center of the life course. This raises questions about the impact of uncertainty about the future on agency and coping over time. Institutions created over the twentieth century to equalize opportunities for social mobility and well-being and to protect citizens from derailing experiences of income and health decline have been retrenched in the United States, and increasingly in other countries where the forces of population aging and globalization are eroding the capacity to sustain these institutions (Hacker 2006). Financial, health and longevity risks have been long associated with older populations (Shuey and O'Rand 2004), but new risks face younger populations for sustained periods of the life course.

The erosion of these institutions elevates the responsibilities of individuals to be more future oriented and vigilant regarding their prospective futures. A tradition of research in social psychology on time perspectives and their influences on human cognition, motivation, and agency provides the opportunity to understand these processes in the future. Carstensen's (Carstensen et al., 1999; Carstensen 2006; Carstensen et al., 2003) socioemotional selectivity theory proposes that the life course is associated with the increasing motivation to derive emotional meaning from life and the decreasing motivation for knowledge acquisition and goal achievement. This pattern produces age differences in the regulation of emotions, coping, and the cognitive processing of attention and memory. These differences are probably brought about by shifting time horizons with age, but can also be provoked by unexpected or uncontrollable events such as illnesses, job losses, and wars that affect the individual sense of control and elicit emotional reactions. When time is limited, as in the case of older age, or when time is an immanent threat of the unknown, as in the case of illness or unpredictable life conditions, emotional responses override goal-seeking.

Giddens (2003) argues that under the conditions of uncertainty associated with modern life, what is required is reflexive life planning. If the life course includes increasing pressures to manage risks, then variations across individuals in future time perspectives and in the propensities to plan and defer gratifications in anticipation of future risks should be better understood. These are not new interests in social psychology, but they have achieved a new salience in the context of social change and its life course implications.

Role Complexity, Conflict, and Identity

A final frontier of social psychological research addresses the question of how social roles retain their meanings for individuals in the face of increasingly frequent role transitions and the management of multiple changing roles over time. Role theory has been central to social psychology and life course research for over half a century. However, its relevance for the modern life course is problematic. Roles are normatively defined expectations for behaviors associated with major statuses in the life course that are prevalent in the population and long-lived over the life course.

Social roles are losing their permanency and power to control the behaviors of their incumbents. Gender roles are especially problematic in modern societies. Gender as a general status construct that represents different life experiences and life outcomes remains a powerful idea; however, gender roles as relatively resilient sets of expectations that predict men's and women's behaviors with respect to work and family activities are losing their validity in life course research. Changes in the organization of the family are especially relevant for understanding the decline of role explanations.

Among the most important long-term trends over the past century is the change in the division of family labor (Gornick and Meyers 2003). Work life and family life are no longer easily separable life domains. Social forces have pulled women out of the home as labor market opportunities have emerged for them and as wage stagnation and occupational shifts have limited men's opportunities for achievement in traditional work roles. These market trends in combination with declining public safety nets that support families have generated rather ad hoc, as opposed to normative, solutions to the maintenance of families. Nonstandard hours of work, makeshift child care arrangements, and various forms of "income and social support packaging" have made parents social innovators of new family "roles."

A similar argument has been made regarding age roles. Riley, Kahn, and Foner (1994) advocated a shift in the view of the life course from a strictly age-differentiated sequence of major irreversible normative transitions to a more age-integrated conception over a decade ago. They and their colleagues argued that social institutions predicated on strong assumptions regarding the age-grading of social roles at the end of the twentieth century lagged behind actual demographic patterns of longevity and healthy life expectancy that challenged assumptions about age. Rather, they argued that transitions in education, work, family, and leisure could occur across the life span with highly variable timing. Persons at the oldest ages could be full-time workers, family heads, students, and active civic participants fulfilling all the expectations of traditional adult roles reserved for those middle ages. The extension of active life expectancy at the turn of the century supports these claims, although the variability among the elderly is as diverse as that observed across age groups over the life span.

Conclusions

The life course presents opportunities and challenges for social psychology. The opportunities reside in the dynamic changes observable in lives over time—and especially in the current period of history in which so many social changes exert forces on individual lives. How individuals manage multiple transitions, uncertainties and risks, and experiences of gains and losses are still largely unexplained social patterns. How identities survive and change in response to these changing social environments is still a matter of speculation.

The challenges of understanding these processes reside principally in the quality and frequency of observations of lives over time. Cross-sectional and experimental studies are useful in identifying correlations among life course experiences and personal perceptions and behaviors. However, the persistence or change of social psychological attributes can best be understood and explained by following lives over time. The observation of lifelong processes requires longitudinal data that are prospective and follows individuals in real time as much as possible. In the absence of these data, detailed life histories can be instructive but limited to memories and retrospective accounts.

References

Aldwin, C. M., A. Spiro III, and C. L. Park. 2006. Health, behavior and optimal aging: a life span developmental perspective. Pp. 85–104 in J. E. Birren and K. W. Schaie (Eds.), *Handbook of the Psychology of Aging,* 6th Edition. New York: Academic Press.

Ardelt, M. 2000. Still stable after all these years? Personality stability theory revisited. *Social Psychology Quarterly* 63: 392–405.

Barrett, A. E. 2000. Marital trajectories and mental health. *Journal of Health and Social Behavior* 41: 451–464.

Bengtson, V. 2001. Beyond the nuclear family: The increasing importance of multigenerational relationships in American Society. *Journal of Marriage and the Family* 63:1–16.

Berg, I. and A. L. Kalleberg (Eds.). 2001. *Sourcebook of labor markets: Evolving structures and processes.* New York: Kluwer/Plenum.

Bernhardt, A., M. Morris, M. S. Hancock, and M. A. Scott. 2001. *Divergent paths: Economic mobility in the new American labor market.* New York: Russell Sage.

Bongaarts, J. 2004. Population aging and the rising cost of public pensions. *Population and Development Review* 30:1–23.

Bond, J., S. Peace, F. Dittmann-Kohli, and G. J. Westerhoff. 2007. *Ageing in society: European perspectives on gerontology.* 3rd Edition. London: Sage Publications.

Brugman, G. M. 2006. Wisdom and aging. Pp. 445–476 in J. E. Birren and K. W. Schaie (Eds.), *Handbook of the Psychology of Aging.* 6th Edition. New York: Academic Press.

Carstensen, L. L. 2006. The influence of a sense of time on human development. *Science* 312: (June 30): 1913–15.

Carstensen, L. L., H. H. Fung, and S. T. Charles. 2003. Socioemotional selectivity theory and the regulation of emotion in the second half of life. *Motivation and Emotion* 27: 103–123.

Carstensen, L. L., D. M. Isaacowitz, and S. T. Charles. 1999. Taking time seriously: A theory of socioemotional sensitivity. *American Psychologist* 54: 165–181.

Caspi, A., D. J. Bem, and G. H. Elder, Jr. 1989. Continuities and consequences of interactional styles across the life course. *Journal of Personality* 57: 375–406.

Caspi, A., B. W. Roberts, and R. L. Shiner. 2005. Personality Development: Stability and change. *Annual Review of Psychology* 56: 453–484.

Conger, R. D. and M. B. Donnellan. 2007. An interactionist perspective on the socioeconomic context of human development. *Annual Review of Psychology* 58: 175–199.

Crimmins, E. and Y. Saito. 2001. Trends in disability free life expectancy in the United States, 1970–1990: Gender, racial and educational differences. *Social Science and Medicine* 52: 1629–1641.

Crosnoe, R. and G. H. Elder Jr. 2003. From childhood to the later years: Pathways of human development. *Research on Aging* 26: 623-54.

Dannefer, Dale. 2003. Cumulative advantage/disadvantage and the life course: Cross fertilizing age and social science theory. *Journal of Gerontology—Social Sciences* 58B, S327–338.

DiPrete, T. A. & Eirich, J. M. 2006. Cummulative advantage as a mechanism for inequality: A review of theoretical and empirical developments. *Annual Review of Sociology* 32: 271–298.

Elder, Glen H. Jr., 1999. Children of the Great Depression: *Social Change in Life Experience*. 25th Anniversary Edition. Boulder, Co: Westview Press (originally published in 1974, University of Chicago Press)

———. 1986. Military times and turning points in men's lives. *Development Psychology* 22: 233–245.

Elder, G. H. Jr., Bem, D., and A. Caspi. 1990. Studying lives in a changing society: Sociological and personological explorations. Pp. 201–247 in Studying persons and Lives, ed. A. I. Rabin, R. A. Zucker, R. A. Emmons, and S. Frank (Eds), New York: Springer.

Elder, G. H. Jr. and E. C. Clipp. 1988a. Combat experience and emotional health: Impairment and resilience in later life. *Journal of Personality* 57: 311–341.

———. 1988b. Wartime losses and social bonding: Influences across 40 years in men's lives. *Psychiatry* 51: 177–198.

Elder, G. H. Jr., M. K. Johnson, and R. Crosnoe. 2003. The emergence and development of life course theory. Pp. 3–19 in J. T. Mortimer and M. J. Shanahan (Eds). *Handbook of the Life Course*. New York: Kluwer/Plenum.

Elder, G. H. Jr. and A. M. O'Rand. 1995. Adult lives in a changing society. Pp. 452–475 in K. S. Cook, G. A. Fine, and J. S. House (Eds.), *Sociological Perspectives in Social Psychology*. Needham Heights, MA: Allyn and Bacon.

Elder, G. H. Jr., E. K. Pavalko, and T. J. Hastings. 1991. Talent, history, and the fulfillment of promise. *Psychiatry* 54: 251–267.

Elman, C. and A. M. O'Rand. 2002. Perceived labor market insecurity and the educational participation of workers at midlife. *Social Science Research* 31: 49–76.

———. 2004. The race is to the swift: Childhood adversity, adult education and wage attainment. *American Journal of Sociology* 110: 123–160.

Freese, J., J-C. A. Li, and L. D. Wade. 2003. The potential relevances of biology to social inquiry. *Annual Review of Sociology* 29: 233–256.

Giddens, Anthony. 2003. *Runaway world*. New York: Routledge.

Gornick, J. C. and M. K. Meyers. 2003. *Families that work: Policies reconciling parenthood and employment*. New York: Russell Sage.

Hacker, J. S. 2006. *The great risk shift: The assault on American jobs, families, health care, and retirement—and how you can fight back*. New York: Oxford University Press.

Hallinan, M. T., (Ed.). 2000. *Handbook of the Sociology of education*. New York: Kluwer/Plenum.

Hamil-Luker, J. and A. M. O'Rand. 2007. Gender differences in the link between childhood socioeconomic conditions and heart attack risk in adulthood. *Demography* 44: 137–158.

Hayward, M. D. and B. K. Gorman. 2004. The long arm of childhood: The influence of early-life social conditions on men's mortality. *Demography* 41(1): 87–107.

Hitlin, S. 2006. Parental influences on children's values and aspirations: Bridging two theories of social class and socialization. *Sociological Perspectives* 49: 25–46.

Hughes, M. E. and A. M. O'Rand. 2004. *The lives and times of the baby boomers*. New York: Russell Sage.

Jacobs, J. A. and R. B. King. 2002. Age and college completion: A life history analysis of women age 15–44. *Sociology of Education* 75: 211–230.

Jacoby, S. M. 2001. Risk and the labor market: Societal past as economic prologue. Pp. 31–60 in I. Berg and A. L. Kalleberg (Eds.), *Sourcebook of labor markets: Evolving structures and processes,* New York: Kluwer/Plenum.

Lachman, M. E. and S. I. Weaver. 1998. The sense of control as a moderator of social class differences in health and well-being. *Journal of Personality and Social Psychology* 74: 763–773.

Lesthaeghe, R. 1995. The second demographic transition in western countries: An interpretation. Pp. 17–62 in K. O. Mason and A.-M. Jensen. (Eds.), *Gender and family change in industrialized countries,* Oxford, UK: Clarendon.

Mason, K. O. and A.-M. Jensen, (Eds.). 1995. *Gender and family change in industrialized countries.* Oxford, UK: Clarendon.

McLanahan, S. 2004. Diverging destinies: How children are faring under the second demographic transition. *Demography* 41: 607–627.

McLeod, J. D. and E. P. Almazan. 2003. Connections between childhood and adulthood. Pp. 391–411 in J. T. Mortimer and M. J. Shanahan. (Eds.), *Handbook of the Life Course.* New York: Kluwer/Plenum.

Mirowsky, J. and C. E. Ross. 2003. *Education, social status and health.* New York: Aldine de Gruyter.

Moen, P. and P. Roehling. 2005. *The career mystique: Cracks in the American dream.* Lanham, MD: Rowman and Littlefield.

O'Rand, A. M. and Hamil-Luker, J. 2005. Processes of cumulative adversity: Childhood disadvantage and increased risk of heart attack across the life course. *Journal of Gerontology-Social Sciences* 60B (Special Issue II): 117–124.

Palloni, A. 2006. Reproducing Inequalities: Luck, wallets and the enduring effects of childhood health. *Demography* 43: 587–616.

Parnes, H. and D. Somers. 1994. Shunning retirement: Experience of men in their seventies and eighties. *Journal of Gerontology—Social Sciences* 49B: S117–S124.

Pearlin, L. I., S. Schiemann, E. M. Fazio, and S. C. Meersman. 2005. Stress, health and the life course: Some conceptual perspectives. *Journal of Health and Social Behavior* 46: 205–219.

Quinn, J. 1997. Retirement Trends and Patterns in the 1990s: The end of an era? Pp. 10–14 in *Public Policy and Aging Report.* Washington, DC: National Academy of Aging.

Richards, M. 2004. Assisted reproduction, genetic technologies and family life. Pp. 478–498 in J. Scott, J. Treas and M. Richards (Eds.) The Blackwell Companion to the Sociology of Families. Oxford: Blackwell.

Riley, M. W., R. L. Kahn, and A. Foner, (Eds.). 1994. *Age and structural lag.* New York: Wiley.

Salari, S. and W. Zhang 2006. Kin keepers and good providers: Influence of gender socialization on well-being among USA birth cohorts. *Aging & Mental Health* 10: 485–496.

Schnittker, J. and McLeod 2005. The social psychology of health disparities. *Annual Review of Sociology* 31: 75–103.

Shanahan, M. J. 2000. Pathways to adulthood in changing societies. *Annual Review of Sociology* 26: 667–92.

Shanahan, M. J., S. M. Hofer, and L. Shanahan. 2003. Biological models of behavior and the life course. Pp. 597–622 in J. T. Mortimer and M. J. Shanahan (Eds.), *Handbook of the Life Course.* New York: Kluwer/Plenum.

Shuey, K. M. and A. M. O'Rand. 2004. New risks for workers: Pensions, labor markets and gender. *Annual Review of Sociology* 30: 453–477.

Singh-Manoux, A., J. E. Ferrie, T. Chandola, and M. Marmot. 2004. Socioeconomic trajectories across the life course and health outcomes in midlife: Evidence for the accumulative hypothesis. *International Journal of Epidemiology* 33: 1072–1079.

Uhlenberg, P. and M. Mueller. 2003. Family context and individual well-being: Patterns and mechanisms in life course perspective. Pp. 123–148 in J. T. Mortimer and M. J. Shanahan (Eds.), *Handbook of the Life Course.* New York: Kluwer.

14

*Anybody's Son Will Do**

Gwynne Dyer
Freelance journalist and columnist

You think about it and you know you're going to have to kill but you don't understand the implications of that, because in the society in which you've lived murder is the most heinous of crimes . . . and you are in a situation in which it's turned the other way round. . . . When you do actually kill someone the experience, my experience, was one of revulsion and disgust.

I was utterly terrified—petrified—but I knew there had to be a Japanese sniper in a small fishing shack near the shore. He was firing in the other direction at Marines in another battalion, but I knew as soon as he picked off the people there—there was a window on our side—that he would start picking us off. And there was nobody else to go . . . and so I ran towards the shack and broke in and found myself in an empty room.

There was a door which meant there was another room and the sniper was in that—and I just broke that down. I was absolutely gripped by the fear that this man would expect me and would shoot me. But as it turned out he was in a sniper harness and he couldn't turn around fast enough. He was entangled in the harness so I shot him with a .45 and I felt remorse and shame. I can remember whispering foolishly, "I'm sorry" and then just throwing up. . . . I threw up all over myself. It was a betrayal of what I'd been taught since a child.

—William Manchester

Yet he did kill the Japanese soldier, just as he had been trained to—the revulsion only came afterwards. And even after Manchester knew what it was like to kill another human being, a young man like himself, he went on trying to kill his "enemies" until the war was over. Like all the other tens of millions of soldiers who had been taught from infancy that killing was wrong, and had then been sent off to kill for their countries, he was almost helpless to disobey, for he had fallen into the hands of an institution so powerful and so subtle that it could quickly reverse the moral training of a lifetime.

*Excerpted from *War* (New York, Crown Publishers)

The whole vast edifice of the military institution rests on its ability to obtain obedience from its members even unto death—and the killing of others. It has enormous powers of compulsion at its command, of course, but all authority must be based ultimately on consent. The task of extracting that consent from its members has probably grown harder in recent times, as the gulf between the military and the civilian worlds has widened. Civilians no longer perceive the threat of violent death as an everyday hazard of existence, and the categories of people whom it is not morally permissible to kill have broadened to include, in peacetime, the entire human race. Yet the armed forces of every country can still take almost any young male civilian and in only a few weeks turn him into a soldier with all the right reflexes and attitudes. Their recruits usually have no more than twenty years' experience of the world, most of it as children, while the armies have had all of history to practice and perfect their techniques. . . .

Human beings are fairly malleable, especially when they are young, and in every young man there are attitudes for any army to work with: the inherited values and postures, more or less dimly recalled, of the tribal warriors who were once the model for every young boy to emulate. The anarchic machismo of the primitive warrior is not what modern armies really need in their soldiers, but it does provide them with promising raw material for the transformation they must work in their recruits.

Just how this transformation is wrought varies from time to time and from country to country. In totally militarized societies—ancient Sparta, the samurai class of medieval Japan, the areas controlled by organizations like the Liberation Tigers of Tamil Eelam today—it begins at puberty or before, when the young boy is immersed in a disciplined society in which only the military values are allowed to penetrate. In large modern societies, the process is briefer and more concentrated, and the way it works is much more visible. It is, essentially, a conversion process in an almost religious sense—and as in all conversion phenomena, the emotions are far more important than the specific ideas.

> When I was going to school, we used to have to recite the Pledge of Allegiance every day. They don't do that now. You know, we've got kids that come here now, when they first get here, they don't know the Pledge of Allegiance to the flag. And that's something—that's like a cardinal sin. . . . My daughter will know that stuff by the time she's three; she's two now and she's working on it. . . . You know, you've got to have your basics, the groundwork where you can start to build a child's brain from. . . .
>
> —USMC drill instructor, Parris Island recruit training depot, 1981

Many soldiers feel the need for some patriotic or ideological justification for what they do, but which nation, which ideology, does not matter: men will fight as well and die as bravely for the Khmer Rouge as for "God, King, and Country." And although the people who send the soldiers to war may have high national or moral purposes in mind, most of the men on the ground fight for more basic motives. The closer you get to the front line, the fewer abstract nouns you hear.

What really enables men to fight is their own self-respect, and a special kind of love that has nothing to do with sex or idealism. Very few men have died in battle, when the moment actually arrived, for the United States of America or for the cause of Communism, or even for their homes and families; if they had any choice in the matter at all, they chose to die for each other and for their own vision of themselves.

> Once you get out there and you realize a guy is shooting at you, your first instinct, regardless of all your training, is to live. . . . But you can't turn around and run the other way. Peer pressure, you know? There's people here with you that have probably saved your life or will save your life in the future; you can't back down.
>
> —USMC Vietnam veteran

> This is going to sound really strange, but there's a love relationship that is nurtured in combat because the man next to you—you're depending on him for the most important thing you have, your life, and if he lets you down you're either maimed or killed. If you make a mistake the same thing happens to him, so the bond of trust has to be extremely close, and I'd say this bond is stronger than almost anything, with the exception of parent and child. It's a hell of a lot stronger than man and wife—your life is in his hands, you trust that person with the most valuable thing you have. And you'll find that people who pursue the aphrodisiac of combat or whatever you want to call it are there because they're friends; the same people show up in the same wars time and again.
>
> —Capt. John Early, ex-U.S. Army, Vietnam; ex-mercenary, Rhodesia

John Early is an intelligent and sensitive man who became a combat junkie ("I'm a contradiction in terms, and I can't explain it") and as such he is a rarity. For most men, the trust and intimacy of a small unit in combat never compensate for the fear and revulsion. But the selfless identification of the soldier with the men in his unit is what makes armies work in combat, and the foundations must be laid in peacetime. "Fighting is a social art, based upon collective activity, cooperation and mutual support," an Israeli soldier observed. "This utter reliance on others is an integral part of the effort to meet the enemy irrespective of odds, and it largely determines men's willingness to risk their lives in pressing the attack. . . . In short, there is rarely brotherhood in facing death when there is none in peace."

The way armies produce this sense of brotherhood in peacetime is basic training, a feat of psychological manipulation on the grand scale which has been so consistently successful and so universal that we fail to notice how remarkable it is. In countries where the army must extract its recruits in their late teens, whether voluntarily or by conscription, from a civilian environment that does not share the military values, basic training involves a brief but intense indoctrination whose purpose is not really to teach the recruits basic military skills but rather to change their values and their loyalties. "I guess you could say we brainwash them a little bit," admitted a U.S. Marine drill instructor, "but they're good people."

The duration and intensity of basic training depend on what kind of society the recruits are coming from, and on what sort of military organization they are going to. It is obviously quicker to train men from a martial culture than from one in which the dominant values are civilian and commercial, and easier to deal with volunteers than with reluctant conscripts. Conscripts are not always unwilling, however; there are many instances in which the army is popular for economic reasons.

In early modern Europe, for example, military service was always intensely unpopular with the mass of the population, and most soldiers were drawn from the most deprived and desperate groups on the margins of society. That changed suddenly in the nineteenth century, with conscription—and at the same time, surprisingly, military service became extremely popular. The fervent nationalism of the nineteenth century had something to do with it, but meat probably had even more.

In the army, the conscripts were fed meat every day and were issued two pairs of boots and a change of underwear—which was more than most of them had back on the farm or in the back streets of the cities. Most armies in the Third World still benefit from this kind of popularity today and have five or ten applicants for every available place (in some countries it is necessary to bribe the recruiter to get in). But even in the modern industrialized nations, where the average civilian's living standard has long since overtaken that of the private soldier and the white heat of nationalism has subsided somewhat, armies have no difficulty in turning recruits, whether conscripts or not, into soldiers.

A more complex question is what kind of soldier (or sailor, or airman) the recruit must now be turned into. This is usually seen mainly in relation to the increased requirement for technical knowledge brought about by modern weapons, but that is not really a problem of basic training. The real crux of the issue is the kind of social environment the recruit will eventually have to fight in.

For all of military history down to less than a century ago, the environment was invariably the same: an extremely crowded one, with his comrades all around him. In a Roman legion, on the gun deck of a seventeenth-century warship, or in a Napoleonic infantry battalion, the men fought close together, and the presence of so many others going through the same ordeal gave each individual enormous moral support—and exerted enormous moral pressure on him to play his full part. So long as you drilled the recruit to the point of boredom and beyond in the use of his sword, cannon, or musket; instilled in him a loyalty to his legion, ship, or regiment; and put him in mortal fear of his officers, he would probably perform all right on the day of the battle.

To a very large extent the crews of modern ships and aircraft (and even tanks)—all the men who fight together from inside machines—are still living in the same social environment, though the crowds have thinned out noticeably. And when men go into battle in the presence of their peers, the same principles of training will still produce the same results. But for the infantry, who fought shoulder to shoulder all through history, the world has been turned upside down.

Even in World War I, infantrymen could still usually see their whole company in an attack, but the dispersion forced on them by modern firepower has reduced the group who will actually be within sight or hearing of each other in a typical position to ten men or fewer—and even they will probably be spread out over a considerable area. For the foot soldier, the battlefield has become a desperately lonely place, deceptively empty in appearance but bristling with menace, where he can expect neither direct supervision by his officer or NCO in combat, nor the comforting presence of a group of other men beside him.

The more sophisticated forms of infantry basic training have now recognized that fact, and in the latter phases of the training they place far greater stress on "small-group dynamics": building the solidarity of the "primary group" of five to ten men who will be the individual's only source of succour and the only audience of his actions in combat. Far greater dependence must now be placed on the individual soldier's initiative and motivation than ever before, and so armies have to try harder. In the United States, where the contrast between the austerity, hierarchy, and discipline of military life and the prevailing civilian values is most extreme, basic training—the conversion of young civilians into soldiers—is given a greater emphasis than almost anywhere else. The U.S. Army, which reckons that all its members could, under some circumstances, find themselves in a combat zone, insists on seven weeks' basic training, followed by advanced individual training in a specific trade—and the U.S. Marine Corps gives twelve weeks of basic training to every man and woman who joins the Corps.

The Marines are a very old-fashioned organization (the last of the U.S. armed forces to get its hands on any desirable piece of new weapons technology) that clings to the belief that every Marine must be a qualified combat rifleman first, even if his subsequent specialty will be cooking or supply. The USMC is also an elite assault force, whose battle doctrine accepts the necessity, on occasion, of trading casualties for time. The entire orientation of the Marine Corps is toward the demands of combat: it informs everything the Corps does.

This makes the Marines atypical of contemporary armed forces in the United States or anywhere else, which generally consist of very large numbers of pseudo-military personnel doing technical, administrative, and even public relations jobs, surrounding a much smaller combat core. The Marines are almost all core. But for this very reason they are an ideal case study in how basic training works: they draw their recruits from the most extravagantly individualistic civilian society in the world and turn them into elite combat soldiers in twelve weeks.

It's easier if you catch them young. You can train older men to be soldiers; it's done in every major war. But you can never get them to believe that they like it, which is the major reason armies try to get their recruits before they are twenty.

Young civilians who have volunteered and been accepted by the Marine Corps arrive at Parris Island, the Corps's East Coast facility for basic training, in a state of considerable excitement and apprehension. Most are aware that they are about to undergo an extraordinary and very difficult experience. But they do not make their own way to the base; rather they trickle into Charleston airport on various flights throughout the day on which their training platoon is due to form, and are held there in a state of suppressed but mounting nervous tension until late in the evening. When the buses finally come to carry them the seventy-six miles to Parris Island, it is often after midnight—and this is not an administrative oversight. The shock treatment they are about to receive will work most efficiently if they are worn out and somewhat disoriented when they arrive.

The basic training organization is a machine, processing several thousand young men every month, and every facet and gear of it has been designed with the sole purpose of turning civilians into Marines as efficiently as possible. Provided it can have total control over their bodies and their environment for approximately three months, it can practically guarantee converts. Parris Island provides that controlled environment, and the recruits do not set foot outside it again until they graduate as Marine privates twelve weeks later.

> They're allowed to call home, so long as it doesn't get out of hand—every three weeks or so they can call home and make sure everything's all right, if they haven't gotten a letter or there's a particular set of circumstances. If it's a case of an emergency call coming in, then they're allowed to accept that call; if not, one of my staff will take the message. . . .
>
> In some cases I'll get calls from parents who haven't quite gotten adjusted to the idea that their son had cut the strings—and in a lot of cases that's what they're doing. The military provides them with an opportunity to leave home but they're still in a rather secure environment.
>
> —Captain Brassington, USMC

For the young recruits, basic training is the closest thing their society can offer to a formal rite of passage, and the institution probably stands in an unbroken line of descent from the lengthy ordeals by which young males in tribal societies were initiated into the adult community of warriors.

Basic training is not really about teaching people skills; it's about changing them so that they can do things they wouldn't have dreamt of otherwise. It works by applying enormous physical and mental pressure to men who have been isolated from their normal civilian environment and placed in one where the only right way to think and behave is the way the Marine Corps wants them to. The key word the men who run the machine use to describe this process is *motivation.*

> I can motivate a recruit and in third phase, if I tell him to jump off the third deck, he'll jump off the third deck. Like I said before, it's a captive audience and I can train that guy; I can get him to do anything I want him to do. . . . They're good kids and they're out to do the right thing. We get some bad kids, but you know, we weed those out. But as far as motivation—here, we can motivate them to do anything you want, in recruit training.
>
> —USMC drill instructor, Parris Island

The first three days the raw recruits spend at Parris Island are actually relatively easy, though they are hustled and shouted at continuously. It is during this time that they are documented and inoculated, receive uniforms, and learn the basic orders of drill that will enable young Americans (who are not very accustomed to this aspect of life) to do everything simultaneously in large groups. But the most important thing that happens in "forming" is the surrender of the recruits' own clothes, their hair—all the physical evidence of their individual civilian identities.

During a period of only seventy-two hours, in which they are allowed little sleep, the recruits lay aside their former lives in a series of hasty rituals (like being shaven to the scalp) whose symbolic significance is quite clear to them even though they are deliberately given no time for reflection, nor any hint that they might have the option of turning back from their commitment. The men in charge of them know how delicate a tightrope they are walking, though, because at this stage the recruits are still newly caught civilians who have not yet made their ultimate inner submission to the discipline of the Corps.

> Forming Day One makes me nervous. You've got a whole new mob of recruits, you know, sixty or seventy depending, and they don't know anything. You don't know what kind of a reaction you're going to get from the stress you're going to lay on them, and it just worries me the first day.
>
> Things could happen, I'm not going to lie to you. Something might happen. A recruit might decide he doesn't want any part of this stuff and maybe take a poke at you or something like that. In a situation like that it's going to be a spur-of-the-moment thing and that worries me.
>
> —USMC drill instructor

But it rarely happens. The frantic bustle of forming is designed to give the recruit no time to think about resisting what is happening to him. And so the recruits emerge from their initiation into the system, stripped of their civilian clothes, shorn of their hair, and deprived of whatever confidence in their own identity they may previously have had as eighteen-year-olds, like so many blanks ready to have the Marine identity impressed upon them.

The first stage in any conversion process is the destruction of an individual's former beliefs and confidence, and his reduction to a position of helplessness and need. Three days cannot cancel out eighteen years—the inner thoughts and the basic character are not erased—but the recruits have already learned that the only acceptable behaviour is to repress any unorthodox thoughts and to mimic the character the Marine Corps wants. Nor are they, on the whole, reluctant to do so, for they want to be Marines. From the moment they arrive at Parris Island, the vague notion that has been passed down for a thousand generations that masculinity means being a warrior becomes an explicit article of faith, relentlessly preached: to be a man means to be a Marine.

Most eighteen-year-old boys have highly romanticized ideas of what it means to be a man, so the Marine Corps has plenty of buttons to push. And it starts pushing them on the first day of real training: the officer in charge of the formation appears before them for the first time, in full dress uniform with medals, and tells them how to become men.

> You have made the most important decision in your life . . . by signing your name, your life, your pledge to the Government of the United States, and even more importantly, to the United States Marine Corps—a brotherhood, an elite unit. . . . You are going to become a member of that history, those traditions, this organization—if you have what it takes.
>
> All of you want to do that by virtue of your signing your name as a man. The Marine Corps says that we build men. Well, I'll go a little bit further. We develop the tools that you have—and everybody has those tools to a certain extent right now. We're going to give you the blueprints, and we are going to show you how to build a Marine. You've got to build a Marine—you understand?
>
> —Captain Pingree, USMC

The recruits, gazing at him with awe and adoration, shout in unison, "Yes, sir!" just as they have been taught. They do it willingly, because they are volunteers—but even conscripts tend to have the romantic fervour of volunteers if they are only eighteen years old. Basic training, whatever its hardships, is a quick way to become a man among men with an undeniable status, and beyond the initial consent to undergo it, it doesn't even require any decisions.

> I had just dropped out of high school and I wasn't doing much on the street except hanging out, as most teenagers would be doing. So they gave me an opportunity—a recruiter picked me up, gave me a good line, and said that I could make it in the Marines, that I have a future ahead of me. And since I was living with my parents, I figured that I could start my own life here and grow up a little.
>
> —USMC recruit

> I like the hand-to-hand combat and . . . things like that. It's a little rough going on me, and since I have a small frame I would like to become deadly, as I would put it. I like to have them words, especially the way they've been teaching me here.
>
> —USMC recruit

The training, when it starts, seems impossibly demanding for most of the recruits—and then it gets harder week by week. There is a constant barrage of abuse and insults aimed at the recruits, with the deliberate purpose of breaking down their pride and so destroying their ability to resist the transformation of values and attitudes that the Corps intends them to undergo. At the same time the demands for constant alertness and for instant obedience are continuously stepped up, and the standards by which the dress and behaviour of the recruits are judged become steadily more unforgiving. But it is all carefully calculated by the men who run the machine, who think and talk in terms of the stress they are placing on the recruits: "We take so many c.c.'s of stress and we administer it to each man—they should be a little bit scared and they should be unsure, but they're adjusting." The aim is to keep the training arduous but just within most of the recruits' capability to withstand. One of the most striking achievements of the drill instructors is to create and maintain the illusion that basic training is an extraordinary challenge, one that will set those who graduate apart from others, when in fact almost everyone can succeed.

There has been some preliminary weeding out of potential recruits even before they begin training, to eliminate the obviously unsuitable minority, and some people do "fail" basic training and get sent home, at least in peacetime. The standards of acceptable performance in the U.S. armed forces, as in most military organizations, tend to rise and fall in inverse proportion to the number and quality of recruits available to fill the forces to the authorized manpower levels. But there are very few young men who cannot be turned into passable soldiers if the forces are willing to invest enough effort in it. Not even physical violence is necessary to effect the transformation, though it has been used by most armies at most times.

> Our society changes as all societies do, and our society felt that through enlightened training methods we could still produce the same product—and when you examine it, they're right. . . . Our 100 c.c.'s of stress is really all we need, not two gallons of it, which is what it used to be. . . . In some cases with some of the younger drill instructors it was more an initiation than it was an acute test, and so we introduced extra officers and we select our drill instructors to "fine-tune" it.
>
> —Captain Brassington, USMC

There is, indeed, a good deal of fine-tuning in the roles that the men in charge of training any specific group of recruits assume. At the simplest level, there is a sort of "good cop/bad cop" manipulation of the recruits' attitudes towards those applying the stress. The three younger drill instructors who accompany each "serial" through its time in Parris Island are quite close to the recruits in age and unremittingly harsh in their demands for ever higher performance, but the senior drill instructor, a man almost old enough to be their father, plays a more benevolent and understanding part and is available for individual counselling. And generally offstage, but always looming in the background, is the company commander, an impossibly austere and almost godlike personage.

At least these are the images conveyed to the recruits, although of course all these men cooperate closely with an identical goal in view. It works: in the end they become not just role models and authority figures, but the focus of the recruits' developing loyalty to the organization.

> I imagine there's some fear, especially in the beginning, because they don't know what to expect. . . . I think they hate you at first, at least for a week or two, but it turns to respect. . . . They're seeking discipline, they're seeking someone to take charge, 'cause at home they never got it. . . . They're looking to be told what to do and then someone is standing there enforcing what they tell them to do, and it's kind of like the father-and-son game, all the way through. They form a fatherly image of the DI whether they want to or not.
>
> —Sergeant Carrington, USMC

Even the seeming inanity of close-order drill has a practical role in the conversion process. It has been over a century since mass formations of men were of any use on the battlefield, but every army in the world still drills its troops, especially during basic training, because marching in formation, with every man moving his body in the same way at the same moment, is a direct physical way of learning two things a soldier must believe: that orders have to be obeyed automatically and instantly; and that you are no longer an individual, but part of a group.

The recruits' total identification with the other members of their unit is the most important lesson of all, and everything possible is done to foster it. They spend almost every waking moment together—a recruit alone is an anomaly to be looked into at once—and during most of that time they are enduring shared hardships. They also undergo collective punishments, often for the misdeed or omission of a single individual (talking in the ranks, a bed not swept under during barracks inspection), which is a highly effective way of suppressing any tendencies toward individualism. And, of course, the DIs place relentless emphasis on competition with other "serials" in training: there may be something infinitely pathetic to outsiders about a marching group of anonymous recruits chanting, "Lift your heads and hold them high, 3313 is a-passin' by," but it doesn't seem like that to the men in the ranks.

Nothing is quite so effective in building up a group's morale and solidarity, though, as a steady diet of small triumphs. Quite early in basic training, the recruits begin to do things that seem, at first sight, quite dangerous: descend by ropes from fifty-foot towers, cross yawning gaps hand-over-hand on high wires (known as the Slide for Life, of course), and the like. The common denominator is that these activities are daunting but not really dangerous: the ropes will prevent anyone from falling to his death off the rappelling tower, and there is a pond of just the right depth—deep enough to cushion a falling man, but not deep enough that he is likely to drown—under the Slide for Life. The goal is not to kill recruits, but to build up their confidence as individuals and as a group by allowing them to overcome apparently frightening obstacles. . . .

If somebody does fail a particular test, he tends to be alone, for the hurdles are deliberately set low enough that most recruits can clear them if they try. In any large group of people there is usually a goat: someone whose intelligence or manner or lack of physical stamina marks him for failure and contempt. The competent drill instructor, without deliberately setting up this unfortunate individual for disgrace, will use his failure to strengthen the solidarity and confidence of the rest. When one hapless young man fell off the Slide for Life into the pond, for example, his drill instructor shouted the usual invective—"Well, get out of the water. Don't contaminate it all day"—and then delivered the payoff line: "Go back and change your clothes. You're useless to your unit now."

"Useless to your unit" is the key phrase, and all the recruits know that what it means is "useless *in battle*."

> I've seen guys come to Vietnam from all over. They were all sorts of people that had been scared—some of them had been scared all their life and still scared—but when they got in combat they all reacted the same—99 percent of them reacted the same. . . . A lot of it is training here at Parris Island, but the other part of it is survival. They know if they don't conform—conform I call it, but if they don't react in the same way other people are reacting, they won't survive. That's just it. You know, if you don't react together, then nobody survives.
>
> —USMC drill instructor, Parris Island, 1982

He felt that way even though he had been told repeatedly that doing this job might require that he die. The knowledge may not really have struck home—eighteen-year-olds will not truly believe in the possibility of their own deaths until and unless they see combat and live long enough to understand what is going on—but the Marine Corps does not avoid the question. On the contrary, it puts a considerable effort into telling the recruits why they must, under certain circumstances, throw their lives away. It happens in the latter part of their training, when the emphasis is shifting increasingly to how Marines should behave in combat, and though they may not understand the logic that makes the individual's self-sacrifice good for the organization, they are by then more than ready to understand it emotionally. . . .

It is certainly the way the Marine Corps wants its men to behave in combat, for the severely practical reason that men will be more willing to risk their lives if they are confident that the others in their unit will take equally great risks to save them if they get in trouble. But the practical necessities and the romantic vision of soldiering are inextricably mixed. In battle the unit will become the only important thing in the infantryman's universe; nothing outside it matters, and no sacrifice for the other men in it is too great. . . .

Only the experience of combat itself will produce such devotion and selflessness in men, but basic training is the indispensable foundation for it. Despite the ways in which it has been altered to take into account the changes in the battlefields soldiers now inhabit and the societies they serve, basic training has remained essentially the same, because it works with the same raw material that's always there in teenage boys: a fair amount of aggression, a strong tendency to hang around in groups, and an absolutely desperate desire to fit in. Soldiering takes up a much bigger part of your life than most jobs, but it doesn't take a special kind of person: anybody's son will do.

There is such a thing as a "natural soldier": the kind of man who derives his greatest satisfaction from male companionship, from excitement, and from the conquering of physical and psychological obstacles. He doesn't necessarily want to kill people as such, but he will have no objections if it occurs within a moral framework that gives him a justification—like war—and if it is the price of gaining admission to the kind of environment he craves. Whether such men are born or made, I do not know, but most of them end up in armies (and many move on again to become mercenaries, because regular army life in peacetime is too routine and boring).

> Most mercenaries are there because of their friends . . . and they're there because they feel important, and it makes them feel good to win, because they're playing a game. . . . It's a very exuberant feeling, combat.
>
> There's a euphoric effect whenever you make contact with an enemy unit or you're ambushed and you can feel the volume of fire start to build up, and you know that the decisions you make have to be absolutely correct because if they're not somebody's going to be killed or maimed, and that's a tremendous responsibility.
>
> You stay scared, all the time. When you're on patrol you never ever know what's going to happen, and that heightens your senses. You're extremely aware; it's almost like you can feel the texture of the air around you, and it just makes you feel extremely alive, and a lot of people like that. . . .
>
> —Capt. John Early

But men like John Early are so rare that they form only a modest fraction even of small professional armies, mostly congregating in the commando-type special forces. In large conscript armies they virtually disappear beneath the weight of numbers of more ordinary men. And it is these ordinary men, who do not like combat at all, that the armies must persuade to kill. Until only a generation ago, they did not even realize that persuasion was needed. . . .

Men will kill under compulsion—men will do almost anything if they know it is expected of them and they are under strong social pressure to comply—but the vast majority of men are not born killers. It may be significant, in this regard, that the U.S. Air Force discovered during World War II that less than 1 percent of its fighter pilots became "aces"—five kills in aerial combat—and that these men accounted for roughly 30 to 40 percent of all enemy aircraft destroyed in the air, while the majority of fighter pilots never shot anybody down. Fighter pilots almost all flew in single-seat aircraft where nobody else could observe closely what they were doing, and as late as World War II they could often see that inside the enemy aircraft was another human being. It may be that the same inhibition that stopped most individual infantrymen from killing their enemies also operated in the air. On the whole, however, distance is a sufficient buffer: gunners fire at grid references they cannot see; submarine crews fire torpedoes at "ships" (and not, somehow, at the people in the ships); nowadays pilots launch their missiles from much farther away at "targets."

> I would draw one distinction between being a combat aviator and being someone who is fighting the enemy face-to-face on the ground. In the air environment, it's very clinical, very clean, and it's not so personalized. You see an aircraft; you see a target on the ground—you're not eyeball to eyeball with the sweat and the emotions of combat, and so it doesn't become so emotional for you and so personalized. And I think it's easier to do in that sense—you're not so affected.
>
> —Col. Barry Bridger, U.S. Air Force

But for the infantry, the problem of persuading soldiers to kill is now recognized as a centrally important part of the training process. That an infantry company in World War II could wreak such havoc with only about one-seventh of the soldiers willing to use their weapons is a testimony to the lethal effects of modern firepower, but once armies realized what was actually going on, they at once set about to raise the average. Part of the job can be done by weapons training that actually lays down reflex pathways that bypass the moral censor. The long, grassy fields with bull's-eyes propped up at the end give way to combat simulators with pop-up human silhouettes that stay in sight only briefly: fire instantly and accurately and they drop; hesitate and they disappear in a couple of seconds anyway. But conditioning the reflexes only does half the job; it is also necessary to address the psychological reluctance to kill directly. These days soldiers are taught, very specifically, to kill.

Almost all this work is done in basic training. The reshaping of the recruits' attitudes toward actual violence begins quite early in the training, with an exercise known as "pugilsticks." Recruits are matched up in pairs, helmeted and gloved, given heavily padded sticks, and made to fight each other in a style that would certainly cause numerous deaths if not for all the padding. And the rhetoric of the instructor makes it clear what is required of them.

> You have got to be very aggressive! Once you've got your opponent on the run, that means you go on and strike with that first killing blow. Recruit, you don't stop there! Just because you made contact that don't mean you stop. You don't cut him no slack! Don't give him room to breathe, stay on top of him . . . keep pumping that stick. That means there should be nothin' out here today but a lot of groanin,' moanin,' a lot of eyeballs fallin'—a lot of heads rollin' all over the place.

Later, the recruits spend much of their time practicing with the weapons that will really be the tools of their trade: rifles, bayonets ("cut on the dotted line"), grenades, and the like. With those weapons, of course, there is no dividing recruits into teams and letting them behave as they would in real combat. But if you can't actually blow your enemy up in basic training, you can certainly be encouraged to relish the prospect of his demise, and even the gory manner of it.

> Well, first off, what is a mine? A mine is nothing more, privates, than an explosive or chemical substance made to destroy and kill the enemy. . . . You want to rip his eyeballs out, you want to tear apart his love machine, you want to destroy him, privates, you don't want to have nothing left of him. You want to send him home in a Glad Bag to his mommy!
>
> Hey, show no mercy to the enemy, they are not going to show it on you. Marines are born and trained killers; you've got to prove that every day. Do you understand?
>
> —Lecture on the use of mines, Parris Island, 1982

And the recruits grunt loudly with enthusiasm, as they have been taught, although most of them would vomit or faint if they were suddenly confronted with someone whose genitals had been blown off by a mine. Most of the language used in Parris Island to describe the joys of killing people is bloodthirsty but meaningless hyperbole, and the recruits realize that even as they enjoy it. Nevertheless, it does help to desensitize them to the suffering of an "enemy," and at the same time they are being indoctrinated in the most explicit fashion (as previous generations of soldiers were not) with the notion that their purpose is not just to be brave or to fight well; it is to kill people.

> The Vietnam era was, of course, then at its peak, you know, and everybody was motivated more or less towards, you know, the kill thing. We'd run PT in the morning and every time your left foot hit the deck you'd have to chant "Kill, kill, kill, kill." It was drilled into your mind so much that it seemed like when it actually came down to it, it didn't bother you, you know? Of course the first one always does, but it seems to get easier—no easier, because it still bothers you with every one that, you know, that you actually kill and you know you've killed.
>
> —USMC sergeant (Vietnam veteran), 1982

Most of the recruits have never seen anybody dead (except laid out in a coffin, perhaps) before they arrive at Parris Island, and they still haven't when they leave. But by then they also half-inhabit a dream world in which they have not just seen dead people, but killed them themselves, again and again. And it's all right to do it, because they've been told again and again, by everyone they respect, that the enemy, whoever he may be, is not really a full human being like themselves; it is permissible and praiseworthy to kill him. . . .

So what are we to make of the fact that men can so easily be turned into killers? There is the consoling fact that most men are so daunted by the enormity of killing another human being that they avoid it if they possibly can. If armies succeed in tricking them into doing it by modern training methods, moreover, a huge subsequent burden of guilt is laid on those soldiers who did what they were asked: it is now widely suspected that the high rate of combat participation in Vietnam was directly responsible for the extremely high rate of "post-traumatic stress disorder" among American veterans of that war.

Nevertheless, if the inhibition against killing can be removed in most people by a little routine psychological conditioning, then we still have a lot to worry about. War has been chronic for most of the time since we moved into the mass civilizations around ten thousand years ago. Is it an inevitable part of civilization? And does it, perhaps, go even deeper than that?

Section V

Social Structural Approaches to Social Psychology

15

*Race and Emotion Management in the Undergraduate College Classroom**

Roxanna Harlow
McDaniel College

Anxious about teaching my first college class, the first advice I received as a new instructor was that teaching had its emotional peaks and valleys. Some days are great and you leave on an emotional high and others are more difficult and you leave feeling discouraged. Whatever the case, I was told by an experienced teacher, do not get too excited about the highs or too down about the lows. Try to stay balanced. What was interesting about this advice was that he did not discuss the pragmatics of teaching or suggest effective teaching techniques. Instead, he recommended ways for me to think about and manage the emotional experiences I would face in the classroom. He gave me advice on the emotion work involved in teaching.

Although the college classroom has been studied and discussed in various ways (see, for example, Gallop 1997; Hendrix 1998; Jacobs 1999; Statham et al. 1991), few people talk about it, other than anecdotally, as an emotional space where professors' statuses (such as race, gender, sexuality, and so forth) shape their affective experiences in the classroom as they negotiate roles, expectations, and power dynamics through interaction with students. For example, research has shown that black professors experience academia differently from their white colleagues, particularly in regard to role conflict, isolation, and a lack of respect and legitimacy as scholars (Aguirre 2000; Baker 1991; Banks 1984; Fields 1996; Menges and Exum 1983; Phelps 1995; Sinegar 1987; Smith and Witt 1993). But what we know less about is how a professor's race influences his or her experience in the *classroom*. When teaching

***Author's note:** This research was supported by a grant from the Society for the Psychological Study of Social Issues. I thank Brian Powell for comments on earlier drafts.

is discussed, it is typically mentioned briefly and/or treated as a minor factor in the professor's routine.

Some researchers have found that black and white professors' experiences in the classroom indeed are different (Hendrix 1995; Moore 1996; Rains 1995). However, it is unclear from their studies whether these experiences are due primarily to race or to gender, and the emotional component of teaching goes mostly unexplored. Here I examine how race shapes professors' perceptions and experiences in the undergraduate college classroom, how they manage the emotional demands from these experiences, and how the management process affects the nature of their job overall.

Emotional Labor and Management

Most jobs require us to deal with our emotions in some way (e.g., holding back anger at a customer or boss). However Hochschild (1983) distinguishes between this type of emotion work and emotional labor. Emotion work is the process of handling our daily, personal emotions; emotional labor involves evoking, performing, and managing emotions that are a required aspect of a job or occupation (e.g., always being cheerful as a flight attendant to evoke feelings of comfort from passengers). Emotion management is the process of handling emotions in both personal (emotion work) and professional (emotional labor) spheres.

Emotional labor and management can be understood as a form of impression management (Goffman 1959; Wood 2000). According to Goffman (1959), impression management is the process through which people project a self-image that is consistent with how they want to be seen by others. Goffman believed that the ability to mask one's true emotions while providing the appropriate emotional display is the true test of a high-quality social performance. Professors can appreciate Goffman's insight here. College teaching requires extensive emotional labor: professors try to perform and evoke emotions such as enthusiasm and excitement while also managing or suppressing their own immediate feelings and moods (Bellas 1999; Harlow 2002). These performances are affected, however, by the degree to which students and teachers begin their relationship with a mutual acceptance of the professor's status and identity.

Identity and Affect Control Theory

Identity theory states that our behavior is directly connected to our self-concept, and our self-concept is in part shaped by the way that people respond to us when we interact (Stryker 1992). According to this theory, we all have multiple identities that are arranged hierarchically: that is, some identities are more relevant than others from situation to situation, and we behave in ways that reflect those identities. For professors in the classroom, their identity as teacher tends to be one of the most important at that moment, and they behave in certain ways so as to reinforce that identity through interaction. But what if interactions with students do not confirm their identity (because of constant challenges to the professor's knowledge or status, for example)? According to affect control theory, when our conception of self is not confirmed, we experience emotional tension that is eliminated by defining the situation differently, or changing our behavior (Heise 1989).

Burke (1991), in his discussion of "the control-system view of the identity process" (p. 838), explains how people minimize the emotional distress that occurs when one's identity (the identity standard) is not confirmed by feedback from others (inputs). To resolve the inconsistency, one changes her or his behavior (outputs) in an effort to alter people's responses (inputs) in a way that is consistent with one's self-defined identity (identity standard). Burke explains that matching one's identity standard with others' inputs can involve a complex cycle of interactions. Ultimately, however, these two must match; otherwise high levels of stress result. In this chapter I seek, in part, to explain what self-definitions professors are trying to establish with their classroom performances, and how these vary by race. If the definitions are not confirmed through interactions with students, what are the emotional consequences for professors, and how are they managed?

Race is what Cohen (1982) defines as a diffuse status characteristic. That is, even though a particular status may be irrelevant to a task, persons of high status are considered more competent. Therefore black professors' identity performances may involve providing "proof" in any number of ways to justify their presence in a high-status position. As Rakow (1991) observes, the statuses of white, male, and professor are all high, and thus are compatible and even anticipated. For African Americans,[1] however, their racial status is inconsistent with their faculty status; therefore they may find themselves doing "tiring 'identity work'" (Rakow 1991:10) in order to reconcile students' perceptions with their own. The findings presented here show that race affects the amount and type of work professors do in the classroom; it creates emotion work and labor for black professors beyond that required of their white peers.

Data and Methods

From February through November 1999, I (an African American female) conducted 58 in-depth interviews with 29 white and 29 African American faculty members at a large midwestern state university with a 91 percent white student population. Twenty-six respondents were female; 32 were male. They included 22 assistant professors, 27 associate professors, and 9 full professors, ranging in age from 30 to 65 with a mean age of 44. Eighteen of the men and 6 of the women taught in traditionally applied fields such as business and health science; 14 men and 20 women were housed in the humanities or social sciences. I included only full-time tenure-track faculty members who taught at least one undergraduate course. I excluded professors in the school of music because students are evaluated differently there. I targeted faculty members acculturated in the United States so that respondents' understandings of race and racial dynamics would be comparable. The sample selection was based on the population of black professors meeting the above criteria. I then matched them with white participants of similar gender, rank, and department or area of study.

[1]In this study, the terms *black* and *African American* are used interchangeably to refer to black people acculturated in the United States.

Findings

Racial Differences in Professors' Perceptions

"Race doesn't matter, but . . ." The black faculty members in my sample were aware of the negative stereotypes associated with their racial group, and often commented on the continued existence of racial problems in society today. Despite this racial awareness, almost half of the black professors were reluctant to claim that their race mattered to students, or that race influenced their classroom experience in any negative way. Problems related to racial issues were often internalized ("It's my own fault for thinking about it too much") or downplayed altogether (see Table 15.1). For example, one professor stated, "Race is always an issue," but then went on to emphasize regional differences that he felt

TABLE 15.1 ***Self-Reported Classroom Experiences, by Race and Gender***

	% of African American Professors			*% of White Professors*		
	Men (n = 16)	*Women (n = 13)*	*Total (N = 29)*	*Men (n = 16)*	*Women (n = 13)*	*Total (N = 29)*
Initially Downplayed or Internalized Their Racialized Classroom Experiences[a]	50	31	41	n/a	n/a	n/a
Believe Students Immediately Notice Their Racial Status	75	92	83	6	0	3
Believe Students Question Their Intellectual Authority (Competency/ Qualifications)	94	54	76	6	8	7
Feel They Must Prove Their Competence/ Intelligence	56	54	55	6	15	10
Received Inappropriate Student Challenges to Intellectual Authority	44	23	34	0	15	7
Racial Double Standard (White Advantage)	50	77	62	25	8	17

[a]This experience is not applicable to white professors because, for the most part, they did not interpret their classroom work in a racialized way.

were more important. He explained, "Just in general, getting over the, if you will, racial divide, I really haven't had any problems like that here. I just try to understand my students" (Respondent 25: black male).

On a general level, race was "always an issue," but this professor wanted to make clear that he personally had no problem with a "racial divide." Similarly, after pondering the effect of race on his teaching, another professor stated, "Uh, the race thing? In the sense that I'm aware that I'm black, but—I'm not sure . . . but I don't really think that it's going to make a difference in the classroom" (Respondent 23: black male). Although these two professors expressed doubts about the significance of their race in the classroom, they also both believed that as soon as they stepped into the classroom, students were surprised by their race and/or noticed it immediately (see Table 15.1).

The data, then, produced seemingly contradictory statements about the effect of race on these professors' classroom experiences. After downplaying it initially, they then proceeded to explain how, in fact, race mattered significantly. Most of these professors felt that students stereotyped them: 76 percent of the black professors reported that students questioned their competency, qualifications, and credibility (see Table 15.1).

In essence, most black professors felt that their classes always contained at least some students who questioned their status of professor. For example, immediately after Respondent 23 stated that he did *not* think his race made a difference in the classroom, he went on to explain that he *had* been concerned about his race because most of the students were white and had never seen a black professor before, especially in his discipline. As a result, he made an extra effort to appear qualified and knowledgeable because he would otherwise be challenged.

Similarly, after being asked, "Do you think your race or gender affects students' positive or negative views of you?" Respondent 25, who had said he had no problems with the "racial divide," added:

> Undoubtedly. Now exactly how, I'm not totally sure . . . but I did have a very, very interesting experience, though, my first semester with a black student. . . . And he said to me after about the third lecture of the class . . . "Dr. [name], I'm so glad that you're here. I've never had a black professor before. And you're competent too." Well, I was glad that he was glad to see me . . . but his statement "and you're competent too" was very interesting coming from him. Now if that was coming from him, just think of what maybe some white kid from some rural farm town in [the state] is thinking when I stand up in front of him, [who] doesn't know me from Adam. (Respondent 25: black male)

Like Respondent 23, this faculty member may not have had problems with the racial divide, but he believed that his race did influence how students viewed him and his ability to teach. Although these responses from black professors initially sounded contradictory, the contradiction is resolved when understood in the context of a management strategy (to be discussed later), which enabled them to function effectively day to day.

In contrast to the black professors, some white male professors downplayed their intellectual presence in order to seem more approachable to students:

> I think that initially the main thing one's doing is not trying to make oneself seem knowledgeable because they're going to think that [I'll be that way] as a professor. I think it's a matter of trying to make oneself seem approachable and accessible, so for me there's a certain element of calculated self-deprecation. (Respondent 47: white male)

This difference in classroom reality for black and for white professors was illustrated in part by faculty members' reports of students' challenges to their classroom authority.

"I really do know what I'm talking about." Although few men of either race reported concerns about their physical authority in the classroom (the right to be in charge, organize the course, assign materials, and discipline students), black men reported that students resisted their intellectual authority—that is, their knowledge and competency (see Table 15.1). This was particularly the case for black assistant professors.

Black women also felt that their competency was questioned, but overall they were more likely to report challenges to their physical rather than their intellectual authority.[2] Young black women at the assistant and associate levels were the most likely to report challenges to both their competence and their control over the classroom. Explaining this dynamic, Respondent 34 (black female) noted that students do not usually see black people in positions of power, especially black women. As a result, they may doubt black women's academic and leadership capabilities. Commenting on the social structural factors shaping students' often unconscious attitudes about blackness, femininity, and intelligence, this professor went on to explain how looking young simply exacerbated the problem for such women.

This question of competency was an issue even for professors who taught predominantly nonwhite classes and/or classes on race-related topics. For example, when asked, "When students see you're their professor, what do you think they're thinking?" Respondent 32 (black female) replied, "So when I walk into the class, they know it's a class dealing with black people. I walk in as a black professor. I think to some degree it probably legitimates the content." The remainder of her response was surprising, however:

> And I think when I walk in there, other things go through their minds. Probably whether or not I'm good, whether or not I'm tough, whether or not this is going to be a blow-off class for them, whether I'm an affirmative action professor, whether I'm going to be one of these attitudes kind of professor, whether I'm going to be a racist professor, whether I'm going to be the kind of professor who makes white people feel bad about what has happened to black people in America.[3]

Despite the course topic, this professor believed that her race triggered for students negative stereotypes about black people (in regard to competence and browbeating about racism), and black women in particular (in regard to anger and attitude). Another professor similarly explained that his blackness gave him credibility in teaching race related topics. At the same time, however, he added that even black students will doubt his intellectual competency,

[2]Describing the "cult of true womanhood," Hill-Collins noted that " 'true' women possessed four cardinal virtues: piety, purity, submissiveness, and domesticity" (1991:71). Thus, although black women (like black men) felt that students doubted their competence, they also struggled, in ways that the men did not, with issues of authority in regard to classroom presence (physical authority) as they tried to balance students' expectations of "submissiveness" and "domesticity" with power and control.

[3]Several black professors used the term *affirmative action professor* or *affirmative action hire* to indicate that students thought they were unqualified. This is not to say that they themselves equated affirmative action with a lack of qualification. They seemed aware, however, that many students viewed affirmative action as the hiring of unqualified people of color.

so he states his credentials on the first day of class in an effort to counteract the negative stereotypes that students of all races have internalized (Respondent 30: black male).

The black professors' responses on these issues differed sharply from those of white faculty members. In reply to the question "When students see you're their professor, what do you think they're thinking?" one professor stated that she had never thought about it before, but they may wonder if she is a graduate student because she is female and looks young (Respondent 21: white female). Similarly, another professor responded, "I'm not sure I know exactly. I think I probably look a little young . . . but otherwise, I don't think that there's much about me that really makes me stand out specifically . . . I don't think I make a very striking first impression or anything" (Respondent 28: white male).

Responses such as "I don't know" or "I never thought about that before" were common among white faculty members answering this question; these were followed by comments on how their age (and, in the case of women, their gender) might play a role in what students thought. White professors usually did not have to anticipate students' reactions to their race, though such anticipation was commonplace for black professors. In contrast to the black faculty members, most white faculty members, especially white males, took students' confidence in them for granted: 76 percent of black professors felt that students called their qualifications into question, in contrast to only 7 percent of white professors (see Table 15.1).

The white professors also had hardly considered how their racial status might shape students' personal and professional evaluations of them. When asked, "Do you feel that your race or gender affects students' positive or negative views of you?" white women were most likely to focus on their gender alone. White men often overlooked the crediting[4] aspects of both their gender and their race. For example, in response to the above question, a professor replied:

> Ohhh, I don't think so. I don't think so. I mean, it probably helps to be a white male but it's really hard to know. You know, the only reason why it may help is that they see me in them . . . they look at me and say, well, this guy is kinda like me, so—I have no proof of that and I really have no way of knowing if that's really even to any great advantage. (Respondent 31: white male)

Although these professors were skeptical that there was any benefit to being a white male, many of the black faculty members in my sample felt that in fact it was a great advantage.

"That's Wrong": Challenges and Impression Management

To resist negative stereotyping, the black professors in my sample often performed competence and authority by projecting a strict, authoritative demeanor, making students aware of their professional achievements, and (for black women) reminding students to call them doctor or professor rather than by their first name, Ms. or Mrs. Although women were more likely than men

[4]Goffman (1963) defines a stigma as a discrediting attribute. It is difficult to fully understand the process of devaluing certain characteristics, however, without discussing how we come to value other characteristics. Crediting attributes, then, add or have the potential to add value or credibility to a person or a group of people. This concept is useful for understanding the relational nature of stigma, and how the valued and the devalued are integrally tied together. Jason Jimerson originally named and conceptualized this idea in personal discussions.

to describe their classroom style as authoritative, this distinction broke down along racial lines: 69 percent of white female respondents reported that they were authoritative in the classroom, while all of the black women did so. Among the men, 44 percent of the black professors considered their style to be authoritative, in contrast to only 19 percent of the white respondents (see Table 15.2). In addition, 69 percent of black women felt that they had to remind students to call them doctor or professor, but only 31 percent of white women reported doing so.

In spite of their efforts to demonstrate competency, black professors reported more challenges to their intellectual authority than did their white colleagues (see Table 15.1). In most of these challenges, as described by the professors, students questioned their knowledge directly or indirectly in a way that was inappropriate or disrespectful. The challenges included arguments on basic points of the discipline (e.g., a student might argue that the sociological imagination is not defined as the professor defined it), questioning the validity of

TABLE 15.2 ***Self-Reported Presentation and Evaluation, by Race and Gender***

	% of African American Professors			*% of White Professors*		
	Men (n = 16)	*Women (n = 13)*	*Total (n = 29)*	*Men (n = 16)*	*Women (n = 13)*	*Total (N = 29)*
Authoritative	44	100	69	19	69	41
Reminds Students to Call Them by Their Appropriate Title	13	69	38	0	31	14
Evaluated by Students as Cold/Mean/Intimidating	0	62	28	0	15	7
Evaluated by Students as Too Hard/Demanding	44	62	52	19	38	28
Felt Physically Threatened by a Student	0	31	14	0	8	3
Validation Regarding Classroom Performance Is Internal	56	46	52	19	0	10
Classroom Problems Decline with Age	25	54	38	6	54	28

lecture material, and more indirect forms of resistance. Describing a challenge by a white student, one professor stated:

> First of all, he simply thought he knew everything, and that he certainly couldn't learn anything from me. And [he] went so far as to say, when I was trying to explain something, . . . "That's wrong, that's just wrong, that's not true." . . . This is very, very difficult because at the same time, you can't go off on him because you've got to be respectful and you've got to be this professional person and stuff, but it's very, very hurtful, you know, particularly from someone who was not an excellent student. (Respondent 45: black male)

While this professor was trying to manage his anger, he was also managing the frustration and "hurt" caused by the doubts to his competency.

In addition to direct challenges such as this, black professors discussed how students challenged them in indirect ways. In one account, a black female professor explained that a student doubted the veracity of her class lecture material. The student then asked a white male professor in the discipline if the lecture was accurate. Once the information was confirmed, the student came back and told his professor that he'd doubted what she said, but the other professor validated it. She went on to say that "some students don't believe what I have to say and they will have to go and ask somebody white before they believe it" (Respondent 32: black female). Although the student did not challenge her knowledge directly in class, the fact that he went to a white male professor in her discipline to confirm her information was an indirect challenge to her knowledge and intellectual authority over the class and the material. She added that she believed such double-checking of her material was quite frequent.

Consequences of Racialized Classroom Experiences

"I have to be perfect." For most of the black professors, one consequence of the challenges to their intellectual authority was a need to prove their competence to students (see Table 15.1). They were particularly conscious about doing well because they did not want to reinforce negative attitudes about black people's intelligence. This pressure to be a racial model often manifested itself in overpreparation and in a hyperawareness of speech patterns or mistakes of any kind. One professor stated:

> Given that I'm the only one [black female], you start to think, well God, you know, are people lookin' at what I do? And they've never seen a black female teaching in [the department]. [The discipline is] for white males. . . . So you always have that doubt. And it makes you a little nervous. Makes you want to do that much better so that you don't have to worry about it. (Respondent 19: black female)

Another professor explained:

> When I first started teaching, I felt as though I had to be almost perfect. . . . And even the first couple of years here, if I would misspeak in terms of making a mistake, I always felt as though students would stereotype me, so I always felt as though I couldn't make a mistake. . . . And I just think that if we have more black faculty members who are here, Latino and otherwise, I could feel increasingly the freedom to not be perfect. (Respondent 33: black male)

These professors felt pressure not only to prove individual competence, but also, as reflected in the above quotes, to be perfect for the whole race because people might interpret any negative personal performance as a reflection on African Americans overall.

"If I were white . . ." In addition to the pressure to be perfect, black professors were coping with the frustration of receiving what they viewed as differential treatment by students: 62 percent of black professors raised the issue of a racial double standard (see Table 15.1). Overall they had the sense that white professors automatically commanded students' respect while black professors had to earn it. Respondents also felt that white professors were thought to be smarter, less biased, and more legitimate as faculty members. A black male professor explained that when he doesn't start off the semester by stating all of his credentials, he gets more students challenging him (Respondent 42: black male). As the only non-white professor in his department, he felt that the double standard lay in the need to prove his competence unlike his white colleagues. Consistent with his belief, the white professors in my sample tended to report that their intellectual authority over classroom material was assumed and taken for granted.

Another professor commented as follows on the double standard:

> There are many black professors here at [school] that think there's like a tax, OK—a black tax—on their course evaluations. So like say if they got a 2.5 on their evaluation. That's equivalent to like a 2.8 for a white professor of comparable quality. That may be true and it may not be true; I don't really know.[5] (Respondent 25: black male)

Although he expressed his doubts about the existence of a "black tax," this respondent implied, at the very least, that the presence of such a double standard on evaluations was not implausible.

In addition to the frustration from a racial double standard, some black professors felt that their white colleagues did not understand how much their classroom experiences differed:

> Students expect the traditional hierarchy of society to prevail in the class. That is, white male on the top, and a black woman on the bottom. And they can't get ready for the fact that a black woman is teaching this class! And that the [white male teaching assistants] are not in charge. . . . You know, I think that if I were white, that I wouldn't have to go through those sorts of things in my classroom . . . but at every turn I have to remind students that I am the professor. I'm not just the instructor . . . I have a PhD . . . I have to tell students, "Look. I graduated *summa cum laude*, I got my master's and my PhD . . . I published these books and these articles . . ." to let them know that you know, I may be black, but what you think about in terms of what it means to be black is not necessarily what I am, if it's a negative perception . . . being uneducated and being illiterate and not able to think and basically being an affirmative action kind of a person. So those are the kinds of things that I think make my job more difficult. Much more difficult. And it's unfortunate that the so-called standardized evaluation process that we have been using in colleges and universities [does] not

[5]At this university, the items on the course evaluations are scored on a scale from 0 (lowest) to 4 (highest).

> take these things into consideration. In fact, if you raise [the subject], the college will look at you like you're crazy because they don't deal with that. And they're actually being honest because they don't understand the sheer level of complexity on the part of the professor and the student in dealing with these kinds of issues. So I'm not blaming my colleagues. I'm just saying they're really very ignorant {*pause*} about what goes on in my classes, and the extent to which I have to use measures above and beyond what they have to use to even survive in the classroom. (Respondent 15: black female)

As stated, some black professors sensed that people did not *get it.* They felt that many did not understand how being black made teaching a different job for them than if they were white.

"The Angry Black Woman": Intersections of Gender and Race

While research has shown that white female faculty members struggle for respect and authority in the college classroom (Baker and Copp 1997; Harlow 2002; Martin 1984; Statham, Richardson, and Cook 1991),[6] black women confronted the burden of negotiating both femaleness and blackness. One respondent replied as follows to the question "Do you feel that your race or gender affects their positive or their negative views of you?":

> I definitely believe that there's something to this business about me being angry and not opening up. I'm just so aware of this whole black woman as, you know, angry person kind of myth. Somehow that we're like 70 percent attitude. . . . But at the same time, I'm like look, I'm not gonna be skinnin' and grinnin' sambo every day. . . . I think they don't allow me the room to be serious, and I really do think that's about the "angry black woman with much attitude" myth, you know? . . . I do feel like some students expect that I'm gonna be more maternal, and if I don't live up to that, then the only place that's familiar to them that they can go in terms of judgments is "Oh, then she must have an attitude." So I'm not like "Oh come here, honey, let me hug you, feel my bosom" kind of thing, right . . . but I really do feel like I don't have options. That there are these sort of two caricatures of black womanhood that they're familiar with, and that somehow I have to work within those. (Respondent 9: black female)

In other words, in the case of black women who do not fulfill the "motherly" expectation and who spend time doing serious work in class, students may interpret their seriousness or businesslike approach within the framework of stereotypical images of black femininity: that is, that black women are angry and have an attitude. Although both white and black women reported efforts to avoid being seen as mean or cold, black female faculty members were more likely to report students actually characterizing them as mean, cold, or intimidating on their evaluations. Black women also were more likely to report receiving physical or verbal threats by students (see Table 15.2).

[6] I also found that women's emotional labor in the classroom is more extensive than men's. Emotional labor due to gender, however, functions differently than emotional labor due to race. This essay focuses only on the racial differences.

Emotion Management Strategies

For many professors, especially women, age and experience reduced some of the problems they faced in the college classroom (see Table 15.2). Negative constructions of blackness endure, however, so black professors had to rely on long-term strategies to manage the racial component of teaching.

"I don't care what other people think." As stated earlier, many black professors initially downplayed the effects of their race in the classroom; doing so helped them manage the overall frustration of a double standard due to racism. By reconceptualizing a group problem such as racism as a problem unique to an individual's pedagogical strategies, black professors gained a greater sense of control over their classrooms and felt less like prisoners of students' negative social conditioning. One professor explained that some of his black peers faced racial difficulties in the classroom, but he did not experience this problem:

> And I say this from the perspective of some of my peers, particularly black professors that I'm familiar with from all around the nation. Quite frankly they have a difficult time, some of 'em, dealing with large white classrooms. . . . Some of that, in my opinion, is not just the problem of dealing with a lot of white students. The problem is themselves! If they would just be themselves and stop trying to live up to some ideal that they think other people are looking for, they'd be fine in a lot of occasions. . . . I know [that] a lot of the white majority students, [when] they see a young black professor, they're gonna try 'em, OK. It's just that simple. . . . The question is, you know, is there a center there? Are you centered enough to just know that you have a job to do, and just go ahead and do it, and be yourself, and that should be enough, and if it's not, well, you're probably in the wrong profession. (Respondent 25: black male)

On the one hand, this repondent acknowledged a racial problem that extends beyond the individual black professor ("white majority students, they see a young black professor, they're gonna try 'em"). At the same time, however, he emphasized that such classroom dynamics did not pertain to him ("I say this from the perspective of some of my peers"). Thus it was a problem that ultimately depended on how an individual "centered" himself or herself, even though he heard such comments from black professors everywhere. With this interpretation, he managed individually what would otherwise have been an insurmountable structural problem.

The idea of "just doing my job," "centering," and "looking internally" was common among most of the black faculty members (see Table 15.2). Many explained that as long as they did their job well, their race would ultimately be irrelevant to students. By adopting this attitude, they decreased the emotion management involved in worrying about stereotyping, credibility, and so forth. Explaining how he felt at the start of a new semester, one professor stated:

> When I walk into the classroom, I'm excited to get things started, and I feel very, very confident about my skills . . . and I don't worry about other people's politics anymore. Kind of like I have an internal focus, rather than an external focus about what other people think about me. It's more important how I feel about me. *I finally came to rest with that* (emphasis added). (Respondent 8: black male)

This professor later expressed pride in his new degree of emotional control in the classroom. Not only did he have to learn to reject consistently negative images of himself, but he also had to learn how to suppress his anger in order to teach effectively.

Another professor explained that she *wanted* to stop caring about students' perceptions, but was continuing to struggle with this difficult form of emotion management. In reply to a question about how much she enjoyed teaching, she stated:

> I really try to do it the best way that I can do it. But sometimes it's pretty difficult because I just get tired of dealing with these issues. And I feel that I've been put upon. And I feel that [because] I have to deal with issues that other people don't have to deal with. . . . So I should just forget about it and go into the classroom and do the best job that I can. And that's what I try to do. But some days it is really a challenge. . . . Some of my colleagues just go into class and talk, and that's it. (Respondent 15: black female)

Frustrated by the fact that she could not, like her white colleagues, simply go into class and lecture without concerns about racism, stereotyping, and challenges, this respondent realized that she had to stop caring so much about students' views. At the same time, she observed that just doing the best job she could while ignoring her emotions was extremely difficult.

Analysis and Discussion

Consistent with findings by Feagin and Sikes (1994), many black faculty members were reluctant to say that their race mattered in the classroom, and looked for other reasons to explain their racialized experiences.[7] Ultimately, however, they expressed frustration about what they considered to be students' challenges to their intellectual authority. Despite this frustration, black professors also discussed how their race was beneficial to them in the classroom. Many noted that black students were often happy to see that they had a black professor. In addition, they felt that their race increased their legitimacy when they were teaching on racial topics. According to their reports, however, this legitimacy had rigid boundaries.

Students might feel that African American professors bring their personal experiences to topics of race, thus providing an "authentic" understanding of the issue. Yet at the same time, these professors discussed how their race might detract from their credibility in regard to students' perceptions of their *intellectual* knowledge of the material: that is, the scholarly, "objective" assessment of racial issues. Thus, although students might accept as legitimate certain experiential knowledge transmitted by the professor, black professors simultaneously might face doubts of their competency regarding their intellectual interpretations of the course material. Adding to the professors' frustration was the fact that both white and nonwhite students doubted their academic abilities.

Research by Chambers, Lewis, and Kerezsi (1995) adds credence to the view that students question black professors' competency. They found that white students generally continue

[7]Half of the black men at some point downplayed the effect of their race in the classroom, but only one-third of the black women did so. This difference may exist because black women faced both gender and race discrimination, and so were less likely to downplay racial factors when the gender issues they faced were so widely acknowledged. Therefore their discussion of gender difference also integrated race: they discussed the experience of being *black* women in the classroom.

to perceive African Americans negatively, particularly when "situations involve close social contact . . . or when African Americans are not cast in stereotypical roles" (p. 55). In addition, after Hendrix (1998) interviewed students to explore the influence of race on professors' credibility, she found that overall, black professors were considered less credible than white professors, particularly when the course subject was not directly connected to their race.

Because of doubts about credibility, I found a heightened concern, particularly among black assistant professors, about making a mistake in class. Their responses were consistent with findings by Aguirre (2000), who argued that because of nonwhite faculty members' small numbers and minority status, white students view them solely as affirmative action hires (which they interpret incorrectly as unqualified hires). These perceptions by students, whether conscious or unconscious, contribute to an environment in which faculty members of color may feel that they must "be overachievers in a context where [w]hite faculty are not themselves overachievers" (Aguirre 2000:72).

As a result of this pressure to overachieve, "minority faculty may perceive themselves as occupying a contradictory role in the academic workplace—outsiders but expected to be model citizens in academe," as they try to prove that they are equal to white faculty members (Aguirre 2000:51). The extensive physical and emotional impression management involved in convincing students of their competence and their right to be in charge would be eliminated if students identified immediately with the professor and associated that identity with intellect and professionalism. In this study, most white professors did not mention challenges to their competency, a sign that they did not need to constantly prove and project intellectual authority.

In contrast to their white colleagues, a mistake in class by black professors could be interpreted as incompetence; such an interpretation reinforces negative stereotypes and reflects negatively on black people as a whole. Not only did black professors carry the weight of knowing that their performance might symbolize the potential of an entire racial group, but also many had white colleagues who might not have noticed or acknowledged the differences in their jobs due to race. Most of the white professors in the sample did not note the possibility of racial differences in the classroom.

Being a credit to the race, while also experiencing the frustration of a racial double standard as well as denials from white colleagues that such a double standard exists, requires black professors to manage both personal and professional emotions far more extensively than their white peers. This is particularly the case for younger black professors. Because they have less experience, they may struggle harder than their seasoned colleagues to win a sense of control over their ability to be effective. This challenge is intensified by the feeling that their knowledge as professors is already devalued because they are black. This dynamic is complicated further by gender: the black female respondents reported the effects of both gender and racial stereotypes as they worked to maintain their physical and intellectual presence in the classroom.

To be effective in the classroom, black professors had to learn how to manage the frustration of a racial double standard and the pressure of representing an entire racial group. Trying not to care about students' stereotypical views emerged as a key management strategy. If they could ignore this type of negative student feedback, the professors could gain a greater sense of control over the emotional and physical labor of the classroom.

If (as stated by identity theory) our conception of self is shaped by responses from others through interaction, and if our behavior is influenced by our desire to have our identity reinforced (Stryker 1992), then professors' classroom performances are in part an effort to reinforce, through students, an identity as a good, knowledgeable professor. Many black faculty members, however, reported that such an identity was not reinforced for them through students, in part because of broader cultural understandings of blackness as inferior. Therefore, to function effectively in the classroom, they had to diminish or even eliminate the importance of interaction with students for defining and confirming their identity as teacher.

Thus, the data showed that more than half of the black faculty members engaged in *selective identity construction*. This process can be defined as selectively incorporating responses from interactions that confirm one's identity while rejecting responses that do not, regardless of the significance of that interaction in reinforcing one's self-concept. For example, in spite of the importance of the teacher identity in the classroom, many of the black professors learned to ignore identity cues from interactions with students that challenged their identity as a professor. Instead they developed and reinforced their teacher identity through other means: positive interactions with students; interactions with friends, family, and peers; and internal strength. They rejected interactions that contradicted their self-concept while maintaining an internal focus so that their professor status was validated from within, not just by students.

This process of maintaining an internal focus, however, involves extensive emotion management. According to affect control theory, as stated earlier, when our conception of self is not confirmed, we adjust our definition of a situation or change our behavior so as to relieve the resulting emotional tension (Heise 1989). The black professors who were the most satisfied with teaching, however, worked to ignore those emotional cues altogether instead of paying attention to the cues and trying constantly to change their behavior in order to correct students' perceptions of them. These professors learned to suppress and (in some cases) ultimately eliminate feelings of frustration, anger, or inadequacy in order to diminish the importance of those student interactions; thus students' responses would no longer be integral to shaping their identity as a professor.

Instead of adjusting their actions or the definition of the situation to change how they felt, as affect control theory would predict, these professors learned how to change how they felt in an effort to change, at some point, the definition of the situation. That is, by ignoring the emotions caused by negative interactions with students, and by focusing solely on confirming their identity internally, they hoped, through their display of confidence and competence, to ultimately change how students viewed them and regarded black professors in general.

Once this emotion management has been accomplished, the emotional labor in the classroom becomes much easier because one can focus on projecting excitement, enthusiasm, and friendliness without the need also to manage fear, frustration, and anger. When a professor can focus solely on the traditional aspects of the job, her or his feelings of enjoyment, relaxation, and confidence can increase, with the effect of potentially undermining students' negative stereotypes about blackness. Contrary to Burke's (1991) notion of the identity process, selective identity construction saves professors from experiencing high levels of stress, even when students' perceptions (inputs) do not match professors' self-concepts (the identity standard). Although these black professors viewed racism as a systemic problem, by constructing their professorial identity selectively, they were able to lessen the individual-level effect of race bias in order to function effectively in the classroom.

Conclusion

When black and white faculty members teach, they function in disparate realities. White professors operate in a social space where whiteness is crediting and privileged, but is invisible and thus taken for granted; African American professors function in a space where blackness is discrediting and devalued. The findings reported here suggest that these social and cultural understandings of blackness and whiteness consequently shape the way that black and white professors experience the college classroom and understand, interpret, and manage those experiences. Black professors' work in the classroom is different and more complex than that of their white colleagues because negotiating a devalued racial status requires extensive emotion management; thus an increased amount of work is required to be effective. Because these results are based on faculty experiences at a large, predominantly white university, further research is needed in settings that differ in size, region, and racial composition. In addition, an exploration of the classroom experiences of other nonwhite and international faculty members would be instructive.

The reality for many African American professors is that there will always be students who question their competency, credentials, and ability to teach and assess students' work. This reality, combined with the weight of representing the entire race, can be emotionally draining, particularly for young faculty members who may spend hours going over lectures so as not to be anything less than perfect or totally prepared. To manage the frustrations resulting from a racial double standard, and to be effective in the classroom, the black respondents learned to stay cognizant of existing racial barriers in society while diminishing the importance of those barriers on an individual level in order to prevent racism from debilitating them in their everyday lives.

References

Aguirre, Adalberto. 2000. *Women and Minority Faculty in the Academic Workplace*. San Francisco: Jossey-Bass.

Baker, Fostenia. 1991. "A Study of Black Faculty Perceptions of Hiring, Retention and Tenure Processes in Major White Universities." PhD dissertation, Department of Educational Leadership, George Washington University, Washington, DC.

Baker, Phyllis and Martha Copp. 1997. "Gender Matters Most: The Interaction of Gendered Expectation, Feminist Course Content, and the Pregnancy in Student Course Evaluations." *Teaching Sociology* 25: 29–43.

Banks, William. 1984. "Afro-American Scholars in the University." *American Behavioral Scientist* 27: 325–338.

Bellas, Marcia L. 1999. "Emotional Labor in Academia: The Case of Professors." *Annals of the American Academy of Political and Social Science* 561: 96–110.

Burke, Peter. 1991. "Identity Processes and Social Stress." *American Sociological Review* 56: 836–849.

Chambers, Tony, Jacqueline Lewis, and Paula Kerezsi. 1995. "African American Faculty and White American Students: Cross-Cultural Pedagogy in Counselor Preparation Programs." *Counseling Psychologist* 23: 43–62.

Cohen, E. G. 1982. "Expectation States and Interracial Interaction in School Settings." *Annual Review of Sociology* 8: 209–235.

Feagin, Joe and Melvin Sikes. 1994. *Living with Racism*. Boston: Beacon.

Fields, Cheryl. 1996. "A Morale Dilemma." *Black Issues in Higher Education* 13: 22–23, 25–26, 28–29.

Gallop, Jane. 1997. *Feminist Accused of Sexual Harassment*. Durham, NC: Duke University Press.

Goffman, Erving. 1959. *The Presentation of Self in Everyday Life*. Garden City, NY: Anchor Books.

———. 1963. *Stigma*. New York: Simon and Schuster.

Harlow, Roxanna. 2002. "Teaching as Emotional Labor: The Effects of Professors' Race and Gender on the Emotional Demands of the Undergraduate College Classroom." PhD dissertation, Department of Sociology, Indiana University, Bloomington.

Heise, David. 1989. "Effects of Emotion Displays on Social Identification." *Social Psychology Quarterly* 52:10–21.

Hendrix, Katherine. 1995. "Professor Perceptions of the Influence of Race on Classroom Dynamics and Credibility." Presented at the annual meetings of the Western States Communication Association, February 10–14, Portland, OR.

———. 1998. "Student Perceptions of the Influence of Race on Professor Credibility." *Journal of Black Studies* 28: 738–763.

Hill-Collins, Patricia. 1991. *Black Feminist Thought*. New York: Routledge.

Hochschild, Arlie R. 1983. *The Managed Heart*. Berkeley: University of California Press.

Jacobs, Walter. 1999. "Learning and Living Media Culture in the College Classroom: An Autoethnography of a Possible Postmodern Space." PhD dissertation, Department of Sociology, Indiana University, Bloomington.

Martin, Elaine. 1984. "Power and Authority in the Classroom: Sexist Stereotypes in Teaching Evaluations." *Signs* 9: 482–492.

Menges, Robert and William Exum. 1983. "Barriers to the Progress of Women and Minority Faculty." *Journal of Higher Education* 54: 123–144.

Moore, Valerie Ann. 1996. "Inappropriate Challenges to Professional Authority." *Teaching Sociology* 24: 202–206.

Phelps, Rosemary. 1995. "What's in a Number? Implications for African American Faculty at Predominantly White Colleges and Universities." *Innovative Higher Education* 19: 255–268.

Rains, Frances. 1995. "Views from Within: Women Faculty of Color in a Research University." PhD dissertation, Department of Educational Leadership and Policy Studies, Indiana University, Bloomington.

Rakow, Lana. 1991. "Gender and Race in the Classroom: Teaching Way Out of Line." *Feminist Teacher* 6: 10–13.

Sinegar, Lee Alton. 1987. "Coping with Racial Stressors: A Case Study of Black Professors in White Academe." PhD dissertation, Department of Counseling, George Washington University, Washington, DC.

Smith, Earl and Stephanie Witt. 1993. "A Comparative Study of Occupational Stress among African American and White University Faculty: A Research Note." *Research in Higher Education* 34: 229–241.

Statham, Anne, Laurel Richardson, and Judith Cook. 1991. *Gender and University Teaching*. Albany, NY: SUNY Press.

Stryker, Sheldon. 1992. "Identity Theory." Pp. 871–76 in *Encyclopedia of Sociology*, edited by Edgar Borgatta and Marie Borgatta. New York: Macmillan.

Wood, Elizabeth Anne. 2000. "Working in the Fantasy Factory: The Attention Hypothesis and the Enacting of Masculine Power in Strip Clubs." *Journal of Contemporary Ethnography* 29: 5–31.

16

Double Consciousness: The Souls of Black Folks

W. E. B. DuBois

O water, voice of my heart, crying in the sand,
All night long crying with a mournful cry,
As I lie and listen, and cannot understand
The voice of my heart in my side or the voice of the sea,
O water, crying for rest, is it I, is it I?
All night long the water is crying to me.

Unresting water, there shall never be rest
Till the last moon droop and the last tide fail,
And the fire of the end begin to burn in the west;
And the heart shall be weary and wonder and cry like the sea,
All life long crying without avail,
As the water all night long is crying to me.

—Arthur Symons

Between me and the other world there is ever an unasked question: unasked by some through feelings of delicacy; by others through the difficulty of rightly framing it. All, nevertheless, flutter round it.

They approach me in a half-hesitant sort of way, eye me curiously or compassionately, and then, instead of saying directly, How does it feel to be a problem? they say, I know an excellent colored man in my town; or, I fought at Mechanicsville; or, Do not these Southern outrages make your blood boil? At these I smile, or am interested, or reduce the boiling to a simmer, as the occasion may require. To the real question, How does it feel to be a problem? I answer seldom a word.

1

And yet, being a problem is a strange experience,—peculiar even for one who has never been anything else, save perhaps in babyhood and in Europe. It is in the early days of rollicking boyhood that the revelation first bursts upon one, all in a day, as it were. I remember well when the shadow swept across me. I was a little thing, away up in the hills of New England, where the dark Housatonic winds between Hoosac and Taghkanic to the sea. In a wee wooden schoolhouse, something put it into the boys' and girls' heads to buy gorgeous visiting-cards—ten cents a package—and exchange. The exchange was merry, till one girl, a tall newcomer, refused my card,—refused it peremptorily, with a glance. Then it dawned upon me with a certain suddenness that I was different from the others; or like, mayhap, in heart and life and longing, but shut out from their world by a vast veil. I had thereafter no desire to tear down that veil, to creep through; I held all beyond it in common contempt, and lived above it in a region of blue sky and great wandering shadows.

That sky was bluest when I could beat my mates at examination-time, or beat them at a foot-race, or even beat their stringy heads. Alas, with the years all this fine contempt began to fade; for the worlds I longed for, and all their dazzling opportunities, were theirs, not mine. But they should not keep these prizes, I said; some, all, I would wrest from them. Just how I would do it I could never decide: by reading law, by healing the sick, by telling the wonderful tales that swam in my head,-some way. With other black boys the strife was not so fiercely sunny: their youth shrunk into tasteless sycophancy, or into silent hatred of the pale world about them and mocking distrust of everything white; or wasted itself in a bitter cry, Why did God make me an outcast and a stranger in mine own house? The shades of the prison-house closed round about us all: walls strait and stubborn to the whitest, but relentlessly narrow, tall, and unscalable to sons of night who must plod darkly on in resignation, or beat unavailing palms against the stone, or steadily, half hopelessly, watch the streak of blue above.

2

After the Egyptian and Indian, the Greek and Roman, the Teuton and Mongolian, the Negro is a sort of seventh son, born with a veil, and gifted with second-sight in this American world,—a world which yields him no true self-consciousness, but only lets him see himself through the revelation of the other world. It is a peculiar sensation, this double-consciousness, this sense of always looking at one's self through the eyes of others, of measuring one's soul by the tape of a world that looks on in amused contempt and pity. One ever feels his two-ness,—an American, a Negro; two souls, two thoughts, two unreconciled strivings; two warring ideals in one dark body, whose dogged strength alone keeps it from being torn asunder.

3

The history of the American Negro is the history of this strife,—this longing to attain self-conscious manhood, to merge his double self into a better and truer self. In this merging he wishes neither of the older selves to be lost. He would not Africanize America, for America has too much to teach the world and Africa. He would not bleach his Negro soul in a flood of white Americanism, for he knows that Negro blood has a message for the world. He simply wishes to make it possible for a man to be both a Negro and an American, without being cursed and spit upon by his fellows, without having the doors of Opportunity closed roughly in his face.

4

This, then, is the end of his striving: to be a co-worker in the kingdom of culture, to escape both death and isolation, to husband and use his best powers and his latent genius. These powers of body and mind have in the past been strangely wasted, dispersed, or forgotten. The shadow of a mighty Negro past flits through the tale of Ethiopia the Shadowy and of Egypt the Sphinx. Throughout history, the powers of single black men flash here and there like falling stars, and die sometimes before the world has rightly gauged their brightness. Here in America, in the few days since Emancipation, the black man's turning hither and thither in hesitant and doubtful striving has often made his very strength to lose effectiveness, to seem like absence of power, like weakness. And yet it is not weakness,-it is the contradiction of double aims. The double-aimed struggle of the black artisan—on the one hand to escape white contempt for a nation of mere hewers of wood and drawers of water, and on the other hand to plough and nail and dig for a poverty-stricken horde—could only result in making him a poor craftsman, for he had but half a heart in either cause. By the poverty and ignorance of his people, the Negro minister or doctor was tempted toward quackery and demagogy; and by the criticism of the other world, toward ideals that made him ashamed of his lowly tasks. The would-be black savant was confronted by the paradox that the knowledge his people needed was a twice-told tale to his white neighbors, while the knowledge which would teach the white world was Greek to his own flesh and blood. The innate love of harmony and beauty that set the ruder souls of his people a-dancing and a-singing raised but confusion and doubt in the soul of the black artist; for the beauty revealed to him was the soul-beauty of a race which his larger audience despised, and he could not articulate the message of another people. This waste of double aims, this seeking to satisfy two unreconciled ideals, has wrought sad havoc with the courage and faith and deeds of ten thousand thousand people,—has sent them often wooing false gods and invoking false means of salvation, and at times has even seemed about to make them ashamed of themselves.

5

Away back in the days of bondage they thought to see in one divine event the end of all doubt and disappointment; few men ever worshipped Freedom with half such unquestioning faith as did the American Negro for two centuries. To him, so far as he thought and dreamed, slavery was indeed the sum of all villainies, the cause of all sorrow, the root of all prejudice; Emancipation was the key to a promised land of sweeter beauty than ever stretched before the eyes of wearied Israelites. In song and exhortation swelled one refrain—Liberty; in his tears and curses the God he implored had Freedom in his right hand. At last it came,—suddenly, fearfully, like a dream. With one wild carnival of blood and passion came the message in his own plaintive cadences:—

> *"Shout, O children!*
> *Shout, you're free!*
> *For God has bought your liberty!"*

6

Years have passed away since then,—ten, twenty, forty; forty years of national life, forty years of renewal and development, and yet the swarthy spectre sits in its accustomed seat at the Nation's feast. In vain do we cry to this our vastest social problem:—

> *"Take any shape but that, and my firm nerves*
> *Shall never tremble!"*

7

The Nation has not yet found peace from its sins; the freedman has not yet found in freedom his promised land. Whatever of good may have come in these years of change, the shadow of a deep disappointment rests upon the Negro people,—a disappointment all the more bitter because the unattained ideal was unbounded save by the simple ignorance of a lowly people.

8

The first decade was merely a prolongation of the vain search for freedom, the boon that seemed ever barely to elude their grasp,—like a tantalizing will-o'-the-wisp, maddening and misleading the headless host. The holocaust of war, the terrors of the Ku-Klux Klan, the lies of carpet-baggers, the disorganization of industry, and the contradictory advice of friends and foes, left the bewildered serf with no new watchword beyond the old cry for freedom. As the time flew, however, he began to grasp a new idea. The ideal of liberty demanded for its attainment powerful means, and these the Fifteenth Amendment gave him.

The ballot, which before he had looked upon as a visible sign of freedom, he now regarded as the chief means of gaining and perfecting the liberty with which war had partially endowed him. And why not? Had not votes made war and emancipated millions? Had not votes enfranchised the freedmen? Was anything impossible to a power that had done all this?

A million black men started with renewed zeal to vote themselves into the kingdom. So the decade flew away, the revolution of 1876 came, and left the half-free serf weary, wondering, but still inspired. Slowly but steadily, in the following years, a new vision began gradually to replace the dream of political power,—a powerful movement, the rise of another ideal to guide the unguided, another pillar of fire by night after a clouded day. It was the ideal of "book-learning"; the curiosity, born of compulsory ignorance, to know and test the power of the cabalistic letters of the white man, the longing to know. Here at last seemed to have been discovered the mountain path to Canaan; longer than the highway of Emancipation and law, steep and rugged, but straight, leading to heights high enough to overlook life.

9

Up the new path the advance guard toiled, slowly, heavily, doggedly; only those who have watched and guided the faltering feet, the misty minds, the dull understandings, of the dark pupils of these schools know how faithfully, how piteously, this people strove to learn. It was weary work. The cold statistician wrote down the inches of progress here and there, noted also where here and there a foot had slipped or some one had fallen. To the tired climbers, the horizon was ever dark, the mists were often cold, the Canaan was always dim and far away. If, however, the vistas disclosed as yet no goal, no resting-place, little but flattery and criticism, the journey at least gave leisure for reflection and self-examination; it changed the child of Emancipation to the youth with dawning self-consciousness, self-realization, self-respect. In those sombre forests of his striving his own soul rose before him, and he saw himself,—darkly as through a veil; and yet he saw in himself some faint revelation of his power, of his mission. He began to have a dim feeling that, to attain his place in the world, he must be himself, and not another. For the first time he sought to analyze the burden he bore upon his back, that dead-weight of social degradation partially masked behind a half-named Negro problem. He felt his poverty; without a cent, without a home, without land, tools, or savings, he had entered into competition with rich, landed, skilled neighbors. To be a poor man is hard, but to be a poor race in a land of dollars is the very bottom of hardships. He felt the weight of his ignorance,—not simply of letters, but of life, of business, of the humanities; the accumulated sloth and shirking and awkwardness of decades and centuries shackled his hands and feet. Nor was his burden all poverty and ignorance. The red stain of bastardy, which two centuries of systematic legal defilement of Negro women had stamped upon his race, meant not only the loss of ancient African chastity, but also the hereditary weight of a mass of corruption from white adulterers, threatening almost the obliteration of the Negro home.

10

A people thus handicapped ought not to be asked to race with the world, but rather allowed to give all its time and thought to its own social problems. But alas! while sociologists gleefully count his bastards and his prostitutes, the very soul of the toiling, sweating black man is darkened by the shadow of a vast despair. Men call the shadow prejudice, and learnedly explain it as the natural defence of culture against barbarism, learning against ignorance, purity against crime, the "higher" against the "lower" races. To which the Negro cries Amen! and swears that to so much of this strange prejudice as is founded on just homage to civilization, culture, righteousness, and progress, he humbly bows and meekly does obeisance. But before that nameless prejudice that leaps beyond all this he stands helpless, dismayed, and well-nigh speechless; before that personal disrespect and mockery, the ridicule and systematic humiliation, the distortion of fact and wanton license of fancy, the cynical ignoring of the better and the boisterous welcoming of the worse, the all-pervading desire to inculcate disdain for everything black, from Toussaint to the devil,—before this there rises a sickening despair that would disarm and discourage any nation save that black host to whom "discouragement" is an unwritten word.

11

But the facing of so vast a prejudice could not but bring the inevitable self-questioning, self-disparagement, and lowering of ideals which ever accompany repression and breed in an atmosphere of contempt and hate. Whisperings and portents came borne upon the four winds: Lo! We are diseased and dying, cried the dark hosts; we cannot write, our voting is vain; what need of education, since we must always cook and serve? And the Nation echoed and enforced this self-criticism, saying: Be content to be servants, and nothing more; what need of higher culture for half-men? Away with the black man's ballot, by force or fraud,—and behold the suicide of a race! Nevertheless, out of the evil came something of good,—the more careful adjustment of education to real life, the clearer perception of the Negroes' social responsibilities, and the sobering realization of the meaning of progress.

12

So dawned the time of Sturm und Drang: storm and stress to-day rocks our little boat on the mad waters of the world-sea; there is within and without the sound of conflict, the burning of body and rending of soul; inspiration strives with doubt, and faith with vain questionings. The bright ideals of the past,—physical freedom, political power, the training of brains and the training of hands,—all these in turn have waxed and waned, until even the last grows dim and overcast. Are they all wrong,—all false? No, not that, but each alone was over-simple and incomplete,—the dreams of a credulous race-childhood, or the fond imaginings of the other world which does not know and does not want to know our power. To be really true, all these ideals must be melted and welded into one. The training of the schools we need to-day more than ever,—the training of deft hands, quick eyes and ears, and above all the broader, deeper, higher culture of gifted minds and pure hearts. The power of the ballot we need in sheer self-defence,—else what shall save us from a second slavery? Freedom, too, the long-sought, we still seek,—the freedom of life and limb, the freedom to work and think, the freedom to love and aspire. Work, culture, liberty,—all these we need, not singly but together, not successively but together, each growing and aiding each, and all striving toward that vaster ideal that swims before the Negro people, the ideal of human brotherhood, gained through the unifying ideal of Race; the ideal of fostering and developing the traits and talents of the Negro, not in opposition to or contempt for other races, but rather in large conformity to the greater ideals of the American Republic, in order that some day on American soil two world-races may give each to each those characteristics both so sadly lack. We the darker ones come even now not altogether empty-handed: There are to-day no truer exponents of the pure human spirit of the Declaration of Independence than the American Negroes; there is no true American music but the wild sweet melodies of the Negro slave; the American fairy tales and folk-lore are Indian and African; and, all in all, we black men seem the sole oasis of simple faith and reverence in a dusty desert of dollars and smartness. Will America be poorer if she replace her brutal dyspeptic blundering with light-hearted but determined Negro humility? or her coarse and cruel wit with loving jovial good-humor? or her vulgar music with the soul of the Sorrow Songs?

13

Merely a concrete test of the underlying principles of the great republic is the Negro Problem, and the spiritual striving of the freedmen's sons is the travail of souls whose burden is almost beyond the measure of their strength, but who bear it in the name of an historic race, in the name of this the land of their fathers' fathers, and in the name of human opportunity.

* * *

14

And now what I have briefly sketched in large outline let me on coming pages tell again in many ways, with loving emphasis and deeper detail, that men may listen to the striving in the souls of black folk.

17

*Gender Matters Most: The Interaction of Gendered Expectations, Feminist Course Content, and Pregnancy in Student Course Evaluations**

Phyllis Baker
University of Northern Iowa

Martha Copp
East Tennessee State University

In this paper, we explore undergraduate students' contradictory expectations of a woman professor (Dr. Baker) who taught a feminist course. Over the course of three semesters teaching the same class, the professor got pregnant and carried her child to term. Using qualitative and quantitative teaching evaluation data from this course, we analyze how students' reactions to their professor shifted depending on their professor's capacity to fulfill their gendered expectations. We also examine how the interactions between students' gendered expectations, their reactions to feminist course content, and their responses to their pregnant professor influenced the students' teaching evaluations of Dr. Baker.

*We would like to thank Sharon Hays, Sherryl Kleinman, Sherry Nuss, Roger Sell, and anonymous reviewers for their helpful comments on this paper. Would also like to thank Cynthia Jacob-Chien and Robert Hunter for preliminary research assistance. This paper was first read at the annual meetings of the Midwest Sociological Society, held in St. Louis, MS on March 11, 1994. Address correspondence to: Phyllis Baker, Department of Sociology and Anthropology, University of Northern Iowa, Cedar Falls, IA 50614-0513; e-mail: BAKER@UNLEDU; Martha Copp, Department of Sociology and Anthropology, East Tennessee State University, Johnson City, TN 37614-0644; e-mail: COPP@ETSU.ETSU-TN.EDU. Order of authorship is alphabetical.

Over the past three decades, unprecedented numbers of women have entered the male-created and male-dominated university professoriate in the United States. Even when women's presence in academia seems commonplace, students, colleagues, and administrators set barriers for women professors by implicitly or explicitly assuming that faculty positions are best held by men (Friedman 1985; Martin 1984; Rakow 1991). Because universities continue to be male-dominated institutions, deep-seated biases against women emerge via gender pay gaps for professors and promotion rates that favor men (Caplan 1995; Johnsrud 1993; Slater 1995). Women faculty members also may experience this "chilly climate" (Hall and Sandler 1984) in their relationships with students and in their subsequent teaching evaluations. Because women's culturally defined gender status clashes with their occupational status as professors (Hodge et al. 1964; Hughes 1971; Statham et al. 1991), students may hold contradictory and unrealistic expectations of them. These contradictions may make it hard for women faculty members to receive outstanding teaching evaluations, because students judge women by their gender performance (West and Zimmerman 1987) first, and by their teaching second.

In this paper, we analyze the complexities of students' gendered expectations by considering what happens when a woman professor (Dr. Phyllis Baker, coauthor) teaches a course with controversial (feminist) content and then becomes pregnant. We examine the interactions between students' gendered expectations, their reactions to feminist course content, and their responses to their pregnant professor. By analyzing qualitative and quantitative data from Dr. Baker's teaching evaluations over three terms, we will show that when students' gendered expectations of their professor were fulfilled, they rated her teaching highly, even though she taught from a feminist perspective and was pregnant. We will also show that when students' gendered expectations failed to be met, their willingness to tolerate feminist material and Dr. Baker's pregnancy practically disappeared, and many students berated Dr. Baker in their teaching evaluations.

In addition to analyzing students' situational reactions to Dr. Baker and her teaching, we explore how Dr. Baker's colleagues interpreted the students' evaluations. We bring our discussion to a close by addressing the implications of our findings. In that section, we suggest that faculty members address students' expectations by directly encouraging them to question gender assumptions. We also provide a useful critique of the assumptions about how professors "profess" that are built into teaching evaluations and their implications for tenure and promotion decisions. Although our paper focuses on one professor teaching one course, we put forth explanations that we hope others, especially women and minorities, will examine for themselves.

Literature Review

When women faculty members enter the classroom, gender, feminist course content, and pregnancy serve as potential and powerful liabilities. Most crucial are the gendered expectations students bring to their relationships with women professors. Researchers argue that contradictory student expectations of women faculty members arise because "women are supposed to be warm, friendly, supportive and deferential, yet professionals are supposed to be objective, neutral, authoritative, and able to offer constructive criticism" (Martin 1984:486).

As Edwin Schur (1983:51) pointed out, "[W]omen are often subjected to norms that contradict one another. As a consequence their efforts to conform to one standard may be treated as deviance when viewed from the opposing [standard]."[1] Not only do students maintain contradictory expectations of women professors, but they also expect different things from women than they do from men. Students expect more sympathy, concern, and leniency from women professors than from men (Bernard 1964; Statham et al. 1991). Gender plays a crucial and sometimes deleterious role in the student-female professor relationship.

Feminist course content may add to a woman professor's liabilities when students perceive the material and the professor as "sexist" and "unfair," which means biased against men (Rakow 1991). Several researchers report angry and defensive reactions from students toward feminist professors (Culley 1985; Davis 1992; Ito 1992; Maher and Tetreault 1994; Neitz 1985). Margo Culley (1985) found that when she taught large introductory courses on women's issues students denied the existence of gender inequality and then insinuated that she hated and blamed men. Francis A. Maher and Mary Kay Tetreault (1994:238) described how one woman sociology professor's students criticized her "as a 'griping,' 'offensive,' 'man-hating feminist' " in their written evaluations of her teaching. While these and other reactions may be attributed to a backlash against feminism that swept across college campuses in the United States (Deay and Stitzel 1991; Faludi 1991; Kamen 1991), they also signal students' strong ambivalence toward women professors as the messengers of feminism during a time when feminism is particularly unpopular.

In addition to gender and feminist course content, pregnancy may diminish women professors' good standing in the classroom. Because many people stereotype pregnant women as emotionally unbalanced and physically uncomfortable (Kleinplatz 1992), students might assume that a pregnant professor is easily agitated, rude, and sickly.

Bringing these different conditions—gendered expectations, feminist course content, and pregnancy—together in the classroom may produce strong reactions in students and lead them to view their woman professor as deviant. For this reason, students may give their professor negative evaluations as a way to punish her for violating their gendered expectations (Schur 1983). The connection to teaching evaluations is demonstrated when students positively evaluate teachers who conform to their gendered expectations. Statham et al. (1991) found that the more women and men professors adhered to gender-appropriate teaching styles, the higher students evaluated them. In her study of how students define professors' ideal traits, Rubin (1981:974) surmised that "students may be judging male and female professors on separate issues" having more to do with gender than teaching competence. And in his thorough review of the research on students' evaluations of men and women college teachers, Feldman (1993:178) stated that "part of what students view in their teachers—including any differences they see between male and female teachers—they may have actually helped to encourage or to 'produce' by their own expectations and demands." Hence, we argue that gender, feminist course content, and pregnancy affect student evaluations of women professors.

[1]Whenever professors differ from the white male heterosexual norm, they must contend with how others perceive their differences and hope that their characteristics will not be perceived as liabilities (Bronstein 1993; Bronstein et al. 1993; Ginorio 1995; Henry 1993–4; Johnsrud 1993; Rakow 1991).

Setting and Background

The setting for our study, the University of Northern Iowa (UNI), is a state university of approximately 11,000 students, most of whom are academically well prepared, instate residents. Iowa is a rural, agricultural state with a traditional, democratic populace and an excellent public school system. Although UNI students' beliefs seem to vary widely, many hold traditional values, stopping short of right-wing conservatism. Most students work hard and act respectfully toward professors regardless of their opinions about the work assigned to them.

Our course evaluation data spanned three terms—spring, summer, and fall 1992—of a general education course entitled "Women, Men, and Society" taught by Dr. Baker. During this time period, Dr. Baker became pregnant and carried her child to term. The course was taught in two different classroom contexts. In the spring and fall terms the class met at the same time of day in a large lecture hall, followed a lecture format, and drew approximately 200 students each time. The tone of the classroom was "traditional," in that Dr. Baker directed the class without sharing control with the students. During the summer term, the class met in a small classroom, incorporated much discussion, and drew 23 students. In comparison to the large lecture class, this small class was intimate and informal in tone.

Each time Dr. Baker taught the large lecture course, she used the same materials, made similar requirements, and wrote similar multiple-choice examinations, with minor fine-tuning. When she taught the smaller class, she used the same course materials but presented them more informally and replaced multiple-choice examinations with essay examinations. Regardless of the classroom context, Dr. Baker taught from a feminist perspective and made the sociological material more understandable by providing personal examples from her everyday life or from the students'. Additionally, so that students would gain a positive appreciation of women who perform multiple roles (e.g., combining work and family), Dr. Baker found one occasion each semester to bring her daughter to class.

Data and Analysis Strategies

The teaching evaluation instrument used in all UNI classes contained two parts. In the first part, students responded to ten statements on a Likert scale ranging from one to seven, with one being "strongly disagree" and seven being "strongly agree." In the second part, students voluntarily wrote remarks about the course and the teacher. The quantitative portion of the evaluation instrument asked students to rate the professor's knowledge of the subject, preparation for class, organization of the course, general attitude, accessibility, clarity of explanation, interest and enthusiasm, fairness of testing and grading, stimulation of learning, and clarity of purposes and objectives. The students were also asked to assign the professor an overall grade. Means were calculated for each evaluation item. For the written comment portion of the evaluation, students could write whatever they wanted in the ample space provided. Students' comments were then typed by work-study students and the professor received a copy for her records.

We analyzed both the quantitative and the written portions of the evaluations. For the quantitative data, we carried out a non-parametric test of the differences between each semester's evaluation item means. To analyze the qualitative portion of the evaluations, both authors read the written comments several times, then discussed them collectively. We next wrote memos on their content and emotional tone (See Lofland and Lofland 1995:186–97). We chose a simple coding scheme of identifying the comments that were clearly positive and clearly negative for each term. We coded comments as clearly positive when students indicated that the professor and/or the course were excellent to good; we coded comments as clearly negative when students expressed dislike or disapproval of the professor and/or the course. We excluded vague comments. We also excluded comments that merely articulated pleasure or displeasure with an examination, a book, a topic, and so on. One author did the initial coding and the other double-checked it for accuracy; thus, we jointly confirmed the number of positive and negative comments. By excluding vague comments and verifying the coding, we believe that our findings accurately reflect the content, tone, and incidence of positive and negative comments for each term.

Quantitative Findings

Ninety-nine students in the spring term filled out the teaching evaluation questionnaire, 22 in the summer, and 124 in the fall. Mean scores for each evaluation item were lowest in the fall semester and highest in the summer (see Table 17.1 and Figure 17.1).

Although the instructor and the feminist course content remained the same, the item means differed greatly from one semester to the next. Because the evaluation item means were based on ordinal-level rather than interval-level data, the nonparametric "sign test" provided a valid test of the differences in scores between each semester (Gibbons 1993). The sign test estimates the probability of observing a specific number of positive and negative differences between each semester's evaluation item means.

TABLE 17.1 ***Means and Standard Deviations for Students' Evaluation Scores, by Term***

	Spring 1992 (N = 99)		*Summer 1992 (N = 22)*		*Fall 1992 (N = 124)*	
Evaluation Item	*Mean*	*SD*	*Mean*	*SD*	*Mean*	*SD*
1 Knowledge	6.141	.888	6.682	.466	5.887	1.152
2 Preparation	5.949	.957	6.455	.582	5.855	1.209
3 Organization	5.768	1.188	6.364	.710	5.694	1.252
4 Attitude	5.131	1.509	6.136	.919	4.718	1.678
5 Accessibility	4.929	1.437	6.045	.976	5.105	1.447
6 Clarity	5.626	1.244	6.318	.700	5.258	1.464
7 Interest/Enthusiasm	6.265	.954	6.81	.393	6.048	1.256
8 Fairness	5.394	1.413	6.455	.782	5.210	1.677
9 Stimulated Learning	5.263	1.580	6.409	.717	4.790	1.691
10 Objectives Clear	5.515	1.344	6.318	.819	5.161	1.653
11 Grade on 4-Point Scale	3.143	.857	3.727	.445	2.842	.992

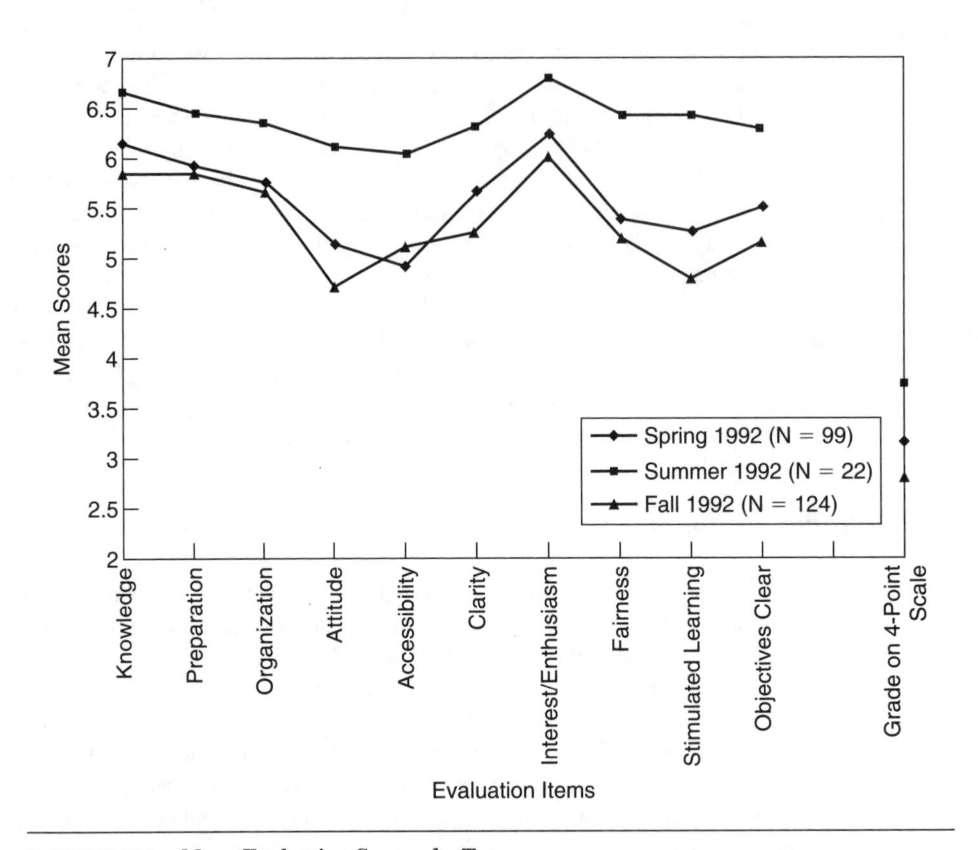

FIGURE 17.1 ***Mean Evaluation Scores, by Term.***

If students' reactions to Dr. Baker did not differ appreciably in the spring, summer, and fall semesters, then the differences in the mean scores would be evenly distributed about zero (that is, positive and negative outcomes would be equally likely to occur). Yet, if students' evaluations between the spring and fall semester took a negative shift, then the number of negative outcomes would greatly exceed the number of positive outcomes. And if students' evaluations during the summer took a positive shift compared to the spring or fall, then the number of positive outcomes would greatly exceed the number of negative outcomes.

Table 17.2 reports the number of positive and negative differences in means between each semester. The spring-fall comparison yielded 10 negative outcomes and one positive outcome, with $p < 0.006$ for a one-tailed test. The comparisons between spring-summer and summer-fall yielded zero negative and 11 positive outcomes, with $p < 0.0005$ for a one-tailed test. Thus, the fall semester evaluation item means were significantly lower than the spring semester, and the summer scores were significantly higher than either the spring or the fall.

We compared the summer term with the spring and fall semesters despite the large difference in class sizes. Some readers might consider this an inappropriate comparison, thinking that class size would outweigh any other influence on students' evaluations. Many

TABLE 17.2 ***Between-Semester Differences in Mean Scores***

Item	*Fall-Spring*	*Summer-Spring*	*Summer-Fall*
1	–.254	+.541	+.795
2	–.094	+.506	+.600
3	–.074	+.596	+.670
4	–.413	+1.005	+1.418
5	+.176	+1.116	+.940
6	–.368	+.692	+1.060
7	–.217	+.545	+.762
8	–.184	+1.061	+1.245
9	–.473	+1.146	+1.619
10	–.354	+.803	+1.157
11	–.301	+.584	+.885
Sign Test:	$p < 0.006$ (one-tailed probability)	$p < 0.0005$ (one-tailed)	$p < 0.0005$ (one-tailed)

instructors believe that classroom size strongly influences students' teaching evaluations (the larger the class, the lower the evaluations). Yet published findings are inconsistent, especially when evaluation items ask students to rate the instructor's presentation skills rather than to rate her or his sensitivity and social interaction skills (Feldman 1984; Hamilton 1980; Marsh et al. 1979; Sidanius and Crane 1989; Whitten and Umble 1980). If class size matters in this study, then its influence occurs mainly through how well Dr. Baker could enact (or appear to enact) a gender-appropriate teaching style. As we will argue more in the next section, being able to demonstrate one's sensitivity, warmth, and friendliness toward students is much more difficult in a large class than in a small one. Students' comments provide a better opportunity to examine this question, so we will turn to them next.[2]

Qualitative Findings and Interpretations

In this section, we first provide an overview of the positive, negative, and miscellaneous comments Dr. Baker received each term. Following our brief discussion regarding the meaning of the different proportions of positive and negative comments, we analyze the conditions that shaped students' comments and provide examples of their transformations over time.

[2]Evaluations of Dr. Baker's teaching by her colleagues are consistently very good. For example, in a 1993 letter, the head of Dr. Baker's department stated that in the "Women, Men, and Society" course Dr. Baker presented the material clearly and confidently, that she had "explored and adopted teaching methods designed to enhance learning in a large group lecture," and that she "provided a scholarly and productive class to her students." In an evaluation letter written by her departmental assessment committee, the authors wrote that they "found Dr. Baker to be well prepared, very knowledgeable, and felt that her presentations were clear and interesting. She seemed confident and at ease. It appeared to both of us that she had good rapport with the students."

The proportion of students' positive and negative comments vary remarkably from one semester to the next (see Table 17.3 for a summary). We found striking disparities that parallel the significant differences in the quantitative data. Table 17.3 shows that the proportion of positive comments grew significantly in the summer and dropped significantly in the fall when Dr. Baker taught the large lecture class in late pregnancy. Likewise, it shows that the proportion of negative comments doubled from the spring to the fall semester. Chi-square tests of the observed frequencies of students' comments are reported in Table 17.3.

We argue that three conditions influenced students' evaluations of Dr. Baker. Students' expectations about and perceptions of Dr. Baker's gender performance, their reactions to the feminist course content, and their responses to Dr. Baker's pregnancy interacted to produce strong differences in their comments over the spring, summer, and fall terms. Depending on how well Dr. Baker could fulfill students' gendered expectations, students reacted differently to the feminist course content and to her pregnancy. Their comments reflect these differences in number, tone, and content. Thus, teaching a large class from a feminist perspective while visibly pregnant exaggerated the contradictions in students' expectations for a woman professor. The more severe the contradictions in students' expectations, the harsher their comments. Yet when Dr. Baker taught the small, intimate class, she unwittingly fulfilled students' gendered expectations of her as a woman; consequently, students' comments were over whelmingly positive. By fulfilling their gendered expectations, students' negative reactions to feminism and Dr. Baker's pregnancy all but disappeared.

Next, we will provide a term-by-term discussion of the content of students' comments. We start with the spring 1992 comments when Dr. Baker became pregnant but not visibly so. Independently of the other terms, we discuss the effects of gender and feminist course content on students' evaluations of Dr. Baker. Then we turn to the fall 1992 written comments, when Dr. Baker entered her last trimester of pregnancy, and compare those comments with the spring comments. Finally, we report on students' comments from the summer 1992 course taught between the spring and fall terms.

TABLE 17.3 ***Numerical Summary of Written Comments, by Code***

	Spring 1992 N = 52		*Fall 1992 N = 57*		*Summer 1992 N = 20*	
Comment Code	n	%	n	%	n	%
Positive	21	40	19	33	18	90
Negative	11	21	25	44	1	5
Other	20	38.5	13	23	1	5
Total	52	100	57	100	20	100

Comparison of frequencies:

1. All Semesters: Chi-square = 27.12, df = 4, $p = 0.00002$
2. Spring and Fall: Chi-square = 6.81, df = 2, $p = .0331$
3. Spring and Summer: Chi-square = 14.37, df = 2, $p = .0008$
4. Summer and Fall: Chi-square = 19.1, df = 2, $p = .0001$

Spring Term 1992

Of the 99 students who completed the spring 1992 evaluations, 52 wrote comments. According to our analysis, 21 comments were clearly positive (40% of the total written comments) and 11 were clearly negative (21% of the total written responses). Students' positive comments emphasized three themes. First, and most commonly, students reported experiencing raised consciousness. For example, a student wrote, "I really enjoyed this course and feel it opened my eyes a great deal to the role women and men play and the discrimination that takes place."[3] Another said, "I think you have changed my generally conservative attitude towards women being 'oppressed'." For the second positive theme, students said that they found the course and the professor interesting and enjoyable. Comments that comprised the third theme were those that judged Dr. Baker to be a concerned teacher who was well-versed in the subject matter. In one such comment, a student wrote, "Dr. Baker is both approachable and knowledgeable. She is a concerned and thorough instructor." By saying that their consciousness had been raised regarding gender inequality and by commenting that Dr. Baker acted concerned and approachable, these students were saying that, overall, Dr. Baker and her course met or exceeded their expectations. By praising her for showing concern and being approachable, these students communicated that Dr. Baker fulfilled their gendered expectations.

The students who commented negatively perceived Dr. Baker in a different light. Their negative comments followed two themes: lack of consideration and professor bias. Two students criticized Dr. Baker for not showing them enough consideration. One student complained about the amount and times of Dr. Baker's customary office hours and another reported that she or he would appreciate it if the professor gave less work and "realized there are other classes than just this one." Both of these comments fall into the category of showing sensitivity to students. Given the large class size and the lecture format that minimized teacher-student interaction, demonstrating sensitivity to each student would be difficult (Crawford and MacLeod 1990; Feldman 1984; Sidanius and Crane 1989). Yet a convincing case can be made that in large lecture classes, students expect a female professor to be more empathic and considerate than a male professor. Bennett (1982) found that students negatively evaluate women professors who fail to provide the extra support that they expect from women. Because "the supportive traits of concern, friendliness, and understanding are regarded highly for women professors [by their students]" (Rubin 1981:972), criticisms involving any of these traits signal students' failed gender expectations. These students thought Dr. Baker was not doing a good job because she did not go out of her way to accommodate them. We believe that Dr. Baker fulfilled gendered expectations for those students who perceived her as concerned and approachable but did not fill gendered expectations for others.

Charges of professor bias can be seen in seven negative comments that variously referred to Dr. Baker as a "male basher," said she was "biased," or characterized the class this way. For example, a student wrote, "After the first unit, this class became a men bashing class since most things were blamed on men and illustrated how women accepted the role handed to them." Another student commented, "The only problem I have is that sometimes [Dr. Baker] tends to present opinions as facts and allows this to make a male-bashing session."

[3]Student comments have been quoted in their original form.

Other students reported that "[Dr. Baker] seems to be biased against men." These negative comments convey important reactions to Dr. Baker and to the feminist course content.

Published accounts by other feminist professors support our findings. Mary Jo Neitz (1985) argued that students react negatively to feminist course content because male students do not think that women's oppression exists and female students think that oppression once existed but no longer affects them. Inequality strikes them as incorrect or exaggerated. Alternatively, privileged students may question structural inequality because they believe that differences between women and men are due to individual circumstances (see Bohmer and Briggs 1991) and because they believe that inequality should be resolved individually rather than collectively (Renzetti 1987). Nancy J. Davis (1992:234) told the story of a male student who left during the middle of her class covering feminist movements and "walked around to the front entrance and shouted in at [her]: 'She's a dyke!'' This experience, along with other reports of negative student reactions toward feminist women professors (Culley 1985; Ito 1992; Maher and Tetreault 1994; Neirz 1985) suggests that students may react negatively to both the feminist content and the professor.

Thus, perhaps some students claimed that Dr. Baker was male-bashing or biased because they did not like having a woman explain to them how people in our society favor men at the expense of women. Especially if they believed that professors should display objectivity (Martin 1984), then a woman lecturing on gender inequality reveals her "bias" and violates the professional stereotype. Consequently, the students who claimed that the course was biased or male-bashing said more than that they disagreed with the feminist perspective of the course. They implied that Dr. Baker lacked the objectivity to comment on gender in society. As a woman, a member of an oppressed group, they may have perceived her as exaggerating the extent of gender inequality. Rather than simply disagree with the perspective, students responded negatively toward Dr. Baker as a professor.

Students' expectations of women professors are contradictory because the low status of women clashes with the high status of professors. When Dr. Baker taught a large lecture class, contradictions in the students' expectations were heightened because she could not provide a convincing display of support, concern, and friendliness to each student. Furthermore, students' responses to the feminist course content interacted with their gendered expectations so that they perceived their professor as biased, rather than the objective professional they expected.

Fall Term 1992

During fall 1992, Dr. Baker taught the large lecture class almost exactly the same way, but under a new condition—advanced pregnancy. As the quantitative portion of the evaluations showed, students gave Dr. Baker significantly lower scores. Of the 124 students evaluating Dr. Baker, 57 wrote comments: 19 (33% of the total written comments) were clearly positive and 25 were clearly negative (44% of the total). Comparing the fall term to the spring term, the number of positive comments dropped from 40 percent to 33 percent, and the number of negative comments more than doubled from 21 percent in the spring to 44 percent in the fall.

The positive comments reflected no definite pattern or theme, unlike those from the spring term. Only one student made a comment about her or his consciousness being raised. Other statements contained the perception of Dr. Baker as fair and easy to relate to or said that the course was interesting. For example, a student stated, "She's a pretty cool teacher. Fair and listens." In other comments, students noted that they liked their professor's demeanor. One student wrote, "I liked your sense of humor and you were very personable." Although the positive comments reflected that some students liked Dr. Baker, their tone lacked the enthusiasm found in the spring term.

Unlike the amorphous positive comments, the negative comments exhibited distinct themes that paralleled the spring term. Twenty-two of the 25 negative comments (88% of the negative comments and 38% of all comments) called Dr. Baker biased and a male basher or claimed that she was rude. Many of the negative comments exuded a tone of sharp disapproval, which struck us as qualitatively different from the spring term.

As during the spring term, many students responded to the feminist course content by claiming that Dr. Baker was biased or a male basher, but their tone seemed more hateful. As a mild criticism, one student wrote, "I got the feeling that all males were complete jerks and that women were the superior race." Several other students showed little restraint. For example, one student alleged that

> This class is about women, men, and society—its not a class for male bashing and total concentration on how women are mistreated. Believe it or not Dr. Baker—women are not discriminated in every aspect of life. We all got tired of hearing Dr. Baker bitch about how bad women have it and all she does is rip on men.

And another student wrote bluntly: "Far too biased, do you hate men?" Thus, although the comments about male-bashing and professor bias resembled those in the spring term, they shifted to an angry and hateful tone and doubled in number.

Unlike the spring term, a second theme in the students' negative comments was rudeness. Students harshly criticized Dr. Baker when they claimed that she was "rude." One student reported, "I feel Dr. Baker was rude at times, constantly a ego maniac, a definate (sic) male basher." Importantly, several of these students believed that the source of rudeness was Dr. Baker's pregnancy. The following two quotations demonstrate this point: "I feel Dr. Baker was very rude and negative to all of her students. I feel you had PMS during your pregnancy" and "When I had interactions with Dr. Baker she was rude. She yelled at me for answering the way I did on a test. I don't think she should have been teaching while pregnant because she was moody and crabby." In a third such example, a student claimed that the pregnancy sabotaged Dr. Baker's work performance: "I think Dr. Baker was irritable because of her pregnancy and this effected her teaching ability and her effectiveness in class." Negative comments like these came as a surprise to Dr. Baker; we surmise that the students perceived Dr. Baker in a dramatically different light than others did in previous semesters.

Because these students mentioned Dr. Baker's pregnancy in their claims that she was rude and crabby, we assume that they held stereotypical beliefs about pregnancy—that pregnancy is a time of emotional up heaval and physical discomfort (Kleinplatz 1992). As a result, students who reacted negatively to Dr. Baker's pregnancy thus assumed she was physically uncomfortable and rude.

Teaching a large class in a formal (professorial) manner while visibly pregnant may have created an extreme interaction between students' gendered expectations for women professors and their assumptions about pregnancy and pregnant women. With scant opportunities to interact personally with students in the large class, Dr. Baker had little chance to show sensitivity and concern to each student. Thus, students could have transformed Dr. Baker's authoritative "professing" into rude behavior that contradicted their expectations of her as a woman. In addition, pregnancy lowered Dr. Baker's status as a woman even further at the same time that it contradicted her high status as a professor. Balin (1988:293–94, 300) argued that pregnant women enter a "liminal" phase in which interactions with others puts them "betwixt and between' particular social roles and positions" and also "disempowers" and "deauthorizes" them. If students believed as Balin suggested, then they could have viewed a very pregnant woman teaching assertively as presumptuous, given her lowly status. Rather than respond favorably to her as a professor, students may have seen Dr. Baker as disempowered and undeserving of authority.

Unfairness to students was the last theme in the negative comments. As we mentioned earlier, once each semester Dr. Baker brought her daughter to class. In the previous spring semester, this occasion elicited no comments from the students. Because no mention was made in the evaluations nor was there an observable reaction during the class, Dr. Baker assumed that this was a benign activity. In the fall semester, an occasion arose on an examination day that required Dr. Baker to bring her sick daughter to class or else postpone the examination without proper notice. After the examination, several students complained to the department head that this event was unfair. Some students, who may or may not have been part of that group, also complained in their written evaluations. One student wrote, "The first test was very unfair & [Dr. Baker] had NO RIGHT to have her kid running around." We note that even though Dr. Baker's daughter sat fairly quietly at the front of room coloring during the examination, in some students' eyes, she disrupted the class and "ran around" during the test. Another student wrote that "Dr. Baker ... exhibited some sort of power trip during a test period when her daughter was present." And a third student complaining about the presence of Dr. Baker's daughter wrote. "Mrs. Baker should have more respect for students if she wishes to get some respect [from] us." The occasion in the spring semester when Dr. Baker brought her daughter to class was not an examination day; thus, we cannot easily compare how pregnancy transformed students' reactions. Yet no students from the spring term made any mention of this visit in their written comments.

With her daughter's presence in the fall class, Dr. Baker appeared to students not only as a woman and a professor, but as a mother, too. Bringing her daughter on an examination day, when pregnant with her second child, enraged some students who perceived Dr. Baker as violating the norm for how a professor should treat her students. Moreover, the students scolded her as a mother (as "Mrs." Baker). This event may have encouraged some students to think that Dr. Baker put her daughter's needs first. A common belief in our society is that "when a woman undertakes the responsibility of parenthood, she subordinates her own needs, desires, or priorities to the welfare of the child" (Laws 1979:126). Students may have interpreted this event as evidence that Dr. Baker put her parental responsibilities above her professorial obligations, failing to put students' special examination-day needs first (even as she tried to honor the class schedule).

In this situation of multiple contradictions, students' assumptions about pregnancy, their perceptions of Dr. Baker as a woman, mother, and professor, and their perception of feminism as male-bashing created an intense interaction effect. This interaction helped produce students' strongly negative evaluations. Compared to the spring term, the fall term comments are striking in that they doubled in number and became harsh, especially for those students who interpreted Dr. Baker's actions as rude and who resented her daughter's presence during the examination. As with the quantitative data, the qualitative data reveal significant shifts in students' comments.

Summer Term 1992

In stark contrast to the spring and fall terms, Dr. Baker had a positive experience teaching the same course to a small class of 23 students in the summer. In the summer term, 20 out of 23 students provided written comments in their teaching evaluations. Dr. Baker received 18 clearly positive comments (90% of the total written comments) and one moderately negative comment (5% of the total written comments). Students' strongly positive evaluations seemed tied to Dr. Baker's greater capacity to fulfill their expectations of her in an intimate classroom setting. Unlike the spring term, Dr. Baker was visibly pregnant (in her second trimester), although she was not as big as she would become in the fall term.

Compared to other terms, the proportion of positive comments during the summer term more than doubled from the spring (40% in the spring to 90% in the summer) and nearly tripled what Dr. Baker would receive in the fall (33%). Positive comment themes in the summer term paralleled the content of the spring term, but contained warmer and more enthusiastic praise. Most students asserted a newfound sense of raised consciousness. One student wrote that the class "makes a person more aware of the issues and their own beliefs, actions, and prejudices." Another declared that he or she had "come to look at the world just a little differently." Comments that the class was interesting and enjoyable comprised a second theme. In a third theme, students characterized Dr. Baker as concerned and knowledgeable. For example, one student wrote, "She is so concerned for us and it is quite obvious." Another stated, "Dr. Baker has taken a personal interest in her students and knows all of our names." The pleased tone of these comments differs sharply from the spring and fall terms. These positive comments indicate two different ways that Dr. Baker reached the students. Students' statements about experiencing raised consciousness indicated an open-minded, rather than negative, response to the feminist course content. And the comments stating their professor's concern and personal interest in students (knowing all their names) demonstrates that Dr. Baker was fulfilling students' gendered expectations.

Unlike the spring and fall terms, the summer term had only one comment that can be construed as negative. A student wrote, "Dr. Baker does a great job of making herself clear—she gives good illustrations. However, sometimes she seems to present the girl's side more than the man's and appears to be sexist toward women." This comment lacks the hostile tone of the fall comments, but it reflects how some students interpreted feminist course content as biased. Importantly, the summer comments lacked any charges of male-bashing and rudeness.

If students' charges of bias or male-bashing stemmed only from the feminist course content, then any course Dr. Baker taught from a feminist perspective would elicit the same reactions. The one summer student who commented that Dr. Baker was biased by "presenting the girl's side more than the man's" signaled some disagreement with feminism by failing to use equivalent language to refer to women and men. Yet it seems unlikely and simplistic to presume that all of the other students held pro-feminist beliefs. We think that the summer students' comments were overwhelmingly positive because the conditions governing the course affected how they viewed Dr. Baker as a woman. The primary form of classroom interaction, discussion, freed Dr. Baker from "professing" in the traditional (authoritarian) sense as she taught the class. In this small class, which met every day, students interacted frequently and informally with their professor. Because Dr. Baker learned their names and recognized them as individuals, she could fulfill students' gendered expectations for a concerned, friendly, sympathetic woman professor far easier than she could for a large class. Thus, within the context of an intimate, informal course, Dr. Baker could better fulfill students' gendered expectations. This, in turn, made other conditions like the feminist course content less salient.

Likewise, students' perceptions of and expectations about a pregnant professor were also transformed in this setting. If pregnancy evoked negative reactions in the fall, why did summer students react so positively to Dr. Baker? The summer term's classroom conditions minimized an authoritarian professor role and reduced the likelihood of contradictions between students' expectations for women and for professors; it also led students to perceive Dr. Baker's pregnancy in a different and positive light. Most students expressed supportive interest in her pregnancy during the summer term. Because they frequently asked about Dr. Baker's pregnancy and received positive answers, we think that if they started the course believing that pregnant women felt moody and physically exhausted, they soon learned otherwise. In an informal situation where pregnancy was addressed openly and without embarrassment, Dr. Baker challenged and transformed common stereotypes. Hence, because students' expectations of pregnant women were altered and Dr. Baker could more easily fulfill their gendered expectations, students responded positively in their evaluations.

Summary

Gendered expectations of Dr. Baker as a professor were prominent in students' written evaluations and in our overall interpretation of their comments. When gendered expectations of their professor were met, students did not find fault with Dr. Baker for being pregnant or teaching from a feminist perspective. However, when students' expectations for Dr. Baker as a woman were unmet, students' written comments became negative and hostile and the content of their comments often touched on professor bias, male-bashing, and rudeness, which students attributed to the feminist course content and to Dr. Baker's pregnancy. This means that students' expectations interacted differently under certain conditions. In the small summer class, when Dr. Baker was best able to meet students' gendered expectations, students were more open to a feminist perspective and to Dr. Baker's pregnancy. But in the large fall class, when Dr. Baker was least able to present herself as a concerned, warm, and friendly woman to each student, students' failed gender expectations interacted with their views of feminism and Dr. Baker's pregnancy, and their comments took a sharply negative turn. Thus, the meanings students attached to their professor depended chiefly on how the situation constrained both their interaction with her and their perception of her gender performance.

Implications

Based on our analyses of the student evaluation data, three sets of implications warrant attention. First, we address concerns for women faculty members and those who want to encourage students to question their closely held assumptions about gender. Second, we speak to faculty members who are involved in promotion and tenure decisions. Third, we discuss issues that surround students' contradictory expectations of professors.

Women professors (both those who choose to become parents and those who choose not to) may take steps to ensure that students do not give poor evaluations due to their unrealistic expectations. In a study of how students evaluated women professors, Martin (1984) found that, at least in male students' eyes, women academics who balanced stereotypically feminine and masculine characteristics were perceived as highly effective professors. And in their study of professors' teaching styles, Statham et al. (1991:100,128–9) noted that women professors, more than men, divulged information about themselves and talked about "personal issues in their students' lives" as a way "to establish their authority without violating sex-appropriate behavioral norms." These researchers suggest that women professors who succeed in the classroom do so by negotiating and minimizing contradictions in students' expectations.

We object to advising women professors to adapt to students' beliefs about gender roles and constantly manage how authoritative or "masculine" they appear. Nor do we think that women professors should strive to be more nurturing toward students or manufacture concern for students simply to meet their gendered expectations. Instead, as sociologists and feminists, we believe that the contradictions raised by what students expect in a woman, a professor, and a mother deserve to be discussed and analyzed by our students, not scribbled unreflexively on evaluations. We believe that professors should continually encourage students to link who they are to how they see the world around them, which includes their teachers. Students need to understand the expectations that they take for granted and question their purposes. Traditional lecture courses with high enrollments that limit student discussion provide probably the most difficult setting for achieving these goals.

The second set of implications concerns how teaching evaluations are used in promotion and tenure decisions. What happens to professors when some students' potent criticisms are taken literally? In Dr. Baker's case, can we assume that she acted rudely, as students said? No, we cannot—other factors influenced students' perceptions of Dr. Baker, and we need to take their charges of rudeness in that context. That some students defined pregnancy as a liability in the classroom or disagreed with Dr. Baker's gender performance does not mean that the whole class shared this belief or that Dr. Baker was even rude in the first place, as evidenced by many positive evaluations.

By failing to consider students' subjectivity as such, colleagues may promote gender bias in the university. For example, colleagues on Dr. Baker's professional assessment committee took the students' comments at face value. Because her pregnancy was mentioned negatively by some students, committee members concluded that Dr. Baker was at fault. In her yearly evaluation letter, they "explained" the negative comments of the fall term by stating that Dr. Baker was "not feeling well." By taking some students' comments at face value the committee exercised two forms of bias. First, they transformed pregnancy into an illness (Rothman 1989) rather than treating it as a normal process. And second, by blaming her, even mildly, the committee tacitly confirmed the students' stereotypical assumption that pregnant women are rude and irritable.

To prevent this kind of injustice, faculty members involved in tenure and promotion decisions need to consider students' gendered expectations of women and men professors. They also need to consider how classroom conditions constrain a professor's ability to fulfill students' expectations. Cranton and Smith (1986) make the sensible point that interpreting evaluations without considering other factors biases the interpretations; this opens the possibility for inappropriate tenure and promotion decisions regarding teaching efforts. Martin (1984), Rubin (1981), and Statham et al. (1991) report some of the problems professors experience when students maintain different sets of expectations for women and men professors and warn that administrators and colleagues should take this into account during the tenure and promotion process. In order to evaluate women and men faculty members fairly, gender must be taken into consideration—particularly students' gendered expectations. Many times, however, faculty are evaluated by teaching criteria under the presumption that they are gender-neutral, without considering that students hold different expectations of women and men.

Our analyses have led us to further question assumptions about social interaction built into the teaching evaluations that influence tenure and promotion decisions. Course evaluations assume that the professor "controls" the class and likewise controls what goes on in students' heads. All that needs to be evaluated is how she or he "led" the class. This assumption denies that students and professors engage in joint interactions (Blumer 1969) to create meaning. And it denies that teaching is a negotiated activity. What students think and do in class matters just as much to the success of the class as how the professor acts and thinks. Thus, our evaluations need to consider the ways that students work jointly with or against their teachers and the social conditions that contribute to this situation.

Our arguments in this paper identify a fundamental problem: Standard course evaluations assume that students and professors only relate to each other as one-dimensional characters in a "standard" classroom, rather than as multifaceted people in varied social settings. Students' judgments of professors are more than just an assessment of the professor's teaching abilities; what students learn about their professors as people, including their social roles, influences students' expectations and ultimately their evaluations. Likewise, as we have argued, the classroom as a social setting influences how students and professors relate to each other. By defining what does and does not matter about the professor and omitting the social context of the class, standard course evaluations exclude the meanings that are attached to social interaction. Consequently, on paper, all professors become one-dimensional characters who teach in irrelevant contexts. Taking these assumptions altogether, tenure and promotion committees may assume falsely that teaching evaluations are accurate, objective summaries of a professor's teaching performance and that no deeper interpretations are necessary.[4]

Our last implication concerns issues that surround students' contradictory expectations of professors. We want to learn how pliable students' expectations are in teacher-student relationships. For example, has the situation Dr. Baker experienced as a pregnant professor occurred under different circumstances for others? If Dr. Baker exhibited different attributes (conservatism, lesbianism, religiosity), would students' resulting comments look more hopeful, alarming, worrisome, or simply outrageous?

Because students' expectations shift depending on the situation and on how the professor presents herself or himself, faculty members who violate the white male, able-bodied stereotype must also experience students' contradictory expectations regarding gender, race, ethnicity, sexual orientation, and physical abilities. We want to understand what occurs for

[4]Tally and Timmer (1992:78) point out a deeper problem: Undergraduates may not even share the same definitions of the terms that administrators and faculty choose so carefully for evaluation because "many abstract conceptual categories are meaningless" to students.

other people, because their accounts are rarely published. Sharing highly critical student evaluations or talking about problematic interactions with students may be difficult and upsetting for professors to do, especially before achieving tenure. We call on others to share their experiences of handling complicated and multiple contradictions in the classroom, and we call for further research on the dynamics and ideologies of professor-student relationships.

References

Balin, Jane. 1988. "Sacred Dimensions of Pregnancy and Birth." *Qualitative Sociology* 11:275–301.

Bennett, Sheila Kishler. 1982. "Student Perceptions and Expectations for Male and Female Instructors: Evidence Relating to the Question of Gender Bias in Teaching Evaluation." *Journal of Educational Psychology* 74:170–79.

Bernard, Jessie. 1964. *Academic Women*. University Park, PA: The Pennsylvania State University Press.

Blumer, Herbert. 1969. *Symbolic Interactionism: Perspective and Method*. Englewood Cliffs, NJ: Prentice-Hall.

Bohmer, Susanne and Joyce L. Briggs, 1991. "Teaching Privileged Students about Gender, Race, and Class Oppression." *Teaching Sociology* 19:154–63.

Bronstein, Phyllis. 1993. "Challenges, Rewards, and Costs for Feminist and Ethnic Minority Scholars." *New Directions for Teaching and Learning* 53:61–70.

Bronstein, Phyllis, Esther D. Rothblum, and Sondra E. Solomon. 1993. "Ivy Halls and Glass Walls: Barriers to Academic Careers for Women and Ethnic Minorities." *New Directions for Teaching and Learning* 53:17–31.

Caplan, Paula J. 1995. *Lifting a Ton of Feathers: A Woman's Guide to Surviving in the Academic World*. Toronto: University of Toronto Press.

Cranton, Patricia A, and Ronald A. Smith, 1986. "A New Look at the Effect of Course Characteristics on Student Ratings of Instruction." *American Educational Research Journal* 23:117–28.

Crawford, Mary and Margo MacLeod. 1990. "Gender in the College Classroom: An Assessment of the 'Chilly Climate' for Women." *Sex Roles* 23:101–22.

Culley, Margo. 1985. "Anger and Authority in the Introductory Women's Studies Classroom." Pp. 209–17 in *Gendered Subjects: The Dynamics of Feminist Teaching*, edited by Margo Culley and Catherine Portuges. Boston, MA: Routledge and Kegan Paul.

Davis, Nancy. 1992. "Teaching about Inequality: Student Resistance, Paralysis, and Rage." *Teaching Sociology* 20:232–38.

Deay, Ardich and Judith Stitzel. 1991. "Reshaping the Introductory Women's Studies Course: Dealing Upfront with Anger, Resistance, and Reality." *Feminist Teacher* 6(1):29–33.

Faludi, Susan. 1991. *Backlash: The Undeclared War against American Women*. New York: Crown.

Feldman, Kenneth A. 1984. "Class Size and College Students' Evaluations of Teachers and Courses: A Closer Look." *Research in Higher Education* 21(1):45–116.

———. 1993. "College Students' Views of Male and Female College Teachers: Part II—Evidence from Students' Evaluations of Their Classroom, Teachers." *Research in Higher Education* 34:151–211.

Friedman, Susan. 1985. "Authority in the Feminist Classroom: A Contradiction in Terms?" Pp. 203–8 in *Gendered Subjects: The Dynamics of Feminist Teaching*, edited by Margo Culley and Catherine Portuges. Boston, MA: Routledge and Kegan Paul.

Gibbons, Jean Dickinson. 1993. *Nonparametric Statistics: An Introduction*. Newbury Park, CA: Sage.

Ginorio, Angela B. 1995. *Warning the Climate for Women in Academic Science*. Washington, D.C.: Association of American Colleges and Universities.

Hall, Roberta and Bernice R. Sandler. 1984. "Out of the Classroom: A Chilly Campus Climate for Women?" Washington, DC: Project on the Status and Education of Women, Association of American Colleges.

Hamilton, Lawrence C. 1980. "Grades, Class Size, and Faculty Status Predict Teaching Evaluations." *Teaching Sociology* 8:47–62.

Henry, Annette. 1993–1994. "There Are No Safe Places: Pedagogy as Powerful and Dangerous Terrain." *Action in Teacher Education* 15(4):1–4.

Hodge, Robert W., Paul M. Siegel, and Peter H. Rossi. 1964. "Occupational Prestige in the United States, 1925–1963." *American Journal of Sociology* 70:290–93.

Hughes, Everest. 1971. *The Sociological Eye: Selected Papers*. Chicago: Aldine-Atherton.

Ito, Kinko. 1992. "Reflections of an Oriental Southern Belle Teaching Sociology in Arkansas." *Teaching Sociology* 20:170–72.

Johnstud, Linda. 1993. "Women and Minority Faculty Experiences: Defining and Responding to Diverse Realities." *New Directions in Teaching and Learning* 53:3–16.

Kamen, Paula. 1991. *Feminist Fatale: Voices from the "Twentysomething" Generation Explore the "Women's Movement."* New York: Primus Library of Contemporary America.

Kleinplatz, Peggy Joy. 1992. "The Pregnant Clinical Psychologist: Issues, Impressions, and Observations." *Women and Therapy* 12:21–37.

Laws, Judith. 1979. *The Second X: Sex Role and Social Role*. New York: Elsevier.

Lofland, John and Lyn H. Lofland. 1995. *Analyzing Social Settings: A Guide to Qualitative Observation and Analysis*. 3rd ed. Belmont, CA: Wadsworth.

Maher, Frances and Mary Kay Tetreault. 1994. *The Feminist Classroom*. New York: Basic Books.

Marsh, Herbert W., Jesse U. Overall, and Steven P. Kesler. 1979. "Class Size, Students' Evaluations, and Instructional Effectiveness." *American Educational Research Journal* 16(1):57–69.

Martin, Elaine. 1984. "Power and Authority in the Classroom." *Signs* 9:482–92.

Neitz, Mary Jo. 1985. "Resistance to Feminist Analysis." *Teaching Sociology* 12:339–53.

Rakow, Lana. 1991. "Gender and Race in the Classroom: Teaching Way Out of Line." *Feminist Teacher* 6(1):10–13.

Renzetti, Claire M. 1987. "New Wave or Second Stage? Attitudes of College Women Toward Feminism." *Sex Roles* 16:265–77.

Rothman, Barbara Katz. 1989. *Recreating Motherhood*. New York: Norton.

Rubin, Rebecca. 1981. "Ideal Traits and Terms of Address for Male and Female College Professors." *Journal of Personality and Social Psychology* 41:966–74.

Schur, Edwin M. 1983. *Labeling Women Devians: Gender, Stigma, and Social Control*. Philadelphia, PA: Temple University Press.

Sidanius, Jim and Marie Crane. 1989. "Job Evaluation and Gender: The Case of University Faculty." *Journal of Applied Social Psychology* 19:174–97.

Slater, R.B. 1995. "The Gender Pay Gap: Where Women Academics Come Up Short on Pay Day." *The Monthly Forum on Women In Higher Education*. 1(3):23–27.

Statham, Anne, Laurel Richardson, and Judith Cook. 1991. *Gender and University Teaching: A Negotiated Difference*. Albany, NY: State University of New York Press.

Talley, Kathryn D. and Doug A. Timmer. 1992. "A Qualitative Methods Exercise: Student and Faculty Interpretations of Classroom Teaching." *Teaching Sociology* 20:75–79.

West, Candace and Don Zimmerman. 1987. "Doing Gender." *Gender and Society* 1:125–51.

Whitten. Betty J. and M. Michael Umble. 1980. "The Relationship of Class Size, Class Level, and Core Versus Non-core Classification for a Class to Student Ratings of Faculty: Implications for Validity." *Educational and Psychological Measurement* 40:419–23.

18

*Emotion Norms, Emotion Work, and Social Order**

Peggy A. Thoits
Vanderbilt University

An experiment by Dutton and Aron (1974) is often used in psychology textbooks to illustrate the role of cognition in emotional experience. The study was intended to demonstrate that physiological arousal can be misattributed to the wrong cause. Men who were approached by an attractive experimenter after crossing a suspension bridge over a deep gorge were more likely to indicate romantic or sexual interest in the experimenter, in contrast to men who had crossed a low wooden bridge over a stream. Dutton and Aron concluded, consistent with Schachter's two-factor theory of emotion (Schachter and Singer 1962), that emotions are in part determined by available cognitive cues, not by physiological reactions alone.

The idea that our perceptions affect our experiences has a long and honorable tradition in sociology, too. But the results of the Dutton and Aron study (1974) are sociologically interesting for other reasons. If one conducts a quick thought experiment, substituting an attractive *male* experimenter approaching *women* who have just traversed a swaying or a stable bridge, one arrives at a different set of probable results: Women would be less likely to misattribute their state of arousal to romantic or sexual interest in the male experimenter. It is more socially acceptable for women to admit fear than for men; it is more socially acceptable for men to show open interest in the opposite sex than for women. In short, the original experiment "worked" because it was grounded in shared social norms about gender-appropriate emotional behaviors—norms taken for granted by the experimenters. Bringing these implicit norms to the forefront and elaborating their implications for interpersonal behavior, societal organization, and group survival is sociology's ongoing contribution to the interdisciplinary

*This paper was presented at Feelings and Emotions: The Amsterdam Symposium, Amsterdam, The Netherlands, June 13–16, 2001 and appeared in 2004 *Feelings and Emotions: The Amsterdam Symposium*, edited by Antony S. R. Manstead, Nico H. Frijda, and Agneta H. Fischer. New York: pp. 359–378 Cambridge University Press, 2004.

dialogue about the nature and functions of emotion and affect. The purpose of this chapter is to highlight the personal and social origins and consequences of emotion norms in group life.

Hochschild (1979) introduced the concept of "emotion norms," an umbrella term covering two important subsets of social rules, "feeling norms" and "expression norms." Feeling norms indicate the range, duration, intensity, and/or targets of emotions that are appropriate to *feel* in specific situations ("You're supposed to be happy at a wedding," "You shouldn't feel so guilty about that," "It's time for you to let go of your anger"). Expression rules guide appropriate *displays* of emotion in given situations (e.g., passionate kissing in public is improper, big boys shouldn't cry, one should show gratitude for a gift).[1] Hochschild argued that both types of emotion—private, subjective experiences and public, observable expressions—were subject to social rules and social control.[2]

If affects are indeed governed by social norms (as a wealth of evidence reviewed here will show), this observation has several implications. First, because emotion norms (like all norms) are social constructions, they will vary in content over time, cultures, and contexts, both reflecting and sustaining the social structures in which they develop. Second, because emotion rules (like all rules) are learned, children and adults undergo emotional socialization and are subject to pressures to conform. Third, because individuals are motivated to seek approval and avoid sanctions, they will hide, transform, or otherwise manage emotions that occasionally violate emotional expectations (as they hide occasional rule-breaking behaviors). Fourth, such efforts at emotional conformity (like efforts at behavioral conformity) have functional social consequences. Finally, because some individuals refuse or fail to obey emotion norms (as they do other norms), "emotional deviants" (Thoits 1985) will be labeled, stigmatized, and subjected to social control, or, under some conditions, they may become agents of social change. How emotion norms are produced by and themselves help to produce social order and social change in these ways are elaborated further in this chapter.

Most sociological research on emotion examines one or more of the implications listed above, which generally center on the causes or consequences of adherence to and deviations from societal feeling and expression norms. Those who investigate the determinants of emotional conventions usually take a social construction of reality approach (e.g., Cancian 1987; Denzin 1990; Illouz 1997); those who study consequences typically emphasize the adaptive functions of emotional regulation and conformity (e.g., Cahill 1999; Clark 1997). Because symbolic interactionist theory merges constructionist and functionalist thinking, this approach tends to dominate sociological research on affect in sociology.

Briefly, symbolic interactionism views self and society as reciprocally related; individuals are both products and producers of social order (McCall & Simmons 1978; Stryker and Statham 1985). Through social interaction, people learn to categorize themselves and others, learn the behavioral expectations attached to their own and others' role identities, and are motivated to meet others' expectations in order to gain approval and rewards. When actors conform to others' expectations in their identity performances, they are in effect

[1]Expression norms correspond to what Ekman (Ekman et al. 1982) termed "display rules."

[2]In contrast, Ekman (e.g., Ekman et al. 1982) and others consider basic emotions to be innate reactions to environmental stimuli, free from cultural or social regulation; only emotional displays are socially controlled. The evidence reviewed here will indicate otherwise.

maintaining the social order. This is the structural-functionalist aspect of the theory: society shapes (i.e., socializes) the self, and the well-socialized self in turn sustains society.

But the self is not simply a social product. The possibility of social construction or social change also resides in human nature. Symbolic interactionists assume that humans are creative, spontaneous creatures, capable of exerting choice and self-determination when circumstances allow. Improvisation is a routine feature of daily life, making possible the renegotiation of identity meanings and behavioral expectations. New norms, values, beliefs, and behaviors are among the many potential innovations, that, if widely adopted by other people, can be constructed or changed.

Where do emotions and emotion norms fit in such thought? To role identities are attached not only behavioral expectations, but expectations for feelings and expression. These norms are part of the broader emotion culture acquired in social interaction. Well-socialized actors are motivated to abide by these emotion norms but are not always able to do so. The structural origins of dissident feelings, how those feelings are reworked to meet social expectations, and the consequences of conforming and deviant emotions for self and society are thus fodder for sociological inquiry.

The Social Construction of Emotions, Emotion Culture, and Emotion Norms

Because emotion norms both reflect and shape people's affective experiences, it may be useful to clarify the sociological view of emotions, in general. Within anthropology, psychology, and sociology, disagreements persist regarding whether emotions are cultural constructions or cultural universals. Despite such debates, a majority of sociologists have adopted a middle-of-the-road approach to the issue of emotional hardwiring (e.g., Kemper 1987; Thoits 1985). Drawing from evolutionary psychologists, they acknowledge the innate, biological basis of the primary or basic emotions (e.g., fear, anger, sadness, happiness, disgust) and the adaptive functions of these emotions for the survival of the species (Ekman et al. 1982). Drawing from anthropology and social history, sociologists recognize that the meanings of emotions, even basic ones such as anger and sadness, have varied across places, peoples, and time (e.g., Kleinman and Kleinman 1985; Levy 1984; Shweder 1994; Stearns and Stearns 1986). For example, Levy (1984) and Kleinman and Kleinman (1985) observed that bereaved Tahitians and Chinese adults who were uprooted during the Cultural Revolution, respectively, "hypercognized" (overemphasized) the somatic aspects of grief and depression and "hypocognized" (ignored) the affective components of these states, complaining that they were sick, overcome with fatigue, drained of energy, and so forth, rather than sad. Stearns and Stearns' (1986) historical research showed that as the industrial revolution transformed the nature of work (creating more service, managerial, and professional jobs) and altered the meaning of family life (from the locus of farm livelihood to an emotional haven from an impersonal, highly competitive world), middle-class Americans came to view angry feelings as disruptive and insisted on anger control at work and at home. Research showing differences in subjective experience across cultures and time convinced sociologists that not only emotion norms but also the meaning of emotional experiences themselves were cultural constructs, at least in part (few would claim that emotions are *solely* social constructions).

Focusing on the socioculturally malleable aspects of emotion, then, sociologists have contributed to this interdisciplinary body of research by more closely examining both the content of "emotion culture" (Gordon 1989) and their structural origins. Emotion culture consists of beliefs about the nature, causes, distributions, value, and dynamics of emotions in general as well as of specific feelings, such as love, anger, and jealousy. In western emotion culture, for example, emotions are thought to be bodily reactions to external stimuli, women are viewed as more emotional than men, negative emotions are regarded as undesirable, intense affective states are thought to dissipate with time, and some feelings (infatuations, lust) and emotional displays (tantrums) are believed to be characteristic of the young but not the very old. These tenets and many others, including norms regarding situationally appropriate feelings and emotional displays, constitute a large body of folk knowledge, passed from one generation to the next.

Sociologists have traced changes in emotion culture, including changes in emotion norms, to changes in social structure. Structure can be broadly described as the ways in which human relationships are organized. It is a truism to observe that culture reflects social structure, but structural patterns are also products of culture. It is almost impossible to disentangle cultural and structural influences at a single point in time. However, longitudinal studies allow an examination of the interplay between the two forces. Typically, structural arrangements alter more quickly than cultural ideologies or norms, so that beliefs about what "ought" to be thought, felt, or done by societal members lag behind what they actually think, feel, or do. These differential rates of change in patterned behaviors and in beliefs help to unravel the reciprocal relations between structure and culture.

As an example, Lofland (1985) has argued that the intensity and duration of grief experiences have increased over the twentieth century as social arrangements have changed. Specifically, as infant mortality has plunged and life expectancy has lengthened, bereavement has become less frequent in people's lives, so each death carries greater emotional impact. Family size has shrunk and nuclear families increasingly live separately from kin, making emotional attachments among coresident family members more intense, again augmenting the impact of loss. Leisure time has increased and bigger homes allow greater privacy, giving individuals more opportunities to withdraw and brood upon loss, lengthening the duration of grief. In short, demographic shifts and alterations in the structure of family life have intensified and prolonged the bereavement experience.

Note that Lofland describes changes in subjective *experiences* over time, rather than changes in emotion norms or emotion culture per se. However, recurrent individual experiences tend to become emotional conventions, or norms. People develop expectations about the intensity and duration of grief based on their own and the often-observed experiences of others, and these expectations (norms) are passed on to others. The demographic and structural trends described by Lofland should not only be associated with self-reported grief experiences, but also with changes in norms regarding how much grief is "normal" and how long it should persist, stated in self-help books and texts for bereavement counselors, for example.

Changes in romantic love norms have also been analyzed structurally. Cancian (1987) has shown that historical changes in American women's roles have "feminized" the meaning and manifestations of love and have generated competing cultural models of commitment to love relationships. Briefly, in shifting the location of work from farm to factory, the industrial revolution polarized gender roles. Men became the primary breadwinners, while women became the socioemotional specialists, responsible for the home and family members' emotional well-being. Love and loving thus became culturally linked with females and femininity. However, structural trends over the last fifty years have increased women's economic and political independence, shifting the balance of power in relationships and forcing men to take more responsibility for maintaining love and affection. This more equalized sharing of the "work" of maintaining relationships has resulted in more androgynous cultural models of committed love. In the "independence model," individuals make long-term commitments only after developing strong, independent selves ("I have to find myself first"). In the "interdependence model," individuals achieve self-development through the process of sustaining a commitment. Evidence supports the existence of these two ideological models in contemporary American emotion culture (Cancian 1987; Cancian and Gordon 1989).

These and other studies (e.g., Stearns and Stearns 1986) suggest that structural changes indeed alter cultural ideologies about emotion. Although emotion culture typically reflects and reinforces social structures, cultural content may also be deliberately shaped by "culture-producing institutions" (Denzin 1990), especially the mass media. Illouz (1997) has demonstrated that western images of romantic love (associated with youth, beauty, freedom, pleasure, and intimacy) and romantic practices (candlelight dining, going dancing, traveling to isolated, exotic settings) are products of advanced capitalism. In ads, films, TV shows, and novels, the ritual consumption of luxuries and sexual intimacy in isolated settings are repeatedly associated with romance. So deeply ingrained in the American psyche are these images that couples automatically use them to characterize their most intimate and authentic romantic experiences. Although Illouz's interviewees are clearly aware that their concepts are a product of consumer culture, they still internalize and actualize these cultural fabrications in their subjective experiences of and normative expectations for romantic love.

Hochschild (1983) has offered perhaps the most influential observations of the effects of capitalist structure on emotion culture and affective experience, in her pioneering study of Delta flight attendants. Hochschild argued that the postindustrial shift in Western nations toward service economies (i.e., based more on the provision of services and less on the production of food and goods) has generated demands for workers skilled in self-presentation and emotional control. In service work, profit generally depends on pleasing the customer or client, so employers exert economic control over employees' emotional self-presentations with warnings, firings, promotions, and pay raises. In Hochschild's terms, such jobs involve "emotional labor." For "service with a smile" to be profitable, however, smiles must be genuine—one must smile and "really mean it." Thus, not only workers' expressive displays but also their private feelings become commodities to be exchanged for a salary or wage. To meet companies' demands for "genuine" feelings, employees routinely engage in "emotion work" or "emotion management" to produce those feelings, risking, Hochschild suggests, eventual self-alienation or a persistent sense of inauthenticity.

In sum, emotional ideologies and norms not only spring from existing social arrangements that repeatedly evoke particular emotional experiences in societal members, but also these may be deliberately created to justify and/or serve the goals of small groups, specific companies, whole industries, or entire social systems. It is important to note that because industrial and postindustrial societies are highly complex, emotion cultures are also likely to be complex. Any one society may contain multiple, overlapping, and potentially conflicting emotional ideologies, and, within them, a great diversity of emotion norms that individuals can use to interpret, evaluate, and justify their own and others' feelings and expressions.

Emotional Socialization

Emotion culture is transmuted into behavior, and hence into social structure, through the process of socialization. Emotional socialization is the acquisition of the emotional knowledge, values, and skills that are appropriate to a person's age, gender, race/ethnicity, social class, and so on. In contrast to psychologists, who largely have focused on *how* children learn the meaning of feelings and expressive displays (e.g., operant conditioning, modeling), or *when* in the developmental process various aspects of this knowledge are acquired, sociologists have focused on *what* children and adults learn in the process of emotional socialization. The transmission of normative content is important because emotion norms not only define situationally appropriate feelings and displays, but also are intended to impel experience and action ("you *should* feel this," "you *must not* show that"). Understanding normative content, then, should better predict individuals' affects and behaviors.

Only a few studies have examined the emotion norms that are taught to children or adolescents (Leavitt and Power 1989; Pollak and Thoits 1989; Simon, Eder, and Evans 1992). Most sociological research on emotional socialization has focused instead on adults who are entering new social roles (spouse, parent, employee) and acquiring the values, skills, and knowledge needed to perform them. An avalanche of these studies analyzed emotional socialization on the job, following in Hochschild's (1983) ground-breaking footsteps.

Studies of supermarket clerks (Tolich 1993), fast food and sales workers (Leidner, 1993), and the like confirmed and elaborated Hochschild's observations that sales and service employees are explicitly admonished to smile and are trained in techniques of suppressing and transforming unacceptable emotions. However, many other occupations, particularly professional ones (e.g., psychiatrists, physicians, mortuary directors, paralegals, attorneys, wedding consultants), require their practitioners to adhere to specific emotion norms, and they transmit techniques for handling improper feelings (although emotional socialization is often informal and implicit). For example, medical students learn that it is important to maintain a stance of affective neutrality toward patients through watching and imitating the comportment and practices of their instructors and advanced peers (Hafferty 1988; Smith and Kleinman 1989). Even skilled laborers, such as high steel ironworkers, receive informal socialization in the dominant emotion norms of their occupation (never show fear, never lose emotional control) and implicit training in emotion management (Haas 1977). In short, a multitude of studies show emotional socialization to be an important aspect of occupational training for workers in a wide variety of jobs, not just sales and service.

Taken together, studies of adult emotional socialization on the job raise a set of more general issues. First, virtually all studies showed that despite extensive training in the emotion norms of their occupations, workers often had difficulties experiencing or expressing the emotional states that were expected of them.[3] Why do well-socialized individuals sometimes feel or display what they shouldn't or *not* feel or display what they should? Second, studies showed that people employed a broad array of strategies to bring their actual feelings

[3]Several investigators point out that problematic relationships with supervisors and coworkers are also key sources of inappropriate emotions and emotion management efforts on the job (Lively, 2000; Morris & Feldman, 1996; Pugliesi, 1999). So clients or customers are not the only causes of emotional norm violations in the occupational realm.

back in line with normative expectations. Do emotion management strategies relate systematically to individuals' structural circumstances? Third, some investigations suggested that frequent or prolonged emotion management efforts could damage individuals' psychological well-being. Are attempts at emotional conformity truly damaging? Research on "emotion work" has suggested answers to these questions.[4]

Emotion Work: Causes, Patterns, and Consequences

Causes of Discrepant Emotions

Hochschild (1983) implied a structural answer to the question of the origins of non-normative feelings, observing that the organization of air travel changed dramatically over the decades, creating a "speed up" and intensification of job demands for flight attendants. Cabins are crowded, flights are delayed, passengers must receive meals in shorter amounts of time, and attendants take the brunt of passengers' tempers, sexism, and occasional drunken unruliness. These highly stressful conditions of work differ considerably from the relaxed conditions in which the company emotion norms for flight attendants were originally developed.

A more general principle is suggested here. When structural conditions are complex, multifaceted, and/or highly demanding, but the norms which apply to those situations are simple and clear, individuals are more likely to experience inappropriate emotions (Thoits 1985). People react emotionally to cues in an immediate situation, but these reactions conflict with norms that apply to the modal or idealized situation. Although such structural strains are commonly found in occupational settings, they have been well documented in other adult role domains, particularly parenting (e.g., Frude and Goss 1981).

Other structural causes can be cited. People who hold multiple roles may experience inappropriate feelings due to conflicting emotional expectations attached to those roles (Thoits 1985). Parents at work with a sick child at home are an example. Anxiety or upset about the child is perfectly acceptable, even required, for parents, but these feelings are improper and distracting at work. Similar conflicts may be experienced by individuals who were raised in two cultural traditions with competing emotion norms. Periods of structural change can also make non-normative feelings more common. When social arrangements are varied or in flux, individuals experience new, unexpected, or unusual life transitions (e.g., acquiring or becoming a stepparent, "coming out of the closet"). Because these transitions are not ritualized (unlike graduations, weddings, and retirements), they lack well-defined norms for behavior *or* emotion. Lacking standards against which to evaluate their emotional reactions, people worry that their feelings are somehow wrong (Thoits 1985). Alternatively, emotional reactions that were appropriate in one time period may become unacceptable in another—for example, possessive jealousy became a forbidden emotion among hippies during the sixties countercultural revolution.

[4]The term "emotion work" or "emotion management" is more inclusive than "emotional labor." Emotion work occurs not only on the job but also in other domains of life, as people try to align their feelings with normative expectations attached to the situation. Emotional labor refers to emotion work performed on the job in order to meet company standards.

Finally, regardless of structural causes, people's innate or spontaneous emotional reactions to environmental stimuli can conflict with existing emotion norms. Individuals may react to certain foods with disgust, to heights with paralyzing fear, or to the sight of an amputee with horror, but be expected not to have these reactions at all or to mask them. Such emotional conflicts are especially common in occupations that require workers to perform acts that most people have been taught to regard as forbidden or taboo: killing, butchering, handling dead or naked bodies, touching genitals, cleaning up blood and feces, and so forth. In these jobs, innate *and* well-socialized reactions to forbidden and/or disgusting tasks must be suppressed or transformed through emotion work.

Strategies of Emotion Management

Studies clearly show that inappropriate emotions are distressing to those who experience them. Interestingly, research along this line has focused almost exclusively on parents (Graham 1981; Power and Krause-Eheart 1995; Taylor 2000). For example, mothers excoriate themselves when they lose their tempers at their babies and conclude, sometimes from a single episode of anger, that they are bad parents (Graham 1981). That one must love and never be angry at one's child are strongly held parental norms.

Such norm violations motivate well-socialized actors to attempt to alter their feelings or displays, not just to hide them. Studies of emotion management have focused on parents' emotion-management strategies (e.g., Frude and Goss 1981; Graham 1981) or, following Hochschild's lead again, on strategies used by workers in a dizzying array of occupations, from beauty salon operators (Gimlin 1996) and sheltered workshop supervisors (Copp 1998) to trial attorneys (Pierce 1995), among many others. Several patterns are evident in this literature.

In occupations that require emotional detachment (e.g., physician, funeral director, police officer), individuals engage in "cognitive work" (Hochschild 1979), reframing a situation so it elicits the proper emotional state. For example, medical and mortuary personnel distance themselves by reconceptualizing patients' bodies as objects, viewing patients' problems as scientific or mechanical problems to be solved, discussing their work in neutral technical language, and joking about harrowing or disgusting situations (Cahill 1999; Hafferty 1988; Pogrebin and Poole 1995; Smith and Kleinman 1989).

In occupations requiring the feeling and display of positive or pleasant emotions (e.g., mothers, table servers), individuals often resort to "bodily work"(Hochschild 1979), altering their physiological states with deep breathing, alcohol or drugs, exercise, and the like. Mothers and waiters temporarily leave the situation, vent their true feelings in private to other personnel, and manipulate their physiological reactions to change their states (e.g., Frude and Goss 1981; Lively 2000). However, flight attendants are an exception; they rely more on cognitive strategies and expression management, perhaps because airplanes have no "backstage" areas to which attendants can retreat and vent (Lively 2000).

Finally, in occupations in which workers must show and/or inspire negative emotions in other people (e.g., bill collectors, trial attorneys), "expression work" predominates, persistently performing a desired state in order to generate and feel it (Hochschild 1983; Pierce 1995; Sutton 1991). For example, bill collectors behave as though they were irritated or angry, the process of playacting generates arousal, and they become more convincingly intimidating in the process (see Thoits 1996).

Jobs involving emotional labor require workers not only to regulate their own feelings (self-management) but also to influence the emotions of their clients or customers (interpersonal emotion management). Researchers have dwelled on self-management processes because they are ways of indirectly evoking desired states in others. Attention has only recently turned to direct forms of interpersonal emotion management—techniques that actively manipulate other people's emotions (Cahill and Eggleston 1994; Francis, Monahan and Berger 1999; Leidner 1993; Lively 2000; Thoits 1996).

Perhaps not surprisingly, actors often apply to others strategies that work for themselves (Thoits 1986). For example, Lively (2000) studied the process of "reciprocal emotion management" among paralegals. For a distressed coworker, paralegals cognitively reframed the stressful situation, encouraged her to vent, took her out for a drink or a walk, and so on. Francis (1997) showed that support groups for the divorced and the bereaved manipulated members' cognitions about themselves and their circumstances in order to change their feelings. Francis also investigated the use of humor as an interpersonal emotion management tool in medical settings (Francis et al. 1999), finding that jokes usually reduced tension in audiences when offered by status equals, but often failed or offended when exchanged between patients and physicians. Goading and inducing physical exertion were other ways to elicit emotions in other people deliberately (Thoits 1996), while demands for expression control dampened intense emotions in others (Whalen and Zimmerman 1998).

Although studies of interpersonal emotion management strategies are still few in number, future research will likely show that the strategies that emotion "managers" most frequently employ vary systematically with structural circumstances and intended emotional states, just as they do for techniques that individuals use on themselves. Understanding how other people's emotions can be directly manipulated should help to explain how such crucial group phenomena as cohesion, cooperation, and loyalty happen, as well as causes of conflict, discrimination, injustice, and cruelty.

The Consequences of Emotional Labor

A number of authors have warned that workers who engage in frequent self- or other-focused emotion management efforts may suffer from self-alienation, a sense of inauthenticity, or emotional "burnout" (Maslach 1982). The evidence at present is mixed. Emotional labor has been linked to several negative outcomes, including sexual problems, emotional and physical exhaustion, lowered self-esteem, insensitivity to the distress of others, self-alienation, job dissatisfaction, and increased psychological distress (Hochschild 1983; MacRae 1998; Pierce 1995; Pogrebin and Poole 1995; Power and Krause-Eheart 1995; Pugliesi 1999; Wharton 1996). On the other hand, Tolich (1993) observed that checkout clerks experienced their emotional performances as both self-alienating (due to a loss of autonomy) *and* liberating (as an assertion of competence). Lively (2001) found that paralegals took great pride in their ability to maintain self-control in the face of stressful demands. Workers who frequently manage others' emotions report a sense of empowerment or self-enhancement (Leidner 1993; Stenross and Kleinman 1989).

Firm conclusions cannot be drawn from studies that differ so greatly in research methods, outcome indicators, and types of emotional labor examined, but it is clear that emotion work on the job does not inevitably damage workers' sense of authenticity or well-being. A key condition may be the degree to which employees view their self-focused and other-focused emotion management efforts as effective. Emotion-management failure is painful and undermines individuals' identities and self-esteem (Graham 1981; MacRae 1998; Power and Krause-Eheart 1995; Taylor 2000). Success likely has positive effects.

Virtually all of the research on emotion work reviewed here suggests that most people are strongly motivated to conform to the emotion rules of their industry or culture; they put real effort into transforming their actual feelings or expressions into those that are expected. People conform because they are socialized to seek social approval and other rewards, and/or they do so because they want to avoid sanctions that are attached to persistent or egregious rule-violations (gossip, reprimands, firing, etc.). Regardless of people's motivations, emotional conformity has important social consequences, beyond those for individuals themselves. Three broad classes of outcomes have been discussed: the maintenance of the social order, the reproduction of social inequality, and the generation of social solidarity.

Social Functions of Emotional Conformity and the "Role-Taking Emotions"

Obviously, when people alter their spontaneous feelings or expressions to meet normative requirements, they are sustaining, rather than challenging or changing, the existing social order. Less obvious, however, is the fact that when people conform to emotional expectations, they are also reproducing status inequalities that are embedded in that social order. This is because emotional expectations and the emotional skills necessary to meet those expectations are distributed differentially by social status.

Cahill (1999) introduced the concept of "emotional capital" to refer to the sum total of an individual's emotional knowledge and skills. (Emotional capital thus includes the acquisition of emotion culture, as well as abilities to understand, display, regulate, and transform one's own and others' emotions. Thus, it is highly similar to what psychologists have termed "emotional intelligence" [Salovey and Mayer 1989].) People accumulate different amounts and kinds of emotional capital, depending on their status characteristics, such as age, gender, race/ethnicity, and social class. Because different social positions (e.g., entertainers, athletes, day care workers) require specific types of emotional knowledge and skills, persons with appropriate forms of emotional capital tend to select and be selected for those positions differentially, which in turn maintains the inequalities tied to those positions. This process is most evident in the occupational realm. "People occupations" attract and hire female and middle-class workers who have been trained to attend closely to emotions and to manage feelings (Hochschild 1983). Working-class boys who have been encouraged to master and mask their fears select and are selected for high-steel ironwork as a career (Haas 1977). Sons and daughters of funeral directors have sufficient prior experience in coping with death and dead bodies to follow in their parents' footsteps (Cahill 1999). Differential selection sustains the gender and social class composition of these occupations, and this stratification in turn perpetuates cultural expectations about the emotionality and emotional skills of specific social groups (again, culture and social structure are mutually reinforcing).

The reproduction of social inequality that occurs at the social system level can also be observed within organizations. Lively (2000, 2001) and Pierce (1995) reported that mostly female paralegals are expected to show deference and support to predominantly male attorneys and clients, while frequently being demeaned, insulted, or ignored in return. Paralegals transform their frustrations with a variety of emotion work strategies (e.g., they view attorneys and clients as spoiled children) and interpret their ability to maintain a pleasant demeanor as an indicator of their professionalism and competence. Ironically, however, by reworking the negative feelings caused by their devalued status in the law firm and by seeing this as a marker of their own moral superiority and professionalism, paralegals help to perpetuate rather than challenge their place in the firm's hierarchy.

Clark (1990) describes these hierarchy-maintaining processes as "micropolitics"—the losing, gaining, or keeping of power, rank, standing, or "place." Emotions are indicators of relative social standing; high-status individuals receive respect and liking, low-status persons are offered contempt or hate. Individuals deliberately manipulate other people's emotions in order to sustain, usurp, upset, or withhold social placement from some and to convey it to others (or themselves). In short, micropolitical emotional exchanges and manipulations are crucial aspects of the creation and perpetuation of social inequality, and the success of these acts depends on individuals' relative possession of the requisite emotional capital.

Emotional capital not only includes knowledge of emotion culture and skill at managing one's own and others' emotions, but also the ability to experience what have been called the "self-conscious emotions" (Tangney 1999) or the "reflexive role-taking emotions" (Shott 1979), such as shame, guilt, embarrassment, pride, and vanity. These "social emotions" result from evaluating the self from the perspective of other people and finding oneself at fault or favored. Guilt and embarrassment cause individuals to engage in reparative behaviors to restore a positive self-image in their own and others' eyes (Shott 1979; Tangney 1999). Pride (self-approval derived from others' approval) encourages behaviors that conform to social norms and values (Barrett 1995; Tangney 1999).[5] In general, then, the reflexive role-taking emotions motivate efforts to conform to social rules, helping, again, to maintain the social order.

Role-taking skills allow the acquisition of other social emotions, the prosocial affects of empathy, sympathy, and pity (Clark 1997; Shott 1979). Empathic role-taking emotions are evoked by "mentally placing oneself in another's position and feeling what the other feels [empathy] or what one would feel in such a position [sympathy]" (Shott 1979, p. 1324). The capacity for these feelings is another key form of emotional capital. Sensitivity to the emotions of others makes one better able to anticipate and meet people's normative expectations and better able to manipulate others' emotions for their benefit or one's own gain. Obviously, such skills are marketable in a service-based economy.

More fundamentally, empathic emotions help to produce social solidarity. Research consistently shows that empathy prompts helping behavior (Eisenberg and Fabes 1990; Shott 1979). (By acting to relieve the distress of another, one's own vicarious distress is alleviated.) Helping behavior in turn generates positive emotions in the recipient (gratitude, liking), forges or reinforces social bonds, creates obligations to reciprocate in kind, and improves the overall welfare of the group (Clark 1997). Perhaps because empathy and sympathy are so crucial for the production and maintenance of social solidarity, they are governed by a set

[5]Shame has less desirable social consequences, prompting social withdrawal and angry and aggressive reactions toward people who are thought to share one's negative view of the self (Tangney 1999; Scheff 1988).

of norms that closely regulate their exchange (e.g., one should not make false claims or too many claims to sympathy, one should reciprocate others' sympathy) (Clark 1997).

In sum, social order, social inequality, *and* social cohesion are byproducts of individuals' emotional capital.

Emotional Deviance and Social Change

Although analysts tend to focus on the positive adaptive functions of individuals' role-taking emotions and their efforts at emotional conformity, these outcomes are by no means determined. Emotion management efforts sometimes fail (Copp 1998; Hochschild 1983; Thoits 1986, 1996). Emotion work failure is probable when structural strains that generate inappropriate emotions are recurrent or persistent, or when emotion-management assistance from others is lacking (Lively 2000; Thoits 1986). When one or both of these conditions occur, emotion work attempts may be unsuccessful, and individuals will suffer from prolonged or repeated undesirable feelings and expressive displays, that is, from *emotional deviance* (Thoits 1986).

There have been few empirical examinations of the consequences of emotional deviance. However, three theoretical possibilities have been raised: Individuals who display persistent inappropriate affect may be labeled by observers as emotionally disturbed (Pugliesi 1987; Thoits 1986), they may label themselves as disturbed (Thoits 1986), or they may seek out similar others to validate their deviant feelings as understandable and justifiable and pursue social change (Wasielewski 1985).

With respect to attributions of disorder, emotional deviance plays an important role in clinicians' and laypersons' recognition of psychological problems (Thoits 2000). As the various editions of the Diagnostic and Statistical Manual of Mental Disorders (DSM) have become more specific over time in their criteria for diagnoses, multiple references have appeared to "inappropriate affect," emotions "far out of proportion to reality," emotional displays that are "intense," "excessive," or "flat," and the like (American Psychiatric Association 1994). In fact, violations of emotion norms are essential defining criteria for roughly 30 percent of the disorders listed in DSM-IV (Thoits 2000). Ordinary adults, too, associate odd or inappropriate emotional behaviors with mental illness (Link et al. 1999; Pugliesi 1987). When presented with descriptions of individuals reacting typically to common life troubles and individuals displaying classic DSM-IV symptoms of major depression and other disorders, a nationally representative sample of adults made sharp distinctions between conventional and deviant emotional states (Link et al. 1999). Thus, both clinicians and laypersons connect deviant emotional reactions to psychiatric disturbance.

Given such associations, persons who persistently or repeatedly exhibit deviant feelings and/or expressive displays are likely to be labeled mentally ill by other people and forced into treatment, or alternatively, well-socialized actors may label themselves as in need of treatment and seek it out (Thoits 1985). Labeling results in the social control of deviant members of society and/or their emotional resocialization in treatment, thus preserving current social understandings and avoiding social disruption.

However, in special circumstances, deviant emotional states may be validated by others and become motivations for pursuing social change. People often seek out similar others who are experiencing the same problematic situations and feelings—self-help groups help to fill this need (Coates and Winston 1983). Individuals are usually comforted to know that others have had the same feelings and understand them. Typically, too, self-help groups instruct members in methods of achieving emotional "health" or "recovery" (e.g., Francis 1997). In these ways, self-help groups act to maintain conventional emotion norms and restore individuals to conventional feelings and behaviors (Thoits 1985). However, when individuals' deviant emotional reactions are in response to injustice or oppression, these shared feelings may be crucial in the transformation of similar others into counternormative peer groups, deviant subcultures, or protest movements. A charismatic leader who manipulates and legitimates the feelings and the new emotion norms of the group may facilitate social change (Wasielewski 1985) . In short, because individuals are not determined by the structures or cultures in which they live, but can exercise agency, creativity, and autonomy, they may, in unjust or oppressive circumstances, redefine their deviant feelings as valid and proceed to use these new normative understandings to persuade others to pursue social change.

Concluding Commentary

Traditionally in sociological thought, self and society have been linked through social roles (Stryker and Statham 1985). In sociological approaches to affect, however, emotion norms bridge the gap between the individual and group. Individuals acquire knowledge of emotion culture, including emotion norms, and develop a variety of emotional skills. With such emotional capital, social actors try to meet cultural standards for feelings and expression, and in the process, they re-create and sustain existing social arrangements, inequalities, and solidarities. However, individuals also introduce modifications or new twists in appropriate emotions or displays that may be validated and adopted by others, initiating a process of social change. Social structural arrangements, in turn, generate recurrent emotional experiences that become expectable, conventional, and eventually normative—part of the emotion culture that individuals absorb. In short, emotion norms and the emotion work processes that maintain them are intermediate theoretical mechanisms linking macro- and microlevel phenomena.

This interplay between society and the individual perhaps is best seen in studies of the causes and consequences of emotional labor, a topic that has preoccupied sociologists and may increasingly grab the attention of historians, anthropologists, and social psychologists, given global shifts from preindustrial and industrial societies to service- and information-dominated economies. Observing such trends, one might ask whether pressures to conform to emotion norms for pay will produce widespread self-alienation and social estrangement, or might such emotional abilities become sources of efficacy and pride? Is the concept of emotion *work* itself simply a product of Western culture, which celebrates the value of individual freedom from constraint? In cultures that elevate collectivism, might people locate their authentic selves in their conformity to others' emotional expectations?[6] These are only a few of the kinds of questions that are raised when emotion norms—and the emotion management processes that sustain or change them—become a central focus of analysis.

[6]I am grateful to Batja Mesquita for suggesting the latter two interesting questions.

References

American Psychiatric Association. (1994). *Diagnostic and statistical manual of mental disorders: DSM-IV*. Washington, DC: American Psychiatric Association.

Cahill, S. E. (1999). Emotional capital and professional socialization: The case of mortuary science students (and me). *Social Psychology Quarterly, 62*, 101–116.

Cahill, S. E. and Eggleston, R. A. (1994). Managing emotions in public: The case of wheelchair users. *Social Psychology Quarterly, 57*, 300–312.

Cancian, F. M. (1987). *Love in America: Gender and self-development*. New York: Cambridge University Press.

Cancian, F. M., and Gordon, S. L. (1989). Changing emotion norms in marriage: Love and anger in U.S. women's magazines since 1900. *Gender & Society, 2*, 308–342.

Clark, C. (1990). Emotions and micropolitics in everyday life: Some patterns and paradoxes of "place". In T. D. Kemper (Ed.), *Research agendas in the sociology of emotions* (pp. 305–333). Albany: State University of New York Press.

———. (1997). *Misery and company: Sympathy in everyday life*. Chicago: University of Chicago Press.

Coates, D., and Winston, T. (1983). Counteracting the deviance of depression: Peer support groups for victims. *Journal of Social Issues, 39*, 169–194.

Copp, M. (1998). When emotion work is doomed to fail: Ideological and structural constraints on emotion management. *Symbolic Interaction, 21*, 299–328.

Denzin, N. K. (1990). On understanding emotion: The interpretive-cultural agenda. In T. D. Kemper (Ed.), *Research agendas in the sociology of emotions*, (pp. 85–116). Albany: State University of New York Press.

Dutton, D. G., and Aron, A. P. (1974). Some evidence for heightened sexual attraction under conditions of high anxiety. *Journal of Personality and Social Psychology, 30*, 510–517.

Eisenberg, N., and Fabes, R. A. (1990). Empathy: Conceptualization, measurement, and relation to prosocial behavior. *Motivation and Emotion, 14*, 131–149.

Ekman, P., Friesen, W. V., and Ellsworth, P. (1982). What are the similarities and differences in facial behavior across cultures? In P. Ekman (Ed.), *Emotion in the human face*, 2d ed. (pp. 128–143). Cambridge: Cambridge University Press.

Francis, L. E. (1997). Ideology and interpersonal emotion management: Redefining identity in two support groups. *Social Psychology Quarterly, 60*, 153–171.

Francis, L. E., Monahan, K., and Berger, C. (1999). A laughing matter? The uses of humor in medical interactions. *Motivation and Emotion, 23*, 155–174.

Frude, N., & Goss, A. (1981). Maternal anger and the young child. In N. Frude (Ed.), *Psychological approaches to child abuse* (pp. 52–63). Totawa, NJ: Rowman & Littlefield.

Gimlin, D. (1996). Pamela's place: Power and negotiation in the hair salon. *Gender & Society, 10*, 505–526.

Gordon, S. (1989). The socialization of children's emotions: Emotional culture, exposure, and competence. In C. Saarni and P. Harris (Eds.), *Children's understanding of emotions* (pp. 319–349). New York: Cambridge University Press

Graham, H. (1981). Mothers' accounts of anger and aggression towards their babies. In N. Frude (Ed.), *Psychological approaches to child abuse* (pp. 39–63). Totawa, NJ: Rowman & Littlefield.

Haas, J. (1977). Learning real feelings: A study of high steel ironworkers' reactions to fear and danger. *Work and Occupations, 4*, 147–170.

Hafferty, F. W. (1988). Cadaver stories and the emotional socialization of medical students. *Journal of Health and Social Behavior, 29*, 344–356.

Hochschild, A. R. (1979). Emotion work, feeling rules, and social structure. *American Journal of Sociology, 85*, 551–575.

———. (1983). *The managed heart: Commercialization of human feeling*. Berkeley: University of California Press.

Illouz, E. (1997). *Consuming the romantic utopia: Love and the cultural contradictions of capitalism*. Berkeley: University of California Press.

Kemper, T. D. (1987). How many emotions are there? Wedding the social and the autonomic components. *American Journal of Sociology, 93*, 2, 263–289.

Kleinman, A., and Kleinman, J. (1985). Somatization: The interconnections in Chinese society among culture, depressive experiences, and the meanings of pain. In A. Kleinman and B. Good (Eds.), *Culture and depression: Studies in the anthropology and cross-cultural psychiatry of affect and disorder* (pp. 429–490). Berkeley: University of California Press.

Leavitt, R. L., and Power, M. B. (1989). Emotional socialization in the postmodern era: Children in day care. *Social Psychology Quarterly, 52*, 35–43.

Leidner, R. (1993). *Fast food, fast talk: Service work and the routinization of everyday life*. Berkeley: University of California Press.

Levy, R. I. (1984). Emotion, knowing, and culture. In R. A. Shweder & R. A. Levine (Eds.), *Culture theory: Essays on mind, self, and emotion* (pp. 214–237). Cambridge: Cambridge University Press.

Link, B. G., Phelan, J. C., Bresnahan, M., Stueve, A., and Pescosolido, B. A. (1999). Public conceptions of mental illness: Labels, causes, dangerousness, and social distance. *American Journal of Public Health, 89*, 1328–1333.

Lively, K. J. (2000). Reciprocal emotion management: Working together to maintain stratification in private law firms. *Work and Occupations, 27*, 32–63.

———. (2001). Occupational claims to professionalism: The case of paralegals. *Symbolic Interaction, 24*, 343–365.

Lofland, L. (1985). The social shaping of emotion: The case of grief. *Symbolic Interaction, 8*, 171–190.

MacRae, H. (1998). Managing feelings: Caregiving as emotion work. *Research on Aging, 20*, 137–160.

Maslach, C. (1982). *Burnout: The cost of caring*. Englewood Cliffs, NJ: Prentice-Hall.

McCall, G. J., and Simmons, J. L. (1978). *Identities and interactions*. New York: Free Press.

Morris, J. A., and Feldman, D. C. (1996). The dimensions, antecedents, and consequences of emotional labor. *Academy of Management Review, 21*, 986–1010.

Pierce, J. L. (1995). *Gender trials: Emotional lives in contemporary law firms*. Berkeley: University of California Press.

Pogrebin, M. R., and Poole, E. D. (1995). Emotion management: A study of police response to tragic events. In M. G. Flaherty and C. Ellis (Eds.), *Social perspectives on emotion*, Vol. 3 (pp. 149–168). Stamford, CT: JAI Press.

Pollak, L. H., and Thoits, P. A. (1989). Processes in emotional socialization. *Social Psychology Quarterly, 52*, 22–34.

Power, M. B., and Krause-Eheart, B. (1995). Adoption, myth, and emotion work: Paths to disillusionment. In J. G. Flaherty and C. Ellis (Eds.). *Social perspectives on emotion*, Vol. 3 (pp. 97–120). Stamford, CT: JAI Press.

Pugliesi, K. (1987). Deviation in emotion and the labeling of mental illness. *Deviant Behavior, 8*, 79–102.

———. (1999). The consequences of emotional labor: Effects on work stress, job satisfaction, and well-being. *Motivation and Emotion, 23*, 125–154.

Salovey, P., and Mayer, J. D. (1989). Emotional intelligence. *Imagination, Cognition, and Personality, 9*, 185–211.

Schachter, S., and Singer, J. (1962). Cognitive, social and physiological determinants of emotional state. *Psychological Review, 69*, 379–399.

Scheff, T. J. (1988). Shame and conformity: The deference–emotion system. *American Sociological Review, 53*, 395–406.

Shott, S. (1979). Emotion and social life: A symbolic interactionist analysis. *American Journal of Sociology, 84*, 1317–1334.

Shweder, R. A. (1994). "You're not sick, you're just in love": Emotion as an interpretive system. In P. Ekman and R. A. Davidson (Eds.), *The nature of emotion: Fundamental questions* (pp. 32–45) Oxford: Oxford University Press.

Simon, R. W., Eder, D., & Evans, C. (1992). The development of feeling norms underlying romantic love among adolescent females. *Social Psychology Quarterly, 55*, 29–46.

Smith, A. C. and Kleinman, S. (1989). Managing emotions in medical school: Students' contacts with the living and the dead. *Social Psychology Quarterly, 52*, 56–69.

Stearns, C. Z., and Stearns, P. N. (1986). *Anger: The struggle for emotional control in America's history*. Chicago: University of Chicago Press.

Stenross, B. and Kleinman, S. (1989). The highs and lows of emotional labor: Detectives' encounters with criminals and victims. *Journal of Contemporary Ethnography, 17*, 435–452.

Stryker, S., and Statham, A. (1985). Symbolic interaction and role theory. In G. Lindzey & E. Aronson (Eds.), *Handbook of social psychology*, 3d ed. (pp. 311–378). New York: Random House.

Sutton, R. I. (1991). Maintaining norms about expressed emotions: The case of bill collectors. *Administrative Science Quarterly, 36*, 245–268.

Tangney, J. P. (1999). The self-conscious emotions: shame, guilt, embarrassment and pride. In R. Dalgleish and M. Power (Eds.), *Handbook of cognition and emotion* (pp. 541–568). New York: John Wiley.

Taylor, V. (2000). Emotions and identity in women's self-help movements. In S. Stryker and T. J. Owens. (Eds.), *Self, identity, and social movements* (pp. 271–299) Minneapolis: University of Minnesota Press.

Thoits, P. A. (1985). Self-labeling processes in mental illness: The role of emotional deviance. *American Journal of Sociology, 92*, 221–249.

———. (1986). Social support as coping assistance. *Journal of Consulting and Clinical Psychology, 54*, 416–423.

———. (1996). Managing the emotions of others. *Symbolic Interaction, 19*, 85–109.

Thoits, Peggy A. (2000). *Emotion and psychopathology: A sociological point of view*. Paper presented at the International Society for Research on Emotions, Quebec City, Quebec, Canada, August.

———. (2004). "Emotion Norms, Emotion Work, and Social Order," pp. 000 in Antony S. R. Manstead, Nico H. Frijda, and Agneta Fischer (eds.) Feelings and Emotions: *The Amsterdam Symposium, 2001*. Cambridge, UK: NY: Cambridge University Press.

Tolich, M. B. (1993). Alienating and liberating emotions at work: Supermarket clerks' performance of customer service. *Journal of Contemporary Ethnography, 22*, 361–381.

Wasielewski, P. L. (1985). The emotional basis of charisma. *Symbolic Interaction, 8*, 207–222.

Whalen, J., and Zimmerman, D. H. (1998). Observations on the display and management of emotion in naturally occurring activities: The case of "hysteria" in calls to 9-1-1. *Social Psychology Quarterly, 61*, 141–159.

Wharton, A. S. (1996). Service with a smile: Understanding the consequences of emotional labor. In C. L. MacDonald and C. Sirianni (Eds.), *Working in the service society* (pp. 91–112). Philadelphia, PA: Temple University Press.

19

The Influence of Involvement in Extracurricular Activities on Perceived Popularity

Raechel Lizon and Mikaela Dufur
Brigham Young University

Any visitor to a junior high or high school can tell within a few minutes which students are top dogs and which students are being hounded. A student's place in a school's social structure can determine whether school is viewed as something to be embraced or escaped. Since students spend a third or more of their daily lives in school, popularity becomes a major aspect of adolescent life (Eder 1985; Kinney 1993; Merten 1996). Popular students are defined as students "who are most influential in setting group opinions, and who have the greatest impact on determining the boundaries of membership in the most exclusive social groups" (Adler et al. 1992:172). Thus, popularity is a type of social prestige and refers to a student's place in the social hierarchy. It is often based on name recognition, clique membership, athletic ability, and appearance (Adler et al. 1992; Kinney 1993). During adolescence, popularity and social identity become increasingly important. Adolescents are more aware and concerned than preadolescents with how others perceive them, and they report that peer perceptions influence their feelings of social and self worth (O'Brien and Bierman 1988). Adolescents also internalize rejection from their peers, viewing it as an indicator of personal inadequacy (O'Brien and Bierman 1988).

Popularity among adolescents isn't merely a matter of who is asked to the prom or burns a yearbook to repress painful high school memories. Research suggests that peer rejection is related to incidences of school violence. Students who are rejected by their peers and report lower levels of popularity are more likely to experience victimization and bullying by other students (Perren and Hornung 2005). Studies suggest that this rejection can lead to aggressive behavior, school violence, lower academic performance, and delinquent behavior (Leary et al. 2003; Perren and Hornung 2005). In extreme cases, research shows a link between unpopularity and rejection by peers with school shootings (Leary et al. 2003).

What makes a student popular? Although we often think of the stereotypes of popular jocks and unpopular nerds, little research has actually examined the relationships between participation in extracurricular activities and adolescent popularity and social structures. In fact, involvement in extracurricular activities is linked to a number of positive outcomes for teenagers, including lower rates of delinquency (Hoffmann and Xu 2002; Landers and Landers 1978), higher academic achievement (Broh 2002), higher self-esteem (Holland and Andre 1987; Marsh and Kleitman 2002), and higher educational aspirations (Darling et al. 2005). We might expect that the influence of extracurricular activities would extend to issues of popularity and social hierarchies, but few studies explicitly consider the relationship between participation in extracurricular activities and students' perceptions of popularity.

It's easy to see how participation in some activities is a measure of popularity—for example, students who are elected to offices or to be homecoming queen must hold considerable status and visibility in order for people to vote for them. But can participation in extracurricular activities make a student more or less popular? Studies suggest that involvement in extracurricular activities is a mechanism that allocates varying levels of status and esteem to participants (Merten 1996). These varying levels of prestige create status categories that both enhance and limit a student's ability to gain social recognition. These categories then shape the social structure and processes in a school, reinforcing the hierarchical structure of student peer groups. Since studies suggest that participation in extracurricular activities affects the formation of status hierarchies, understanding how extracurricular activities influence perceived popularity levels can provide valuable insight into the formation and maintenance of adolescent social identity and adolescent social systems.

In addition, the ways students react to cliques and rejection may vary by their sex. Male students who are unable to gain popularity with their peers are more likely to react with aggressive behavior. Some studies suggest that for male students, peer acceptance and popularity are gained through avenues of normalized masculinity, which are characterized by "hypermasculine identification, athletics, fighting, distance from homosexuality, dominant relationships with girls, socioeconomic status, and disdain for academics" (Klein 2006: 53). However, few avenues are available to males who cannot achieve acceptance and popularity through these traditional markers of stereotypical masculinity (Klein 2006). Consequently, some rejected males turn to extreme forms of violence as a display of hypermasculinity in an attempt to gain status with their peers (Klein 2006). Returning to our example of school shootings, there is evidence that at least some shooters recognize the ways their actions play into these notions of masculinity. One accused student explained that after shooting his peers at school he felt more "popular" because "I was feeling proud, good, and more respected" (Klein 2006: 56). Thus, unpopular male students may engage in school violence as a means of obtaining status among their peers. The emergence of both scholarly studies and popular books and movies on the phenomenon of "Queen Bees" and "Mean Girls" demonstrates girls are highly skilled at using information, allies, and lines of communication to solidify their own popularity and undercut their peers' social standing (cf. Merten 1996; Wiseman 2002). It is possible that boys and girls use participation in extracurricular activities in different ways when assessing popularity and social status.

In this study, we address these issues by examining whether students who are involved in extracurricular activities are more likely to identify themselves as popular. Because some studies suggest that different types of extracurricular activities result in varying outcomes, we also analyze whether this relationship varies based on the type of extracurricular activity in which the student is involved (Broh 2002; McNeal 1995); in addition, we investigate whether these effects are different for boys and girls. We also utilize Cooley's concept of the looking-glass self to explain why adolescents are concerned about how their peers view them, as well as social identity theory and social categorization theory to provide explanations for how extracurricular activities function as a system that creates ingroups and outgroups.

The Looking Glass and Adolescent Self-Concept

Cooley's concept of the looking-glass self helps explain why the perceived opinion of peers is an important factor in an individual's self-concept. Cooley ([1902] 1983) suggests that individuals view themselves as a reflection of how others see them. This occurs as a person imagines how he/she appears to their peers, and what type of judgment or evaluation their peers are making of the person. This imagination then results in a positive or negative feeling. For example, if an individual imagines that another person would evaluate her positively, this can result in a positive self-feeling. In contrast, if an individual imagines that a peer would evaluate him negatively, it can result in negative self-feelings. Since research suggests that adolescents value the opinion of their peers highly, an imagined negative judgment by peers can result in negative self-feelings (O'Brien and Bierman 1988). Thus, students who perceive themselves as unpopular with their peers are more likely to experience negative self-feelings.

However, this can vary based on whether the person desires the positive approval of the peer group he/she is imagining. Cooley states ([1902] 1983), "The thing that moves us to pride or shame is not the mere mechanical reflection of ourselves, but an imputed sentiment, the imagined effect of this reflection upon another's mind. This is evident from the fact that the character and weight of that other, in whose mind we see ourselves, makes all the difference with our feelings" (184). Thus, an individual's positive or negative evaluation does not depend solely on the imagined evaluation of the other. Instead, the relationship between the individual and the other must be considered. If the individual values the opinion of the other person, then an imagined positive judgment results in positive self-feelings. However, if the individual does not value the opinion of the other, then an imagined positive judgment may result in negative self-feeling. Thus, students may take more seriously the opinions they imagine coming from adolescents higher in the social hierarchy.

Social Identity Theory and Adolescents' Assessment of Group Membership

How, then, do adolescents determine whose judgments are meaningful to them, or which opinions they value? Social identity theory suggests a tendency toward group membership and exclusion among adolescents. Turner (1999) notes that individuals use categorization to understand the world around them. When individuals come into contact with an unknown other, they seek to place a label on the other as a means of understanding the social environment. Through this identification process, similar others are placed in the ingroup category while dissimilar others are viewed as members of an outgroup. Since individuals gain elements of their self-identity through group interaction, delineation between ingroups and outgroups is an important element of self-esteem[1] maintenance. Social identity theory suggests that it is through comparison that self-esteem is maintained. Self-esteem is increased when an individual compares the perceived positive attributes of their ingroup with the perceived negative attributes of the outgroup. Thus, when adolescents label a peer as unpopular, they are creating a less valued outgroup to which they can favorably compare themselves. This allows the adolescents to maintain or bolster their self-esteem and self-identity. In addition, such tendencies create a social hierarchy that helps teens understand which imagined judgments are to be given more weight.

Social categorization theory suggests that ingroup bias can be created by merely the knowledge that distinct groups exist (Turner 1975). Thus, those in the ingroup are accepted while those in the outgroup are devalued simply because there is an awareness of differing groups. This process occurs because individuals begin to view group membership as an important part of their self-concept and identity (Tajfel 1972). Merely participating in or being excluded from extracurricular activities is one way in which such distinct groups are created. However, there is a psychological need for the ingroup to be evaluated as positive in comparison to the outgroup so that positive social identity can be maintained since individuals begin to classify themselves, not based on personal characteristics, but based on group identity (Turner 1999). Stereotypes about the outgroup then may develop, increasing the distinction between groups and causing greater discrimination. Thus, for students who perceive themselves as popular to maintain their positive self-identity, they must distinguish an outgroup with less valuable characteristics, thereby creating a group of social outsiders. In fact, adolescents who are unpopular with other students tend to be viewed as social outsiders and are often excluded from social interaction (Adler and Adler 1995; Kinney 1993). To accomplish this, labels that help to create categories, such as participation in particular extracurricular activities, may be imbued with positive or negative judgments.

In addition, exclusion of unpopular students is often used to define group membership boundaries (Adler and Adler 1995). Students avoid unpopular social outsiders because they fear they will be associated with the lower social status of those individuals. However, some students are able to overcome the stigma of unpopularity as they interact with more social groups. This is possible, in part, because participation in activities can change perceptions about both individuals and groups (Kinney 1993). Higher-status students may increase the social prestige of an activity by joining, raising the popularity of other students in the group. If students who were previously unpopular can join a higher status group, they are then perceived as being more popular. On the other hand, if a number of unpopular youths join a group, their influx may lower the social status of the overall group.

[1]While popularity and self-esteem are interrelated concepts, popularity differs from self-esteem. Popularity is based on how an individual is perceived by others socially (Adler et al. 1992; Kinney 1993). Even self-perceived popularity is based on how individuals feel others perceive them—not on whether the individuals value themselves. In contrast, self-esteem is an "individual's positive or negative attitude toward the self as a totality" (Rosenberg, Schooler, Schoenbach, and Rosenberg 1995: 141). Thus, popularity is based on others estimation of social worth, while self-esteem is person's self-assessment of value. Consequently, an individual may have high levels of self-esteem and low levels of popularity or vice versa.

Thus, well-managed involvement in extracurricular activities may be an important way students can improve their social position, as such activities can provide an entrance into new social groups and access to higher status. Through this process, unpopular students who are observant about how extracurricular activities enhance or hurt social status are able to use participation to increase their school social position. However, students who do not participate in high-status extracurricular activities are more likely to be viewed as unpopular because they do not obtain the higher status group association that participation often brings. Therefore, students who are involved in extracurricular activities may be viewed as more popular by their peers, while students who are not involved in extracurricular activities may be viewed as less popular since they are more likely to lack high status group association.

However, although students who participate in extracurricular activities tend to feel more integrated into the social structure at school, not all extracurricular activities have the same effects on academic outcomes (Broh 2002; McNeal 1995; Ziblatt 1965). Participation in different extracurricular activities may have divergent effects on students' perceived popularity, as well. For example, McNeal (1995) found that involvement in sports decreases a student's chances of dropping out of school, while involvement in academic and vocational activities has little influence on dropping out. This may occur because athletes develop more social connections with other students and feel more attached to the school social environment than do students in other activities. In addition, Sandstrom and Coie (1999) found that students who are initially rejected by their peers are more likely to be accepted after participating in extracurricular activities, especially if they displayed aggressive behaviors like those found in sports. Other studies also indicate that popularity is based partially on a student's athletic ability (Adler et al. 1992; Kennedy 1995). It stands to reason, then, that students in the athletic ingroup reap the benefits of higher placement in the social hierarchy at school. They are then able to assume more positive imagined judgments from students who rank lower in the social structure, increasing their own self-image and popularity. While the idea that people sporting athletic letter jackets might be considered popular likely comes as little surprise to anyone who has ever attended a high school, the fact that this pattern seems common does not explain its roots.

One possible explanation for why all extracurricular are not created equal is the influence of gender. Studies suggest that the influence of extracurricular activities on positive academic outcomes varies for males and females (Videon 2002). In a qualitative study, Merten (1997) found that for females, participation in certain high-status extracurricular activities such as cheerleading and drill-team were means of gaining popularity with peers. Females often gained status through participation in activities that highlighted glamour and appearance (Adler et al. 1992; Merten 1997). However, males often gained popularity by participating in activities that highlight strength and aggression such as sports (Adler et al. 1992). Thus, it appears that when an extracurricular activity emphasizes stereotypical gender roles, it increases perceived popularity more than if the activity does not reinforce existing gender stereotypes.

We test three ways participation might be related to extracurricular activities. First, participation may create links between and visibility among students; if this is true, we would expect that participation in any extracurricular activity would increase students' popularity. By contrast, participation in higher-status activities, such as athletics, might allow students to imagine more positive judgments from other students, increasing both their self-image and their position in the social hierarchy; thus, we test the possibility that effects of participation on popularity vary by activity. Finally, we explore the possibility that participation in activities that reinforce gender stereotypes benefits students because such activities allow their peers to categorize their activities using behavioral and social cues they have already been trained to understand. This may create different categories and hierarchies for boys and girls, affecting the imagined responses from others. Students may assume more positive judgments when they are participating in activities considered "appropriate" for their sex. We investigate whether boys and girls receive different returns in popularity to certain activities.

Data and Methods

For this study, we use the National Education Longitudinal Study (NELS), which provides a nationally representative sample of eighth-grade students. It contains detailed questions on participation in extracurricular activities and perceptions of popularity. We use responses from the first wave of data collection conducted in 1988, which comprises a sample of 10,938 eighth-grade students. In this study, the dependent variable is the self-reported popularity level of the student, while the key independent variables are measures of the students' participation in extracurricular school activities. Our models also include control variables for race, socioeconomic status, and gender, since research suggests that these variables are related to extracurricular activity participation levels (Holland and Andre 1987; Kennedy 1995; Ziblatt 1965). We used ordinal logistic regression to test these hypotheses (for more details on the analyses, see Lizon 2007). To test whether the effects of extracurricular participation might vary by group, we also performed analyses that allowed us to examine whether the influence of participation on popularity worked differently for boys and girls. For example, will boys who play sports gain more popularity than girls who do, or will boys in cheerleading be considered as popular as female cheerleaders? We also asked this question about potential differences by race and socioeconomic status.

Findings

Table 19.1 displays the results of the model using participation in extracurricular activities to predict perceived popularity. Activities that have a significant relationship with popularity are in bold. After controlling for race, sex, and socioeconomic status (SES), twelve extracurricular activities are significantly related to perceived popularity levels. Participation in varsity sports, intramural sports, cheerleading, computer club, science club, dance, drama, honor society, newspaper, yearbook, band, and student government are significantly associated with popularity. Involvement in sports and some performance activities are related to higher popularity levels even in the presence of controls, while participation in band, science club, and computer club persist as negative predictors of popularity. With the exception of science and computers, participation in specific subject clubs tends to be unrelated to student popularity levels. In addition, higher SES students think themselves significantly more popular than lower SES students. Also, males perceive themselves, on average, as significantly more popular than

TABLE 19.1 ***Model Summary of Participation in Extracurricular Activities and Perceived Popularity***

Positive Relationship	*Negative Relationship*
Varsity sports	**Computer club**
Intramural sports	History club
Cheerleading	**Science club**
Foreign language club	Vocational education club
Dance	**Band**
Drama	Other topic club
Honor society	Speech & Debate
Newspaper	
Yearbook	
Student government	

(Statistically significant relationships are bolded)

females. Whereas African American students have higher perceived popularity levels than non-Hispanic white students, Asian/Pacific Islander students perceive themselves as less popular than white students. However, the relationship between ethnicity and perceived popularity is not statistically significant for Native American and Hispanic students.

We also tested whether extracurricular participation brings the same returns in popularity to all groups, or if some groups benefit more than others. In six cases, we found that some groups benefit more—or are hurt more—by participating in certain activities. For example, we had asked whether playing sports would have the same benefits for boys and girls. In fact, participation in varsity sports increases the popularity of both boys and girls, perhaps because it increases their visibility in the school. However, we found that boys gain more in popularity by playing sports than girls do (Figure 19.1). Gender is also significant when considering participation in band. Popularity drops much more sharply for female students who participate in band than for male students who participate in band (Figure 19.2).

The effects of extracurricular activity participation vary somewhat by ethnicity, as well. Participation in honor society increases the self-reported popularity of Asian students more than it increases the self-reported popularity of non-Hispanic white students. For African American students, participation in cheerleading does not increase perceived popularity as much as it does for white students. However, African American students who participate in drama gain more in perceived popularity than white students do. In addition to sex and race, socioeconomic status also influences how self-reported popularity levels are affected by participation in extracurricular activities. Higher SES students gain more in popularity from involvement in cheerleading than lower SES students. These findings suggest that students' self-reported popularity levels are influenced in different ways by participation in extracurricular activities. Both the type of activity and the characteristics of the student influence how involvement in extracurricular activities is related to perceived popularity levels.

What do these findings tell us about how participating in extracurricular activities affects popularity? We proposed three tests: First, that any participation would increase popularity. This

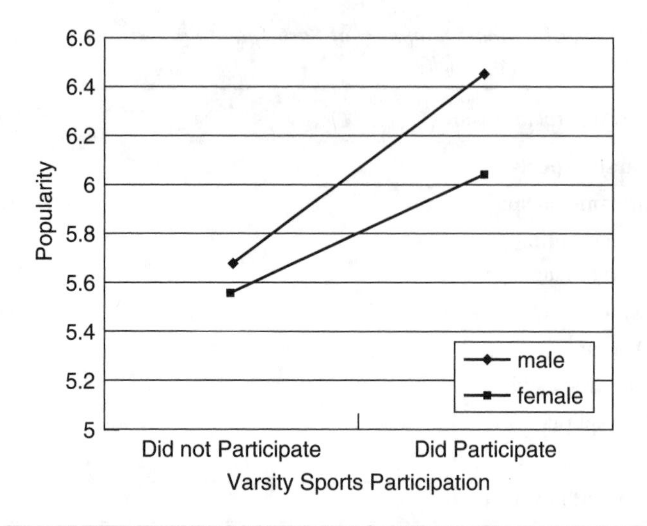

FIGURE 19.1 ***The Influence of Participation in Varsity Sports on Perceived Popularity.***

is not necessarily true, as not all activities are the same when it comes to increasing popularity. Participating in a few activities, notably band and computer and science clubs, is associated with lower perceived popularity. In addition, participation in several other activities had no significant effect—positive or negative—on popularity. The second test did show that some activities, notably sports and some performance activities, are associated with increasing popularity for all groups. Involvement in all types of sports, including varsity sports, intramural sports, and cheerleading, is associated with higher levels of perceived popularity. Participation in varsity sports has the strongest affect on perceived popularity levels while involvement in

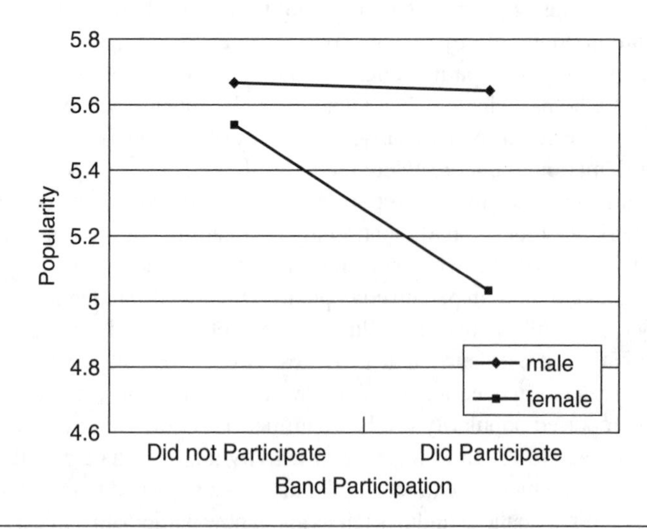

FIGURE 19.2 ***The Influence of Participation in Band on Perceived Popularity.***

dance, drama, computer club, honor society, yearbook and newspaper have lesser affects on perceived popularity levels. Taken together, these patterns show that there is a hierarchy of social categories associated with extracurricular activities that adolescents use to understand their social world. Finally, boys and girls do follow somewhat different paths to popularity, with boys receiving greater returns to athletics and girls paying a greater price for being in the band. Along with findings about ethnicity and SES, this suggests that status characteristics make a difference in the ways involvement in extracurricular activities is translated into popularity.

Discussion

Our analysis of almost eleven thousand adolescents shows that students who participate in school government, intramural sports, varsity sports, cheerleading, dance, drama, honor society, newspaper, and yearbook report higher levels of popularity, while students who participate in computer and science clubs and band perceive themselves as less popular. However, many people still recovering from junior high school could have reported that, with fewer complicated statistical models. Why do different activities lead to such different results in popularity—and why do these particular activities increase or decrease popularity? Social identity theory provides an explanation for these differences. Let's examine three specific cases to unravel how ingroups, group identity, and status affect these activities.

For students to be involved in school government, their peers must vote them in to their position; peer acceptance is often a prerequisite to participation. Thus, this activity allows highly popular students to associate on a regular basis, increasing group identity and commonly shared bonds. Consequently, this helps solidify the ingroup. In addition, participation in school government brings valuable social and personal rewards. School government officers often enjoy time out of class, leadership retreats, recognition at assemblies, power to decide how school resources are spent, and a voice in what social activities the school will host. Since there are a limited number of positions, this scarcity increases the status of students who are able to gain these valuable rewards. Given that adolescents esteem more highly individuals who are viewed as obtaining scarce high-status symbols, students who are able to obtain the valuable rewards associated with student government are more likely to be popular. Coupling the imagined positive judgment that comes along with this greater esteem with actual empirical evidence of popularity in the form of being voted into a position of power by peers allows student government officers to internalize the message that they hold a great deal of status in a school's social hierarchy.

Involvement in varsity sports also brings certain social rewards. Varsity sports allow students to be highly visible among their peers while highlighting socially desirable attributes such as athleticism, fitness, and winning (Adler et al. 1992; Kennedy 1995; Merten 1997). Varsity sporting events also are more likely to have a high profile with a relative large numbers of spectators. Thus, students involved in varsity sports are more likely to be observed doing socially desirable or prestigious activities by their peers. Also, varsity sports are often connected with important school events. For example, at many schools the football game is a highlight of Homecoming Week, which provides athletes with recognition from other students, community members, and the local press. Therefore, varsity sports allow students to participate in highly desirable activities while being viewed by a large peer audience.

Moreover, varsity sports create a clique or ingroup of like-minded students who gain status by exclusion. A relatively small number of students are capable of making the team while others are excluded because of their perceived lack of skill. This selection system constructs an ingroup and outgroup—those who can make the team and those who cannot. Thus, the elite ingroup that shares socially valued characteristics is distinguished from the larger outgroup that does not possess this same level of athleticism. Consequently, participation in varsity sports brings a ready-made ingroup of similar others, a less desirable outgroup, and socially desirable rewards.

In contrast to student government and varsity sports, participation in computer or science clubs is not an exclusive activity. Instead, such clubs generally have open enrollment, and any student can participate. Thus, involvement in this activity does not establish a clear ingroup and outgroup since any number of students can join or leave at any time. Computer or science club students may develop less solidarity because they are not usually working as a group toward a common goal. Instead, students often work in opposition to each other as opponents during computer games or on projects for judged science competitions. This reduces the group solidarity and ingroup identity of the students. In addition, computers are sometimes considered to be involved in lower visibility and lower prestige activities. Consequently, those who participate become associated with a lower prestige group. Students outside computer club are likely to attach this negative label to *all* students involved in the club, even though there may be little ingroup solidarity or homogeneity within the club itself. Because other students do not view this activity as prestigious, participation is actually negatively related to perceived popularity levels.

Another reason participation in computer or science clubs may be related to lower levels of perceived popularity is that it may attract students who reject mainstream definitions of prestige and popularity. Students who are unpopular in school sometimes bond together into an outgroup that seeks new definitions of value while rejecting mainstream definitions, so they can maintain their self-esteem (Kinney 1993). These students may be rejecting the activities of the popular group and creating a group where less popular students are accepted. However, these new definitions of popularity are exclusive to their less popular group and so these students are not viewed as gaining mainstream popularity.

The activities that are related to higher popularity levels might be explained in part by the ability of extracurricular activities to increase the visibility of participants. Studies suggest that a major factor of adolescent popularity is being "known" (Kinney 1993). This refers to a student's social visibility or how high profile the student is in the school social environment (Kinney 1993). Students who are more known are considered higher in the social hierarchy. Thus, time spent on almost any moderate to high prestige extracurricular activity will increase the visibility of the student and consequently their perceived popularity level. Many activities provide opportunities for students' names to be presented to the public. Students involved in drama will often have fliers promoting their plays with the specific names of those playing the leading roles while students involved in newspaper will have their name on the article byline, making their visibility more like those of students in sports or performance activities. Activities such as these increase how well a student is "known" by other students, thus influencing their perceived popularity levels.

In addition, these activities also allow participants to interact with the student body in a socially prestigious manner. For example, students who are involved in newspaper and yearbook interact with the student body by conducting interviews, photographing events, and meeting with many groups as they cover different stories or topics. Students on the newspaper staff often decide who will be photographed and written about in the school community and whether the activity will be presented from a positive or negative perspective. This increases both the visibility and the interaction with various groups that the student experiences. Since popular students report participating in more social groups and have a wider variety of friends than other students, participation in extracurricular activities allows them to strengthen their ties with a wider range of students. Also, proximity and familiarity often lead to friendship formation and acceptance. Thus, popularity levels are influenced by what activities a student participates in and how prestigious or visible those activities are, because it allows student to build connections and friendships with others.

This research suggests that student self-reported popularity levels are related to the types of activities students participate in and the visibility of those activities. When activities are high profile and exclusive, offering scarce social and personal rewards, they are more likely to be associated with higher perceived popularity levels since these activities automatically define a desirable ingroup and a less desirable outgroup. Conversely, low profile, less prestigious, and more inclusive activities are associated with lower perceived popularity levels since involvement often attaches a stigmatized label to participants. This suggests that extracurricular activities can function as a system that allocates scarce popularity resources to members of the student body based on what socially desirable characteristics they possess.

In addition, these patterns work differently for boys and girls. Males who are involved in varsity sports show higher self-reported popularity than female students who are involved in varsity sports. In contrast, females who participate in band report lower levels of popularity than males who participate in band. These differences can be explained by the varying sources of popularity for male and female students. The source of male popularity is often performance based, whereas the source of female popularity is often appearance based (Adler et al. 1992). Since male adolescents gain social prestige through athletic ability and performance, varsity sports enhance male popularity levels more than female popularity levels because they provide males with success in "idealized models of masculinity" (Adler et al. 1992: 170). Varsity sports are avenues of normalized masculinity that accentuate the gender stereotype of the idealized male as aggressive, competitive, and strong (Adler et al. 1992; Klein 2006). In contrast, open competition is often viewed as a less socially acceptable for female adolescents. Instead, female adolescents often engage in more covert forms of competition that emphasize interpersonal relationships or personal appearance (Merten 1997). Consequently, when girls are involved in varsity sports, it does not highlight socially valued gender appropriate characteristics to the same extent that it does for boys. Thus, males gain more perceived popularity from involvement in varsity sports than females.

The effect of participation in band for males and females can be explained in a similar manner. Although band participation is related to lower perceived popularity for males, females who participate in band report greater unpopularity than males who participate in band. For female adolescents, popularity is often based on wearing expensive and in-style clothes and physical attractiveness (Adler et al. 1992; Eder 1985; Merten 1997). Females obtain social prestige by gaining the attention of popular boys (Merten 1997). However, when girls participate in band they often wear uniforms that do not allow them to stand out from other band members. Thus, they are less able to gain positive attention from others. Also band uniforms may remain the same for multiple years and many resemble military outfits. Consequently, these uniforms may be viewed as unstylish by peers. Since the source of female popularity is often appearance or the ability to attract the attention of high prestige boys, girls who participate in band are less able to gain popularity through these avenues when wearing band uniforms that do not distinguish them from other participants (Merten 1997). Thus, activities that reinforce stereotypes or interaction processes students already use have stronger effects on popularity than activities that do not.

In addition to these differences by gender, there are also differences by race. Asian American students who participate in honor society have higher self-reported popularity than students of other ethnicities who participate in honor society. This may be explained by the emphasis and high prestige that is placed on academic achievement by many Asian Americans. Asian Americans are more likely to place a higher value on education and have higher academic aspirations than students of other ethnicities (Goyette and Xie 1999; Kao 2000). Since NELS popularity levels are self-reported, Asian American students who participate in honor societies are more likely to view membership as prestigious. Consequently, Asian American students are more likely to associate participation in honor societies with higher levels of perceived popularity. In addition to influencing self-reported popularity levels for Asian American students participating in honor society, race is also a significant factor when evaluating the perceived popularity of African Americans who participate in drama and cheerleading. However, further research is needed into why participation in cheerleading and drama has different affects on the self-reported popularity of African American students than it does on the self-reported popularity of students of other ethnicities.

In addition to these differences based on race, there are also differences based on SES. Higher SES students who participate in cheerleading report higher perceived popularity than lower SES students who participate in cheerleading. Cheerleaders are often stereotyped as high status, well-dressed, in-style, and attractive students (Eder 1985; Merten 1996). However, if a cheerleader does not fit this stereotype, they experience lower popularity levels (Merten 1996). Since higher SES students have more financial resources to acquire the current and rapidly changing in-style trends, they are more able to fit the stereotype of a cheerleader than lower SES students. These financial resources provide higher SES cheerleaders with the chance to obtain greater social prestige through new clothes and expensive accessories. Taken together, these patterns suggest that when extracurricular activities reinforce existing social stereotypes they have a stronger effect on perceived popularity.

These relationships between extracurricular activities and popularity provide a deeper understanding of how school social groups gain and maintain solidarity and social status. However, further research is needed to examine what other factors influence student popularity. While some extracurricular activities allow for a large degree of self-selection, others do not—joining a sports team generally requires being selected by adults in charge and at least some degree of skill. Joining a cheerleading squad or student government is often a case of the rich getting richer, with students who already enjoyed considerably visibility and popularity receiving additional evidence of their social position. Future research might benefit from studying the more subtle differences between activities any student may join, such as computer club or intramural sports. In addition, some students may intentionally choose not to participate in any formal activities or to limit their peer interaction to a small number of close friends, perhaps with few detrimental effects to their overall well-being.

Since not all students participate in extracurricular activities, future studies should examine how these students achieve their position in the social hierarchy and what factors influence their social position.

References

Adler, Patricia A. and Peter Adler. 1995. "Dynamics of Inclusion and Exclusion in Preadolescent Cliques." *Social Psychology Quarterly* 58:145–162.

Adler, Patricia A., Steven J. Kless, and Peter Adler. 1992. "Socialization to Gender Roles: Popularity among Elementary School Boys and Girls." *Sociology of Education* 65:169–187.

Broh, Beckett A. 2002. "Linking Extracurricular Programming to Academic Achievement: Who Benefits and Why?" *Sociology of Education* 75:69–95.

Cooley, Charles Horton. [1902] 1983. *Human Nature and the Social Order*. New Brunswick, NJ: Transaction Books.

Darling, Nancy, Linda L. Caldwell, and Robert Smith. 2005. "Participation in School-Based Extracurricular Activities and Adolescent Adjustment." *Journal of Leisure Research* 37:51–76.

Eder, Donna. 1985. "The Cycle of Popularity: Interpersonal Relations among Female Adolescents." *Sociology of Education* 58:154–165.

Goyette, Kimberly and Yu Xie. 1999. "Educational Expectations of Asian American Youths: Determinants and Ethnic Differences." *Sociology of Education* 72(1):22–36.

Hoffmann, John P. and Jiangmin Xu. 2002. "School Activities, Community Service, and Delinquency." *Crime and Delinquency* 48:568–591.

Holland, Alyce and Thomas Andre. 1987. "Participation in Extracurricular Activities in Secondary School: What Is Known, What Needs to Be Known?" *Review of Educational Research* 57:437–466.

Kao, Grace. 2000. "Group Images and Possible Selves among Adolescents: Linking Stereotypes to Expectations by Race and Ethnicity." *Sociological Forum* 15(3):407–430.

Kennedy, Eugene. 1995. "Correlates of Perceived Popularity among Peers: A Study of Race and Gender Differences among Middle School Students." *Journal of Negro Education* 64:186–195.

Kinney, David A. 1993. "From Nerds to Normals: The Recovery of Identity among Adolescents from Middle School to High School." *Sociology of Education* 66:21–40.

Klein, Jessie. 2006. "Cultural Capital and High School Bullies: How Social Inequality Impacts School Violence." *Men and Masculinities* 9(1):53–75.

Landers, Daniel and Donna Landers. 1978. "Socialization via Interscholastic Athletics: Its Effects on Delinquency." *Sociology of Education* 51:299–303.

Leary, Mark R., Robin M. Kowalski, Laura Smith, and Stephen Phillips. 2003. "Teasing, Rejection, and Violence: Case Studies of School Shootings." *Aggressive Behavior* 29:202–214.

Lizon, Rachel. 2007. "The Influence of Involvement in Extracurricular Activities on Perceived Popularity." Unpublished Master's Thesis, Brigham Young University, Provo, UT.

Marsh, Herbert W. and Sabina Kleitman. 2002. "Extracurricular School Activities: The Good, the Bad, the Nonlinear." *Harvard Educational Review* 72:464–515.

McNeal, Ralph B. 1995. "Extracurricular Activities and High School Dropouts." *Sociology of Education* 68:62–80.

Merten, Don E. 1996. "Burnout as Cheerleader: The Cultural Basis for Prestige and Privilege in Junior High School." *Anthropology and Education Quarterly* 27:51–70.

———. 1997. "The Meaning of Meanness: Popularity, Competition, and Conflict among Junior High School Girls." *Sociology of Education* 70:175–191.

O'Brien, Susan F. and Karen Linn Bierman. 1988. "Conceptions and Perceived Influence of Peer Groups: Interviews with Preadolescents and Adolescents." *Child Development* 59:1360–1365.

Perren, Sonja and Rainer Hornung. 2005. "Bullying and Delinquency in Adolescence: Victims' and Perpetrators' Family and Peer Relations." *Swiss Journal of Psychology* 64(1):51–64.

Rosenberg, Morris, Carmi Schooler, Carrie Schoenbach, and Florence Rosenberg. 1995. "Global Self-Esteem and Specific Self-Esteem: Different Concepts Defferent Outcomes." *American Sociological Review* 60(1):141–156.

Sandstrom, Marlene Jacobs and John Coie. 1999. "A Developmental Perspective on Peer Rejection: Mechanisms of Stability and Change." *Child Development* 70:955–966.

Tajfel, Henri. 1972. "Social Categorization." Pp. 272–302 in *Introduction a la Psychologie Sociale*. Volume 1, edited S. Morcorici. Paris: Larousse.

Turner, John C. 1975. "Social Comparison and Social Identity: Some Prospects for Intergroup Behaviour." *European Journal of Social Psychology*, 5: 5–34.

———. 1999. "Some Current Issues in Research on Social Identity and Self-Categorization Theories," in *Social Identity*. Eds. Naoi Ellemers, Russell Spears and Bertjan Doosje. Oxford: Blackwell.

Videon, Tami M. 2002. "Who Plays and Who Benefits: Gender, Interscholastic Athletics, and Academic Outcomes." *Sociological Perspectives* 45(4):415–444.

Wiseman, Rosalind. 2002. *Queen Bees and Wannabes: Helping Your Daughter Survive Cliques, Gossip, Boyfriends, and Other Realities of Adolescence*. New York: Crown Publishers.

Ziblatt, David. 1965. "High School Extracurricular Activities and Political Socialization." *Annals of the American Academy of Political and Social Science* 361:20–31.

20

Contact in Context: Whites' Attitudes toward Interracial Marriage

Bryan R. Johnson
Pennsylvania State University

Cardell K. Jacobson
Brigham Young University

ABSTRACT
Using data from a *New York Times* poll conducted in 2000, we analyze whites' approval of interracial marriage by examining the contexts in which whites have contact with blacks. The contexts can be ordered by the type of contact they provide, from close and personal to distant or hierarchical. The results of our analysis show that the type of contact engendered by a variety of contexts is important in determining attitudes toward interracial marriage. The contacts in most of the social settings are associated with friendship; the social structural contexts of age, gender, income, political party, and region are all related to approval of interracial marriage even when friendship is controlled statistically.

Acceptance of interracial marriage has increased substantially over the past few decades (Schuman et al. 1997). The actual rates of intergroup marriage also have increased, though they remain low (Heaton and Jacobson 2000; Qian 1997; Schuman et al. 1997). While early research focused on interracial marriage as a proxy for understanding race relations and acceptance of other groups (e.g., Gordon 1964), more recent studies have found that intermarriage still evokes an emotional response from many whites and some members of minority communities (Herring and Amissah 1997; Pettigrew 1997; Yancey 2001). Still other research has found stronger opposition to black-white marriage than to marriage between other groups (Herring and Amissah 1997; Lewis and Yancey 1995; Spickard 1989). Thus, in many ways, intermarriage remains the ultimate break with traditional racial norms. The examination of attitudes toward interracial marriage remains important and provides an important focal perspective on intergroup relations.

In this essay we use data from a recent national poll to examine whites' attitudes toward interracial marriage. We employ the contact hypothesis as a theoretical framework and develop hypotheses about the types of social settings that are likely to influence these attitudes. Essentially we maintain that social structures either impede or facilitate acceptance of other groups and affect positions on interracial marriage. As Bobo and Fox (2003) argue in their overview of the special edition of *Social Psychology Quarterly* on race and racism, mainstream sociological research has examined many of the structural manifestations of racism and discrimination, but "the micro processes necessarily embedded in these structural analyses are still largely unaddressed" (p. 319). We attempt to further the analysis of such microprocesses by examining how contexts of interracial contacts and friendships are related to attitudes about interracial marriage.

The Social Contact Hypothesis

Social contact between groups is commonly viewed as a critical and ameliorative factor in improving intergroup relationships. As Allport stated in 1954, the contact hypothesis claims that under specific conditions, contact with members of different racial groups can promote positive and tolerant attitudes toward other groups (Pettigrew 1998). As applied to marriage, the contact hypothesis asserts that the chance for members of different groups to intermarry depends primarily on their opportunities to meet and interact socially. Only under favorable conditions, however, can pertinent information about other groups be obtained, synthesized, and formulated into positive reactions so that good relationships develop. In such conditions, interracial friendships evolve, and romantic relationships and intermarriage become more probable. Thus, positive contact and favorable attitudes toward members of other groups become important precursors to intermarriage.

According to Allport's classic theoretical formulation, positive outcomes to social contact occur only (1) in cooperative events, (2) among participants of equal status, (3) between those who hold common goals, and (4) with those who have supportive authority. More recent research on the positive effects of cooperation has confirmed these predictions (see, for example, Aronson et al. 2002; Desforges et al. 1997; Hewstone and Brown 1986; Powers and Ellison 1995; Sigelman and Welch 1993).

Other factors also affect outcomes. Knowing one individual from another group is insufficient. Sigelman and Welch (1993), for example, found that the racial views of whites whose circle of friends included one black person closely paralleled the views of whites with no black friends. Yancey (1999) found that whites' hostility toward blacks only declines when blacks and whites of equal status share a wide variety of contacts. Intergroup relations are enhanced most fully when the contact is intimate, personal, and friendly, and, ideally, involves several individuals of the other group (Desforges et al. 1997; Hewstone and Brown 1986; Pettigrew 1997). Under these conditions, attitudes about other groups become more general and are not identified with just one or a few individuals. Thus friendship appears to be a critical factor affecting interracial attitudes, motives, and, most likely, approval of interracial dating.

Contact within Social Structures

Contact, however, occurs within social structures. Blau and his colleagues identified a number of macro- and intermediate-level factors that affect rates of intergroup marriage (Blau 1977, 1994; Blau, Blum, and Schwartz 1982), such as relative group size, geographical separation, segregation within those areas, and the age structure of local areas.

Other intermediate-level social structures present individuals with opportunities to meet people from different groups. Such structures can facilitate, modify, or impede the development of intergroup relationships (Kalmijn 1998; Kalmijn and Flap 2001; Powers and Ellison 1995; Yancey 1999). We focus on contact that occurs in four social settings: educational settings, religious institutions, residential neighborhoods, and the workplace. Each provides opportunity for contact, but the type of contact varies in the degree of intimacy.

Most scholars who have examined the effects of education on racial attitudes have found a positive relationship between education and interracial tolerance (e.g., Sandefur and McKinnel 1986; Schoen et al. 1989; St. Jean and Parker 1995; Tinker 1982; Wilson and Jacobson 1995). Although intergroup contact within educational institutions often remains less than ideal for improving racial attitudes (see, for example, Schaefer 1996), these institutions nevertheless provide opportunities for increased intergroup contact and acceptance that may not exist elsewhere in society. The increased approval may result from at least two aspects of education: learning greater tolerance and equal-status contact with members of different groups.[1] In the few previous detailed analyses of attitudes about interracial marriage, approval of interracial marriage is greatest among the college educated. Other evidence of this correlation between education and racial tolerance confirms that education is associated positively with higher rates of intermarriage (Heaton and Jacobson 2000; Jacobs and Labov 2002; Kalmijn 1993; Qian 1997; Sandefur and McKinnel 1986; Tucker and Mitchell-Kernan 1990). Thus we expect education to be associated with greater approval of interracial marriage among whites.

Intergroup contact also may occur in religious institutions. Like education, religion can provide both contact and positive injunctions about acceptance of others. Religions almost universally promote tolerance of others and of other groups. Assessments of religion's effect on prejudice are ambiguous, however. Some authors indicate that religiosity is associated with high racial prejudice; others find religiosity to be related weakly, if at all, to racial attitudes. Still others emphasize that intrinsic or personal religiosity is associated negatively with prejudice, while extrinsic or social religion has a positive association with prejudice (see Batson et al. 1993; Hunsberger 1995). More recently, Yancey (1999, 2001) found that those who attend segregated churches possess significantly more stereotypical attitudes than those who attend integrated churches. The mere presence of members of other groups does not necessarily

[1]Numerous authors also have commented, however, that middle-class students learn how to mask racial prejudices.

lead to contact, however. Some may choose not to have contact, and the presence of large numbers of members of other groups actually may present a racial threat to some persons (see Bobo 1983; Bobo and Kluegel 1993; Quillian 1996; Taylor 1998). Nevertheless, we expect whites in religious institutions to show greater support for interracial marriage than do others.

Residential neighborhoods, the third arena we examine, also present the possibility of contact. Neighborhoods tend to consist of individuals of similar socioeconomic backgrounds; this suggests that egalitarian relationships can exist among neighbors (Yancey 1999). Sigelman and Welch (1993) also found that whites' contacts with blacks in their neighborhood served as a source of information about blacks. Other residential studies indicate that whites living in integrated housing projects develop favorable attitudes toward blacks at a faster rate than whites who live in segregated projects (see Pettigrew 1998; Yancey 1999). Powers and Ellison (1995) found that the contact which occurs in racially integrated neighborhoods reduces opposition to intimate forms of interracial contact, specifically interracial dating.

Other empirical studies, however, have not shown positive attitudinal change to be correlated with residential interracial contact. Yancey (1999) notes that lack of support for residential integration can "exacerbate racial hostilities" rather than alleviate them. Quillian (1996) and Taylor (1998) also report that whites who live in places with high concentrations of blacks are more likely than others to hold prejudicial attitudes. Thus we expect neighborhoods to be associated less closely with support for interracial marriage than are educational and religious institutions.

The workplace is the fourth social setting believed to affect interracial attitudes (Kalmijn and Flap 2001; Powers and Ellison 1995). Much of the contact between groups in the workplace is hierarchical, however. As Reskin, McBrier, and Kmec (1999) observe, sex and racial composition are highly variable in organizations, and fewer than half of workplaces include one or more black employees. Furthermore, although individuals may live in integrated neighborhoods or work together, they often lead separate lives. As in neighborhoods, we expect contact in the workplace to be associated less closely with support for interracial marriage than contact in educational and religious institutions.

Contextualizing the Contact Hypothesis

In sum, since each of these social structures shows considerable variation, we expect that religious and educational institutions will have greater potential to create ameliorative environments than will neighborhoods or workplaces. The contact that occurs in educational and religious settings is more likely to be close, personal, sustained, and egalitarian and to involve cooperative tasks than the contact that occurs in neighborhoods and workplaces. Although the workplace provides individuals with opportunities for contact with members of other groups, such contact is often hierarchical, distant, and impersonal. And though neighborhoods allow contact, individuals may be quite isolated within the area. Thus we expect contact in these two settings to be related less strongly to attitudes about interracial marriage than contact in educational and religious institutions.

Additional Factors Related to Intermarriage: Control Variables

As noted earlier, friendship appears to be a critical influence on attitudes about other groups and approval of interracial dating (Pettigrew 1997; Powers and Ellison 1995; Yancey 1999). Bonilla-Silva (2003) presents compelling evidence that whites inflate reports of their friendship with blacks and that whites "promote" black acquaintances to "good friends" when interviewed. Though the degree of contact reported may be inflated, we use the amount of self-reported contact as a control variable.

Friendship is likely to be an intervening variable between social contexts and attitudes. Self-selection also may operate: those who hold favorable attitudes about other groups are more likely to enter racially mixed situations. Thus we use friendship as a control variable in order to assess more accurately whether the social structures themselves are conducive to more tolerant attitudes.

Age and gender also are related to attitudes about race. Older people tend to be less tolerant of others in general and of interracial marriage in particular. Gender differences in attitudes about interracial marriage also have been found (e.g., Johnson and Marini 1998; St. Jean and Parker 1995: Wilson and Jacobson 1995). Hughes and Tuch (2003), however, show that the differences are much smaller and more inconsistent when the comparisons include both traditional demographic and socialization variables. The magnitude and the direction of the influence vary for different groups, and gender differences in attitudes toward intermarriage sometimes are less pronounced than other variables such as age and education (Wilson and Jacobson 1995). In the analysis that follows, we control statistically for both age and gender in order to more accurately test the relationship of the four contexts to attitudes about interracial marriage.

Finally, we control for three other variables: income as a measure of social status, political party identification as a weak but important measure of political conservatism or liberalness, and region. With these variables controlled statistically, we can better assess the relationship of the social settings to approval or disapproval of interracial marriage.

Data

The data for this analysis were taken from a national survey conducted by the *New York Times* (2000) and archived at the Inter-University Consortium for Political and Social Research at the University of Michigan. This special poll on race relations was based on telephone interviews conducted between June 21 and June 29, 2000. Unfortunately, blacks were not asked questions about contact with other groups, so the analysis that follows is based only on the 1,107 white adults who participated.[2]

[2]A companion article to this one that reports the analysis of black attitudes is published in the *Journal of Black Studies* in March 2006. That analysis showed that although several variables are related to African American attitudes about interracial marriage, only friendship remained important when all the variables were examined together in the analysis. Blacks who had more friendships were more likely than other blacks to support interracial marriage, supporting the contact hypothesis.

The sample of telephone exchanges was selected randomly by computer from a complete list of more than 42,000 active residential exchanges across the United States. Within each exchange, random digits were added to form a complete telephone number; thus access to both listed and unlisted numbers was possible. Within each household, one adult was designated by a random procedure to be the respondent. Sampling was adjusted to account for household size, number of telephone lines in the residence, geographic region, sex, age, marital status, and education.

Table 20.1 presents a comparison of the *New York Times* data (whites only) with the General Social Survey (GSS) data from 1998 and 2000 (also whites only). The *New York Times* sample appears to be quite comparable to the GSS sample except that the former includes slightly fewer respondents with incomes less than $15,000 and with low educational levels, and slightly more Republicans.

The survey asked a variety of questions about race, including questions about the conditions under which respondents had contact with blacks. Respondents were asked directly whether they approved or disapproved of interracial marriage. Previous surveys, such as the GSS, often relied on indirect measures of attitudes toward interracial marriage, using questions that sometimes elicited reactions to governmental intervention, as well as attitudes about intermarriage (St. Jean 1998).

The residential contact variable was measured by asking white respondents: "About how many of the people who live in the immediate area around your home are black?" The interracial religious attendance variable asked: "How many people at your church or synagogue are black?" Occupational contact was measured with the question "About how many of the people you work with are black?" Response categories for each of the questions were "none," "a few," "about half," or "almost all." Because few whites selected "almost all" for any of the questions, these responses were combined with responses of "about half" to create the category "half or more."

Approximately 45 percent of the respondents did not go to church or went only a few times a year. Thirty-six percent of the respondents were out of the workforce, either retired or not employed. Those who did not attend church and those not actively working were not asked about the amount of contact they experienced in those settings. To retain cases and still assess the effects of the other independent variables for these individuals, we assigned them to a "zero contact" category. We then created an additional "dummy" variable to account for employment status (0 = unemployed, 1 = retired, 2 = working). We did the same with church attendance. This procedure allows us to control for the differences in levels of religious service attendance and involvement in employment while retaining cases in the analysis. Then we can ascertain the effect of the two independent variables for those who actually attend religious services and participate in the workforce.

Education was measured as the last grade of school completed by the respondents, from less than high school to postgraduate work or degree. Approximately one-third of the sample had completed high school, and just over one-fifth had completed college. The detailed frequencies for educational achievement are presented in Table 20.1. We treat education as interval-level data. Males account for 43 percent of the sample (coded 1), and females 57 percent (coded 0). Age ranges from 18 to 93 years, with a mean age of 48.4. A number of respondents refused to provide their specific age, but reported their age in the "age group" question. Thus we use "age group" in the analysis.

Finally, income is coded on a five-point scale from 1 (less than $15,000) to 5 (more than $75,000). Because it is a control variable, we treat it as interval data. About 6 percent

TABLE 20.1 ***Descriptive Characteristics of Samples and Variables: New York Times and General Social Survey***

Variable	*1998–2000 General Social Survey (%)* *N = 4,479*	*2000 New York Times Sample (%)* *N = 1,107*	*2000 New York Times Approval of Interracial Marriage (%)*
Income			
Under $15,000	16.0	8.9	52.3
$15,000–$30,000	20.5	20.9	62.6
$30,001–$50,000	21.9	28.2	70.5
$50,001–$75,000	15.0	18.2	73.3
Over $75,000	14.4	17.9	77.5
Political Party Identification			
Republican	36.3	43.5	62.8
Independent	18.2		
Don't know/other	2.0	13.9	73.1
Democrat	43.1	42.6	74.8
Education			
Less than high school graduate	16.5	7.1	53.4
High school graduate	29.7	32.1	63.2
Some college or trade	27.6	24.0	67.4
College graduate	14.8	21.5	72.9
Postgraduate	11.4	14.9	84.5
Sex			
Male	44.2	43.0	70.0
Female	55.8	57.0	67.8
Age group			
18–29	25.2	13.5	18.5
30–44	33.1	32.3	38.1
45–64	27.7	34.0	32.3
Over 64	14.0	19.9	10.7

TABLE 20.1 ***Continued***

Variable	*1998–2000 General Social Survey (%)*	*2000 New York Times Sample (%)*	*2000 New York Times Approval of Interracial Marriage (%)*
	N = 4,479	*N = 1,107*	
N by Region			
195, Northeast		17.6	69.9
298, North central		26.9	67.9
390, South		35.2	61.0
224, West		20.2	82.0

Notes: Ages range from 18 to 93, with a mean of 48.4. The social contact variables (attend church with blacks, blacks in workplace, and blacks in neighborhood) range from 0 to 2, with means of .76, .87, and .98, respectively.

of the sample refused to state their income; we impute this value from other variables known to be related to income.[3] Political party identification was coded "Republican" (43.5%), "don't know" (13.9%), and "Democrat" (42.6%); Democrat is the reference category. Descriptive characteristics of the sample and specific questions are presented in Table 20.1.

The response categories to the question about approval of interracial marriage were "approve" (coded 1) and "disapprove" (coded 0). Sixty-nine percent of whites said they approved of interracial marriage; the approval rate is somewhat higher in the west (82%) and somewhat lower in the south (61%). Seventy-nine percent of blacks in the sample said they approve of interracial marriage, but because questions about contact with whites were not asked of blacks, our analysis is limited to the responses of the whites in the sample.

Whites' approval of interracial marriage in this sample is slightly higher than in other national polls, but the other polls are slightly older. According to the *Washington Post* poll of July 1998, for example, 52 percent of respondents in a national sample said marriage between blacks and whites was always acceptable; an additional 23 percent said it was "acceptable in some situations, but not others." The January-February 1997 Gallup Poll found that 64 percent of respondents approved of marriage between blacks and whites. A survey conducted by Knight Ridder in May of the same year, asking the same question, reported that 63 percent of respondents approved of interracial marriage (percentages from Roper Poll Center online). Thus the results from the *New York Times* poll appear to be consistent with those of other polls.

Analysis

We use logistic regression to analyze the data. With this approach we can assess the odds that an individual approves of intermarriage as a function of both categorical (sex, political party, employment status, work with blacks, blacks in neighborhood, attend church with

[3]See the original article for details on imputing missing data.

blacks, and region) and continuous (education, age, income, frequency of church attendance, friendship) independent variables. Logistic regression also is more appropriate than ordinary least squares for the analysis of a dichotomous (either yes or no) independent variable. Age, sex, region, income, political party identification, and interracial friendship (having friends and guests of another race and visiting those of another race) were included as control variables.

The friendship variable is a summation of four friendship or contact variables: having friends of another race, having guests of another race, visiting persons of another race, and socializing with friends of another race. All four variables are related significantly to approval of interracial marriage (see Table 20.2). When all variables are included in the analysis, however, only visiting and socializing remain significant. All four variables share considerable variation, so when they are regressed against approval of interracial marriage only two of the four variables remain significant. A factor analysis revealed that these four items loaded on a single factor ranging from .68 to .77 (with a possible range of 0.0 to 1.00, see Table 20.3).[4] Thus we summed the four items and used the cumulative score (all scored yes or no) as our friendship variable. The resulting scale ranges from 0 to 4, reflecting the degree of contact with blacks reported by whites.

TABLE 20.2 ***Relationship of Friendship Variables to Approval of Interracial Marriage (Logistic Regression)***

Variable	*Bivariate*		*Multivariate*	
	B	*p*	*B*	*p*
Socialize with another race	.93	.001	.40	.02
Visit those of another race	1.21	.001	.91	.001
Have guests of another race	.90	.001	.27	.13
Have friends of another race	.71	.001	.15	.80

TABLE 20.3 ***Factor Analysis of Friendship Items***

	Factor Loadings	
Item	*Principal Components*[a]	*Principal-Axis Factoring*[a]
Socialize with another race	.77	.68
Visit those of another race	.73	.61
Have guests of another race	.77	.68
Have friends of another race	.68	.54

[a] Eigenvalue = 2.18.

[4]For details of this analysis and goodness-of-fit statistics, see the original article in *Social Psychology Quarterly*.

Results

Results for Control Variables

Gender is not related significantly to approval of interracial marriage, and inclusion of gender in the analysis did not affect the remainder of the variables. All other control variables are related significantly[5] to approval of interracial marriage. For each categorical increase in age (increments of fifteen years), the odds[6] that whites in the sample approve of interracial marriage decrease by 49 percent (.51 instead of 1.00); this result occurs with all the other variables included in the model (see the results for age under control variables in the last column of Table 20.4). For each categorical increase in income (in increments of $15,000), the odds of approving of interracial marriage increase by approximately 18 percent (note the figure of 1.18 in the last column for income). The odds that Democrats approve of interracial marriage are 72 percent higher than the odds for Republicans. The odds of approving of interracial marriage for those without a political party identification are 2.4 times higher than the odds for Republicans.

As we noted earlier, studies of interracial marriage have long found higher rates of interracial marriage in the west and lower rates in the south (see, for example, Heaton and Jacobson 2000; Heer 1966). Here we also find a higher approval rate in the west than in the South. The northeast and the north central regions fall in the middle of the distribution (see Table 20.1). The west is the reference category in the analysis presented in Table 20.4. The odds that individuals from the northeast and north central regions approve of interracial marriages are somewhat lower than those for individuals from the west. The difference between the west and the north central region is statistically significant; the odds ratio is .60, indicating lower approval. Southerners also are significantly less likely than westerners to approve of interracial marriage: the odds ratio for those from the south is .32, substantially below the 1.00 we would expect if no regional differences are present. Finally, as expected, the friendship or interracial socializing variable also is related significantly to approval of interracial marriage. After we account for the effects of the other independent variables in the model, each one-unit increase in the friendship scale is associated with a 34 percent increase in the odds of approving of interracial marriage. As in other studies (e.g., Pettigrew 1997; Sigelman and Welch 1993; Yancey 1999), friendship appears to be critical in affecting attitudes toward intermarriage.

[5]The term "significant" is used to estimate the importance of a variable in a statistical model. Typically this is done by examining the variable's p-value. A p-value indicates how often an estimated statistical value would be expected to occur by chance alone, if it were truly zero in the population. A common approach in determining statistical significance in empirical research is to use $p < 0.05$ as the cut-off value. Following this approach, variables with values falling below the 0.05 threshold are considered significant, whereas those falling above this threshold are not (Hoffmann 2004).

[6]As implied by the name, an odds ratio is merely the ratio of two odds. An odds ratio is simply two odds that are compared to determine if one of the groups in the analysis has a higher or a lower odds of a particular binary outcome. An odds ratio greater than one indicates a positive association between an independent variable and a dependent variable. Conversely, a number between zero and one indicates a negative association between variables. As would be expected, an odds ratio equal to or close to one indicates that the odds of an outcome are the same for the groups being compared (Hoffmann 2004).

TABLE 20.4 ***Logistical Regression of Social Settings on Approval of Interracial Marriage, without and with Social Friendship Variable***

	Without Friendship[a]			*With Friendship*[a]		
Independent Variables	*Beta*	*p*	*Odds Ratio*	*Beta*	*p*	*Odds Ratio*
Education	.28	.001	1.32	.27	.001	1.30
Frequency of church attendance	–.18	.004	.835	–.16	.01	.86
Attend church with blacks	.54	.003	1.71	.41	.03	1.50
Employment status	–.24	.10	.79	–.22	.13	.80
Work with blacks	.20	.19	1.22	.13	.40	1.14
Blacks in neighborhood	.13	.32	1.14	–.01	.99	.99
Control Variables						
Age	–.75	.001	.47	–.67	.001	.51
Region						
West (reference)[b]						
Northeast	–.50	.07	.61	–.32	.25	.72
Northcentral	–.69	.01	.50	–.51	.05	.60
South	–1.25	.001	.29	–1.15	.001	.32
Income	.15	.04	1.16	.17	.02	1.18
Political party identification						
Republican (reference)[c]						
Don't know	.81	.002	2.24	.75	.01	2.13
Democrat	.54	.001	1.72	.54	.002	1.72
Friendship with blacks				.29	.001	1.34
Constant	2.27	.001	9.702	1.44	.01	4.22

[a] $N = 976$.

[b] Without friendship, Wald = 29.65, $p < .001$; with friendship, Wald = 27.12, $p < .001$.

[c] Without friendship, Wald = 15.22, $p < .001$; with friendship, Wald = 13.86, $p < .001$.

Results for Contexts

After all variables are included in the analysis (including the control variables age, region, income, attendance, political party, and friendship), persons not in the workforce do not differ significantly from those in the workforce in their approval of interracial marriage ($p = .13$). Whites' association with blacks in the workplace also is not related significantly to attitudes toward interracial marriage ($p = .40$). Similarly, residential composition is not significant in the full model ($p = .99$). These results are presented in Table 20.4. Possible reasons for these outcomes are explored more fully in the discussion section.

As expected, however, education is a significant predictor of favorable attitudes toward interracial marriage ($p < .001$). After controlling for the effects of the other independent variables in the analysis, each one-year increase in education is associated with a 30 percent (1.30 in the last column of Table 20.4 for education) increase in the odds of approval ($p < .001$).

The results for religion are mixed. After controlling for the effects of the other variables, each categorical increase in church attendance (ranging from "never" to "every week") is associated with a 14 percent *decrease* in the odds of approving of interracial marriage ($p = .01$). Among those who attend church, however, the congregation's racial composition is an important factor in support for interracial marriage: the odds of approval among those who attend with a few blacks are about 50 percent higher than among those who attend all-white congregations. Further, the odds of approval among those who attend church with 50 percent or more blacks are approximately twice as great as among those who do not attend church with any blacks ($p = .03$).

Discussion

As anticipated, the context of interracial interactions contributes significantly to whites' attitudes regarding interracial marriage, and probably to whites' attitudes about race in general. Further, this occurs even when friendship, age, region, church attendance, political party, and income—all of which are associated significantly with racial attitudes—are controlled for statistically. In other words, the structural factors or arenas of contact exert a significant effect over and beyond the control variables used in the model.

On the basis of the results, the contexts can be ordered along a social contact continuum ranging from cooperative and egalitarian (cohesive) at one end to superficial and hierarchical (noncohesive) at the other end. Below we discuss each of these contexts in greater depth.

Religious Settings

In our analysis, religion showed mixed but important effects. Those who do not attend church are generally more supportive of interracial marriage than those who do. For those who attend with blacks, however, support for interracial unions increases as the proportion of blacks increases. Racial separation in religious settings is likely to reflect some individuals' preference. The separation also is likely to reflect neighborhood segregation and the traditional pattern of separate worship that has existed throughout this country's history. Under these circumstances, separate worship is associated with lower support for interracial marriage.

Where integrated churches exist, however, they are probably characterized by relationships of relatively equal status (see Powers and Ellison 1995). Moreover, members of different races are likely to cooperate as they perform religious duties sometimes required in their churches. Under these conditions, integrated religious institutions appear to meet a sufficient number of the conditions specified by the contact hypothesis to produce positive attitudes about interracial contact and intermarriage.

Educational Settings

As expected, increased education is also associated with favorable attitudes toward interracial marriage in the white sample. Again, we obtained these effects even when we included all the control variables in the model. The results were strongest for those with college and graduate degrees: the odds of approval are roughly three times higher among these individuals than among those with only a high school education. Colleges and universities appear to provide an atmosphere of tolerance and acceptance; at the same time they supply opportunities for cooperative, equal-status contact. Our findings further suggest that educational settings can offer favorable social contacts and ideas that are conducive to positive attitudes toward intergroup marriage. The effects for education, however, are less pronounced than those for integrated religious institutions.

Residential and Occupational Settings

Neighborhoods and workplaces are not significantly related to attitudes toward racial intermarriage, once the other variables are controlled statistically. We suggest two probable explanations for the lack of these relationships. First, neighborhoods and workplaces often do not offer the type of contact required to form opinions either supporting or opposing interracial marriage. Although these settings afford whites the opportunity to interact with blacks, the contact is not sufficiently cooperative or intimate to lead to positive attitudes. At the same time, however, the contact may not be sufficiently competitive or superficial to reinforce negative stereotypes and prejudicial attitudes.

Our second explanation for these nonsignificant results is that countervailing trends may be at work in these environments. Some whites have cooperative, equal-status, personal relationships with other groups in these settings; others probably do not. Still others may have contact with members of other groups, but only in competitive or hierarchical relationships. Also, as Yancey (1999) and Sigelman and Welch (1993) observe, whites' contact with members of other races does not necessarily increase support for black-white social interaction.

The *New York Times* survey does not provide fuller details about the extent or quality of the contact in these settings. Further research and contextual data are needed in order to clarify when contact in these institutions leads to greater support for interracial marriage.

The Critical Role of Friendship

Although this research focuses more on contact than on actual friendship, the latter appears to be a critical component of the former. We incorporated friendship into the analysis mainly to control for extraneous factors. Although it accounts for these possible effects statistically, it also has an interesting effect on two of the context variables. When the constrained model without the friendship scale is compared with the full model, which includes the friendship scale, integrated religious service attendance and region show considerable variation.

In the simple model, attending church with blacks is highly significant ($p = .003$), but drops to the .03 level when friendship is included in the model (the difference is significant at the .02 level). Furthermore, the odds of approving of interracial marriage decrease by approximately 13 percent when friendship is included in the analysis. Friendship shares a significant amount of variance with interracial religious settings; this finding provides further justification for including the friendship measure as a control for outside factors. The effect and magnitude of the religious contexts of contact also can be teased out more efficiently and more effectively when friendship is included in the model; without this control variable, the influence of interracial religious attendance on attitudes would appear to exert a much larger effect than it actually does.

Region has a similar relationship to racial attitudes when the friendship scale is included in the full model. In the unconstrained model, all categories (except the northeast) differ significantly from the west. When friendship is included in the full model, the northeast is not significantly different from the west, but the strength of the odds ratios increases for each category of region with friendship included. Again, these effects illustrate the importance of friendship in the formation of racial attitudes and approval of interracial marriage.

Conclusion

We used two streams of research literature—literature about the social contact hypothesis and about factors associated with acceptance of intergroup marriage—to develop a conceptual model about the effect of social contexts on attitudes toward interracial unions. We tested the model using data from a nationally representative poll conducted by the *New York Times* in 2000. In this essay we have argued that the social structure or context of contact is a critical factor in understanding and explaining attitudes toward interracial marriage, and we specified four arenas in which such contacts make these attitudes either more or less favorable.

Our primary conclusion is that attitudes toward interracial marriage are influenced in different ways in various social arenas. These effects occur even when friendship, a critical variable in the formation of racial attitudes, is controlled statistically. These environments can be ordered on a cohesive dimension, characterized in terms of the amount of intimate, personal, and egalitarian contact they are likely to provide. Religious and educational institutions appear to offer sufficient positive contact to improve attitudes about interracial marriage. On the other hand, our results also suggest that neighborhoods and workplaces, once other variables are included in the analysis, either do not furnish sufficient contacts or do not provide the type of contact needed to produce positive attitudes. Another possibility is that these latter settings provide a mixture of positive and negative contacts that is insufficient to affect attitudes.

The results presented here are based on self-reported contact. Questions about multiple types of contact in one setting were not included in the *New York Times* questionnaire, and the data do not allow a further examination of these effects. Future research that provides a more detailed analysis of the context of contact may be able to tease out these differences.

Unfortunately the *New York Times* survey did not ask blacks about their contact with whites. The authors of the survey may have assumed that because of the relative group sizes, almost all blacks have contact with whites, or they may have believed that such questions would be offensive to black Americans. Powers and Ellison (1995) and Ellison and Powers (1994), using the now-dated National Survey of Black Americans, show that blacks' contact with whites varies greatly across social settings. Analyses of data from other racial and ethnic groups would allow generalization of the contact hypothesis to such groups, and could clarify the effects of contextual factors in the study of interracial attitudes and relationships.

Although we have examined only the relationship between the four arenas and attitudes about interracial marriage, similar results are likely to be found for other institutions and for other attitudes and interracial behaviors. The relationship of individual characteristics such as education, gender, education, and region to racial attitudes has been documented in many previous studies, but less attention has been given to contextual variables. As suggested by Bobo and Fox (2003), we have yet to examine the microprocesses present in many social structures that facilitate good race relations.

References

Allport, Gordon. 1954. "The Religious Context of Prejudice." *Journal for the Scientific Study of Religion* 5:447–57.

Aronson, J., C. B. Fried, and C. Good. 2002. "Reducing the Effects of Stereotype Threat on African American College Students by Shaping Theories of Intelligence." *Journal of Experimental Social Psychology* 38:125–138.

Batson, C. Daniel, Patricia Schoenrade, and W. Larry Ventis. 1993. *Religion and the Individual: A Social Psychological Perspective*. New York: Oxford University Press.

Blau, Peter M. 1977. *Inequality and Heterogeneity*. New York: Free Press.

———. 1994. *Structural Contexts of Opportunities*. Chicago: University of Chicago Press.

Blau, Peter M., Terry C. Blum, and Joseph E. Schwartz. 1982. "Heterogeneity and Intermarriage." *American Sociological Review* 47:45–62.

Bobo, Lawrence D. 1983. "Whites Opposition to Busing: Symbolic Racism or Realistic Group Conflict?" *Journal of Personality and Social Psychology* 45:1196–1210.

Bobo, Lawrence D. and Cybelle Fox. 2003. "Race, Racism, and Discrimination: Bridging Problems, Methods, and Theory in Social Psychology Research." *Social Psychology Quarterly* 66:319–332.

Bobo, Lawrence D. and James R. Kluegel. 1993. "Opposition to Race-Targeting." *American Sociological Review* 58:443–464.

Bonilla-Silva, Eduardo. 2003. *Racism without Racists: Color-Blind Racism and the Persistence of Racial Inequality in the United States*. Lanham, MD: Rowman and Littlefield.

Desforges, Donna M., et al. 1997. "Role of Group Representativeness in the Generalization Part of the Contact Hypothesis." *Basic and Applied Social Psychology* 19:183–204.

Ellison, Christopher G. and Daniel A. Powers. 1994. "The Contact Hypothesis and Racial Attitudes among Black Americans." *Social Science Quarterly* 75:385–400.

Gordon, Milton. 1964. *Assimilation in American Life*. New York: Oxford University Press.

Heaton, Tim B. and Cardell K. Jacobson. 2000. "Intergroup Marriage: An Examination of Opportunity Structures." *Sociological Inquiry* 70:30–41.

Heer, David M. 1966. "Negro-White Marriages in the United States, 1960 and 1970." *Journal of Marriage and the Family* 36:246–58.

Herring, Cedric and Charles Amissah. 1997. "Advance and Retreat: Racially Based Attitudes and Public Policy." Pp. 121–143 in *Racial Attitudes in the 1990s: Continuity and Change*, edited by Steven A. Tuch and Jack K. Martin. Westport, CT: Praeger.

Hewstone, Miles and Rupert Brown. 1986. "Contact Is Not Enough: An Intergroup Perspective on the Contact Hypothesis." Pp. 1–44 in *Contact and Conflict in Intergroup Encounters*, edited by Miles Hewstone and Rupert Brown. Oxford: Blackwell.

Hoffmann, John P. 2004. *Generalized Linear Models*. Boston: Pearson.

Hughes, Michael and Steven A. Tuch. 2003. "Gender Differences in Whites' Racial Attitudes: Are Women's Attitudes Really More Favorable?" *Social Psychology Quarterly* 66:384–401.

Hunsberger, Bruce. 1995. "Religion and Prejudice: The Role of Religious Fundamentalism, Quest, and Right-Wing Authoritarianism." *Journal of Social Issues* 51:113–129.

Jacobs, Jerry A. and Teresa G. Labov. 2002. "Gender Differentials in Intermarriage among Sixteen Race and Ethnic Groups." *Sociological Forum* 17:621–646.

Johnson, Monica Kirkpatrick and Margaret Mooney Marini. 1998. "Bridging the Racial Divide in the United States: The Effect of Gender." *Social Psychology Quarterly* 61:247–258.

Kalmijn, Matthijs. 1993. "Trends in Black/White Intermarriage." *Social Forces* 72:119–146.

———. 1998. "Intermarriage and Homogamy: Causes, Patterns, Trends." *Annual Review of Sociology* 24:395–421.

Kalmijn, Matthijs and Henk Flap. 2001. "Assortative Meeting and Mating: Unintended Consequences of Organized Settings for Partner Choices." *Social Forces* 79:1289–1312.

Lewis, Richard and George Yancey. 1995. "Biracial Marriage in the United States: An Analysis of Variation in Family Member Support." *Sociological Spectrum* 15:443–462.

New York Times. *New York Times Race Poll,* June 2000 [MRDF], ICPSR version. Ann Arbor, MI: Inter-University Consortium for Political and Social Research.

Pettigrew, Thomas F. 1997. "Generalized Intergroup Contact Effects on Prejudice." *Personality and Social Psychology Bulletin* 23:173–185.

———. 1998. "Intergroup Contact Theory." *Annual Review of Psychology* 49:65–85.

Powers, Daniel A. and Christopher G. Ellison. 1995. "Interracial Contact and Black Racial Attitudes: The Contact Hypothesis and Selectivity Bias." *Social Forces* 74:205–226.

Qian, Zhenchao. 1997. "Breaking the Racial Barriers: Variations in Interracial Marriage between 1980 and 1990." *Demography* 34:263–276.

Quillian, Lincoln. 1996. "Group Threat and Regional Change in Attitudes toward African-Americans." *American Journal of Sociology* 102:816–860.

Reskin, Barbara, Debra McBrier, and Julie Kmec. 1999. "The Determinants and Consequences of Workplace Sex and Race Composition." *Annual Review of Sociology* 25:335–361.

St. Jean, Yanick. 1998. "Let People Speak for Themselves: Interracial Unions and the General Social Survey." *Journal of Black Studies* 28:398–414.

St. Jean, Yanick and Robert E. Parker. 1995. "Disapproval of Interracial Unions: The Case of Black Females." Pp. 341–351 in *American Families: Issues in Race and Ethnicity,* edited by Cardell K. Jacobson. New York: Garland.

Sandefur, Gary D. and Trudy McKinnel. 1986. "American Indian Intermarriage." *Social Science Research* 15:347–371.

Schaefer, Richard T. 1996. "Education and Prejudice: Unraveling the Relationship." *Sociological Quarterly* 37:1–16.

Schoen, Robert, John Wooldredge, and Barbara Thomas. 1989. "Ethnic and Educational Effects on Marriage Choice." *Social Science Quarterly* 70:617–629.

Schuman, Howard, Charlotte Steeh, Lawrence Bobo, and Maria Krysan. 1997. *Racial Attitudes in America: Trends and Interpretations*. Cambridge, MA: Harvard University Press.

Sigelman, Lee and Susan Welch. 1993. "The Contact Hypothesis Revisited: Black-White Interaction and Positive Racial Attitudes." *Social Forces* 71:781–795.

Spickard, Paul R. 1989. *Mixed Blood: Intermarriage and Ethnic Identity in Twentieth-Century America*. Madison: University of Wisconsin Press.

Taylor, Marylee C. 1998. "How White Attitudes Vary with the Racial Composition of Local Populations: Numbers Count." *American Sociological Review* 63:512–535.

Tinker, John N. 1982. "Intermarriage and Assimilation in a Plural Society: Japanese-Americans in the United States." *Marriage and Family Review* 5:61–74.

Tucker, M. Belinda and Claudia Mitchell-Kernan. 1990. "New Trends in Black American Interracial Marriage: The Social Structural Context." *Journal of Marriage and the Family* 52:209–218.

Wilson, Deborah S. and Cardell K. Jacobson. 1995. "White Attitudes toward Black and White Interracial Marriage." Pp. 353–367 in *American Families: Issues in Race and Ethnicity,* edited by Cardell K. Jacobson. New York: Garland.

Yancey, George. 1999. "An Examination of the Effects of Residential and Church Integration on Racial Attitudes of Whites." *Sociological Perspectives* 42:279–304.

———. 2001. "Racial Attitudes: Differences in Racial Attitudes of People Attending Multiracial and Uniracial Congregations." *Research in the Social Scientific Study of Religion* 12:185–206.

21

Attribution of Responsibility for Wrongdoing in Organizations: A Cross-Disciplinary Approach with Applications

Jeannine A. Gailey
Texas Christian University

Matthew T. Lee
The University of Akron

Imagine that you are serving on a jury in a case involving multiple defendants, including doctors, scientists, nurses, administrators, and even a government agency. The prosecution asks you to consider the evidence presented and to find all of the above guilty for their participation in secret radiation experiments in which unwitting human "guinea pigs" were subjected to lethal doses of radiation. The defense argues that criminal responsibility cannot be determined based on the evidence because there are too many players involved, each one lacking the required *mens rea* (guilty mind) due to the compartmentalized nature of the agency. You have heard the evidence presented by both sides and realize that this is not a clear-cut case of A harmed B; instead it's a case that involves multiple organizations and levels within those organizations, various individuals and a variety of motives.

How do you decide which factors are important for determining who or what to hold responsible? Should only the knowledge or foresight of the people within the organization be considered? Or should you also consider the intentions of the people involved? What about the morality of the situation given the prevailing social context? Or who initially caused the events? What about finding the government agency itself guilty? Can an organization commit a crime? All of these issues will probably effect how you determine the outcome of the case, but scholars know little about how each of these factors interact to affect attributions of responsibility (AOR) in organizational settings.

In recent years, scholarly attention and research on AOR has declined because compartmentalized research agendas have stifled advances in knowledge. We argue that the only way to move the field forward is to provide a synthesis in the form of a cross-disciplinary model of AOR for wrongdoing in organizations. This model, situated in psychological, sociological, and organizational literatures, provides a theoretical basis for the consistent measurement of concepts and inclusion of appropriate variables in research on AOR in organizational settings. The model we present has legal implications that are important for understanding how the general public (i.e., potential jurors) assigns guilt and for identifying which factors are relevant when wrongdoing occurs in organizations. Therefore, after we present the model and provide a brief overview of the literature, we also apply aspects of the model to understand three real-world cases of organizational wrongdoing. First, we begin by defining the terminology that we use throughout the chapter.

We use the term organizational "wrongdoing," instead of "crime" or "deviance," because organizations are frequently involved in acts that are not violations of extant criminal codes, but could still be considered by specific audiences (e.g., civil juries, consumers, the general public) to be morally reprehensible or blameworthy in some way (Gailey and Lee 2005a; Hamilton and Sanders 1995). We also argue that the term deviance is too broad because it incorporates both positive and negative actions (see Spreitzer and Sonenshein 2004). Therefore, the model we present is useful for cases of wrongdoing by individuals acting on behalf of the organization to further organizational, not (exclusively) personal interests (Gailey and Lee 2005a). This excludes some acts, such as wrongdoing committed by an individual against an organization (e.g., embezzlement, see also Braithwaite 1985) or individualistic crimes that takes place in an organizational setting (e.g., violence among coworkers).

We define "responsibility" as falling along a burden-of-proof continuum (Gailey and Lee 2005a). Social responsibility is at the least restrictive end, with public disapproval and in some cases outrage loosely tied to prevailing legal standards of guilt or blameworthiness. At the other end is criminal culpability, which is based on the strictest standard of guilt "beyond a reasonable doubt." Between these two extremes is the intermediate standard of "preponderance of evidence" used by the civil justice system.

"Attributions" are judgments about one's perceptions of why an act occurred, rather than causal perceptions of the act per se. The question for attribution scholars relates to what relevant outsiders *believe* was important during the act, not what forces actually generated an outcome. A number of individual and social factors shape perceivers' beliefs. Sociologists typically examine the context of the situation, because the actor may give information or offer explanations that influence the judgments made by an observer (Hamilton and Hagiwara 1992). Psychological social psychologists, however, tend to view responsibility as a cognition or a decision made by an individual. Most previous research in psychology has focused on how research participants attribute responsibility to either accidental or intentional outcomes. We argue that attention on the actor as an individual overshadows contextual and organizational considerations and that the focus on the intentions of an actor is not always warranted.

Despite a great deal of research on attributions, a review of the social science literature on AOR with regard to wrongdoing reveals important limitations. The first involves a lack of integration of insights across disciplines, as well as subdisciplines within psychology. Although sociological and psychological studies on the topic share a common foundation in Heider (1958), they have not built on cross-insights since branching off from his classic work. In fact, studies of AOR for wrongdoing often fail to incorporate insights from the larger body of work on attribution theory. While scholars across disciplines acknowledge and cite one another's work, they do not use it to inform their methodology or analysis.

Because of the lack of integration, there are inconsistencies in the measurement of AOR. Sociologists (Gailey and Lee 2005b; Hamilton and Sanders 1995) generally ask audiences how "responsible" an actor is for an event, using a continuum of "not at all responsible" to "completely responsible." By contrast, some psychologists use various concepts such as blame, causation, and responsibility interchangeably, while others argue that these are not equivalent and that responsibility is a multidimensional concept (Critchlow 1985; Gebotys and Dasgupta 2001; Shaver 1985). The lack of consistency in the measurement of responsibility is a direct result of merely acknowledging research from other disciplines but not building on it.

The second limitation involves the fact that the organization studies literature has been overlooked in AOR research. The rise of the organizational, as opposed to the individual, actor is perhaps the defining characteristic of contemporary society (Coleman 1982). As legal scholars have pointed out, this development has had important ramifications for all aspects of social life, including AOR (Stone 1975). Both the AOR and organizational studies literatures could benefit tremendously by incorporating one another's work.

The third gap in the literature results from a disorganized approach to the topic. For example, an examination of the impact of variables such as the audience's sex has not yielded significant differences with regard to attributing responsibility in the sociological literature (Gailey and Lee forthcoming; Sanders and Hamilton 1987), but psychological studies have found such differences (Krulewitz and Nash 1979; McDonald 1995). This contradictory finding, among others, may be an artifact of distinct research designs and the model that we propose might represent a possible solution.

The Cross-Disciplinary Model of AOR

Although not comprehensive, the model shown in Figure 21.1 incorporates insights from the three perspectives mentioned earlier. It also provides a basis for future tests of AOR with a parsimonious set of variables most relevant to wrongdoing in organizational settings.

The three boxes on the left side of Figure 21.1 contain sets of variables that previous research has identified as affecting some aspect of responsibility attributions. In the *actor characteristics* box, we list key concepts regarding the actor (i.e., the person[s] engaged in wrongdoing) that the literature has indicated should affect how audiences assign responsibility. Most, but not all, of the variables in the actor characteristics box have been studied in the psychological literature, and a few have been the focus of sociological studies, but they have not been tested systematically against each other, nor against the variables listed in the other two boxes. The *audience characteristics* box indicates the variables that are specific to the audience; that is,

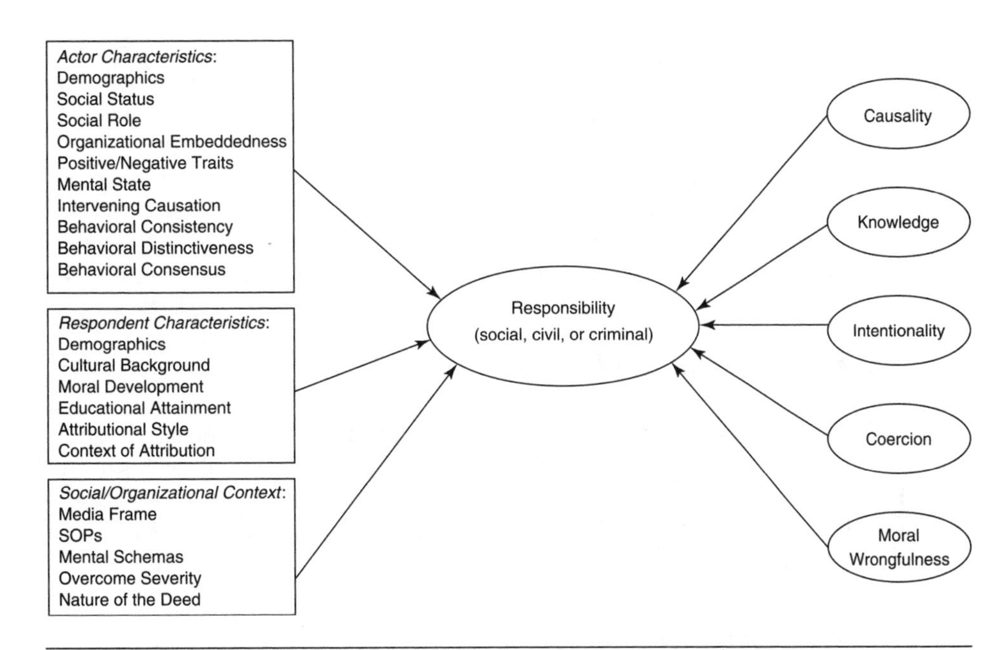

FIGURE 21.1 ***Cross-Disciplinary Model of Attribution of Responsibility for Wrongdoing in Organizations**Adapted from Galley and Lee (2005)***

the outsiders who attribute responsibility for the actor's wrongdoing. In research studies, these outsiders are often participants in experiments. Like the actor characteristics variables, audience characteristics have been investigated in an ad hoc manner in isolation from each other. The variables listed in the *social/organizational context* box are external to both the actor and the audience. For example, organization- or industry-specific standard operating procedures (SOPs) and mental schemas are "external" to the actor in the sense that they are features of the organization or social context. Although numerous studies of organizations have manipulated outcome severity and the nature of the action, few have examined the effect of media portrayals, and to our knowledge, only two studies have operationalized variables from the organizational studies literature (Paternoster and Simpson 1996; Simpson and Piquero 2002).

The concepts displayed in the boxes on the left of Figure 21.1 may moderate or mediate each other if they are tested together. For example, audiences from different cultural backgrounds may have differing views about the role of organizational/institutional forces, and these culturally bound perspectives may influence the importance that audiences attach to "internal" actor characteristics such as age, race, and gender. Therefore, the listed variables will influence each other to some extent, but how strongly is still unknown.

Conceptualization of Responsibility

Shaver (1985) proposes five dimensions of responsibility, which he argues perceivers consider before attributing responsibility: causality, knowledge, intentionality, coercion, and moral wrongfulness. These dimensions have been important in previous research which has indicated that characteristics of the defendant affect how jurors determine some dimensions of responsibility (i.e., "blameworthiness"), but not others (i.e., "guilt"; see Gleason and Harris 1976). By using Shaver's conceptualization of responsibility, we can examine findings of fact while still addressing features that are relevant within the U.S. civil and criminal justice systems, as well as social responsibility broadly defined. In the following section we review a small portion of the literature that has examined some of the concepts we included in Figure 21.1 in order to demonstrate their importance and significance to our model (for a more thorough review, see Gailey and Lee 2005a). We also apply the model to three real-world cases to help illustrate how select variables affect AOR.

Literature Review and Application

In the psychological tradition, AOR research has covered a range of issues. Although it addresses wrongdoing only occasionally, this tradition has implications for AOR involving both positive and negative outcomes. We first discuss actor characteristics from both the psychological and sociological literatures, followed by a real-world case to illustrate their importance.

Actor Characteristics

AOR researchers commonly manipulate the characteristics of actors in scenarios presented to research participants or survey respondents, such as demographic characteristics (sex, gender, race, age, SES), positive/negative traits, mental state, and intentions, among others that we include in the actor characteristics box found in Figure 21.1. Regarding an actor's positive/negative traits, a large body of research has found that our interpretations of others' behavior depends, for example, on whether we initially receive favorable or unfavorable information about them (Asch 1946). If we know or think that someone is intelligent, we may interpret his or her subsequent behavior as daring rather than reckless. Similarly, other researchers have found that variables such as sex, socioeconomic status, and race all influence how perceivers attribute responsibility (Gleason and Harris 1976; Hansen and O'Leary 1985; Kleinke and Baldwin 1993; Stewart 1980).

Kelley's (1973) theory of attributions builds on the above assumptions. If an act is consistent with previous behavior, audiences are more likely to attribute causality or responsibility to the person rather than to some external cause, such as having a bad day. Building on these ideas, Fincham and Shultz (1981) examined events that occur between a behavior and a consequence in order to understand more clearly the conditions under which audiences use the concept of intervening causation to generate judgments of causation, blame, and restitution in cases of wrongdoing. Not surprisingly, findings indicate that audiences tend to attribute less responsibility to acts that are involuntary or that have unforeseeable consequences.

The sociological AOR literature is much more limited regarding actor characteristics than that of psychology. Hamilton's (1983) "roles-and-deeds" model focuses on how the actor's social role and/or social status influence perceiver's AOR for wrongdoing. The "nature of the deed" refers to the act for which an actor potentially may be held responsible—different acts entail different judgments of responsibility—and is part of the social context identified in Figure 21.1. In determining judgments about responsibility, different roles seem to provide audiences with differing criteria of strictness in terms of the level of intent necessary for declaring "guilt." In other words, it is not what you did, but what you did given who you are and the social context that determines which sanctioning rules apply. For example, an authority figure issuing an order may be seen as more responsible than a subordinate who follows that order. Sociologists have focused on the actor's status, role (the actor's position in the organization and whether the actor is autonomous, obedient, or conforming) and hierarchy (the organization's power structure) (Hamilton 1986; Hamilton and Sanders 1995; Sanders and Hamilton 1997).

Sociologists have devoted little attention to individual actor characteristics such as race, age, gender, and socioeconomic status (Myers 1980; also see Sanders and Hamilton 1987). Myers (1980), however, did examine some of these actor characteristics as well as social contexts in order to determine whether AOR is constrained by the situation surrounding criminal actions, but she was interested in individual wrongdoing, not organizational. Using data from verdicts of real trials her results indicated that the actor's employment status influenced how jurors assign responsibility, but race, sex, and age do not. Myers also found that the victim's marital status and age, as well as the severity of the consequences of the act, are important predictors of AOR. Her conclusions suggest that future research in AOR focus on the social psychological question of whether and to what end attributions are constrained and shaped by context.

Application of the "Actor Characteristics" Box: The Interaction of Social Status, Social Role, and Organizational Embeddedness in the Case of the Cold War Human Radiation Experiments. Having reviewed some of the more important variables associated with actor characteristics, we now provide an illustration of how these variables may affect AOR in a real-world case of organizational wrongdoing involving Cold War human radiation experiments. The discussion that follows does not explore all of the complicated interrelationships among all possible factors that might have played a role in responsibility attributions. Rather, we highlight the role of three variables from the first box in Figure 21.1 that we believe to be particularly important in the current case.

Imagine that a stranger has just walked up to you, jabbed a hypodermic needle into your arm, and injected you with what she believed would be a lethal dose of a highly toxic, but not fully understood substance. How would you feel? Perhaps like a victim of a violent crime, say, attempted murder, or at least criminal assault? Suppose that you later learned that the reason that you were injected with this dangerous substance was the stranger's simple curiosity to learn about its health-related effects. There is probably not a prosecutor in the country who would fail to press charges against the perpetrator upon learning the facts of your case. But what if the assailant was a respected member of the medical community—in other words, of high status? And what if the doctor was acting under orders from a legitimate authority—in other words, in an obedient social role? And finally, what if this doctor was part of a vast, secret, government-funded research program focused on issues of national security? Would these actor characteristics make a difference to you, or to a given prosecutor?

Consider the case of Albert Stephens. In May 1945, the same week that Germany announced its surrender in World War II, Albert Stevens arrived at the University of California Hospital (UCH) in San Francisco. Albert was a fifty-eight-year-old, unemployed house painter who was misdiagnosed with terminal stomach cancer by doctors at UCH.

Possibly because of his grim diagnosis, scientists from the Manhattan Project—the top-secret military program that developed the atomic bombs dropped on Hiroshima and Nagasaki—selected Albert to become a subject in their ongoing research into the effects of a highly radioactive substance (plutonium) on human beings. On May 14, without his knowledge or consent, Albert was injected with what scientists who participated in the experiment called a "carcinogenic dose" or a "lethal textbook dose" of plutonium (Welsome 1999:92, 94). Scientists lacked precise data on where plutonium might settle in the body or how fast it might be excreted through urine or feces, and they hoped that studying Albert—at least until the cancer or the plutonium killed him—might provide them with information that would be useful in protecting the health of the atomic workforce. To their surprise, after doctors removed what appeared to be a large cancerous growth in Albert's abdomen, they discovered that he did not have stomach cancer after all.

In the wake of this revelation, doctors did not inform Albert that he was cancer-free, and they certainly had no interest in disclosing that they had injected him with a lethal dose of plutonium without his knowledge or consent. Albert was ultimately discharged from the hospital and government-funded medical personnel offered to pay Albert to collect his own urine and feces in jars, which would be retrieved on a weekly basis from a shed behind his house. Government scientists analyzed the samples in order to continue to track the excretion of plutonium over the years. According to Albert's son, Albert believed that this procedure was related to his operation for stomach cancer, and his family was happy that he was receiving free medical care because he was unemployed and did not have health insurance. Albert's family believed that he was receiving effective treatment for his stomach cancer because he lived two decades longer than doctors expected. Fortunately for Albert, the doctors were wrong about both the lethality of the plutonium, as well as his cancer. Fortunately for the doctors involved in the experiment, their social status, obedient role, and organizational embeddedness shielded them from prosecution (our hypothetical stranger would not have been so lucky).

More generally, despite the fact that Nazi doctors were convicted of crimes against humanity by the Allies in 1947 (two years after Albert's plutonium injection) for using people as subjects in harmful experiments without their voluntary, informed consent, none of the thousands of human radiation experiments conducted in the United States ever resulted in criminal prosecutions—not even for simple assault. Embeddedness in a Nazi organization neutralized the exculpatory effects of social status and social role, whereas embeddedness in U.S. governmental organizations bolstered the mitigating effects of these variables, highlighting the complexity that results from interactions of the variables in the first box of Figure 21.1.

Audience Characteristics

Psychological research has identified a number of audience characteristics that influence AOR, although these findings depend on other contextual factors and various conceptualizations of responsibility. We include the more widely studied traits in Figure 21.1. We focus on audience members' sex, gender, and attributional style as representing the types of variables that psychologists have found to be important because these variables have exerted effects on AOR across numerous studies, although most did not involve organizational wrongdoing.

Psychological studies have found a strong correlation between attributions and the attributor's sex (Crittenden and Wiley 1980; Hansen and O'Leary 1985; McDonald 1995). Krulewitz and Nash (1979) examined AOR in a study on perceptions of sexual assault, to learn whether the attributor's sex, the nature of the victim's resistance, and the outcome of the assault would affect how audiences attributed responsibility. Women attributed greater responsibility to the victim than men did, but the attributor's sex did not affect AOR for the assailant. Thus, in attributing responsibility audiences rely in some circumstances not only on the deed itself, but also on sex-role stereotypes (Krulewitz and Nash 1979).

It is possible that measuring a person's gender, instead of biological sex, would produce more valid results. Although no studies have tapped this dimension, the literature on moral development suggests that AOR scholars might find gender a useful variable to include in analyses (Gilligan 1982; Kohlberg 1981). Gender affects understandings of responsibility; given cultural and temporal variations in sex roles, we argue that an integrated model of AOR would benefit from including a more sophisticated measure than an attributor's biological sex or a dichotomous gender scale.

In addition to sex and/or gender, the audience member's attributional style is a powerful predictor of AOR (Henry and Campbell 1995). For example, people with an external locus of control (meaning that they attribute events in their life to luck rather than merit, see Rotter 1974) may be more likely to attribute responsibility to factors outside the actor. Similarly, the attributional effects of a relatively stable "causal schema" (Kelley 1973) or "underlying cognitive structure" (Martinko 1995:10) may persist even after controlling for situational and control variables. For example, one study found that audience members who exhibited a positive explanatory style attributed absenteeism to external factors, while audience members who had a strong Protestant work ethic were more likely to cite internal factors (Judge and Martocchio 1995). The contributions from psychology complement the sociological literature.

Sociological research on audience characteristics specifies the conditions under which environmental influences proposed by Heider (1958) are important. Although Sanders and Hamilton (1987) found that demographic differences could not account for variations in AOR, Hamilton and Hagiwara (1992) demonstrated that social negotiations, accounts, excuses, and justifications may be used to diminish or even eliminate perceptions of responsibility for wrongdoing.

Although some demographic factors do not seem to predict attributions by audience members in sociological studies, cultural background and educational attainment are both important (Hamilton and Sanders 1983; Sanders and Hamilton 1997). One study included the impact of the legal culture and economy of three countries (the United States, Japan, and Russia) while controlling for individual differences such as stratification, education, and social class (Hamilton and Sanders 1996). The results showed that social class has little relation to assigning responsibility to actors in organizations. Concerning education, however, audience members with higher educational attainment were more likely to attribute responsibility to obedient actors within the organization, possibly because highly educated people are more likely to have careers that are more autonomous. With regard to culture, American audiences' opinions about obedience to orders had implications for corporate accountability, but Japanese and Russian audiences' beliefs did not. This finding is not surprising: a large body of literature reports that group members of Eastern origin have a very different social and intellectual history than Westerners, and this difference affects processes of causal attribution and responses to social circumstances and situations (Nisbett 2003). Below we illustrate how one audience variable (educational attainment) affects AOR in a case of military wrongdoing.

Application of the "Audience Characteristics" Box: Educational Attainment and the My Lai Massacre. The My Lai massacre involved a series of atrocities that occurred in 1968 during the Vietnam War in the village of My Lai (Kelman and Hamilton 1989; see also http://www.pbs.org/wgbh/pages/frontline/programs/transcripts/714.html). Briefly, U.S. soldiers killed roughly five hundred unarmed Vietnamese civilians, largely women and children. Other crimes perpetrated by the soldiers included rape, torture, and the mutilation of bodies (including cutting off body parts to keep as trophies). Although the crimes were both well documented and horrific, only one soldier was convicted and punished by the U.S. military justice system: Lieutenant William Calley. Initially sentenced to life in prison for his role in the murders of approximately one hundred Vietnamese villagers, both for giving orders to shoot unarmed prisoners captured at My Lai and for pulling the trigger himself, Calley served only three years on house arrest before being paroled. This lenient sentence, combined with the fact that no other soldiers were even convicted, raises a number of important issues for AOR theorists, not the least of which is the interference in the military justice process by then-president Richard Nixon. As with the human radiation experiments, the social status, social role, and organizational embeddedness of the soldiers undoubtedly influenced the outcomes of the criminal investigation. Public opinion about the soldiers certainly played a powerful role as well, as the American public overwhelmingly supported Calley and the other soldiers.

However, our current interest in the My Lai case is to illustrate the role of educational attainment in AOR. In a national survey of the American public about the My Lai massacre, conducted shortly after Calley's conviction was announced in 1971, researchers learned that 79 percent disapproved of Calley's conviction and 67 percent believed that most people would kill unarmed civilians under similar circumstances. In fact, only 33 percent claimed that they themselves would not pull the trigger. In other words, audiences did not want to hold the soldiers responsible for acts they believed most Americans would carry out under similar circumstances. But not all audience members agreed. Researchers discovered several demographic variables that distinguished likely shooters from nonshooters. Among these were sex, prior military experience, and region of residence. But the strongest predictor of self-reported refusal to shoot unarmed civilians was educational attainment (Kelman and Hamilton 1989). Those who are well educated are more comfortable challenging authority figures and are therefore less likely to follow orders that they perceive to be unlawful. It is also possible that those with higher educational attainment are not as quick to dehumanize others. Blindly following orders and dehumanizing enemies seem to be essential ingredients in massacres like the one at My Lai. Regardless of how one interprets the finding, the implications for AOR cannot be overstated: attributors with higher educational attainment, on average, are more likely to hold participants in massacres responsible for their crimes.

This underscores the point that simply knowing the facts about a particular case of wrongdoing, including the characteristics of the actors discussed in the previous section, will not be enough to predict the outcome of the AOR process. One must also know something about characteristics of the audience doing the attributing. The educational attainment of a society's members clearly plays an important role in how that society's social control systems distribute blame for wrongdoing.

Organizational Features and Media Representations

In addition to cultural and contextual factors, we have good reason to believe that audiences' responsibility attributions are influenced by media representations of cases of wrongdoing and other organizational features. Most people learn about organizational crime from the mass media; also, because individuals rarely have enough information to form opinions independently on public issues, they are often at the mercy of the media, not only for information but also for interpretation (Graber 1980). Furthermore, the criminal justice system assumes that exposure to media coverage biases potential jurors in criminal cases. In effect, a media frame may institutionalize a particular causal explanation for a negative individual and/or organizational outcome, thus taking "ownership" of the social construction of public problems and influencing how audiences attribute responsibility (Gusfield 1981:10).

Although some variants of attribution theory have been applied to organizational contexts (see Martinko 1995), most involve self-attributions, and few have investigated AOR by outsiders for actors involved in organizational wrongdoing. AOR studies have yet to model one of the most dominant features of bureaucratic life: the restriction of decision-making opportunities by processes that generate outcomes from unreflective action (Laroche 1995). This oversight is significant because the ubiquity of unreflective action in organizations bears directly on a number of dimensions of responsibility, notably intentionality and moral wrongfulness (see Figure 21.1).

Organizational scholars have produced an immense literature explicating the complex manner in which institutional logics and cognitive schemas contribute to unreflective actions (DiMaggio 1997; Jackall 1988; Powell and DiMaggio 1991). The influence of these factors potentially cuts across social roles and even transcends the "focal organization" that historically has provided the social location for responsibility claims (Lee and Ermann 1999). Furthermore, institutional logics are an important source of causal schemas that make up a person's attributional style and on which observers rely to make sense of events such as organizational wrongdoing (see Gioia 1991).

The extent to which audiences perceive and understand how institutional logics transform "decisions" into unreflective actions and convert moral issues into routine procedures absent of moral implications is likely to determine how extensively perceivers attribute responsibility to the other variables displayed in Figure 21.1 (see Laroche 1995; Lee and Ermann 1999). It is possible that a juror who has experienced this process firsthand by working in a bureaucracy will be more likely to acquit corporate defendants for actions stemming from institutional logic. In such a case, the acquittal may appear to be the result of the defendant's ability to utilize the corporation's deep pockets for a strong legal defense. However, it may relate more closely to the juror's ability to "take the role of the other."

The important point is that persons in organizations rarely make decisions based on unrestricted "free will" because one or more institutional logics are operating (Jackall 1988). Such logics regularize the behavior of individuals by setting the parameters of thought and prohibiting certain courses of action. To take one concrete example, in the 1970s the automobile recall coordinator for Ford Motor Company was interested in recalling the Pinto due to a potential safety concern, but the data that he and others collected failed to meet organizational standard of evidence for initiating such a recall. As a result, there was no "decision" to be made: recall was not an option because that determination must be based on organizational criteria rather than personal preference (Lee and Ermann 1999). More generally, actors may believe that they are making decisions, but in many cases, the institution has provided behavioral scripts, also known as standard operating procedures (SOPs), and cognitive frameworks for understanding behaviors, known as mental schemas, that guide behavior and determine what choices are expected or unthinkable (DiMaggio 1997; Powell and DiMaggio 1991). Scripts and schemas constitute the building blocks of institutional logics and demonstrate the ways in which organizational actions transcend individual decisions or preferences.

Our brief review of the relevant literatures suggests that structural influences on organizational wrongdoing may be institutional, organizational, sociological, and/or psychological. This view implicates multiple, "nested" (Friedland and Alford 1991:242) levels of analysis, which may include institutionalized, industrywide social conventions (e.g., the use of cost/benefit analysis, see Lee and Ermann 1999), the presence of a virtuous or nonvirtuous culture in a specific organization (Haines 1997), and social-psychological factors such as cognitive schemas and behavioral scripts (see Gioia 1991). We contend that a cross-disciplinary model of AOR for organizational wrongdoing must incorporate factors at each of these levels. In the section that follows, we illustrate how media frames influenced the outcome of the Enron case.

Application of the "Social/Organizational Context" Box: Media Frames and the Enron Case. As we discussed earlier, AOR is often affected by how the media constructs the facts of a case. For a case such as the collapse of Enron, the effects of media frames are unavoidable, despite the best efforts of the criminal justice system to select unbiased jurors without preconceived notions about the defendant. There can be little doubt that the media attention to egregious cases of organizational wrongdoing at the turn of the twenty-first century, of which Enron is probably the most infamous, played a key role in corporate executives such as Enron's former CFO Andrew Fastow agreeing to accept long prison sentences as part of plea agreements. In the words of one scholar, Fastow and others were rightly "afraid to face an angry, punitive jury" that had been primed by a steady diet of negative publicity about the case and about corporate wrongdoing more generally (Rosoff 2007:519). Insisting on a trial proved to be a mistake for former Enron CEO Jeffrey Skilling: he was sentenced to twenty-four years in prison for fraud, compared with Fastow's ten-year term.

The prosecution in Skilling's case drew on the dominant media portrayal of the Enron debacle: that Skilling and others at Enron hid the truth from shareholders. For example, in his closing statement the lead prosecutor argued that Skilling's case was "so simple":

> It's black-and-white. Truth and lies. The shareholders, ladies and gentlemen . . . buy a share of stock, and for that they're not entitled to much but they're entitled to the truth. . . . They're entitled to be told what the financial condition of the company is. They are entitled to honesty, ladies and gentlemen. (quoted in Gladwell 2007)

In other words, Skilling withheld vital information that prevented shareholders from making an informed choice about investing in Enron—he kept secrets in violation of the law. But there is a complexity here that is missing from the fraud frame promoted by the media and the prosecution. According to a recent revisionist account, much of the material used to frame the Enron scandal as a fraud came from public filings to the U.S. Securities and Exchange Commission (SEC) from Enron itself. The problem, according to Malcolm Gladwell (2007), was not too little information, but too much. The length and complexity of Enron's accounting documents allowed the company to hide in plain sight the fact it was not making money for years. For example, the company had not paid income tax in four out of its last five years because it had no real income to report. Much of its profits were tied up in projected future earnings, not real dollars, a fact the company reported in its filings with the SEC and Internal Revenue Service (IRS). Reporters finally "broke" the case by simply reading the public documents.

During the years that Enron's stock soared above its competitors, all of the important watchdog groups—external auditors, the financial press, and the popular news media—ignored the obvious fact that the company had no viable business model. Without exception, these "outsiders" served as cheerleaders for the company. Enron had in fact bribed key reporters with exorbitant payments for "consulting," leading one observer to quip that the company had "turned *muckrakers* into *buckrakers*" (Rosoff 2007:516). Investigative journalism was reduced to "rewriting Enron press releases" (Rosoff 2007:514). Does the fact that Enron's financial shell game was an open secret mitigate the criminal blameworthiness of executives like Jeff Skilling? Perhaps the answer to this question is always somewhat dependent on the social context in which it is asked. Given the highly charged atmosphere surrounding his trial, a conviction may have been a forgone conclusion. We are not implying that Skilling was actually innocent. However, his lengthy prison sentence is suggestive of our broader point that the attribution of responsibility does not occur in a social vacuum.

Discussion and Conclusions

Our review of the AOR literature has revealed several theoretical and methodological gaps. One is a lack of interdisciplinary communication. The second is a disorganized approach to the topic, which has resulted in inconsistent measurement of responsibility. The third is a theoretical issue. Not only do sociologists and psychologists need to incorporate insights from each other's work; they also will benefit by including factors derived from organization studies. Concerning practical application, AOR research based on our model has much to contribute to our understanding of how jurors assign guilt—that is, criminal or civil responsibility. If an organization is involved in a case of wrongdoing, jurors sometimes are asked to determine whether the organization and the individual, or both, are guilty (or financially responsible in civil cases), regardless of any contextual factors that may have influenced or facilitated the crime or wrongdoing.

The problem is that the law does not correspond well to the way the average juror attributes responsibility: some jurors may be influenced by contextual factors at an unreflective level, which may decrease the likelihood of accountability. This is illustrated by the widespread public support for Lieutenant Calley discussed in our application for the audience characteristic box of our integrated model. The research that we reviewed suggests that people consider factors such as role requirements, situational pressures, and social conventions before determining responsibility. Yet because these factors are not reflected in legal definitions of crime, accountability for untoward outcomes is reduced, particularly in organizations (Hamilton 1980). American corporations and/or organizations often are not held responsible for harming large numbers of people (Simon 1996). In cases like Enron, the opposite outcome can occur when media frames turn from laudatory to accusatory. Research derived from the model we propose may help us understand more clearly such disparate results, and learn what factors influence people when they are asked to attribute responsibility, the first step toward social and legal change.

The purpose of this chapter was to review and synthesize three literatures with implications for AOR for wrongdoing: psychology, sociology, and organizational studies. The model proposed provides a starting point for a research agenda that generates more theoretically comprehensive tests of propositions derived from AOR research. Such work could help revitalize an interesting and important area of social science scholarship, and a field with important legal implications in a society increasingly defined by both organizational dominance and organizational wrongdoing. Without a cross-disciplinary model, researchers are likely to continue to test these factors independently, which limits practical applications, particularly to the legal system.

References

Asch, Solomon E. 1946. "Forming Impressions of Personality." *Journal of Abnormal and Social Psychology,* 59:177–181.

Braithwaite, John. 1985. "White Collar Crime." *Annual Review of Sociology,* 11:1–25.

Coleman, James S. 1982. *The Asymmetric Society*. Syracuse, NY: Syracuse University Press.

Critchlow, Barbara Press. 1985. "The Blame in the Bottle: Attributions about Drunken Behavior." *Personality and Social Psychology Bulletin,* 11:258–274.

Crittenden, Kathleen S. and Mary G. Wiley. 1980. "Causal Attribution and Behavioral Response to Failure." *Social Psychology Quarterly,* 43:353–358.

DiMaggio, Paul. 1997. "Culture and Cognition." *Annual Review of Sociology,* 23:263–287.

Fincham, Frank D. and Thomas R. Shultz. 1981. "Intervening Causation and the Mitigation of Responsibility for Harm." *British Journal of Social Psychology*, 20:113–120.

Friedland, Roger and Robert R. Alford. 1991. "Bringing Society Back In: Symbols, Practices, and Institutional Contradictions." Pp. 232–263 in *The New Institutionalism in Organizational Analysis*, edited by Walter Powell and Paul DiMaggio. Chicago: University of Chicago Press.

Gailey, Jeannine A. and Matthew T. Lee. Forthcoming. "Media Influences and the Assignment of Responsibility for Wrongdoing in Organizational Settings." *Sociological Focus*.

———. 2005a. "An Integrated Model of Attribution of Responsibility for Wrongdoing in Organizations." *Social Psychology Quarterly,* 68: 338–358.

———. 2005b. "The Impact of Roles and Frames on Attributions of Responsibility: The Case of the Cold War Human Radiation Experiments." *Journal of Applied Social Psychology*, 35:1067–1088.

Gebotys, Robert J. and Bikram Dasgupta. 2001. "Attribution of Responsibility and Crime Seriousness." *Journal of Psychology,* 121:607–613.

Gilligan, Carol. 1982. *In a Different Voice: Psychological Theory and Women's Development.* Cambridge, MA: Harvard University Press.

Gioia, Dennis. 1991. "Pinto Fires and Business Ethics: A Script Analysis of Missed Opportunities." *Journal of Business Ethics*, 11:379–389.

Gladwell, Malcolm. 2007. "Open Secrets: Enron, Intelligence, and the Perils of Too Much Information." *New Yorker* (January 8). Retrieved on 2/24/07 from http://www.newyorker.com/fact/content/articles/070108fa_fact.

Gleason, James M. and Victor A. Harris. 1976. "Group Discussion and Defendant's Socio-Economic Status as Determinants of Judgments by Simulated Jurors." *Journal of Applied Social Psychology*, 6:186–191.

Graber, Doris A. 1980. *Crime News and the Public*. New York: Praeger.

Gusfield, Joseph R. 1981. *The Culture of Public Problems: Drinking-Driving and the Symbolic Order.* Chicago: University of Chicago Press.

Haines, Fiona. 1997. *Corporate Regulation: Beyond "Punish or Persuade."* New York: Oxford University Press.

Hamilton, V. Lee. 1980. "Intuitive Psychologist or Intuitive Lawyer? Alternative Models of the Attribution Process." *Journal of Personality and Social Psychology*, 39:767–772.

———. 1986. "Chains of Command: Responsibility Attribution in Hierarchies." *Journal of Applied Social Psychology*, 16: 118–138.

Hamilton, V. Lee and Shigeru Hagiwara. 1992. "Roles, Responsibility, and Accounts across Cultures." *International Journal of Psychology*, 27:156–179.

Hamilton, V. Lee and Joseph Sanders. 1983. "Universals in Judging Wrongdoing: Japanese and Americans Compared." *American Sociological Review*, 48:199–211.

———. 1995. "Crimes of Obedience and Conformity in the Workplace: Surveys of Americans, Russians, and Japanese." *Journal of Social Issues*, 51:67–89.

———. 1996. "Corporate Crime through Citizens' Eyes: Stratification and Responsibility in the United States, Russia, and Japan." *Law and Society Review*, 30:513–475.

Hansen, Ranald D. and Virginia E. O'Leary. 1985. "Sex-Determined Attributions." Pp.67–99 in *Women, Gender and Social Psychology*, edited by Virginia E. O'Leary, Rhoda Kesler Unger, and Barbara StrudlerWallston. Hillsdale, NJ: Erlbaum.

Heider, Fritz. 1958. *The Psychology of Interpersonal Relations*. New York: Wiley.

Henry, John W. and Constance Campbell. 1995. "A Comparison of the Validity, Predictiveness, and Consistency of Trait Versus Situation Measure of Attributions." Pp. 35–52 in *Attribution Theory: An Organizational Perspective*, edited by Mark J. Martinko. Delray Beach, FL: St. Lucie Press.

Jackall, Robert. 1988. *Moral Mazes: The World of Corporate Managers*. New York: Oxford University Press.

Judge, Timothy A. and Joseph J. Martocchio. 1995. "Attributions Concerning Absence from Work: A Dispositional Perspective." Pp. 97–124 in *Attribution Theory: An Organizational Perspective*, edited by Mark J. Martinko. Delray Beach, FL: St. Lucie Press.

Kelley, Harold H. 1973. "The Process of Causal Attribution." *American Psychologist*, 28:107–128.

Kelman, Herbert C. and V. Lee Hamilton. 1989. *Crimes of Obedience: Toward a Social Psychology of Responsibility and Authority*. New Haven, CT: Yale University Press.

Kleinke, Chris L. and Michael R. Baldwin. 1993. "Responsibility Attributions for Men and Women Giving Sane versus Crazy Explanations for Good and Bad Deeds." *Journal of Psychology*, 127:37–50.

Kohlberg, Lawrence. 1981. *The Philosophy of Moral Development: Moral Stages and the Idea of Justice.* San Francisco, CA: Harper and Row.

Krulewitz, Judith E. and Janet E. Nash. 1979. "Effects of Rape Victim Resistance, Assault Outcome, and Sex of Observer on Attributions About Rape." *Journal of Personality*, 47:557–574.

Laroche, Herve. 1995. "From Decision to Action in Organizations: Decision-Making as a Social Representation." *Organization Science*, 6:62–75.

Lee, Matthew T. and M. David Ermann. 1999. "Pinto 'Madness' as a Flawed Landmark Narrative: An Organization and Network Analysis." *Social Problems*, 46:30–50.

Martinko, Mark J. Ed. 1995. *Attribution Theory: An Organizational Perspective*. Delray Beach, FL: St. Lucie Press.

McDonald, Don Michael. 1995. "Fixing Blame in N-Person Attributions: A Social Identity Model for Attributional Processes in Newly Formed Cross-Functional Groups." Pp. 273–288 in *Attribution Theory: An Organizational Perspective*, edited by Mark J. Martinko. Delray Beach, FL: St. Lucie Press.

Myers, Martha A. 1980. "Social Contexts and Attributions of Criminal Responsibility." *Social Psychology Quarterly*, 43:405–419.

Nisbett, Richard E. 2003. *The Geography of Thought: How Asians and Westerners Think Differently . . . and Why.* New York: Free Press.

Paternoster, Raymond and Sally Simpson. 1996. "Sanction Threats and Appeals to Morality: Testing a Rational Choice Model of Corporate Crime." *Law and Society Review*, 30:549–583.

Powell, Walter and Paul DiMaggio. 1991. *The New Institutionalism in Organizational Analysis.* Chicago: University of Chicago Press.

Rosoff, Stephen M. 2007. "The Role of the Mass Media in the Enron Fraud: Cause or Cure?" Pp. 513–522 in *International Handbook of White-Collar and Corporate Crime*, edited by Henry N. Pontell and Gilbert L. Geis. New York: Springer.

Rotter, Julian B. 1974. "Internal-External Locus of Control Scale." Pp. 227–234 in *Measures of Social Psychological Attitudes*, edited by John P. Robinson and Phillip R. Shaver. Ann Arbor, MI: Institute for Social Research.

Sanders, Joseph and V. Lee Hamilton. 1987. "Is There a 'Common Law' of Responsibility? The Effect of Demographic Variables on Judgments of Wrongdoing." *Law and Human Behavior*, 11:277–297.

———. 1997. "Distributing Responsibility for Wrongdoing Inside Corporate Hierarchies: Public Judgments in Three Societies." *Law and Social Inquiry*, 21:815–855.

Shaver, Kelly G. 1985. *The Attribution of Blame: Causality, Responsibility, and Blameworthiness.* New York: Springer-Verlag.

Simon, David R. 1996. *Elite Deviance.* New York: Allyn and Bacon.

Simpson, Sally S. and Nicole Leeper Piquero. 2002. "Low Self-Control, Organizational Theory, and Corporate Crime." *Law and Society Review*, 36:509–547.

Spreitzer, Gretchen M. and Scott Sonenshein. 2004. "Toward the Construct Definition of Positive Deviance." *American Behavioral Scientist,* 47:828–847.

Stewart, John. 1980. "Defendant Attractiveness as a Factor in the Outcome of Criminal Trials: An Observational Study." *Journal of Applied Social Psychology,* 10:348–361.

Stone, Christopher D. 1975. *Where the Law Ends: The Social Control of Corporate Behavior.* New York: Harper & Row.

Welsome, Eileen. 1999. *The Plutonium Files: America's Secret Medical Experiments in the Cold War*. New York: Dial Press.

22

*Social Structure and Psychological Well-being**

Catherine E. Ross and John Mirowsky

University of Texas, Austin

If social status affects well-being, the question is why. What might explain associations between structural conditions and people's feelings of psychological and physical well-being? In this chapter, we develop a paradigm in which social status shapes well-being by way of mediators that explain why social statuses might influence distress; moderators that delineate the circumstances under which a social status is more or less psychologically harmful; and their combination, which we call structural amplification. First we define the concept of psychological well-being versus distress. Then we present evidence linking social inequality to distress. We focus on socioeconomic status (education, work, and income), gender, and family status. The root cause of socioeconomic inequality is educational attainment: it shapes the kinds of jobs people can get, their income and economic hardship, the kinds of neighborhoods they can afford to live in, and almost every other aspect of people's daily lives. In the next section, we give examples of what we consider the core mediator, or link, between social status and well-being, the sense of personal control. We also introduce the concept of trust. In the third section, we discuss the core conditions under which education has a more or less beneficial effect on well-being. We present the theory of resource substitution which posits that education is most important to the well-being of people who are otherwise disadvantaged, like women. In the final section, we link the concepts of mediators and moderators and present the concept of structural amplification. Here we focus on how neighborhoods shape the sense of personal control and trust.

*Parts of this chapter appeared in "Social Structure and Psychological Functioning: Distress, Perceived Control and Trust." by Catherine E. Ross and John Mirowsky. Pp. 411–447 in *Handbook of Social Psychology*, edited by John DeLamater. NY: Kluwer-Plenum. 2003.

Social Structure, Cognitions, and Emotions

Psychological distress, including depression, anxiety, and anger, are emotions or feelings. We call the negative end of the emotion continuum psychological distress, and the positive end, psychological well-being. The cognitions—thoughts, perceptions, or worldviews—we cover include the sense of personal control and trust. At the other end of the continuum, are the sense of powerlessness and mistrust.

Cognitions link social structure to emotions. Distress is generated by objective conditions of disadvantage. This disadvantage, inequality, strain, burden, and hardship must be perceived to be felt as distressing. Research has identified the sense of personal control as an important link between individuals' place in the stratification system and their psychological well-being. Perceived powerlessness is generated by objective conditions of powerlessness and leads to distress. Despite recent interest in trust, less is known about the structural determinants of trust and whether trust mediates the impact of social structure on psychological well-being. Theory suggests it does. Theoretically, mistrust is generated by disadvantage, threat, and powerlessness and leads to distress.

Psychological Distress

Defining and Measuring Psychological Distress

Depression and Anxiety. Distress is an unpleasant subjective emotional state. It takes two major forms. The first is depression: feeling sad, demoralized, lonely, hopeless, worthless, wishing you were dead, having trouble sleeping, crying, feeling everything is an effort, and being unable to get going. The second is anxiety: being tense, restless, worried, irritable, and anxious. Depression and anxiety each take two forms: mood and malaise. Mood refers to the feelings such as the sadness of depression or the worry of anxiety. Malaise refers to bodily states, such as the listlessness and distraction of depression or the autonomic ailments (headaches, stomachaches, dizziness) and restlessness of anxiety. Depression and anxiety—both mood and malaise—are related in two ways: the maps of their social high and low zones are very similar, and a person who has one also tends to have the others (although not necessarily at the same time). Table 22.1 shows some examples of symptoms of depression and anxiety, separating mood and malaise.

Depression and anxiety are especially useful indicators of the subjective quality of life. Depression and anxiety are highly correlated: People who suffer from one usually also suffer from the other. They are the most common types of psychological problems, experienced by everyone to some degree at some time. Maps of their emotional high and low zones tell us a great deal about the nature of life in different social positions. However, there are other types of emotional distress that have received less attention. One is anger.

Anger. Anger is another unpleasant emotional state also highly correlated with depression. People who feel angry often feel depressed. Weissman and Paykel (1974) first described women who were depressed, partly because of being powerless and dependent *vis-à-vis* their husbands. The women got angry at their husbands, took it out on their children, and

TABLE 22.1 ***Items from Indexes of Depression, Anxiety, and Anger***

Respondents are asked, "How often in the past month have you ____". Responses are recorded as never (0), almost never (1), sometimes (2), fairly often (3), or often (4). Alternatively, respondents are asked, "Now I'm going to read a list of different feelings that people sometimes have. After each one I would like you to tell me on how many days you have felt this way during the last week. On how many days have you ____?" (0–7).

1. DISTRESS
a. DEPRESSION
i. Mood
Felt sad[a]
Felt lonely[a]
Felt you couldn't shake the blues[a]
Felt depressed[b]
Been bothered by things that don't usually bother you[b]
Wondered if anything was worthwhile anymore[c]
Felt that nothing turned out for you the way you wanted it to[c]
Felt completely hopeless about everything
Felt worthless
Thought about taking your own life
ii. Malaise
Felt that everything was an effort[a]
Felt you just couldn't get going[a]
Had trouble keeping your mind on what you were doing[a]
Had trouble getting to sleep or staying asleep[a]
Didn't talk to anyone or talked less than usual[b]
Felt no interest in anything or anybody
Felt tired all the time
Had poor appetite
iii. Positive affect
Enjoyed life[b]
Felt hopeful about the future[b]
Felt happy[b]
b. ANXIETY
i. Mood
Worried a lot about little things[c]
Felt anxious, tense, or nervous[c]
Felt restless or fidgety[c]
ii. Malaise
Had dizziness[c]
Had shortness of breath when you were not exercising or working hard[c]
Had your hands tremble[c]
Had your heart beating hard when you were not exercising or working hard[c]
Suddenly felt hot all over[c]

(continued)

TABLE 22.1 *Continued*

- **c.** ANGER
  - **i.** Mood
    - Felt annoyed with things or people[d]
    - Felt angry[d]
  - **ii.** Behavioral
    - Yelled at someone[d]

[a] from the short version of the Center for Epidemiological Studies Depression Scale (Modified CES-D) (Mirowsky and Ross 1990; Ross and Mirowsky 1984).

[b] From the CES-D (Radloff 1977).

[c] Modified version of symptoms from the Langner index (1962).

[d] From the anger scale (Mirowsky and Ross 1995, 1996; Ross and Van Willigen 1996).

Researchers can use the level of generality or specificity relevant to their research question. At a general level, for example, a distress index can include depression and anxiety, mood and malaise, and positive affect (scored in reverse). At more specific levels, researchers can distinguish between depression and anxiety, and further between depressed (or anxious) mood and malaise; and anger.

then felt guilty, which makes them even more depressed. Recently a few sociologists have begun to look more systematically at social structure and anger (Ross and Van Willigen 1996; Schieman 1999, 2000).

In the "social structure and psychological distress" model, distress is a consequence of social problems, not the problem itself (Mirowsky and Ross 2003). Socially structured inequality, disadvantage, stress, and hardship have broad-reaching consequences for psychological well-being, affecting various types of distress (Aneshensel et al. 1991; Pearlin 1989). However, most research on the emotional consequences of inequality has used depression as the indicator of distress. By focusing on a particular problem—depression—Aneshensel and her colleagues argue, researchers do not adequately test a sociological model. Conditions of inequality and disadvantage theoretically result in higher levels of all types of distress, including anger (Mirowsky and Ross 1995).

Most sociological research ignores anger, and on the other hand, most research on anger takes a medical model approach. In a medical model, anger is the problem itself. Anger as a health problem has entered the medical literature by way of specification of the components of type A personality. Research indicates that the constellation of behaviors known as type A is not uniformly bad for health: Hostility and anger increase the risk of heart disease, but competitive, hard-driving, goal-oriented behavior does not (Appel et al. 1983; Thomas 1989). In this model, anger is treated a maladaptive emotion with negative health consequences. Thus, people who are "too hostile" are given suggestions to reduce anger like "taking time out," "distracting yourself," and "thought stopping" (Consumer Reports on Health 1994). The medical model ignores structural strains—the relative risks of anger structured by one's social environment. Nowhere does it suggest that the social situation that produced the anger could be modified, for example, by providing affordable child care to families with children or encouraging fathers to share child care responsibilities with mothers (Ross and Van Willigen 1996).

This model prevails in spite of the fact that conceptualizations of anger suggest that it is likely caused by social inequality. Anger is a social emotion. It results from the assessment of inequality in social situations or relations, from perceptions of having been unjustly treated, or from perceptions of a violation of a fair social contract (Averill 1983; Novaco 1985; Tavris 1982). Anger, therefore, may be useful in the study of structural determinants of psychological well-being because it may be the result of an individual's assessment of inequality, often as it is played out in interpersonal relations in the family. Theoretically, inequality produces frustration and anger. Studying anger may allow researchers to identify objective conditions perceived as inequitable by individuals. Social patterns of anger may contain a message about patterned social inequalities.

Distress and Well-being as a Continuum. Well-being and distress are opposite poles on a single continuum: More well-being means less distress and more distress means less well-being. Well-being is a general sense of enjoying life and feeling happy, hopeful about the future, secure and calm. Lack of these positive feelings is related to depression and anxiety. It is useful to think of a continuum from happy and fulfilled at the well-being end to depressed and anxious at the distress end.

The fact that well-being and distress are opposite poles of the same emotional dimension seems obvious. Yet, some researchers say that positive and negative affect are distinct dimensions of mood, and not just opposite poles (e.g., Bradburn 1969). The reason given is that the negative correlation between measures of well-being and of distress is not perfect (not –1.0). Depending on how well-being and distress are measured, the estimated correlation ranges from –.50 (Ross and Mirowsky 1984) to near zero (Bradburn, 1969). These correlations seem to suggest that well-being and distress are at least partially independent moods. There are two reasons why the negative correlation between well-being and distress is less than perfect, even though they are opposite poles of a single dimension of mood. The first is random measurement error. There is always a certain amount of randomness in the processes of communicating and recording. By our estimate, the correlation that is corrected for random error is approximately –.70 (Ross and Mirowsky 1984).

The second reason the correlation is less than perfect is that some people express their feelings less than others. Differences in expressiveness crosscut differences in mood. The worse a person's mood the less well-being and more distress he or she reports, but the less expressive a person is the less of both he or she reports. By our estimate, differences in expressiveness account for 30 percent of the nonrandom differences in reported well-being and distress. Differences in mood account for the other 70 percent. Differences in expressiveness are easy to take into account, and investigations show they have little effect on the results of studies. Women are more expressive than men, but this does not account for the higher levels of anxiety and depression reported by women (Mirowsky and Ross 1995). Other sociodemographic differences in expressiveness are not as great as that between the sexes, and do not account for the social patterns of distress. Well-being increases and distress decreases with greater education and income, with fewer personal losses and economic hardships, and with marriage. Well-being and distress have opposite sociodemographic patterns because they are opposite ends of the same continuum.

Satisfaction Is Distinct from Psychological Well-being. Satisfaction is not a part of psychological well-being. Well-being and distress are the poles of one dimension; satisfaction and discontent are the poles of another. Satisfaction implies a convergence of aspiration and achievement that reflects resignation as much as it does accomplishment. Whereas distress often results from deprivation, dissatisfaction results from deprivation relative to one's expectations. Although the two may often go together, the instances in which they do not are important to sociological theory. For example, education increases expected income and thus increases both well-being and satisfaction with one's income; but among people in the same income bracket, higher education increases well-being but decreases satisfaction with that level of income (Mirowsky 1987). The most advantaged have the highest expectations, which tends to reduce satisfaction with a given level of achievement, while simultaneously enhancing the sense of well-being (Ross and Van Willigen 1997).

Social Statuses that Generate Distress

We focus on three social statuses that generate distress: gender, family status, and socioeconomic status. The fourth main status—age—is addressed elsewhere (Mirowsky and Ross 1999). These social patterns of psychological distress can be summarized as follows: (1) women are more distressed than men; (2) married people are less distressed than the unmarried, but those with children at home are somewhat more distressed than nonparents; and (3) the higher one's socioeconomic status (education, job, and income) the lower one's level of distress.

Gender

Surveys find that women report higher average levels of depression and anxiety than men (Aneshensel 1992; Mirowsky and Ross 1995, 2003). Women also rate their health worse and have more physical impairments than men, although they live longer (Ross and Bird 1994). The evidence that women are more distressed than men seems compelling, yet the pattern has been questioned since the 1970s when it was first uncovered by Walt Gove and his colleagues, and it continues to be questioned today (Dohrenwend and Dohrenwend 1976, 1977; Gove and Clancy 1975; Ritchey et al. 1991; Rieker and Bird 2000; Seiler 1975). Two perspectives question whether women are really more distressed than men. We call them the *response-bias view* and the *gendered response view* (Mirowsky and Ross 1995). According to the response-bias view, women are more aware of their emotions, more likely to talk about emotions to others, to be open and expressive, and to think that discussing personal well-being is acceptable rather than stigmatizing. Thus, when women and men are questioned about depression and anxiety, the women report it more. According to the gendered-response theory, women respond to the ubiquitous stress of life with somewhat different emotions than men. In particular, women might feel anxious and depressed where men feel agitated and angry.

As the evidence will show, women genuinely suffer greater distress than men, and that the difference in distress reflects and reveals women's comparatively disadvantaged social standing. It is not simply that women express their emotions more freely than men, and thus appear more distressed. Nor is it simply that women respond to stressors with different emotions than men, and surveys ask more questions about responses typical of women than about those typical of men. Women do express emotions more freely than men, and women express distress somewhat differently than men. However, expression does not explain the difference in distress. In fact, the more the analyses adjust for differences in expression, the *greater* the gap in distress found between women and men. Furthermore, contrary to gendered-response theory, women feel more angry than men, not less (Conger et al. 1993; Mirowsky and Ross 1995).

Women are more likely to express their feelings than men by two measures (Mirowsky and Ross 1995). First, we asked people a direct question about how much they agreed with the statement "I keep my emotions to myself." Men were more likely to agree than women that they keep their emotions to themselves. Second, we used an unobtrusive measure, the tendency to report both positive emotions (happiness) and negative emotions (sadness), using a confirmatory factor method that adjusts for the actual content of happiness and sadness. Women are more likely to express emotions regardless of content. The unobtrusive measure of expressiveness is associated with reports of various types of distress, including depressed mood (sadness), absence of positive mood (happiness), anxiety, anger, and malaise. Contrary to expectations, though, people who say they keep their emotions to themselves actually report more distress of all types, not less. Maybe keeping one's emotions to oneself is distressing in the long run because it precludes supportive responses from other people. Most important, adjustment for two measures of expressiveness does not account for sex differences in distress. On the contrary, adjustment for the tendency to express emotions leaves the gender gap intact. In most cases, the gap in distress favoring men increases. Even though women are more expressive than men, their expressiveness does not account for their high reported levels of distress.

According to the gendered-response theory, men and women experience the same amount of stress but differ in the nature of their emotional responses to stress (Aneshensel et al. 1991; Dohrenwend and Dohrenwend 1976, 1977; Rosenfield 1999). Where men get angry and hostile, women get sad and depressed. Evidence for the gendered response perspective requires two findings: 1) women have higher levels of depression; men have higher levels of anger, and 2) people with high levels of anger have low levels of depression. Findings do not support gendered-response theory. First, women are more angry than men, not less (Conger et al. 1993; Mirowsky and Ross 1995; Ross and Van Willigen 1996). Second, people with high levels of depression are more angry, not less angry. Depression and anger are positively correlated. If men avoided depression by becoming angry, anger and depression would be negatively correlated. Anger doesn't substitute for depression. Anger accompanies depression.

In fact, all types of distress go together. Depression, anger, anxiety, lack of happiness, and malaise are all positively correlated. Different types of distress do not substitute for one another. Women and men do not face equal levels of frustration, stress, and disadvantage, but simply respond to ubiquitous stress in different ways. Women have more of all types of distress.

Thus far we have focused on distress. Distress is an unpleasant subjective state consisting of emotions and feelings that cause pain and misery. A focus on misery and suffering seems justified on its own, without reference to other values. People would rather not be distressed. It is worse to feel sad, demoralized, lonely, worried, tense anxious, angry, annoyed, run down, tired, and unable to concentrate or to sleep than to feel happy, hopeful about the future, and to enjoy life. Women are more distressed than men. But what about behaviors like heavy drinking, illegal drug use, or antisocial behavior? Are they substitutes for depression, anxiety, anger, unhappiness, and malaise that women experience? Do men avoid depression by these behaviors?

The distinction between emotional (or affective) problems like depression, anxiety, and anger, and behavioral problems, like heavy drinking, raises the possibility that gendered response may occur across realms of disorder, even though it does not occur within the emotional realm. Women get depressed, anxious, and angry; but men abuse alcohol and illegal drugs, and engage in antisocial behavior more frequently than women (Aneshensel et al. 1991; Ross 2000). Symptoms from different realms should *not* be combined—they represent inherently distinct phenomena that may be interrelated but should not be confounded. Distress is a problem for the person who suffers it. Antisocial behavior, drinking, and drug use may be correlated with distress, but are not themselves distress. In some cases such as antisocial behavior or alcoholism, the behaviors may be at least as much a problem for other people as for the person himself. However, the question remains whether women feel more distressed than men because the men transform their frustrations into behavioral disorder.

Two things must be true for transrealm gendered response to explain women's greater distress. First, some type of behavioral disorder must reduce distress. If a behavior does not lower distress, then it cannot account for lower male levels of distress. On this count, there is little or no support for transrealm gendered response. Studies find that depression *in*creases with the level of antisocial behavior, alcoholism, and drug abuse, which are the main problems found more commonly in men than in women (Boyd et al. 1984). One study finds that men who drink heavily, use opiates, and smoke cigarettes have higher levels of depression than those who do not, although marijuana use only correlated with depression when it was used to cope with problems (Green and Ritter 2000). Men and women who drink heavily and engage in behavior that gets them in trouble with the law have higher levels of depression than those who do not (Ross 2000). Heavy drinking, illegal drug use, and other lawless behaviors are not substitutes for depression. Engaging in these behaviors doesn't protect men from turning stress and frustration inward upon themselves. On the contrary, people who drink and engage in antisocial activities have higher levels of depression than those who do not. When we take heavy drinking and lawless behavior into account, the gender gap in depression does not decrease; it increases by about 40 percent (Ross 2000). This means that heavy drinking and lawless behavior do not explain why men have lower levels of depression than women. On the contrary, if women drank and engaged in illegal activities as much as men do, women's depression levels would be even higher than they are now. (Furthermore, although men use illegal drugs more frequently than women, women are more likely than men to use prescribed psychoactive drugs—over one woman in five compared with less than one man in ten [Verbrugge 1985].)

Men's destructive behaviors do not account for their low levels of depression. In fact the men who drink heavily, use illegal drugs, and engage in antisocial behavior have higher levels of depression than the men who don't. Women certainly would not protect themselves from getting depressed if they turned their stress and frustration outward; it would lead to even more depression. Depression accompanies anger, hostility, violence, illegal activity, use of drugs, and heavy drinking; it does not substitute for it.

Women are more distressed than men. Measured as sadness, demoralization, hopelessness, anxiety, worry, malaise, and anger, women experience distress about 30 percent more frequently than men (Mirowsky and Ross 1995). It is not simply that they are more likely to express their feelings. It is not simply that men and women respond differently to the ubiquitous stress of life. Women's and men's lives differ, and this difference puts women at higher risk of distress. Theories of gender inequality or gender-based exposure to social stressors explain women's elevated distress as the consequence of inequality and disadvantage (Mirowsky and Ross 2003). Different positions in the social structure expose individuals to different characteristic amounts of hardship and constraint. Women's positions at work and in the family disadvantage them compared with men.

Compared with men, women face more economic dependency, restricted opportunities for paid employment, lower earnings, less power at work and at home, more routine and unfulfilling work, more conflict between work and family obligations, and unfairness in the division of household labor (Mirowsky 1985; Reskin and Padavic 1994; Ross and Wright 1998), all of which increase distress. In 1999, men aged twenty-four to sixty-five were more likely to be employed than women: 87.5 percent compared with 72.8 percent. Among the college-educated, 93 percent of men were employed compared with 81.9 percent of women. Among persons with a college degree in 1999, women earned $31,452, on average, compared with men's earnings of $55,057 (whites: $31,406 compared with $56,620; blacks: $31, 952 compared with $42,539) (U.S. Bureau of the Census 2000). Women, employed or not still do the majority of domestic work although fathers now participate in child care more than ever before (Bianchi 2000). Women's greater burden of demands and limitations creates stress and frustration, manifesting in higher levels of distress. This idea was first proposed by Gove and his colleagues, who, along with others, found that employed women—whose lives were more like men's—were less distressed than homemakers (Gove and Tudor 1973). We later found that couples who share both the economic responsibilities and the domestic responsibilities for housework and child care also share much the same level of psychological well-being, and are less distressed than other couples (Ross et al. 1983). An analysis of the factors that increase the husband's domestic work shows that when husbands do more, the higher the wife's earnings, and when they do less, the more their own earnings exceed the wife's. Thus, equality in the division of labor at home, which provides psychological benefits to the husband and wife, depends on their economic equality in the workplace (Ross et al. 1983).

Compared with men, women are less likely to be employed, more likely to be employed part time rather than full time, have lower earnings, less fulfilling work, and more economic hardship, aspects of socioeconomic status, which as we discuss next, increase distress. However, young women's levels of education now equal men's (U.S. Census 2000). Since education is the source of socioeconomic status, the gap between men's and women's levels of distress may close in the future, although thus far evidence for this trend is equivocal (Mirowsky 1996).

Socioeconomic Status

High socioeconomic status improves psychological well-being. Low socioeconomic status increases psychological distress (Kessler 1982; Link et al. 1993; Mirowsky and Ross 1995, 2003; Pearlin et al. 1981; Ross and Huber 1985; Ross and Van Willigen 1997).

High socioeconomic status is also associated with self-reported good health, high levels of physical functioning, less chronic disease, and lower mortality (Mirowsky, Ross, and Reynolds 2000; Reynolds and Ross 1998; Ross and Wu 1995; Williams and Collins 1995). Some people are exposed to more social stressors and fewer resources to deal with them. They are the poor and poorly educated; unemployed, employed part time, or working at menial and unfulfilling jobs; and living in poor and rundown neighborhoods where crime is a constant threat. Some people have fewer problems and more resources to solve them. They are the well-to-do and well educated, working at challenging and fulfilling jobs and living in pleasant neighborhoods.

Socioeconomic status indicates a person's relative standing in the distribution of opportunity, prosperity, and standing. It broadly refers to one's place in the unequal distribution of socially valued resources, goods, and quality of life. It is typically measured by education, work, and income. People with college educations, employed at good jobs, with high incomes have high socioeconomic status. Although there is some value in looking at overall standing, there is more value to keeping each component separate. Education, income, and work indicate different underlying concepts. Education is the accumulated knowledge, skills, values, and behaviors learned at school (called human capital), in addition to being a credential that structures employment opportunities. Income and economic hardship indicate economic well-being. Work is productive activity (paid or not). Furthermore, education, employment, and economic resources are not on the same causal level. Education is the key to people's position in the stratification system; it decreases the likelihood of being unemployed, increases the likelihood of full-time employment, and gives people access to good jobs with high incomes. Part of education's effect on psychological well-being is mediated by employment status, work and economic resources, but some is a direct benefit of schooling (Ross and Van Willigen 1997).

Employment, especially full-time employment, is associated with higher levels of psychological (and physical) well-being (Pearlin et al. 1981; Reynolds and Ross 1998; Ross and Mirowsky 1995; Ross and Van Willigen 1997). Job qualities also affect psychological well-being. Although some researchers studying stratification looks at occupational prestige, this is not really the most important thing about jobs to psychological well-being. The two most important aspects of work to well-being include autonomy and creativity are work that is autonomous, free from close supervision, and provides opportunities for workers to make their own decisions, and work that is creative, nonroutine, involves a variety of tasks, and gives people a chance for continued learning and development decreases distress (Ross and Drentea 1998; Ross and Van Willigen 1997; Ross and Wright 1998). Autonomous and creative work give workers the chance to use their skills in the design and implementation of the their own work, and it gives them the freedom to use thought and independent judgment in doing different things in different ways rather than doing the same thing in the same way in a process designed and controlled by others (Kohn and Schooler 1982). These qualities of work decrease distress directly and in part by way of boosting people's sense of personal control.

Low income is distressing mostly because it increases economic hardship (Reynolds and Ross 1998), and economic hardship itself is more than a function of income. Low levels of education, marriage, and children in the home all decrease economic hardship directly, apart from income (Mirowsky and Ross 1999), and low levels of education further deprive people of the problem-solving resources needed to cope with the stresses of economic hardship. Ross and Huber (1985) find a synergistic effect on economic hardship of low education and low income, each making the effect of the other worse. Economic hardship increases psychological distress; the chronic strain of struggling to pay the bills and to feed and clothe the children takes its toll in feelings of depression and malaise (Conger et al. 1992; Ge et al. 1992; Pearlin et al. 1981; Reynolds and Ross 1998; Ross and Huber 1985; Ross and Van Willigen 1997).

Family Status

Compared with married people, the single, divorced, and widowed have higher levels of depression, anxiety, and other forms of psychological distress, they have more physical health problems as indicated by acute conditions, chronic conditions, days of disability, and self-reported health, and their death rates are higher (Mirowsky and Ross 2003; Ross 1995; Ross et al. 1990; Umberson and Williams 2000; Waite and Gallagher 2000). The one exception to the consistent, positive effects of marriage concerns young adults: very young adults who get married do not experience lower depression levels than those who remain single (Horwitz and White 1991). The positive effect of marriage on well-being is strong and consistent, and selection of the psychologically healthy into marriage or the psychologically unhealthy out of marriage cannot explain the effect. Some think that marriage protects men's psychological well-being more than women's (Riessman and Gestel 1985), but recent evidence shows men's advantage over women in psychological well-being is as large or larger among the single, divorced, and widowed (Simon 2002).

Social support and economic resources likely explain why marriage is associated with psychological well-being. Compared with being unmarried, marriage provides emotional support—a sense of being cared about, loved, esteemed, and valued as a person (Ross 1995). Married people also have higher household incomes and lower levels of economic hardship than the nonmarried. Social support and a lack of economic hardship improve psychological well-being (House et al. 1988; Ross et al. 1990).

Children, however, do not improve parents' psychological well-being, measured as the absence of depression, anxiety, and psychophysiological distress. People with children at home do not have higher levels of well-being than nonparents (Mirowsky and Ross 2003). In many instances, parents—especially mothers—are more psychologically distressed than nonparents. Children at home either increase psychological distress or have an insignificant effect on well-being. The stress of parenthood is felt at home: Kandel and her colleagues, for instance, found that children at home increase depression, but parents whose children have left home are less depressed than the childless of the same age (Kandel et al. 1985).

What are the processes by which children affect parents' distress? Two explanations stand out—economic hardship and the demands of child care. Children in the home lead to economic hardship, increasing depression for both men and women (Ross and Huber 1985). At the same level of family income, a family with children feels more economic pressure than one without children (Mirowsky and Ross 1999). The chronic strain of struggling to pay the bills and to feed and clothe the children takes its toll in feelings of depression and anger (Pearlin et al. 1981; Ross and Huber 1985; Ross and Van Willigen 1996).

Children greatly increase the total amount of domestic work, especially for women. In the household, mothers do a disproportionate amount of child care—much of it in the form of housework like cooking, cleaning, and doing laundry—which increases depression (Kessler and McRae 1982; Ross et al. 1983). Furthermore, mothers typically manage the child care arrangements, and thus are further exposed to the difficulties of arranging care for the children while the parents are at work, which also increases depression (Ross and Mirowsky 1988). Inequity in the distribution of housework and child care is a primary means by which gender inequality is perpetuated in the home, increasing depression and anger among women (Glass and Fujimoto 1994; Lennon and Rosenfield 1992; Ross and Van Willigen 1996). According to the gender inequality perspective, women are not more *vulnerable* to the stressors of parenthood, although some researchers argue that women are more affected by parenthood because the role is more salient to them (Simon 1992), but rather that women are more *exposed* to the stressors of parenthood than are men.

Sense of Control

A sense of personal control links social structure to emotional well-being (Mirowsky and Ross 2003). Perceived control occupies the central position in a three-part model in which social statuses shape perceptions and beliefs, which, in turn, affect emotional well-being. In this section we describe the social causes and emotional consequences of perceived control versus powerlessness. Perceived powerlessness is generated by objective conditions of powerlessness and leads to distress.

Of all the beliefs about self and society that might increase or reduce distress, belief in control over one's own life may be the most important. Seeman placed the sense of powerlessness at the top of his list of types of subjective alienation, defining it as, "the expectancy or probability, held by the individual, that his own behavior cannot determine the occurrence of the outcomes, or reinforcements, he seeks" (Seeman 1959: 784). Alienation is any form of detachment or separation from oneself or from others. Powerlessness is the separation from important outcomes in one's own life or an inability to achieve desired ends. Perceived powerlessness is the cognitive awareness of this reality. Powerlessness, as a social-psychological variable, is distinct from the objective conditions that may produce it and the distress an individual may feel as a consequence of it.

Defining and Measuring the Sense of Personal Control

The sense of personal control is a learned, generalized expectation that outcomes are contingent on one's own choices and actions. People with a high sense of control report being effective agents in their own lives; they believe that they can master, control, and effectively alter the environment. Perceived control is the cognitive awareness of a link between efforts and outcomes. On the other end of the continuum, perceived powerlessness is the belief that one's actions do not affect outcomes. It is the belief that outcomes of situations are determined by forces external to one's self such as powerful others, luck, fate, or chance. People with a sense of powerlessness think that they have little control over meaningful events and circumstances in their lives. As such, perceived powerlessness is the cognitive awareness of a discrepancy between one's goals and the means to achieve them. Perceived control and powerlessness represent two ends of a continuum, with the belief that one can shape conditions and events in one's life on one end of the continuum, and the belief that one's actions cannot influence events and circumstances at the other (Mirowsky and Ross 2003).

The importance of perceived control is recognized in a number of social and behavioral sciences, where it appears in several forms with various names. In sociology researchers build on themes of perceived powerlessness versus control. As a result, many of the constructs used by sociologists overlap, and they are not seen as very distinct. Concepts related to personal control appear under a number of different names in addition to perceived powerlessness and control, notably mastery (Pearlin et al. 1981), personal autonomy (Seeman 1983), the sense of personal efficacy (Downey and Moen 1987; Gecas 1989), instrumentalism (Wheaton 1980), and personal agency (Thoits 2006), and at the other end of the continuum, fatalism (Wheaton 1980) and perceived helplessness (Elder and Liker 1982). In psychology concepts closely related to the sense of personal control include internal locus of control, self-efficacy, and helplessness. Psychologists are more likely than sociologists to focus on differences among related concepts, but these concepts also overlap some with the sense of personal control.

The sense of personal control (Mirowsky and Ross 2003) overlaps with the personal control component of Rotter's locus of control scale, which includes questions like "when I make plans I can make them work" or "I have little influence over the things that happen to me." Compared with persons with an external locus of control, those with an internal locus of control attribute outcomes to themselves rather than to forces outside of themselves (Rotter 1966). However, the concept of personal control refers to *oneself*, not others, and it is *general*, not realm-specific. Thus, unlike Rotter, we exclude beliefs about the control others have over their lives and realm-specific control, like political control, from the concept. For instance, we do not consider questions from the Rotter scale like "the average citizen can have an influence in government decisions" or "there will always be wars" to be measures of the sense of personal control since they do not refer to oneself, and they are realm-specific.

The Mirowsky-Ross measure of the sense of personal control balances statements claiming and denying personal control, and balances statements in which the outcome is positive and negative, as shown in Figure 22.1 (1991). This eliminates defense, self-blame, and agreement bias from the measure. Defense is the tendency to claim control over good outcomes but deny control over bad outcomes. Self-blame, the opposite, is the tendency to claim control over bad outcomes but not good. Agreement is the tendency to simply say "yes" to survey questions, irrespective of content. Because of our balanced 2×2 design, none of these tendencies biases the measure of personal control.

Heuristics in Psychology and Sociology

The most useful research on the links between social structure, perceptions of control, and emotional outcomes synthesize the strengths of psychology and sociology—as did Rotter and Seeman—while avoiding the pitfalls. Both Rotter (1966) and Seeman (1959) recognized that perceived powerlessness—the major form of subjective alienation—and external locus of control were related concepts. In fact, Rotter derived the concept of locus of control

Personal Control

	Successes	Failures
Control	(1) I can do anything I set my mind to. (2) I am responsible for my own successes.	(1) My misfortunes are the result of mistakes I have made. (2) I am responsible for my failures.
Lack of Control	(1) The really good things that happen to me are due to luck. (2) If something good is going to happen to me, it will.	(1) Most of my problems are due to bad breaks. (2) I have little control over bad things that happen to me.

FIGURE 22.1 ***Indicators of the Sense of Personal Control (Mirowsky and Ross 1991).***

from the sociological concept of alienation, stating "the alienated individual feels unable to control his own destiny" (Rotter 1966:263). The roots of current concepts lie in their early interdisciplinary work.

Each discipline has a heuristic, or working assumption, which greatly simplifies reality to provide a base from which to proceed with research. In the extreme, psychology assumes that beliefs come out of people's heads without reference to social conditions, whereas sociology assumes that there is nothing *but* social structure. Sociologists too often discount the ways in which perceptions mediate the effects of social position on well-being; psychologists too often discount the influence of social structure on perceptions. Both links are crucial to understanding the processes by which social position affects psychological well-being.

Sociologists sometimes imply that social structure has consequences for individual behavior or well-being without reference to individual beliefs or perceptions (Braverman 1974). Erikson (1986) critiques sociologists who think that bringing in social psychological mediating variables somehow makes theory less structural. "There are those," says Erikson, "who argue that one ought to be able to determine when a person is alienated by taking a look at the objective conditions in which she works. The worker exposed to estranging conditions is alienated almost by definition, no matter what she says she thinks or even what she thinks she thinks. That view . . . has the effect of closing off sociological investigation rather than the effect of inviting it. Alienation, in order to make empirical sense, has to reside somewhere in or around the persons who are said to experience it" (1986:6). The association between the objective condition and the subjective perception is an important empirical question; one that must be investigated, not assumed.

Some psychologists, on the other hand, discount the effects of social position, instead claiming that perceptions of control are as likely to be illusory as to be based on reality.

Levenson says that a belief that one controls important outcomes in one's life is *unrelated* to the belief that others, chance, fate, or luck control the outcomes (Levenson 1973; see Lachman 1986 for a review). Brewin and Shapiro (1984) contend that a perceived ability to achieve desirable outcomes is unrelated to a perceived ability to avoid undesirable ones. In both cases, people supposedly fail to see a connection, and the realities of life do not suggest one. Implicitly, these views deny the effects of social structure on the sense of control. Levenson's view suggests that education, prestige, wealth, and power do not shift the locus of real control from others and chance to oneself. Brewin and Shapiro's view suggests that the real resources available for achieving success are useless for avoiding failure. The empirical basis for these claims is small and often insignificant correlations between internal and external control and control over good and bad outcomes. Next we discuss the biases in their scales created by agreement tendencies and defensiveness that produce these results.

Control, Defense, and Acquiescence. Responses to questions about personal control capture the concept of interest and two other cross-cutting concepts—the tendency to agree and self-defense. Some people tend to agree with statements irrespective of content. Agreement tendency can make it appear as if internal and external control are uncorrelated (as in Levenson, 1973). Some people are more likely to believe that they control the good outcomes in their lives than that they control the bad ones (self-defense); others take more responsibility for their failures than for their successes (self-blame) (as in Brewin and Shapiro 1984). Agreement tendencies and the tendency toward self-defense or self-blame cross-cut the concept of interest and bias measures unless they balance agreement and defense. Thus, measures of personal control ideally should balance defensiveness and agreement tendencies to achieve unbiased measures. The Mirowsky-Ross measure of the sense of control (1991) is a two-by-two index that balances statements about control with those about lack of control, and statements about success (good outcomes) with those about failure (bad outcomes). It is shown in Figure 22.1. Interestingly, Rotter's locus of control scale used a forced-choice format to solve the problem of acquiescence, but his logic apparently was lost when researchers switched to Likert scales. Likert scales are much more efficient in surveys, and are more acceptable to respondents who dislike being forced to choose one of two extremes. Likert scales allow degrees of agreement with each statement. However, Likert scales should balance control and lack of control over good and bad outcomes to ensure validity.

Social Statuses that Generate a Sense of Control

Objective Power and Perceived Control

Belief in external control is the learned and generalized expectation that one has little control over meaningful events and circumstances in one's life. As such, it is the cognitive awareness of a discrepancy between one's goals and the means to achieve them. Beliefs about personal control are often realistic perceptions of objective conditions. An individual learns through social interaction and personal experience that his or her choices and efforts are usually likely or unlikely to affect the outcome of a situation. Failure in the face of effort leads to a sense of powerlessness, fatalism, or belief in external control, beliefs that can increase passivity and result in giving up. Through continued experience with objective conditions of powerlessness and lack of control, individuals come to learn that their own actions cannot produce desired outcomes. In contrast, success leads to a sense of mastery, efficacy, or belief in internal control, characterized by an active, problem-solving approach to life (Mirowsky and Ross 2003).

Sociological theory points to several conditions likely to produce a belief in external control. First and foremost is powerlessness. Defined as an objective condition rather than a belief, it is the inability to achieve one's ends or, alternatively, the inability to achieve one's ends when in opposition to others. The second is structural inconsistency, which is a situation in which society defines certain goals, purposes, and interests as legitimate and desirable and also defines the proper procedures for moving toward the objectives but does not provide adequate resources and opportunities for achieving the objectives through legitimate means. The third is alienated labor, a condition under which the worker does not decide what to produce, does not design and schedule the production process, and does not own the product. The fourth is dependency, a situation in which one partner in an exchange has fewer alternative sources of sustenance and gratification than the other. The fifth is role overload, a situation in which expectations of others imply demands that overwhelm the resources and capabilities of the individual. Although these conditions are not exhaustive, they all point to the generative force of various forms of social power. In looking for the sources of perceived powerlessness, researchers have looked for variables associated with conditions of powerlessness, structural inconsistency, alienated labor, dependency, and role overload.

Among the major sociodemographic correlates of the sense of personal control are: 1) socioeconomic status, especially education and its consequences for work and income; and 2) gender, and its consequences for work and family statuses and interactions. (The third—age—is addressed elsewhere—see Mirowsky and Ross 1999, for one.)

Socioeconomic Status

High socioeconomic status is associated with a sense of personal control (Mirowsky and Ross 1983, 2003). Looking at specific components of socioeconomic status (SES) separately, education, employment (especially full-time employment), income, lack of economic hardship, and autonomous and nonroutine work each decrease the sense of powerlessness and increase the sense of control, adjusting for the other components.

Education is the key to a person's place in the stratification system. It shapes the likelihood of being employed at a good job with a high income, and it boosts the sense of control as a direct consequence of schooling. Education raises the sense of personal control because it helps people successfully prevent problems, or solve them if prevention fails, to achieve their goals, and to shape their own lives (Mirowsky and Ross 1998, 2005). Through education, one develops capacities on many levels that increase one's sense of personal control. Schooling builds human capital—skills, abilities, and resources. Education develops the habits and skills of communication: reading, writing, inquiring, discussing, looking things ups, and figuring things out. It develops basic analytic skills such as observing, experimenting, summarizing, synthesizing, interpreting, classifying, and so on. Because education develops the ability to gather and interpret information and to solve problems on many levels, it increases control over events and outcomes in ones life. Moreover, in education, one encounters and solves problems that are progressively more difficult, complex, and subtle. The process of learning builds problem-solving skills and confidence in the ability to solve problems. Education instills the habit of meeting problems with attention, thought, action, and persistence. Thus, education increases effort and ability, the fundamental components of problem solving (Wheaton 1980). For these reasons, high levels of education are associated with a sense of personal control (Mirowsky and Ross 2003). Finally, education serves as an avenue to good jobs and high incomes. Thus it marks the social power that helps provide control over circumstances of life (Ross and Wu 1995).

Jobs are important for a number of reasons. Low-status jobs produce a sense of powerlessness because the job, and the opportunities and income it provides, are seen as barriers to the achievement of life goals (Wheaton 1980). Jobs that are substantively complex (especially in work primarily with information and people rather than with things) increase the sense of personal control and psychological self-directedness (Kohn and Schooler 1982; Ross 2000). Jobs that provide autonomy—freedom from close supervision and participation in decision making—increase the sense of personal control (Bird and Ross 1993; Kohn and Schooler 1982; Ross and Mirowsky 1992). Together substantively complex, nonroutine, creative, interesting, autonomous work signals control over one's own work, which increases perceived control (Mirowsky and Ross 2003).

In sum, theory strongly predicts a positive relationship between SES and the sense of control, and research strongly supports the prediction. Most aspects of SES, including high levels of education, income, autonomous and creative work, and employment itself are significantly associated with high perceived control. SES may also help explain gender differences in perceptions of control.

Gender, Work, and Family

Theory suggests that women have a lower sense of control over their lives than men as a result of economic dependency, restricted opportunities, role overload, and the routine nature of housework and women's jobs. Past evidence indicates that women have a lower sense of control than men, but sometimes the difference is insignificant (Ross and Bird 1994; Ross and Mirowsky 1989). We examine the empirical evidence for expectations based on our theory of personal control. Then we return to the original question of whether women have a lower sense of control over their lives than do men, and the circumstances under which they do and do not.

Paid and Unpaid Work. Women are more likely to do unpaid domestic work; men are more likely to work for pay. Compared with not working for pay, employment is associated with status, power, economic independence, and noneconomic rewards, for both men and women. For women who are exclusively housewives, domestic work is done without economic rewards, without the opportunity for advancement or promotion for work well done, and, because it is often invisible, routine, devalued, and taken for granted, without psychological rewards. People employed for pay have a greater sense of control over their lives than others. Perceived control over one's life is the expectation that one's behavior affects outcomes, and working for pay likely produces a mental connection between efforts and outcomes. Furthermore, homemakers are economically dependent, which may decrease one's sense of control and increase the perception that powerful others shape one's life. Both economic dependency and the disconnection between work and rewards theoretically decrease perceived control among unpaid domestic workers compared with paid workers. Empirical evidence indicates that employed persons have a higher sense of control than the nonemployed overall (Ross and Mirowsky 1992), and that the employed have a higher sense of control than homemakers specifically (Bird and Ross 1993; Ross and Drentea 1998; Ross and Wright 1998). Elder and Liker (1982) found that elderly women who had taken jobs forty years earlier, during the Great Depression, had a higher sense of self-efficacy and lower sense of helplessness than women who remained homemakers.

Work and Family Interactions. Overall, employment is associated with a high sense of personal control, but not all jobs are alike, nor are all household contexts of employment. Critical combinations of low pay, nonautonomous working conditions, and heavy family demands (conditions faced disproportionately by women) may negate the positive influence of employment on control. Ross and Mirowsky (1992) find, first, that the difference in perceived control between employed and nonemployed depends on job conditions, including job autonomy and earnings (job authority, promotion opportunities, and job prestige are not significant). As job autonomy and earnings increase among the employed, their sense of control relative to that of the nonemployed increases. Second, household labor modifies the effect of employment on the sense of control. The higher one's responsibility for household work, the less the association between employment and control (Ross and Mirowsky 1992). Responsibility for household work greatly decreases the sense of control associated with employment. (Household work does not decrease perceived control in itself; among people who are not employed, household work slightly increases the sense of control). Similarly, Rosenfield (1989) finds that the role overload of mothers who are employed at full-time jobs increases the sense of powerlessness and thus increases depression. Third, the greater the household income from sources other than one's own earnings, the less the association between employment and perceived control (Ross and Mirowsky 1992). The lower the household income available from other sources, the greater the sense of control associated with having a job compared with not having one. Although other household income increases the sense of control, it decreases the positive effect of one's own employment on the sense of control.

The sense of control predicted for the employed who have low earnings and autonomy (a standard deviation below average) and major responsibility for household chores (a standard deviation above average) is actually lower than the average sense of control than among people who are not employed. At the other extreme, the sense of control predicted for the employed with high earnings and autonomy and low responsibility for household chores is very high, much higher than among the nonemployed.

Job autonomy, earnings, responsibility for household work, and other family income combine to make the association between employment and the sense of control greater for most men than for most women. Men have higher autonomy and earnings, less responsibility for household work, and lower amounts of other household income. Because of the differences in these factors, employment increases the expected sense of control most for married males, followed by nonmarried males, then nonmarried females, and finally married females.

For married women, the typical combination of low pay, low autonomy, high responsibility for household chores, and high family income other than personal earnings nearly negates the positive association between employment and the sense of control.

Reexamining Gender. Theory predicts that women have a lower sense of control than men. Adult statuses disadvantage women in terms of objective powerlessness, economic dependence, routine and unfulfilling work, and role overload. Women's positions at work, in households, and in the interactions between the two spheres provide empirical support for explanations of why women would have lower perceived control than men. Women's jobs pay less, provide less autonomy, and are frequently combined with household responsibilities that produce role overload. These conditions are associated with low personal control. On the other hand, some research does not find significant differences between men and women in their levels of personal control. These results mean that 1) something else, as yet unidentified, about women's lives offsets the negative conditions, and increases perceived control, 2) under some, as yet unidentified, conditions women have higher levels of control than do men. Identifying these conditions is a fruitful area for research. The fact that non-married women who have household incomes on par with married women (an unusual group) have high levels of personal control hints at a route for future research. Another fruitful path relates to age. Younger generations of women have work and education levels more equal to men's, which produces a smaller gap in perceived control between young men and women than older men and women (Ross and Mirowsky 2002).

Consequences of the Sense of Personal Control

People with high levels of personal control have low levels of psychological distress (Mirowsky and Ross 2003). Distress tends to be elevated among people who believe they have little influence over the things that happen to them, what is going to happen will happen, we might as well decide what to do by flipping a coin, and success is mostly a matter of getting good breaks. In comparison, distress is low among those who believe that when they make plans they can make them work, misfortunes result from the mistakes they make, there is really no such thing as luck, and what happens to them is their own doing. A meta-analysis of ninety-seven psychological studies, indicates strong and consistent evidence that a belief in external, as opposed to internal, control is associated with increased distress (Benassi et al. 1988).

In addition to its direct, demoralizing impact, the sense of not being in control of the outcomes in one's life can diminish the will and motivation to actively solve problems. Wheaton (1985) argues that fatalism decreases coping effort. Belief in the efficacy of environmental rather than personal forces makes active attempts to solve problems seem pointless: "What's the use?" The result is less motivation and less persistence in coping and, thus, less success in solving problems and adapting. Taking Wheaton's arguments a step further, the fatalist has a reactive, passive orientation whereas the instrumentalist has a proactive one. Instrumental persons are likely to search the environment for potentially distressing events and conditions, to take preventive steps, and to accumulate resources or develop skills and habits that will reduce the impact of unavoidable problems (for example, driving carefully, wearing a seat belt, and carrying accident insurance). When undesired events and situations occur, the instrumental person is better prepared and less threatened. In contrast, the reactive, passive person ignores potential problems until they actually happen, making problems likely to occur and leaving the person unprepared when they do. Furthermore, passive coping, such as trying to ignore the problem until it goes away, fails to limit the consequences of the problems. Thus, the instrumentalist is constantly getting ahead of problems whereas the fatalist is inevitably falling behind. The theoretical result is a magnification of differences: fatalists suffer more and more problems, reinforcing their perceived powerlessness and thus producing escalating passivity in the face of difficulties, and more and more distress.

Together, perceived powerlessness and distress negatively impact health. Emotional distress worsens health, and poor health in turn is distressing (Aneshensel et al. 1984). Furthermore, perceived control shapes health apart from distress. People with high levels of personal control are effective forces in their own lives. According to the theory of personal control, control's benefit lies in effectiveness (Mirowsky and Ross 1986). Instrumental persons are likely to accumulate resources and to develop skills and habits that prevent avoidable problems and reduce the impact of unavoidable problems. One consequence is better health. The sense of personal control improves health in large part by way of health-enhancing behaviors. Compared with people who feel powerless to control their lives, people with a sense of personal control know more about health, they are more likely to engage in healthy behaviors like quitting smoking, exercising, walking, maintaining a normal weight, and drinking moderately, and, in consequence, they have better self-rated health, better physical functioning, fewer illnesses, and lower rates of mortality (Mirowsky and Ross 1998; Seeman and Seeman 1983).

Summary

Looking broadly at theory and findings, we see that a sense of mastery and control are associated with achievement, status, education, employment, income, and work that is autonomous, unsupervised, complex, and creative, whereas fatalism and a sense of powerlessness are associated with failure, barriers to achievement, dependence, poverty, disadvantage, economic hardship, poor health and physical impairment, heavy family demands, work overload and work/family conflict, and work that is simple, routine, and closely supervised. People in higher socioeconomic positions tend to have a sense of personal control and people in lower socioeconomic positions a sense of personal powerlessness. This produces socioeconomic and gender differences in distress. Patterns of perceived control also help explain some of the beneficial effects of marriage relating to better economic circumstances of the married, but the rest of marriage's beneficial effect is probably due to social support. The sense of powerlessness can be depressing and demoralizing in itself, but worse than that it can undermine the will to seek and take effective action. As a result, the disadvantaged have a triple burden: First, they have more problems to deal with; second, their personal histories are likely to have left them with a sense of powerlessness; and third, that sense of powerlessness discourages them from martialing whatever energy and resources they do have in order to solve their problems. The result for many is a multiplication of despair.

What kinds of social resources could moderate these distress-producing disadvantages? We think education is key.

Conditions that Moderate the Influence of Social Status on Distress

Education, Gender, and Resource Substitution

Because education indicates human capital, it is a unique resource in the path to well-being. In school people learn to read, write, analyze, communicate, negotiate, solve problems, look things up, figure things out, plan, persevere, trust others, work with colleagues, and develop ideas. These skills and abilities learned in school help people control their own lives. High personal control helps people cope actively and flexibly, to avoid problems, and to prepare for those that cannot be avoided. Education is a critical resource because it is a resource itself, and the learned effectiveness it indicates helps people generate other resources.

"Resource substitution" states that education's influence on well-being is greater for the disadvantaged than it is for the more advantaged (Ross and Mirowsky 2006). Women's disadvantaged status means that they generally have fewer socioeconomic resources than men: They face more economic dependency, restricted opportunities for full-time employment, routine and unfulfilling work, and lower earnings. Women may therefore depend more heavily on education for well-being. Resource substitution exists when having multiple resources makes outcomes less dependent on the presence of any specific resource. Resources can substitute for one another; one can fill the gap if the other is absent, and each has less of an effect if the other is present. As a consequence, the effect of having a specific resource is greater for those who have fewer alternative resources.

This means that the very people who need other resources most in order to cope with their disadvantaged conditions or statuses are the least likely to have them. Thus, when resources substitute, disadvantages multiply. People with the most resources are less dependent on any one of them for their well-being. More resources, alternatives, choices, and options make any one resource less critical. People with the fewest resources are most dependent on any one resource for their well-being. The absence of alternative resources means women are especially dependent on education for well-being. Women with low levels of education will suffer more than will men for the very reason that they have fewer alternative resources to call on. On the other hand, women with college degrees will likely have levels of well-being as high as men's.

Resource substitution models take a general form. When poor physical or mental health, like depression, is the outcome, they imply a negative effect of education, a positive effect of disadvantaged status, and a negative interaction between education and disadvantaged status.

Education, Human Capital, and Well-being. Education has qualities that go beyond those of other resources because it indicates resourcefulness, or the ability to meet situations effectively. As human capital, education shapes the ability to create resources and to turn existing things into resources. A person's education is part of the person, rather than being external to the person like friends and family, neighborhood, or income. The skills and knowledge learned in school are inalienable—they cannot be taken from those who have it (Mirowsky and Ross 2005). Like education, the sense of personal control is a resource that inheres in the person. In contrast, resources external to the person such as a supportive relationship, a nice house in a good neighborhood, a welfare check, a job, or a paycheck can be lost.

Human capital is the productive capacity developed, embodied, and stocked in human beings themselves. An individual who acquires an education can use it to solve a wide range of problems because schooling builds skills and abilities on several levels of generality. On the most general level, education teaches people to learn. It develops the ability to write, communicate, solve problems, analyze data, develop ideas, and implement plans. It develops broadly useful analytic skills such as math and logic, and, on a more basic level, observing, experimenting, summarizing, synthesizing, interpreting, classifying, and so on. In school one encounters and solves problems that are progressively more difficult, complex, and subtle. The more years of schooling the greater the cognitive development, characterized by flexible, rational, complex strategies of thinking. Higher education teaches people to think logically and rationally, see many sides of an issue, and analyze problems and solve them.

Education also develops broadly effective habits and attitudes such as dependability, motivation, effort, trust, and confidence. In particular the process of learning creates confidence in the ability to solve problems. Education instills the habit of meeting problems with attention, thought, action, and perseverance. Apart from the value of the skills and abilities learned in school, the process of learning builds the confidence, motivation, and self-assurance needed to *attempt* to solve problems. Thus education increases effort, which, like ability, is a fundamental component of problem solving. Because education develops competence on many levels, it gives people the motivation to shape and control their lives. In contrast, the poorly educated may not posses the resources necessary to achieve their goals, which produces a sense of powerlessness, fatalism, and helplessness. Education increases learned effectiveness and the sense of personal control; its absence produces learned helplessness.

People with higher levels of education have lower levels of depression than those with less education, and the negative association of education with depression is greater for women (Ross and Mirowsky 2006). Women with less than a college degree have much higher levels of depression than do men. Among persons with a college degree, the gender gap that favors men is near zero. Higher education is associated with less depression for both sexes, while also narrowing the gap between men and women. Low levels of education disadvantage women more than men. But at high levels of education, women's depression levels are as low as men's. On average, women's depression levels exceed men's. Education reduces depression for both men and women, but more so for women. (See Figure 22.2.) This is largely because education increases both men's and women's sense of personal control, but it increases women's more. Because education has a greater impact among women than men, it can close the gap between them, and the gender gap in depression is near-zero among men and women with college degrees or higher. Since women now earn the majority of college degrees, education could close the gender gap in depression in future generations.

Trust

Defining and Measuring Trust and Mistrust

Trust is a belief in the integrity of other people. Trusting individuals expect that they can depend on others. They have faith and confidence in other people. Mistrust, the opposite of trust, is the cognitive habit of interpreting the intentions and behavior of others as unsupportive,

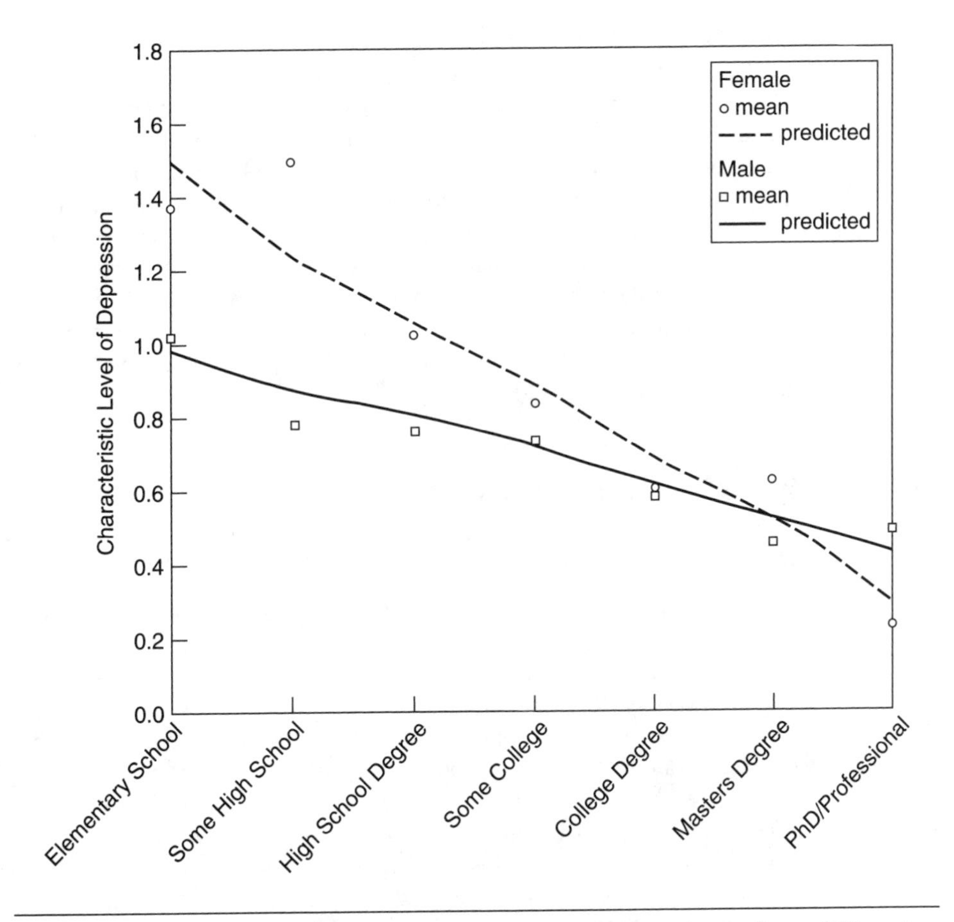

FIGURE 22.2 ***Mean and Predicted Characteristic Levels of Depression by Sex and Education, Adjusting for Age and Race (Ross and Mirowsky 2006).***

self-seeking, and dishonest (Mirowsky and Ross 1983). Mistrust is an absence of faith in other people based on a belief that they are out for their own good and will exploit or victimize you in pursuit of their goals. Mistrusting individuals believe it is safer to keep their distance from others, and suspicion of other people is the central cognitive component of mistrust (Kramer 1999). Trust and mistrust express inherently social beliefs about relationships with other people. Trust and mistrust embody learned, generalized expectations about other people's behaviors that transcend specific relationships and situations (Barber 1983; Gurtman 1992; Mirowsky and Ross 2003).

One short mistrust scale sums the number of days in the past week respondents "felt it was not safe to trust anyone," "felt suspicious," and "felt sure everyone was against you" (Mirowsky and Ross 1983, 2003). This scale only asks about the mistrust end of the trust-mistrust continuum, which is a limitation, although it has the advantage of being a likert scale. The General Social Survey includes three forced-choice questions about trust: "Do you think most people would try to take advantage of you if they got a chance, or would they try to be fair?" (Coded take advantage vs. fair) "Would you say that most of the time people try to be helpful, or that they are mostly just looking out for themselves?" (Coded helpful vs. look out for themselves), and "Generally speaking would you say that most people can be trusted or that you can't be too careful in dealing with people?" (Coded can trust vs. can't be too careful) (Brehm and Rahn 1997; Paxton 1999). Respondents do not like forced-choice questions, and forced dichotomies also eliminate real variation in beliefs. Likert scales indicate respondents are not very mistrusting, but forced-choice scales indicate that respondents do not endorse statements that others are fair and helpful, either (Mirowsky and Ross 1983; Paxton 1999). More work is needed on the development of trust scales. Despite interest in trust and mistrust, little research has been done on the structural causes of mistrust. Recently we developed and tested a theory about social structure and trust, described next (Ross et al. 2001).

Social Statuses that Generate Mistrust

Scarce Resources, Threat, and Powerlessness

Mistrust and trust imply judgments about the likely risks and benefits posed by interaction. How do people make decisions about interaction when it is uncertain whether other people can be trusted? Three things theoretically influence the level of trust: scarce resources, threat, and powerlessness (Ross et al. 2001). Where the environment seems threatening, among those who feel powerless to avoid or manage the threats, and among those with few resources with which to absorb losses, suspicion and mistrust seem well founded. Mistrust makes sense where threats abound, particularly for those who feel powerless to prevent harm or cope with the consequences of being victimized or exploited. Furthermore, for people with few resources, the consequences of losing what little one has will be devastating. Those with little cannot afford to loose much, and need to be vigilant in defense of what little they have. If so then mistrust will be more common among persons who live in threatening environments; among individuals who feel powerless to prevent or deal with the consequences of harm; and among the disadvantaged, who live in disadvantaged neighborhoods with high levels of threat, and who have few individual resources to make up for any losses.

Disorder, Powerlessness, and the Structural Amplification of Mistrust

Through daily exposure to a threatening environment, where signs of disorder are common, residents come to learn that other people cannot be trusted (Ross et al. 2001). Neighborhoods with high levels of disorder present residents with observable signs and cues that social control is weak (Skogan 1990). In these neighborhoods, residents report noise, litter, crime, vandalism, graffiti, people hanging out on the streets, public drinking, run-down and abandoned buildings, drug use, danger, trouble with neighbors, and other incivilities associated with a breakdown of social control. In neighborhoods with a lot of disorder, residents often view those around them with suspicion, as enemies who will harm them rather than as allies who will help them.

Neighborhood disadvantage is associated with mistrust because of the disorder common in these neighborhoods. Residents of disadvantaged neighborhoods—where a high proportion of households are poor and mother-only—have significantly lower levels of trust because these neighborhoods often have high levels of disorder (Ross et al. 2001).

Neighborhood disorder also reinforces a sense of powerlessness that makes the effect of disorder on mistrust even worse. Perceived powerlessness is the sense that one's own life is shaped by forces outside ones control. Its opposite, the sense of personal control, is the belief that you can and do master, control, and shape your own life. Exposure to uncontrollable, negative events and conditions in the neighborhood in the form of crime, noise, vandalism, graffiti, garbage, fights, and danger promote and reinforce perceptions of powerlessness. In neighborhoods where social order has broken down, residents often feel powerless to achieve a goal most people desire—to live in a clean, safe environment free from threat, harassment, and danger (Geis and Ross 1998; Ross et al. 2001).

The sense of powerlessness reinforced by a threatening environment amplifies the effect of that threat on mistrust, whereas a sense of control would moderate it. At heart, individuals who feel powerless feel awash in a sea of events generated by chance or by powerful others. They feel helpless to avoid undesirable events and outcomes, as well as powerless to bring about desirable ones. Individuals who feel powerless may feel unable to fend off attempts at exploitation, unable to distinguish dangerous persons and situations from benign ones, and unable to recover from mistaken complacency. In contrast those with a sense of personal control may feel that they can avoid victimization and harm and effectively cope with any consequences of errors in judgment. Neighborhood disorder signals the potential for harm. Some people feel they can avoid harm, or cope with it. Neighborhood disorder generates little mistrust among individuals who feel in control of their own lives, but a great deal among those who feel powerless.

Thus mistrust emerges in disadvantaged neighborhoods with high levels of disorder, among individuals with few resources who feel powerless to avoid harm (Ross et al. 2001). Mistrust is the product of an interaction between person and place, but the place gathers those who are susceptible and intensifies their susceptibility. Specifically, disadvantaged individuals generally live in disadvantaged neighborhoods where they feel awash in threatening signs of disorder. Among individuals who feel in control of their own lives, neighborhood disadvantage and disorder produce little mistrust. However, neighborhood disorder impairs residents' ability to cope with its own ill effect by also producing a sense of powerlessness. Neighborhood disorder destroys the sense of control that would otherwise insulate residents from the consequences of disorder. Thus, the very thing needed to protect disadvantaged residents from the negative effects of their environment—a sense of personal control—is eroded by that environment. This is an instance of what we call structural amplification.

Structural Amplification

Structural amplification exists when conditions undermine the personal attributes that otherwise would moderate their undesirable consequences. The situation erodes resistance to its own ill effect. More generally, it exists when a mediator of the association between an objective condition and a subjective belief or feeling also amplifies the association. The mediator of an undesirable effect is also a magnifier of that effect.

Mediators link objective social conditions to subjective beliefs and feelings. Mediators are a consequence of an exogenous (or independent) variable and a "cause" of a dependent variable. They explain patterns. Modifiers condition associations between objective statuses and subjective beliefs or feelings, making the associations between exogenous and dependent variables stronger or weaker, depending on their level. Modifiers sometimes moderate effects, lessening the ill effects of disadvantaged or threatening conditions, but in structural amplification, modifiers amplify ill effects, making them worse. Most important, in structural amplification, modifiers are also linked to social conditions. Here a sense of powerlessness amplifies the association between neighborhood disorder and mistrust, but the perception of powerlessness does not just come out of people's heads without reference to social conditions. A sense of powerlessness is also a consequence of neighborhood disorder. When modifiers of the association between a social condition and mistrust result from the condition itself, this produces structural amplification.

Individual Disadvantage

Disadvantaged individuals live in disadvantaged neighborhoods, so research on neighborhoods and trust must take into account individual characteristics in order to establish that neighborhoods affect mistrust over and above the characteristics of the individuals who live there. Individual disadvantage also influences mistrust. Older people, whites, employed persons, those with high household incomes, and the well educated are more trusting than younger persons, nonwhites, those with low incomes, and those with less education. In terms of family status, single parents have the highest levels of mistrust, followed by single people without children, married parents, and married persons without children. Individuals with low incomes, little education, the unemployed, minorities, young people, or single parents may lack the resources that encourage trust. In general individual socioeconomic disadvantage correlates with mistrust, with one exception. Men hold advantaged statuses compared with women, but men are significantly more mistrusting than women. Why men have lower levels of trust than women despite their more advantaged status is not clear. Possibly, men's relationships are less supportive and more competitive and exploitive than are women's (Turner and Marino 1994). To the extent that men interact mostly with other men, mistrust may be warranted. In general, disadvantaged individuals are more mistrusting as a consequence of their individual disadvantage and because they live in disadvantaged neighborhoods with high levels of disorder.

Individual disadvantage is also associated with perceived powerlessness. Persons with low incomes, lower levels of education, nonwhites, and those who are not married report more personal powerlessness than do people with high incomes, education, whites, and married persons. Adjustment for perceptions of powerlessness and the way that powerlessness amplifies the harmful effect of neighborhood disorder on mistrust largely explains the effects of income, education, and race on mistrust. Low household income, minority status, and low educational attainment show the same pattern, which we describe for the case of income: People with low incomes live in neighborhoods with high levels of disorder; they feel a greater sense of personal powerlessness partly as a direct result of their individual disadvantage and partly as a result of the threatening neighborhoods in which they live; and their perceptions of powerlessness make the effect of neighborhood disorder on mistrust even worse. This amplification of disadvantage largely explains the impact of low household income, education, and minority status on mistrust (Ross et al. 2001).

Emotional Consequences of Mistrust

The ability to form positive social relationships depends on trust. It allows pairs of individuals to establish cooperative relationships whenever doing so is mutually beneficial. Coleman emphasizes trust as an element of social capital, because trusting social relationships help produce desired outcomes. Sampson and his colleagues also emphasize trust in their definition of collective efficacy: the mutual trust and social bonds among neighbors that are likely to be effective in decreasing crime (Sampson et al. 1997). People who trust others form personal ties and participate in voluntary associations more often than do mistrusting individuals (Brehm and Rahn 1997; Paxton 1999). Trusting individuals are themselves more trustworthy and honest and are less likely to lie and harm others so that they create and maintain environments of trustworthiness—without which the social fabric cannot hold. Trusting people enter relationships with the presumption that others can be trusted until they have evidence to the contrary. Because trusting individuals can form effective associations with others, the presumption of trust can be an advantageous strategy, despite the fact that expecting people to be trustworthy is risky (Molm et al. 2000).

In contrast, the consequences of mistrust can be far-reaching and severe. Mistrust can interfere with the development, maintenance, and use of social support networks. Trust allows pairs of individuals to establish cooperative relationships whenever doing so is mutually beneficial. Mistrusting individuals, on the other hand, may not seek social support when in need, may reject offers of such support, and may be uncomfortable with any support that is given. Furthermore, mistrusting individuals help create and maintain the very conditions that seem to justify their beliefs. Their preemptive actions may elicit hostile responses, and their diminished ability to participate in networks of reciprocity and mutual assistance may have several consequences: without allies they are easy targets of crime and exploitation, when victimized or exploited they cannot share their economic or emotional burden with others, and by not providing aid and assistance to others mistrusting individuals weaken the community's power to forestall victimization and exploitation and to limit its consequences (Mirowsky and Ross 1983).

Mistrust represents a profound form of alienation, one that has progressed from a sense of separation from others to one of suspicion of others. Furthermore, the cognitive habit of interpreting the intentions and behavior of other people as unsupportive, self-seeking, and dishonest can develop into paranoia, especially under conditions of powerlessness and socioeconomic disadvantage. Paranoia is an even more profound rift with others than is mistrust. Individuals may go from a more general belief that people are manipulative and may harm them in pursuit of goals, to a more specific belief that they have been singled out as a target for persecution. "When other people in one's life have become a hostile army, social alienation is at its deepest" (Mirowsky and Ross 1983:238). Theory suggests that mistrust is associated with depression and anxiety because it implies severed social relationships.

Conclusion

Some conditions rob people of control over their lives. Disadvantage, joblessness, dependency, oppressive work, not finishing high school, poverty, and neighborhood disorder ingrain a sense of powerlessness that demoralizes and distresses. The most destructive situations hide from people in the fact that everyone has a choice. However constricting the situation, it is better to try to understand and solve the problems than it is to avoid them or bear them as the inevitable burden of life. In the path to well-being, education is key: it supplies individuals with real control over their lives, improves choices, resources, and opportunities, and helps overcome other disadvantages.

References

Aneshensel, Carol. 1992. "Social Stress: Theory and Research." *Annual Review of Sociology* 18:15–38.

Aneshensel, Carol S., Ralph R. Frerichs, and George J. Huba. 1984. "Depression and Physical Illness: A Multiwave, Nonrecursive Causal Model." *Journal of Health and Social Behavior* 25:350–371.

Aneshensel, Carol S., Carolyn M. Rutter, Peter A. Lachenbruch. 1991. "Social Structure, Stress, and Mental Health: Competing Conceptual and Analytic Models." *American Sociological Review* 56:166–178.

Appel, Margaret, Kenneth Holroyd, and Larry Gorkin. 1983. "Anger and the Etiology and Progression of Physical Illness." Pp. 73–85 in *Emotions in Health and Illness: Theoretical and Research Foundations*, edited by L. Temoshok, C. Van Dyke, and L. Zegans. New York: Grune and Stratton.

Averill, James R. 1983. "Studies on Anger and Aggression: Implications for Theories of Emotion. *American Psychologist* 38:1145–1160.

Barber, B. 1983. *The Logic and Limits of Trust*. New Brunswick, NJ: Rutgers University Press.

Benassi, Victor A., P. D. Sweeney, and C. L. Dufour. 1988. "Is There a Relationship between Locus of Control Orientation and Depression?" *Journal of Abnormal Psychology* 97:357–366.

Bianchi, Suzanne M. 2000. "Maternal Employment and Time with Children: Dramatic Change or Surprising Continuity?" *Demography* 37:401–414.

Bird, Chloe E. and Catherine E. Ross. 1993. "Houseworkers and Paid Workers: Qualities of the Work and Effects on Personal Control." *Journal of Marriage and the Family* 55:913–925.

Boyd, Jeffrey H. et al. 1984. "Exclusion Criteria of DSM-III: A Study of Co-occurrence of Hierarchy-Free Syndromes." *Archives of General Psychiatry*. 41:983–989.

Bradburn, Norman M. 1969. *The Structure of Psychological Well-Being*. Chicago: Aldine.

Braverman, H. 1974. *Labor and Monopoly Capital: The Degradation of Work in the Twentieth Century*. New York: Monthly Review Press.

Brehm, John and Wendy Rahn. 1997. "Individual-Level Evidence for the Causes and Consequences of Social Capital." *American Journal of Political Science* 41:999–1023.

Brewin, C. R. and D. A. Shapiro. 1984. "Beyond Locus of Control: Attribution of Responsibility for Positive and Negative Outcomes." *British Journal of Psychology* 75:43–49.

Coleman, James S. 1988. "Social Capital in the Creation of Human Capital." *American Journal of Sociology* S95–S120.

Conger, Rand D. et al. 1992. "A Family Process Model of Economic Hardship and Adjustment of Early Adolescent Boys." *Child Development* 63:526–541.

Conger, Rand D., Frederick O. Lorenz, Glen H. Elder, Ronald L. Simmons, and Xiaojia Ge. 1993. "Husband and Wife Differences in Response to Undesirable Life Events." *Journal of Health and Social Behavior* 34:71–88.

Consumer Reports on Health. 1994. "Is Hostility Killing You?" *Consumers Union* 6:49–50.

Dohrenwend, Bruce P. and Barbara S. Dohrenwend. 1976. "Sex Differences in Psychiatric Disorder." *American Journal of Sociology* 82:1447–1459.

———. 1977. "Reply to Gove and Tudor." *American Journal of Sociology* 82:1336–1345.

Downey, G. and Phyllis Moen. 1987. "Personal Efficacy, Income and Family Transitions: A Longitudinal Study of Women Heading Households." *Journal of Health and Social Behavior* 28:320–333.

Elder, Glen H. and Jeffrey K. Liker. 1982. "Hard Times in Women's Lives: Historical Influences across Forty Years." *American Journal of Sociology* 88:241–226.

Erikson, Kai. 1986. "On Work and Alienation." *American Sociological Review* 51:1–8.

Ge, Xiaojia et al. 1992. "Linking Family Economic Hardship to Adolescent Distress." *Journal of Research on Adolescence* 2:351–378.

Gecas, Viktor. 1989. "The Social Psychology of Self-Efficacy." *Annual Review of Sociology* 15:291–316.

Geis, Karlyn J. and Catherine E. Ross. 1998. "A New Look at Urban Alienation: The Effect of Neighborhood Disorder on Perceived Powerlessness." *Social Psychology Quarterly* 61:232–246.

Glass, Jennifer and Tetsushi Fujimoto. 1994. "Housework, Paid Work, and Depression among Husbands and Wives." *Journal of Health and Social Behavior* 35:179–191.

Gove, Walter R. and Kevin Clancy. 1975. "Response Bias, Sex Differences, and Mental Illness: A Reply." *American Journal of Sociology* 81:1463–1472.

Gove, Walter R. and Jeannette F. Tudor. 1973. "Adult Sex Roles and Mental Illness." *American Journal of Sociology* 78:812–835.

Green, Brian E. and Christian Ritter. 2000. "Marijuana Use and Depression." *Journal of Health and Social Behavior* 41:40–49.

Gurtman, M. B. 1992. "Trust, Distrust, and Interpersonal Problems: A Circumplex Analysis." *Journal of Personality and Social Psychology* 62:989–1002.

Horowitz, Allan and Helene Raskin White. 1991. "Becoming Married, Depression, and Alcohol Problems among Young Adults." *Journal of Health and Social Behavior* 32:221–237.

House, James, Debra Umberson, and K. Landis. 1988. "Structures and Processes of Social Support." *Annual Review of Sociology* 14:293–318.

Kandel, Denise B., Mark Davies, and Victoria H. Raveis. 1985. "The Stressfulness of Daily Social Roles for Women: Marital, Occupational, and Household Roles." *Journal of Health and Social Behavior* 26:64–78.

Kessler, Ronald C. 1982. "A Disaggregation of the Relationship between Socioeconomic Status and Psychological Distress." *American Sociological Review* 47:752–764.

Kessler, Ronald C. and James A. McRae. 1982. "The Effect of Wives' Employment on the Mental Health of Married Men and Women." *American Sociological Review* 47:216–227.

Kohn, Melvin and Carmi Schooler 1982. "Job Conditions and Personality: A Longitudinal Assessment of Their Reciprocal Effects." *American Journal of Sociology* 87:1257–1286.

Kramer, Roderick M. 1999. "Trust and Distrust in Organizations: Emerging Perspectives, Enduring Questions." *Annual Review of Psychology* 50:569–598.

Lachman, M. E. 1986. "Personal Control in Later Life: Stability, Change, and Cognitive Correlates." Pp. 207–236 in *The Psychology of Control and Aging*, edited by M. M. Baltes and P. B. Baltes. Hillsdale, NJ: Lawrence Erlbaum Associates.

Langner, Thomas S. 1962. "A Twenty-two Item Screening Score of Psychiatric Symptoms Indicating Impairment." *Journal of Health and Human Behavior*. 3:269–276.

Lennon, Mary Clare and Sarah Rosenfield. 1992. "Women and Mental Health: The Interaction of Job and Family Conditions." *Journal of Health and Social Behavior* 33:316–327.

Levenson H. 1973. "Multidimensional Locus of Control in Psychiatric Patients." *Journal of Consulting and Clinical Psychology* 41:397–404.

Link, Bruce G., Mary Clare Lennon, and Bruce P. Dohrenwend. 1993. "Socioeconomic Status and Depression: The Role of Occupations Involving Direction, Control, and Planning." *American Journal of Sociology* 98:1351–1387.

Mirowsky, John. 1985. "Depression and Marital Power: An Equity Model." *American Journal of Sociology* 91:557–592.

———. 1987. "The Psycho-Economics of Feeling Underpaid: Distributive Justice and the Earnings of Husbands and Wives." *American Journal of Sociology* 92:1404–1434.

———. 1996. "Age and the Gender Gap in Depression." *Journal of Health and Social Behavior* 37:362–380.

Mirowsky, John and Catherine E. Ross. 1983. "Paranoia and the Structure of Powerlessness." *American Sociological Review* 48:228–239.

———. 1984. "Mexican Culture and Its Emotional Contradictions." *Journal of Health and Social Behavior* 25:2–13.

———. 1986. "Social Patterns of Distress." *Annual Review of Sociology* 12:23–45.

———. 1990. "Control or Defense? Depression and the Sense of Control Over Good and Bad Outcomes." *Journal of Health and Social Behavior* 31:71–86.

———. 1991. "Eliminating Defense and Agreement Bias from Measures of the Sense of Control: A 2 × 2 Index." *Social Psychology Quarterly* 54:127–145.

———. 1995. "Sex Differences in Distress: Real or Artifact?" *American Sociological Review* 60:449–468.

———. 1998. "Education, Personal Control, Lifestyle, and Health: A Human Capital Hypothesis." *Research on Aging* 20: 415–449.

———. 1999. "Well-being across the Life Course." Pp. 328–347 in *A Handbook for the Study of Mental Health*, edited by Allan V. Horowitz and Teresa L. Scheid. Cambridge: Cambridge University Press.

———. 2003. *Social Causes of Psychological Distress*. New York: Aldine. Transaction.

———. 2005. "Education, Learned Effectiveness, and Health." *London Review of Education* 3:205–220.

Mirowsky, John, Catherine E. Ross, and John R. Reynolds. 2000. "Links between Social Status and Health Status." Pp. 47–67 in *The Handbook of Medical Sociology* (5th ed.), edited by Chloe E. Bird, Peter Conrad, and Allen M. Freemont. Upper Saddle River, NJ: Prentice Hall.

Molm, Linda D., Nobuyuki Takahashi, and Gretchen Peterson. 2000. "Risk and Trust in Social Exchange: An Experimental Test of a Classical Proposition." *American Journal of Sociology* 105:1396–1427.

Novaco, Raymond W. 1985. "Anger and Its Therapeutic Regulation." In *Anger and Hostility in Cardiovascular and Behavioral Disorders,* edited by M. A. Chesney and R. H. Rosenman. Hemisphere: New York.

Paxton, Pamela. 1999. "Is Social Capital Declining in the United States? A Multiple Indicator Assessment." *American Journal of Sociology* 105:88–127.

Pearlin, Leonard I., Morton A. Lieberman, Elizabeth G. Menaghan, and Joseph T. Mullan. 1981. "The Stress Process." *Journal of Health and Social Behavior* 22:337–356.

Radloff, Lenore. 1977. "The CES-D Scale: A Self-report Depression Scale for Research in the General Population." *Applied Psychological Measurement*. 1:385–401.

Reskin, Barbara F. and Irene Padavic. 1994. *Women and Men at Work*. Thousand Oaks, CA: Pine Forge Press.

Reynolds, John R. and Catherine E. Ross. 1998. "Social Stratification and Health: Education's Benefit beyond Economic Status and Social Origins." *Social Problems* 45:221–247.

Rieker, Patricia P. and Chloe E. Bird. 2000. "Sociological Explanations of Gender Differences in Mental and Physical Health." Pp. 98–113 in *Handbook of Medical Sociology* (5th ed.), edited by Chloe E. Bird, Pater Conrad, and Allen M. Fremont. Upper Saddle River, NJ: Prentice Hall.

Riessman, Catherine Kohler and Naomi R. Gerstel. 1985. "Marital Dissolution and Health: Do Males or Females Have Greater Risk?" *Social Science and Medicine* 20:627–635.

Ritchey, Ferris J., Mark La Gory, and Jeffrey Mullis. 1991. "Gender Differences in Health Risks and Physical Symptoms among the Homeless." *Journal of Health and Social Behavior* 32:33–48.

———. 1989. "The Effects of Women's Employment: Personal Control and Sex Differences in Mental Health." *Journal of Health and Social Behavior* 30:77–91.

———. 1999. "Splitting the Difference: Gender, the Self, and Mental Health." Pp. 209–224 in *Handbook of the Sociology of Mental Health*, edited by Carol S. Aneshensel and Jo C. Phelan. New York: Plenum.

Ross, Catherine E. 1991. "Marriage and the Sense of Control." *Journal of Marriage and the Family* 53:831–838.

———. 1995. "Reconceptualizing Marital Status as a Continuum of Social Attachment." *Journal of Marriage and the Family* 57:129–140.

———. 2000. "Neighborhood Disadvantage and Adult Depression." *Journal of Health and Social Behavior* 41:177–187.

Ross, Catherine E. and Chloe E. Bird. 1994. "Sex Stratification and Health Lifestyle: Consequences for Men's and Women's Perceived Health." *Journal of Health and Social Behavior* 35:161–178.

Ross, Catherine E. and Patricia Drentea. 1998. "Consequences of Retirement Activities for Distress and the Sense of Personal Control." *Journal of Health and Social Behavior* 39:317–334.

Ross, Catherine E. and Joan Huber 1985. "Hardship and Depression." *Journal of Health and Social Behavior* 26:312–327.

Ross, Catherine E. and John Mirowsky. 1984a. "Components of Depressed Mood in Married Men and Women: The Center for Epidemiologic Studies' Depression Scale." *American Journal of Epidemiology* 119:997–1004.

———. 1988. "Child Care and Emotional Adjustment to Wives' Employment." *Journal of Health and Social Behavior* 29:127–138.

———. 1989. "Explaining the Social Patterns of Depression: Control and Problem–Solving—or Support and Talking." *Journal of Health and Social Behavior* 30:206–219.

———. 1992. "Households, Employment, and the Sense of Control." *Social Psychology Quarterly* 55: 217–235.

———. 1995. "Does Employment Affect Health?" *Journal of Health and Social Behavior* 36:230–243.

———. 2002. "Age and the Gender Gap in the Sense of Personal Control." *Social Psychology Quarterly* 65:125–145.

———. 2006. "Sex Differences in the Effect of Education on Depression: Resource Multiplication or Resource Substitution?" *Social Science & Medicine* 63:1400–1413.

Ross, Catherine E., John Mirowsky, and Karen Goldsteen. 1990. "The Impact of the Family on Health: The Decade in Review." *Journal of Marriage and the Family* 52:1059–1078.

Ross, Catherine E., John Mirowsky, and Joan Huber 1983. "Dividing Work, Sharing Work, and In-Between: Marriage Patterns and Depression." *American Sociological Review* 48:809–823.

Ross, Catherine E., John Mirowsky, and Shana Pribesh. 2001. "Powerlessness and the Amplification of Threat: Neighborhood Disadvantage, Disorder, and Mistrust." *American Sociological Review.* 66:568–591

Ross, Catherine E. and Marieke Van Willigen. 1996. "Gender, Parenthood and Anger." *Journal of Marriage and the Family* 58:572–584.

———. 1997. "Education and the Subjective Quality of Life." *Journal of Health and Social Behavior* 38:275–297.

Ross, Catherine E. and Marylyn P. Wright. 1998. "Women's Work, Men's Work, and the Sense of Control." *Work and Occupations* 25:333–355.

Ross, Catherine. E. and Wu, Chia–ling. 1995. "The Links between Education and Health." *American Sociological Review* 60:719–745.

Rotter, Julian B. 1966. "Generalized Expectancies for Internal vs. External Control of Reinforcements." *Psychological Monographs* 80:1–28.

Sampson, Robert J., Stephen W. Raudenbush, and Felton Earls. 1997. "Neighborhoods and Violent Crime: A Multilevel Study of Collective Efficacy." *Science* 277:918–924.

Schieman, Scott. 1999. "Age and Anger." *Journal of Health and Social Behavior* 40:273–289.

———. 2000. "Education and the Activation, Course, and Management of Anger." *Journal of Health and Social Behavior* 41:20–39.

Seeman, Melvin. 1959. "On the Meaning of Alienation." *American Sociological Review* 24:783–791.

Seeman, Melvin and Teresa E. Seeman. 1983. "Health Behavior and Personal Autonomy: A Longitudinal Study of the Sense of Control in Illness." *Journal of Health and Social Behavior* 24:144–159.

Seiler, Lauren H. 1975."Sex Differences in Mental Illness: Comment on Clancy and Gove's Interpretations." *American Journal of Sociology* 81:1458–1462.

Simon, Robin W. 1992. "Parental Role Strains, Salience of Parental Identity and Gender Differences in Psychological Distress." *Journal of Health and Social Behavior* 33:25–35.

———. 2002. "Revisiting the Relationships among Gender, Marital Status, and Mental Health." *American Journal of Sociology* 107:1065–1096.

Skogan, Wesley G. 1990. *Disorder and Decline.* Berkeley: University of California Press.

Tavris, Carol. 1982. *Anger: The Misunderstood Emotion*. New York: Simon & Schuster.

———. 2006. "Personal Agency in the Stress Process." *Journal of Health and Social Behavior* 47:309–323.

Thomas, Sandra. 1989. "Gender Differences in Anger Expression: Health Implications." *Research in Nursing and Health* 12:389–398.

Turner, R. Jay and Franco Marino. 1994. "Social Support and Social Structure: A Descriptive Epidemiology." *Journal of Health and Social Behavior* 35:193–212.

Umberson, Debra and Kristi Williams. 2000. "Family Status and Mental Health." Pp. 225–253 in *Handbook of the Sociology of Mental Health,* edited by Carol S. Aneshensel and Jo C. Phelan. New York: Plenum.

U.S. Bureau of the Census. 2000. "Profile of the Nation's Women." www.census.gov.

Verbrugge, Lois M. 1985. "Gender and Health: An Update on Hypotheses and Evidence." *Journal of Health and Social Behavior*. 26:156–182.

Waite, Linda and Gallagher, Maggie. 2000. *The Case for Marriage*. New York: Doubleday.

Weissman, Myrna M. and Eugene S. Paykel. 1974. *The Depressed Woman.* Chicago: University of Chicago Press.

Wheaton, Blair. 1980. "The Sociogenesis of Psychological Disorder: An Attributional Theory." *Journal of Health and Social Behavior* 21:100–124.

———. 1985. "Models for the Stress-Buffering Functions of Coping Resources." *Journal of Health and Social Behavior* 26:352–364.

Williams, David R. and Chiquita Collins. 1995. "U.S. Socioeconomic and Racial Differences in Health: Patterns and Explanations." *Annual Review of Sociology* 21:349–386.

About the Contributors

Phyllis Baker (with Martha Copp) is an assistant professor of sociology at the University of Northern Iowa. She studies battered women from a qualitative perspective and has articles in press on this research. She also published a book, *Bored and Busy: An Analysis of Formal and Informal Organization in the Automated Office* (information from her 1999 article in *Teaching Sociology*).

Martha Copp (with Phyllis Baker) is an assistant professor of sociology at East Tennessee State University. A qualitative researcher, her current work explores heterosexual socialization in adults with developmental disabilities and emotion management in the workplace. She is coauthor of *Emotions and Fieldwork* (information from her 1999 article in *Teaching Sociology*).

Mikaela Dufur (with Raechel Lizon) is an assistant professor of sociology at Brigham Young University. Her interests in social psychology focus on the ways social institutions such as the family, education, and labor markets influence child and adolescent identity formation and social interactions. She is particularly interested in the ways parents, teachers, and students interpret and transmit gendered symbols and expectations. Her work has appeared in *Social Forces, Journal of Marriage and the Family*, and *Sociological Perspectives*.

Gwynne Dyer has worked as a freelance journalist, columnist, broadcaster and lecturer with a Ph.D. in Military and Middle Eastern History from the University of London. Source: http://www.gwynnedyer.net/

Glen H. Elder, Jr., (with Angela O'Rand) is Howard W. Odum Distinquished Professor of Sociology and Research Professor of Psychology at the University of North Carolina at Chapel Hill. He has been involved in the development of life course studies as a field of inquiry, and is currently investigating pathways of risk and resilience into the young adult years, as well as the relationship between life transitions and health in the middle years.

Diane Felmlee is Professor, Vice Chair, and Director of Graduate Studies in the Sociology Department at University of California, Davis. Her interests within social psychology include close relationships, social networks, gender, and mathematical modeling, and she regularly teaches courses on those topics. A recent paper of hers, published in *Social Forces* (2001), investigates the effects of social networks on relationship breakup, i.e., "No Couple is an Island." Her current work examines the social psychological contextual factors that influence the stability and instability of intimate couples over time, with research funded by a National Science Foundation grant on dynamic modeling (with Ferrer & Widaman). In this new project she conceptualizes a couple as a dynamic, dyadic system that evolves daily, sometimes in surprising ways.

Jeannine A. Gailey's (with Michael Lee) research focuses on attributions of responsibility for organizational wrongdoing and gender and deviance, specifically masculinity using a social psychological framework. She has coauthored manuscripts in these areas for *Social Psychology Quarterly, Journal of Applied Social Psychology*, and *Deviant Behavior*. Her most recent research focuses on the attribution of responsibility for organizational wrongdoing, eating disorders, and the relationship between deviance and masculinity. She is currently an Assistant Professor of Criminal Justice at Texas Christian University. She holds a B.A. in psychology from Mount Union College, as well as an M.A. and Ph.D. both in Sociology from the University of Akron.

Marcie Goodman is an Assistant Professor of Sociology at Weber State University in Ogden, Utah. She is designated as primary instructor in this discipline for the WSU satellite campus in Layton, Utah (Davis Center). Dr. Goodman completed a BA in History and an MS in Sociology from Brigham Young University, and a Ph.D. from the University of Utah, where she continues an adjunct association. Her areas of specialization, along with Social Psychology, are Historical Sociology, Theory, Race, Class, and Gender Studies, and Research Methods. Her focus is primarily in teaching, and she has conducted classes in over two-dozen sociological subject areas. She is a regular contributor to social science curriculum development at Western Governor's University, a non-profit institution for competency-based online learning located in Salt Lake City. Additionally, she teaches on a volunteer basis in United States Family History, American Migration Patterns, and Southern Genealogical Records.

Roxanna Harlow is an associate professor of sociology and coordinator of the African American Studies minor at McDaniel College. With interests in race and ethnicity, education, and pedagogy, she teaches *Society and the Individual, Race and Ethnic Relations in the U.S., Sociology of Education, Intersections of Race, Class, and Gender, and Introduction to Sociology*. Noted in the *Chronicle of Higher Education*, she has published her work on race and the college classroom in *Social Psychology Quarterly*. She has also published research on differential responses by race to the 9/11 attacks, and pedagogical strategies for teaching sociology. She has also done numerous presentations on issues of multiculturalism, race, gender, identity, and the classroom.

Scott M. Hofer (with Michael Shanahan and Stephen Vaisey) is Professor of Human Development and Family Sciences and Director, Psychosocial Core, Center for Healthy Aging Research at Oregon State University. He received his Ph.D. in Psychology from University of Southern California in 1994 and held postdoctoral positions at the University of Manchester and the Center for Developmental and Health Genetics at the Pennsylvania State University. His research examines the role of aging and health on changes in cognitive functioning, in interaction with demographic and psychosocial influences, involving collaborations with national and international researchers on longitudinal studies on aging. His research has been funded by NIA, NIMH, and NICHD and he is an Associate Investigator on research networks in Australia, Sweden, and the United Kingdom. He is currently leading the development of an international collaborative network for the coordinated and integrative analysis of longitudinal studies on aging (IALSA).

Christine Horne is Associate Professor of Sociology at Washington State University. Her research focuses on social norms—in particular, their emergence and enforcement. She teaches undergraduate courses in sociological theory and introductory social psychology. Her work has appeared in journals such as *Social Psychology Quarterly, Social Forces*, and *Sociological Theory*. She is co-editor of *Theories of Social Order* (with Michael Hechter) and *Experimental Studies in Law and Criminology* (with Michael Lovaglia).

James House is the Angus Campbell Collegiate Professor of Sociology and Survey Research. He has appointments with the Survey Research Center at the Institute for Social Research and is a Professor of Sociology at the College of Literature Sciences and Arts at the University of Michigan. He also holds an appointment as a Professor of Epidemiology at the School of Public Health & a Faculty Associate with the Institute of Gerontology. He is the 2007 winner of the Social Psychology Section's Cooley-Mead Award given annually to a member of the ASA who has made significant lifetime contributions to sociological social psychology.

Bryan Johnson (with Cardell Jacobson) Bryan Johnson is a doctoral candidate in Marketing at the Smeal College of Business, Pennsylvania State University. He earned BS and MS degrees in Sociology from Brigham Young University. His current line of research bridges Sociology and Marketing by examining the impact of social structure on consumption. He is currently investigating how the use of social capital in the marketplace impacts consumption experiences. His research also addresses the interaction between social structure and persuasion attempts, as well as issues of race in consumer behavior.

Matthew T. Lee's (with Jeannine Gailey) research focuses on organizational deviance, as well as the relationship between immigration and crime; he has co-authored papers in these areas for *Criminology, Social Psychology Quarterly, Social Problems, Sociological Quarterly, Sociological Focus, Social Science Quarterly*, and *International Migration Review*. His book *Crime on the Border: Immigration and Homicide in Urban Communities* (LFB Scholarly 2003) disputes the conventional wisdom that immigration increases crime and instead develops an alternative account known as the immigration revitalization perspective. His most recent research addresses the attribution of responsibility for organizational deviance and he is in the process of co-authoring a book on altruism. He is currently an Associate Professor of Sociology and Conflict Management Fellow at The University of Akron. He holds a BA in Psychology from Kent State University, as well as an MA in Criminology and a Ph.D. in Sociology from the University of Delaware.

Raechel Lizon (with Mikaela Dufur) is a sociology graduate student at Brigham Young University. Her social psychology research interests include the formation and maintenance of adolescent social groups, the influence of peer rejection and acceptance on social identity, and the effect of social identity on self-esteem.

George J. McCall (with J.L. Simmons), Ph.D., Harvard, 1965, is Professor Emeritus of Sociology and Public Policy Administration at the University of Missouri-St. Louis. As that joint affiliation suggests, he has there served as an applied sociologist-in program evaluation, conflict resolution, and violence—while retaining his primary identification as a sociological social psychologist. Throughout a career at UMSL and at several Big Ten universities, the Federal government, and three South African universities, McCall has published frequently on self, identity, interaction, and personal relationships. Those publications began with the here-excerpted book, *Identities and Interactions*, that served to introduce the concepts of role-identity and of the self as intersecting systems of identities. His most recent publications along these lines include: "The Me and the Not-Me: Positive and Negative Poles of Identity" (pp. 11–26 in *Advances in Identity Theory and Research*, edited by Peter J. Burke, Timothy J. Owens, Richard Serpe, and Peggy A. Thoits. New York: Kluwer Academic-Plenum Press, 2003); "Interaction" (pp. 327–348 in *Handbook of Symbolic Interactionism*, edited by Larry T. Reynolds and Nancy J. Herman. Walnut Creek, CA: AltaMira Press, 2004); and "Symbolic Interaction" (pp. 1–23 in *Contemporary Social Psychological Theories*, edited by Peter J. Burke. Stanford, CA: Stanford University Press, 2006).

Bernard N. Meltzer, Professor Emeritus at Central Michigan University, has taught and written chiefly within the symbolic interactionist frame of reference. His publications have dealt with the following topics: the dying concept of "personality", chance and human conduct, deception in everyday life, the concept of "mind", sources of embarrassment, verbal ambiguity: the case of puns, encouraging serendipity, the emergent element in human behavior, forms of resentment, "Have a nice day!" (phatic communication), symbolic interactionism and psychoanalysis, etc.

John Mirowsky (with Catherine Ross) is Professor in the Department of Sociology and the Population Research Center at the University of Texas in Austin. He studies social aspects of health and well-being, particularly as they develop over the life course. His recent publications include *Education, Social Status, and Health* and the second edition of *Social Causes of Psychological Distress*, both co-authored with Catherine E. Ross and Published by Aldine-Transaction.

Gil Richard Musolf is Professor of Sociology at Central Michigan University. He teaches two undergraduate courses, Sociological Theory and Social Psychology, and two graduate courses, Classical Sociological Theory and Contemporary Sociological Theory. He has published in a number of journals, among them: *The Sociological Quarterly, Symbolic Interaction, Sociological Inquiry, Studies in Symbolic Interaction, Journal of Contemporary Ethnography, Contemporary Justice Review*, and *The Social Science Journal*. His text *Structure and Agency in Everyday Life* is in its second edition. He recently contributed the chapter, "The Chicago School," for the *Handbook of Symbolic Interactionism.*

Angela M. O'Rand (with Glen Elder) is Professor of Sociology at Duke University. She has published extensively on life course processes related to gender, education, work history, economic status and health. She is particularly interested in modeling lifelong processes to determine the cumulative effects of diverse life course trajectories on aspect of well-being in mid to late life.

Catherine E. Ross (with John Mirowsky) is a Professor in the Department of Sociology and the Population Research Center at the University of Texas. She is a structural social psychologist. She teaches Sociology of Mental Health and Sociology of Health and Illness. Her research examines the effects of socioeconomic status, work, family, and neighborhoods on men's and women's physical and mental health, and their sense of control versus powerlessness. Recent publications include "Neighborhood Disadvantage, Disorder, and Health." *Journal of Health and Social Behavior* 2001 (with John Mirowsky), "Powerlessness and The Amplification of Threat: Neighborhood Disadvantage, Disorder, and Mistrust" *American Sociological Review* 2001 (with John Mirowsky and Shana Pribesh), and "Sex Differences in the Effect of Education on Depression: Resource Multiplication or Resource Substitution?" *Social Science & Medicine* 2006 (with John Mirowsky).

Michael Shanahan (with Scott Hofer and Stephen Vaisey) is an Associate Professor of Sociology at the University of North Carolina at Chapel Hill. He is interested in theory and methods of life course sociology (a sub-discipline of social psychology) and their application to the study of adolescence and the transition to adulthood, and to links between genetic factors and behavior. He is the co-author (with Ross Macmillan) of a book about the life course, *Beyond the Sociological Imagination: Biography, Context, and Contingency*, to be published in the summer of 2007 by Norton & Company. He also co-edited (with Jeylan Mortimer) *The Handbook of the Life Course* (2003, Kluwer-Plenum).

J.L. Simmons (with George McCall), Ph.D., Iowa, 1962, died in 2003 in St. Louis, where he had resumed at UMSL an academic career earlier abandoned in California. Simmons was widely known for his writings on deviance, but (with McCall) he also contributed significantly to sociological social psychology, including not only the here-excerpted *Identities and Interactions* but also such other joint publications as *Social Psychology: A Sociological Approach* (New York: Free Press, 1982); and "Levels of Analysis: The Individual, The Dyad, and the Larger Social Group" (pp. 56–81 in *Studying Interpersonal Interaction*, edited by Barbara Montgomery and Steve Duck. New York: Guilford Publications, 1991).

Lynn Smith-Lovin is Robert L. Wilson Professor of Sociology in the Trinity College of Arts and Sciences at Duke University. She received the 2006 Cooley-Mead Award and the 2005 Lifetime Achievement Award in the Sociology of Emotions. Her research examines the relationships among social association, identity, action and emotion. Her current projects involve an experimental study of justice, identity and emotion as well as research with Miller McPherson on an ecological theory of identity (both funded by the National Science Foundation). Recent publications include "Social Isolation in America" in the June 2006 *American Sociological Review* and "The Strength of Weak Identities" in the June 2007 *Social Psychology Quarterly*. She has served as President of the Southern Sociological Society, Vice-President of the American Sociological Association, and Chair of the ASA Sections on the Sociology of Emotion and on Social Psychology.

Peggy A. Thoits is the Elizabeth Taylor-Williams Distinguished Professor of Sociology and Research Professor of Social Medicine at the University of North Carolina, Chapel Hill. Her research interests focus on stress, coping, and social support processes in mental health and illness; the effects of holding multiple roles on psychological well-being; and the conditions under which individuals label themselves as having psychological problems. She applies emotions theory in all three of these research areas, paying special attention to the causes and consequences of emotional deviance, i.e., persistent or repeated violations of emotion norms that both clinicians and lay persons recognize as psychological problems or emotional disturbances.

Jonathan Turner is Distinguished Professor of Sociology at the University of California, Riverside. He received his Ph.D. from Cornell University in 1968. He is primarily a general theorist, seeking to develop abstract theories and models of social processes. He has developed theories on social processes at the micro-, meso-, and macro-levels of social reality, from theories of interpersonal processes and emotions at the micro level of face-to-face interaction through theories of organizations and ethnic relations at the meso or middle level of reality to theories of institutional stratification systems at the macro level of reality, and beyond to world system dynamics where inter-societal processes unfold. He is not a social psychologist, per se, but instead a theorist who at times studies micro social processes of face-to-face interaction. His major works that explore micro social processes are *A Theory of Social Interaction* (1988), *Face-to-Face: Toward a Theory of Interpersonal Behavior* (2002), and *Human Emotions: A Sociological Theory* (2007). These works contain in their bibliography his articles and chapters in books on micro social processes.

Steven Vaisey (with Michael Shanahan and Scott Hofer) is a Caroline H. and Thomas S. Royster, Jr. Fellow and Ph.D. candidate in sociology at the University of North Carolina at Chapel Hill. His main research interests lie at the intersection of cultural sociology, social psychology, and cognitive science. Methodologically, he has developed statistical techniques for combinatorial and fuzzy set analysis and is also devising new ways to measure unconscious cultural schemas using qualitative interview data. His dissertation explores the origins and consequences of the moral worldviews of American teenagers.

Robert Young is Professor of Sociology and Chair of Sociology and Anthropology at the University of Texas at Arlington. He teaches courses in the area of social psychology, including a graduate seminar in social psychology and undergraduate courses on The Social Psychology of Crime and Individual and Society. His research focuses on social cognition and social interaction processes. Recent publications in these areas include: *Understanding Misunderstandings* (University of Texas Press 1999), "Guilty Until Proven Innocent: Conviction Orientation, Racial Attitudes, and Support for Capital Punishment" (*Deviant Behavior*, vol. 25, 2004), and "Expectancy Narratives and Interactional Contingencies" (*Symbolic Interaction*, forthcoming).